D1229232

Writing & Fighting the Confederate War

The Letters of Peter Wellington Alexander
Confederate War Correspondent

Edited by William B. Styple

William B. Styple

Belle Grove Publishing Co.

Belle Grove Publishing Co.
P. O. Box 483
Kearny, N. J. 07032
email: bellegrove@worldnet.att.net
website: bellegrovepublishing.com

Copyright © 2002 by William B. Styple

All rights reserved.

No portion of this book may be reproduced in any form or by electronic means, without permission in writing from the publisher.

ISBN: 1-883926-14-9 SC
ISBN: 1-883926-15-7 HC

Library of Congress Control Number: 2002105076

This book is the second volume in the **Writing & Fighting the Civil War** Series

Volume One—Writing & Fighting the Civil War, Soldier Correspondence
 to the New York Sunday Mercury, ISBN 1-883926-13-0, Published Sept. 2000.

Table of Contents

Foreword

Once again William B. Styple scores a high-five with the Civil War community. In the past he has shared with us as author or editor/compiler a number of critically acclaimed titles. The last off the press in June 2000 was *Writing and Fighting the Civil War: Soldier Correspondence to the New York Sunday Mercury*. He also teamed with Brian Pohanka to co-author, direct and produce the Echoes of the Blue & Gray video series.

This time Styple again employs his talents as a sleuth and researcher to give us *Writing & Fighting the Confederate War: The Letters of Peter Wellington Alexander, Confederate War Correspondent*. Unlike his past endeavor, Styple's latest focuses on the Confederacy and its life and death as seen and experienced by Peter Wellington Alexander, its observant special correspondent for the *Savannah Republican*.

On occasions, during the Fredericksburg Campaign and on the march to Gettysburg, when Alexander was ill with "camp fever", friend and protégé Capt. Virgil A. S. Parks filled in providing a soldier's view to the *Republican* as "V. A. S. P." Unfortunately Parks lost his life at Gettysburg.

As heretofore, as with the *Sunday Mercury* book, Alexander's correspondence expanded my Civil War horizons. Alexander spends much of the war in Richmond and in the field with the Army of Northern Virginia and its predecessor, the Army of the Potomac. He also travels west to spend key time with Albert Sidney Johnston's and P. G. T. Beauregard's Army of the Mississippi in the late winter and spring of 1862. He writes as an eyewitness of Shiloh and the siege of Corinth. By mid-summer he is back in Virginia.

Like the very best of today's war correspondents, Alexander seemingly has a sixth sense to be where the action is. This despite articles deemed to be too critical of the Richmond government that occasionally results in denial by the bureaucracy of his credentials to visit the armies.

His views of Confederate politicians and military leaders are candid. Readers will observe that, long before Brandy Station and Gettysburg, he is a Jeb Stuart critic. Since most of his readers are Georgians, activities of military and political leaders and soldiers from the Empire State are highlighted. This is refreshing because of the high profile given to Virginians by the widely quoted Richmond press.

A dedicated Confederate partisan, Alexander, even in the new government's darkest days, sought in his writings to boost morale that there was light at the end of the tunnel. Too bad that he never found the time to write his contemplated history of the Confederacy.

The Civil War as reported by Peter Wellington Alexander provides a welcome perspective of the conflict as seen by a journalist. So again we are indebted to Bill Styple for making this resource available.

Edwin C. Bearss
Historian Emeritus
National Park Service

Preface

"His life was a historic one"—so began the obituary of Peter Wellington Alexander, former Confederate War Correspondent. In the autumn of 1886, newspapers throughout the southern United States eulogized their esteemed colleague, taking great care in memorializing the passing of another hero of the Lost Cause. This particular hero was different in some respects, for he never led a cavalry charge, commanded a battery, or even shouldered a musket. During the War Between the States, his weapon was not the sword but the pen, and in a time when so many lives were freely given for country and cause, Peter Wellington Alexander was honored as someone who gave his country more than most.

Under the bylines "P. W. A." or simply "A.," Alexander wrote nearly 800 dispatches from the scenes of conflict for the Savannah *Republican*, Atlanta *Southern Confederacy*, Mobile *Advertiser & Register*, Richmond *Dispatch*, and even the *Times* of London. His panoramic letters vividly describe the bloodstained battlefield, the forced march, the lonely camp, the suffering hospital, and the corrupt halls of government. By the second year of the war, Alexander's letters were so widely copied and read throughout the South that "P. W. A." became a household name.

As the war progressed, few southern leaders, military or political, held as much influence in the Confederacy as did Peter Wellington Alexander. In a letter written shortly after the battle of Antietam, Alexander painted the ragged condition of Lee's footsore veterans. This letter created such a sensation in the Confederacy that the resulting public contributions of food, clothing and cash helped sustain Lee's army through the winter of 1862-'63. Alexander's letter did more for the army, as one newspaper noted, "than all the legislation passed by Congress in the past year." Another important contribution to the cause was Alexander's revelations of incompetence, militarily or otherwise. Although fiercely Confederate, Alexander spared no offender. His personal integrity and dutiful courage compelled him to criticize any incompetence or injustice if he felt it hampered the war effort.

Whether as an eyewitness to some of the Civil War's bloodiest battles—Manassas, Shiloh, Antietam, Gettysburg—or describing the privations of the common soldier, Alexander proved himself an able chronicler of events. Not overly given to propagandizing, Alexander knew he was recording history and frequently mentioned the "future historians" who may consult his work. In his battlefield correspondence, he took great care to describe events not only in the broad perspective of field commanders but also in the restricted views of the soldier in the ranks. Occasional inaccuracies, which are understandable due to the fog of war, were in most cases rectified by Alexander in follow up correspondence. Above all, Alexander faithfully portrayed the common soldier as the true heroic figure of the war; never failing to stand up for the grunts whose sufferings and sacrifices went unnoticed as generals fought for headlines. This caused Alexander to become idolized by soldiers and civilians alike and led him to achieve celebrity status throughout the South, earning the sobriquet "the Prince of Correspondents."

At the close of the conflict, Alexander was urged by many to write a comprehensive history of the Confederacy, or at the very least, publish his wartime correspondence in the form of a book; unfortunately, he had failed to maintain an archive of his work. Alexander looked to his former readers for assistance, and through advertisements placed in southern newspapers, he collected his old correspondence.   He also asked former Confederate commanders to allow him to examine their military and personal papers; a few complied. Alexander eventually assembled a massive archive of letters, documents, scrapbooks, manuscripts, and newspapers, totaling nearly 7,500 items. However, for reasons unknown, he never turned this material into a book. Fortunately, his archive was preserved and is now housed in the collections of Columbia University's Rare Book and Manuscript Library. Serving as a primary source, Alexander's letters are invaluable to all students of the Civil War: for as a war correspondent, he has few equals; as a chronicler of the Confederacy, he stands alone.

I have selected over 200 letters for this book, basing my selection on their importance, content, and ability to guide the reader through the conflict. I have made all effort to preserve the integrity of the Alexander correspondence: the letters appear under their original headline and in the order in which they were written, along with their publication date; places, dates and names appear in brackets; any original editorial comments appear in braces; my editorial comments appear in italics. Misspellings whether by Alexander or the paper's typesetter, have been left uncorrected and without a *sic*.

It is with great pleasure that I would like to thank all of those who have assisted me in the preparation of this volume. My sincere thanks to Sonia Krutzke, Jack Fitzpatrick, Brian Pohanka, Ed Bearss, Tom Brown, Doug Reed, Jim Nevins, John Valori, Jeffrey Wert, Horace Mewborn, Bernard Crystal and the librarians at the Columbia University Rare Book and Manuscript Library, Seton Hall University, University of Georgia, and the Kearny Public Library.   Special love to my wife Nancy, and children Kimberlee and Bradford.

Beginnings

Peter Wellington Alexander, son of Peter and Mary Marks Alexander, was born on March 21, 1825 in Elbert County, Georgia. Very little is known about his early life; the only family history is a 1910 letter by his widow, Marie Theresa Shorter Alexander, in which she sparingly records a few biographical facts about her late husband. According to Marie Theresa, young Peter attended "the best schools in his neighborhood," preparing himself for entrance to the University of Georgia at Athens. While studying English composition, Alexander surpassed his fellow students as a writer and in other academic respects as well. He finished near the top of the class of 1844; second only to the famous orator and future Confederate States senator, Benjamin H. Hill—whom Marie Theresa described as "one of Mr. Alexander's most loyal and devoted friends." Upon graduating, Alexander decided to take a course in law and remained in Athens for that purpose until conclusion of the term. Being admitted to the bar in 1845, Alexander proceeded to Savannah to establish his law practice. In order to supplement his income, Alexander wrote political articles for the Savannah *Republican*—the leading "organ" of the Whig party in Georgia. These articles illuminated Alexander's ability as a writer, and eventually he rose to the position of editor-in-chief of the *Republican* from 1853-1857. The editorship resulted in much stress due to overwork, and Alexander's physician ordered him to give up the daily operations of the newspaper and consider moving inland to a different climate to improve his health. Alexander left Savannah and made Thomaston, Georgia his home.

On July 4, 1860, the United States of America celebrated its 84th birthday. The "peculiar institution" of Slavery was practiced in fifteen of its thirty-six states, and political debate over whether to expand slavery into the new territories or abolish the practice entirely had been a divisive topic for decades.

In disagreement over the results of the presidential election of 1860, the State of South Carolina seceded from the United States on December 20, declaring itself free and independent from the old Union. Talk of a Confederacy of Cotton States was fast becoming reality as other slave states began to contemplate secession. Mississippi, Florida and Alabama soon followed South Carolina's example. It wasn't just sectional politics anymore; the United States began to fragment.

Although Peter Wellington Alexander firmly believed any state had the constitutional right to secede from the Union, he was a most decided anti-secessionist. "Mr. Alexander felt that the grievances under which the South suffered should have been fought out in Congress," Marie Theresa recalled, "and always contended that we should not have given up the Flag, which belonged equally to the South as to the North." Despite his Unionist feelings, Alexander was appointed a delegate to the convention meeting at the State Capital at Milledgeville during the third week of January 1861. Alexander went feeling assured that he would vote against the act of secession, but upon arrival he realized that the secessionists were no longer in the minority. "They fought it bitterly," said Marie Theresa, "but the anti-secessionists were hopeless of preventing what they considered the suicide of the State; they at last signed the ordinance of secession knowing that if it was to be it was most desirable that it should be unanimous." Peter Wellington Alexander's signature was second to last on the list— immediately preceding the signature of Alexander Stephens, the future Vice-President of the Confederate States.

On January 19, 1861, Georgia became the fifth state to leave the Union. Louisiana and Texas soon followed suit.

On Monday, February 4, a convention of six of the seven seceded states met in Montgomery, Alabama to discuss unification and by Friday a constitution was adopted. The following day, former U. S. Senator and Secretary of War Jefferson Davis was unanimously elected as Provisional President of the Confederate States of America. In short, it took from December 20, 1860 to February 4, 1861—forty-six days—to shatter a country that had existed for nearly 85 years and begin a civil war that would kill 2% of its population.

Any hope of political compromise died when the shooting war began on April 12, 1861 with the Confederates firing on the United States flag at Fort Sumter in Charleston Harbor. With war commenced, the States of Virginia, Arkansas, Tennessee, and North Carolina chose to side with the Confederacy. On May 20, the Provisional Congress of the Confederacy voted to move their capital from Montgomery, Alabama to Richmond, Virginia and to convene there on July 20. Editors of the Northern press urged President Abraham Lincoln to forward the army to Richmond, arrest all traitors and prevent this convention.

Throughout the North American continent, men-of-arms, followed by war journalists, made their way to Virginia for a showdown.

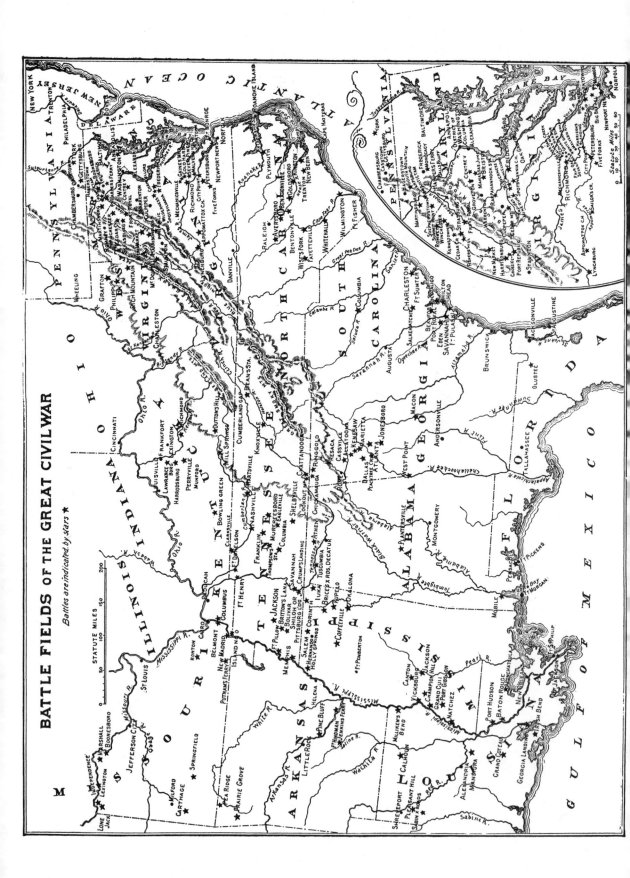

BATTLE FIELDS OF THE GREAT CIVIL WAR

Battles are indicated by Stars ★

1861

Never give up the fight

On June 7, 1861, Peter Wellington Alexander, special Virginia Correspondent for the Savannah Republican, *and the Atlanta* Southern Confederacy *arrived in the Capital of the Confederate States of America with war clouds darkening.*

Our Correspondent arrives in Virginia

RICHMOND, Virginia, June 9, 1861 [6-15-61]

The Old Dominion is one vast camp. Not only have thousands of her own sons buckled on their armor, but tens of thousands of the very flower of the chivalry of the South have rushed to her rescue. Not a train enters her borders from the West or the South that does not swell the gathering hosts. They come up from the wilds of Arkansas and Texas, from gallant Tennessee, Louisiana, Mississippi and Alabama, and foremost of all, from intrepid Georgia and South Carolina. But one spirit animates the moving legions, and that is to wash out the footprints of the invader with his own blood. There can be no such thing as peace so long as a single Abolitionist remains upon the soil.

It would be imprudent to enter into details as to our military operations. Correspondents and newspapers, as well as readers, must be patient, and learn to be content with the conviction that our civil rulers and military leaders are equal to the emergency, and that they are backed up by as gallant a set of men as ever trod the earth. Such information as it would be prudent to publish, I shall be glad to communicate to you from time to time. It should never be forgotten, however, that secrecy is one of the chief elements of military success.

The opinion is gaining ground, that it is no part of the present programme of the Federal Government to attack Norfolk; at least not until the reduction of Richmond. It is believed that a large force will be directed against the State from Ohio; another similar force from Pennsylvania; while a third *corps d'armee* will attempt to cut it way from Alexandria, and a fourth from Old Point Comfort. This last division will leave Norfolk to the left and proceed up the Peninsular between James and York Rivers, aided by a naval force. Having secured Richmond, their idea is that they will have a better footing upon which to commence negotiations for the settlement of boundaries. It is my judgment, that they would take the West bank of the Potomac for a boundary line in the North East, and the Southern line of Missouri in the North-West, and the Southern bank of the Ohio River in the North, should Kentucky come with us, *which she will do.*

Indeed, I believe that the Federal Government would settle upon this boundary now but for the political necessity that is upon them. The Republican party desire to retain their hold upon power, and to justify themselves before the Northern people, and this, they very well know, is impossible to do without first exasperating and misleading the people, and making them believe we are wrong and deserve a good thrashing, whether we get it or not. Personal and party ambition is at the bottom of the war, just as it was the moving cause of the last war that Mr. [Prime Minister William] Pitt engaged against Napoleon.

President Davis, mounted upon a snow-white charger, reviewed, yesterday afternoon, the Louisiana battalion of Washington Artillery, one of the finest bodies of soldiery on the continent. The President sits on his horse most cheerfully, and has the air of a thorough-bred chieftain. His appearance excited great enthusiasm and applause.

P. W. A.

RICHMOND, June 11, 1861 [6-15-61]

We heard rumors in town this morning of an attack early yesterday morning, upon the Yankees at Newport News, by the Confederate forces under Gen. [John B.] Magruder, late Major in the U. S. Army. It had been whispered about the city for some days, that orders had been sent to Gen. Magruder to make such an attack, and we now learn, both by way of Yorktown and Suffolk, that heavy and continued firing was heard at an early hour yesterday morning, in the direction of Newport News. It is further stated that the enemy's tents are no longer visible, though their fires were left burning. No other particulars have yet reached us. It may be that the whole rumor is without foundation.

I was present yesterday afternoon at Howard's Grove, when President Davis, accompanied by Gov. [John] Letcher, reviewed the 1st Georgia Regiment, Col. [James N.] Ramsey. At the conclusion of the review, the President, sitting on his splendid white charger, addressed the regiment in a few soul-stirring words, in the course of which he paid them, and the gallant State from whence they came, a high compliment. Col. Ramsey called for three cheers for the Warrior President, which were given by the regiment with a heartiness that almost made the ground tremble beneath our feet. Though not the usual way of manifesting respect in military circles, still, it seemed to gratify the President, who gracefully bowed his acknowledgments.

Gov. Letcher, a round-headed, fussy-looking sort of personage, was introduced to the Regiment by Col. Ramsey, when he availed himself of the occasion to inform them, that he should accompany the regiment and the other forces ordered to the north-western part of the State.

It is said that the 1st Georgia Regiment has done more hard work than any regiment in the service. It was the first to reach Pensacola, and from the day of their arrival until that of their departure, they were engaged, almost without intermission, in throwing up sand batteries, building bomb-proof magazines, and drawing heavy cannon from a fourth to a half mile through the deep sand and burning sun. This service has rendered them a hardy, athletic, sunburnt set of fellows, equal to any emergency, and capable of thrashing double their number of bluenoses out of their boots. I was present when Col. Ramsey read out the order to proceed over the mountains to Phillippi. He added a word or two of patriotic remark, and concluded by pointing his bony finger to the northwest and saying, "There is the road to the enemy—to-morrow we march." The remark seemed to electrify the regiment, who sent up a shout that would have made old Abe tremble in his shoes, if he could have heard it.

It is not thought here that there will be any general engagement for some weeks. Neither side is fully prepared, though they both have sufficient forces in the field to get up a grand affair. Volunteers, however, require time to drill and to become equipped for active duty, and especially in time required in organizing the commissary's and quarter-master's departments. There will be more or less skirmishing every day or two, and it may be that some of these skirmishes will lead to a general battle at some of the many points where the hostile forces are in close proximity to each other; as, for instance, in the direction of Newport News, Manassas Gap and Harper's Ferry. When the contest begins in earnest, the fighting will be rapid and bloody.

I do not believe I have mentioned yet the names of the several officers who are in command at the important points along the frontier. Gen. [Benjamin] Huger, the best officer in the ordnance department of the late U. S. Army, has charge of the forces in and about Norfolk. Gen. Magruder, who was a Major, and one of the finest officers in the late service, has command at Yorktown. Gen. [Pierre G. T.] Beauregard at Manassas Gap; Gen. [Joseph E.] Johnston at Harper's Ferry, and Gen. [Robert S.] Garnett at Phillippi. There was no better officers in the late army than Johnston and Garnett. It is understood that for the present, Maj.

Gen. [Robert E.] Lee is chief in command of all these forces, though it is reported that all orders of a general nature proceed directly from the President. Whether the President will take the field is not yet certainly known, though such is the general belief. He keeps his own councils; and, as a general rule, when you hear that he is *going* to do a thing, you may set it down as untrue. His intentions are only known by what he *has already done.*

While at Craney Island, below Norfolk, last week, I saw a large number of free negroes at work upon the batteries, and was told that 300 had volunteered their services from Petersburg alone. They are doing good service, for which they receive ample compensation. The abolition forces along the line of the Potomac steal and entice away all the slaves that come within their reach, and then put them to hard work, in the face of all their fair promises.

P. W. A.

RICHMOND, June 12, 1861 [6-15-61]

I am glad to inform you that later intelligence from Yorktown, received this afternoon, confirms the previous reports in regard to the affair at Bethel Church. Full particulars have not yet come to hand, or, if they have, they are in the possession of the authorities, and have not been given to the public. Nor has the exact number of the killed and wounded on the enemy's side been ascertained; but a gentleman just from the scene of the action tells me that the enemy lost about 70 killed, and about 200 wounded. The Yankees were shrewd, or humane enough—I can't tell which—to remove their dead and wounded as fast as the disastrous circumstances of the battle would allow them; otherwise, we might have obtained more precise information as to the casualties of the day.

Among the killed, was Capt. Waldrop [Maj. Theodore Winthrop], of the famous New York Seventh Regiment. As you are aware, his Regiment had returned to New York from their champagne—I mean their campaign—in Washington. His sword, with patriotic inscriptions upon its shining steel, is now in Richmond, as well as his pistols, epauletts, &c.

The most remarkable part of the affair, is the fact that we lost only one man—named [Henry W.] Wyatt—and had but few wounded.

The following, just to hand from Yorktown, contains interesting details not before received:

YORKTOWN, June 11, 1861.

An engagement, lasting four hours, took place yesterday (Monday) between five regiments of the troops from Old Point, and 1,100 Confederate troops, consisting of Virginians and North Carolinians, under General Magruder, at Bethel Church, York county. Before telling you of the battle, I will give you some circumstance preceding it. About two weeks ago, a party of 300 Yankees came up from Hampton, and occupied Bethel Church, which position they held a day or two and then retired, leaving written on the walls of the Church several inscriptions, such as, "Death to Traitors!" "Down with the Rebels!" &c. To nearly all of these the names of the writers were defiantly signed, and all the pensmen signed themselves as from New York except one, who was from "Boston, Mass., U. S." To these excursions into the interior, of which this was the boldest, Gen. Magruder determined to put a stop, and accordingly filled the place, after the Yankees left, with a few companies of his own troops. In addition to this, he determined to carry the war into the enemy's country, and on Wednesday [June 5] last, [Capt. Robert] Standard's battery of the Howitzer Battalion, was ordered down to the Church, where it soon was joined by a portion of Brown's battery of the same corps. The North Carolina Regiment, under Colonel [Daniel H.] Hill, was also there, making in all about 1,100 men, and seven Howitzer guns.

On Saturday last [June 8] the first excursions of considerable importance was made. A detachment of 200 Infantry and a Howitzer gun under Major [George] Randolph, and one of 70 infantry and another Howitzer under Maj. James Lane, of the N. C. Regiment, started different routes to cut off a party which had left Hampton. The party was seen and fired at by Maj. Randolph's detachment, but made such fast time that they escaped. The troops under Maj. Lane passed within sight of Hampton, and as they turned up the road to return to Bethel, encountered the Yankees, numbering about 90, who were entrenched behind a fence in the field, protected by a high bank. Our advance guard fired on them, and in another moment the

North Carolinians were dashing over the fence in regular French (not New York) Zouave style, firing at them in real squirrel hunting style. The Yankees fled for their lives, after firing about three minutes without effect, leaving behind them three dead and a prisoner. The fellow was a stout, ugly fellow from Troy, N. Y. He said that he had nothing against the South, but somebody must be soldiers, and he thought he had as well enlist. None of our men were hurt.

This bold excursion, under the very guns of the enemy, determined the authorities at Old Point to put a stop to it and clear us out of Bethel. This determination was conveyed to us by persons who came from the neighborhood of the enemy. On Monday morning [June 10] about 600 Infantry and two guns, under Gen. Magruder, left the camp and proceeded towards Hampton; but after advancing a mile or two, received information that the Yankees were coming in large force. We then retired, and after reaching camp the guns were placed in battery, and the infantry took their places behind their breastwork. Everybody was cool, and all were anxious to give the invaders a good reception.

About 9 o'clock the glittering bayonets of the enemy appeared on the hill opposite, and above them waved the Star Spangled Banner. The moment the head of the column advanced far enough to show one or two companies, the Parrott gun of the Howitzer Battery opened on them, throwing a shell right into their midst. Their ranks broke in confusion, and the column, or as much of it as we could see, retreated behind two small farm houses. From their position a fire was opened on us, which was replied to by our battery, which commanded the route of their approach. Our firing was excellent, and the shells scattered in all directions when they burst. Within our encampment fell a perfect hailstorm of canister shot, bullets and balls. Remarkable to say, not one of our men was killed inside of our encampment. Several horses were slain by the shells and bullets.

Finding that bombardment would not answer, the enemy, about 11 o'clock, tried to carry the position by assault, but met a terrible repulse at the hands of the infantry as he tried to scale the breastworks. The men disregarded sometimes the defences erected for them, and, leaping on the embankment, stood and fired at the Yankees, cutting them down as they came up. One company of the New York Seventh Regiment, under Captain Winthrop, attempted to take the redoubt on the left. The marsh they crossed was strewn with their bodies. Their Captain, a fine looking man, reached the fence, and, leaping on a log, waved his sword, crying, "Come on boys; one charge, and the day is ours." The words were his last, for a Carolina rifle ended his life the next moment, and his men fled in terror back. At the redoubt on the right, a company of about 300 New York Zouaves charged one of our guns, but could not stand the fire of the infantry, and retreated precipitately.

During the charges the main body of the enemy, on the hill, were attempting to concentrate for a general assault, but the shell from our Howitzer Battery prevented them. As one regiment would give up the effort, another would be marched into position, but with no better success, for a shell would scatter them like chaff. The men did not seem able to stand fire at all.

About one o'clock, their guns were silenced, and a few moments after their infantry retreated precipitately down the road to Hampton.

Our Cavalry, numbering three companies, went in pursuit, and harassed them down to the edge of Hampton. As they retreated, many of the wounded fell along the road and died, and the whole road to Hampton was strewn with haversacks, overcoats, canteens, muskets, &c., which the men had thrown off in their retreat.

After the battle, I visited the position they held. The houses behind which they had been hid had been burnt by our troops. Around the yard were the dead bodies of the men who had been killed by our cannon, mangled in the most frightful manner by the shells. The uniforms on the bodies were very different, and many of them are like those of the Virginia soldiery. A little farther on we came to the point to which they had carried some of their wounded, who have since died. The gay looking uniforms of the New York Zouaves contrasted greatly with the paled, fixed faces of their dead owners. Going to the swamp through which they attempted to pass to assault our lines, presented another bloody scene. Bodies dotted the black morass from one end to the other.

I saw one boyish, delicate-looking fellow lying on the mud, with a bullet hole through his breast, his hand was pressed on the wound from which his lifeblood had poured, and the other was clenched in the grass that grew near him. Lying on the ground was a Testament which had fallen from his pocket, daubed with blood. On opening the cover I found the printed inscription, "Presented to the defenders of their Country, by the New York Bible Society." An U. S. flag was also stamped on the title page.

Among the haversacks picked up along the route were many letters from the Northern States, asking if they liked the Southern farms, and if the Southern barbarians had been whipped out yet.

The force of the enemy brought against us was 4,000, according to the statement of the six prisoners we took. Ours was 1,100. Their loss in killed and wounded must be nearly 200. Our loss is one killed and three wounded. The fatal case was that of a North Carolinian who volunteered to fire one of the houses behind which they were stationed. He started from the breastwork to accomplish it, but was shot in the head. He died this morning at the hospital.

The Louisiana Regiment arrived about one hour after the fight was over. They are a fine looking set of fellows.

As there was a force enough at Old Point to send up to Bethel and surround us, we took up the line of march and came up to Yorktown, where we now are.

P. W. A.

Official casualties for the battle of Bethel Church: Federals, 18 killed, 53 wounded, and 5 missing for 76 casualties; Confederates, 1 killed and 7 wounded.

RICHMOND, June 17, 1861 [6-21-61]

The most notable feature in the news of to-day, is the evacuation of Harper's Ferry by the Confederate forces under General Johnston, and their withdrawal in the direction of Winchester. This last named place is the principal town in Frederick county, and the point of junction of the Harper's Ferry Railroad, and the Alexandria, Loudon & Hampshire Road, leading to the Westward. It is considered by military authorities to be an important strategic point, the occupation of which is deemed indispensable to the complete maintenance of our ultimate line of defense. Previous to the abandonment of Harper's Ferry, the bridge, which is represented to have cost near $1,000,000 was burned, and the armory and other public buildings destroyed. The provisions and ammunition were removed, as, I presume, the heavy guns were.

Not being a military man, I am unable to give you the reasons which influenced the authorities to order the evacuation of this important point. A glance at the map will satisfy any intelligent mind, however, that Harper's Ferry was too far in advance for a line of defense, having Manassas Junction for its center. Had the Potomac been our line of defense, then the possession of the Ferry would have been of the first importance. As it is, it was of but little use to us, except as a basis for offensive operations, which as I am informed, constitutes no part of our present military policy. Besides, the Federal forces were threatening Romney, with the view to the ultimate occupation of Winchester, in which event, they would have had Harper's Ferry, as it were, in a sack, from which there would have been no escape. It is true, they might not have been able to reduce the place, so thoroughly was it fortified, yet they could have starved our forces into submission. It would have been impossible, moreover, without occupying Winchester, for us to have prevented the junction of the column led on from the West by Gen. [George B.] McClellan, and that led down from Pennsylvania by Gen. [Robert] Patterson; and having united their forces, the fall of Harper's Ferry would have been only a question of time.

But whether my speculations be reasonable or the reverse, I am satisfied that if the place has really been abandoned—and all the reports concur in saying it has been—the reasons for it are good and sufficient. The Government, as well as our military operations, has been conducted with great tact and sagacity, and my confidence in their prudence and wisdom, is unlimited. This confidence is shared by the army and the public generally, as far as I have been able to learn. And it is well that it is so; for it strengthens the hands of those in authority and enables them to give all their attention and energies to the enemy.

You would be amused to read the accounts in the Northern papers of the late brilliant battle at Bethel Church. They were not prepared for such a reverse and they offer an excuse for their defeat. Some of them say that their supply of ammunition having become exhausted, Gen. [Ebenezer] Pierce (who was in command of their motley regiments) was forced to fall back. In the next breath they charge him with incompetencey, and even accuse Gen. [Benjamin] Butler of great negligence in not having taken the command himself. Some go so far as to charge the whole disaster to the inordinate vanity of the latter, who is ever seeking occasions to get his name before the public. They try also to conceal the number of their dead and wounded, while they exaggerate our losses most ridiculously. They set down our forces, which were only 1,100, at twice their real number, and say that we had a number of concealed batteries of rifled cannon. The New York *Times* speaks of Butler and Pierce as two Massachusetts barristers, who ought to be dismissed to their special pleadings and demurrers—the petty warfare of the bar, at which they are expert, and competent military men assigned to the command whose movements are not regulated by a desire to pave the way to the Presidency.

P. W. A.

The much-desired contest between the two armies of the North and South seemed imminent. With Federal forces occupying Alexandria, Virginia, a Confederate army—the Army of the Potomac, nearly 15,000 strong, began to assemble at Manassas Junction, only 20 miles from Washington, D. C.

Our Correspondent going to the Seat of War

RICHMOND, June 25, 1861 [6-30-61]

I have just returned from the War Office where I went to get a pass or permit, to proceed to Manassas. Just think of a citizen of the Empire State of the South, "Native, and to the manor born," having to procure a ticket before he can be allowed to move about in the good Old Dominion, where the bones of his ancestors repose! And yet your correspondent dare not complain. Indeed, this precaution on the part of our military authorities, is rendered necessary, by the fact, that there is a large number of spies scattered throughout the State. With few exceptions, these spies are men of Northern birth, but who have heretofore removed to Virginia, and are now residing here. A large portion of the population about the Navy Yard at Norfolk, and the Armory at Harper's Ferry, and especially in the Western part of the State, is made up of emigrants from the Free States. They constitute a majority of the inhabitants in some of the North-Western counties; and hence the rebellion in that section, under the lead of Carlisle and the Wheeling convention. You have already seen the [West Virginia] Declaration of Independence which that tory convention has issued. They proceed upon the assumption that the legal authorities of the State, by withdrawing the commonwealth from the Union, have abdicated their offices and left them vacant; and hence they have appointed a Governor and Lieut. Governor, and are proceeding to organize, if not anew for the whole State, then for one they propose to create out of a few disaffected counties beyond the Blue Ridge.

At last accounts, there was a good prospect that this nest of traitors would soon be dispersed. Gen. Garnett was within a few miles of Philippi, and I have heretofore informed you that Gen. [Henry A.] Wise's legion was gathering along the crests of the mountains, ready to pounce upon the enemy. The impression is gaining ground here, that there is too much surplus hemp in Virginia, any way, and that some of it might be used to advantage. The authorities here, however, are rather slow coaches—I mean the State authorities. There is a score of traitors here in Richmond, right under the nose of the Governor, and they might be detected if the proper efforts were made. The members of the Convention are busily engaged in ventilating their peculiar theories about the famous resolutions of '98; while many of the "first families" are devoting no small part of their time to "the wild hunt after office." Under these circumstances, one need not be surprised that some things are not done that should be done. But the advent here of the President and his Cabinet, has infused new life into the public service; and the consequences is, that resident traitors and Hessian soldiers will have to make tracks soon.

There is reason to believe that the Washington Government would be glad to enter upon negotiations for peace, if they were not afraid of the demon they have conjured up in their midst. The commercial, shipping, manufacturing and monied classes are ripe for peace; but the infamous politicians and mendacious newspapers, which control the multitude, and the vast army of mendicants in the shape of contractors, purveyors, and office-hunters, will not consent. Lincoln and [William] Seward have raised a whirlwind which they can neither ride nor control. [Horace] Greeley is already threatening them with the power behind the throne.

And yet your correspondent believes we shall have peace by Christmas, and for the simple reason, that the North is too poor to carry on the war. The people there have had a large trade, and have made a good deal of money; but, with the loss of the South, they are very much in the condition of a planter with a hundred slaves and no land to work them upon. They make nothing of consequence to export, except breadstuffs, and then only when the crops are short in England and along the Baltic and Black seas. With the exception of iron, they produce but little of the raw material of which their manufacturers are composed. They cannot compete with European manufacturers, and we, who have heretofore taken ninety-nine-hundredths of their surplus wares and fabrics, are now buying nothing from them. Nor are they importing anything worth naming, as their own papers admit. And, with the loss of Southern trade and Southern cotton, their ships, as well as their cotton mills, must be idle. Where, then, is the money to come from to carry on this war?

You need not look to Mr. Lincoln's forthcoming message to ascertain the future policy of his Government. That will be full of big talk, you may be sure. If you desire to get at the true feeling and intention of the Government, you should look to the report of the Secretary of the Treasury—not the surface, or the mere verbiage, or hostile tone of the report, but to the literal meaning of it, when stripped of its outside trappings. If he recommends the establishment of a National Bank, or a resort to direct taxation, or any other feasible plan for raising large sums of money, then you many rest satisfied that the Government means *war*—otherwise, it will be for peace.

But my permit lies before me, and my landlady has filled my haversack with three days rations, and, like Gen. Beauregard, I shall proceed to extend my lines in the direction of the enemy. Having promised some of my friends a *scalp*, I must proceed to redeem the pledge. It may be that your correspondent will lose his own scalp in the undertaking. Well, a man should learn to give as well as take. So, here goes.

P. W. A.

FAIRFAX COURT HOUSE, June 28, 1861 [7-3-61]

Leaving Richmond yesterday morning, I arrived at Manassas Junction, the headquarters of General Beauregard, at 2 P. M. A slight investigation satisfied me that the Junction was not the place for one to cast his tent who desired to witness a battle; and, therefore, following the example of the army, I advanced my lines to this place, twelve miles nearer to the enemy. It is fourteen miles from Fairfax to Alexandria, and fifteen miles on a direct line to Washington City. The advanced posts of Hessians are not exceeding six miles from where I now sit; and their drums can be distinctly heard from my window, as they beat their evening and morning calls. This letter is written, therefore, as it were from the mouth of the enemy's guns.

It sends the blood through the heart in a more tumultuous flow, when one reflects that he is separated from the hated despot who would blast his native land, by a space of only fifteen miles. How the patriot longs to clear the intervening distance by a bound, and to throttle the tyrant upon his blood stained throne! Nominally, Mr. Lincoln is a republican President—really he is a despot, the violator of his country's laws, the usurper of its rights and liberties, and the base and beastly oppressor of the people. The honored seat of the peerless Washington has become the throne of a fanatical and ignorant barbarian, who has banished all law and destroyed every right. Many a gallant heart looks wistfully towards the Potomac, and beats all the more rapidly as the happy day approaches when the order shall be given to advance. Depend on it, if the line of march be taken up, there will be no retreat until the vultures shall have been driven out of the temple of liberty.

You will not expect me to enter into particulars in a letter from this place, either as to the number and disposition of our forces, or their future movements. Indeed, very little is known as to the plans of Gen. Beauregard, who possesses in an eminent degree the military virtue of silence. One can only judge of his intentions by what he does, and our convictions in this regard are the result rather of a logical process than of any positive information. A somewhat inquisitive person approached the General some days ago, in the vain hope of extracting something, when he curtly replied, that if his own coat knew what his intentions were, he would throw it into the fire and burn it up. I can only promise, therefore, to give you such general news, as it would be proper to communicate. If anything decisive should occur, I will endeavor to supply you with full and readable information, should the fortunes of the battlefield leave me a survivor.

On our arrival here last night, we heard of one of those daring exploits for which the present campaign is distinguished. The heroes were two Texans—Colonel B. Frank Terry, a large planter, and the brother of the famous Judge [David] Terry of California, and Capt. T. S. Lubbock, a brother of the Lieutenant-Governor of Texas. They had just arrived here, and this was the first time they had been out. They proceeded to within four miles of Alexandria, where, from the top of a hill, they had a full view of the Potomac and Washington City. They gradually picked their way in between two advance posts, and descrying a vidette before them, they made a bold dash at him. The Lincolnite turned his horse's head towards Alexandria, and putting spurs to him, made all possible haste to escape. Nothing daunted, the rangers engaged in the pursuit. Colonel Terry, who had the fleetest horse, was evidently gaining upon the "flying Dutchman," and the race was becoming decidedly interesting, when Captain Lubbock discovered the picket camp and called to his companion to beware; but it was now too late; and besides, the Colonel could not control his impetuous horse, (a new one and not well trained which he had purchased in Richmond,) and ere he was aware of it, he had dashed into the little camp and flushed up the enemy as if they had been a flock of partridges. They stood aghast at the apparition; but on the frightened Yankee fled, and on the stalwart Colonel rushed their horses at the top of their speed. At length, getting within 150 paces of him, the Colonel brought down his rifle upon him, but owing to the awkwardness of his horse, the shot did not take effect. Intent, however, upon bagging his game, and forgetful of himself, he pulled down upon him once more with his navy pistol at a shorter distance—and seeing him fall upon his horse's neck, he turned his own and went in pursuit of the squad of five whom he had surprised at their camp. Three of them had fled; the other two—an old United States Dragoon and a Zouave, he and his companion captured, and with them, a fine horse and all their arms—all of which they brought into Fairfax last night. Col. Terry is six feet three inches in height, and though an exceedingly quiet and modest man, one might fancy that he does not look unlike a thunderbolt when in full pursuit of an enemy.

P. W. A.

Interesting Sketch of Jackson and the Killing of Ellsworth
MANASSAS JUNCTION, Virginia, July 10, 1861 [7-15-61]

I have returned from Fairfax Court House, the advanced post of the Confederate forces in the direction of Alexandria, to this place, the head-quarters of Gen. Beauregard, and shall proceed by the first train to Richmond, whither I go to procure stationery, which is not to be had anywhere in the country, and to lay certain matters before the authorities. You cannot get so much as a sheet of any kind of writing paper either at Fairfax village or this place, and ten days ago I wrote to Richmond, and then sent a telegram, to have a supply forwarded to me by Express; but nothing has been heard of the parcel up to this time. One is surprised that the merchants do not keep such articles on hand. They have been asked again and again to do so, and perhaps about the time the army moves from this region, the miserable old fogies will have made up their minds and laid in a supply, which, it is hoped, they will have on hand the balance of their lives.

Before leaving Fairfax, I called to pay my respects to Mrs. Susan M. Jackson, the widow of James W. Jackson, the martyr who fell in Alexandria on the 24th of May, in the cause of Southern liberty. She resides in a neat little cottage near the Court House, provided for her by Maj. Henry W. Thomas who married a sister of her husband. She received me with great kindness, and spoke with deep emotion of the generosity of the Southern people towards herself and family. She has three lovely children with her—all daughters—of the ages of thirteen, ten and seven, one of whom is said to bear a striking resemblance to her father. Mrs. Thomas has two daguerreotypes of the hero, one of which was taken while he was at work in his garden with his hat, coat and vest off. It is a very striking face, and bears abundant evidence of gallantry and unshrinking courage. He has the eye of an eagle. His features are bold and striking, and his hair is thick and stiff, and stands up like Gen. Andrew Jackson's, as if in defiance of all the hats in the world. No physiognomist can look upon the "counterfeit presentment" without feeling that he was every inch a hero, and that his was as gallant a spirit as was ever offered up in defense of his country's flag. You will be glad to learn that his likeness will be multiplied in duetime by every means of art, so that every one may obtain a copy who desires it.

There are certain facts connected with the life and death of Jackson which I have never seen in print, and which cannot fail to interest your readers. He was born in Fairfax county near the Potomac River, and was 38 years old the 8th of May [1861]. He married his wife in Kentucky, while on a visit to his brother who resides in that State, and some few years thereafter he removed to Fairfax Court House, where he continued to live until December. He was the life of the village—a generous, open-hearted fellow, wholly unselfish, a great lover of children and young people, always took sides with the weaker party, spake his own mind freely though not offensively, scorned everything that was little and mean, and feared no man living or dead. You will not be surprised to hear that such a man did not accumulate much of the "thrift that follows fawning." Fond of society, he leased the Marshall House in Alexandria, fitted it out with new furniture and table ware, and removed there the first of the present year.—He is the same man who cut down the Lincoln pole in Occoquan, in the adjoining county of Prince William, last summer.

Jackson was asleep in the second story where [Col. Elmer E.] Ellsworth entered his house (about daybreak) and proceeded to the roof to take down his flag. The servant who aroused him, told him that the house was full of Lincoln men, and that some of them had gone up after the flag, and begged him not to leave his room. He rose immediately, and slipping on his pants, seized his double barreled shot gun at the head of his bed, and had reached the first turn in the stairway leading to the third story, where he met Ellsworth coming down with the flag wrapped around him and followed by a number of Zouaves. Without uttering a word—it was enough that his flag had been taken down—Jackson shot him through the heart, the load carrying a part of the flag like a piece of patching into the heart itself where it was afterward found. One of the Zouaves fired almost at the same instant upon Jackson, who was standing a little below and looking up the stairway. The ball of the Zouave struck him just between the eyes on the bridge of the nose, and passed out at the back of his head. Though in the very article of death, the hero returned the fire of the enemy as he was falling, but without effect, the load passing near his head, burying itself in the wall above.

Notwithstanding he was down and dead, the cowardly rascals rushed upon him, one stabbing him with a bowie knife in the stomach, and another driving his bayonet through his body and actually pinning it to the floor. In this position the corpse was kept from early dawn until 11 o'clock, before any of his friends or even his family were allowed either to see it or remove it. At one time it was seriously discussed among the enemy whether they should not cut the body into pieces and burn it.

At length orders came from Washington to allow the corpse to be removed. It was taken to Fairfax Court House, and thence to the old family homestead where he was born, near which his aged mother still resides, and thence beneath the trees under which he gamboled in his infancy, and near the classic Potomac in whose waters it was his want to bathe, he was buried by the side of his father. The old homestead now belongs to a Mr. Cutts, a Northern man, who has voluntarily fled from the State and taken up arms against the South. The family burying ground was reserved at the time of the sale.

Will not the generous people of the South rescue the birthplace and grave of its heroic son from the thread of the cowardly traitor who now owns it, and present it to his wife and children? His wife has not the means to purchase it; for all the furniture and other property which they had in Alexandria were burned or broken to pieces by the enemy. What better use could the money which our people are raising for their relief, be applied, than to that of the humble farm where the hero now sleeps as a permanent home for his stricken widow and weeping orphans?

P. W. A.

On July 18, a Federal reconnaissance-in-force clashed with Confederate infantry along Bull Run near Blackburn's Ford, Va.

Our Correspondent Arrives at Manassas
ARMY OF THE POTOMAC,
MANASSAS JUNCTION, July 20, 1861 [7-26-61]

I arrived here late this afternoon, having left Richmond early this morning and been on the road nearly the whole day. The use of the road for the past few days has been surrendered up almost entirely to the military authorities, and so great is the demand for transportation by the War Department, that it is with difficulty that the trains can manage to get through under less than ten to twelve hours.

As the great battle of the campaign will, in all probability, have been fought and decided before this reaches you, it will not be amiss, especially since the fact is already known to the enemy, to say that General Johnston has arrived here from Winchester with the greater part of his forces recently stationed at that place. What is the precise number of the troops brought with him, I am unable to say. Some of them are still on the road, and are expected to get in sometime to-night. Among those who reached here to-day, were the 7th, 9th, and 11th Georgia Regiments, under Colonel [Francis S.] Bartow, [Lucius J.] Gartrell and [Edward R.] Goulding, the brigade under the command of Col. Bartow. I have not been able to see any one who is attached to the brigade, owing to the lateness of the hour at which I arrived, but I learn that all three of the regiments were, immediately upon their arrival, ordered forward to an advanced position upon Bull's Run, near Union Mills, where the Alexandria & Manassas Railroad crosses the creek. That they will give a good account of themselves in the great battle that is impending, you may feel perfectly assured.

Gen. Johnston ranks Gen. Beauregard, and consequently he will succeed to the command, at least nominally, in the approaching conflict. This seems to have occasioned some regret among the troops who have been stationed here, since Gen. Beauregard has had all the labor of arranging the camp, perfecting the works and preparing the ground for what we all believe will be a great victory. It would be impossible, however, for any officer to supersede him in fact, though he may be outranked under the rules of the War Department. Whatever may be the result, therefore, to "little Beaury" will belong the honor, now and hereafter.

In addition to the forces brought down by Gen. Johnston, I learn that 2,300 men arrived here this morning from Aquia Creek under command of Brig. Gen. [Theophilus] Holmes. They marched across the country a distance of 30 miles since yesterday morning. This force is composed chiefly of Tennesseeans, with some companies from Arkansas. The men are said to look very much as if they would not ask for more than one bite at a Yankee.

It is generally conceded that Patterson has moved down the Potomac from Martinsburg to the relief of Gen. [Irvin] McDowell, and that he took with him his entire force. The number of the enemy now before us cannot be less than 75,000. That Gen. [Winfield] Scott will risk such an army in the hands of either McDowell or Patterson, or both of them, is not believed for one moment. When the great contest does take place, he will take the command of the Federal forces himself. If he does not, it will be because he expects defeat. Our own forces are believed to be at least a third less than those which are arrayed against us.

The impression prevails here that there will be a grand battle to-morrow, and that we will be the attacking party this time. I have been here too short a time to venture an opinion myself, but I should not be surprised if, in the next few days, we did not witness a series of active operations, culminating by or before the middle of next week in a pitched battle, in which all the forces on both sides will be engaged.

I have said nothing thus far of the battle of Bull's Run, for the reason that you will find, in the Richmond papers of this morning, and especially the *Examiner*, a better account of it than I could possibly give you. A few facts may be mentioned, however, that will not fail to interest your readers. The first is, that the battle was opened by [Thomas W.] Sherman's famous battery, under the protection of whose fire the enemy's infantry advanced upon our lines. Nearly all the shells passed over our men and exploded beyond them. Not so with the New Orleans Washington Artillery which was opposed to Sherman's battery, and whose guns did horrible execution. Indeed, it is believed that but for the precision and destructiveness of their fire, the enemy would have approached nearer and in greater numbers, and that our victory would have been greater than it was. The Federal battery changed its position fifteen times during the engagement, and at last left the field minus one of its guns which we captured, together with 501 small arms.

Soon after getting here, I encountered a little drummer boy of fourteen summers from Lynchburg, who says he went over the field soon after the battle with the hope of getting a revolver. He examined the pockets of a score or more of the dead without finding a solitary "red," his only trophy being an odd looking dirk with a buckhorn handle and a due bill for seven dollars from one Dutchman to another.

Another lad, a marker for the Alexandria Rifles, appearing upon the field, was ordered to the hospital by his Captain as a place of safety. The little fellow was not pleased with the order, though he obeyed it, but when the battle began to wax warm, he stole back and seizing the gun of a disabled soldier he succeeded in killing one Hessian and wounding the second.

Some of the officers have furnished their servants with revolvers, and it is asserted to be a fact that these negroes made several captures during the fight on Thursday. One of them, Dick Langhorn, from Lynchburg; a strapping big fellow, shot down one man, his ball taking effect through the shoulder; and when all his barrels had been discharged, he rushed upon another whom he knocked down with his pistol. Seizing the two by the collars, he started to carry them to his master, when one of them showed some disposition to resist; whereupon Dick turned to him and said: "See here, Massa, you'd better come 'long, or dis here nigger will hurt you, see ef he don't." Seeing the d—l in Dick's eye, he submitted, and the two were carried prisoners to the Colonel of the Regiment, the Eleventh Virginia.

[Col. Wade] Hampton's Legion and the 13th Mississippi Regiment have just arrived, and the 11th Mississippi is expected some time to-night. A few days would increase our forces materially. North Carolina is sending up some of the finest regiments I have seen, and about three a week.

P. W. A.

Official casualties for the July 18 skirmish at Blackburn's Ford: Federals, 19 killed, 38 wounded, and 26 missing; Confederates losses were 15 killed, 53 wounded. Three days later, the armies met again.

The Battle of Manassas
ARMY OF THE POTOMAC
Manassas, July 22, 1861 [7-27-61]

Yesterday, the 21st day of July, 1861, a great battle was fought and a great victory won by the Confederate troops. Heaven smiled on our arms, and the God of battles crowned our banners with laurels of glory. Let every patriotic heart give thanks to the Lord of Hosts for the victory He has given His people on His holy day, the blessed Sabbath.

Gen. Johnston had arrived the preceding day with about half of the force he had, detailed from Winchester, and was the senior officer in command. He magnanimously insisted, however, that Gen. Beauregard's previous plan should be carried out, and he was guided entirely by the judgement and superior local knowledge of the later. While, therefore, Gen. Johnston was nominally in command, Beauregard was really the officer and hero of the day. You will be glad to learn that he was this day advanced from a Brigadier to the rank of full General. But to the battle.

At half-past six in the morning, the enemy opened fire from a battery planted on a hill beyond Bull's Run, and nearly opposite the center of our lines. The battery was intended merely to "beat the bush," and to occupy our attention, while he moved a heavy column towards the Stone Bridge, over the same creek, upon our left. At 10 o'clock, another battery was pushed forward, and opened fire a short distance to the left of the other, and near the road leading North to Centreville. This was a battery of rifled guns, and the object of its fire was the same as that of the other. They fired promiscuously into the woods and gorges on this, the Southern side of Bull's Run, seeking to create the impression thereby that our center would be attacked, and thus prevent us from sending reinforcements to our left, where the real attack was to be made. Beauregard was not deceived by the maneuver.

It might not be amiss to say, that Bull's Run, or creek, is North of this place, and runs nearly due east, slightly curving around the Junction, the nearest part of which is about 3 ½ miles. The Stone Bridge is some seven miles distant, in a northwesterly direction, upon which our left wing rested. Mitchel's ford is directly North, distant four miles, by the road leading to Centreville, which is seven miles from the Junction. On our right is Union Mills, on the same stream, where the Alexandria and Manassas railroad crosses the Run, and distant four miles. Proceeding from Fairfax Court House, by Centreville, to Stone Bridge, the enemy passed in front of our entire line, but at a distance ranging from five to two miles.

At 9 o'clock, I reached an eminence nearly opposite the two batteries mentioned above, and which commanded a full view of the country for miles around, except on the right. From this point I could trace the movements of the approaching hosts by the clouds of dust that rose high above the surrounding hills. Our left, under Brigadier-General [Nathan G.] Evans, [Thomas J.] Jackson and [P. St. Geo.] Cocke, and Col. Bartow, with the Georgia Brigade, composed of the 7th and 8th regiments, had been put in motion, and was advancing upon the enemy with a force of about 15,000 while the enemy himself was advancing upon our left with a compact column of at least 50,000. His entire force on this side of the Potomac is estimated at 75,000. These approaching columns encountered each other at 11 o'clock.

Meanwhile, the two batteries in front kept up their fire upon the wooded hill where they supposed our center lay. They sent occasional balls, from their rifled cannon, to the eminence where your correspondent stood. Gens. Beauregard, Johnston and [Milledge] Bonham reached this point at 12, and one of these balls passed directly over and very near them, and plunged into the ground a few paces from where I stood. I have the ball now, and hope to be able to show it to you at some future day. It is an 18-pound ball, and about 6 inches long. By the way, this thing of taking notes amidst a shower of shells and balls is more exciting than pleasant. At a quarter past 12, Johnston and Beauregard galloped rapidly forward in the direction of Stone Bridge, where the ball had now fully opened. Your correspondent followed their example, and soon reached a position in front of the battlefield.

The artillery were the first to open fire, precisely at 11 o'clock. By half-past 11, the infantry had engaged, and there it was that the battle began to rage. The dusky columns which had thus far marked the approach of the two armies, now mingled with great clouds of smoke, as it rose from the flashing guns below, and the two shot up together like a huge pyramid of red and blue. The shock was tremendous, as were the odds between the two forces. With what anxious hearts did we watch the pyramid of smoke and dust! When it moved to the right, we knew the enemy were giving way; and when it moved to the left, we knew that our friends were receding. Twice the pyramid moved to the right, and as often returned. At last, about two o'clock, it began to move slowly to the left, and thus it continued to move for two mortal hours. The enemy was seeking to turn our left flank, and to reach the railroad leading hence in the direction of Winchester. To do this, he extended his lines, which he was enabled to do by reason of his great numbers. This was unfortunate for us, as it required a corresponding extension of our own lines to prevent his extreme right from outflanking us—a movement on our part which weakened the force of our resistance along the whole line of battle, which finally extended over a space of two miles. It also rendered it more difficult to bring up reinforcements, as the further the enemy extended his right, the greater the distance reserve forces had to travel to counteract the movement.

This effort to turn our flank was pressed with great determination for five long, weary hours, during which the tide of battle ebbed and flowed along the entire line with alternate fortunes. The enemy's column continued to stretch away to the left, like a huge anaconda, seeking to envelope us within its mighty folds and crush us to death; and at one time it really looked as if he would succeed. But here let me pause to explain why it was our reinforcements were so late in arriving, and why a certain other important movement miscarried.

The moment he discovered the enemy's order of battle, Gen. Beauregard, it is said, dispatched orders to Gen. [Richard S.] Ewell, on our extreme right, to move forward and turn his left or rear. At the same time he ordered Generals [D. R.] Jones, [James] Longstreet and Bonham, occupying the center of our lines, to cooperate in this movement, but not to move until Gen. Ewell had made the attack. The order to Gen. Ewell unfortunately miscarried. The others were delivered, but as the movements of the center were to be regulated entirely by those on the right, nothing was done at all. Had the orders to Gen. Ewell been received and carried out, and our entire force brought upon the field, we should have destroyed the enemy's army almost literally. Attacked in front, on the flank and in the rear, he could not possibly have escaped, except at the loss of thousands of prisoners and all his batteries, while the field would have been strewed with his dead.

Finding that his orders had in some way failed to be executed, Gen. Beauregard at last ordered up a portion of the forces which were intended to co operate with General Ewell. It was late, however, before these reinforcements came up. Only one brigade reached the field before the battle was won. This was led by Gen. E. K. Smith, of Florida, formerly of the United States army, and was a part of General Johnston's column from Winchester. They should have reached here the day before, but were prevented by an accident on the railroad. They dashed on the charge with loud shouts and in the most gallant style. About the same time, Maj. [Arnold] Elzey coming down the railroad from Winchester with the last of Johnston's brigades, and hearing the firing, immediately quit the train and struck across the country, and as a gracious fortune would have it, he encountered the extreme right of the enemy as he was feeling his way around our flank, and with his brigade struck him like a thunderbolt, full in the face. Finding he was about to be outflanked himself, the enemy gave way after the second fire. Meanwhile, Beauregard rallied the center and dashed into the very thickest of the fight, and after him rushed our own brave boys, with a shout that seemed to shake the very earth. The result of this movement from three distinct points, was to force back the enemy, who began to retreat, first in good order, and finally in much confusion. At this point the cavalry were ordered upon the pursuit. The retreat now became a perfect rout, and it is reported that the flying legions rushed past Centreville in the direction of Fairfax, as if the earth had been opening behind them. It was when Gen. Beauregard led the final charge, that his horse was killed by a shell.

We captured thirty-four guns, including Sherman's famous battery, a large number of small arms, thirty wagons loaded with provisions, &c., and about 700 prisoners. Among the latter, were Col. [Michael] Corcoran, of the New York Irish Zouaves, Hon. Mr. [Alfred] Ely, member of Congress, from New York, Mr. [Edward] Carrington, of this State, a nephew of the late Wm. C. Preston, who had gone over to the enemy, and thirty-two Captains, Lieutenants, &c. We came near bagging the Hon. Mr. [L. S.] Foster, Senator from Connecticut.

The official reports of the casualties of the day have not yet come in, and consequently it is impossible to say what our loss is. I can only venture an opinion, and that is, that we lost in killed, wounded and missing, about 1,500—of which about 400 were killed. The enemy's loss was terrible, being at the lowest calculation, 3,000.

Thus far I have said but little of the part taken by particular officers and regiments; for the reason that I desire first to obtain all the facts. Nor have I said anything of the gallant seventh and eighth regiments from Georgia. This part of my duty is most melancholy. It may be enough to say, that they were the only Georgia regiments here at the time, that they were among the earliest on the field, and in the thickest of the fight, and that their praise is upon the lips of the whole army, from Gen. Beauregard on down. Col. Gartrell led the seventh regiment, and Lieutenant-Colonel [William] Gardner the eighth, the whole under the command of Col. Bartow, who led them with a gallantry that was never excelled. It was when the brigade was ordered to take one of the enemy's strongest batteries, that it suffered most. It was a most desperate undertaking, and followed by the bloodiest results. The battery occupied the top of a hill, on the opposite side of Bull's Run, with a small piece of woods on the left. Descending the valley along the Run, he proceeded under cover of the hill to gain the woods alluded to, and from which he proposed to make a dash at the battery and capture it. On reaching the woods, he discovered that the battery was supported by a heavy infantry force, estimated at 4,000 men. This whole force, together with the battery, was turned upon the eighth regiment, which was in the van, with terrible effect. Indeed, he was exposed on the flank and in front to a fire that the oldest veterans could not have stood. The balls and shells from the battery, and the bullets from the small arms, literally riddled the woods. Trees six inches in diameter, and great limbs were cut off, and the ground strewn with the wreck. It became necessary to retire the eighth regiment, in order to re-form it. Meanwhile, Col. Bartow's horse had been shot from under him. It was observed that the forces with which his movement was to be supported had not come up. But it was enough that he had been ordered to storm the battery; so, placing himself at the head of the seventh regiment, he again led the charge, this time on foot, and gallantly encouraging his men as they rushed on. The first discharge from the enemy's guns killed the regimental color-bearer. Bartow immediately seized the flag, and again putting himself in the front, dashed on, flag in hand, his voice ringing clear over the battlefield, and saying, "On, my boys, we will die rather than yield or retreat." And on the brave boys *did* go, and faster flew the enemy's bullets. The fire was awful. Not less than 4,000 muskets were pouring their fatal contents upon them, while the battery itself was dealing death on every side.

The gallant Eighth Regiment, which had already passed through the distressing ordeal, again rallied, determined to stand by their chivalric Colonel to the last. The more furious the fire, the quicker became the advancing step of the two regiments. At last, and just when they were nearing the goal of their hopes, and almost in the arms of victory, the brave and noble Bartow was shot down, the ball striking him in the left breast, just above the heart. His men rallied around him, and finding him mortally wounded and that the forces that had been ordered to support their charge had not yet come up, they gradually fell back, bearing him in their arms and disputing every inch of ground. I learn that they would never have retired but for the orders which were given in consequence of the non-arrival of the supporting force. It appears that the order to support our charge, like that to Gen. Ewell, miscarried—a failure which had nearly cost us two of the best regiments in the army. Col. Bartow died soon after he was borne from the field. His last words, as repeated to me, were: "they have killed me, my brave boys, but never give up the ship—we'll whip them yet." And so we did!

The field officers of the Seventh Regiment escaped except Col. Gartrell who received a slight wound. All the superior officers in the Eighth Regiment, except Maj. Cooper, were killed or wounded. Lieut. Col. Gardner had his leg broken by a musket ball, and Adjutant [John] Branch was killed. Capt. [Columbus] Howard of the Mountain Rangers from Merriwether county was also killed. But I shall not go into a statement of the killed and wounded preferring in delicate and painful a matter to await the official report, which I hope to get to-morrow, when I shall have more to say about our heroic regiments. I will add just here, that our loss in officers was very great. Among others may be mentioned Gen. [Bernard] Bee, Lieut. Col. [B. J.] Johnson of Hampton's Legion, and Col. [F. J.] Thomas of Gen. Johnston's Staff, and others. Gen. Jackson was wounded in the hand, and Col. [C. Roberdeau] Wheat of the New Orleans Tigers was shot through the body. Col. [Egbert] Jones of the 4th Alabama Regiment it is feared was mortally wounded. The regiments that suffered most and were in the thickest of the fight, were the 7th and 8th Georgia, the 4th Alabama, 4th South Carolina, Hampton's Legion, and 4th Virginia. The New Orleans Washington Artillery did great execution.

If we consider the numbers engaged and the character of the contest, we may congratulate ourselves upon having won, one of the most brilliant victories that any race of people ever achieved. It was the greatest battle ever fought on this continent, and will take its place in history by the side of the most memorable engagements. It is believed that General

Scott himself was nearby, at Centreville, and that he directed as he had planned the whole movement. Gen. McDowell was the active commander upon the field.

President Davis arrived upon the field at 5 o'clock just as the enemy had got into full retreat. His appearance was greeted with shout after shout, and was the equivalent to a reinforcement of 5,000 men. He left Richmond at 7 in the morning.

But "little Beaury" against the world.

P. W. A.

The Magnitude of the Triumph
HEADQUARTERS OF THE ARMY OF THE POTOMAC,
MANASSAS, July 25, 1861 [7-31-61]

This is the fourth day since the great battle of Stone Bridge, and yet there is scarcely a man in the Army of the Potomac who fully appreciates the magnitude of the victory achieved by our men. Every hour fresh information is being received, which compels us to alter and add to our figures, as to the tremendous loss of the enemy in killed, wounded, missing and prisoners, and of arms, baggage and provision wagons, ammunition, camp equipments, and the outfit of an army. What was considered a success on Sunday night, is now known to be one of the greatest and most complete triumphs ever won by one army over another. If therefore, I am obliged to alter my figures in each successive communication, you should not ascribe it to negligence or recklessness in statement, but to the fact that each succeeding hour brings to light some fresh incident or additional particular.

The enemy commenced to retreat in good order, but he had not proceed far along the turnpike (which is very straight) that leads to Centreville and Fairfax, before [Capt. Del] Kemper's battery, from Alexandria, followed in pursuit, and from each succeeding hill sent a plunging fire into the ranks of the retreating army. This battery was served with great skill, and did immense damage. Meanwhile, the first regiment of Virginia cavalry, Col. Stewart [J. E. B. Stuart] commanding, engaged in the pursuit. They rushed upon the rear of the flying army with uplifted swords and deafening shouts, hewing them down and dispersing them into the woods and fields, as far as Centreville. At this point a brigade, which had been pushed forward from our center, saluted them with a deadly fire. The panic, by this time, had seized the whole army, officers, privates, amateur Congressional fighters and newspaper correspondents, all; and a perfect stampede ensued. They rushed down the turnpike, and through the fields and woods, as if a stream of burning lava had been pursuing them; and the broken, frightened and demoralized multitude never did stop until they got to Alexandria, a distance of thirty miles from the battlefield. Many of them even went on to Washington. The road, as far as Centreville, was strewn with their dead; and along the entire route to Alexandria, were to be seen great piles of baggage, arms and accoutrements that had been thrown away, broken carriages and wagons, riderless horses, and wounded and disabled fugitives.

The panic was not confined to the soldiery, but extended to the authorities at Washington; and gentlemen from that city and Alexandria say we might have driven the enemy out of both places on Monday without firing a gun, if we had continued the pursuit. Even the Washington *Star* admits the utter rout of the Federal forces. It says there is no use in trying to conceal the truth, and that the defeat and rout of its army has had but one parallel in history, and that is the battle of Waterloo. It calls upon Congress to vote another 100,000 men, and another $100,000,000. They will certainly find it necessary to raise fresh troops, for those who met us on Sunday will never do it again.

I have seen a number of prisoners, including several surgeons who are in attendance upon the enemy's wounded. They assure me that the rank and file of the Federal army had no dream that there would be a battle of Sunday morning. The idea had been inculcated among them that we would fall back upon their first appearance, as we did (for strategic reasons) at Harper's Ferry and Fairfax. Gen. McDowell issued a general order, before they left Centreville, in which he stated that the army would proceed to Manassas Junction, where they would take dinner and stay all night. Next morning they would take up the line of march for Richmond, where they would arrive by the end of the week. It was expected that there would be a little skirmishing, but nothing more, and that the bridges along the route would be destroyed. To meet this latter difficulty, he had brought with him a corps of carpenters, with their tools, and several wagonloads of bridge timber, which had been prepared, and was ready to be put up. Among our captures, were these tools and timber.

They tell me, also, that the army was accompanied by Senators [Henry] Wilson, of Massachusetts, Foster of Connecticut, [Henry] Anthony and [James] Simmons of Rhode Island, and [Lyman] Trumbull, of Illinois, Ely, of New York, and other members of the House, whose names they did not remember, who went along to add éclat to the triumphal march of the grand army from Washington to Richmond. These gentry, including a corps of correspondents and telegraphists from New York and Washington, were provided with horses, buggies, carriages, liquors and cigars, and indeed with a full outfit for a dainty taste of camp life in the "rebel provinces." Mr. Ely was captured, and it is now known, beyond all doubt, that Senator Foster was killed in his carriage by a shell, during the retreat. It is equally well known that we came near bagging the other Congressmen also.

One may imagine with what pleasurable anticipation these carpet knights with kid gloves and peg top pantaloons, set out from Washington and brought up the rear of the invading army, but what stretch of imagination will ever be able to comprehend the wild fright and frantic horror with which they headed the retreat and reappeared in the streets of the Federal Capital? As they marched out, a triumphant army led the way; as they fled back, a panic-stricken rabble came thundering at their heels, crushing and tramping each other in their headlong fright, and more terrible in their cowardly fright than in their boastful valor. "Verily, how have the mighty fallen!" They went clad in purple and gold; they came back in sackcloth and ashes.

It is impossible even now to give a correct statement of the prisoners taken; for they are still being brought in from the woods; or of the number of guns and small arms taken, or of the vast piles of provisions, munitions and ammunition captured. The number of baggage and provision wagons which we got is estimated at 150. These were heavily laden with supplies for the march to Richmond. Among other things that fell into our hands, was a handsome camp chair which was addressed to Gen. Winfield Scott, Richmond, Va. The chair will probably be taken on to Richmond by order of Little Beaury, and will await the arrival there of Gen. Scott.

The Northern papers are fruitful in excuses for the disaster which has overtaken the Federal arms. Some attribute it to our terrible "masked batteries" which crowded every hill; whereas we did not have a solitary piece of ordnance in five miles of the battlefield, except our flying artillery. Others ascribe their defeat to our overwhelming numbers, which is equally false; for the most moderate calculation puts down the enemy's forces at three times those of the Confederates. Another fellow, who is cuter than all the rest, says that a prodigious column of Confederate cavalry, 5,000 strong, appeared upon a hill of indefinite dimensions, and forming in the shape of a V, with the sharp end towards the Federal lines, they advanced, and just when they got up to them, the terrible V opened in two parallel lines, disclosing in their midst a frowning battery of 32 pounders, which mowed down their ranks like grass. All such statements are false. The truth is, it was a fair stand-up fight—such as the *Tribune* professed to desire—and it took place upon an open field of the enemy's own choosing.

The battle was a decided success, and was fought with distinguished gallantry by all our troops who participated in it. It is but just to say, however, that the Fourth Alabama, Seventh and Eighth Georgia, Fourth South Carolina, Hampton's Legion, Sixth North Carolina, and the Eleventh and Seventeenth Virginia, did the hardest fighting, suffered most and bore the brunt of the battle. Colonel [Joseph B.] Kershaw's and Col. [E. B.] Cash's (South Carolina) Regiments came into the action late, but did most effective service in the pursuit which they continued nearly to Centreville. Gen. E. K. Smith's Brigade, a portion of Gen. Johnston's Winchester forces, reached Manassas during the battle, and rushed to the field, a distance of seven miles, through the broiling sun, at double quick. As they neared the field, from a double quick, they got fairly to running, their eyes flashing, the officers crying out, "on boys, to the rescue," and the men shouting at the top of their voices. When Gen. Johnston saw Smith, he exclaimed, "the Blucher of the day has come." They soon arrived in front of the enemy, and with a shout that might be heard from one end of the battlefield to the other, they were launched at the adversary like a thunderbolt. They delivered but two fires when the enemy began to give way, and in a few minutes he was in full retreat. The Brigade is composed of one Tennessee and one Mississippi regiment, and a battalion from Maryland. As they rushed into the fight, I could but recall, with an appreciation I never felt before, the words of Holy writ— "as terrible as an army with banners."

I do not believe that I have informed you in any of my previous letters, that Col. [James] Cameron, of one of the Pennsylvania [79th N. Y.] regiments, had been killed, and that his brother, Lincoln's Secretary of War, had sent a friend—one Arnold Harris, a lobby member about Washington—to ask for his body. As he did not come under a flag of truce, Gen. Johnston ordered him into custody and sent him to Richmond. The Republican Secretary chose to ignore the existence of our authorities and the rank and position of our officers, by sending a verbal message and without a flag, just as the ministers of King George were wont to act towards Gen. Washington and the Continental Congress during the first revolution, and therefore our officers chose to send the aforesaid Mr. Harris to prison.

I have just heard that five more of Ellsworth's Zouaves—Old Abe's pet lambs—were captured to-day in the woods near Centreville, one of whom was Col. [Noah] Farnham, the successor of Ellsworth. He had been wounded, and the others remained behind to take care of him.

There are some additional facts touching the death of the lamented Bartow and the part which the 7th and 8th Georgia Regiments performed in the great battle of the 21st, which I have obtained from eye-witnesses, and which cannot fail to interest your readers. Col. Bartow fell when he was leading the Seventh in a charge upon [James] Ricketts' battery, not Sherman's. Lieut. W. P. Moon, of the Atlanta Confederate Volunteers, J. T. Lindley, of the Cobb county Confederate Guards, J. L. Dobbs of the same company, and a Virginian, picked him up and bore him off to the rear. His last words, uttered when they started off with him, as reported to me, were: "Boys, they have killed me, but never give it up." They carried him seventy-five or a hundred yards from where he fell, and laid him down; but the bullets fell so thick about him that they removed him further down the hill, where they procured some water. He drank a little, and then seemed to try to speak, but was not able. They then applied the canteen to his lips a second time, but he was unconscious and could not swallow the water. Laying him back, he died almost immediately, and without a struggle. They took off his gloves and placed them and a cartridge box under his head for a pillow. He did not live more than twenty minutes after he fell. When I first saw him, about ten o'clock at night, his face wore the smile of victorious satisfaction that led me, for a moment, to doubt the reality of his death. Hearing of his fall, Gen. Johnston sent a detachment to bring his body to headquarters, which was done, and on the following day, by order of President Davis, his remains were taken to Richmond to Mrs. Bartow. His sword, which had been previously broken by a ball, was saved, and yesterday I succeeded in getting his belt.

While on a visit yesterday to the Seventh Regiment, I had the satisfaction to examine their flag. It has fourteen bullet holes in it, and the flagstaff was struck in four places. After Col. Bartow's fall, Lieutenant [E. F.] Paxton of Virginia asked leave, the color bearer being wounded, to carry the flag. His request was granted, and he and W. L. Norman, one of the color guards, of DeKalb county, were the first to place it upon the captured battery. Eli W. Hoyle of the Atlanta Confederate Volunteers, was the first to mount the battery.

There is another incident which deserves public mention, and which shows of what kind of stuff the Georgia boys are made. Wm. DeJarnett of the Rome Light Guard, having been slightly wounded and left behind, concealed himself in the bushes. The Second Rhode Island Regiment passed by, without seeing him, but Col. [John] Slocum who commanded the regiment and who came on behind it, discovered him in the bushes. Attempting to draw his pistol he said, "your life, you rebel." For some reason he could not get out his pistol easily, and seeing DeJarnett level his musket at him, he cried out, "don't shoot." But the Georgian did shoot and killed him too. He then took to his heels through the thicket, and the regiment sent a shower of bullets after him but to no effect. I saw Slocum's grave to-day in a little cabbage garden by the side of the road not far from the battlefield, and also found their Maj. [Sullivan] Ballou of the same Regiment who had his leg shot off.

But I must stop; for if I were to go on to tell all the gallant acts of our boys, my supply of paper would soon be exhausted. All the officers in both Regiments, and every man in the ranks, did their whole duty. Major Cooper is the only field officer in the Eighth, and Col. Jas

F. Cooper, the only one in the Seventh, who escaped injury. Col. Gardner, who had his leg broken by a minnie ball, is now at a farm house, near this place, and doing very well. Major [John] Dunwoody, of the Seventh, received a slight wound in the shoulder, while his horse received four shots without being killed.

I send herewith a list of the casualties in the Eighth Georgia Regiment. There were only 550 men in the Regiment when it went into action, owing to sickness and other causes, and yet 32 were killed, 151 wounded, and 11 are missing—194 in all. More than one out of every three. In the Oglethorpe Light Infantry, Col. Bartow's old Company, only 16 men out of 87 escaped without a wound or mark of some kind, either upon their bodies or their clothing.

There is still another fact I cannot forbear to record. After the terrible fire to which the Eighth Georgia had been exposed, and which they received with the immobility of marble statues, Gen. Beauregard passed the little remnant of the Regiment that was still left, and which was ready to strike another blow; and raising his cap with undisguised admiration and sympathy, he said, "Eighth Georgia, I salute you." What a scene, and how much it implied!

P. W. A.

Further Details

HEADQUARTERS OF THE ARMY OF THE POTOMAC,
Manassas, July 27, 1861 [8-1-61]

It would really seem that one would never get through with the task of describing the great battle of Stone Bridge. There are so many interesting incidents connected with it, so many individual acts of heroism, so many phases in which the mighty struggle may be viewed, and, I regret to add, so many conflicting accounts from different parts of the field, owing to the different standpoints from which it was witnessed, that the labor of preparing a reliable and consistent account would appear to be almost interminable. I hope, however, to be able to conclude what I may have to say of the battle in this and subsequent letters. This letter will be devoted to a narrative of certain facts and details, which I have not yet alluded to, and my next will contain some account of the character and appearance of the battlefield by sunlight and by moonlight.

Your readers will be rejoiced to learn, that the wounded in the 7th and 8th Georgia Regiments, as well as the Regiments from other States, are receiving every attention that skill and sympathy can suggest. Most of them have been removed down the railway to Culpepper Court House, Orange Court House, Warrenton, Gordonsville and Richmond, and many of them are quartered with private families, where they are the recipients of the kindness and most assiduous attentions. Dr. J. F. Alexander, of Atlanta, the Surgeon of the 7th, and Dr. H. V. Miller, of Rome, the Surgeon of the 8th, and their active assistants, have nobly and efficiently performed the painful duties of their offices. I was with them for half an hour during the battle, and saw our wounded and crippled friends as they were brought back to a little clump of trees where they had established a temporary hospital. Never did men labor more successfully or indefatigably, and never did martyrs endure the tortures of the stake with more patience, and fortitude than our suffering men exhibited under the painful operations to which they submitted. I saw legs and feet taken off, arms and ghastly gashes sewed up rapidly and yet skillfully, and that too almost upon the very border of the battlefield; and yet scarcely a groan escaped the lips of the heroic sufferers. I arrived at the conclusion from what passed before my eyes, that next to a skillful field officer, the most important man on the day of battle is the Surgeon.

I have already related some of the gallant exploits of our Georgia boys. Doubtless there are many others, if I had time and opportunity to trace them up. Chs. M. Harper, of the Miller Rifles, (Floyd co.) is the hero of one of those daring feats which, while they deserve to be handed down to posterity, will serve to illustrate the prowess of the Southern army. During the dreadful fight in which the immortal Eighth was engaged, he became separated from the Regiment and was finally taken prisoner by a squad of seven federalists. He submitted gracefully and voluntarily shared with them the contents of his canteen. When one of his own Regiment passed within hailing distance, he would call to him to fall in, as it was all over with them. In this way and by the activity of his captors, some six or eight Georgians were captured. At length Harper, having tipt the wink to his comrades, turned to his captors and said: "Gentlemen, one good turn deserves another, and as you have taken us prisoners, we now take you prisoners—yield or die." At the same time he and his friends pulled down their guns upon them. The Yankees thinking prudence the better part of valor, submitted with equal grace to their altered fortunes, and were marched off by our boys and delivered to Gen. Beauregard.

I have already informed you that the grand army was accompanied by a number of Congressmen and other dignitaries. It now appears that several ladies were induced to grace the triumphal march by their presence—among others two daughters of Senator Wilson of Massachusetts, and Miss Weed, a daughter of Thurlow Weed. This last lady had been especially requested to accompany the expedition, and to plant the flag of the Union upon the Capitol in Richmond. *That* Weed perished, miserably nipped by the untimely frost of Manassas.

I have some curious and instructive envelopes picked up on the field of battle after the enemy's flight. One is embellished with the figure of a woman bearing aloft the Stars and Stripes, and underneath these words taken from the letter of Secretary [John A.] Dix to the collector at New Orleans:

"If any one attempts to haul down the American flag, shoot him on the spot."

Another is ornamented with the head of Washington, and below occurs the words:

"Preserve the land of Washington."

"We unfurl the glorious Stars and Stripes."

"We redeem the soil of the Old Dominion."

To the right and above occurs this direction—"From the Second Regiment Connecticut Volunteers."

But it would require a sheet of fools-cap to describe the several varieties the enemy left behind in his flight. All of them contained some allusion to the war, and were designed to inculcate a feeling of devotion to the Union, or vengeance upon the pestiferous rebels.

The men on both sides assure me that their thirst during the battle was indescribable. They were seen to stop during the hottest of the fight, and pick blackberries to cool their parched tongues. Cold coffee or tea is much better than water, and will slake thirst much quicker, and at the same time refresh one, as I know from experience. If the soldier would fill his canteen with either one of these beverages when he goes out to fight, he would ever afterwards use it on such occasions in preference to water. I would mention in this connection, for the purpose of showing the completeness of the enemy's equipment, that a number of gutta percha drinking tubes were found, about three feet long, and having a mouth piece at one end and a filter twice the size of a lady's thimble at the other. The muddiest water, when drank through one of these tubes, is perfectly clear when it reaches the lips. The tube is flexible, and can be easily carried about the person.

P. W. A.

Official losses for the Battle of First Manassas/Bull Run: Federals, 460 killed, 1124 wounded, 1,312 missing for 2,896; Confederates, 387 killed, 1,582 wounded, and 13 missing for 1,982.

Our Correspondent's Sickness and the Cause of It

RICHMOND, Virginia, August 8, 1861 [8-16-61]

It is a cause of much regret to me, that anything should have occurred to prevent me from completing, at an earlier day, my account of the great battle of Manassas. I went out early in the morning, after a scant breakfast, did not return until one o'clock that night, had nothing to eat in the meantime except a cracker, and altogether must have walked through the hot sun and heavy dew at least twenty miles. In addition to this, I went over the battle-field on Wednesday following, when the effluvia arising from the enemy's dead, many of whom still remained unburied, and the scores of dead horses scattered over the field, was most offensive and sickening; and my surprise is equaled only by my gratitude, that my attack, though sharp, was no worse. My physician informs me that he has been called to see a number of patients who were present at the battle, and whose illness he can ascribe no other cause but that of the great mental and physical excitement under which they labored during the fight. It was this individual concern which every man felt in the mighty struggle, no less than the vast social and political interests at stake, that rendered every soldier a hero, inspiring his heart and nerving his arm to deeds that have no parallel in the world's previous history. Every man felt that it was upon his own shoulders the tremendous issue rested, and that unless he did his part faithfully, victory would never crown our banners.

I shall never forget my own feelings from 3 to 4 o'clock on the day of battle. As you are already aware, the enemy, by a well conducted feint upon our extreme left, at Stone Bridge, succeeded in throwing the main body of his forces across Bull's Run, two and a half miles further up, at Sudley's Ford, and was moving down upon our rear when his movement was discovered. This compelled us to fight him, not upon our original line, which runs nearly East and West along Bull's Run, but upon a new line of the enemy's own choosing, and nearly at right angles to the first, running almost North and South. So weak was our force upon the extreme left, and so heavy the enemy's that the Confederates gradually fell back, though disputing every inch of ground, until 3 o'clock, when they ceased their retrograde movement and stood, from one end of the line to the other, like a wall of rock, against which the enemy beat and struggled in vain. There were no masked batteries or field works on either side, and the field was as new to our men, most of whom had but recently arrived and never saw it before, as it was to the adversary. The battle had been raging from 11 o'clock, and now extended along a line of two miles, and over an undulating country interspersed with grain fields, thickets and patches of woods.

We all felt that the decisive hour had arrived. We knew, too, that an empire trembled in the balances, and that the lives, the fortunes and the liberties of ourselves and of generations yet unborn, were the mighty stake for which the bloody handed combatants were playing. *Would* a just and righteous God, who loves the right and hates the wrong, give the day against us? Who shall say that no prayer went up that day from the field of battle? That one hour, full of agony and doubt, seems even now almost a lifetime. If the question had been whether the spectator should be torn by wild beasts, or made the happiest being in the universe, his suspense could not have been more painful and agonizing.

Half past 3 o'clock arrives, and still the combat rages; and still the wounded come pouring back, some on litters and some hobbling by the side of friends, and still (which is better than all) our men stand as firm as the Blue Ridge whose lofty summits loom up in the blue distance. An aid-de-camp comes dashing by, and I inquire of him, what of the day? "God only knows," is his whispered reply; and, adding that the General desired every man, whether wounded or not, who could bear an arm to fall into line, he galloped on to another part of the field. Some of us turned to and rallied the slightly wounded, and those who had been separated from their commands and fought out, and such spectators as were in reach. We were soon equipped with the arms of those who had been disabled, and felt grateful for an opportunity to strike one blow for the holiest of causes, and if need be, to go down in one common wreck with our brothers. It was evident that the commanding Generals felt that the day was still in doubt, or that they desired a general rally and a bold dash along the whole length of our lines. At the time I thought it was the former.

But I will not prolong the account. Just at this time Gen. Smith rushed in with his splendid brigade; Gen. Beauregard and Johnston made a bold dash at the center, and Gen. Evans with two fresh regiments from South Carolina did the same on the right. The earth fairly trembled beneath the mighty shock. The enemy reeled and staggered like a stunned giant, and began to retire and flounder among the thickets and hills, when Heaven smote him with a panic that sent him wailing and gnashing his teeth along the road and through the woods and fields towards Washington—a broken, ruined and terrified rabble.

There were not then, nor has there been since, any noisy rejoicings or unseemly demonstrations among our troops. They bore themselves with a modesty characteristic of the brave, and chastened by the reflection that the victory had cost us many of the noblest spirits in all the land. This was especially observable in the 7th and 8th Georgia Regiments, whose manly grief at the loss of their chivalric commander and many of their brave comrades was truly touching.

Having procured Dr. Miller's ambulance, a party of us started to look for the body of Col. Bartow. It was a melancholy search, and extended far into the night. The moon was shining, however, and afforded sufficient light for our purpose. But who can describe the awful sights its pale beams disclosed to us during that night's rambles among the hills? The mangled forms, the ghastly wounds and gleaming faces of the dead; the beseeching cries of the wounded; the torments and contortions of the dying—who can depict them! The first man I encountered was a youth of twenty summers who had been killed by a minnie ball, which entered the temple just in front of the ear and passed out on the other side. It was a monster ball, and made a hole through which we could almost see. We next came upon a great heap of the enemy's dead, and among them some wounded who were still alive. It was here that the gallant 4th Alabama Regiment had covered themselves with glory. An appeal was made to us by a wounded man from New York for water. An Alabamian, also wounded, interposed and begged that we would give the New Yorker water; for, he added, "when I was shot down, a member of a New York Regiment went to the hollow, and filled my canteen with water, and brought it to me." Of course we did what we could to render the poor fellow as comfortable as possible.

But on we move among the dead, turning over first one man and then another, to see whether he be not the one for whom we are searching. As this one is turned over we discover that all the lower part of his face has been carried away by a shell. This one has an arm torn away, that one a leg, and the one further has lost his entire head. At one place we find a leg and nothing else; at an other, the scattered fragments of a body. By this branch, we find a poor fellow who, having crawled to the water's edge, drank his fill, and died. We could see, by the bloody track, that another had vainly tried to reach the water, but died before he got to it. Near the stream stood a horse, one of whose forelegs had been carried away by a cannon ball. He groaned most piteously.

Meanwhile, we learn that Col. Bartow's body had been found and carried in by another party. So, we fill our ambulance with the wounded, and send them in to the hospital. By 10 o'clock, all our wounded had been cared for, and we turn our footsteps back to the hospital. Three of us who started on foot finally got lost. Again we traverse the battlefield, and again are our ears saluted by the cries and groans of the wounded and dying. At length, my companions, having encountered friends who were uncertain whether they wound return to the hospital that night, I struck out alone into the road leading to Manassas, (seven miles distant) and along which the battle had raged furiously during the latter part of the day. I soon came upon heaps of the enemy, where the dead and wounded, and torn and mangled horses lay one upon another. A wounded Irishman, from Minnesota, saw me by the moonlight, and begged, "for the love of the holy St. Patrick," that I would give him "so much as one mouthful of water." It was a great trial. I had been out since early morning without anything to eat but one cracker, and it was four or five hundred yards back to the branch; but I remembered what the wounded Alabamian had said, and went and got it for him. Nay, I should have gone any way. Having taken off the coat of a dead soldier, and folded it, and made a pillow for him, and placed the canteen of water within his reach, I bade the poor fellow to be of good cheer, and left him among his dead companions. You may be sure he never ceased to ask the blessing of the holy Virgin upon me as long as I could hear him.

Further on, I encountered a small party, one of whom was an old man, whose white locks gleamed in the moonlight, and another was a young woman, who leant upon his arm. What could they be looking for at this late hour, in this dread place? Was it for a son who had fallen in battle, or for the husband of this young wife? As I reached the top of the hill, and turned to take a last look at the field, I heard a woman's scream far down the road, which told too plainly for whom they were searching. She had found *him*, but whether dead or wounded, I could not tell. God have mercy upon the young wife, and upon the stricken hearts, throughout our land, whose loved ones now sleep the sleep of death.

I had desired to give you some account of my visit to the field on Wednesday following the battle, and of what I there saw, but must forbear, lest you and your readers become weary. If, in this letter, I have had to deal a good deal with what I saw and felt myself, you, and such of your readers as know me, will not ascribe it to egoism, but to a desire to present them, as faithfully as possible, the great battle of Manassas, in all its lights and shades.

P. W. A.

The Battle of Manassas, July 21, 1861—Sad Sights
RICHMOND, VIRGINIA, August 12, 1861 [8-17-61]

I promised to give you some account of the battlefield of Manassas as seen by moonlight and by sunlight. The first part of the promise has been redeemed—the latter, much to my regret, remains to be performed. It is anything but an inviting theme. One soon becomes accustomed to the presence of the dead and the dying—to headless bodies, torn and trembling limbs, and the cries and struggles of the wounded. His blood once up, he may even become indifferent to danger—to the dread shock of battle, "the clash of resounding arms," the leaden hurricane sweeping and crashing among the broken bones and mangled bodies of the contending hosts. The battlefield is not without its sublimity as well as its terror. The long line of glittering bayonets, the roll of a thousand drums, the wheeling and rushing of squadrons, the huge columns of dust and smoke that shoot up like great pyramids from the plains below, the incessant roar of artillery and musketry, the great balls and shells that rush screaming through the air like winged devils escaped from the regions of the damned—there is something in all this to stir the blood, to inspire the heart, nerve the arm, and to make one desire to end his life amid the mighty din and uproar. But when the conflict is over and the blood has resumed its accustomed flow, there is something repulsive at least to me in the sight of a battlefield.

It commenced to rain early on Monday morning—the day after the battle—and continued to pour down in torrents all that day and night. Tuesday the sun came out, and it was very hot, as it was on Wednesday, when I made up my second visit to the field. All of our wounded that could be found, were cared for on Sunday night, though many of them were exposed to the drenching rain on Monday, their tents not having arrived. This was no disadvantage, however, as the rain served to keep down fever and prevent mortification. On Monday our dead were buried or boxed up and sent home for internment, and many of the enemy's wounded were brought in and attended to. All Tuesday was devoted to burying the dead on the other side, and yet the work had not been half finished when I arrived on the field Wednesday morning. So intolerable was the stench arising from the dead, and especially from the horses, that our men had been compelled to suspend their humane labors. I did hear that some of the prisoners we had taken, were subsequently sent out and ordered to finish the work, which they did, though reluctantly.

It was a sad sight—the battlefield, that day. The enemy's dead still lay scattered in every direction, and the silent vulture had begun to circle above them. They were well clad, and were larger and stouter men than ours. Nearly all of them were lying upon their backs, some of them with their legs and arms stretched out to the utmost. Many had their feet drawn up somewhat, while their arms, from the elbows, were raised and the hands rather closed, after the fashion of boxers. It was a singular and yet the prevailing attitude.—Most of them had sandy or red hair, and I have observed that this is the predominant color among our own soldiers. Those who were not killed instantly, had almost invariably torn open their shirt collars, and loosened their clothing about the waist. There was another mark in addition to this, by which we could tell whether their death was sudden or lingering. It was the color of the face. If the body had time to become cool and quiet before death, the corpse was pale, though not so much so as those who die from disease.—Those who were killed instantly, however, and while heated and excited, were purple and black in the face.

Such of the poor wretches as had been buried, were placed in long ditches or trenches, sometimes twenty or thirty in the same trench. Of course, it was impossible to procure coffins or boxes for them. They were laid away in the same attitude in which they were found, and in which their bodies and limbs had become stiff and rigid—one with arms and legs stretched out—another bent nearly double—a third with his hands raised, as described above. One poor fellow had died with his arm clasped around a small tree, and others with their hands clasped tightly about their muskets, or such twigs or roots as were in their reach. One was found with his Bible opened upon his breast. Some had their hands crossed and the whole body composed after the manner of a corpse. A few were found upon whom there was not the least wound or mark. Whether they had died from sunstroke, or from exhaustion, or simple fright, it was impossible to say, though probably it was from the first cause.

Thus dying, and thus buried, their dust will soon commingle, and to mortal vision be come one undistinguishable mass. Whether it shall be blown about this pendent globe by the winds of heaven, or scattered by the wheels of Time in its remorseless sweep to that goal to which everything is hurrying, or whether it shall continue to repose quietly where it now sleeps, it is not for us to determine. We only know that this dust shall be gathered together on the morning of the resurrection, and that the spirits which animated it in this life will be summoned before the Judgement Seat to give an account of the deeds done in the body, chief among which will be their wicked invasion of Southern homes and alters. Having performed the duty required of us by humanity, we may well leave the rest to that dread Judge whose protecting kindness has been around us and over us in all our troubles.

I was glad to see that most of our own dead had been buried upon the battleground— many of them where they had fallen. In some instances, those belonging to the same company or regiment were gathered up and buried near each other, each little hillock being marked by a board or stone with the name of the hero cut upon it. What more fitting cemetery could be found for the gallant dead than the field which has been sanctified by their precious blood and rendered forever immortal by their deeds of valor! I can sympathize with the tender sentiment that would gather up the honored ashes of its loved ones, and transport them for internment in the old family burying-ground in the far South; and yet, I can but admire that stern patriotism—if it may be thus called—which would prefer the torn and bloody plains of Manassas to the proudest mausoleum below the sun.

And to the heroes who fell upon those plains—who would exchange their lot in this life and that which is to come, for that of the beastly-tyrant who would crush us beneath his heel! To me, there has always seemed to be a species of religion in the feeling which prompts a man to forsake father and mother, wife and child, and go forth in defense of the liberties of his country. He who falls in such a cause, never falls too soon. The blood thus spilt, one may hope will not be an unacceptable sacrifice before the Lord of Hosts, the friend of the weak, and the avenger of the wronged and oppressed. We may not claim that the spirits of the fallen brave are caught up in chariots of fire, and borne to realms where there shall be no more drawing of the sword and no more oppression; and yet, we may be allowed to indulge the belief, that it is no sin in the sight of Heaven for a man to defend the graves of his ancestors and the sanctity of his hearth stone, and even to lay down his life in so holy a cause.

But enough. When the future historian comes to the chapter devoted to the battle of Manassas, he will say, if he tells the truth, that our soldiers were well handled by the officers, and that the infantry, the cavalry, and the artillery, were maneuvered skillfully and successfully. He will say, also, and with emphasis, that the day was carried, and the victory won, by the unflagging pluck and dogged courage of our men. Many of these men were young, and, as it were, just from the breasts of their mothers; and yet, neither Caesar's legions, nor the Old Guard of Napoleon, nor the Grenadiers of Frederick the Great, ever fought better, or charged more gallantly, or retired more doggedly. All honor, then, now and hereafter, to the last syllable of recorded time, to the heroes of Manassas!

P. W. A.

Peace Speculations

RICHMOND, August 15th, 1861 [8-20-61]

Since the battle of Manassas, the public has been favored with a good deal of speculation in regard to the prospect of peace. One can hardly pick up a newspaper, or encounter a friend on the streets, that this does not furnish the prevailing topic of the day. Shall we have peace soon? What effect is the great victory of the 21st of July likely to have upon the further progress of the war? Will there be more fighting? and if so, will it consist of mere skirmishes, to be followed by an early restoration of peace, or must we prepare for another great battle, and for a protracted war?

These are interesting questions, and full of importance to the Southern people. I ventured the opinion, some weeks previous to the late battle, that with energy and promptness on our side, the war might be virtually ended by Christmas. I have seen no reason, since the battle, to change that opinion, but many to strengthen it. I stated, also, that the Federal Congress would vote all the men and money that Mr. Lincoln might call for, but that the people themselves would never furnish the money, nor would the Government ever be able to borrow it. I see no cause to change this opinion. On the contrary, every day's revelations demonstrate the utter bankruptcy of the Northern Government. The wealth of the North is a sham and a humbug. It consists chiefly of railways, ships, machine shops, manufacturing establishments and brick and mortar, which of themselves produce nothing, or but little. All this vast machinery, imposing enough upon paper, *creates* nothing, and is useful only in moving and manipulating what others produce. Just now, this kind of property is of but little value in providing the means of carrying on the war. Where, then, is the North to get its money to pay its army? The people have it not; and if they had, recent developments show that they would be slow to lend it to a rickety concern as the Federal Government. Can it be borrowed abroad? The very last arrival from Liverpool brings the intelligence that it cannot. The London *Times*, the most influential paper in the world, and which is almost always a true reflex of the British mind, says: "It would be dangerous for England to have anything to do with the American loan;" and the London *Herald*, the organ of Lord Derby, discountenances all efforts to negotiate it. If the English will not touch the loan, will the capitalists on the continent do it? They will not.

The truth is, the whole fabric of Northern finance and commerce rests upon sand; and now that the winds of revolution have commenced to blow and the rains to fall upon it, the structure is about to topple in the dust. This is equally true of its social fabric, and of its present disgraced and corrupt government. The earth is trembling beneath them, and the whole rotten concern is threatened, politically, financially and socially, with the fate of Sodom and Gomorrah.

A great war cannot be prosecuted without credit or money. The North has neither. But will the men who are to fight their battles and subjugate us be forthcoming? I do not believe they will. Not 5,000 out of the 75,000 three months' volunteers have reenlisted, since the expiration of their term. The recruiting of the regular army has absolutely ceased, and but very few fresh volunteers are offering. But for the regiments that had tendered their services previous to the disastrous battle of Manassas, and which are therefore committed and cannot retreat, the Government at this time would be without force enough, other than the regulars, to do garrison duty. The men who fled Manassas will never fight us again, and the accounts which they will disseminate throughout the abolition States will deter others from taking their places. The prisoners we took say that the Confederates fought like devils, and you may be sure that those who escaped, and some of whom never stopped until they got to New York, will represent us to be "half horse and half alligator"—monstrous centaurs—huge beasts, with seven heads and seven horns—who would think nothing, any morning at breakfast, of drinking a gallon of blood, and devouring the shank of a Yankee, with a few coals of fire thrown in by way of pepper to season it. The most reliable accounts from Washington inform us that the number of recruits returning home far exceed those who are arriving, and that great uneasiness prevails in the city, not only among the people, but in the highest official circles. If they do not see the handwriting upon the wall, it is only because their hearts have been hardened and their eyes blinded, that they may be damned.

The question recurs then, will the war be a long one or a short one? For myself I believe that the *contest* was decided upon the Plains of Manassas, though the war may be protracted for some months longer, and we may have to fight one or more battles, before the enemy will consent to make peace. The disgraceful rout of the Federal army, the consternation throughout the North, the reluctance with which new volunteers come forward, the imposition of enormous taxes, the impending bankruptcy of the manufacturing and commercial classes, and the destruction of all kinds of business, coupled with the early recognition of our independence by England and France, and the raising of the blockade, all point conclusively to the fact that if we do our own duty promptly and faithfully, the war will be of short duration. Everything depends, however, upon the zeal and energy with which we act; for the gods help only those who help themselves. A great peace movement has already been started in the North, and it is growing in volume and strength every day, the ultimate result of which will be, with prudence and firmness on our part, to transfer the Government from the hands of the wretches who are now using it as an engine of oppression, to those of more conservative sentiments and more national views. There may be much blood shed before all this is accomplished, not only between the North and the South, but between the northern people themselves; but that such will be the final denouncement, there can be but little room for doubt.

P. W. A.

Evils in Our Army

RICHMOND, Virginia, August 20, 1861 [8-25-61]

There is a growing evil in some of our Regiments which calls for exposure and condemnation. You will be surprised to hear that it is dueling. An intelligent and reliable friend informs me, that he knows of two duels now on the tapis between volunteers from Georgia. I have heard of similar affairs among the troops from other States. I know nothing whatever of the parties to these quarrels—neither their names nor the regiments to which they belong, nor the counties from whence they came. What I may have to say, therefore, can have no personal reference to the gentlemen engaged.

A volunteer is a person who freely and of his own accord offers his services to his Government to defend its territory and maintain its rights and honor upon the field of battle, if necessary even unto death. When he enters the army, he binds himself as a soldier and a man of honor to square his conduct by the rules and regulations adopted for the government of the army. He obligates himself to obey those who are in authority, to do whatever he may be commanded to do, to go wherever he may be ordered, to advance, retreat, fight or run, or do whatever else his official superiors may think is best. In other words, during the term of his enlistment, he parts with all control over himself, and transfers to the Government all his faculties and energies, mental and physical, subject only to the terms of the law in such cases made and provided.

There is another obligation he takes upon himself, which, though not expressed, is implied, and of equal force with the foregoing. It is, to inflict all the injury he can, under the rules of war, upon the enemy, and to promote, in all proper ways, the welfare of his own Government, its people and its army. If any one infringes upon his own rights, whether he be a private and below him, or an officer and above him, he has a full, complete and ample remedy. The rules of the army, which he agreed to observe when he entered it, provide a suitable tribunal where his wrongs may be promptly vindicated and his rights respected and enforced.

What right, then, has any soldier, whether private or officer, who has thus disposed of himself to his Government, to send a challenge or to fight a duel during the term of his enlistment? He has volunteered in the service of the Government, and has taken up arms against the enemies of that Government. Nay—as in this war—he is fighting in the sacred cause of liberty, and against a corrupt, licentious and vindictive enemy. All that man or woman holds dear is at stake. Before the volunteer stands the armed foe of his country. Will he move himself forward to meet that foe, as he has bound himself to do, or will he turn aside, and for some trivial, technical offence of a private nature, seek the life of his brother volunteer in the same holy cause? If the wrong be slight, a brave man may overlook it. If it be gross and grievous, there is the court-martial—let him apply to that. If is be of a character that cannot be reached by that tribunal, let him adjourn the quarrel until the common enemy shall be beaten back and the national wrongs vindicated. But if he must fight—if he must have blood, and can't wait—then, in the name of all that is rational and patriotic, let him strike at the foe in front, and not at the brother on his right hand or his left.

With an enemy in the field, no man should be tolerated in the army one day who would send, bear, or accept a challenge. He is no friend to his country, but its enemy. He makes war upon its friends. He thirsts for blood of its soldiers, and so far as he is concerned, leaves the enemy free to burn, to pillage and to murder. What more can the enemy do? What more does he do?

There is another evil which requires correction, but which has gone too far, I fear, to be entirely extirpated. I allude to the practice of carrying side arms by volunteers. The musket and the bayonet are the true weapons of the soldier. They are the best, too—the best for offense and for defense. All other weapons are in the way, are seldom used, frequently lost, and instead of adding to, really detract from the effectiveness of the soldier. I made special inquiry among the men who were engaged in the battle of Manassas, and I could not hear of a single instance where a pistol or bowie knife had been used, except one. In the exceptional case alluded to, a regiment had been ordered to fall back, and a captain of one of the companies who was reluctant to retire, fired off his revolver at the enemy, three hundred yards distant, by way of expressing defiance. It is rare that the approaching forces get near enough to each other to justify a resort to side arms, and when they do, no other weapon ever invented is equal to the bayonet. It is said that there is no instance on record, where an army has ever successfully withstood a bayonet charge properly directed and made with determination. Raw volunteers, however, who do not appreciate the great value of this weapon when they get into close quarters, are liable to be thrown into inextricable confusion by relying upon their revolvers, which are of as little use against a well directed charge, as so many pop-guns would be in staying the onward sweep of an avalanche.

But the greatest evil arising from this practice is the constant bloodshed to which it leads. Scarcely a week passes that we do not hear of a difficulty, involving life or limb, all of which can be traced to this wretched practice. I do not mean that these things occur in camp and after the soldier has taken his position in the army. It is on the road, and at many stations, and especially at this and other points where he is halted for a week or two before entering into active service, and where he can get any quantity of the meanest kind of liquor. A drunken soldier, with a revolver stuck in his belt on one side and a bowie knife in the other, is about as fit to go at large as an infuriated maniac; and the authorities ought to see to it, that no more men be suffered to enter the service unless they leave all such weapons at home, where they may be needed. A pistol is a part of a horseman's equipment, but it is not a legitimate weapon in the hands of the infantry.

P. W. A.

Skirmishes
ARMY OF THE POTOMAC
Manassas, August 28, 1861 [9-3-61]
I can only send you a short letter to day. Indeed, there is but little to write about at this advanced post—that is, but little that it would be proper to communicate. There are collisions every day or two between scouting parties, resulting sometimes in loss of life, and the capture of one or more prisoners. An affair of this sort came off yesterday, near Fall's Church, seven miles north east of Fairfax Court House, in which three or four Confederates were wounded. We took six or seven prisoners, and probably killed and wounded some of the enemy; but as he left the field, we could not ascertain the extent of his casualties. Col. Stuart, of the Virginia cavalry, was in command of our forces. The enemy had about 400 engaged, or rather present; for it did not amount to an engagement. It is expected that a similar, though rather more important affair, would take place to-day.

The enemy is very restless and uneasy. The impression prevails, beyond the Potomac, that Johnston and Beauregard will move upon Washington soon; and, in consequence of it, the enemy, for the past few days, has been throwing out strong scouting parties, for the purpose of feeling our lines, and ascertaining where the main body of our forces are posted. He wishes to provoke us to a development of our strength, in order to ascertain in what direction we are likely to move.

This policy of the adversary will fail. Such officers as Johnston and Beauregard are not likely to be thrown off their guard in that way. They understand the game too well, to suffer the enemy to trick them into showing their hands before they are ready. I do not say whether they will move upon Washington soon or not, nor, indeed, whether they will do so at all. They keep their own counsels. But, should they decide to move, they will do it when they get ready, and not before.

I regret to say there is a great deal of sickness in the army. This is not a healthy country at this season of the year. The remark applies to all the counties bordering on the

Potomac, from the Great Falls down. The Presidents of the United States have found it necessary, for several years past, to retire from Washington during the months of August and September, on account of the insalubrity of the climate.

There are other reasons, however, for the unhealthiness of the army, and chief among them, is the want of proper police regulations in the camps. In plain English, the camps are not kept clean. This I know, from personal observation. In many of the regimental camps, the messes are in the habit of throwing refuse bread, scraps, and parings of meat, and pieces of bones, watermelon rinds, green corn cobs, and all the greasy remains of the cooking department, just outside of their tents, and where, under the constant alternation of sunshine and rain, they are sure to become an early source of pestilence and death. The men seldom sweep their tents or air their blankets; while many of the camps are never swept at all. The result of this negligence and inattention, is a heavy list of the sick.

When I ask the officers about it, they excuse themselves by saying it is impossible to enforce the necessary hygienic discipline among volunteers.

Neither the company officers nor the men, they say, will submit to those sanitary regulations, without which, it is impossible to preserve the health of the command. This plea, to my certain knowledge, is not well founded. There is the first Regiment Georgia Regulars, Col. [Charles] Williams, and the 15th Georgia Volunteers, Col. [Thomas] Thomas, where the most rigid rules are enforced, and cheerfully obeyed by all the officers and men. The camps are swept daily, and all refuse matter of every description is carried beyond the lines and burnt. The result is, these regiments enjoy almost a complete exemption from all kinds of disease, except those of an infectious character, which cannot well be guarded against in camp, and such as are incident to a change of water. Col. Thomas' regiment is fresh in the service, and has to run the gauntlet of the measles, colds, and bowel affections; but, beyond such disorders, it is exceedingly healthy. Colonel Williams', which served some three months on Tybee Island, and has become inured to camp life, is singularly healthy. In a certain Mississippi regiment on the contrary, where every man is permitted to do as he likes, two-thirds of the entire command is on the sick list, whilst the deaths have reached as high as nine on one day. You will not be surprised to hear that the Colonel of the regiment is now under arrest.

Who is responsible for all this sickness? Clearly, the Commander-in-chief is not entirely blameless. The whole army is subject to his orders, and bound to yield with proper obedience, or be punished.

P. W. A.

Pleasant Autumn
ARMY OF THE POTOMAC
Manassas, Sept. 1, 1861 [9-7-61]

Autumn has set in, and with its advent comes pleasant weather—the first for many weeks. With occasional intervals of sunshine and blue skies, we have had clouds and rain almost incessantly throughout the month of August. When the weather was good, it did not last long enough for the earth to become dry and the water courses to resume their accustomed channels; and hence, the great increase of sickness in the camps. For the past three days, however, the weather has been delicious, and the temperature delightful. The air is soft, and balmy, and elastic, and already our sick list has begun to diminish. I rode out to several of the camps yesterday, and wherever I went I saw numbers of the sick who had crawled out from their tents to enjoy the glorious sunshine and the pure, health-giving breeze, as it swept down from the distant summits of the Blue Ridge. Their pale cheeks and trembling limbs told how much they had suffered. But not a murmur escaped their lips; they bore all their sufferings, and privations, and hard living in camp, with the patience and fortitude that ever characterize the brave.

One poor fellow, whose ears were so thin and bloodless that you could see the sunlight thro' them, was seated upon his blanket propped up against a tree. In his hand he held a letter which he had just finished reading, and which, it was evident, had aroused all the tender sensibilities of his nature. Perhaps it was from his mother in the far South, whose yearning heart and daily prayers had followed him in all his marches and counter-marches since she last pressed him to her beating heart. It may be that she had heard of the great battle of Manassas, and of his narrow escape and heroic daring, and the letter may have contained some expression of the maternal pride and deep gratitude which agitated her bosom. It may be, too, that in it she had breathed a prayer for his future safety, and had asked God to protect her darling boy amid the dangers of the battle, and to return him to her when the contest shall have ended.

Perhaps the letter was from one who was still dearer to him, if possible, than mother or father—for his eye looked supernaturally bright and tender, as he held the delicately traced sheet between his wasted fingers. Possibly it was written by some bright-eyed, sunny-headed girl, whose last whispered word to him, as he bade her adieu, sent a thrill of joy through every fibre of his heart. What his thoughts were, no one could divine, except that they were not of an unpleasant character. If one might judge, however, from outward appearances, his mind had run far into the future—to a time, perhaps, when this war should be over, and when he should have a little cottage among the trees upon the hillside, with clustering vines and sunny walks, lowing herds and snowy cotton fields, and when this same bright-eyed, sunny-headed girl should be there with her sweet smile and cheerful voice to welcome him *home* when his day's toil was over. Possibly she had ventured to hint, in her timid way, that she, too, longed for the return of the dove of peace; but why she desired it, doubtless she had not said, though he well knew the reason.

Alas! who can tell how many hearts there are in all this broad land that have been stricken by this horrid war! The loved ones who have been slain in battle or fallen from pestilence—the painful separation of families, the long and weary marches, the dangers of the battle field and camp, and the suspense and anxiety at home—how much suffering all these bitter consequences of the unnatural conflict have produced. How many eyes have they filled with tears, how many hearts with sorrow! Who shall say that the authors of this iniquitous war shall not be punished in this life and that which is to come for all this suffering? To us of the South, there is no alternative left but to defend our homes and the graves of our ancestors. The war is not of our seeking—it was forced upon us. And although our brave brothers may be slain upon the field and our friends may weep and suffer at home, now that the struggle is upon us, in the language of the lamented Bartow, we shall "never give up the fight," until victory perches upon our standard, or the last man of us has been cut down.

But we must leave the soldier to his letter and the pleasant thoughts it has given him. His dream may not last long. Ere this reaches you, it may be broken by the "cannon's deep roar," and the tramp of armed legions rushing to the conflict. His cheek may be still paler when the battle has ended, and some rude board on the banks of the Potomac may point the writer of that letter to the spot where his wasted form reposes. The air is thick with rumors, and from my tent I can see couriers galloping to and fro along every road and over every hill. The Generals are silent; the transportation wagons have been gathered in groups around each regimental camp; orders have been given to the men to reduce their baggage, and to keep cooked and always on hand three days' rations. All these things portend the coming storm.

P. W. A.

ARMY OF THE POTOMAC
MANASSAS, September 5, 1861 [9-13-61]

I did not write you yesterday on account of my absence at the battlefield, where I went to witness the erection, by the Eighth Georgia Regiment, of a marble shaft upon the spot where Col. Bartow fell. The Seventh, Eighth and Eleventh Georgia Regiments were present in full force; also the Kentucky Regiment and a detachment from the Ninth Georgia Regiment. These regiments composed the brigade commanded by Colonel Bartow at Winchester, though only two of them (the Seventh and Eighth) arrived in time to participate in battle, the others having been detained by an accident of the railroad. The officers and band of the First Georgia Regulars, a portion of Gen. [Robert] Toombs' staff, and detachments from the Second and Fifteenth Georgia Volunteers, with a large concourse of other persons, including visitors here and soldiers attached to other Confederate regiments, were present. Brigadier-General Samuel Jones, who succeeded Col. Bartow in command of the Second Brigade, was also in attendance with his entire staff. There were a few ladies on the ground, one of whom, it will be no indelicacy to say, was Mrs. Branch, of Savannah, whose heroic son, Adjutant John Branch, now sleeps upon the immortal field where we stood; while another son, Sanford Branch, was taken prisoner at the side of his dead brother and is now in Washington; and a third, Hamilton Branch, still stands his ground in the glorious Eighth, determined under the favor of Providence to avenge the death of the one and the imprisonment of the other. It was peculiarly appropriate that this body should have been present on such an occasion. The intrepid commander whose heroism we had met to commemorate, in all his brigade had no truer men than the BRANCHES—none who loved him more, and none whom he loved more. Many of their comrades came up to pay their respects to this mother of Georgian Gracchii, each one of whom had some kindly recollection of her sons to relate, or some manly virtue to rehearse.

The several regiments formed in a hollow square around the spot where the column was to be planted. Gen. Jones and staff, and other field officers and visitors, took their positions within the square. The band of the First Georgia Regulars, the best I have heard in Virginia except perhaps the band of the New Orleans Washington Artillery, played a beautiful and touching requiem, after which the Rev. Mr. Jones, Chaplain of the Eighth Georgia, offered up an exceedingly appropriate prayer. Gen. Jones then stepped forward and said that Vice President [Alexander] Stephens who had been at Manassas for some days in attendance upon his brother, Lieutenant-Colonel Linton Stephens, and Gen. Toombs had been invited to be present and deliver addresses on the occasion; but that the former had been called to Richmond, and that the latter was laboring under a temporary indisposition which prevented his attendance. Under these circumstances, the Hon. Mr. [Thomas J.] Semmes, the Attorney-General of Louisiana, who was accidentally present, had consented to make some remarks. Mr. Semmes, having been introduced by Gen. Jones, proceeded to deliver a very chaste and becoming eulogium. He said that he had not had any warning of what would be expected of him; but he stood upon the Plains of Manassas, and the name of *Bartow* was now a household word in Louisiana and throughout all this broad land, and he felt that if he could but give expression to the emotions of his own heart, he should not fall far below the requirements of the occasion. I have been promised a copy of his remarks, however, and shall not do the speaker the injustice to attempt a report of them from memory.

Major Cooper, of the Eighth, was about to give an order in regard to the further conduct of the ceremonies, but feeling overcome by the recollections of the day of battle and of the man at whose side he had fought, he said he could not refrain from adding a word to what had already been so eloquently and appropriately said. His speech was short, and was the speech of a soldier. Like a good musket ball, it went straight to the mark, and to the hearts of all present. Indeed, I saw many wet eyes around that marble shaft yesterday—great diamond tear drops upon rough bearded cheeks, that never have and never will blanche in the presence of an enemy.

The column was planted in its place by Gen. Jones, Mr. Semmes, Col. [T. H.] Taylor, of the Kentucky Regiment, Maj. Cooper, and other officers, each one of whom threw a spadeful of earth around it. Mrs. Branch, Mrs. Semmes, of New Orleans, and Miss Mary Cook, of Alabama, also threw in each a spadeful, as did all the members of the Oglethorpe Light Infantry, (Col. Bartow's old company,) and hundreds of others who desired to testify their admiration of the fallen hero.

The shaft, which is round and plain, rises about five feet above the ground, and is a foot in diameter. It was made round to prevent visitors to the field from chipping off pieces of the marble, to carry with them home as relics of the field of the dead. The inscription is exceedingly simple and appropriate. It is in these words:
"Francis S. Bartow.
They have killed me, boys,
But never give up the fight."
Altogether it was a solemn ceremony. Around us spread the torn and bloody battlefield, which but a few weeks before had been the scene of the fiercest conflict ever waged upon the Western Continent. It now lay calm and quiet, its plains and hills and valleys reposing in the autumnal sunlight, and its blasted verdure once more rejoicing in its wonted freshness. The overthrown fences, and the timberless trees through which the iron and leaden

hailstorm had sped, and the new-made graves where sleep alike the vanquisher and the vanquished, are all that is left to tell that here the children of glory had met the invader, and had overthrown him. Upon a hill in the center of this scene, and upon which Sherman's famous battery was stationed, and around which the storm raged fiercest—here it was that the hero fell, flag in hand, in the very arms of victory; and here it was that the marble shaft containing his dying words was planted. That shaft now points its white finger from the plains of glory below, upward to those supremer and more heavenly plains where the brave who fall in their country's cause, shall rest from their struggles and be crowned with chaplets of immortal green. Long after that marble shall have crumbled into dust, and until the sun and stars which now beam and blaze around the throne of God, shall have been stricken from the skies, the PLAINS OF MANASSAS and the name of BARTOW shall not be absent from the lips of the sons and daughters of men.

The cenotaph erected and the ceremony over, I went with Lieut. Moon, of the Atlanta Confederate Volunteers, to the spot to which Col. Bartow was borne after he was shot, and where he breathed his last. An error occurred in one of my former communications in regard to the persons who carried him off the field; and as the men who performed the sad duty as well as the entire command feel desirous that each one's part, however humble, should be rightly understood, I am glad of an opportunity to make the correction. The persons, then, who bore him off were Lieut. Wm. P. Moon, private E. L. Morton, of the Dekalb Light Infantry and privates J. F. Lindley and J. L. Dobbs, of the Cobb County Confederate Guards, and all of the Seventh Regiment. They carried him about one hundred and fifty yards to the rear, and laid him down under a cedar tree, some of the limbs of which were torn off by pieces of shell. I cut a walking cane from a branch that shaded him where he died, and requested Lieut. Moon to have the spot marked. He says that Col. Bartow seemed to be looking at them and smiling all the time up to the moment of his death.

I heard yesterday, for the first time, of a remark made by Lieut. Col. Gardner, of the 8th, after he had been shot down and taken prisoner, which deserves to be recorded in brass. The regiment, after holding their ground against fearful odds for a long time, were finally compelled to fall back, and the enemy coming up, found Col. Gardner lying on the ground. An officer rather disposed to exult over their partial success, said to him in substance: "Sir, your army better yield. We are driving you back. We have 50,000 men on the field and heavy reserves coming up. Stop this effusion of blood, and surrender, or we shall sweep you from the face of the earth." Col. Gardner indignantly replied: *"Never! but we will give you such a fight as this every day from here to the Gulf of Mexico."* What Georgian does not feel proud of the brother who, though wounded and lying flat on his back in the midst of exulting foes, thus bearded them to their faces and bade their whole army defiance?

P. W. A.

General Albert S. Johnston
ARMY OF THE POTOMAC
Manassas, September 8, 1861 [9-15-61]

Gen. Albert S. Johnston, as you have doubtless already announced, arrived in Richmond two days ago by the overland route from California. The Richmond *Examiner* say, the opinion prevails in military circles that General Johnston should be sent to Missouri, where it is thought his splendid abilities could be turned to the greatest advantage for the public service. While I do not take issue with the *Examiner* as to what may or may not be the judgement of military men as to the proper field for this officer, it is but just to say that there is a very general desire in this quarter, that he should be placed at the head of the Army of the Potomac.

The forces now here are divided into two *corps d'armee*. The first corps is commanded by Gen. Beauregard, and the second by Gen. Joseph E. Johnston. The latter being the ranking officer by seniority of appointment, would be entitled, under the rules of the War Department, to take supreme command in case of battle. Before his departure from Winchester, his corps was designated the army of the Shenandoah, and the distinction is kept up, I understand, since his arrival here, Gen. Beauregard's division being known as the Army of the Potomac. I have disregarded this distinction in my letters heretofore, having dated such of them as were written here, from the Army of the Potomac.

Bonaparte said that one poor General was better than five good ones with a divided and equal command. This saying might have received a most disastrous illustration upon the Plains of Manassas, but for the good sense of the officers in command. During the thickest of the fight, it is said that Gen. Johnston sent word to Beauregard to bring up his reserves. Little Beaury returned word that it was his (B.'s) fight, and for Johnston to bring them up. They met and arranged the matter in ten seconds, and General Johnston brought up the reserves. This was creditable to both parties. Had they been different men, the battle might have been lost upon a point of precedence.

Gen. Albert S. Johnston, however, is generally conceded to be the finest field officer in the Confederate States, if not on this continent. Gen. [Zachary] Taylor considered him the first man in the army, and it is known that Gen. Scott and the officers of the old army looked upon him as "the coming man" among the younger men in the service. He is thoroughly posted in the details in every department of the army; and what is of vastly more importance, *he knows what to do with volunteers*. A short time after leaving West Point, he retired to private life, and did not re-enter the army for several years. In the meantime, he mingled freely with the people, and now understands their feelings and dispositions as well as any man in or out of the army. This, I fear, is not true of his namesake.

A rule may be a very good one when applied to the regular service, into which men enlist for the pay, and yet be very unwise when applied to volunteers, and especially such volunteers as make up the Confederate Army. Indeed, the regulations of the War Office were adopted for the government of regulars—men who were fished up from the lowest walks of life, and who fought for money. An attempt to engraft these regulations upon the volunteer system, would not be more unwise than an effort to govern white men by the same rules that our people adopt for the management of their slaves. This distinction between volunteers and regulars is not always fully appreciated by officers in the regular service. Gen. Albert S. Johnston, however, is believed to be an exception to this rule; and it is for this reason that many sagacious men would like to see him placed in command of the chief division of the army.

A portion of the Southern press, as you have doubtless observed, has been clamorous ever since the battle of Manassas for greater severity in our treatment of the prisoners now in our possession. They exaggerate the treatment shown to Confederate soldiers confined at Washington and Fort LaFayette, and then call upon the President to mete out the same measure to the Yankees in our hands. An eye for an eye, and a tooth for a tooth, is their doctrine; and very good doctrine it is, if their premises were only right. If the Federal authorities should cause a single one of our men to be executed, I should say, hang up ten of the enemy. But they will not touch a hair of the head of one of them. They dare not do it.

Neither our cause nor our Government will lose anything by the course it is pursuing. Two wrongs never make a right. Let us do right ourselves, and we may well appeal alike to the judgement of men and heaven. The wicked flee when no man pursueth, but the righteous are bold as a lion. This was shown in the cowardly rout of the enemy at Manassas when no man pursued. We profess to conduct the contest upon the principles of civilized warfare, and not upon a narrow, vindictive and barbarous system. This policy is having a salutary effect upon the Northern mind, even in New England, and especially in the North-West. It is strengthening the hands of our friends beyond the Susquehannah and Ohio, and adding volume and power to the peace movement.

In the North-west the war is becoming unpopular. Newspapers, public meetings and political conventions do not hesitate to express the growing condemnation by the people of the policy of the administration. Sentiments are daily avowed in Cincinnati and Chicago which, if expressed in Philadelphia and New York, would secure the author a cell in Fort LaFayette. If the war should continue much longer, the North-West will imitate the South and set up for itself. Cincinnati, in a free State, is sounder to-day than Louisville in a slave State.

Our policy in view of these facts, is an obvious one. While we prosecute the war with the utter vigor, we should be careful to do nothing that would hurt our cause among the civilized nations of the earth, or check the ground-swell that now convulses and distracts the Northern mind. I have met intelligent persons who even doubt the policy of attacking

Washington. An aggressive movement on our part just at this time, they seem to apprehend, would have a tendency to re-unite the people, and stop the disintegration which has commenced. While this may be at least partially true, the better opinion would appear to be, that the seizure of the Federal City, and the planting of the Stars and Bars upon the dome of the Federal Capitol, would strike terror into the Northern heart, demoralize their public authorities, and bring discredit upon their Government throughout the world.

P. W. A.

McClellan's Plans
ARMY OF THE POTOMAC
Near Centreville, Va., September 14, 1861 [9-20-61]

The affair alluded to in my last letter [Sept. 12] as having occurred near Munson's Hill, in front of Arlington, got sadly turned around before it reached our headquarters. Instead of getting the worst of it ourselves, as at first reported, it now appears that the enemy were the sufferers, and that we escaped wholly unhurt.

Gen. Longstreet, who is in command of our forces in the vicinity of Munson's Hill, having ascertained that the enemy was moving in considerable force up the river, in the direction of Vienna, dispatched Col. [J.E.B.] Stuart, of Maryland [1st Va. Cav.], with a small force of 300 infantry, 100 cavalry and 2 guns, to observe his movements, and, if possible, to hold him in check until a larger force could be sent up. The enemy's force, as we afterwards learned from the prisoners we took, consisted of three regiments of infantry, 200 cavalry and 8 guns. Col. Stuart managed to head off the force and get his two pieces into position before they were aware of his movements. The first intimation they had of his presence was conveyed to them by two well-directed shots from his guns. The salutation was unexpected and produced great consternation in the ranks of the enemy, who immediately began to fall back in much disorder. He doubtless imagined that he had encountered one of those "infernal masked batteries," for which this region is so famous. The affair lasted but a short time, and the enemy fired but few shots; and they seemed to be directed at random. Six men were left dead upon the field, and four prisoners were taken. It is said that Gen. McDowell [Isaac I. Stevens] led the Federal forces. The object of the expedition is not known, but it is believed that it was sent out to reconnoiter our lines in that direction, and to ascertain, if possible, the strength and position of our forces.

This belief is strengthened by the events of yesterday. We hear that the enemy pushed forward a column, yesterday morning, in the direction of Fairfax Station, and another towards Munson's Hill, and that he drove back our pickets and captured Munson's Hill. The report is probably exaggerated. I have no doubt that McClellan, with a view to occupy our attention, and to ascertain our position and strength at various points along our lines, found it necessary to throw forward reconnoitering parties in considerable force. But I cannot believe that he means to offer us battle. If he intended to attack our lines, he should have done it ten days ago, when he might have sallied out from his entrenchments in force and given us a good deal of trouble before our forces could have been concentrated in sufficient strength to repel the attack. He has shown but little enterprise. With his entrenchments to fall back upon, he might with entire safety have engaged us at several points. He has not waited too long. His fear is that Johnston and Beauregard will seek to cross the river above Washington, and move down between Baltimore and the capital. To prevent the execution of what he supposes their programme to be, he has sent considerable reinforcements up the river on the Maryland side; and lest we should attack him at Arlington and Alexandria, on the Virginia side, he has likewise increased his forces at those points. Meanwhile, in order more effectually to checkmate the movement to cross the river, he seeks to engage our attention by pushing forward such reconnoitering parties as those alluded to above.

It would be injudicious to speculate upon the probable plans of our officers, further than to state what the enemy imagines them to be. All doubt will be cleared up in due season—possibly before this letter reaches your readers.

Gen. [Joseph] Johnston moved his headquarters yesterday to Fairfax. Gen. Beauregard moved to the same place the day before. I do not believe I have mentioned in any of my former letters that Prince [Camille A. J. M.] Polignac of France, has received an appointment upon Gen. Beauregard's staff, with the rank of Lieutenant-Colonel. He is a grandson of the famous Prince Polignac who was imprisoned at Ham for his fidelity to Charles X. He is reputed to be in close communication with Louis Napoleon, and upon terms of intimacy with Count Morny. It is to him we are indebted for the insertion in the Paris journals, last Spring, of various friendly notices of the Confederate Government. He comes highly recommended by our friends in Paris. He is about thirty years old, and exceedingly plain and unpretending. His family has enjoyed the title of Prince for five hundred years.

Capt. E. Porter Alexander, of Washington, Ga., formerly of the U. S. Army, is another member of Gen. Beauregard's staff. I am unacquainted with him, but learn that he is looked upon as one of the most promising young officers in the army. That such is Gen. B.'s opinion, may be inferred from the fact that he has made him his Ordnance Officer and Chief of Artillery—an exceedingly responsible and important position.

Several revolvers and razors, and one gold watch, have been found since we came to this place. The man upon whose farm we are encamped, says a letter was picked up after the federal army left, which one of the men had written to his wife, but lost before he had an opportunity to post it. He informed her that he had selected his farm just above Centreville, and that it was one of the finest he ever saw. He bids her to have everything in a state of readiness to bring the family down as soon as the war shall have blown over. I should not be surprised if the poor, deluded simpleton were not now in undisturbed possession of a little farm upon the field of Manassas.

Another letter was found upon the person of a dead soldier, by a man in Extra Billy Smith's Regiment, and by him forwarded to a member of Congress at Richmond, where it was seen by several members. It was from a wife to her husband. She informed him that she would in a few weeks present him with the hope of a family, upon which occasion she would require the services of a nurse. She desired him, therefore, as soon as the Grand Army reached Richmond, to procure a smart, handy young white girl, about sixteen years old, and send her on immediately. She did not want a poor girl, nor one belonging to a second-rate family—none but one of the F. F. Va. (first families of Virginia) would fill the bill.

One may laugh at these things now, and yet how plainly do they show the deceits which the Federal Government and its officers have practiced upon their army, the motives which induced the men to enter the service, and the doom in reserve for us if they had been successful.

P. W. A.

A Retrospect
ARMY OF THE POTOMAC
Near Fairfax, Va., September 23, 1861 [9-27-61]

Nine weeks ago, yesterday, the battle of Manassas was fought. The Confederates won the victory; but where are its fruits? Has the Government—has the commanding General—done the best that could be done? If they have then the country ought to be satisfied. If they have not, the country may overlook, though it will not forget, the short coming.

Our effective force here is very little, if any greater than it was two weeks after the battle. The number of regiments is considerably larger, but owing to sickness, it may well be doubted whether the number of fighting men is much greater. Our means of transportation have been increased, and the Commissariat department is somewhat better supplied. Our supply of ammunition is ample, and a number of field batteries have been organized and brought into service. Another object of great importance, which it would be imprudent to name at this time, has been accomplished. Meanwhile, the moral effect of the victory in the United States has been most beneficial, while its political effect in Europe has been all we could desire. A wholesome lesson has been administered to the enemy, and European nations have been taught to look upon the Confederate Government as a fixed fact—a power in the earth which will make itself felt and respected. This much, at least, has been accomplished.

On the other hand, time has been given the enemy to supply the places of his retiring regiments, to re-organize his demoralized forces, to recruit his broken columns, and to recover, in part, at least, from the panic with which he was seized at Manassas. He has had time, also, to surround his capital both on the Virginia and Maryland sides, with defensive works of the most formidable character, and to accumulate vast amounts of provisions, clothing, ammunition and stores of every kind. It may be doubted whether the works this side of the river can be carried, except at a sacrifice of life too great for the object to be accomplished. No apprehensions need be entertained as to the result of a conflict on the open field. Behind entrenchments, however, and protected by fortifications, the enemy may stand his ground against equal numbers and inflict heavy loss. But should our men ever get near enough for him to see their gleaming eyes, neither his breastworks nor the Potomac River will be sufficient to stay his flight.

Such is the debit and credit account of the battle of Manassas. The reader must decide for himself upon the wisdom of the policy that has been pursued. That we could and should have entered Washington ten days after the battle, is now conceded upon all sides. Indeed, it has seemed to me that the way has been left open to us at any time since the 21st July. If Napoleon had been at the head of our forces, or any other commander who possessed their confidence, and understood the aggressive spirit of the volunteer, the Army of the Potomac would to-day have been thundering at the gates of Philadelphia and New York. And yet, I do not wish to be understood as finding fault with Johnston and Beauregard. The latter yielded up command the day after the battle, and since that time Johnston has had the direction of affairs. He is believed to be a good strategist, and he certainly possesses great coolness and courage. He knows, too, that the Government is in its infancy—that, like a child beginning to walk, we are just taking our first steps among the nations of the earth—that the whole world looked upon us with more or less distrust, and that many of our own people even felt some misgiving as to the result. In view of these facts, and knowing how much depended upon success in our first endeavors, he may have felt that he could not be too cautious, and that even where the chances were in favor of success, it was hazarding too much to make the attempt unless he were doubly sure of victory. An empire is the stake, and the happiness and liberties of unborn generations tremble upon his shoulders!

It may be presumption in a mere civilian to criticize the military movements of the army. Thus far, you will bear me witness, I have abstained from doing so. And even now, I wish to be understood as merely expressing the opinion of one who disclaims all pretensions to military science. I certainly do not sympathize with those whose daily cry is "On to Washington." We have all seen the disastrous results of a similar utterance on the other side of the Potomac—"On to Richmond." There are abuses and defects in the army, which I shall claim the privilege of exposing at the proper time. But, for the present, I am willing to trust our officers. They are in a position to judge what is wisest to be done. There is but one proviso I would insist upon, and that is the Army of the Potomac must winter in Washington and Baltimore, or make an effort to do so. Short of this, neither the army nor the country will be satisfied.

P. W. A.

In Statu Quo
ARMY OF THE POTOMAC
Fairfax Court House, October 1, 1861   [10-11-61]

There has been no change in "the situation" since my last letter. Our picket force remains on the line to which it was retired on the night of the 27th ultimo. The enemy has occupied the line of hills which we abandoned, including Munson's, Mason's and Upton's hills. I am not advised whether Gen. McClellan has ordered these elevations to be fortified, but it is probable he will do so at an early day, as it is considered a blunder on his part not to have done it previous to our occupation of them.

President Davis arrived at Fairfax last evening, and is now staying at Gen. Beauregard's headquarters. I do not think that his visit portends anything in regard to the movements of the army. His health is quite feeble, and the visit may have been undertaken for recreation as much as for anything else. He desired, too, doubtless, to confer with the officers in command, and to examine and inspect for himself, the position and condition of our forces.

He was received with great enthusiasm by the troops at Fairfax, among whom as with the whole army, he is exceedingly popular. Tho' considerably fatigued by the trip from Richmond, I understand that he rode out this morning, and appeared to be quite refreshed.

The cause of the recent attack made upon Vice President Stephens, by the Richmond *Examiner*, is to be sought for in the precarious condition of Mr. Davis' health. It is feared that the President may not live through his term of office—in which event Mr. Stephens, as the Vice President, would succeed to the Chief Magistracy of the Confederacy; and hence the desire to supercede him by a man better suited to the purposes of the authors of the attack. It is speculation upon the probabilities of the death of Mr. Davis before the expiration of his Presidential term. The utter groundlessness of the objections urged against Mr. Stephens is conclusive upon the point.—The expressed willingness to take Gen. Toombs or Mr. [Howell] Cobb, also of Georgia, does not relieve the instigators of the attack; for behind and above all other objections brought against Mr. Stephens, is one which proves that this readiness to accept those gentlemen is affected and not real. I allude to the doctrine of sectional interests and equality, under which these defamers of the great Georgia claim, that it would be unjust to take both the President and Vice President from the cotton States.

Thus you see that this sectional monster, having seven heads and ten horns, is already beginning to show itself in our young Confederacy. Already we hear of Cotton States and Border States. There never was a more fatal policy than that which recognizes sections and sectional interests in the same Confederacy and under the same Government. It is ruinous alike in States and Confederacies. We have all seen what it led to in the United States. We have also seen that the policy produced the same deadly fruit in this State. Here there is a Western Virginia and a Tidewater or Eastern Virginia—and the one is now warring against the other with all the animosity of alien enemies. Nothing but the coolness and courage of Gen. [Felix] Zollicoffer has prevented a similar conflict in Tennessee, where there is an East Tennessee, and a Middle and West Tennessee. The doctrine prevailed in Kentucky and Missouri, and there, too, sectional animosities have culminated in sectional war, and brother now clamors for the blood of brother.

There was a considerable party opposed to the accession of the so-called border States, on account of the dissimilarity between them and the more Southern States, and the inordinate love of office among the Virginians. The course pursued by the *Examiner* and its coadjutors, is not calculated to reduce the numbers of that party. On the contrary, if persevered in, is more likely to operate unfavorably upon the destinies of down-trodden Maryland. If we are to have geographical parties—if the new Confederacy is to be divided into Cotton States and Border States—or, in plain English, into Northern States and Southern States—and our rulers are to be selected and our Government administered with a view to the imaginary local interests of particular geographical divisions, in contradistinction to the welfare of the whole country, then the sooner we know it the better, and the sooner a second secession takes place the better. The moment we admit that there are different interests in the Confederacy which call for partial and sectional treatment, that moment we sow the seeds of our own dissolution.

But I have wandered from the subject. The attack upon Mr. Stephens has been followed by a terrible rebound. From every State and locality a voice of rebuke has been heard—clearly showing, what his friends in Georgia already well know, that no man in all the land enjoyed in a greater degree the confidence and affection of the whole people.

P. W. A.

The Army to Fall Back

ARMY OF THE POTOMAC

Fairfax Court House, October 10, 1861 [10-18-61]

There is no change to report in the position of affairs. I have heard of nothing to change the opinion expressed in my last letter, that the Confederates would fall back at an early day behind Bull Run. On the contrary, many things have come to my knowledge to confirm this opinion. Of course, much depends upon the movements of the enemy; for we are ready to receive him here or at Bull Run.

A line of pickets is stretched from Fortress Monroe to Kansas; yet, we manage to now and then to procure Northern Newspapers by way of the underground railroad. The last batch received brings us news that McClellan has been ordered to St. Louis in place of [John C.] Fremont lately called to Washington for trial; and that Gen. [John] Wool, who has been superseded at Fortress Monroe by Gen. [Joseph] Mansfield, will succeed McClellan in the command at Washington. Such is the rumor in Washington, Baltimore and New York. That such rumors afloat, and that they have created no little excitement beyond the Potomac, there can be doubt; but I am unable to say how much foundation there is for them, especially in regard to McClellan.

We hear further, that much dissatisfaction exists among the bankers in Wall Street and throughout the North, on account of the hesitating policy of McClellan. It is reported that they frankly admit, that neither they nor the country can stand a long war; and they claim that when they agreed to furnish means for the prosecution of the war, it was only on condition that short work should be made of it. These accounts are confirmed in substance by Maj. Gen. [G. W.] Smith and Brig. Gen. [Mansfield] Lovell, who lately arrived here from New York, where they enjoyed the best possible facilities for getting reliable information. They represent the distress prevailing in the North, growing out of the derangement of commerce, the stagnation of business, the shortness of the grain crop, and the uneasiness of capitalists, to be almost terrible.

Five days hence (the 15th of October) is the time by which the second installment of $50,000,000 of the federal loan is to be paid. It may be that Wall Street is availing itself of the exigencies of the Government to extort from it greater vigor in the future prosecution of the war. And it may be that Johnston and Beauregard have lain idle along the Potomac, in part at least, for the reason that an active campaign here might have stimulated the efforts of Northern capitalists to assist their Government. It is evident that Mr. Lincoln can do but little without their cooperation. The money kings are not the least powerful potentates in the land. Indeed, we hear they went so far on a recent occasion as to demand an early movement forward, and that Gen. McClellan replied that he would resign rather than undertake it. Sensible to the last.

We are sorry to give up Fremont in the West; for his brutal policy and incompetency were of incalculable benefit to the Confederate cause, in uniting the people of Missouri and Kentucky. We feel somewhat reconciled to the change by the announcement that Gen. Wool has been transferred to Washington. He and Gen. Scott, between whom there is a quarrel of long standing, will not be able to get on in harmony.

McClellan is the best officer, after Gen. Scott, the enemy has. He has conducted the campaign since his advent into Washington with great skill. He has managed to set rumors afloat in Richmond and the army of the Potomac, that he had an army of 150,000 men—that he would soon cross the river and attack us with a force of 100,000 troops—and that large fleets were about to sail from Northern ports to ravage our coasts and burn our cities. The object of all this bluster was to distract our councils, to divert from the Potomac, Kentucky and Missouri the reinforcements intended for those points, and to alarm the people along the whole Southern coast.

How far McClellan has succeeded in his plans, it is not for me to declare. I can only say we have good reason to conclude that he has no such force about Washington as he would have us believe. Since the battle of Manassas, 67,000 troops have passed through Baltimore on their way to Washington and points in Maryland. Nearly all the three months volunteers have returned home, and the regulars are scattered along the line from Fortress Monroe to St. Louis. The forces, then, at and about Washington, cannot exceed much, if any, 75,000 men, many of who are disabled by sickness. I cannot now give you my reasons for speaking so positively as to numbers.

I have said, and still believe, that an active and offensive policy after the battle of Manassas, would have been the best; yet I am frank to confess that the opposite policy pursued by Johnston and Beauregard has not been without its good results. If what we hear through the Northern press be true, then we are whipping the enemy by standing still. Their expenses are enormous, being about $8,500,000 per week. No nation can stand such a drain as this long. Hence, the clamors of the bankers and capitalists against McClellan. The prospect of the most frightening suffering among the poorer classes this winter, only complicates the difficulties of the Government. Ships are rotting at their wharves, factories are idle, mechanics are out of employment, the poor are clamoring for bread, and bankers are restive and uneasy. The whole country groans and staggers under the mighty load which now presses its bended back. Meanwhile, our march is onward in Kentucky and Missouri.

We had a visit yesterday from Sir James Ferguson, a member of the British Parliament. He was an officer in the Crimean War, is about thirty-five years of age, and possesses great intelligence. He brings letters to Gen. Toombs, Gen. Beauregard and others. I suspect that his visit has been made for the purpose of examining for himself into the actual condition of affairs in this country, with a view to the question of the recognition of our independence and the raising of the blockade by the British Government. He expects to return in time for the assembling of Parliament this winter. He seems to understand the differences between the Yankee and Western man, and between the Southerner and both of them. He expressed himself without reserve and in the most friendly terms towards the Confederate States, and says he has been most favorably impressed with the bearing, the spirit and the intelligence of our volunteers. He represents that a large majority of the English people, and of Middle and Lower Canada are animated by the most friendly sentiments towards us. Western Canada, the refuge of escaped negroes, is more or less hostile in its feelings. Lord [R. B. P.] Lyons gave him a passport to cross the Potomac, which Mr. Seward countersigned, on the written condition that he should not visit the insurrectionary States. This aroused his British spirit; whereupon, he returned the passport to Mr. Seward and came around by the Western route.

P. W. A.

Waiting for the Enemy
ARMY OF THE POTOMAC
NEAR CENTREVILLE, October 18, 1861 [10-27-61]

I have nothing new that it would be proper to report in regard to the position of the Army of the Potomac. Your readers must be satisfied with the general statement that we are encamped in line of battle, and ready and eager to meet the foe. If he will but come out, with the smiles of Providence on our side we shall whip him. Many a brave fellow may go down before the rushing tide of the battle, but yield we never shall, let the invader's forces be ever so large.

In visiting the various Georgia regiments near me, yesterday and day before, I found large numbers of the brave fellows busily engaged in writing letters. The impression is very general, that there will be a great battle soon, and they were writing what they believe might be their last letters to the dear friends at home. They look this danger before them square in the face; and yet their last prayer at night and their first wish in the morning, is that they may be led forth to battle.

Looking from my tent, there is a sea of canvass spread out before the eye—a wilderness of tents—conspicuous among which may be seen those of the Georgia Regulars, and the second, seventh, eighth, ninth, eleventh, and fifteenth regiments of Georgia Volunteers. We stand, as it were, side by side, our arms interlocked and ready, if needs be, to go down, but never back. The torn and tattered flags of the seventh and eighth, still float to the breeze, and "we tread no step backwards," is the sentiment that animates every heart.

No troops throughout the whole army stand higher than the Georgians. In dauntless courage, resolute purpose, daring impetuosity, and good order, they have no superiors, and but few equals. Such is the judgement of the army.

It is believed that our Generals are fully informed of the plans of McClellan. His ostentatious transfer, in the daytime, of large bodies of troops to this side of the Potomac, has deceived nobody. His strategy was good enough—only it was understood. Vainly did he imagine, when he so confidently pushed his men forward in front, that we did not have an eye upon another man he was getting ready to move in a different direction.

Ought not a monument to be erected to a man who would, in 12 hours, ride one hundred miles and surmount the greatest obstacles, to communicate important intelligence? The campaign upon the Potomac abounds in feats of the rarest romance and daring, from which the poet and novelist will weave many a thrilling story for the entertainment of future generations. I had thought before this war, that with the last survivors of the old Revolutionary struggle, the manhood and womanhood of the land had died out; but how much mistaken were all of us who entertained such an opinion. No age or country ever produced a race of women more loyal and self sacrificing, or men more heroic and dauntless.

The Federals are in much trouble about our movement. Professor [Thaddeus] Lowe was up the greater part of the day, yesterday, in his balloon. It could be distinctly seen from our camp, a distance of twenty miles from Alexandria.

OCTOBER 19th, 9 A.M.

It is eight miles to the post office at Manassas, and frequently it is not without difficulty that we can get our letters there to be posted. Failing to send forward the foregoing yesterday, I have opened it to give you the latest news up to this hour.

McClellan has sent out scouting parties as far as Fairfax, seven miles from Centreville, and is advancing his picket forces very cautiously, at lest they should encounter a masked battery. He has also sent scouts as far up the railroad as Fairfax Station, at which place the Confederates had destroyed all the depot buildings before we left.

It is reported that Gen. [Nathaniel] Banks has crossed the Potomac at Conrad's ferry (below Harpers Ferry and the mountains,) with 20,000 men, and that he will move down upon our left from that point. Gen. Evans is near Leesburg watching his movements, though with a greatly inferior force. From Centreville to Conrad's ferry, it is twenty-five or thirty miles, and to Leesburg about twenty.

A strong naval force has been fitted out at Annapolis, the object of which is to destroy our batteries at Aquia Creek and above, and to co-operate with the attacking columns higher up. In other words, the opinion prevails that the Federals will advance upon us from these points simultaneously, viz: from Conrad's ferry above, Alexandria in the centre, where their heaviest forces are posted, and Aquia Creek and Occoquan below. Many officers still doubt however, whether he will come as far as Centreville. The demonstrations on the left and in the center may be merely points to cover the movement against the batteries on the river below. A few days will probably remove all doubts.

A battle being imminent, Col. Thomas W. Thomas addressed his regiment (the 15th Georgia) after morning drill, day before yesterday. I send you a copy of it, and you will agree with me that nothing could be more to the point..

Eighty years ago today the battle of Yorktown was fought.

P. W. A.

{ADDRESS of Col. Thomas to the 15th Regiment, Georgia Volunteers, after morning drill, on the 17th of Oct., 1861, at the camp near Centreville.}

Soldiers: The appearances surrounding us indicate we will have a fight in a few days; perhaps in one day. We have been mistaken so often, however, that I will not venture to prophesy with perfect certainty.

I, like yourselves, have never been in battle. It will be a novel sensation to me as to you. But by inquiry among those who have seen and felt it, I have learned something that perhaps would be useful and interesting to you. The great object our enemies seem to have in view, is to invent some means, or to find some plan, by which they can kill us without being hurt themselves. If we adopt some method to circumvent this single feature of their tactics, they are helpless, and we have them at our mercy. The sole thing, therefore, necessary is to go up close. We are told some of the rifles in your hands will kill a man half a mile. Don't you believe it; it's all stuff. No gun will kill a man that far, and if they could, no one could hit a man three hundred yards with certainty. You go up within a hundred yards or less, and then your marksmanship will tell. Get close to them; stand firm; aim well, and not a single regiment they have will stand before you five minutes.

But their artillery—their terrible big guns. We hear they have two hundred of the finest pieces of artillery in the world. Well, I hope it is true; we want those guns; we are entitled to them; we know how to use them, and they don't, and Providence never, intended that fine cannon, nor anything else, should be held by those who understand not their use. After diligent inquiry, I can hear of but one single man on our side killed by their cannon at the battle of Manassas Plains. Providence fought with us at Manassas. He will fight with us again, if we are brave. He loves valor, and He loves a valiant soldier. He will help us, but he will not drop cannon down to us out of the skies. He expects to help us by putting it into the hearts of our enemies to bring the cannon in our reach, and then He expects us to take them.

Another marked feature of the fight, if we get into one, you will find is the whistling of the shells. Our enemies have succeeded admirably in constructing a harmless instrument which makes a curious and unpleasant noise, and it has this wonderful peculiarity; it seems to be coming straight at every man who hears it. Now, we know it can't be coming at but one man, or at most two; and the truth is, it is coming at nobody. You have nothing to do but to pay close attention to your hind sight, and the whistling of the shells will after a little become rather a small matter in the grand drama you are acting. The man who hears thunder is never struck by the lightning. The great implement of death in war you hold in your hands, the musket or the bayonet—and your enemies have none better of more terrible.

Another feature in the fight will be the falling of the killed and wounded. It is a trying thing to a man to see his friends fall by his side, and our first impulse is to carry him to the rear. But remember, the best way to save your wounded friend is not for five or six to leave the ranks, and thus weaken and break your line. This will insure his destruction and your own by the trampling and bayonets of your enemies. Your wounded friends ought to be in the rear, and you ought to be between them and the foe. Now, the plainest and most effectual way to do this is to close up your ranks and advance on the enemy.

Soldiers, you fight for your liberty, your country, your wives and your children. You cannot afford to be defeated. Your fate would be hewers of wood and drawers of water to an enemy you abhor. Your enemies are bought with a price—fifty dollars per head bounty, and large pay induce them to enter the ranks to destroy your rights. Can you yield to such a foe? With one powerful blow let us crush them and return home to our families and firesides.

On October 21, Federal General Charles Stone made a reconnaissance-in-force across the Potomac River near Leesburg, Virginia. The resulting battle brought another Bull Run-style defeat for the Federals and boundless jubilation for the Confederates.

Glorious Victory!
ARMY OF THE POTOMAC
Centreville, Oct. 22, 1861 [10-27-61]

The weather has been disagreeable and unfavorable for field operations for some days, and this morning we have a sharp "Nor-wester," accompanied by a driving mist that is anything but pleasant. It reminds one of the weather we sometimes have in Georgia just before Christmas. The men are cutting and hauling wood over the muddy roads, or standing round the campfires with their blankets thrown over their shoulders, and drying first one side and then the other. The horses are gathered about the wagons, and drawn up and shivering in the cold wind and rain. Now and then a courier may be seen dashing down the turnpike clad in an oilcloth suit, and his head inclined in the direction from which the wind blows and the mist comes. Just at this point a detachment of seventy men from this brigade passes my tent, each man with a spade or axe upon his shoulder, and going forward to a point where we are throwing up some earthworks. Each brigade furnishes a similar detachment every day. Meanwhile the sentinels may be seen upon the distant hilltop and along the valleys, pacing their solitary rounds and keeping constantly in motion to make themselves warm. It is a cold day, and yet not so cold out that one's heart warms towards the brave fellows who, day and night, in storm and sunshine, stand sentinel between us and a merciless foe.

It is just such weather as makes one desire to be seated in a soft chair, beside a cheerful fire in a cozy little room, with a good book to read. But such pictures of the imagination only render the reality the more cheerless; at least they do not contribute anything to that frame of mind which is necessary to the preparation of an interesting letter. I can keep neither my hands nor my feet warm; for my tent is wet and the ground is damp and cold.

The entire country from Manassas to the Potomac has been stripped of forage, and there is not even straw to be had, except in the most limited quantities, to scatter in the tents. The fencing has been destroyed and the rails used for firewood; barns and hay-ricks have been emptied; cattle pens and sheep folds have been exhausted; wagons and teams have been impressed, orchards stripped, farms cut up by newly made roads, and the whole country ravaged as if a fire had swept over it. Many of the inhabitants have been compelled by necessity of abandon their homes and retire back into the country, where their families would be out of immediate danger and convenient to supplies for their support. It is but just to add, that the Confederates have paid for everything their necessities have forced them to take.

What is true of Fairfax county, will be found to be equally true of North-western Virginia, Kentucky, Missouri, and all other neutral States and districts. Neutrality is the worst policy that any people can adopt.

GLORIOUS VICTORY.—10 o'clock, A.M.—We have just received news of a most brilliant affair of yesterday at Leesburg, 20 miles above us. Gen. Evans, who is stationed near that place with a brigade, was attacked early in the morning by a column of 10,000 men, under Gen. [Charles] Stone. The Confederate force numbered 2,500, and yet they achieved a most splendid victory. The fight was continued at intervals throughout the day, and was so hot that nobody could be spared to bring the glorious news. Gen. Stone intended to take the Confederates by surprise; and in order to make his chances doubly sure, he brought with him a force of four to one, with a full and complete compliment of artillery.

The exact results of the engagement have not been ascertained, but the most reliable accounts to hand state that we took 50 privates and 19 officers prisoners—that we drove the entire force back pell mell into the river, and that in attempting to cross, 300 of them were drowned. Among the killed, was Gen. [Edward] Baker, Senator from Oregon, whose body was pierced by 5 different balls. The number of killed and wounded is not yet known. The prisoners were started back last night, to get them out of the way, lest the enemy renew the attack. Reinforcements have already been sent up to meet such a contingency.

We could hear the firing from our camp, but it was generally supposed that the enemy was engaged in artillery practice. I had nearly forgotten to say, that Gen. Evans took 3 pieces of artillery, and it is supposed a number of small arms.

2 o'clock, P.M.   Further particulars of the battle of Leesburg have just come to hand. The battle was fought about one mile from Leesburg, and between that place and the Potomac, which is about 2 miles from the town. The enemy had crossed at Edward's Ferry, in boats, flats and skiffs.—His force, as already stated, was about 10,000 men, and ours about 2,500. We took 520 prisoners, including 19 officers, among whom were Col. [William] Lee, of the old United States Army. We took 3 pieces of artillery, about 600 small arms, several wagon loads of provisions, and considerable amount of ammunition and clothing.—The enemy's loss in killed and wounded is estimated at between 4 and 500; ours at 300. In addition to this, the enemy lost some 300 who were drowned in crossing the river. They rushed into the boats and other craft upon which they had crossed to this side, and many of them being crowded and overloaded, sunk or upset. When the courier left last night, the Confederates were driving the Federals back at every point, and inflicting the most terrible punishment.

Gen. Evans is known in the army by the name of "Shanks." All honor to Shanks for the brilliant victory of Leesburg.

In haste,   P. W. A.

Official losses for the Battle of Leesburg or Ball's Bluff: Federals, 49 killed, 158 wounded, 714 missing—many presumed drowned for 921 casualties; Confederates, 36 killed, 117 wounded, 2 missing for 155 casualties.

The Leesburg Fight
ARMY OF THE POTOMAC
Centreville, October 29, 1861 [11-5-61]

No official account of the battle of Leesburg has yet been published. I am compelled therefore, not having been present myself, to rely upon the accounts given by persons who witnessed the fight, and such apparently well authenticated statements as reach me through other channels. If, under circumstances, I should be led into error, your readers who have accompanied me thus far in this campaign, will readily excuse me. It is impossible always to sift the truth from falsehood. This is especially the case in camp, where many thousands of men are thrown together from all parts of the country, who are unknown to each other and easily imposed upon by rumors which they have no opportunity to investigate. It is safe to say, that here as elsewhere, the wheat bears but a small proportion to the chaff.

The most satisfactory account I have had of the battle was given to me by the Rev. Dr. Stiles of Georgia, who has two sons under Gen. Evans, and who was present and witnessed the greater part of it. The enemy had sent over the previous night a portion of his forces, who crossed a little above Leesburg at Mason's Island, and concealed themselves in the woods. Others crossed at Edward's Ferry, somewhat below Leesburg. The fight commenced early in the morning, and consisted of a series of skirmishes, until about 4 o'clock in the afternoon, when it became general. The enemy took shelter in the woods and thickets, and seldom showed himself upon the open field. This compelled our men to enter the woods and flush them up after the fashion of deer hunters whose habit it is to scour every thicket and cover where the game might find a hiding place. Late in the day when the Federals had been driven out, the fight became hot and furious, owing to the superiority of their numbers. The 8th Virginia regiment behaved with the greatest gallantry, and was more than a match for three times its numbers. The Mississippians fought well also, as they always do. The cavalry took but little part, and our battery, which had been posted on the flank to prevent reinforcements from coming up by the two roads, did not fire a gun. The enemy made good use of his artillery, especially in affording protection to his troops while they were crossing the river; and whenever they were driven back to the river, during the fight, those from the other side were brought to bear upon our men with considerable effect.

But the Federals could not stand close quarters nor cold steel, and finally were driven back to the river at a place where the bluff varies from twenty to sixty feet in height. Down this bluff they rushed, like the herd of swine into which the unclean spirits had entered. Mr. Stiles estimates the number drowned at 450. They crowded the boats and flats in such numbers as to sink and upset them, and whole loads went down together. Many tried to swim across and were lost, and others were taken in a state of nudity, who had stripped for the same purpose. The scene is represented to have been terrific and the fright and consternation of the poor wretches as indescribable. Some were leaping down the precipice' some were stripping and rushing into the water; others were crowding into the sinking boats and screaming in the death agony as they sunk into a watery grave; others, again, sought a hiding place under the cliffs and among the rocks. In the meantime, the enemy on the opposite side, unable to keep up their artillery fire, lest they should destroy their own friends, looked on in awe, whilst the Confederates pressed forward and smote the flying and affrighted rabble as with the sword of an avenging spirit.

Late Northern papers just to hand vainly endeavor to break the force of this terrible blow. They affect to consider it a very small affair—only "a reconnaissance party in force" on their part. They say that their missing are coming in, and that Gen. McClellan is entirely satisfied with the results of the movement, since his only object, the ascertainment of our position and strength in that quarter, has been fully accomplished. The mendacious simpletons are easily satisfied.

P. W. A.

Northern News
ARMY OF THE POTOMAC
CENTREVILLE, November 3, 1861 [11-10-61]

A batch of Northern papers has just come to hand by the underground railroad. I have not had an opportunity to make extracts from them, but I hand you below a statement of the more important news which they bring us. You will agree with me that the news is important, as well to the world at large as to ourselves and the Northern people.

Imprimis; the New York *Tribune* contains a telegram from Washington, which states that Gen. Scott will retire from the army in ten days from the date of the dispatch. His pay as Lieutenant-General will be continued to him as heretofore, in accordance with an act of the Federal Congress passed at its late extra session. The telegram further states, that there has never been a settlement between Gen. Scott and the War Department since the Mexican War—the General claiming that there was a balance due to him, and the Secretary of War claiming that the balance was due the Department. Well, it appears that the matter has been recently investigated, and that the balance has been ascertained to be in Gen. Scott's favor. This balance is to be paid at once, and his pay as Lieutenant-General is to be continued during life. In other words, the schemers of the Federal Government have bought the old man off. He was too infirm, too slow and cautious, and perhaps too honest, for their purposes. McClellan will probably succeed to the supreme command. No one is likely to regret the change sooner than the Northern people themselves. Gen. Scott was incomparably the ablest military man they had. No army was ever better fitted out and equipped than the one he sent to the Plains of Manassas; and the stratagem which enabled it to cross Bull Run and attack our flank was perfect. But the old hero's caution does not jump with the fanaticism of the North. The result is, he has been retired, (a polite word for dismissed and disgraced), just as McClellan will be when reverses shall have taught him the virtue of prudence.

The papers alluded to above bring us other intelligence of an important character. They state that the great naval expedition—the invincible Armada of the North—had sailed from Fortress Monroe on Wednesday last, 30th October. They publish also the instructions of the Secretaries of the Navy and War Departments to the commanders of the expedition. The instructions to Commodore [Samuel] Dupont, who commands the fleet, are full and explicit, and contain specific directions as to the manner in which the squadron shall approach the shore, and the several brigades and batteries shall be landed. The instructions to the officer in charge of the land forces are equally explicit. The entire programme is given, except the particular spot to be attacked and occupied.

These last instructions embrace some points of vital interest to the Southern people. The Secretary of War refers to the correspondence between himself and General Butler at Fortress Monroe, upon the question of the proper disposition to be made of such slaves as may be taken or may come in voluntarily, belonging to rebellious citizens, and says that the General in command will be governed by the principles laid down.

P. W. A.

A Scouting Expedition
ARMY OF THE POTOMAC
Centreville, November 13, 1861 [11-21-61]

I have not written you the last few days on account of absence on a scouting expedition. There was but little to write about, however, if I had been here, without treading upon forbidden topics. What say you then, to some account of our late expedition? It did not abound in daring exploits, or romantic incidents; and yet, it may serve to give you some idea of the nature of the service in which our troops are frequently engaged.

The order from headquarters was sent out at 11 o'clock at night, and it called for a picket force consisting of three crack regiments and about 600 cavalry. The 1st Georgia Regulars, Lieut. Col. Magill commanding, was one of the regiments designated in the order, and they were required to take with them one day's rations, and to be ready to move at daybreak next morning. The other regiments named in the order were Col. [Ambose P.] Hill, 13th Virginia, and Col. Stuart's [G. H. Steuart] of the Maryland Line. It was understood that the enemy had thrown forward a force beyond his lines in the direction of ——— , and the object of the expedition was to capture or drive it back.

The prospect for a little sharp work was so inviting, that I determined to accompany the Regulars; so I filled my haversack, mounted my horse, and fell into line just as the first flashes of the coming day began to illuminate the eastern horizon. It had rained all the previous day, and the roads were heavy, and in some places almost impassable. But it cleared up during the night, and overhead it was a lovely day. The frost and ice soon disappeared, and the air became genial and elastic as the sun mounted upward to the zenith.

It was a long weary march for such roads as we had to travel. For eight miles we kept the public highway, but after that we followed such cross roads and neighborhood ways as would enable us to pass unobserved. Our route was somewhat semi-circular, the object of Gen. Steuart, who commanded the expedition, being to get in, if possible, between the main body of the enemy and his advanced force. Night found us eighteen miles from camp—the men weary and footsore, but cheerful and eager for the fray. Orders were given to file off into a dense forest near the road, to stack arms for a few hours rest, and to make as little noise as possible. Pickets were immediately thrown out, and scouts dispatched in various directions to observe the movements of the enemy.

Having kindled small fires, the men were soon engaged over the remains of their day's rations. Nearly all of them had brought cooked provisions; while a few were compelled, in the hurry of leaving, to bring a pint or two of flour and a flitch of raw bacon. To a looker-on, the scene was full of interest. The dim forest—the flickering camp fires hid away among the trees and under the hill—the novel occupation of the men, some of whom were bringing in straw and leaves to lie upon, while others were gathering around the fires disposing of their frugal meal, or broiling a piece of bacon upon the end of their ram-rods, or discussing in an undertone the late march and the prospect of an early engagement—the arms stacked near by and reflecting back the light from the burning embers—the officers gathered in little knots and arranging the plans of to-morrow—the horses tied close at hand with saddles on and ready to move at a moment's notice—the consciousness of the proximity of the enemy, and above all, that a short march would bring us to Mount Vernon, the Mecca of every Southern heart, and that the ground upon which we stood had once been trod by Washington—all these things and this consciousness conspired to make it a scene over which the heart and the pencil of the old masters would have warmed and glowed with delight.

But we expect to move soon after midnight; so there is but little time to devote to [fanc]y or of fact. We turn in, then, not to bed, but to leaves and straw. Only a [few brin]g their blankets, as the general understanding was, that we would return [soon.] But with overcoats, comforters, straw, leaves and fire, however, we [had som]e refreshing sleep. The soldier soon learns to sleep anywhere—even upon [the ground] in the rain. An old campaigner told me not long since, that he could sleep [warmly] with nothing but a *sheet* of water to cover with. Be as it may, I managed [it on t]he night in question. The last thing I noticed before going to sleep was a [son of] the Emerald Isle, who was inclined to be somewhat musical. His favorite [was] the famous "Widow [Mother] Machree," which he would hum in a [low, and n]ow and then he would break out in another strain—

"O, she wouldn't and she couldn't and she didn't come at all."

Pat had evidently been taking a "d'hrop o' somethin'," somewhere.

Let me say just here, that the Irish of the South have done, and are doing, their whole duty in this war. Wherever I have seen one, he was not only true to the cause, but ready to seal his devotion to it with his best blood. Pat may be noisy and sometimes a little insubordinate, but his heart is in the right place. He loves liberty and hates oppression and as such, he is the friend of the South and the enemy of the North. His fellow countrymen in the United States have been temporarily led astray, but they are all getting back into the right path, and henceforth but few of them will be found enlisting in the Northern army.

Next morning we were called up at 3 o'clock, by which hour it was expected our scouts would return with full and accurate information as to the exact position of the enemy. They did not get back, however, until daylight, and then they brought news, much to our disappointment that the bird had flown. We had bivouacked near a small cabin, and immediately upon our arrival the previous evening, inquiry was made of the children residing there in regard to their father. They replied that he had gone to hunt the cow—a common excuse among the tory population on the Potomac. As we neared the house about sunset, the mother was seen to come to the door, cast an anxious look up the road by which we were approaching, and then to dart off in the opposite direction, leaving her children, two of whom were quite young, behind her. She did not return until a late hour of the night, and then she pretended she had been frightened by our sudden appearance. The truth was, however, she had carried the news of our arrival to a neighboring conspirator, and he had taken it to a third, and the third had communicated it to the fourth; and thus it went, until the enemy was made aware of our presence.

The intelligence produced no little commotion within the Federal lines, as we learned from our scouts the following morning; but whether the main body was getting ready to attack us or were in full retreat, they could not tell, owing to the darkness and distance. We were ready to fight one to four, as far removed as we were from any supporting force.

We returned by a different route, marching along in front and near the enemy's lines, with the hope of flushing a fresh quarry. We expected him up every moment, but he declined to come out or to be surprised.

But I must stop. We returned in safety, but disappointed at the result of the expedition.

P. W. A.

No Fight, and But Little Prospect of One

ARMY OF THE POTOMAC

Centreville, November 17, 1861 [11-27-61]

It is now the middle of November, and yet McClellan still declines to come out from behind his works and give us battle. For weeks we occupied the range of hills just in front of his fortifications and in full view of his Capital, and there flaunted our flag in the faces of himself and his rulers and defied him to battle. He refused to pick up the glove we had thrown down, and instead of heading an offensive movement, the object of which was to crush out the rebellion, he adopted a defensive policy, and devoted all his time, day and night, to the safety and protection of his Capital. If he refused to fight us at Munson's Hill, where he had his works to fall back upon, will he come out twenty miles to Centreville and measure swords with us upon the open field? You know my opinion upon this point, and it need not be repeated here.

But Johnston and Beauregard are in a position to be better informed than I possibly can be. They have believed for some weeks that McClellan would fight them before the winter set in; and hence they fell back to this place. As he would select the time for the attack, it was entirely proper for them to select the ground upon which they would receive him. I understand they still entertain some hope that they will have the pleasure of seeing him at Centreville; and if not here, then at some other point along our lines. It is not probable that another attempt will be made on our left, as the one already made at Leesburg resulted so disastrously to the Federal arms; but there is some reason to think it not altogether improbable that an attack is contemplated on the right in the direction of the Occoquan or Aquia Creek.

The roads other than the turnpikes are already nearly impassible to artillery and heavy wagons. It is seldom that we have more than two or three dry days together, and the soil when it does rain is very unfavorable for heavy transportation. A recent excursion across the country satisfied me that the period has almost arrived when it will be impossible to conduct offensive operations in the field. I refer, of course, to a general movement looking to the invasion of the country and the permanent occupation of our territory. It would be utterly impossible during the winter season for McClellan to keep his army supplied by wagon trains at a distance of fifty miles from Washington, his base of operations, unless he had a dozen parallel turnpikes all leading to the same point. No man without experience in such matters can form any adequate conception of the immense amount of transportation required for the movement of an army. Not only the tents, camp chests and ordinary baggage have to be transported, but there are the medical and hospital stores, the ammunition, provisions for the men and forage for the trains, all of which have to be carried along. It is seven miles from this place to Manassas, from which we draw our supplies, and yet fifteen wagons are barely sufficient to do the transportation of a single regiment in camps. The hauling of wood is a very heavy item itself. It would not be wide of the mark to say, that the Army of the Potomac consumes daily in cold weather the wood on six or seven acres of land. The consumption in cabins with fire-places would not be so great; and it would be still less in stoves, which, I understand, will be used as far as they can be had.

There is nothing new to report in the position of affairs here. Our men succeed every few days in capturing some of the enemy's pickets, who are immediately sent forward to Richmond and points further South. The weather is becoming disagreeably wet and cold, especially to men in their tents and on the cold ground. The health of the army however, continues to improve, though it is not yet such as we could desire it to be. There has been considerable abatement in the number of cases of typhoid fever, measles and mumps, though the army is not yet free of them. Jaundice is prevailing to a greater extent just now than any other disease.

P. W. A.

On November 8, the U. S. S. San Jacinto *halted the British mail packet* Trent, *and forcibly removed two Confederate diplomats. The resulting international incident—the Trent Affair—threatened war with the United States and Great Britain.*

Capture of Mason and Slidell
Centreville, November 18, 1861 [11-25-61]

You will have heard by telegraph before this reaches you, of the forcible seizure of Mr. [James] Mason and Mr. [John] Slidell, our Commissioners to England and France, on board a British mail steamer in mid ocean. We were disposed here to doubt the correctness of the report, until the receipt this afternoon of the Washington *Star*. That paper confirms the statement, and speaks of the affair as a glorious achievement.

The arrest of Mr. Mason and Mr. Slidell is the most highhanded proceeding between nations at peace, as the United States and Great Britain are, of which I have ever heard or read. It is equivalent to a declaration of war followed up by immediate blow. The Federal Government had no more right, under the law of nations, to arrest an English steamer and forcibly seize and carry away any of its passengers, even though they were its own citizens, than it had to march a regiment into London and seize them at the very gates of the Queen's palace. That the British Government will resent the outrage with all the power at its command, there can, I should think, be no doubt. It is stated that the Federal Captain [Charles Wilkes] who made the arrest, acted under a warrant from the State department—a fact which, if true, precludes the possibility of a disclaimer of the act by the Government. He brought the English steamer to by a shot across her bow, and then boarded her, and violently arrested and brought away our Commissioners against their protests and that of the commander of the ship. Under these circumstances, it is doubtful whether the amplest apology, coupled with the surrender of the prisoners, can prevent an early rupture and resort to arms on the part of Great Britain.

It has been suggested, in explanation of the conduct of the Federal Government, that possibly it may desire a difficulty with England. Conscious of its inability to subdue the rebellious States of the Southern Confederacy, and too proud to acknowledge the fact, it is not impossible that it should invite a rupture with a nation already believed to be friendly to us, knowing that it would be less humiliating to retreat at the proper time from a contest so unequal, than it would be to end the war with an acknowledgment of our independence. It may be also, that Mr. Seward was in his cups when he issued the order for the arrest of the Commissioners; for he is known to have abandoned himself, since the commencement of the war, more freely than ever to the worship of the wine-loving deity. The same may be said of his chief, Mr. Lincoln. But they will never be able, either with wine or water, to wash out the stains that now blacken their guilty consciences.

You have also seen probably a report of the late speech of Mr. Secretary [Simon] Cameron in Washington City. He is reported to have said, that the slaves of the South are loyal to the Union, and that if it be right to place spades in their hands to work upon Federal forts, it is equally right to place muskets in their hands to fight Federal battles. Thus you see the issue of emancipation will soon be made, as I predicted in a former communication. Well, let it come. The Yankees are sure to meet defeat in this last and desperate movement as they have been upon the field of battle.

P. W. A.

Catching Prisoners
ARMY OF THE POTOMAC
Centreville, November 29, 1861 [12-6-61]

If I do not always inform you of the captures made by our pickets, it is because they have ceased to be of much interest on account of their frequency. A fresh batch of prisoners, numbering 32, was brought in yesterday with their horses, arms, &c. They belonged to a company of Pennsylvania cavalry sent out to protect a wagon train which had been dispatched on a foraging expedition in the direction of Vienna. They were taken by a North Carolina company—a part, I suspect, of Col. [Robert] Ransom's regiment of cavalry. The men were exceedingly well dressed, though indifferently mounted, owing to the unfaithfulness of the agents whose duty it was to purchase the horses. One of the prisoners remarked, that their entire company would have escaped if they had been as well mounted as those in front. The idea of making a stand seemed never to have occurred to their minds—the only question being at the speed of their horses.

But my object in alluding to the affair at all, is not so much to give you an account of the capture, as to communicate some statements made by one of the prisoners. He was talking with an intelligent Georgian from Hancock county, and in the course of the conversation he introduced the subject of peace. He inquired what the Confederates said on the subject. The Georgian replied, that they said nothing at all.

Yankee—How is that, sir? Don't your people sometimes discuss the subject?

Georgian—They do not. The North made the war, and we are only defending ourselves and homes. We wage not war against you, and whenever you let us alone, we will lay down our arms, and not before. For this reason we have nothing to say on the subject of peace. We couldn't make peace if we desired to do so, without yielding the whole question, which we shall never do.

Yankee—What would satisfy the South?

Georgian—The South will be satisfied with nothing less than the twelve States that have already seceded, and the right for Kentucky and Maryland to decide by ballot with which side they will cast their lots. Peace might be made on this boundary now, but next spring nothing less than the original fourteen States will satisfy our people. Has anything been said on the subject of peace beyond the Potomac?

Yankee—Yes sir. The subject is discussed freely in the army, both by officers and privates.

Georgian—Well, what do they say?

Yankee—The men are generally in favor of peace, and it is the prevailing opinion that some steps will be taken this winter by our Congress to settle the troubles between the North and South. I guess we shall have to recognize you after all. At least, such is the talk in camp.

Georgian—I shouldn't be surprised if you did. But when is McClellan coming out to fight us?

Yankee—I don't think he will come soon, sir. It was not believed in our lines that there would be another general engagement in this quarter this campaign. There may be engagements between the pickets and outposts, but nothing more. I hope there will be no more such affairs as that at Leesburg. You *butchered* our people there, sir.

Such is the substance of the conversation. You can draw your inferences from it. The man appeared to be candid and sincere, and was much distressed at his condition. He inquired particularly about the reported raising of the "black flag" in Georgia and South Carolina, and seemed much relieved when told he was safe and would be treated kindly. The conversation occurred in the presence of the other prisoners, none of whom expressed any difference in regard to his statements. Some of them appeared to be quite confident, however, that the North would "give us jessie" yet.

There are vague rumors floating about camp, that the enemy will soon advance upon our right in the neighborhood of Evansport and Occoquan. The last letter at hand of Mr. [William H.] Russell to the London *Times*, indicates that as the point likely to be attacked. He was pretty nearly correct in his prediction as to the time the naval expedition would set sail, and it may be that he is right in this instance also.

The weather for two weeks past has been very unfavorable for active operations, and there is no present prospect of improvement. It has rained, snowed or sleeted every day for the last six days. We have not had three consecutive days of sunshine in nearly as many weeks. The weather is exceedingly changeable, and as capricious as a spoilt beauty of eighteen summers. I have known it to rain, clear up, rain again, and then sleet, all in twenty-four hours. The soil does not absorb the water readily, and consequently the earth is cold and damp all the time. Oh, for one day of the glorious sunshine and genial air of dear old Georgia!

Such is the weather. And yet an order was sent out last evening from headquarters requiring an immediate inspection to be made of all the baggage in the army—with a view, it is supposed to its reduction. A return is ordered to be made of all personal baggage above one suit of outer and two of under clothing, and one blanket where there is an overcoat, and two blankets where there is no overcoat. There is but little straw to be had; the tents in many instances are old and dilapidated, and they are too small and crowded to keep fires in them. Where there are but two or three in a tent, the men manage to have a little fire by digging a small hole in the ground and filling it with live coals. The blankets are small and the supply scant; but such as they are, if the men are to be stripped of them, much suffering and sickness will be the certain consequence. They would sooner give up half their rations than their blankets; and yet if an emergency should arise, they would cheerfully burn them to save them from the enemy.

If there be any real ground to expect a battle soon, then the men would cheerfully surrender up the blankets, as they would their lives in defense of their country. But if there be no such prospect, and the baggage is to be sent to Manassas, to be pilfered and to rot from exposure to the weather, then there can be no sort of excuse for such a procedure—baggage sent back from Fairfax six weeks ago—at least, so much of it as has not been stolen—still lies at Manassas, literally rotting from insufficient protection against the weather.

A great many letters and newspapers addressed to persons in the army, fail to reach their destination on account of the manner in which they are addressed. If a person be attached to a General's staff, then they should be directed to the care of that officer. If he belong to a regiment or battery, then they should be addressed to the care of the Colonel of the regiment or the Captain of the battery, with the name of the company to which he is attached. Letters and packages directed otherwise, fail to reach their destination three times out of four. Each regiment has its postmaster, whose duty it is to take to the post-office all letters sent from the regiment, and to receive and distribute such as are intended for the regiment. It would be well if friends at home would observe these directions.

P. W. A.

Expecting a Fight
ARMY OF THE POTOMAC
Centreville, Va., December 4, 1861 [12-12-61]

Almost every body one meets with insists that there will be a great battle here soon. It is contended that the political, no less than the military, necessities of the Federal Government will force McClellan to assume the offensive and to come out upon the open field. It is with the greatest difficulty that he can procure supplies for his men and forage for his teams. The blockade of the Potomac has closed the channel by which the city of Washington and the army have heretofore received the chief part of their provisions, fuel, forage and munitions of war. The surrounding country has been stripped of every pound of meat and meal, and every blade of grass, that could be bought or impressed. The single line of railway leading out of Washington is insufficient to accommodate the enormous demands upon it for transportation. Winter will soon be here; nay, it is already upon us, and transportation by wagon trains will in a short time be impossible.

What, then, can McClellan do but fight? How else will he be able to raise the blockade of the Potomac? It is not a matter of choice with him and his government, but of necessity. The press is clamorous for a forward movement. The bankers and capitalists are clamorous;

the politicians are clamorous; and the Congress, it is believed, will be equally clamorous for another movement in the direction of Bull Run—that dark and bloody Run, more frightful than the ancient Styx, over which the Yankee army has not yet found a Charon skillful enough to transport them. With a fanatical mob shouting at his heels and his men insufficiently provided, what can he do but fight? The Potomac must be unlocked, or the army must suffer. Some of the cavalry horses captured last week by the North Carolinians were so poor, our men turned them loose as too worthless to keep.

Such is the reasoning of those who insist that there must be a fight. In addition to this, refugees from Washington are unanimous in the opinion that a forward movement will be made at an early day. A large number of transportation wagons have been accumulated in Alexandria, and thus Gen. [Edwin] Sumner, with twelve regiments, is reported to be cautiously feeling his way down the river on the Virginia side towards our batteries below. So decisive was this movement considered of the intentions of the enemy, that Gen. Toombs was notified of it by telegraph and advised to return if he desired to be present at the battle. He reached Centreville to-day, with but little hope, however, of meeting the enemy. He is one of the few who are slow to believe that McClellan will fight at all except upon his own judgement. If ready to move, he will come out and give us battle. If not ready, he will not hazard his own reputation and the safety of his army, merely to gratify the clamoring multitude, even though that multitude be composed, in parts of bankers and congressmen.

The prime difficulty with McClellan is a want of confidence in his troops. He has men enough, and arms and artillery enough; but unfortunately for him, his troops have "no stomach for the fight." The prisoners we have taken admit as much. They evince the greatest curiosity to see Bull Run and Beauregard, and I am inclined to think they would go as far to see either as they would any stream or individual on the continent.

Not only the people of the U. States, but foreigners beyond the Atlantic seem to regard Beauregard as the leader of the Army of the Potomac. They seldom speak of any other officer in connection with this division of the Army. He seems to have taken fast hold upon the public mind of the world. Such is emphatically true of the army itself, by whom he is regarded with confidence and admiration. His unaffected loyalty to the cause, his unselfishness, his generous nature and unostentatious manners, together with his brilliant career, have rendered him the idol of his men. It is but justice to say, however, that Gen. Johnston is the commander-in-chief of the Army of the Potomac, and as such, is responsible for its management. He directs, and Beauregard and all others obey. Should a great battle be won, to him will belong chief praise and credit. Should it be lost, upon his shoulders will rest the heavy responsibility. As a strategist, the army put a great confidence in his judgement and sagacity. But I shall have more to say of both of these officers hereafter, and especially of their connection with the campaign on the Potomac. Until then, further remark may be pretermitted.

Accustomed as we are in camp to death in all its forms, there are accidents that some times occur resulting in the loss of life, which startle us by their very strangeness. An accident of this character occurred a few days ago in the Banks County Guards, 2nd Georgia regiment, while out on picket duty. A musket was left leaning against a tree, the butt resting upon the corner of a blanket that had been thrown down at the root of the tree. The owner of the blanket went for it, and taking it up suddenly, the musket was thrown to the ground, and went off, the ball striking a man sitting some twenty paces off, just below the eye, killing him instantly!

A still more startling accident occurred a few weeks since. A man was found dead in his tent one morning, having been pierced to the heart by a large minie ball. No one, not even the friend at his side, had heard the report of a gun during the night, and there were no firearms in the tent. How, then, had he been killed? A bullet hole was found in the side of the tent, through which it was supposed the ball had entered. Some one probably at this distance of several hundred yards, had during the night fired off his minie rifle in the air, and the ball had found a lodgment in the heart of the unconscious sleeper. Was it Chance that directed the fatal ball, or was it guided by an Unseen Hand? He had escaped the leaden hail that was rained upon him on the Plains of Manassas, to fall by a single ball, fired at the dead hour of night, and at a distance so great that the report of the piece was not heard. Any yet, no one who stood upon those Plains on that bloody day can doubt that the Hand which had saved him in the hour of battle had borne him hence in the mid watches of the night.

P. W. A.

No Change
ARMY OF THE POTOMAC
Centreville, December 11, 1861 [12-19-61]

There is no change to report in the relative positions of the two armies since the date of my last letter. The weather is pleasant, and neither army seems to be in a hurry to go into winter quarters. For the past four days, the weather has been as soft and balmy as you ever have it in Georgia. The roads have improved wonderfully in the meantime, and are fast becoming firm and dry. If Gen. McClellan intends to give us battle, now is his time; for he cannot expect better roads or finer weather before next Spring. It might require additional horse power to maneuver artillery in the open field, owing to the late freeze and thaw; but we should have the same difficulty to encounter. A gun that required four horses to move it rapidly and promptly over favorable ground, would now require six or eight horses. This arises in great part from the unfavorable character of the soil for field operations. The water percolates the clay slowly, and remains for the most part in the thin crust of soil overlying the clay, where it is subject to alternate freezes and thaws throughout the winter. Artillery and baggage trains could be transported with considerable ease during a hard freeze; but should a thaw follow soon, it would be impossible to save them in case of disaster to the army.

The troops, however, have not suffered themselves to be seduced by the superb weather of the last few days, but have been busily engaged in rendering their tents as comfortable as possible. Diverse ways and means have been devised for this purpose, some of which are unique and almost amusing. The simplest mode is to dig a small hole in the ground a few inches deep, and fill it with live embers. In this way a tent may be made comfortable in a few minutes, and the embers produce no smoke. Those who desire to have a fire-place large enough to burn wood, dig a hole of the requisite size and shape at the back end of the tent, with a covered flue leading outside, which is topped by two or more flour barrels, the one stuck in the other. Sometimes the tent is cut, and a regular dirt and stick chimney is built. Turf is frequently cut into the form and size of bricks, for which it answers as a very good chimney may be constructed. In some instances the men dig into the sides of the hills and burrow in the ground. If the inequality of the ground be not sufficient for this, they dig down the upper side until it is made even, and then pitch their tents. This protects them against the wind on the side next to the hill. Others again pitch their tents where the ground is flat, and then excavate to the depth of two or three feet inside, and go in and out by dirt steps. A fireplace is cut into one side of the earth wall, which has its vent outside through a chimney constructed of turf or of dirt and sticks. These chimnies are almost invariably topped with barrels. In a few instances a sort of cabin is built of poles and dirt. There are two styles of architecture in vogue, both of which are original and unique. The first can be best described by saying that the cabin, when finished, looks like the steep roof of a house set down on the ground. The second is conical in form, and reminds one of a huge potatoe heap. The poles rest upon the ground and are brought to a point above, and then covered over with brush and mud.

Poor as these contrivances are, the private soldier is unable to participate, except in a slight degree, in the comfort arising from them, in consequence of the smallness of the tents, and the numbers who are crowded into them. But little room is left for a fireplace in a tent of only ten feet square, and in which six or eight men sleep and store all their baggage. In most cases, they are compelled to resort to log fires in the company streets, which do well enough when the weather is dry and calm, but answer very poorly when it is wet and windy. When the army goes into winter quarters, rude but comfortable log cabins will be erected, convenient to wood and water.

Two men belonging to Maj. Wheat's battalion of N. O. Tigers, were executed near this place at 11 o'clock yesterday for mutinous conduct. They were blindfolded, and their hands tied behind them and also to a post, in front of which they were made to kneel. A detachment of 24 men had been detailed to shoot them. Twelve of the guns were loaded with ball cartridges and twelve with blank cartridges, so that the men whose painful duty it was to execute the judgement of the court martial, should each remain in ignorance whether the gun he might fire was charged with ball or not. A priest attended the condemned to the place of execution, and was constant and devoted in his attentions to the last. At length the guns, previously loaded, are handed to the executioners; the vast crowd of spectators become silent; the fatal order is given, and in an instant the poor wretches are launched into eternity!

The execution was attended by an immense crowd, to whom the good priest addressed an admonition at the request of the criminals. Drink had driven them to commit the crime which had cost them their lives, and they desired that others might avoid the rock upon which they had been wrecked. I am glad to add that a general order has since been issued, forbidding the sale of liquors within the lines of the army, either by sutlers or other persons. When men are out on duty at night, or in bad weather, it is well enough to grant them a reasonable allowance of good whisky or brandy; but the vile stuff sold in the camps, frequently at eight and ten dollars per gallon, is unfit for even a brute. A biscuit or canteen of coffee, however, even though cold, will impart more warmth than a glass of brandy; and they contain withal good nourishment, which is indispensable to the proper performance of the duties of the soldier.

I had occasion, not long since to visit the battlefield, and especially the spot where Bartow fell. But few traces remain of the bloody struggle, and a solemn stillness seems to pervade the field. I was surprised to find that the marble shaft which marks the spot where the heroic Georgian fell, was covered with the inscriptions of visitors, and that efforts had been made to obtain pieces of it, as mementos of the man and the field. These inscriptions were written for the most part in pencil, and consisted of the names of the writers, or of some expression of admiration for the gallant dead. One person more ambitious than the rest, had picked his name into the marble with the point of a needle or other sharp substance, and had then filled it in with his pencil. The column is literally covered by these inscriptions, not so much space being left as one might cover with his fingernail.

Col. Bartow's intrepid bearing upon the field, his heroic death, and last words, have produced a profound impression upon the popular heart. I have been assured that even the shoes upon his dead horse's feet (a beautiful gray mare), and several of her teeth, have been removed by persons who wished to obtain some relic of the hero who bestrode her, whilst others have plucked out portions of her mane and tail, and had them wrought into trinkets. All these things bespeak the popular regard and admiration, and reconcile us in some sort to the bad taste, (not to call it by a harsher name,) which could lead strangers to cover his monument with their own names.

As the occasion may not occur again for alluding to the subject, permit me to suggest here, that a mistake has been made in regard to the last words uttered by Col. Bartow. As rendered upon the monument, they were, "They have killed me, boys, but never give up the field." The error occurs in the latter part of the sentence. The words he did utter, as I learned a few hours after his death, and again on the following day, from the men to whom he spoke them, were as follows: "They have killed me boys; but never give it up." This is a terser, stronger and better expression than the first; and what is more, it reminds one of the nervous style of expression common to the author. Never give up the fight, the field, the struggle, the cause—*"never give it up."* Not that field, or any other field, alone was in his mind; but every field, the whole struggle, and the cause itself—all these swept through his swelling heart, and summing the whole in one word, he bade them "never give it up."

P. W. A.

A Crowded City

RICHMOND, Va., December 15, 1861 [12-21-61]

I returned to Richmond two days ago. The city is full of people, even to overflowing. The hotels, boarding houses and lodging establishments, as well as the streets, are crowded to suffocation. Every train, whether from the East, the South or the West, brings a fresh contribution of strangers, and of sick and disabled soldiers seeking hospital accommodations; and each returning train takes back large numbers of men whose furloughs have expired, and of volunteers whom the hospital surgeons have pronounced fit for duty. This alternate ebbing and flowing of the tide of humanity through the streets and hotels, and over the railways, gives to Richmond the appearance of a thrifty, busy and growing city, and adds greatly to the demand upon every department of the Government for subsistence and transportation.

What a huge machine a great army is! What a vast amount of labor and money it requires to move, to subsist and to clothe it! What immense stores of provisions and forage—what numberless wheels and muscles—what coffers of gold—what wonderful supplies of patience, of knowledge, of energy and intellect—what well-springs of courage and patriotism! Many good people imagine when a large array of men have been brought together, and arms put into their hands and ammunition into their cartridge-boxes, that all is done that need to be done. What a mistake! You would scarcely believe it, but *shoes* are more important than arms. Men may fight with clubs and bows, with stones, with their hands; but they can't fight and march without shoes. So with the transportation necessary to move an army, and the food to subsist it. Both are indispensable, and without them but little can be accomplished.

But has the Government done its duty in providing the requisite energy and skill in the various departments of the army? It has not. This is said in no spirit of faultfinding, but for the purpose of pointing out defects in the administration of the army with a view to their correction by those in authority.

And first, in regard to the Quarter-Master's department: It is the duty of this department to provide transportation, fuel and quarters for the men, and forage for the teams and the staff and cavalry horses. The rule adopted in the Army of the Potomac—and the same is true, I presume, elsewhere—has been to impress all the transportation and forage in the counties adjacent to Manassas. Where the owners were willing to part with their teams or provender, they received pay for them; otherwise, they were seized and the owners turned over to the Government for remuneration. There cannot be less than 1,500 to 2,000 wagons, and 6,000 to 8,000 horses, in the service of the Quarter-Master's department for that division of the army. This does not include the horses in the service of field officers and the cavalry regiments, all of which have to be subsisted by the Quarter-Master.

The result of the system adopted, as you will perceive, has been, not only to strip the people of their supplies of corn and hay, and of their wagons and teams, but to deprive them of the means of making another crop. They have neither wagons to do the work of the farm nor horses to draw them, nor feed for such saddle horses and cattle as may have been left them. They have not even bread left for their families. Their fences have been destroyed, and their beef cattle killed and consumed. Under these circumstances, it will be necessary next year for the army to look to other sources for its supplies. The error has been in not procuring the means of transportation from distant points, and leaving the transportation of the surrounding country intact to be used in an emergency. If this had been done, *there would have been no lack of the means to move the army just after the battle of Manassas.* The people within reach could have furnished it in forty-eight hours. As it is, if a great necessity should suddenly arise to move the army rapidly and promptly, it could not possibly be done unless the Quarter-Master had already on hand a sufficient number of wagons which he has not. The same remark will apply to the forage necessary for the support of the teams, and especially to the beef, upon which the army is mainly subsisted. Cattle can be driven; and thus the amount of transportation may be diminished. Hereafter, however, it will be necessary, in the event of a forward movement, to haul all our commissary stores, after having obtained them from distant points, since there will be no cattle left to drive. This error is chargeable to the Commissary department. The present means are insufficient to transport the baggage and Quarter-Master's stores. In the future it will be necessary, also, to transport our supplies of beef, after it has been slaughtered elsewhere. This will require a third more transportation.

At first, drivers were impressed with the wagons. Now, they are detailed from the ranks, of the army—young men who have had no experience in driving, and who complain that they did not enlist to drive wagons. They are required to alternate, and thus every day or two there is a new driver, who is ignorant both of the ability and disposition of the horses, and who soon teaches them bad habits. He takes but little care of the teams, never greases the harness and wagon, and frequently loses the one and turns over and breaks the other. Sometimes, owing to the irregularity of the supply, the horses are fed for a week at a time on shelled corn alone; then on hay, or straw, and but seldom on hay and corn—and sometimes on nothing.

The result is, the mortality among the horses, owing to the want of proper management and feed, is as great as it has been among the troops. This is not all: At the end of twelve months the horses will be entirely worthless. I have seen no horse in a government wagon which I would be willing to give one dollar for at the end of a year's service. Not only is great loss thus sustained by the Government, but the transportation service is rendered less certain and efficient.

If the same mismanagement prevails throughout the army that obtains at Manassas, then the Government sustains a loss in the wear and tear of horses, harness and wagons of $10,000 a day! A similar system upon a plantation would bring the proprietor to ruin in a few years. A simple advertisement inserted in a few newspapers in Virginia, Tennessee, North Carolina and Georgia, would have secured the Government experienced drivers, and all the wagons and mules it could desire. This would have left the farmers in the vicinity of the army in possession of their teams, and thus have enabled them to render efficient service when most needed. In addition to this, newer and stronger wagons might have been procured, as well as a full supply of good mule teams, which are better suited than horses to the heavy work of the army.

The same want of judgment and foresight prevails in the Commissary department. The hides taken from the cattle slaughtered for the use of the army, will shoe the army; the tallow will light the army; while the oil from the feet is sufficient to keep all the harness wagons and artillery in good order. As it is, not half of the hides are saved in proper condition; while four-fifths of the tallow and all the oil are wasted! In the meantime, the Government is paying large sums for shoes, harness and candles. A small outlay would secure the services of a few men who could accompany the army and convert all this tallow into candles, and cure and send forward all the hides. The soldier is entitled to soap, though he seldom gets any, unless he buys it. One man to a regiment would be sufficient, with the means now wasting, to manufacture an ample supply for every person in it.

The administration of the medical department is not only stupid, but brutal. In former letters I have spoken of the ignorance and criminal negligence of regimental surgeons, many of whom have had no practical experience in surgery, and who in a whole year never had as many cases as they are frequently called upon to visit every day in the army. It is to the general administration of the department, however, that I would now invite attention. The supply of medicines is very meager, especially of certain important descriptions. And yet, it is notorious that there are medicines enough in the towns and villages throughout the Confederacy to supply the army and the people. I allude to such standard articles as are necessary in the treatment of those diseases peculiar to the camp. A simple advertisement, such as I have spoken of above, would enable the Government to procure all it may desire. The efforts of the Medical department, however, are limited to Richmond and a few other points, where the prices are highest and the supply smallest. Meanwhile, the best and bravest men who ever drew a sword are dying for want of these medicines! The guilty parties seem to forget that there is a day coming—a Great Day—when official insolence shall be rebuked; when sham patriotism shall be stripped of its cheap trappings, and when professional pretensions shall be called upon to answer for the blood of its victims.

P. W. A.

On December 13, in western Virginia, a Federal army under Gen. R. H. Milroy attacked Confederate forces near Buffalo Mountain.

The Fight at Alleghany
RICHMOND, December 20, 1861 [12-25-61]

The details of the late battle on top of the Alleghany Mountain, in which the 12th Ga. Regiment, Col. [Edward] Johnson, took a conspicuous part, come in very slowly. The object of the enemy was to take the Confederates by surprise, and to cut them off and to destroy them. For this purpose he came with a largely superior force, sufficient advantage to insure even the

Yankees the victory. The truth is, however, it is difficult for them to bring into the field a force large enough to whip a well appointed Southern regiment.

The Georgians behaved with great gallantry, as they have always done when they met the enemy. It is not unusual to hear them spoken of in terms of high praise by strangers on the cars and in the hotels. It was only yesterday I heard an intelligent Virginian say, that the Georgians seemed to be almost omnipresent wherever there was any fighting to be done, and that they never struck a blow that did not leave its mark behind. At Rich Mountain on the retreat of the gallant [R. S.] Garnett; at Manassas, Greenbrier, Hatteras and Pensacola; on top of the Alleghany, and in the late affair in which the Georgia Hussars were engaged—wherever, indeed, they have encountered the enemy, and under whatever disadvantages, they have displayed a courage and fortitude equal to every emergency, and borne themselves in a manner that reflected honor upon themselves and the glorious old commonwealth which they are proud to hail as mother. When this war shall have ended, and the righteous mead of praise shall have been awarded to the brave and faithful, there is not a hill-top in all her wide domain from which a monument should not ascend to record the deeds of her heroic children.

But when will the war be brought to a close? Will it be next year? The contest was virtually decided on the Plains of Manassas, and had the victory there achieved, been followed up with vigor and promptitude, there is reason to believe that it would have been of shorter duration than it now promises to be. Had we marched into Washington, as we might have done, the Federal Government would have dispersed to the winds, and our independence acknowledged by the great powers of the earth. Maryland would have been relieved; and Missouri and Kentucky would have risen when there was no enemy within their borders to prevent; and to-day our lines might have been stretched along the Susquehanna, the Ohio and the Mississippi. This being accomplished, we might well have afforded to adopt the defensive policy; for then we should have all we claim and all we desire.

There are men in high positions of large information, who think that no intelligent opinion can yet be formed as to the probable duration of the war. There are so many conflicting opinions and interests in the North—so much fanaticism, corruption and folly— that it is impossible to say how long the contest will last, what direction it will take, or what proportions it will assume. There are others who think 1862 will be a year of blood, and that with it the active operations of the war will close. The two republics may continue to occupy a hostile attitude, and a kind of border warfare may be waged, until the party at present in power in the United States shall be overthrown, and another party, more disposed to peace, installed in its place. With a new administration, it is thought that peace may be restored, just as the Crimean war was brought to an end upon the death of Emperor Nicholas, its author, and the accession of his son Alexander. Even the obstinate and gouty George III, was brought to consent to the recognition of the independence of the colonies and the restoration of peace. There are others still who predict their hopes of a settlement upon the success of the Democratic party, between whom and the conservative Republicans a future coalition is believed to be improbable. But little importance, however, is attached to this view of the question, as all existing parties at the North may be swept away long before the present storm shall have run its course. We may have to deal with a military dictator—some Northern Cromwell—and not with existing political organizations. Already parties in the North have, in a measure, reversed their former positions. Large hopes were built upon the ancient conservatism of the Democratic organization; and it is believed by many that the defensive policy hitherto pursued by the Confederate Government originated in a desire to aid that party, as being most disposed to peace, in its efforts to regain the power it had lost. I know not how much foundation there is for this opinion. If such views have had any influence upon the conduct of war, I can only say that they have been attended with but little success.

But the time has come when all such hopes, if any such were ever indulged, should be discarded. If we would have peace, we must win it at the point of the bayonet. Blows thick and fast must be given; every energy should be put forth, and every sacrifice made, whether of life or property, that may be necessary to our success. This great FACT should never be lost sight of. The people at home have endured much, and may endure more; but they should remember that the inconveniences and losses which they sustain, are small compared with the privations and sufferings, the sickness and death, of their brothers in the field. While the latter are equal sufferers with themselves in the depreciation of property and the hardships consequent upon the practices of heartless extortioners, they have, in addition, given up all the comforts of home and offered their bodies as a living wall against the invader.

Should war ensue between the U. States and England, the many of the hardships we have to encounter, will pass away. Our ports will be opened to the exportations of cotton and the importation of arms and merchandise; the occupation of the extortioner will be gone, and the North itself, whose aider and abettor he is, will be pleased, as it were, between the upper and nether millstone. The prevailing opinion here is, that the existing troubles between the Federal Government and Great Britain cannot be accommodated without a resort to arms, and many look with confident expectation to an early declaration of hostilities with England. The North will neither surrender Messrs. Mason and Slidell, nor apologize for their capture. The people there have gone stark mad, and, like the Egyptians with Pharaoh at their head, they seem to be crazy enough to push on into a sea of blood that shall swallow them up. Surely Heaven has smitten them with blindness!

The telegraph has already informed you of the death of Col. Terry, who fell gallantly fighting at the head of his regiment of Texan Rangers a few days ago in [Rowlett's Station] Kentucky. He was with the Army of the Potomac until the battle of Manassas, after which he returned to Texas to raise a regiment which he commanded at the time of his death, and it is the same person of whose daring exploits I had frequent occasion to speak in my letters last summer. His death is not simply a great loss to the Confederate service; it is a calamity. He was just in the prime of a noble manhood, of a large and imposing mould, possessing great wealth, and as modest as a woman and brave as Julius Caesar. The honors paid to his remains in Nashville were all deserved.

But there are moral as well as military heroes. There is one in Richmond at this time—a man of great intellect and high position. His health has been indifferent for some days, but he is much better now, and will soon be able to resume his official duties. He may be seen any day when well moving noiselessly about the hospitals where the sick soldiers are sent. He has a kind word for every patient—lingers around their cots, inquires after their wants, and consoles and encourages them by his quiet attentions and brotherly language. His public duties press heavily upon him; yet he finds time to steal away from the crowd that would follow at his heels, and to search out the sufferer. Does not your heart tell you instinctively who this hero of the Hospital is? It is Alexander H. Stephens—of whom it will not be said in the last day, "I was sick, and ye visited me not."

P. W. A.

With the approach of winter, and little prospect for further fighting, Alexander left Virginia and returned to Savannah for Christmas. The Confederacy, baptized with blood, faced another year battling for their independence.

1862

Crisis and Duty

After spending the holidays in Georgia, Alexander quickly returned to Virginia. His contract with the Atlanta Southern Confederacy *having expired, "P. W. A." now wrote exclusively for the Savannah* Republican, *although other newspapers were still permitted, as customary, to copy the correspondence as long as they credited the source.*

Day Breaking in the East
RICHMOND, January 20, 1862 [1-26-62]

I returned to this place two days ago, and should have written you before this, but for the reason that I desired first to procure reliable information in regard to a matter of great public concern. I am glad to have it in my power now to say, that day is beginning to break in the east. At least, it is reported, and I believe it, *that the Independence of the Confederate States will be conceded and recognized by Great Britain and France within the next forty days.* Recent events may precipitate the action of those governments, and our nationality be acknowledged in a very short time. The Trent affair, the brutal insolence of the Northern press and people, the destruction of commerce, and the derangement of financial affairs consequent upon cotton famine, have produced a profound impression in our favor and against the North among European powers. The hopelessness of the contest, so far as the Federal Government is concerned, is now dim and conceded by statesmen abroad, whilst, with few exceptions, the people of Europe are unanimous in their denunciations of the corruption, imbecility and cowardice which mark the Yankee Government and its army.

It is also said, and I think truly, that an intimation was given to our Government some weeks ago, to the effect that the British and French Governments, and probably the Spanish Government also, were favorably inclined towards the Confederate States, and that they were disposed to recognize our independence at an early day. It was thought best, however, as the time was short, to await the inauguration of the permanent Government on the 22nd day of next February. These adventures had left Europe before information had been received there of the unwarrantable seizure of Messrs. Mason and Slidell. This latter occurrence, and the increasing distress occasioned by the withholding of the cotton crop, may, as already intimated, bring about our recognition at an earlier day than that mentioned above.

There is reason also to believe that simultaneous with the acknowledgement of our independence, the blockade will be declared, by the same Powers, to be ineffectual and illegal, and as such, not binding or worthy to be observed. Should the United States resist this proceeding, then there will be war between them and the maritime powers of Europe. Upon the raising of the blockade, the shipment of cotton abroad and the introduction of foreign goods, will commence. A sense of relief will then be experienced throughout the Confederacy. Money will become abundant. An adequate supply of arms and ammunition will be obtained. The occupation of the extortioner—the aider and abettor of the enemy—will be gone, and the Government and the people be placed in a position to conduct the war with vigor and success.

But will the United States stand up to its threat, to consider the recognition of our independence equivalent to a declaration of war? It is unsafe to speculate in advance upon the action of the Federal Government. Its conduct in the Trent affair was so cowardly and despicable, that it were difficult to imagine any depth of disgrace to which it would not descend. There are those, however, who believe that a war with England is not only probable, but even imminent. The excitement in Canada and in the British navy against the United States, is very great; and in the absence of any disposition on the part of either Government to provoke a war, one need not be surprised if an unpremeditated collision on land or sea, should involve the two nations in hostilities almost any day. As with men, so with Governments, when brought face to face; the most trivial occurrence may lead to bloodshed. But more of this and other matters of a cognate nature in a future communication.

I may mention a rumor in this connection, that a committee of Congressmen proceeded to Manassas yesterday, charged with a request to Gen. Beauregard, that he would consent to be transferred to the military department embracing the State of Missouri. Gen. B. is almost indispensable to the Army of the Potomac, and there are many who would regret to see him leave it. It is reported that the President is entirely willing to make the transfer. Of one thing you many feel entirely satisfied to wit: that Gen. Beauregard will do what he believes to be best for the public service. A more loyal and unselfish patriot does not breathe within all the bounds of the Confederacy.

P. W. A.

In a letter written on January 3, 1862 to the Richmond Dispatch, *Confederate War Correspondent William G. Shepardson carelessly informed his readers of the positioning of various brigades in the Manassas Junction area. The publication of this letter incurred the wrath of Gen. Johnston resulting in the issue of General Order No. 98, calling for the expulsion of all newspaper correspondents within the Army of the Potomac. Alexander freely criticized the order, but had no choice and returned to Richmond.*

The Order Against Reporters
RICHMOND, January 25, 1862 [2-1-62]

The general order reported to have been issued by Gen. Johnston, in regard to reporters and correspondents for the press, is the subject of considerable discussion both in and out of the army. I find but few who justify the order, and those few are generally persons who have had some quarrel with the press, or who feel that their performances in politics or in the field have not been duly appreciated and magnified by the chroniclers of the time. I am unwilling to believe that Gen. Johnston was influenced by motives so unjust and unworthy. There are others, however, less charitable, who attribute the order to the fact that Gen. Beauregard has been the subject of frequent and repeated commendations by writers from the army, whilst the author of the order and the commander-in-chief on the Potomac has been passed over in comparative silence. Until the contrary be shown, it is but simple justice to believe, as I do, that he was influenced by no such unworthy considerations, but by a mistaken regard for the public service, and a desire to discharge the duties imposed by the great trust with which he is clothed.

And yet it is impossible to justify the order. According to report, it was issued in consequence of a letter written from Manassas and published in the Richmond *Dispatch*, in which the writer undertook to locate the several brigades in that vicinity, and to specify the particular places where they have taken up their quarters for the winter. Other details are given and other facts mentioned, which, it is but right to say, should never have found a place in a Southern newspaper. But if the correspondent for the Richmond *Dispatch* has committed an indiscretion, why should the correspondents for other papers, be punished for his folly? Why should the innocent be made to suffer for the wrongs of the guilty? Such is not the rule adopted in our tribunals of justice.

That correspondents from the army should be put upon terms is freely admitted. It is asking too much to allow them to enter the lines of the army, and to write and publish what they please. The public good, however, in this, as in all other things, should be the rule of their conduct. So far as my observation has gone, the press of the Confederate States has exercised great prudence in relation to the movements of the great army. Many things have been withheld from publication out of a proper regard for the public service; and yet the next arrival by the underground railroad would bring us Northern papers containing the very information which had been withheld from the Southern people. It is notorious that there are spies at Manassas with uniforms on their backs, and others in Richmond, and possibly in the War Office itself. It is to these lynx eyed agents, and not to writers for the press, that McClellan looks for information. I have no doubt but that the astute Federal General laughed heartily when he heard of Gen. Johnston's order; *just as the latter would have laughed had he heard that McClellan had issued such an order.* No man in the Confederate States is less influenced in his movements by what appears in Northern newspapers, than Gen. Johnston; and it would be folly to suppose that General McClellan, any more than his great opponent, regulates his action by the declarations of the adversary's press. Admitting that correspondents are always well informed, which is far from the fact, they are too reticent, and publish too little, to enable any officer to proceed with safety who should act upon their statements and opinions.

The proper plan would seem to be, to admit professional reporters and correspondents within the lines of the army upon the single condition of their individual responsibility for whatever they write and publish. Let the bounds be defined beyond which they shall not go; and when they pass these bounds, let them be punished like any other transgressor of the rules adopted for the government of the army. To exclude them entirely would be to strike a heavy blow at the freedom of the Press already guaranteed to the people by the fundamental law of the land. Even in despotic France, it has not been found necessary to adopt such a rule as that now proposed. To the Yankee government alone belongs the honor of an attempt to curtail the liberty of speech, and to suppress and suborn the press. I submit that they are not a fit people to set us an example in a matter which so nearly concerns the freedom and welfare of the South.

It is now six months since the battle of Manassas was fought, and yet the official report, just ordered to be published, has not yet been laid before the people. But for the writers who were present and took part in the action, we should still have been in utter darkness as to all the details of that glorious day. The foul slanders and lying representations of the Northern papers would have gone uncontradicted; and the outside world would have formed its judgement accordingly.

But have the people no interest in this matter? Are the rights and interests of the Army distinct and different from those of the people?

Of whom is the Army composed? Of volunteers, the sons and brothers of the people. Who furnishes the vast sums of money required to maintain the Army and the government? The people. To whom does the country itself belong? To the people. When a battle is fought, then shall the people be required to wait in painful suspense for the official report? Must they wait three or six months before they shall be allowed to know whether *their* Army has been victorious, and whether *their* brothers and sons have been killed or wounded?

There are many things which the good of the people and the success of their arms require to be kept secret. Such things should be kept secret. All else, however, should be made known if they desire it. The line should be drawn at the proper place, and any encroachment on either side would be an encroachment upon the rights of the people. Indiscrete publications on the one hand, and the withholding or proper and desirable information on the other, would be equally an encroachment upon their rights.

But admitting there was cause for the order, the remedy is worse than the evil complained of. The people will have news from the army; and to satisfy their demands, the press will be driven to the necessity of relying upon private letters written by volunteers to their families. For the most part, these writers have but little opportunity to collect news, and to winnow the false from the true. The result will be, they will send home the numberless rumors, some of them the silliest and most contradictory, that find their way into camp. In addition to this, being restrained by no such responsibility as that proposed to be placed upon the regular correspondent, they would divulge a thousand things, unintentionally no doubt, that should be kept secret. Thus the evil which Gen. Johnston desires to correct, would only be inflamed and increased by the very means he has adopted to suppress it.

P. W. A.

RICHMOND, January 28, 1862 [2-7-62]

I sent you two days ago, a printed copy of the official reports of General Johnston and Beauregard, of the battle of Manassas. One thing, will strike the impartial reader in perusing these reports, and that is the credit awarded to the Virginians and South Carolinians. But little is said, comparatively, of the forces from other States. It was believed that General Johnston affected the Virginians a good deal, and Gen. Beauregard the sons of the gallant Palmetto State; but it was not to be expected that the Eighth Georgia regiment which did as hard fighting as any and suffered most of all the regiments in the battle, would be passed over with a slight reference in a grave official paper which purported to present an impartial and historical account of the battle. Hampton's Legion, for example, behaved with unsurpassed gallantry, and [Joseph B.] Kershaw's and [E. B.] Cash's regiments fought admirably after they reached the field, which was late. Indeed, Hampton's Legion was not among the first forces to meet the enemy. But the Eighth Georgia entered the battle early in the day, was exposed to a murderous fire for hours, held its position until ordered to fall back, against five times its numbers, and that at a point and an hour upon which everything depended. Every field officer, except one, was either killed or wounded. Out of about 550 men who went into the fight, there were 196 casualties, including killed, wounded and missing. The regiment which suffered most, after the Eighth Georgia, was the Fourth Alabama, which alone is entitled to share with it the bloody honors of the day.

Had the ever-to-be-regretted Bartow survived the fortunes of the field, the part which the Georgians performed would have received more appropriate notice than has been bestowed upon them. Even the Seventh regiment has been denied the honor of having participated in the capture of the celebrated Sherman's or Ricketts' battery. And yet eye-witnesses informed me three days after the battle, that a Georgian was the first to mount the battery, and that the colors of the Seventh were the first to be planted upon the guns. We have never claimed the exclusive honor of taking the battery; but I do insist, in vindication of the truth of history, that the Seventh Georgia regiment participated in the capture equally with the brave Carolinians and Virginians. If it were necessary, a thousand living witnesses could be bro't who would attest to the fact.

I would not impeach, even by implication the fairness and justice of General Johnston and Beauregard; nor would I pluck one leaf from the crowns of glory which grace the brows of the heroic children of Virginia and South Carolina. The latter are entitled to all the credit which has been bestowed upon them, if we except the *exclusive* honor awarded them in regard to the capture of the battery. But I confidently believe, that if Col. Bartow had lived, and Lieut. Col. Gardner's severe wound had not disabled him for many months, a fuller and more earnest representation of the part performed by our gallant brothers, would have been made to Commander-in-Chief, and that thus more ample justice would have been done them.

Gen. Johnston's report is general in its character, and enters into but few details. It is better written, however, than Gen. Beauregard's, which is full of details as to localities and time, which are comparatively undesirable, but meagre and unsatisfactory when he comes to speak of the parts played by individuals and particular forces. An examination of these reports should satisfy even the most skeptical, of the propriety of allowing discreet and intelligent correspondents to accompany the army. The public learnt more of the true character of conflict, of the dauntless courage of the men, and of those acts of individual heroism which electrified the heart of the nation, from the warm and glowing accounts given by writers from the field, than from the long-deferred and formal reports of those in command.

You were notified by a former letter, of the probable transfer of Gen. Beauregard to the West. I now have it in my power to state, that he will proceed at an early day, (rumor says he has already left,) to Columbus, Kentucky, where he will take command of the forces at that important point. The transfer, it is believed, is entirely agreeable to him. He will be succeeded at Manassas by Maj. Gen. Gustavus W. Smith, an accomplished and competent officer.

This reminds me that in nearly all the shop windows on the principal thoroughfares of Richmond, you will find admirable photographs of Gen. Beauregard, and other officers and distinguished personages—including President Davis, Vice-President Stephens, Gens. Johnston, Evans, Bee, Bartow, [Benjamin] McCulloch, and others. They are got up by Messrs. Taylor & Perkins of Augusta, Ga., and are executed in the highest style of the art. Hundreds of these photographs are sold daily, and it will not be long before they find their way into almost every household in the Confederacy. Col. Bartow's is taken in citizen's dress from an old daguerreotype, there being no likeness of him in military costume extant. Those of the President and Vice-President are of life size and very good.

It is now two weeks since the [Maj. Gen. Ambrose] Burnside expedition sailed; and still we are without definite advices of its destination or fate. The prevailing opinion here is, that the greater part of it has been lost. Perhaps, the wish is father to the thought. We have any number of rumors, some plausible enough, and others wild and contradictory—but nothing certain. "Some truth, though dashed and brewed with lies."

Gen. Longstreet arrived here last night from Manassas. Everything was quiet in that quarter when he left.

P. W. A.

RICHMOND, January 31, 1862 [2-9-62]

On my return to this city, I noticed what appeared to be a large pile of soldiers' boxes, at the depot at Wilmington, N. C. There seemed to be several hundred of them piled up under a shed. There were several volunteers on the train, returning from a short visit to their homes—some of whom were bound to Norfolk, some to Yorktown, and others to Manassas and Winchester. I overheard enough of their conversation to learn how it was that so many boxes belonging to soldiers had been left at Wilmington.

Upon the arrival of the train at Wilmington, which is after midnight, the soldier who has been working and struggling along the route to get his box through, is informed that it is impossible for it to go forward then, but that it will be sent on by the next train—say the following day. The box contains such supplies of food and clothing as loving hands at home have prepared for him. His furlough will soon expire, and his stock of money is rapidly diminishing. If he remain over in Wilmington, he must sleep on some friendly door-step, or seek a hotel, where the charges will be disproportionate to his means. If he go on, the box may be lost. What then shall he do? He has allowed himself barely time to get back to camp before the expiration of his leave of absence; so he decides, like a brave soldier, to continue his journey, and trust to the railway authorities to forward his luggage. And that is the last he ever sees of his box.

But this is not all. The railroad companies have agreed to transport soldiers at half price. Well, a poor fellow, who has just recovered from a wound received in defense of his country, finds himself able, after several weeks' confinement, to hobble about upon a pair of crutches. He gets a furlough to go home to recruit his wasted strength. He succeeds, after much effort, in reaching the ticket office, and applies for a through ticket. "You can't have it, sir," says the ticket officer. "Why not?" inquires the man on crutches. The answer is, "We don't sell through tickets to soldiers." So the man on crutches—the man who has volunteered to serve his country, and has actually been disabled in its service—must procure a new ticket from every road over which he may have to pass. He may have lost an eye or a limb in battle, or have just got up from a long and exhausting attack of typhoid fever, and the weather may be inclement and the hour late at night when he changes cars; still, he must grope his way through the darkness and rain, and snow, in a strange place, and thro' bustling crowds of eager men, to the ticket office, or consent to pay an additional sum for his passage. He may be knocked off his frail support by a rushing omnibus or a frantic porter; but what care the railroad officials? He must not only procure a fresh ticket at every change of cars, but he must have his baggage re-checked also.

But a civilian is leaving Richmond at the same time with the man on crutches, and he, too, applies for a through ticket; *and it is furnished him!* Why is this? Why should a discrimination be made against the soldier? I cannot inform you. Wherever I have been, with scarcely an exception, the railroads are so conducted as to give the greatest possible annoyance to the men to whom they are indebted for their protection. Through tickets are cheaper than way tickets; and hence, perhaps, the distinction. An extortioner—the abettor of the enemy—may travel from Manassas to Savannah at a cost of $25. The corpse of a soldier who fell up on the battlefield is charged just double the sum! It was only yesterday that an official of the Virginia Central Road threatened to have the dead bodies of those heroic sons of Savannah, who fell at the battle of Manassas, and which were being carried home for final interment, thrown out of the cars upon the arrival of the train, unless they were removed immediately. They were removed; but if they had not been, and the unfeeling monster had carried out his threat, there is one man in Richm'd who would have been lynched—that's all.

The failure in the connection of the trains on many of the railroads between Savannah and Augusta, and this place, is of such frequent occurrence, as to render it a matter of surprise when the mails get through in due time. The cause of these failures was freely canvassed both by through and way passengers, and it was not uncommon to hear men, living along the line, offer to take bets that we would have to stay over at this or that place. They charged some of the railway men with being interested in the hotels on the way-side; and hence, they said, there was a failure about every alternate day. There are no large bodies of troops passing now north or south, and there is no sort of excuse for these frequent failures. The Columbus, Atlanta and Macon papers reach here at the same time with the *Republican,* and sometimes they anticipate it. The Augusta papers invariably arrive here a day in advance. This is true also, I believe, of the mail going South.

The permanent government of the Confederate States will be inaugurated on the 22nd day of February, the birthday of Washington. It is thought there will be at least two changes in the Cabinet—the State department, and the Post Office Department. The general desire seems to be that the Hon. Wm. C. Rives, of this State, should be called to the State Department. I heard an eminent personage say, a few days ago, that he was the most thorough and accomplished statesman and diplomatist on this continent.

P. W. A.

The Crisis and Our Duty

RICHMOND, February 11, 1862 [2-15-62]

I am no alarmist; this *you* know very well. But if I have gained any credit among your readers for candor and sincerity, I trust they will believe me when I tell them that the crisis of the revolution approaches, and that the time is near at hand when the Confederate States will be required to put forth every energy, or submit to the yoke of the oppressor.

Such is the opinion of the coolest and most sagacious men in Richmond. We are to be weighed in the balances, and that right speedily. Shall we be found wanting? *That* is the question now.

Since the battle of Manassas, we have done little else but brag. We have taunted McClellan with cowardice; we have reviled his government, jeered his army, and thanked God we were not as other men are. We have boasted, in terms amounting almost to blasphemy, that Providence was on our side—forgetting that Heaven helps those only who help themselves. Faith, without works, is of but little value. But who amongst us practices this doctrine now? Is it the government? Is it the people?

Whilst we were heaping reproaches upon the Federal commander-in-chief, and marching up and down in front of his capitol, flaunting our flag in his face, he had the good sense to disregard our taunts and bide his time. He even had the nerve to resist the clamors of Congressmen, bankers, and the whole Northern multitude. It would seem as if his time had nearly come. Nothing but the most energetic and determined action on our part can prevent McClellan from reaping the fruits of his patience and toils.

Will the people take that action? They will if they can only be made to understand their danger. To this end the press, the pulpit, the women of the land, have an important duty to perform. If they are equal to the emergency, and would render their labors available, they must move at once. There is not a day to be lost—not an hour. The six and twelve months' troops have done well; but they can do better—they can enlist for two years or the war. No one believes the war will last two years, unless we fail to do our duty now. There are many men now in the field who, it is believed, would continue there but for the solicitude of parents and friends. A word from the father, mother, or sister, would decide them at once to remain where they are. Shall that word be withheld in Georgia?

They can either enroll themselves in new regiments, or join the old ones as recruits. Many of the old regiments have been thinned by disease and battle, and I understand that two officers from each company have been detailed for the purpose of procuring recruits to fill up their ranks. Captain [George] Dawson, of Green County, who commands a company in the glorious old Eighth, and other officers, are now on their way to Georgia and other States, charged with this urgent duty. The press and the people should render them every facility that can contribute to the early success of their labors.

There are many advantages in joining an old and seasoned regiment. The officers have acquired experience in the discharge of the duties of their respective positions, and the men have learned to take care of themselves. It requires weeks to instruct a raw regiment in the simplest evolutions; whereas fresh recruits, being distributed through the several companies of an old regiment, soon acquire a knowledge of the drill, and readily fall into their proper positions.

But the soldiers now enlisted should not be expected to do all the fighting. There are others still at home who should come to the rescue. The opportunity to do so is now presented.

The people of Georgia are warned; it is for them to turn a deaf ear, or heed the warning. Every dollar should be saved that can be. Every ounce of powder and lead, and every gun and gun flint, should be sent to the field. And for every gun, there should be one soldier in the field, and one at home drilling to take his place should he fall.

I write urgently, for the times are urgent. If we pass the coming summer, the Northern army will break down of its own weight. No nation under the sun can stand a drain of one thousand millions of dollars a year. Our ports will be opened and foreign recognition will come in time, though there is reason to fear that both have been postponed by our recent disasters. So much greater the reason why we should retrieve these disasters, and why there should be no more of them.

The reduction of Fort Henry is still a mystery. There are those who know not whether to attribute it to cowardice or treachery. The enemy ascribes it to the latter. Either is bad enough. We are glad there are some brave spirits among the garrison, who preferred captivity to flight.

P. W. A.

In early 1862, the Confederacy suffered its first reverses. On February 6 Fort Henry on the Tennessee River, threatened by Federal forces under Gen. U. S. Grant, capitulated; ten days later Fort Donelson on the Cumberland River surrendered along with a Confederate army numbering 13,000. Tennessee was in Federal control—a catastrophe for the South. While off the North Carolina coast, a Federal invasion force of 7,500 troops led by Gen. Ambrose Burnside attacked and overran the Confederate defenses on Roanoke Island, capturing more than 2,000 Confederates and successfully gaining a base of operations on the Atlantic coast.

The Late Disasters—Is Anybody to Blame

RICHMOND, VA., February 13, 1862 [2-19-62]

The disaster at Roanoke's Island, and the ascent of the Tennessee river, continue the absorbing topics of comment and speculation. Nobody seems to understand why so much time and labor should have been bestowed upon the works at Columbus and the Mississippi river, and so little upon Fort Henry and the Tennessee. If Fort Henry was reduced by an hour's bombardment, may not Fort Donelson be also? If the Federal gunboats succeeded in penetrating to the head of navigation upon the Tennessee, may they not also, having reduced Fort Donelson, steam up to Nashville by the Cumberland? Of what avail is it to close the front entrance by locks and bars, if we leave the side gate or the back door open? One of Tennessee's most heroic sons—the famous David Crockett—was wont to say, that there were people in the world who, if the front of their jackets were made of fine cloth, did not care if the backs were made of fustian. Do our engineers in the West act upon a like principle?

The reduction of Roanoke Island and the occupation of the waters and fertile corn districts of eastern North Carolina are not less significant and important. If the gateway to the notable old State was worth defending at all, it should have been efficiently and adequately defended. The garrison of the island had but two alternatives before them—success or captivity. Retreat was impossible. I don't wonder that Mr. Secretary [Judah] Benjamin has been sick for the last two or three days.

The Burnside expedition, it is now believed, looks to the seizure of the railway at or near Weldon, and a flank movement against Norfolk. If such be its object, the movement is full of danger to us. You will be of a like opinion if you will but take your map and trace out the line of railway through North Carolina, and the sounds and rivers in the eastern part of that State and Virginia, and then remember that there is a large Federal force at Fortress Monroe ready to co-operate with the expeditionary troops under Gen. Burnside. Some one— perhaps the old Prince Metternich—described Italy as "a geographical expression." The country around Norfolk and Portsmouth is not unlike a sack, the neck of which is Suffolk, which is accessible alike from Albemarle Sound and Fortress Monroe, which are in the bottom of the sack. Nay, such a force would be in position to threaten Richmond itself.

That the enemy has some such plan as this in view, and he will seek to throw a heavy column forward from the lower Potomac, and thus avoid Johnston above and Magruder below, there is much reason to believe. Meanwhile, should either Johnston or Magruder fall back in the direction of this place, the one would be impeded and harassed in the rear by forces from Washington, and the other by forces from Fortress Monroe. I am unable to say whether the James and York are properly defended or not. It is said they are—just as it was said that Roanoke Island and the Tennessee river were.

Such is believed to be McClellan's plan for "forcing Gen. Johnston out of his rat-hole at Manassas," to use the elegant language of the Northern press. If such be his programme, it is not improbable, as was intimated in one of my late letters, that one or more of the greatest battles of the revolution will be fought within twenty miles of Richmond.

The first duty of the people at home is to assist in continuing the six and twelve months' troops in the field, and in filling the places of those who may not re-enlist with fresh recruits. The next, and of equal importance to the first, is to add to the war regiments and bring them up to the proper standard. Nearly all the regiments were too small in the beginning, and they have since been reduced by deaths and discharges. Having done this; the next thing is to raise and equip as many new regiments as possible.

There is not a day to be lost. Whilst the roads are closed to us, the rivers are open to the enemy. If the rain and snow impede our movements on land, they facilitate his on water. He is aware of his advantage and of our exigency, and is moving with all the rapidity and energy possible. He knows he must break down under his present enormous expenditures if they are continued much longer; and his heart beats with fear at each arrival from London and Paris, where he believes our independence will soon be acknowledged and his blockade pronounced illegal. He is mustering all his means and powers, therefore, for the final blow with which he hopes to crush us to the earth. If he fail, the war is over. If he succeed, it is prolonged indefinitely—at least until our freedom is won. Are the people ready for the word? *The enemy is!*

P. W. A.

More Disasters

RICHMOND, February 19, 1862 [2-24-62]

The Federal "anaconda" begins to tighten his coil. The "circle of fire" with which the south was to be surrounded, already illuminates the distant horizons. A bitter foe—smarting under former defeats, jeered at by the world, even distrustful of his own courage—now thunders at our gates, a victorious and multitudinous host!

The weather is bad and the news is bad. The heavens are black above us, and the air is filled with strange sounds—the shouts of a triumphant enemy! The wires have already borne you the evil tidings.

Fort Donelson has fallen. It is a great disaster, and has produced much pain and excitement here. The nation bows its head and smites its breast in bitter sorrow, but, thank God! not in despair. The darkness is relieved at least one cheering gleam—our men brought away "blood on their bayonets." They fought a good fight, and yielded only to overpowering numbers. Like a thief in the night, the enemy chose his own time, and place and mode of attack. He had ample water transportation, and could bring up any number of reinforcements; whilst the Confederates, having waited to see where the thunderbolt would fall, moved only with great difficulty over the heavy roads and through the rich loam of the country.

No details have reached here yet—at least, none have transpired. The war office had intelligence of the disaster Sunday night [February 16], but Mr. Benjamin was afraid to share it with his own people, lest, perhaps, the enemy might hear of it!

No one here underrates the extent of the disasters which have befallen our arms. It were unwise to do so. But nobody thinks of yielding an inch. The brave and the patient are never cast down by misfortune. Washington and his little army were fugitives before a victorious legions for seven years; and when he did stop to deal them a blow, he fled again the moment it was given. If nothing else be left us, may we not do the same? Heaven will come at last to our help, if we be true and faithful.

P. W. A.

On February 22, Alexander left Richmond for Huntsville, Alabama, where it was expected that General Albert S. Johnston would establish his headquarters for the Confederate Army of the Mississippi. But upon learning that a battle was imminent at New Madrid, Missouri and Island No. 10 on the upper Mississippi, Alexander continued west to Memphis, arriving there on March 4.

The Importance of Holding "Island No. 10."
Memphis, Tenn., March 10, 1862 [3-19-62]

We have had no boat from up the river to-day. You have already been advised the enemy had occupied Point Pleasant, some ten miles below New Madrid on the Missouri side of the river. They have fired upon all the boats that have passed for the last two or three days; and it may be they have prevented the passage of the boat due this afternoon. A rumor prevailed yesterday that Com. [George N.] Hollins had shelled the Federals out of the place, but the statement would seem to lack confirmation.

It is of the highest consequence that the Confederates should be able to maintain their present position on the Mississippi river. Island No. 10 is situated just where the boundary line between Tennessee and Kentucky strikes the river, and is a very strong position. There need be no doubt of our ability to hold the Island against the gunboats of the enemy. Hickman, a few miles above on the Kentucky side, is also in our possession, and we hold the eastern bank of the river from that point down to New Orleans and below. It is from the western bank that danger is to be apprehended. Our forces at New Madrid, on the Missouri side, are already besieged, and now an attempt is being made to plant a battery at Point Pleasant on the same side a few miles lower down. The permanent occupation of either of those places by the enemy would cut off communication with Island No. 10 by water, if indeed it did not lead eventually to its abandonment. To prevent such a disaster, it will be found necessary to keep Com. Hollins' gunboats constantly in motion, and possibly to land a heavy force on the western-side of the river, and sweep the enemy back into the country.

Thus you will see how difficult it is to hold the river and both of its banks. Blocking up the channel and occupying one side does not prevent the enemy from seizing points on the other side and stopping our boats by means of his batteries. Nothing but a large land force, in addition to efficient water batteries and a full complement of transportation and gunboats, can enable us to hold the river and prevent the descent of the enemy to Memphis and New Orleans. To do this effectually will require great skill and energy, and an adequate and well-equipped force. That Gens. Beauregard, [Leonidas] Polk and [Braxton] Bragg are equal to the emergency, there need be no doubt. The only ground for apprehension relates to the means at their command. The Federals have been preparing for months for the descent of the river, and they are now ready and amply provided with men, boats, arms, and all kinds of supplies. Unfortunately, the same cannot be said of the Confederates.

Thus you will perceive the absolute necessity of maintaining our position at New Madrid and Island No. 10, and of preserving the integrity of our lines along the Mississippi &

Charleston railway. To do this it becomes necessary for us to keep a strong force at both points. Federal success at either point may lead to the forcing of the Mississippi and the occupation of Memphis, and after awhile of New Orleans—the Mecca towards which the eyes of the Federal army of the West are now wistfully turned. With the control of the Mississippi, we should also lose the control of the White, Arkansas and Red rivers. The loss of these water highways would be a disaster far greater than the fall of Fort Donelson and all the other reverses we have experienced. The possession of the Arkansas river alone, with the Mississippi down to the point of confluence, would render it all but impossible for Gen. [Sterling] Price to maintain himself in Missouri.

I have been thus particular in order that your readers may appreciate the position of affairs in the West, and understand how important it is that we should continue to hold the Mississippi river. Comprehending the exigencies of the situation, the people will the more readily make those efforts, without which success were impossible. The South-west is now one vast camp, and the tread of armed legions may be heard throughout the length and breadth of the great Valley of the Mississippi. Every town and hamlet is responding to the call of the victorious Beauregard, and if arms and ammunition were to be had in the same abundance as volunteers, the advance of the invader would be stayed. We hope to be able to arrest his footsteps any way, and to teach him that his further progress can only be accomplished at a cost of rivers of blood. Never were a people more aroused and resolute than those who live in this magnificent valley. They are turning out nearly their whole fighting population.

Memphis, just now, is overrun by gamblers, garroters and murderers—the foul birds of prey who follow in the wake of an army. An old man, a cigar dealer, doing business in one of the most public streets of the city, was strangled last night, during a thunder storm, and robbed of about $15,000 in specie, the hard earnings of a life of labor and economy. His dead body was not discovered until this morning. Not a day or night passes that some one is not dirked, knocked down, or robbed. In a single street it is reported there are no less than fourteen gambling hells! The vile wretches of whom I speak are supposed to be contributions from New Orleans, Nashville, Mobile and other points, where recent events and the rigid rules adopted for the protection of the country against such characters were found too warm for their comfort. It is the custom of these gentry to decoy soldiers into drinking saloons, where the liquor is drugged, and when the victim is prepared, they proceed to win all the money he has. Let such rascals be hung to the nearest lamppost; they don't deserve a trial. A speedy execution is all they are entitled to.

P. W. A.

With his correspondence now circulating throughout the Confederacy, "P. W. A." achieved a popularity with soldiers and civilians alike; occasionally, his editors printed letters of praise.

Editors of the Savannah *Republican*, March 19, 1862
Dear Sirs:

The gentlemen composing the "Gen. Walker" mess of the Georgia Hussars, Company B, (eight in all) have unanimously agreed to contribute each $1 one dollar per month towards the expense of retaining your correspondent "P. W. A." at the seat of war in the northwest.

We trust that each and all of your subscribers will follow our example, for his letters will furnish to posterity a better written and more reliable history of the war in that quarter than any which will ever be published. Any one of your subscribers who is not willing to respond to your call is not worthy of having a newspaper sent to him, and certainly can feel but little interest in the cause which should excite the mostly lively interest in the breast of every man whose all is at stake in this contest.

You have our most hearty congratulations in possessing as able a correspondent as "P. W. A.", whose merit will be thoroughly appreciated by the generations which follow us.

P. W. A. in Tennessee

MEMPHIS, March 21, 1862 [4-7-62]

There is but little news to communicate to-day.

So far as we are informed, affairs remain without change at Island No. 10 and its vicinity. A rumor has reached town, that the Federals have been digging a canal across the bend in the river from New Madrid to a point above the Island, in order to turn our works at the latter place.

There is another rumor in town, to the effect that Andy Johnson, Mr. Lincoln's Governor of Tennessee, has been killed at Nashville by some loyal son of the South. Though only a rumor, and a vague one at that, I cannot forbear alluding to it here, since I sincerely hope it may be true. So far as Tennessee is concerned, he is the worst enemy we have. He has lent himself to the Federal government for the subjugation of the South, and, if it should be found necessary, he will sacrifice the State government of Tennessee, and the institution of slavery itself, in order to detach the border States from the Confederate cause.

P. W. A.

MEMPHIS, April 2, 1862 [4-8-62]

The surprise of our picket forces at Union City, Monday morning [March 31], and the capture of 75 to 100 men, with all the tents, baggage, and stores of 1,000 men, and some 300 cavalry horses, was most disgraceful. The details will reach you through the city papers, and I have no heart to recapitulate them here.

It is not always in our power to command success in battle. The enemy may have the advantage in numbers, arms, or position, and may compel us to yield him the victory. Under these circumstances, defeat is not disgrace. But not so in case of surprise. There can be no excuse for a surprise, because it is always in our power to prevent it.

My informant tells me that the Federals are sanguine and boastful. They have no idea that we will dare to meet them, but think we will continue to fall back until we are driven into the Gulf of Mexico. They talked just this way when the Grand Army came out to Manassas.

May a just God enable us to give them a similar reception!

P. W. A.

On April 6 the Confederate army under Gen. Albert Sidney Johnston attacked an unsuspecting Federal force under Gen. Ulysses S. Grant near Shiloh Church, Tennessee. Alexander was once again, a witness to history.

The Battle of Shiloh; the First Day's Fight

BATTLEFIELD OF "SHILOH"

Seventeen miles [north] east of Corinth,

Sunday night, April 6, 1862 [4-17-62]

I reached Corinth yesterday, but found it impossible to get a horse to come out to the army, then encamped fourteen miles east of that place, on the road leading to Pittsburg Landing. This landing is four miles below Hamburg on the Tennessee river. I was more fortunate at 10 o'clock this morning, however, and succeeded in procuring a mule and a hard Mexican saddle without any padding in the seat. In this way I reached the field a little after noon.

It was known that the enemy had a heavy force on this side of the river, and that [Maj. Gen. Don C.] Buell was advancing overland from Columbia with a large reinforcing column. In view of these facts, Gens. Johnston and Beauregard determined to give battle before Buell should come up. The army was put in motion on Thursday [April 3], and by Saturday evening our entire force had got into position. It was the intention of our officers to have given battle on yesterday, but some of the regiments were raw, and there was some delay in getting them ready.

We commenced the attack at sunrise this morning. Our order of battle is said to be the strongest known to military science. We advanced in three parallel lines or corps, each one in line of battle. The first or front corps, was led by Major General [William J.] Hardee. Immediately behind him came a full complement of artillery. A thousand yards in his rear followed the second corps or line, led by Major General Bragg. Immediately in his rear came the third corps, being our reserve, commanded by Major General Polk. General Johnston was in supreme command, nobly assisted by Gen. Beauregard.

The artillery was commanded by Brig. Gen. [James] Trudeau, under the orders of General Bragg. General T. distributed his batteries along the roads and upon such open elevations as he could find. The batteries have been handled with consummate skill and effect throughout the day by their respective officers.

The nature of the ground is exceedingly unfavorable for field operations. With the exception of two or three small fields of eight or ten acres each, the battle has been fought wholly in the woods. The woods are quite open, however, much more so than in Georgia; but they nevertheless interfered very much with the evolutions of the army. The ground is rolling, and in many places quite wet and boggy near the water courses, several of which cross the field, and still further impeded the operations of the day.

But Gen. Hardee has encountered the enemy in front. The sun is just rising as his division is hurled against them like a thunderbolt. The enemy was not expecting an attack, as was evident from the condition in which he received us. Indeed, he was not aware of our near presence; he never expected us to attack him, and was doubtful whether we would ever allow him to get near enough to attack us. Hardee "set his squadron in the field" with great judgement, and led them most gallantly throughout the day. I have not been able to come up with him, but hear that he escaped without a scratch.

The enemy was at length driven from his first line of encampments. Meanwhile he recovered from his surprise, and met our onset with firmness and resolution. The fighting now became hot and close, and raged with great violence and fury along our entire front. The right and left wings as well as our center was engaged, and the roar of artillery and the rattle of musketry fairly shook the earth. But on Hardee presses, backed up by Bragg and followed by Polk—each corps rolling onward like succeeding waves of the storm-lashed sea. Hardee's corps advances, but it is done slowly; for the enemy has rallied his forces and is handling them with coolness and spirit. We moved forward as it were by inches, but still we did move, and never at any time during the day did we lose one foot of ground we gained.

At length we reached the center of the enemy's encampment. He yielded his home in the woods with much reluctance, and disputed every foot of ground with courage and resolution. Thus far we have advanced thro' the woods, which are almost destitute of undergrowth. Everywhere the trees bear the marks of the terrible conflict. Limbs were carried away, and in some places trees a foot in diameter were cut off. In a few instances, the long, sharp rifled cannon balls passed entirely through the tree. The traces of the musketry fire are to be seen everywhere upon the trees and bushes, and also in the numbers of the dead and wounded over whom we advanced.

At two o'clock the resistance had increased, and became more obstinate than at any time during the day. Gen. Johnston, in order to make a sure thing of it, placed himself at the head of our attacking force, and led the charge in person. How unfortunate that he should have done so, for at half past 2 o'clock he received a minie ball in his breast, and had his leg badly torn by a shell. He fell, and died soon afterwards, but not until the enemy had given way all along the lines. He died in the arms of Col. Wm. Preston, of Kentucky, his aid and brother-in-law, and former U. S. Minister to Spain, while Gov. [Isham] Harris, of Tennessee, another aid, supported his head.

Thus a brave soldier and skillful officer has gone down before the red tide of battle. He fell in the very arms of victory, with our flag upraised and advancing under the mighty impetus given to our attack by his own individual heroism and daring. Let the Republic do justice to his memory, and repair the grievous wrongs which have of late been heaped upon him.

The fall of Johnston did not in the least discourage our men; for they knew the gallant Beauregard was still left to them, with many other officers of skill and courage. On they press, therefore Bragg has long since brought up his corps, composed for the most part of his seasoned Pensacola troops, and most admirably has he handled them throughout the entire day. Gallant and chivalric, yet cool and sagacious, he knows when and where to plant his terrible blows. Gen. Polk also was many times in the thickest of the fight, and bore himself throughout the battle, whether in the immediate front of the enemy or bringing up his spirit of a Christian warrior. Only a portion of our reserves were ever brought into action, there being no necessity for it.

At half past five the enemy was in full retreat, and hotly pursued by the victorious Confederates. He fled back to the Tennessee, and took shelter under his gunboats and river works, the fire from which was too heavy for our light field batteries. Night, too, had come on, and our army returned to the enemy's camp and are now occupying it. The Federals left their tents standing, together with all their camp equipage, quartermaster and commissary stores, private baggage, medical supplies and considerable ammunition. The attack was so furious—it came so much like the first clap of thunder when the storm begins—and the pursuit so close and unrelenting, that they had no time to remove anything—not even to gather up their records and half-finished letters. The amount of property taken is immense. Our men are now regaling themselves upon the ample supply of excellent food everywhere to be found.

I am unable to speak with certainty of the number of the enemy's forces. One of the first prisoners I encountered (a lieutenant, who formerly belonged to the old army), estimated them at 120,000 men. Others put them down at 100,000; others, again, at 75,000, and some at 50,000. Gen. [Benjamin] Prentiss, who was captured about 5 o'clock, says the Federal army on this side of the river was composed of six divisions, of about 7,500 each, which would make the forces of the enemy engaged about 45,000. They probably exceeded this number, without including the forces on the other side of the river. At no time had we as many men engaged as the enemy.

Nor can I speak with certainty of the number of batteries or prisoners we have captured. It is too early after the battle, and too much confusion prevails, for me to get at the precise facts. The number of prisoners is variously estimated; some say 2,000, and others 4,000; one report has it that one entire brigade has been captured. This is, doubtless, a mistake. Among the prisoners are many officers, and the greater part of the Seventh Iowa Regiment, who lately petitioned the Federal Congress for permission to inscribe upon their banner the victories of Belmont and Donelson.

The number of batteries taken is said to be eighteen, which, allowing six pieces to the battery, would make one hundred and eight guns. It is more probable that parts of eighteen batteries were taken. Several stands of colors were also captured—three by the First Louisiana Regiment alone. I have seen two of them myself, and was present when they were brought in and delivered to Gen. Beauregard. I witnessed also, the arrival and presentation of Gen. Prentiss, who was taken by a staff officer or officers of Gen. Polk, and conducted to the latter, who sent him, with his compliments, immediately to Gen. Beauregard. The following is the substance of the conversation that ensued after they had shaken hands.

Prentiss—Well, sir, we have felt your power to-day, and have had to yield.

Beauregard—That is natural, sir. You could not expect it to be otherwise. We are fighting for our homes, for our wives and children, for generations to come after us, and for liberty itself. Why does your government thus war upon us and seek us upon our own soil?

Prentiss—Our people have never yet been able to bring themselves to consent to see the Union broken up. Such a thing has not entered into our calculations, and cannot.

Beauregard—The Union is already broken and the last man, woman and child in the South will willingly perish before it shall be restored. What force have you had engaged to-day?

Prentiss—Six divisions numbering a little over 7,000 each—the whole not amounting to more than 40,000. Gen. Grant commands, assisted by Gens. [William T.] Sherman, [John] McClernand, [Stephen] Hurlburt, [Lewis] Wallace, and myself. Gen. [C. F.] Smith is sick, and has not been upon the field. My division was the first to receive your attack, and we were not properly supported; if we had been the day might have gone otherwise. There has been mismanagement somewhere. Had I been supported in time, we should have broken your center at the time we stopped your advance.

Beauregard—You are mistaken, General. My order of battle was such, that if you had even penetrated the center of our front line, it would only have been to encounter certain destruction; we would have cut you to pieces. Has Gen. Buell arrived, and what are his forces?

Prentiss—(hesitating).—I do not know where Gen. Buell is, or the number of his forces. I have heard he was at Nashville, and then at Columbia, and also that he was on the road. We do not look for him under forty-eight hours. I fear you will capture the greater part of our army on this side of the river. You have met and overcome to-day the best troops we have.

Beauregard—I am glad to hear it, and trust that the result of this day's work may bring your government to a frame of mind more favorable to peace.

Prentiss—That can hardly be, sir. If your army had pushed on after the battle of Manassas, it might have taken Washington, and overrun the North, and brought us to peace. We had an insufficient supply of arms then, and were not prepared. The muskets purchased in Belgium by [John C.] Fremont were of but little account; you could turn your thumb in the muzzle, the bore was so large. We also procured from England the old arms that have been stored away in London Tower ever since the war with Napoleon in 1815. They are of no value whatever. It is only within the last sixty days that we have become thoroughly efficiently armed. Our supply is now ample, and we cannot be overcome. Your government has made two mistakes—first, in not availing itself of the fruits of the battle of Manassas; and secondly, in waiting until we had become well armed and organized. We have now 250,000 men in camps of instruction, who will be brought upon the field as they may be needed. We do not doubt the final result.

Beauregard—Nor do we. Our cause is just, and God will yet give us the victory.

Prentiss—We know you have able officers and a spirited army to back them, but our confidence is firm. And permit me to add, General, that among all the Confederate officers, no one is so great a favorite with us as yourself. Such is my own feeling, and that of our army and people.

Beauregard—You are very kind, sir; but we have much better officers than I am. Gen. Sidney Johnston and Gen. Joseph Johnston are both my superiors in ability as well as rank. I have served under both of them most cheerfully, and know them well. I care nothing for rank; the good of the country is what I look to.

Other observations were made, but the foregoing embraces the chief points of the interview. Gen. Prentiss was easy and pleasant, and not at all depressed.

P. W. A.

The Battle of Shiloh; the Second Day's Work

BATTLEFIELD OF SHILOH,

Near the Tennessee River,

Monday night, April 7, 1862   [4-18-62]

We have had another day of battle and blood. The fight was renewed this morning at 8 o'clock by the enemy, who had been reinforced during the night; and with the exception of short breathing spells, it raged with tremendous violence and fury until night separated the combatants. The apprehensions expressed in my letter of last night have been realized. Buell did come up this morning, and with him came large reinforcements. But I am anticipating the events of the day. Let me resume the narrative where my last letter left it, and rehearse the varying fortunes of the day in the order of their occurrence. This is necessary to a proper understanding of the battle; and until this general sketch or outline is drawn, it will be impossible to enter into those minor details which constitute an interesting feature in the picture.

Night alone prevented us from reaping the fruits of our brilliant victory of yesterday. It was quite dark when we chased the foe back to Pittsburg Landing, where he sought protection from his gunboats and river works. Had Beauregard possessed the power of Joshua to command the sun to stand still in the heavens for the space of an hour, our victory would have been as complete as that of the great Hebrew warrior. As it was, we expected to be able to capture so much of the Federal army this morning as could not be transferred to the bank of the river last night, unless large reinforcements should come to their relief.

The enemy received the most important aid from his gunboats. Indeed, he is indebted to these gunboats for his escape from certain destruction. They, together with his river works, answered the valuable purpose of fortifications, to which he could retire when beaten on the field. With only our light field pieces, it was impossible to operate at night with any hope of success against these works and boats, or to prosecute during the heavy storm that followed the work of completing the victory. Our forces had reached the river in one or two places as night came on, and in this way had gained some knowledge of the enemy's defences. With this knowledge, and the enemy's driven into close quarters and caught between our lines and the river, there was every reason to believe we would be able to capture the larger part of his forces this morning, provided they were not reinforced during the night or transferred to the other bank of the river.

The boats kept up a constant fire during the night from their heavy guns. It appears that the enemy did not seek to recross the river. Knowing that large reinforcements were at hand, he held his position on the river bank until this morning. Gen. Beauregard knew there was a division of 7,000 men at Crump's Landing, a few miles below Pittsburg, and he gave orders last night to proceed against them this morning, and to capture them. This division succeeded, however, in forming a junction with the forces at Pittsburg, and at 8 o'clock this morning the Federals, thus reinforced, moved out from the river and offered us battle. They must have known that other reinforcements were at hand, and that they would arrive upon the field at an early hour. The fight was renewed about a mile and a half from the river, or midway between the river and the Federal encampment.

The enemy came up to the work with great spirit and resolution. Appeals had doubtless been made to the men during the night, and the repossession of their camp represented to them as a point of honor from which there could be no escape. The attack was directed against our center; and though vigorous and spirited, and not expected, it was repulsed, and the enemy driven back with great slaughter. He rallied again, however, and this time he moved with an increased force upon our right wing. Here, too, he was repulsed and forced to retire. His next attempt was directed against our left wing, his attacks growing more vigorous, and his forces increasing with each succeeding movement. Indeed, it was now evident that he had received large accessions to his ranks, and that we had fresh troops at heavy odds to contend against. But the Confederates nobly did their duty, and the attack on the left was also repulsed. The enemy again retired, but only for a time; for Buell's forces had now come up, and the attack was renewed all along our lines, on the right, center and left. Simultaneously with this, an attempt was made to turn both our wings.

The battle now raged with indescribable fury. I have never heard or imagined anything like the roar of the artillery, and the incessant rattle of the small arms. The deep thunder bass of the one, and the sharp, shrill tenor of the other, intermingled with the shrieks of bursting shells and the whizzing of cleaving rifled cannon balls, was grand beyond description. It was the awful Hymn of Battle rolling upward to the skies and literally shaking the earth beneath. It was a solemn anthem, the notes of which were traced in blood, and uttered from brazen throats, that might have satisfied Mars himself.

The Confederates stood their ground against the furious onset, and for the fourth time the enemy was compelled to retire.

> "As meets the rock a thousand waves—
> So Inisfall met Lochlin."

It was now one o'clock. Our men were greatly exhausted; they had fought eighteen hours, and withal had slept but little, having been engaged much of the preceding night in searching out and taking care of the wounded. It was evident, too, that the enemy had been largely reinforced, and that each succeeding attack was made by fresh troops and overwhelming numbers. In view of these facts, and in order to rest his men, and to prevent an unnecessary loss of life, Gen. Beauregard availed himself of the falling back of the Federals to withdraw his troops to the enemy's line of encampment, where we rested last night. This was about a mile and a half from the point where the fight commenced this morning.

The enemy hesitated for some time, but finally came up and renewed the conflict. He was met with undiminished courage and resolution by the Confederates, who displayed the greatest possible gallantry. The battle raged on, and night alone separated the combatants. At length the enemy fell back, and so did the Confederates, both sides badly worsted and severely punished. Hardee, who commanded the front line or corps, held his ground until the enemy withdrew. Our reserves had been engaged throughout the day, and Polk, Bragg, and Hardee, each in his proper field, had nobly co-operated in the work of the day. They deserve great credit, as do the brigade and regimental officers, and the gallant spirits whom they led to battle. Gen. [John] Breckinridge particularly distinguished himself. Though not a military man by profession, Gen. Beauregard is reported to have said that he displayed great aptitude and sagacity, and handled his brigade with skill and judgement.

Having said thus much, I feel it my duty as a faithful chronicler of the times, to refer to matter here which had a controlling influence upon the fortunes of the day.

Our attack yesterday was so sudden and successful that the enemy found it impossible to remove his quartermaster and commissary stores, or even to save the baggage of the men. The temptation thus offered was too great for our troops to resist. Sunday night large numbers of them, supposing there would be no more fighting, set to work to gather up such spoils as the Federal encampment contained. There were arms, overcoats, caps, shoes, coffee, sugar, provisions, trunks, blankets, liquors, private letters and numberless other things which the enemy had been compelled to abandon. Such of our troops as were engaged in searching out the wounded and dead, or were not restrained by a sense of duty, wandered from their respective camps, and spent much of the night in plundering. Orders had been issued by Gen. Beauregard positively prohibiting anything of the kind, but many of the troops are raw, and officers and men were alike elated at our success; and consequently the necessary steps were not taken to enforce the orders of the commander-in-chief. At an early hour this morning, the men renewed their search after the spoils of victory, and many of them were separated from their commanders when the enemy renewed the battle. Some of them had even started back to their camps, loaded with such articles as they had been able to find.

After deducting the killed and wounded, and those who were engaged in removing the wounded, it would be no exaggeration to say that 5,000 sound and able-bodied men had thus wandered out of line, and took no part whatever in the battle to-day. On the other hand, the enemy had been largely reinforced.

Thus, with a diminished force on our part, we had to meet fresh troops and a more numerous army than that we encountered yesterday. And thus, too, the spoils have prevented us from again driving the enemy back into the Tennessee, notwithstanding great odds in his favor.

It was well enough, while the conflict lasted, that our troops should exchange their smooth bored muskets and shot guns for the splendid arms thrown away by the retreating foe; but there can be no excuse for the disgraceful proceeding to which I have alluded.

The spoils of victory are not less demoralizing than defeat and disaster. Such is the lesson taught by history in all ages of the world, from the time when Achan was reduced by "the wedge of gold," down to the present day. It is hoped that the experience of this day will not be thrown away either by our officers or soldiers.

P. W. A.

The Day after the Battle
Monterey, six miles from Shiloh.
Tuesday morning, 10 o'clock, April 8, 1862 [4-19-62]

Meeting with no opportunity to send forward my letter of last night, I have opened it for the purpose of bringing up the narrative to the present hour.

Neither party has showed a disposition to renew the fight this morning. We have not sought the Federals and they have not sought us. Both sides seem to have had enough of battle. After scowling at each other, like two exhausted pugilists, with bloodshot eyes and bruised and battered bodies, they have turned away, and left the contest still undecided. The Confederates are quietly returning to their lines, and the Federals to theirs. We have burnt a good many of their tents, and brought away a great deal of their baggage and camp property, and all the guns captured on Sunday. The medical stores were to have been removed yesterday, but the renewal of the fight early in the morning, prevented it. We took other guns yesterday, and lost four belonging to [T. J.] Stanford's Mississippi battery. Gen. Breckinridge had ordered the battery to be withdrawn, but the officer in charge waited to fire a few more shot, and thus lost a portion of his guns. We lost no small arms or prisoners that I have heard of, except such old muskets as were thrown aside by our troops for the superior arms left by the enemy. We also brought away a number of wagons and horses, and some ambulances. But no account has yet been taken of our captures, and I forbear entering into further details until reliable data can be obtained.

For the same reason, I shall offer no opinion as to the number killed and wounded on either side. I hope the Confederate loss is not so large as many believe it to be. I am satisfied that the number killed is not in the usual proportion to the wounded. This is owing doubtless, to the protection afforded by the trees.

6 P. M.

The enemy ventured so far this afternoon as to send out a cavalry regiment a short distance in the direction of our lines. General Breckinridge set the Texas Rangers and [Col. Nathan B.] Forrest and his mounted men after them, who captured about fifty prisoners and chased the remainder back and through two regiments of infantry that had come along to support them. In the confusion that ensued among the Federals, they fired upon their own cavalry, and wounded and killed a number of them. Col. Forrest received a shot in the side, which passed around near the spine, making rather an ugly wound. It is not thought to be mortal, however. The entire Federal force engaged immediately fell back in evident disorder.

It would be premature at this time to indulge in speculation upon the results of the two days' battle, out of which we have just emerged. I may be permitted to say, however, that the effect upon the Confederates has been to inspire them with fresh confidence and renewed determination. They have felt of the enemy, and have themselves passed through the fire, and will be the better prepared for a second great battle which is to come off at or near Corinth.

I am not informed as to the extent of the reinforcements which the enemy has received, or of his ability to undertake an early forward movement. He has been badly crippled and cut up, and has lost much valuable property, and many of his best field pieces. Moreover, the roads are in a shocking condition. It rained very hard last night and again to-day, and there is a prospect for more rain to-night. All these things will tend to delay further active operations by either party.

P. W. A.

CORINTH, April 12, 1862 [4-22-62]

Both armies seem to have settled down into a state of quiet. There is more or less skirmishing between the picket and cavalry, in which the Confederates invariably get the best of it. It has rained almost uninterruptedly since the battle, and the condition of the roads is such as to render them impassable to artillery and baggage trains. It is not probable, therefore, that the enemy will undertake any offensive movement of a general character for some days—perhaps not for two weeks.

A complete muster roll of the Federal expedition up the Tennessee, was found on the battlefield. It shows that the enemy had a force at and around the battleground of 61,000 men. This includes the division of Gen. Lewis Wallace at Crump's Landing, four miles below Pittsburg, and which was not engaged until early Monday morning. There were 21 batteries, averaging six pieces to the battery—thus making the number of their guns 126. After deducting the division at Crump's Landing, and allowing 5,000 for the sick, we have a force of 48,500 men. These men we fought on Sunday. The forces opposed to us on Monday, 25,000 of whom were fresh troops, were still larger. Allow 10,000 for the captured, killed, wounded and disabled on Sunday, there would still remain of the original force 38,000 men. Wallace's division of 7,500, and Buell's reinforcements, who came up on Monday, roughly estimated at 17,500—making together 25,000 men—would swell the Federal army opposed to us on Monday to 63,000. These fresh forces doubtless brought with them as many guns as we had captured, which would leave their artillery about as strong on Monday, as it was on Sunday.

It would be improper, perhaps, to offer any estimate of the forces engaged on our side. When all the facts shall have come out, however, there will be found additional reason for the pride we so justly feel in Southern arms and Southern prowess. The Confederate forces were chiefly from Alabama, Mississippi, Louisiana, Texas, Arkansas, Tennessee and Kentucky. Georgia was represented by an excellent battery and a fine cavalry company, and gallant little Florida had a regiment on the field. Georgia, as you know, is very largely represented on other fields. It would be improper to make distinctions, if any really existed; and I am glad to have it in my power to state, as the result of my own personal observation on the field, and from information derived from official sources, that all our troops behaved as men ought to do who are fighting for their hearthstones and for liberty itself. Alabama has just reason to feel gratified with the performance of her heroic children. This is the judgment of all men. And while all the superior officers distinguished themselves, your own Gen. [Jones M.] Withers was among the most heroic and daring, gallantly leading his men in the very thickest of the fight. He escaped, I am glad to say, without a scratch.

The dashing General [Adley] Gladden, who admirably led four of your own regiments, has just breathed his last! A brave officer and noble spirit has gone down, but his name will long live on glory's page.

It is now stated the Gen. Johnston was not struck in the body at all, but that he was wounded in the foot and just above and behind the knee. The ball cut an artery, and he was so far in advance that he bled to death before a surgeon could be brought up! It was a crucial moment, and he placed himself at the head of a brigade, and made a bold dash at the enemy which literally scattered them to the winds. But his life was the price of our success. All honor to the fallen chief! He entered the battle with the resolution to return victorious or die upon his shield. He did both!

The battle abounded in acts of personal prowess and individual gallantry. I have already alluded to such as came to my knowledge, but the weather has been such, and the facilities for visiting the camps, which occupy an area of several miles, are so limited, that I have not found it possible to collect and verify them for publication. Most of them will reach you through private letters, and to them I must refer you for the present.

One thing I urge upon the people at home, and that is to fill up as rapidly as possible the places of the noble dead. Many of the companies and regiments have suffered very heavily; some of them have been decimated, and but few were ever entirely full. Let recruits come forward at once, and take up the arms that have been laid aside by the fallen brave. Another great battle will be fought here soon; if not here, then somewhere in the vicinity of the Tennessee river. But whenever and wherever fought, it must be more or less decisive of the campaign in the Southwest. Cavalry are not wanted; we have too many now. The country is unsuited to this kind of service. Such is the opinion of our best officers; and I doubt whether any more cavalry would be received, if offered.

P. W. A.

Official losses at the Battle of Shiloh or Pittsburg Landing: Federals, 1,754 killed, 8,408 wounded, and 2,885 missing for a total of 13,047; Confederates, 1,723 killed, 8,012 wounded, and 959 missing for a total of 10,694.

MEMPHIS, TENN., April 17, 1862 [5-2-62]

Persons who have arrived here from Nashville and Paducah gives us the Northern version of the battle. The Federal account, published in Nashville, admits a loss of 18,000 in killed, wounded, missing and prisoners. The estimate at Paducah, where boatloads of the wounded were being received, was 20,000. A St. Louis paper, received here and forwarded to Corinth, contains a similar estimate. It was freely admitted that they were badly defeated and cut to pieces on Sunday. On Monday they claim that it was a drawn battle, and, if anything, that they got somewhat the better of it.

The enemy is more liberal than we expected him to be. We had supposed that he would claim a great victory; but the truth got out, doubtless, before the newspaper and telegraph censors had time to concoct a statement that should gloss over the matter. He ought to know what his own loss was, but I cannot bring myself to believe it was anything like 20,000. When they are whipped, the Federals have a way of exaggerating their own losses, by way of excuse and apology for their defeat. They think it is all right enough if they can only show that they were terribly cut to pieces, and lost hundreds and thousands. Such was their conduct immediately after the battle of Manassas; and yet two weeks had not elapsed before they rushed to the other extreme, and run down their losses to a very insignificant figure. They will do the same thing with respect to the battle of Shiloh.

Packages of balls, as you have been informed by telegraph, labeled "poisoned balls," were found among the ammunition abandoned by the enemy. I get my information from an eminent surgeon attached to Gen. Hardee's division, and who had seen and examined the packages. He informed me, also, that the Federal authorities had allowed poisoned quinine to be smuggled across the line, and that it had found its way into the army, where he had analyzed it.

This is in keeping with their practice of wearing breastplates and using telescopic sight on their pieces. Their whole idea of war is to invent some means, or resort to some trick by which they can get the advantage. Such a thing as a fair, open, stand up fight upon anything like equal terms, has never entered their heads since the Grand Army first moved out to Bull Run.

It is to be hoped that our troops will not forget these steel breastplates, and that here after they will aim a little lower. It is a fault common to all volunteers to shoot too high. They load and fire rapidly, and consequently take a coarse sight, which carries their ball over the heads of the enemy. The marks upon the trees furnish abundant evidence of the truth of this statement. Some of these marks were too small for a musket or rifle ball, and the circumstance led me to examine some musket cartridge, which I found in the enemy's encampment. In addition to the usual charge of powder and ball, each of the cartridges contained three large buckshot. First came the powder, then the large round musket ball, and then the buckshot. This fact may account in part for many of the slight wounds received by the Confederate troops.

It is evident that the enemy has a corps of sharp-shooters attached to each of his brigades. Very few of our officers were so fortunate as to come out of the late battle without a mark of some sort, either upon their persons or clothing. If they escaped themselves, their horses were in many instances killed or wounded. Gen. Johnston was killed, and Gens. Hardee, [A. H.] Gladden, [Benjamin] Cheatham, Bushrod Johnson, [Charles] Clark, [John S.] Bowen and others, were wounded. Several regiment officers were also killed and many wounded. All this could not have been accidental. Among our wounded, not heretofore mentioned, was Gov. [George W.] Johnson, the Provisional Governor of Kentucky, who fell into the hands of the enemy. It is feared that his wounds will prove fatal.

It is currently reported that Gen. [George B.] Crittenden has resigned his position in the army. He and Gen. [William] Carroll of this city were suspended from their commands just before the battle, at the instance of Maj. Gen. Hardee, in consequence of their intemperance; and it is supposed that Gen. Crittenden sent in his resignation in consequence of this proceeding. Gen. Carroll was attached to Gen. Crittenden's command. The whole country will approve of the course pursued by Gen. Hardee, while no sober man will regret that Crittenden has left the army. He is one of the cleverest men in the world, and no one questions his courage or loyalty; but his habits are such as to render him wholly unfit to command.

It is reported that the enemy is falling back some distance down the Tennessee river. If this be true, it has been done, probably, for the purpose of uniting with the forces landed on this side of the Mississippi just above Fort Pillow. Possibly, Gen. Buell has discovered that it will be a hazardous undertaking to march from Pittsburg across the country to Memphis. Should the forces lately at New Madrid be able to form a junction with those under Buell somewhere between Mississippi and Tennessee—say at Dresden or Humbolt—the Federals may hope to sweep everything before them, and finally reach this city. A few days will remove all doubt as to their movement.

P. W. A.

MEMPHIS, April 24, 1862 [5-7-62]

I regret to learn that some of my letters have failed to reach you. I have written regularly since the battle of Shiloh. Possibly some of the letters were on the trains captured by the enemy at Decatur and Huntsville. The moment that intelligence reached me of the seizure of the railroad at those points, I changed the direction of my letters and sent them by way of Mobile.

Gen. [Ormsby] Mitchel, in his report of the occupation of Huntsville on Friday, the 11th inst., says: "We captured 200 prisoners, 15 locomotives and a large number of cars, the telegraphic apparatus and offices, *and two southern mails.*"

One of my letters, (perhaps two) was in these mails. One of the mails was coming in this direction, and contained letters, I fear, intended for myself. This is not all. A box of summer clothing sent to me from Atlanta, were also lost. Thus you see, you are not the only one who has been made to suffer by the inroads of the enemy.

The enemy is straining every nerve to bring together an overwhelming force at as early a day as possible. In addition to the reinforcements referred to in my last letter, it is now reported that the greater part of Fremont's command will be sent from Northwestern Virginia to the Tennessee. At this rate, it is possible Gen. [Henry] Halleck may collect an army of 100,000 men.

I may remark here however, that the columns of 100,000 and 200,000 men so often boastfully spoken of by the Federal press, exist only on paper. The entire Federal force in the west does not exceed 150,000 men, one-fourth of whom, as in all volunteer armies, may be set down as unfit for service, by reason of sickness, absence or disability. The proportion of noneffectives in the Federal army of the west is fully up to this figure. We hear that there are 9,000 sick in Nashville, and a northern paper now before me, says there are 5,000 cases of diarrhea in Cairo and Mound City alone—all from Grant's army. The water and climate are quite as fatal as our muskets and artillery. A month hence the mortality will be fourfold greater than it is now.

P. W. A.

MEMPHIS, April 27, 1862 [5-9-62]

Events follow each other with such rapidity, and the mails have become so irregular and uncertain, that it is difficult to prepare a connected narrative of what is transpiring in the West. The city has been in a state of great excitement for some days past, in consequence of the unfortunate condition of affairs at New Orleans. The uneasiness has been greatly increased by the silence of the authorities. Though aware of the advantages gained by the enemy, and that the people along the river and far into the country were excited by the wildest and most painful rumors, they have obstinately refused to allow any dispatches to pass over the wires, or to utter one word to relieve the public anxiety.

A desire to prevent the enemy up the river from getting the news through our newspapers, is the reason assigned for the course pursued by the authorities, who seem never to have supposed that the spies who carry southern papers through the lines, could also carry the news in their heads. An absurd fear of the effect of the intelligence upon our army is another reason urged for withholding the unwelcome tidings. This is simply ridiculous; for the troops, *who are not to blame for any of our reverses*, are better prepared, by reason of their superior fortitude, virtue and courage, to receive disagreeable news, than the short sighted authorities themselves.

If it be true and there can be no doubt of it, that New Orleans has fallen, no human ingenuity will ever be able to relieve the War and Navy Departments of the responsibility. They have had one entire year to put the city and river in a state of defense; and yet we hear that the Federal gunboats, after a few days' bombardment, have passed up to the city. They have had the same time within which to build gunboats and construct river defences that the enemy had; and we have thousands of negroes to do the work. And yet, through the utter inefficiency little was done—so little, indeed, that the chief city in the Confederacy, and the grandest river in the world, with its fertile shores and abounding wealth, have fallen into the hands of our enemies almost without a blow. What are we to think of the chiefs of Departments who permit such things to be done?

The fall of New Orleans necessarily gives the Federals the control of the Mississippi river and all its tributaries, including the Red, the Arkansas, the White, and the St. Francis rivers—at least as far as the gunboats can pass—will soon be lost to us, together with the steamboats, unfinished gunboats, stores and other property that cannot be removed into the interior or destroyed. Memphis and Fort Pillow will fall just as soon as the enemy sees proper to advance up the river.

It is hoped that the cotton and other property within reach of any of the streams I have mentioned, will be forthwith destroyed. Beauregard has already issued an order requesting the planters to apply the torch at once.

What effect the success at New Orleans will have upon the plans of the enemy, if any, I am unable to inform you. Having opened the Mississippi, some suppose Gen. Halleck, instead of risking battle at Corinth, will move down the Tennessee and around into the Mississippi. This, to say the least of it, is doubtful, since a movement of that kind would involve the abandonment of Nashville and Middle Tennessee. The loss of the Mississippi, though a great blow under any circumstances, will be stripped of many of its advantages to the enemy, so long as Beauregard is left unconquered in the field.

Price and [Earl] Van Dorn did not cross the river to this side any too soon. Nearly all of their troops have reached Corinth, or are *en route* to that place. Gen. Halleck is also concentrating an immense force on the Tennessee. The battle may by fought before this reaches you, and upon the result hangs, possibly, the fate of the Southern people.

P. W. A.

In the beginning of May, a reorganized Federal army 120,000 strong under Major General Henry Halleck advanced from Pittsburg Landing toward the Confederates at Corinth, Mississippi.

CORINTH, MISS., May 1, 1862 [5-12-62]

We are in the immediate presence of the enemy, and consequently there is but little that it would be proper to communicate. Besides, the great battle, upon which so much depends, may be fought, and the result announced, before this letter can reach your readers. The railway line from Corinth to Mobile has been surrendered to the military authorities, as indeed have all the lines leading from this place. It is impossible to say, therefore, when my communications will find their way to your office.

It is believed on all hands that the great battle of the South-west will be fought at an early day—possibly this week. It is not supposed that the main body of the enemy's force has left the Tennessee river. Strong reconnoitering parties have been thrown forward, and in this way the Federals have been steadily driving in our pickets and advancing their lines for the last five or six days.

The object of this slow and cautious advance is two-fold; First, to reconnoiter the ground thoroughly, and prepare the roads and bridges for the movement of the army proper; second, to feel our lines as it were, and to ascertain our exact position. When this all have been accomplished, we may expect the enemy to advance in force, provided the weather be auspicious. Everything depends on the weather. If it should be favorable, the battle will be fought in a very few days, if unfavorable, then it may be delayed for some time.

There is considerable sickness in the army. The prevailing diseases are dysentery, pneumonia and measles, with occasional cases of chills and fever. The ground occupied by our encampment about Corinth is low and damp, and has not been dry since Christmas. The sickness in the Federal army is said to be very great.

P. W. A.

CORINTH, MISS., May 12, 1862 [5-19-62]

I fear my letters must prove uninteresting to your readers. There is material enough, if I felt at liberty to use it; but the immediate presence of the enemy, and the existence of spies throughout the country, who catch up and report everything that can be of any possible advantage to their employers, admonish me of the necessity of exercising great reserve and caution. There are some topics, however, which will not lose all the interest that attaches to them, by being withheld for a time.

The more one sees of the hardy Western men who have followed Van Dorn and Price across the Mississippi, the more he is impressed with their martial bearing. It is seldom you find one in anything approaching a uniform. They wear all sorts of garments, cut in all sorts of fashions, with a belt about their waists, a slouched hat stuck upon their heads and their pants in their boots. Yet there is something in their step and manly forms, and in their frank, devil-may-care look, that cannot fail to arrest the attention of one who does not judge by outside appearances alone.

Gen. Price possesses the confidence and affection of his troops to an extent I have never witnessed before. They have several names by which they designate him in camp, such as "Pap," "Dad," "the old Tycoon," "the Fox of the West," &c. He has a kind and respectful word for each one, and is always accessible whether on business or to hear complaints. And yet he is firm and energetic, and controls his men with the greatest ease. He does not find it necessary to surround his headquarters with surly sentinels, nor to call to his side a flock of butterflies in the shape of volunteer aids-de camp. Fancy soldiers, who ride gay horses and wear fine clothes, and who almost invariably return rude answers to respectful inquires, and render themselves generally disagreeable and ridiculous, may be ornamental, but they are seldom useful. Civility is a debt which every man owes to his neighbor. It is a cheap commodity, and yet it goes a long way and smoothes many a rough place. A kind word, especially from those in authority, is like letting another man light his candle by our own, which loses none of its brightness by what the other gains. This Price understands; and hence the strong hold he has upon the heart of his soldiers and his countrymen.

General Halleck, is reported to have sent Price word that he (Price) had the advantage of him in Missouri, on account of his superior knowledge of the country, but that he had him now where he wanted him, and should either capture or whip him soon. "Tell Halleck," was Price's reply, "that he has not men enough to capture me—and as for whipping my boys, I have this proposition to make; He may select 100 of the best men in the whole Northern army, and place himself at the head of them; and I will take the same number of my men as they come and without distinction and will place myself at the head of them; we will go into an open field and fight it out, and for one I'm willing to let the fate of the Southern Confederacy depend on the result." I have not heard that Halleck sent any reply.

P. W. A.

CORINTH, May 17th, 6 a.m. [5-23-62]

It has become so warm and dusty, that I find it necessary to rise early and write my letters before breakfast. We have had no rain for nearly two weeks, and the skies look as if it would continue dry for some time. With hundreds of wagons and thousands of men and horses daily moving about the depot and through the camps, the surface of the earth—a rich, thirsty loam—has been ground into dust, which flies up into one's face at almost every step. I thought it was bad enough at Manassas on the day of the great battle, but it is infinitely worse here. The soil is that peculiar nature, not uncommon in the West, which is quite wet and boggy in the winter, and quite as dry and parched in the summer.

You will not be surprised to hear, therefore, that there is an insufficient supply of water for the army. Indeed, the supply has run so low, and the water is of such an unwholesome character, that many of the regiments have found it necessary to dig wells.

If not too late, allow me to suggest to gardeners and planters about cities and along railroads within two hundred miles of any point where our forces are stationed, to raise as many vegetables, watermelons, cantalopes and fruit, as possible. They cannot do the soldier a greater favor, or do more to service his health, than by adopting this course. If this plan suggested is not adopted, our troops will be compelled to subsist through the hot summer months upon bread and salt meat alone. Fruit, if properly put up, can be sent five hundred miles. And where this cannot be done, let it be dried and put up in sacks. Indeed, everything in the form of food, whether for man or horse, should be carefully husbanded.

P. W. A.

Beauregard realized that he would not be able to hold Corinth, and planned to withdraw down the line of the Mobile and Ohio Railroad. On May 25, to preserve the secrecy of the evacuation, Beauregard ordered all "press correspondents to leave the army on the first train and not to remain within twenty-five miles of Corinth."

ARMY OF THE MISSISSIPPI
Corinth, May 26, 1862 [6-2-62]

This is the last letter I shall be able to send you from this point. Gen. Beauregard has issued an order, requiring all newspaper and other public correspondents to retire from the army. This step has been taken in consequence of the alleged indiscretion of one of the correspondents [Sam Reid] of the Memphis *Appeal*, who writes over the signature of "Sparta." No complaints have been made of anything I have written, or of the letters of other writers from the army. On the contrary, the letters of some of us have been referred to frequently, by persons high in authority, in terms of warm commendation, and information of interesting character has been voluntarily imparted to us that it might be laid before the public. And yet all of us alike, the innocent as well as the guilty, are made to suffer for the sins of one man.

It is believed by some that Gen. Beauregard has been induced to issue this unjust and tyrannical order by Gen. Bragg, the most waspish officer in the army, or by some one of the swarm of guady butterflies who bask in the sunlight of his presence—many of whom are volunteer aids or officers whose merits have not been duly appreciated by the independent writers of the day. The truth is, the characters to whom I allude are the bane of the army. There is hardly a general officer in the service who is not surrounded by a multitude of volunteer aids, with *whip and spur*, (the latest style of riding,) who follow in the train of their chiefs like the tail of a comet, and who, though ornamental, are seldom useful. For the most part, they are young men who have wealthy parents, and who have not the patriotism to enter the ranks and perform the duties of a true man and soldier. They are pert, insolent and impudent; they ride fine horses with gay trappings, use an immense amount of gold lace, swear like a trooper, and render themselves generally disagreeable and ridiculous. This is true not only of volunteer aids, but many of the officers whose heads have been turned by their sudden elevation, and who think they are required to exercise their power every hour in the day, lest somebody forget what "mighty men of valor" they are. These characters are generally known, in the army, by the vulgar but expressive name of "squirts."

Gen. Beauregard, nevertheless, is responsible for the order to which I have alluded, and will so be held by the country and by the historian.

The freedom of the press, though guaranteed by the fundamental law of the land, exists only in name. The military authorities have for some time claimed and exercised the right to inspect all telegraphic dispatches, and to prohibit their transmission over the wires unless they were such as they saw fit to approve. Every telegram I have sent you since my return to this place, had first to be submitted to the Adjutant General, and without whose approval the operators dare not send it. Not content with this imitation of the Lincoln government, they now issue a peremptory order, completely closing the door against all knowledge of the operations of the army, and in effect destroying the newspaper press of the country. Will the people submit to this unwarranted stretch of power? Ought they to submit to it?

A few short months ago Gens. Beauregard and Bragg were condemning the Northern despotism for the very thing they are now doing. The Federal Government was guilty of the outrage of searching the house of the citizen without due process of law, suspending the writ of *Habeas Corpus*, seizing private property, destroying the liberty of the citizen, and exercising a surveillance over the Press, which amounted to a virtual denial of all freedom of thought and speech. The military authorities of the Confederate States are following fast in the footsteps of the infamous tyranny that lords it over an enslaved people beyond the Potomac, and that now seeks to subjugate us to its ruinous rule. We had hoped it would never be said of us, as it has been of our enemies, that freedom was incompatible with success, and that to achieve our liberties, we must first become slaves.

The complaint against the correspondent of the *Appeal* relates to a telegram which he sent to that paper. Before the telegram was sent, it was submitted to the acting Adjutant-General of the army, and by him approved. If blame attaches to any one, therefore, it is the Adjutant, whose duty it was to expunge all news of a contraband character.

I am glad to say the order of expulsion is universally condemned by the army. I have not met with a single individual, officer or soldier, outside of the "charmed circle" alluded to, who approves of the proceeding. It is everywhere looked upon as a blunder, which, like Banquo's ghost, will return in life and in history to plague the authors of it.

When I came to Corinth, the first thing I did was to call upon the Adjutant-General of the army, who gave me permission to visit the camps and to pass in and out of our lines without let or hindrance. I expressed a desire to be placed upon a military footing, to be allowed access to such orders and dispatches as it was proper to publish, and to be held responsible for my conduct like other men in the army. He courteously granted my request, and until his recent illness everything went on smoothly and pleasantly. But unfortunately, it became necessary some days ago for Gen. [Thomas] Jordan (the Adjutant-General) to go into the country on account of sickness. Had he been at his post, I have no idea that such an order, as that complained of, would ever have been issued. He is a soldier, a scholar and a gentleman, and his department is conducted with singular ability and courtesy.

When a correspondent or other person in the army transgresses any of the rules adopted for its government, it is proper that he should be punished; but there is no reason why the innocent should be made to suffer, and especially the people who have been lavish of their means and their blood in support of our cause. This war is the people's war. Their sons and brothers make up the army, and their means, and theirs alone, support and maintain it. And shall they not be allowed to know anything that is transpiring within that army? When their sons are maimed or slain in battle, shall they be denied the poor privilege of seeing a list of the killed and wounded? Is the army to be a sealed book to the country? Even in despotic France and monarchial England, literary men have been encouraged to accompany their armies, and to write freely of their movements; but it has been reserved for free (?) America alone to place a muzzle upon the Press.

Personally, I care nothing for the order. On the contrary, I am glad of an opportunity to return to my home in dear old Georgia. But I do regret its promulgation on account of the army, and the bleeding hearts at home, and General Beauregard himself, whom I have supported and defended for the last twelve months with whatsoever ability I possessed, and that, too, at times when I believed his course at least questionable.

Without the aid of the women, the Pulpit and the Press, the revolution in which we are engaged would long ere this have proved a lamentable failure. I, who have done least of all the writers from the army, can say this without presumption. This fact is patent to all the world, except the arrogant and silly officials in the civil and military service of the Government. And yet a "puff" as long as your finger would purchase from many of them permission to do and say almost what you please.

The truth is, a blunder was committed at Corinth on Thursday last [May 22], when the army marched out to attack the enemy, without having first made proper reconnaissances. The movement was a failure, and it is now feared that the time has passed for *attacking* the enemy, whose position has been rendered next to impregnable. The obnoxious telegram in the Memphis *Appeal* did not reach here until after the enemy had been made aware of it. Any attempt, therefore, to saddle any part of the blame upon the correspondent in question is both unjust and disingenuous. A scapegoat is wanted, however, and this writer has answered the occasion. Unfortunately, General Halleck does not look to the Confederate press for his information of our movements. Spies, dressed in the garb of citizens, enter and leave our lines without much difficulty, and desertions from the twelve months' regiments from the disaffected portions of Tennessee, are not unfrequent. In this way Halleck receives almost a daily report of our movements.

I have written thus plainly, not from any want of respect for Gen. Beauregard, whom I esteem as one of the most loyal and unselfish men of any country or age, but in vindication of the freedom of the Press, and of the rights and respectability of literary men everywhere.

There is but little to communicate in regard to position of affairs here. The Federals are fast closing in around us. It is reported, by an intelligent scout, that they have planted one of their heavy siege guns just across a swamp, and within one mile and a half of our works. Others will, doubtless, be got into position soon. Indeed, it is probable they will begin the work of shelling our camps before the week is out. They have also erected very strong defensive works, to guard against an attack by us.

We must, therefore, go out and fight them in their own strong positions, or submit, be shelled in ours, or prepare to retire from Corinth. No other alternative is left us.

P. W. A.

Alexander's criticism of Beauregard's order received its own share of criticism from some rival newspapers causing the Savannah Republican *to defend their star reporter.*

Our Army Correspondent & His Critics—Savannah *Republican* [6-11-62]

The letters of our Army Correspondent, "P. W. A." concerning Gen. Beauregard's order, excluding correspondents from the Army of the West, have been criticized liberally by a portion of the Press—his positions opposed, but discussed in a spirit of candor and moderation. Another portion of the Press—a very small and insignificant one, which has either not the enterprise or the money to employ correspondents and keep its readers properly informed of public affairs—has given loose rein to private malice and all manner of uncharitableness against our correspondent, seeking to hold him up as a incendiary writer, and a defamer of the leaders of our armies. Such stuff is so ridiculously illogical and unjust, that it became its own best answer, and we have not thought it worth while to trouble ourselves about it. "P. W. A." is beyond the reach of such malicious creatures, and their missiles fall impotent at his feet.

In the meantime, Alexander steams away from the scene of strife.

STEAMER *BEULAH*, ALABAMA RIVER, June 11, 1862 [6-16-62]

Having become satisfied that I could render you but little service by remaining longer in the South-west, and that there was no prospect of anything like a general engagement for some time to come, I decided to return to Georgia, taking the river route from Mobile to Montgomery as the more pleasant.

We have had a pleasant though tedious trip thus far. The Alabama is a very picturesque river, with high, bold bluffs and jutting headlands. The corn along its banks, as far as we have been able to observe, promises an abundant yield. I have not seen an acre of cotton from Mobile to Selma.

Gen. Prentiss and fifty-six other Federal officers captured at Shiloh, got on the boat at this place. They have been confined here, and are now being removed to Atlanta, probably to be exchanged.

Gen. Prentiss readily recognized me, from having seen me at Beauregard's headquarters at Shiloh. He is very inquisitive—what Yankee is not?—and seems quite desirous of getting the latest news. He appears particularly anxious to know whether we have occupied Grenada, Miss., and admits that it seemed to him an important point when he passed it on his way from Corinth. He rather prides himself on the trick he thinks he played upon Beauregard, when he informed him, in reply to an inquiry, that he did not know where Buell was, and did not think he could arrive at Shiloh in less than 48 hours. When I informed him of Buell's statement, in his report, (which he has not seen,) that he reached Savannah on the Tennessee, as early as Saturday night, before the battle, he said yes, he knew it at the time, but thought it but fair to deceive general Beauregard, if he could.

"General Beauregard," he added, "asked me also if we had any works at the river, to which I replied, 'you must consider us poor soldiers, General, if you suppose we would have neglected so plain a duty!' The truth is, however, we had no works at all. Gen. Beauregard stopped the pursuit at a quarter to six; had he used the hour still left him, he could have captured the last man on this side of the river, for Buell did not cross till Sunday night."

The latter opinion is entertained by some of our own officers who were in front at the time the order to cease the pursuit was received. Indeed, I have heard that Bragg and Hardee hesitated about obeying the order, so well convinced were they that Gen. Beauregard would not have issued it if he had been present and understood the exact position of the two armies. Desultory firing was kept up until night by detached parties who were late in receiving the order, and hence many supposed the battle continued until night separated the combatants. According to Buell's report, our shot was falling among the fugitives crouching under the riverbank at the time our troops were called off. Beauregard acted, doubtless, from the best information he had at the time, and he did not think it prudent, after a battle of 12 hours, to expose his men to a fierce cannonading from the Federal gunboats and their supposed river batteries.

You will remember the doubt I expressed, in my report of the interview between Beauregard and Prentiss, of the sincerity of the latter when he came to speak of Buell's whereabouts. His manner indicated that he was prevaricating. So universal is the law to tell the truth, that but few men ever become such adepts in falsehood as to be able to violate it without showing some signs of hesitation or confusion.

P. W. A.

Alexander's critical comments about Beauregard's performance at Shiloh caused even more controversy for himself. A month later, Beauregard's former adjutant general, Thomas Jordan, published a reply entitled: "A Lost Opportunity at Shiloh," in which he disputed Alexander's claim that Beauregard was "duped" by Prentiss.

After regaining his health, Alexander prepared for another campaign.

THOMASTON, Ga., July 3, 1862 [7-7-62]

Mr. Editor: I have received both of your letters asking me to proceed to Richmond and resume my correspondence with the *Republican*. I have not been quite well for a month. Indeed, but few persons who were compelled to drink the unwholesome water at Corinth, escaped entirely. My health is improving daily, however, and I hope it will be fully restored in a few days.

I have been somewhat surprised since my return home, to learn that two or three newspapers in Georgia have been quite industrious in their efforts to bring discredit upon my correspondence from the army. I had not supposed before that my letters were considered of so much consequence as to call for this kind of treatment. You well know that I have not been actuated, in my endeavors to serve the great cause in which we are engaged, by mercenary motives. I did not abandon my business, and give my time, and expose my life, either for the compensation which the *Republican* granted me, or for the purpose of pushing any scheme of my own, or of any other individual. All I required of you was to pay my expenses; the remainder I freely gave to the country. The compensation you allowed me, though most liberal, was not sufficient to meet my actual expenses. In addition to this, one finds it necessary, in his visits to the hospitals and his travels over the railways, if he have any soul to share not only his last crust, but his last dollar also, with the sick and needy soldier. In order to meet these additional demands, and to cover the loss of baggage, &c., I found it necessary occasionally to send letters to a few other papers—my sole object being to serve the cause honestly and faithfully with the Pen, while others were doing it with the Sword.

P. W. A.

Alexander at last returns to Richmond and the business of war reporting, however, General Order No. 98—the order forbidding newspaper correspondents from reporting from the army is still in effect; Alexander must find a way to circumvent the order.

RICHMOND, July 26, 1862 [8-1-62]

I did not reach this city until yesterday, in consequence of the detention of the trains. At no time since the commencement of the war has the pressure upon the railway line from Augusta to Richmond been greater than for the last two weeks. Large numbers of persons, who came on to minister to the necessities of the wounded in the late battles, are returning home, and in many instances taking with them their sick and mutilated friends. Thus the trains going South are crowded with the victims of war in search of quiet and health among their native hills, whilst those coming North are loaded with troops who come to fill their places and to strengthen still further the arm of the Government in the gigantic contest in which it is engaged.

I have not yet visited the battlefield, nor sought to enter the lines of the army. Well informed persons tell me that Gen. Johnston's order in relation to correspondents, issued last fall and reiterated this spring, still remains in force, and that the military authorities continue to conduct the war upon the idea that the desire and anxiety of the people in regard to the fate of their friends and the fortune of our arms, is mere impertinent curiosity and nothing else. It is true, I might evade this order and manage to work my way into the lines, but I may safely presume you do not expect me to do this. A few days at furthest, and I shall be in a position to inform you whether there is any ground to expect a relaxation of the rule.

It would be improper to speculate upon the probable plans of Gen. Lee. The people here feel the greatest confidence in his energy and genius, and have long since dismissed all fears in regard to the safety of their beautiful capital. With the exception of an occasional interchange of shot between pickets near Malvern's Hill, every thing is in a state of quiet on the James river. Gen. [John] Pope, the greatest braggart and liar in the Federal army, has his headquarters in Culpepper Courthouse, thirty miles this side of Manassas, whence he sends out occasional foraging parties, more for the purpose of pillaging, and deluding his own people with the idea that he is about to commence offensive operations, than for anything else. The belief prevails at Washington that Stonewall Jackson has moved up in the direction of Pope's position, and the Federal Sodom and Gemorrah is in great consternation in consequence of the report. Should the Confederate Gideon start after the mendacious boaster, he will get a terrible whipping—that is all. Jackson runs well himself—fortunately, however, not *from* the enemy, but *after* them.

P. W. A.

RICHMOND, July 29, 1862 [8-4-62]

It has been my desire to furnish you a connected and intelligible account of the series of battles fought in front of Richmond just one month ago, especially of the part taken by the troops from your own noble State, but thus far I have not been able to do so. I had hit upon a plan, notwithstanding the prevailing order of Gen. Johnston, which promised to be successful, but simultaneously with my arrival here, a considerable portion of the army was put in motion, and it is now many miles distant. You will not expect me to be more definite. It is sufficient to say, that the first steps towards a realization of the policy referred to by President Davis as the one hereafter to be pursued by the armies of the Confederacy, have been taken, and under circumstances which promise to add additional lustre to the arms of our young Republic. If any of your readers are still at a loss to understand my meaning, I can only say that the best fighter in the Confederate service and the greatest liar in the United States will probably cross swords within a week from this time.

General Pope's army occupies the region of country between Manassas and the Rappahannock river on this side, including Fredericksburg and the surrounding country. His lines extend west from the town of Fredericksburg near the Potomac, to the foot of the Blue Ridge. He holds also the various gaps leading across the Blue Ridge into the valley of the Shennandoah, the scene of Jackson's late brilliant exploits. It is doubtless a part of the Federal plan, that the troops in the valley, under Banks and [Franz] Sigel, shall co-operate with those under the immediate command of Pope in the event of an attack upon either. Such, also, was the plan adopted by the Federal officers in the valley six weeks ago, and yet Jackson managed to attack them in detail and to drive the greater portion of their forces across the Potomac. What he has done once, he can do again.

It is known that McClellan has sent off several transports loaded with troops. They went down the James river, but whether his object is to reinforce Pope or to abandon his present precarious position, it is impossible to say. It must now be evident to the most sanguine Federalist, that McClellan cannot reach Richmond from his present base and with his present force, and that the 300,000 men lately called for by Mr. Lincoln, if they were now in camp, could not be relied on for three months in an aggressive movement. There are intelligent persons, therefore, who consider it not improbable that the "on to Richmond" programme will be abandoned for the present, and that McClellan will transfer the greater part of his forces to the north side of the Rappahannock, for the defense of Washington. A portion of them will be left at Fortress Monroe and another portion at Norfolk; but the remainder, it is believed, will be employed in the defense of the Federal capital.

The recent demonstrations by McClellan and Pope have deceived nobody. We know that neither one of them is in a condition to undertake to march upon Richmond. It is probably a part of their plan to divide our attention between the James river and the Rappahannock, and thus to keep us stationary until they shall have connected their forces and perfected their movements. Be this as it may, the country will be glad to hear that Gen. Lee is not likely to gratify them. He will hardly wait for the new levy to be raised and prepared for the field, or for the "young Napoleon" to repeat his wonderful strategic maneuvers of changing his base by a flank movement.

You have doubtless seen the orders recently issued by President Lincoln and Gen. Pope, in which it is proposed, not only to seize and appropriate all property, real and personal, belonging to the "rebels," that may be necessary for the use of the Federal army, but to introduce into the military and naval service of the United States all such slaves as they may be able to seduce from their masters. Gen. Pope has also notified the male citizens within his lines that they will be required to take the oath, and failing to do so, that they will be escorted to a point south of his lines, not to return again under penalty of death. It would seem that he is envious of Gen. Butler, and not content with being the greatest economist of truth in the Federal dominions, that he now seeks to rival the monster in atrocity and inhumanity. The Northern newspapers justify these proceedings, and affect to discover in them evidence of a disposition to prosecute the war with earnestness and determination. The less successful their arms are, the more bloodthirsty do they become. The people of the South, however, will not be appalled by the open avowal of a policy which has been pursued by Federal officers from the beginning. Nor is it probable that the Northern armies will long have an opportunity to carry out the brutal plans of their government. If it be our future policy to carry the war beyond the border, and wring from an obstinate foe a recognition of our rights, as indicated by the President, all that is necessary to be done is to unleash our brave legions and set them upon the enemy. Whether may be said of the statesmanship in the Cabinet, or the generalship on the field, it must be confessed by all that the men in the army have never failed to perform their part. They have never been wanting in the hour of trial.

P. W. A.

RICHMOND, August 18, 1862 [8-22-62]

You must let me off with a brief letter to-day. I leave by the first train upon which I can get standing room, for Gordonsville and the army beyond, and am much engaged just now looking after my commissary arrangement and securing transportation. No passenger trains run on the road now, and there is not transportation enough for the troops. Some entire divisions have had to march the entire distance.

General Lee went up some days ago and assumed command of the army in person. This is said to be altogether agreeable to Gen. Jackson, who reports to have the greatest confidence in Lee's ability and judgement. It is reported that the bold chieftain of the Shenandoah once remarked that he was willing to fight under any officer who might be placed over him, but as for Lee, he was ready to follow him blindfolded. But enough; it is not probable that I shall be able to communicate with you by telegraph at all from Gordonsville. My letters must be few and brief also, except in the event of a battle. The regulations are such as to leave on a very narrow margin to correspondents from the field.

P. W. A.

RICHMOND, August 19, 1862 [8-23-62]

We are without further particulars of the late battle at Cedar Run. According to the Richmond *Enquirer*, the only troops engaged in the battle, except the Forty-eighth Alabama Regiment, were Virginians. The Hon. Hines Holt, of Georgia, who has just returned from Gordonsville, and whose son (Maj. [B. H.] Holt) commanded the Thirty-fifth Georgia Regiment during the fight, states, on the contrary, that Georgia and Alabama were well represented on the field, and that their troops behaved with their usual gallantry. It is said that Colonel [James] Canty's Alabama command was actively and conspicuously engaged, and that a Georgia Brigade, commanded by Colonel E. L. Thomas, was one of the first on the field and the last to leave it. Among other regiments from the latter State engaged in the fight, he mentioned the Twelfth, Fourteenth, Thirty-fifth and Forty-ninth.

It is reported that the Twelfth Georgia rendered most important service at one point in the battle. Our plan of battle was simple, and as follows: Having ascertained that the enemy occupied a large body of woods, with their artillery in front, General Jackson ordered his own artillery to advance and engage the enemy's, and thus occupy their attention while he sent by a circuitous route an infantry force to attack them on the right and left flanks. The movement was eminently successful, and the defeat of the enemy complete. They discovered our advance on the left, and undertook to outflank the forces sent in that direction, and partly succeeded. Indeed, their unexpected counter movement created considerable confusion in our lines, and but for the firmness and valor of the veteran Twelfth, it is said the day might not have gone so well with us on that part of the field as it did.

I am told that after the fight was over, a shout was heard to go up from the whole battlefield, "Huzzah for the Twelfth Georgia, that stood its ground and saved the day!" I need not tell you that it is regarded as one of the very best regiments in the whole service. It is reported that whenever Georgia troops are sent to Jackson, he tells them that all he requires of them is to do as well as the Twelfth.

You will, probably, receive important news, by telegraph, from the lines of the Rappahannock, before this reaches you. A regard for the success of our arms will not allow me to be more explicit. From all the information at hand, however, I feel authorized to assure you and your readers that our prospects, in that quarter, under the favor of Divine Providence, are all that can be desired.

There seems no doubt that McClellan has sent a portion of his forces to the Rappahannock. Their places will, probably, be supplied by the new regiments raised under the recent call of Mr. Lincoln. McClellan is a good drill master, and, possibly, his government intends to pay him the compliment of establishing a camp of instruction at Berkley, and placing him in command of it. It is not believed that he had more than 55,000 effective men when he reached the James river after his late disastrous defeat. He entered the battles before Richmond with about 90,000 men. Of these, 25,000 (some say 30,000) were killed, wounded and taken prisoners, and about 10,000 straggled off, a portion of whom were deserters, whilst others perished in the swamps of the Peninsula. Burnside's and [James] Shields' divisions, sent to his relief, have since been ordered to the Rappahannock, and now constitute a part of Pope's command. It is not known what other forces have been taken from him and sent to Pope; but put them at 15,000, and then allow 10,000 for his sick. This reduces his present effective force to about 30,000 men; and it may become necessary to send these to Washington by the first of September.

Pope's command consists of five divisions, viz: McDowell's, Bank's, Sigel's, (late Fremont's) Burnside's and Shields'. It is possible that a few regiments have been sent to him from Washington and Baltimore; though in the present excited state of feeling in Maryland, it might not be considered safe to withdraw any part of the forces now stationed there. It is not believed that any portion of the Western army followed Pope to Virginia. It would be safe, therefore, to estimate his present force on the Rappahannock, after deducting his losses in the late battle at Cedar Run, at 45,000 men. It cannot exceed 50,000, and is hardly less than 40,000. Jackson is fully able to meet and dispose of this army.

P. W. A.

Official casualties for the Battle of Cedar Mountain: Federals, 314 killed, 1,445 wounded, and 622 missing for 2,381; Confederates, estimated 1,341 casualties.

Battle of Manassas No. 2.

BATTLEFIELD OF MANASSAS, August 31, 1862 [9-12-62]

Another great battle has been fought on the bloody Plains of Manassas, and once more has Heaven crowned our banners with the laurel of victory. The conflict opened Friday afternoon [August 29], and last night not a Federal soldier remained on the South side of Bull Run, except the prisoners we had taken and those who sleep the sleep that shall know no waking until the great day of Judgment. The people of the Confederate States—those at home no less than the invincible heroes in the field, and the friends of justice and the lovers of liberty everywhere—assuredly have cause for rejoicing and thanksgiving. Never since Adam was planted in the garden of Eden, did a holier cause engage the hearts and arms of any nation; and never did any people establish more clearly their right to be freemen.

I did not arrive in time to witness the battle of Friday, the 29th. Leaving Gordonsville at 9 o'clock that day, on a freight train, I reached Rapidan Station, the present terminus of the railroad, at noon. There I took horse, forded the river; struck for the Rappahannock—forded that river also—got to Warrenton at one o'clock yesterday—rested my horse, and then took the turnpike for the battle-field, fourteen miles distant where I arrived in one hour and fifteen minutes, and just in time to witness, for the second time, the triumph of Confederate arms on these ever memorable plains.

I cannot undertake to give the number of men engaged on either side. It is not probable, however, that the enemy had more than 75,000 troops on the field. Our own forces were considerably less, a large part of the army not having arrived in time to participate in the fight. Longstreet's *corps d'armee* held the right, A. P. Hill's and [Richard H.] Anderson's (late Huger's) divisions the centre, and Jackson's veterans the left. Jackson was the first to reach the plains below the Blue Ridge; Hill came next, and then Longstreet, who entered at Thoroughfare Gap. The enemy occupied the Gap with a full division, and seemed disposed to dispute the passage of our troops; but Toombs' and [George T.] Anderson's Georgia brigades, which led the corps, made a bold dash and soon drove them away with but little loss. That was on Thursday, the 28th. Jackson had brought the enemy to bay between Gainesville and Groveton, two miles from the old battlefield, on the Warrenton turnpike. Knowing this, Longstreet pressed forward, and succeeded in getting into position on the right of the turnpike, in time to hold that part of our lines while Jackson engaged the enemy on the left.

It should have been stated that Longstreet played the enemy a clever trick before he left the South bank of the Rappahannock. Jackson and Hill having moved around by Sperryville above, he made feints at several fords on the Rappahannock as if he would cross over, and thus drew the attention of the enemy to these points, whilst he put his forces in motion and marched rapidly to the northward and around to Gainesville. So successful was the maneuver that a late Northern paper now before me congratulates its readers upon the brilliant victory achieved by the Federals in driving us away from the fords!

The enemy advanced to the attack on Friday. He was probably aware of Jackson's comparative weakness. He soon discovered, however, that a heavy Confederate column (Longstreet's) had got into position on the right, and immediately commenced a retrograde movement. The battle, which was hotly contested for a time, in which the artillery took a prominent part, continued through the afternoon, and resulted in the repulse of the enemy along the entire line. Jackson's forces were chiefly engaged, and behaved with their usual gallantry. The scene of the conflict was just in front of Gainesville and on the left of the Warrenton turnpike as you look towards Washington.

The enemy were driven back to the edge of the old battle-field of Manassas. The Confederates slept on the field, and there awaited a renewal of the attack on yesterday. They were not disappointed, for the enemy again advanced against our left at 2 o'clock, P. M., and engaged Jackson first. By three the engagement became general, and the battle was joined.

Gen. Lee was in command, having come to the front some days ago. But a word of explanation in regard to the field and the position of the combatants,

The Warrenton and Alexandria Turnpike runs nearly Eastward, and the road from Sudley Ford on Bull Run to Manassas Junction North and South. These highways intersect each other in the center of the old battleground. Advancing down the turnpike, our forces faced to the East and in the direction of Washington, while the enemy faced to the West, but not exactly toward Richmond. The line of battle, three miles in length, extended across the turnpike almost at right angles and nearly parallel with and just West of the Sudley road. The battle of Manassas was to be fought over, and the point to be decided was, whether we should advance upon Washington or the enemy upon Richmond. This was the issue, and this the battleground.

We learn from prisoners that Halleck, McClellan and Pope were present. McClellan had brought up his old U. States Regulars, eighteen regiments, under Fitz John Porter, [Samuel] Heintzelman's division, and other corps of his James river army. It was evident that the enemy were confident of victory. They were aware of Jackson's weakness, and of the fact that not more than half of our army had come up; and by precipitating the battle, they hoped to avenge their shameful defeat on the same ground a little more than one year ago. Indeed, we hear that McDowell, the most civilized officer in the Federal service and the commander at Manassas last year, made an urgent appeal to his troops to wipe out the disgrace which then befell their arms, and never to leave the field but as conquerors.

As I have already stated, the enemy opened the battle by an attack upon our left. A heavy column, with a full complement of artillery, was launched against Jackson's veterans, but there, as elsewhere, they encountered a "Stone-wall" as immovable as the Blue Ridge. The onslaught would have been fearful to any other but Confederate troops struggling for the dearest rights known to man. The attack was repulsed, however, and the enemy forced to retire.

In the meantime a heavy force was moved up against A. P. Hill and Anderson in the center, and Longstreet's splendid corps on the right. The attack upon the center was not characterized by much vigor, but on the right it was made by McClellan's Regulars, and was furious. After the first movement against the left was repulsed, Jackson found but little difficulty in advancing his lines. The infantry were very reluctant to engage the stern chieftain again, and their artillery alone resisted him with spirit. But on the right the conflict raged with great violence for more that an hour before we had made any impression upon the serried ranks of the Regulars. When they did yield, it was slowly and in perfect order. It could hardly be called a retreat; we pushed them, as it were, from one elevation to another, gradually following them up and firmly holding the ground they had been forced to abandon.

In this way the contest continued until near sunset, the retrograde movement of the enemy growing more rapid and less orderly as the battle proceeded. Jackson pressed forward vigorously on the left; Hill and [R. H.] Anderson did the same in the center; and as the foe retired faster in that part of the field than on the right, our line finally assumed somewhat the form of a crescent.

Jackson at length bent his line around by the Sudley road, near the church of that name, and about the same time, the center and right reached the old battleground. Then followed as splendid fighting on the part of the Confederates as the world ever saw. As the fact broke upon them that they again stood upon that glorious field, and that the enemy sought a renewal of the decision rendered there one year ago, they swept on as if they were borne onward by the fiat of fate. The eye grew brighter, the arm waxed stronger, and catching the inspiration of the place, and of the children of glory who sleep upon its hills, they sent up shout after shout, that rose high above the mighty din and uproar, and sounded in the ear of the already retreating foe like a sentence of judgement.

About the same time Gen. Toombs, who had been absent under orders, reached the field at the top of his horse's speed. His appearance was greeted with the cheers of ten thousand Georgians in Longstreet's corps. The shouts were caught up along the valley and over the hills as his splendid form swept across the field in the direction of his brigade. He found it at length, and led it immediately forward in the thickest of the fight. Dashing down the hill not far from where Bee and Bartow fell, he got within forty paces of a Federal brigade, which saluted him and his men with a terrific fire. The men called to him to dismount, as otherwise he would certainly be killed. His only reply, uttered in trumpet tones, was: "President Davis can create generals; God only makes the soldier—ON!"

Finally our entire line crossed the Sudley road, and swept past the stone house at the intersection of the roads, the Henry and Lewis houses on the right, on towards Bull Run. But the enemy managed his artillery with great skill and judgement. His firing was superb, and I must admit, superior to our own. His batteries were posted at commanding points, and enabled him to cover the retreat of his infantry by delaying our advance. Night, too, came to his rescue, and to Nature and not his own arms, was he indebted for his escape from utter destruction. The pursuit was kept up until darkness prevented further effort, and the order to halt was given.

The enemy escaped across Bull Run during the night, and morning found him in a hurried retreat, for the second time over the same road and from the same battlefield back to Washington. Thus the issue has been decided for the second time in our favor, and the judgement of July, 1861, stands affirmed before the world. The battle of Manassas has been fought over, and a gracious God and our own right arms have given us the victory.

Gen. Stuart advanced to Centreville and beyond this morning, but saw nothing of the enemy, except stragglers who were waiting to be taken.

It is too early to enter into details, either as to the part performed by individuals or the extent of the victory. Gen. [Thomas] Drayton was not entirely successful in bringing his excellent brigade into action at the time, but otherwise, the battle was a complete success. Every officer and man from Gen. Lee down to the humblest private, with exceptions too unimportant to justify particular notice, performed his whole duty. But our triumph, however, has been purchased at the cost of much precious blood. Our loss has been heavy; not less, I fear, than six or seven thousand. The casualties of the enemy, including killed, wounded, and probably fifteen hundred or two thousand prisoners, will not fall much short of ten or twelve thousand men. Among the slain on the part of the Federals, is Gen. McDowell,* Col. [Fletcher] Webster of Massachusetts, and many other officers; at least such is the report of prisoners. On our side we have to lament the death of Gen. Ewell,* who was wounded yesterday and died this morning. Gens. [William] Mahone and [Micah] Jenkins were wounded—not dangerously; whilst a number of officers were killed, including Col. [John] Means, (formerly Governor,) of South Carolina and Col. [W. T.] Wilson of the Seventh Georgia. Gen. [Roger] Pryor was captured, but soon effected his escape.

Among our captures, are several thousand stand of small arms, thrown away by the flying foe, some eighteen or twenty pieces of artillery, many wagons, a large amount of stores and other valuable property. It is reported that Stuart destroyed 17,000 pairs of shoes, by a sudden descent upon Manassas Junction on Friday, and that Jackson destroyed several railway trains loaded with provisions, after filling his own wagons, the day before.

The strategy of the enemy was clever and deserves attention. He had attacked Jackson on Friday, and were repulsed. He renewed the attack yesterday, and thus sought to create the belief that his chief object was to turn our left. Having, as he supposed, produced this impression upon our right a very heavy force, including the old United States Regulars and other picked troops, under Fitz John Porter and Heintzleman. His object doubtless was to turn our right, throw us back against the Blue Ridge, keep open his communication by the Alexandria and Orange railway, and with Fredericksburg, and his gunboats to the south, and cut us off from the base of our supplies. The conception was excellent, but the execution was faulty.

Bee, Bartow, and others who fell on this field last year, have been amply revenged. The shaft erected over the spot where Bartow perished has been removed by the vandals, but the ground around the place is marked by the Federal dead. The Henry house, which was riddled by the artillery shot of the enemy last year, and where its aged owner, Mrs. Henry, was killed, has also been removed piecemeal by the enemy, and probably sold as relics; but before its very doors, and within its demolished walls, sleep to-day the miserable myrmidons of the North.

Batteries were planted and captured yesterday where they were planted and captured last year. The pine thicket where the Fourth Alabama and Eighth Georgia suffered so terribly in the first battle, is now strewn with the slain of the invader. We charged through the same woods yesterday, though from a different point, where Kirby Smith, the Blucher of the day, entered the fight before. These are remarkable coincidences; and they extend even to my own experience. In the roadway where I relieved a wounded Irishman from Wisconsin late at night last year, I to-day found another Irishman crying for succor. As I rendered it to the first, so I gave it to the second.

Is not the hand of God in all this? Who but He brought us again face to face with our enemies upon these crimsoned plains, and gave us the victory? When before did the same people ever fight two separate battles, upon the same ground, within so short a period? For the second time the God of Battles has spoken by the mouth of our cannon, and told the North to let us go unto ourselves. Will that ill-starred people require Him to repeat the command after the manner of Pharaoh and the purblind Egyptians? We shall see.

P. W. A.

{*Survived the battle.}

Official casualties from the Battle of Second Manassas/Bull Run were: Federals, 1,724 killed, 8,372 wounded, and 5,958 missing for a total of 16,054; Confederates, 1,481 killed, 7,627 wounded, and 89 missing for a total of 9,197 casualties.

Further From the Late Battles

IN FRONT OF FAIRFAX C. H., September 1, 1862 [9-10-62]

I have not yet been able to send off my letter of yesterday. It is sixty-five miles back to Rapidan station, the nearest available post office, and I have found it impossible to obtain the services of a courier to go so far, though I have offered fifty dollars for one. For the same reason, I have not been able to send you a telegraphic account of the late battle. The wires and all the railway bridges from the Rapidan to this point were destroyed by the enemy, and it will require some time to replace them, especially if the present management be continued. In this statement you will concur, when I tell you that the officer charged with the duty of rebuilding the bridge at Rapidan station, goes down to Gordonsville at night, a distance of 18 miles, to sleep!

The battle of Saturday, the 30th, was emphatically a pitched battle. The enemy selected his own ground, chose his own time, and deliberately advanced to the attack. A large part of our forces had not arrived, and consequently, while we were in a condition to accept battle, we would in a few days have been better prepared to offer it. It was a short battle, and yet it was long enough to be violent and bloody while it lasted, and decisive in its results.

True to their lying proclivities, the Federal officers, as late as 5 o'clock Saturday afternoon, claimed the battle as a victory, and so represented it to their Government. The Washington *Star* of that date contained a telegram from Pope, giving an account of the engagement of Friday with Jackson. He informed the General-in-Chief that he had badly whipped "the rebel Jackson," and that, with the reinforcements then at hand, he should crush out the whole army the next day, Saturday.

A subsequent telegram, dated at 5 P.M., two hours after the battle commenced, said that the Federal arms had everywhere been successful up to that hour. The statement was not true at 5 o'clock, and three hours later, it was an unblushing falsehood. One part of the dispatch, giving the result of Friday's fight, may be true, viz: the admission that his losses on that day would reach 8,000 men. If such were his casualties on Friday, they must have been twice as heavy on Saturday.

I find that I must correct the statement made upon the authority of prisoners, that Halleck and McClellan were present on Saturday. Halleck certainly was not there, nor it is believed that McClellan was. Halleck came out to Centreville Sunday (yesterday), and possibly McClellan, who, it is reported has been assigned the chief command of the field. Nor did the enemy retire immediately to Arlington and Alexandria. He remained at Centreville until this afternoon—at least a heavy rear guard did-and was overtaken three hours ago by Jackson's corps, two miles in advance of where I now write. A heavy artillery fire was the first intimation we had here that our advance had encountered his rear guard. Our wounded are now being bro't in, while the cannonading still continues. But let us finish up one battle before we enter upon another.

My position during the fight was somewhat on the right, where the battle seemed to rage with the greatest violence, and this led me to believe that our left and center had quite an easy thing of it. It now appears, however, that the contrary is true, and that the enemy fought with great resolution for two hours both on the left and center. Jackson was pressed very hard at one time, and found it necessary to ask for assistance, but instead of sending it to him, Gen. Lee created a diversion in his favor, which answered the same purpose, by pressing forward our right under Longstreet. The effect was soon perceptible; Jackson was not only relieved, but was enabled to move forward and drive the enemy back in disorder.

The advance of our right and left compelled the enemy to fall back in the center also, and thus our whole line moved forward as the adversary retired. The principle fighting, however, after 5 o'clock, was on the right, where Heintzleman's and Burnside's corps and a heavy force of U. S. regulars contested our advance. Upon the fall of Gen. Ewell, Brig. Gen. [Alexander R.] Lawton, whose brigade composed a part of his forces, took command of his division, and handled it with great judgment and energy.

Had every part of our line on the right been fought with equal energy and resolution, the victory would have been more decisive even than it was. The timely appearance of Toombs, and the brilliant charge he made, had a controlling effect upon the fortunes of the day. Col. [Henry L.] Benning, an officer of rare merit, had charge of the brigade until his arrival. Had Drayton promptly co-operated in the charge, the enemy's line would have been more completely broken, and he would have been driven back upon Bull Run an hour sooner than he was. As it was, one hour of daylight was all we required to utterly disperse the Federal army and capture many guns and thousands of prisoners. Jackson had already reached the Run above, and [John B.] Hood and Toombs, who held the extreme right of Longstreet's corps, were within a few hundred yards of it below, when darkness prevented further pursuit. Napoleon defeated the Austrians at Austerlitz, because, as he said, they did not know the value of an hour. The prisoners we did take were paroled to-day, and sent North by way of Harper's Ferry.

We have two reports to-night. One is, that the whole Federal army remained at Centreville yesterday and up to 2 o'clock to-day. The other is, that the main body continued its retreat toward Washington, and that only a heavy rear guard, disencumbered of wagons and baggage, remained behind to cover the retreat. It was this rearguard, according to the latter report, that we encountered this afternoon. It is not improbable that McClellan, who is now in command, will seek to conduct the retreat as he did at Richmond, by fighting us late in the evening and retiring at night. If he has brought up the remainder of his James river army, he may feel strong enough to give us battle.

It is now (midnight) raining, and has been for several hours. The army has not had a mouthful of bread for four days, and no food of any kind, except a little green corn picked up on the roadside, for thirty-six hours. The provision trains are coming up, but many of the troops will have to go another day without anything to eat. Many of them are also barefooted. I have seen scores of them to-day marching over the flinty turnpike with torn and blistered feet. They bear all these hardships without murmuring, since every step they take brings them that much nearer to bleeding Maryland. As for tents, they have not known what it was to sleep under one since last spring.

I have made but slight reference to the battle of Friday, where Jackson's corps alone was engaged, because I have been able to learn but little about it. The battle Saturday was followed by a rain yesterday, and the army having been put in motion, I have been almost constantly in the saddle ever since. For the present, therefore, I can only say, that the battle was more violent and destructive than I had at first supposed and added new lustre to the arms of the veteran followers of Jackson. The loss on both sides was considerable, but I am not prepared to offer any estimate of them. The prevailing opinion to-day in official quarters was, the enemy's loss in killed on both days was twice as heavy as our own. Our troops seem to have shot with fatal precision.

Some sixty or more citizens of Washington City, who came over to witness the battle were captured, and have been sent on to Richmond. They have been deceived by Pope's dispatch, and came over under the impression that Lee and Jackson were about to be "wiped out."

TUESDAY MORNING, Sept. 2nd.

The affair last evening referred to above, continued through the rain storm until it was quite dark. Our advance under Jackson encountered what we suppose was the rear guard of the enemy, and finally stampeded it.

Major General [Philip] Kearny, of the Federal army, was killed under circumstances, if correctly reported, quite discreditable to his character as a soldier. He was leading a regiment to the attack, and came suddenly and unexpectedly upon the 49th Georgia. He threw up his hands and called out, "Don't shoot, I surrender"—then putting spurs to his horse, attempted to effect his escape. This base trick did not succeed; a well aimed ball from a Georgia rifle hit him in the back and brought him to the ground a dead man.

P. W. A.

Alexander's version of Kearny's death contradicts other eyewitness Confederate accounts; but this is understandable, for Alexander seldom gives credit to the fighting qualities of the Yankee.

Our Army in Maryland

IN FRONT OF FREDERICKTOWN, MD., September 8, 1862 [9-24-62]

As was intimated in my letter of yesterday, {*} the people of Maryland were not expecting to see us on the east side of the Potomac so soon. They would not have been more surprised if an army had dropped down from the sky, than they were when they first beheld the dust-covered columns moving out from the river. They had been waiting for us so long; they had felt so keenly the truth of saying, that "hope deferred maketh the heart sick;" and had been so often deceived and bewildered by the mendacious press and lying authorities of the United States, not only in regard to the achievements of our arms, but as to our disposition and ability to render them assistance, that they had almost given up all idea of ever seeing a Confederate army firmly planted on the soil of Maryland. The authorities had exerted themselves to keep them in utter ignorance of our true intentions and ability. Military forces had been posted along the river and quartered throughout the State, to repress all spirit of inquiry and shut out intelligence; and where these instruments did not succeed, the knife, the halter and dungeon were brought into requisition. Men have been taken from the side of their wives and the caresses of their little ones at the hour of midnight, and hurried off to distant prisons; whilst others have been hunted from their homes and compelled to seek refuge in the swamps and thickets, where they were slain like wild beast, and their bodies hung up by the highways. Women have been imprisoned and forced to flee from burning homes, only to fall into the hated embraces of a brutal soldiery; and mothers and their children have been stopped in the streets and rudely stripped of their bonnets and sashes where they happened to correspond with the colors of the Confederate States. Churches have been defiled and the Ministers of God dragged from the very "horns of the alter." The writ of *habeas corpus*, the freedom of speech, and the sanctity of the domicile, have been wantonly violated or ruthlessly destroyed.

Five days ago Maryland, chained hand and foot, writhed in the arms of the oppressor, like a weeping, trembling virgin who appeals in vain to the mercy of her ravisher. To-morrow she may be free! We have come to strike the fetters from her beautiful limbs and punish her despoiler. We have come to gather in the last tribes of the South and to set a boundary betwixt our adversary and ourselves. This done—as we trust it will be before the snow shall have covered this lovely valley—we shall depart in peace to our own homes among the sunny hills of the free and independent South. But should it be the will of Heaven that the war shall continue yet another year, then we are resolved, by the blessings of God, to maintain the stand we have taken as long as there is a musket left and a hand to wield it. We can never quit Maryland except as conquerors, or a broken, ruined army.

A little more than two months ago, the battles of Richmond were fought and the siege of the city was raised. Since that time the army of the Potomac has fought three pitched battles and seven combats, engaged in numberless skirmishes, (in all of which it was successful over a superior force) marched two hundred miles through a comparatively desolated country, without tents, and in many instances on bare feet and with insufficient food, crossed one large river and several smaller streams, and to-day threatens the capital of an enemy who, seventy days since, was investing our own. This brilliant campaign will strike the scales from the eyes of the people of the North, as it has already torn off the mask from their infamous government. While the former will be dazzled by the light of truth suddenly flashed upon them from our guns, the falsehood, treachery, despotism and folly of the other, like the vile features of Mokanna, when stripped of their veil, can but disgust its deluded followers and bring it to open shame before an indignant world.

We ransack history in vain for a more brilliant campaign than this. Our track from the James river to the Potomac, like the milky way in the skies, is one of unsurpassed brightness and splendor. The rapidity of our movements, the splendor of our triumphs, the valor of our men and the genius of our leaders, will strike the world with amazement. The army has not only driven the invader from our capital and cleared the State of Virginia of his presence, but it is encamped to-day within twenty miles of the Pennsylvania line, and in striking distance of Harrisburg, Baltimore and Washington. Such achievements as these, if they do not extort from foreign governments a formal recognition of our independence, will at least demonstrate to all thinking men our right to be free, and the utter folly of any further attempt at our subjugation.

It may be, as we advance forward, that our line of communications to the rear will be intercepted; nevertheless we expect to be able to maintain ourselves wherever we go. We now hold the Baltimore & Ohio railroad from the Monocacy to Harper's Ferry, and the branch road leading from that place down the valley of the Shenandoah to Winchester. This route will probably be adopted in our communications with the South, instead of the more exposed and inconvenient line to Manassas, and thence across the fords of the Potomac, always subject to be rendered impassable by heavy rains. The enemy did not have time to destroy the railway bridge at Harper's Ferry; but succeeded, I am informed, in removing most of the cars. It is not known what cars were on the Winchester branch at the time of his unpremeditated exit.

We have conflicting reports from Baltimore. It was first said that the enemy were removing all the military stores in the city, and that our friends there had risen to prevent it. To-day we hear that a force, estimated at 30,000 men, was marching in the relief of the city from Washington. Both reports may be true. Gen. Wool is the military commandant of the city. Of course, we do not care how much the enemy divides his forces. If he should send them all to Baltimore, we can but quietly take possession of Washington, and should he concentrate them all in the latter place, the agreeable alternative will be left us to march leisurely down the great Cumberland turnpike and take Baltimore. If he divide them, instead of one, we shall simply take two bites at the cherry; or if we like it better, we may march North to Harrisburg, and take up our winter quarters in the capitol of Pennsylvania.

As we approach the Pennsylvania border, the people appear to be more equally divided in their sentiments. In this and the more southern counties the secessionists are represented to have a decided majority, especially in the large slaveholding districts. Our friends have no doubt that, if left to a fair vote, the State would elect to go with the Confederacy by a large majority. The people at many places received us with shouts and tears and begged us never to leave the State until we shall have released it from the grasp of the tyrant. The young men have already begun to enroll themselves, and we are assured that as soon as the Federal forces scattered over the State shall have been compelled to retire towards Washington, as they will be soon, thousands more will array themselves under our banner. The greatest excitement prevails from the Potomac to the Delaware; and Washington and Baltimore are represented to be in a perfect tremor—the one from fright, the other from joy.

It appears that the Federal draft has only been postponed to the 15th inst., not abandoned. The people say our coming was just in time to save them from the dreadful alternative of either taking up arms against their brethren of the South, or fleeing from their homes. One man told me he evidently believed the finger of God had guided our footsteps and delivered the people through our hands.

The army has been resting to-day along the shady banks of the Monocacy river, cooking, washing and bathing. It is reported that we will move to-morrow, but in what direction I am unable to say. Should we succeed in getting possession of Baltimore, the army will probably go into winter quarters there and in Washington; for the occupation of the former place would insure the fall of the latter. With the Baltimore and Ohio Railroad and the Chesapeake and Ohio Canal already in our possession, and the railway line between Washington, Baltimore and Annapolis, rendered unavailable by our occupation of Baltimore, the circuitous route from New York and Philadelphia around to the Chesapeake Bay, and up the Potomac, would be the only channel left open by which the enemy could receive his supplies. The Potomac is frequently closed to navigation by ice in the winter; but if it were not, and if we should not obstruct it by batteries planted along its banks, still it would be impossible to procure sufficient supplies by this route for the city, and the army quartered there. Whatever be our destination, however, we hope to be able to clothe and shoe the army wherever we may go; but as this is not absolutely certain, the people at home should strain every nerve to provide for the comfort of the troops. The sick and wounded in the rear should be the special objects of their attention, even if we should succeed in furnishing the army in the field.

Fredericktown, near which we are bivouacking, is a place of several thousand inhabitants. All the hats, clothing and shoes in the town have been bought up by the quartermasters or the troops themselves. We have found less trouble about our currency than was expected. The farmers and merchants prefer Maryland or Virginia money in exchange for their produce and wares, but still they are not indisposed to receive Confederate notes at some discount. Those who are unwilling to take them are generally Unionists, who close their stores and barns against us. As we advance away from the Potomac, and the brokers and sharpers come upon the board the trouble will doubtless be increased, unless we are speedily and completely successful. It would have been wise, therefore, for Mr. Secretary [Christopher] Memminger to have made some arrangement with the Virginia banks to supply a sufficient amount of their notes to meet the immediate wants of the army. The plan was suggested to him, and it may be he will yet adopt it.

P. W. A.

{*The letter referred to did not come to hand.—Editors.}

The March of the Confederate Army
NEAR MIDDLETOWN, MD., September 10, 1862 [9-22-62]

Orders were issued last night to move at 5 o'clock this morning. Jackson's corps started first, then [D. H.] Hill's, and finally Longstreet's, which being the right wing of the army, bro't up the rear. The army has marched by the left flank from Richmond into Maryland, and hence Jackson, who commands the left, has headed the column all the way.

To-day, our march lay along the great Cumberland turnpike in the direction of Hagerstown. The dust was intolerable, exceeding anything I have ever seen or imagined. The turnpike proper, or middle of the highway, was completely free from this annoyance; but the dirt-way on either side, over which the wagons, artillery, cavalry and beef cattle proceeded, sent up a suffocating cloud of gray and yellow dust that enveloped the whole army. It has been very warm to-day besides, and this rendered the march still more tiring to the men. But they were prepared for it by the two days of rest they have just had along the banks of the Monocacy.

While passing through Frederick, we were welcomed with many demonstrations of sympathy by the citizens, the women and children taking the lead. It was not an uncommon thing to pass a house with only one window open, and on looking in to see one or more ladies sitting in the back part of the room, waving miniature flags. The people in this part of the State have felt the heel of the oppressor, and hence even in the presence of a Confederate army they find it necessary to be as cautious as possible. They say if they only knew we would not abandon the State, they would throw off every disguise and array themselves on our side at once, with arms in their hands. We encountered a good many Unionists both in the town and country. They conducted themselves with propriety, and were in no wise molested by our soldiery either in person or property. This was in accordance with Gen. Lee's order, a copy of which you will find enclosed herewith. Not a pound of hay nor a piece of wood has been consumed without the owner's consent and full compensation. In this the people have been agreeably surprised; they had heard so much through Federal sources of the lawlessness of our troops, that they were prepared to witness scenes of violence and spoilation wherever the army marched.

The order before leaving the Monocacy, was to cook three days' rations—just sufficient, as the men supposed, to last them to Baltimore, forty miles distant, and the Mecca to which all eyes have been turned since we crossed the Potomac. But the road we have taken does not lead to Baltimore, but directly from it. What does it mean? Is Harrisburg our destination, or Pittsburgh, or Cincinnati?

But the weary men have rolled themselves up in their blankets, and in their dreams are paying pleasant visits to their distant homes; and I must follow their example.

HAGERSTOWN, MD., September 11th.

It has been cloudy and misty too, and consequently, the dust and heat have been less oppressive. We kept on the Cumberland turnpike until we had passed Boonsboro' a short distance, where Jackson and [A. P.] Hill and others took the road to Williamsport, and Longstreet continued along the pike in this direction. One brigade only (Col. [Henry] Benning's late Gen. Toombs') entered Hagerstown to act as a guard, the remainder of Longstreet's corps having stopped three miles short of the town.

Our march, yesterday and to-day, lay across the valleys of the Monocacy and the Catocton, up the beautiful Antietam Creek, and over the continuing lines of the Blue Ridge [South Mountain]. I have never seen a more beautiful and lovely region, or more picturesque and bewitching scenery.

Many of the people of Hagerstown and the adjacent country have fled across the Pennsylvania line, five miles distant, taking with them such effects as they could carry. The fugitives are such as had taken an active part in oppressing and hunting down the Secessionists in this part of the State, and being condemned by their own consciences, they concluded their only safety lay in immediate flight. No pursuit was attempted, and no punishment was mediated against them; we have come, not to punish, but to deliver the people of Maryland. Many of those who fled are known here as Dunkards—a class of persecuting religionists, who wear very long hair and beard. "The wicked flee when no man pursueth."

Those who remained, and who constitute a majority of the town and country, have given us a very cordial reception. They have thrown open their houses to us, and exerted themselves to render up as comfortable as possible. Several Confederate flags were displayed, and the ladies met us at every corner with smiles, bouquets and waving handkerchiefs. The boys hurrahed for Jeff. Davis as lustily as they do in Richmond, and one can almost image he is in the far South. Intelligent citizens tell me there is not a county, even along the Pennsylvania border, that would not, if left to a free choice, cast its lot with the South.

We are standing on the borders of Pennsylvania. Shall we enter the State? An immense majority of the people and the army would answer, yes. But would it be wise? Would it not be better to relieve Maryland, now we are here, than to leave her behind and go into the enemy's country? Is it for revenge that we should march into Pennsylvania? A nation may make war, or continue it when once in, to resent an insult, but never for mere revenge.

HAGERSTOWN, MD., September 12, 1862.

The army did not move to-day as was expected. Jackson and Hill turned off yesterday this side of Boonsboro', and took the road in the direction of Williamsport; since which I have not heard what their movements have been. Possibly there is a remnant of Pope's army down the river, that may have retreated across the mountains from Manassas; and if so, that will account for Jackson's detour towards the Potomac. An occasional report of artillery firing has been heard to-day in the direction of Williamsport and the fords on the river.

There is a strong Southern feeling in this town and vicinity. This may appear the more striking in consequence of the flight of many of the Unionists. A company of recruits arrived this evening from Frederick, and others are coming in singly and in squads from the surrounding country. A recruiting office has been opened here, and a sufficient number have been enrolled to make up a company. Stuart is receiving many additions to his cavalry regiments. It would be better if the recruits would organize themselves into distinct Maryland regiments, elect their own officers, and come into the army as the troops from the other States have done. Our cavalry force is already large enough, unless it were more useful. Last Fall the Federal cavalry numbered more than 50,000 men, and yet they have not been worth the saddles on which they ride. Ours have done better, but their performances have fallen far below the expectations of the public. [John H.] Morgan and Forrest in the West, and Stuart and [Turner] Ashby in the East, and a few other isolated commands, have contributed largely to our success; but with these exceptions, the horses would have been more usefully engaged, if they had been left at home in the plough.

Northern journals are much puzzled by our strategy. They affect to believe that, in crossing the Potomac into Maryland, we have done the very thing they most desired. They will be sure to bag us this time, and thus bring the war to a speedy close. They say also, which is probably true, that our movements into Maryland and towards the Ohio, will stimulate the volunteering business at the North, and impart fresh vigor in the counsels of the government. In spite of all this "sound of fury," however, there are unmistakable symptoms of alarm. Neither the press nor the government can conceal their uneasiness. Washington is in a panic, and so is Harrisburg, and so is the whole North.

September 13th.

The army has not moved yet. Heavy firing was heard in the direction of the Potomac this morning. We are at a loss to understand what it means; we only know that Jackson is there, and that he is a wall of safety wherever he goes.

The Federals are not more puzzled by Gen. Lee's movements than our own people. Hagerstown is not the way to Baltimore from Frederick; nor is it on the direct route to Harrisburg, the capital of Pennsylvania. It does lie, however, on the great Cumberland turnpike leading from Baltimore to Cumberland, and in the direction of Pittsburgh, Columbus and Cincinnati. It was the bill to construct this turnpike by the Federal Government that led to the division of parties into those who favored internal improvements by the Government and those who opposed them. From this place to the Pennsylvania line is about five miles, and to Harrisburg it is about fifty-five miles. Thus you see we are within three days' march of the capital of the Keystone State. We have already cut the Baltimore & Ohio Railroad, and our advance to Harrisburg would enable us to destroy the Pennsylvania Central, one of three great railway lines between the Atlantic and the West. The Baltimore & Ohio and the New York & Erie roads are the other two.

A majority of the Northern papers express the opinion that Gen. Lee has only come into Maryland to procure a supply of food and clothing for his ragged, barefooted and famished army. Others think he is bound for Baltimore; others again for Harrisburg; whilst the New York *Times* would not be surprised if he were to form a junction at Cincinnati or Pittsburgh with Bragg and E. Kirby Smith, take possession of the shops and foundries at Pittsburgh, build gunboats and cast cannon, and by occupying the line from Wheeling up to the Lakes above, separate the West from the North and East, and seek to make terms with the West. All of the cities indicated—Baltimore, Harrisburg and Pittsburgh—are within easy reach of us. To which point will Gen. Lee direct his steps? I do not know; yet I have great confidence in his skill and judgement.

The army has encountered much difficulty since it came into Maryland on account of our currency. At first our friends in Frederick took it freely at a small discount, but in this part of the State, where we must procure our supplies, it is with great trouble we can pass it at all. If it were known that the army would remain in Maryland, the people would receive it freely— at least, they say so. Virginia banks bills pass as currency as the Federal "green-backs." The bills of other solvent Southern Banks pass at a trifling discount.

P. W. A.

Battle of Boonsboro' Gap—Important Movements

BOONSBORO, MD., September 14, 1862 [9-30-62]

Orders were issued yesterday afternoon for the men to cook three days' rations. The enemy was then encamped—a considerable portion of it, at least—in and around Hagerstown, and the prevailing opinion was that we should move forward in the direction of Harrisburg. What Gen. Lee's original intentions were, it were impossible for any one outside of his immediate council to say; but whatever they were, it would not be venturing too far to say they have been temporarily changed by the bold, and apparently confident, advance of McClellan. Instead of marching upon Harrisburg, we turned back upon our track, and moved down the Cumberland turnpike towards Frederick and Baltimore. As the column approached the village of Boonsboro', at the foot of the Blue Ridge, ten miles from Hagerstown, a rapid artillery fire could be heard. The report soon obtained that it was an affair of artillery merely; but as we advanced nearer we could distinctly hear the report of small arms hotly engaged.

Gen. D. H. Hill's corps [division] had crossed the Potomac and come up to the vicinity of Boonsboro', and constituted the rear of the army, which, with the exception of Jackson's, A. P. Hill's and [Lafayette] McLaws' commands, was encamped along the turnpike from Boonsboro' to Hagerstown. He held the Gap in the mountain, therefore, through which the turnpike passed, and was the first to encounter the advancing columns of McClellan. It seems that the Federal commander put his forces in motion as soon as he had definite information that we had crossed into Maryland. His march was rapid, and soon brought him to Frederick, where there was a sharp engagement between the cavalry. He followed on after us through Middletown, and had reached the Boonsboro' Gap in the Blue Ridge, about midway between the villages of Middletown and Boonsboro', when he came upon D. H. Hill's corps, as already stated. This was late last evening.

The position of our forces at this time was not advantageous for a general engagement. Longstreet and Anderson were near Hagerstown, twelve miles from Boonsboro' Gap. Jackson and A. P. Hill had recrossed to the Virginia side and were investing Harper's Ferry, and McLaws held the Maryland Heights opposite Harper's Ferry, from which point he co-operated with Jackson and Hill in the movement against that position. Gen. Lee, therefore, immediately ordered back Longstreet's and Anderson's forces to the relief of D. H. Hill, then engaged near Boonsboro'. The Blue Ridge is not high at this place, though it is broad-backed, the passage across by the turnpike being nearly two miles. The enemy held the mouth of the Gap on the eastern side, and some of the spurs or off shoots of the mountain next to Middletown. We held the western end of the Gap and more than one-half of the mountain. The enemy was in great force; we had only one corps, D. H. Hill's, and some detachments of cavalry. Longstreet and Anderson did not arrive until near 4 P. M., up to which time Hill's corps had maintained the unequal combat single-handed.

It would be proper to premise, that for reasons which will abundantly appear in the course of this narrative, it is utterly impossible at the present to prepare either a full or correct account of the battle fought to-day. The skirmishers were engaged as early as 6 o'clock this morning. From that hour until night the combat lasted with varied success. [Samuel] Garland's brigade was the first to enter the fight, and [George B.] Anderson's, (N.C.) [Roswell] Ripley's, [Robert E.] Rodes' and [Alfred H.] Colquitt's, went in subsequently, and in the order in which their names occur.

Garland was killed about 9 o'clock by a minie ball, which struck him in the breast, as he was gallantly leading a charge. Col. [Vannoy H.] Manning, of the Fifteenth Georgia, of [Thomas] Drayton's brigade, which came up late in the day, was wounded. Beyond these two, I have heard of no other casualties among the officers engaged, though many have, doubtless, been killed or wounded.

There was but one road—the Cumberland pike—by which Longstreet and Anderson could move from Hagerstown to Boonsboro'; consequently the forces got into position slowly after their arrival. Upon reaching the vicinity of the mountain, the several divisions and brigades were sent forward to their proper places, to reach which they had to file off to the right and left by narrow country roads and get up the mountain side as best they could. There were two smaller gaps—one on the right and the other on the left—to which forces were immediately sent forward. For these reasons, it was nearly sunset before the whole of Longstreet's corps got fully into position, though the brigades, first to arrive, had been engaged two hours or more.

Thus, you perceive, that the enemy had not only greatly the advantage of numbers, owing to the absence of a large portion of our troops, but was the first to get into position. When the Confederates would charge down the mountain, they were subjected to a terrific crossfire from the Federal batteries posted on the spurs and elevations on the eastern side, which rendered it impossible to advance. Indeed, for reasons sufficiently apparent upon a perusal of this narrative, I am inclined to believe that the enemy got the best of the fight. They will certainly claim a victory, and subsequent events will give some coloring to the claim.

The troops under D. H. Hill behaved with great gallantry, and none more so than Rodes' brigade of Alabamans, and Colquitt's brigade of Georgians. The former brigade is composed of the Third, Fifth, Sixth, Twelfth, and Twenty-sixth Alabama regiments, and the latter of the Sixth, Twenty-third, Twenty-seventh, and Twenty-eighth Georgia regiments, and the Thirteenth Alabama. Up to this hour I have heard of no casualties among the officers in either command.

The artillery engaged under Hill was [Lieut. Col. A. S.] Cutts' battalion of artillery and [James] Bondurant's (formerly Montgomery's) battery, recruited chiefly in Alabama.

Evans', Jones', Toombs', (except his old brigade and himself had been left at Hagerstown as a guard,) Hood's and other divisions in Longstreet's corps participated in the fight late in the afternoon, with what results I am unable to inform you. The battle continued until eight o'clock at night, each side, with unimportant exceptions, maintaining their original ground.

Jackson, A. P. Hill and McLaws had been sent to operate against Harper's Ferry, where the enemy had between eight and ten thousand troops, which it was their purpose to capture. News had been received that Banks was moving up with a heavy force for the relief of the Federal troops at that point. With a view, therefore, to the concentration of his force, and to insure the reduction of Harper's Ferry, Gen. Lee determined, at 9 o'clock to-night, to abandon his position in front of Boonsboro', and to move down towards the Potomac on our right, which was McClellan's left. The wagon trains were ordered to withdraw to the river at Williamsport above, recross at that place, and move down to Shepardstown on the Virginia side below, just opposite Sharpsburg in Maryland. This movement made it necessary for us to leave our wounded in the hands of the enemy. I fear also that they captured some hundreds of prisoners, men who had fallen asleep or got out of position. The wagon train was cut by a detachment of 1,600 Federal Cavalry, who were not aware of the position of affairs until they struck the road the trains had taken. They stopped long enough to destroy (according to the report,) about seventy ordnance wagons attached to Longstreet's corps. These events, as I have already intimated, will doubtless lead the enemy to claim a great victory over the combined forces of Gen. Lee.

P. W. A.

SHARPSBURG, MD., September 15th.

The movement to this place last night was successfully executed. The army is now in a position where it can be concentrated, or if need be, where relief can be sent to Jackson or Jackson can come to us. The change has rendered it necessary for McClellan to alter his front, and to move down so as to take position between our forces and his Capitol. This we understand he is now doing.

We have rumors from Harper's Ferry which, for the present, I forbear to mention. It is sufficient that Jackson will probably succeed in capturing the entire Federal force at that place. The wagons have recrossed the river at Williamsport, and are now moving down to Shepardstown, three miles from this place.

P. W. A.

SHARPSBURG, MD., September 16, 1862 [9-27-62]

We have just received the gratifying news of Jackson's complete success at Harper's Ferry. He has not only reduced the place, but he has captured, (it is reported,) 8,700 prisoners, an immense quantity of commissary and ordnance stores, thirty odd pieces of field artillery and several siege guns, and all the arms in the hands of the prisoners. Other reports put the number of arms taken at a considerably higher figure, but you will hear from Richmond the correct number before this letter can get through to you. The Federals were chiefly new troops, and were commanded by [Col. Dixon S.] Miles, the officer who was suspended for drunkeness at Centreville during the first battle of Manassas. One rumor has it that they were commanded by a General or Colonel Smith. The prisoners have been paroled and sent on to Washington.

There was but little fighting—indeed, nothing but slight skirmishing. The positions occupied by our forces so completely covered the place, that no avenue of escape was left the enemy. McLaws held the Maryland Heights on this side of the river, and Jackson and Hill invested the place on the Virginia side. The enemy saw their predicament, and were wise enough to submit to an unconditional surrender. The men were marched out and required to stack their arms in presence of our troops drawn up in line to enforce the order, if need be.

Jackson recrossed the river this morning, and reached this place this afternoon. McLaws came up later, and will move into position early to-morrow. I am not informed where A. P. Hill is, but it is reported he was left at Harper's Ferry. Jackson has gone up to the left

There has been heavy artillery firing nearly all day. The combatants are taking up their final positions and feeling of each other, preparatory to a great battle to-morrow. The casualties have been slight on either side. Some of the enemy's shells bursted in this place, but no one of the citizens was killed. Late this afternoon—about sunset—the enemy made a bold dash on the left, with the hope of driving us from a commanding position; but he was disappointed and driven back. This is the only time the infantry have been engaged to-day.

The report that Gen. [William] Loring had crossed the Potomac some days ago, was without foundation. I cannot tell you where he is, for I do not know.

10 o'clock at night.

It seems I was mistaken in one particular in regard to the capture of Harper's Ferry. Instead of being a bloodless victory, I now hear from the most reliable sources that a desperate battle was fought Sunday afternoon on this side of the river at Crampton's Gap in the blue ridge. Gen. Howell Cobb, with his own brigade and about 500 men of Mahone's, was ordered by Maj. Gen. McLaws to occupy the Gap and hold it, if need be, at the cost of every man in his command. It was known that the enemy had sent heavy reinforcements for the relief of Harper's Ferry, and that they were moving up the river on the Maryland side, and in the direction of Crampton's Gap; Jackson and A. P. Hill were on the Virginia side, and it was desirable that these reinforcements should either be driven back or delayed until the reduction of the place could be accomplished. Hence the instructions of General McLaws to Gen. Cobb.

The enemy reached the Gap, 15,000 strong, at 3 P. M. Sunday, and immediately gave battle to Cobb's small force of 2,100. A fearfully unequal and terrific fight ensued. Should the enemy succeed in passing the Gap that afternoon, they would reach Harper's Ferry in time to relieve the beleaguered garrison. The Confederates appreciated the necessities of their position, and freely opposed their bodies a living wall against the hostile host. The battle lasted until night. Cobb was not only forced to give back, but he was flanked on the right and left, and suffered terribly. Indeed his command was almost annihilated, but still his brave troops fought with a desperation and courage which has not been surpassed during the war.

At length night came, and the enemy had not passed the Gap, though he had slowly cut his way through our mutilated ranks. The object of the Confederates had been accomplished; they had delayed the advance of the enemy until it was too late for him to get through Sunday night. Next morning the Federal forces at Harper's Ferry surrendered to the heroic Jackson, but Cobb did the fighting. Let him wear the crown who wins the victory.

I have seen no list of our heavy casualties. It is known, however, that the Hon. John B. Lamar, of Macon, Ga., then brother-in-law and volunteer aid of Gen. Cobb, was killed. His body was saved and taken to the Virginia side. Col. Jefferson Lamar, commanding the "Tom Cobb Legion," in the absence of Col. T. R. R. Cobb, was wounded and fell into the hands of the enemy. It is supposed that he was mortally wounded. The Legion suffered very severely.

But I must close. We are on the eve of a terrible conflict, and heaven only knows what the result will be. From all I see around me, I feel certain that one of the greatest battles of the war will be fought here to-morrow. The enemy are in tremendous force—not less than 140,000 men. The Antietam river is in our front; the Potomac in our rear. If we are defeated, the army must perish; if successful, the stream in front and the Blue Ridge at whose base it flows will prevent any pursuit. It is an awkward position; but the genius of our leaders and the valor of our troops, with the favor of Providence, will yet deliver us. The source of greatest regret is, that we shall probably have to recross the Potomac.

P. W. A.

SHARPSBURG, September 17, 1862 [9-27-62]

9 P. M.—A bloody battle has been fought to-day. It commenced at daybreak and lasted until 8 o'clock at night—fourteen hours. The enemy made the attack, and gained some advantage early in the day on the left, and subsequently on the right, but was finally repulsed with great slaughter. Our own losses have been heavy, including many officers of worth and position.

But I cannot say more at this time. This brief and hastily written note is designed to be the forerunner only of my account of the battle—and is sent now because an opportunity is offered to forward it to the post office at Winchester.

I will only add, that the timely appearance of McLaws on the left, saved the day on that part of the field, and that to Toombs we are indebted for saving it late in the afternoon on the right. Both charges were brilliantly successful. A. P. Hill got up at 2 P. M., and went in at 4, and contributed largely to the success of the day. Nearly all the troops behaved with great spirit.

Again I say—and with this remark I conclude this note—the prospect is, we shall have to return to Virginia.

P. W. A.

The Battle of Sharpsburg

SHARPSBURG, MD., September 18, 1862 [10-4-62]

The fiercest and most hotly contested battle of the war was fought here yesterday. It commenced at early dawn, the enemy being the attacking party, and lasted, with occasional breathing intervals, until it was quite dark. Whether we consider the numbers engaged, the fierceness of the assault, the dogged courage of the Confederates, or the almost unparalleled duration of the fight, it must be regarded as one of the most extraordinary battles of modern times. In no instance, since the revolution was inaugurated, has either party had engaged as many as 100,000 men at any one time. At Richmond, each side had, all counted, perhaps as many as 100,000; but in no one of the series of battles fought around that city was anything like that number engaged, either on the part of the Confederates or the Federals. I had estimated the force of the enemy here at too high a figure, probably; but if it be reckoned at 125,000 men, and our own at two-thirds of that number—say 80,000—we have two tremendous armies, such indeed as have not been seen on any battlefield in this war. The enemy had brought up the last man he could get. The coasts of Virginia, North Carolina, South Carolina and Georgia had been stripped of the troops sent to desolate them. Northwestern Virginia had been abandoned by [Gen. Jacob] Cox and his command, and all the new volunteers, except enough to garrison the works about Washington, had been sent to McClellan. These, with the army he brought from the Peninsula, now recruited and prepared for fresh labors, and Burnside's seasoned corps, gave him an army alike formidable in numbers and material.

His artillery was on a scale commensurate with the great army he commanded. It was really superb, whether we regard the number of batteries engaged and the range and calibre of the guns, or the splendid manner in which they were handled. The men fought well, too— better, in fact than the Federals have ever done before, except at Shiloh; and the new volunteers did shout as well as the older troops. They are of a better class of men, and make up in spirit and intelligence, what they lack in drilling and discipline.

There can be no doubt upon this point; since we took some of them prisoners and know they fought well before they yielded. The Federals, doubtless, had been taught to feel that our movement into Maryland was an invasion of their soil, and that every blow struck within its limits was a blow in defense of their own homes far away in New England and along the banks of the Hudson and the Schuylkill. There are but few, if any, races, however cowardly and despicable, that will not fight the invader of their homes; even the worm we tread upon turns to sting the heel that crushes it to death.

McClellan commanded in person the enemy's right, (our left,) besides exercising a general supervision over the whole field; Burnside on the left, and Sumner in the center. On our side, Longstreet commanded the right wing, Jackson the left, and D. H. Hill the center—the whole being under the calm and watchful eye of Gen. Lee. This order of battle brought McClellan and Jackson face to face, Longstreet and Burnside, and Hill and Sumner. Thus pitted and matched, the battle was opened as soon as there was sufficient light to point a gun, and continued for fourteen long and weary hours. It was dry and dusty beneath, but cloudy and pleasant above. The enemy had availed himself of the darkness of the preceding night to post his batteries at commanding points. This he was the more able to do, since he had subjected us to a heavy cannonade the day before, and thus forced us to develop our lines and positions.

The battle-ground was along the banks of the Antietam river, just in front of Sharpsburg. This lovely stream runs due South along the foot of the Blue Ridge, and empties its crystal waters into the Potomac a short distance above Harper's Ferry. The Confederates held the Western side of the river, except for a short distance on the left and above, where the enemy's lines crossed it, and the Federals held the Eastern side next to the mountain. Indeed, the general configuration of the country, and as well as the positions of the two armies, recalls to mind the Chickahominy and the James river, and the position of the combatants in front of Richmond, except that the enemy had the Blue Ridge to his back here, whilst his lines were thrown forward across the Antietam on our left instead of our right as on the Chickahominy. With this exception, the lines of the enemy closely hugged the East bank of the river, which is shallow, easily fordable except for artillery, and not more than thirty feet in width. On the swelling elevations between the stream and the Blue Ridge the Federal batteries were planted, whilst ours occupied the hills on the Sharpsburg side. The distance from Sharpsburg across to the base of the mountains does not exceed a mile and a half, and the river is about midway between the two. On our right was a wide stone bridge, which it was important that we should hold. The ground was mostly open, but very uneven.

The respective positions of the two armies were equally strong, except in this, that the enemy had his back against the Blue Ridge, which would under almost any circumstances prevent a rout on his part or pursuit in ours.

The battle was opened by McClellan both with artillery and small arms on our left, where a fierce and nearly successful assault was made upon Jackson. Column after column was brought up and hurled against the Stonewall corps, which had been marching and fighting almost daily since it left Richmond, and for two hours or more our ranks were slowly forced back by the overwhelming numbers brought against them. Jackson reached his position the night before when it was quite dark, and consequently was entirely ignorant of the topography of the field. The old Stonewall brigade yielded the ground inch by inch, and Ewell's division, now commanded by Lawton, the best officer probably under Jackson, fought desperately. This division embraces some of the best regiments in the army, including the unconquerable Twelfth Georgia. Our ranks suffered terribly, and many a brave spirit was made to bite the dust. Among others, I may mention Brigadier General Lawton, who received a painful wound in the leg, and Col. Marcellus Douglas, of the Thirteenth Georgia, commanding Lawton's old brigade. Seeing he was mortally wounded, Douglas refused to be removed, preferring, as he said, to die upon the field. His body was subsequently recovered and taken to the Virginia side.

Meanwhile, and almost simultaneous with the attack on the left, Sumner opened a terrific fire on our center, which was followed by a like assault on our right by Burnside's corps. It was an indescribably sublime scene when the tide of fire and smoke swept slowly and majestically from the left down the valley past the center, and on to the extreme right. The solemn Blue Ridge formed an appropriate background to the awful spectacle. The elevations upon which the batteries were planted, were crowned with wreaths of smoke of most fantastic shapes, nearly concealing "the valley of death" below, where the infantry were engaged in a fearful struggle. Each party had, probably, as many as two hundred pieces of artillery on the field, though but little over half that number was brought into action at the same instant, either by the Confederates or Federals. But think of two hundred cannon of every available caliber engaged in deadly conflict at short range! The Federals directed their pieces chiefly at our batteries, and sometimes the latter were so enveloped in smoke from their own discharges, and the bursting shells from the enemy's guns, that they were completely lost to sight. Our own pieces, on the contrary, were pointed at the infantry columns of the Federals, by special order of Gen. Lee. Artillery duels, so called, accomplish little, except to enable the parties to display their gunner ship. In the present instance, the departure from the old rule was productive of most beneficial results, in that the enemy's assaulting columns were repeatedly repulsed by the well-directed fire of our artillerists.

The great object of McClellan was to reach the Potomac on the left, distant not more than a mile and a half from the Antietam, and thus to close us, as it were, in a *cul de sac*. The two streams make a sudden curve towards each other at this point. Knowing that we would hardly attempt to cross the Antietam, along the banks of which, with slight exceptions, the two armies were engaged, he had massed enormous columns on the left and another on the right. Owing to the great inequality of forces engaged, Jackson found it necessary to yield the ground he held at the beginning of the fight, and to call for assistance. Fortunately, McLaws' division had arrived from Harper's Ferry some time during the previous night, and was sent to the relief of Jackson about nine o'clock. It arrived just in a nick of time. The enemy, already badly worsted by Jackson, were compelled to fall back with great slaughter before the impetuous charges of the fresh regiments, until the parties occupied their original positions in the morning. The fighting, however, was continued until night with occasional intervals, though without any particular advantage to either side.

The conflict along the center, was severe, but owing to the nature of the ground was confined chiefly to artillery. Indeed the artillery took an unusually prominent part in the battle in every part of the field. The small arms were not warmly engaged for sometime, early in the day after a few volleys, except on the left. The Washington Artillery behaved splendidly; and so did Cutts' battalion. The former is attached to Longstreet's corps, the latter to D. H. Hill's. The other batteries, and the heavy reserves under Gen. [William N.] Pendleton, performed their parts handsomely also.

The most formidable assault on the right was made about 9 o'clock, and continued until after two. The object of the enemy was to gain possession of a stone bridge just in front of Toombs' division [brigade]; which occupied the extreme right in Longstreet's corps. The Second and Twentieth Georgia, Lieut. Colonel [William] Holmes and Col. [John B.] Cumming commanding, belonging to Toombs' old brigade, and now commanded by Col. Benning, were entrusted with the duty of defending the bridge. The regiments were very much reduced, but they discharged their duty most heroically. Regiment after regiment, and even brigades, were brought up against them; and yet they held their ground, and the bridge too, until they had fired their last cartridge. The men were clamorous for fresh ammunition; for it had now become a point of honor with them to maintain their ground, even if it cost the life of every last one of them. But owing to the furious onslaught made against the entire right wing, it was found impossible to supply them in time; and consequently they had to retire, with the loss even of [D. G.] McIntosh's battery. This was fifteen minutes after two o'clock, when a strong silence, broken only by a random shot, ensued for the space of two hours along the whole front of the army. The accomplished and chivalric Holmes of the Second fell pierced through the body a few minutes before the firing ceased, and died instantly. An effort was made to remove his body but the persons who attempted it were wounded and compelled to leave it on the field. Maj. [Skidmore] Harris assumed the command, and with Col. Cumming of the Twentieth, displayed great coolness and valor. The enemy lay in heaps in front of the bridge, as they did on the left in front of Jackson. An officer who examined the ground over which McLaws and Jackson drove them, says the enemy's dead lay so thick at one place, over an area of three acres, that he could walk over every yard of it on the bodies of the slain!

The silence which followed at a quarter past two o'clock, was all the more profound and impressive from the stunning fire that had raged so furiously since early dawn. Was the enemy content with the possession of the bridge and the ground in front of it? Had both combatants had enough of the bloody work? Or did they stop by mutual consent, in order to allow the exhausted fighters time to receive their breath? For hours the Confederates had been turning their eyes wistfully towards the Potomac, in hopes of seeing the head of A. P. Hill's advancing column. Would the Blucher of the day come up in time?

At length about 3 o'clock, Hill made his appearance and his brigades were quietly distributed along the lines where they were most needed. The enemy were hardly aware of his arrival; for his forces were advanced behind hills and thickets to their proper positions. Everything being ready, the Confederates renewed the conflict at 4 o'clock, and from that hour until night it raged without interruption. The Fifteenth and Seventeenth Georgia, commanded by Col. Millican and Capt. [J. A.] McGregor, and a portion of the Eleventh Georgia, which had just been brought up from the rear, where they had been on detached duty, united in the charge. Col. Millican addressing his men, told them to follow their officers, and if they fell to march forward over their bodies—an injunction that was literally fulfilled, for the brave Colonel was killed, and his command dashed on over him as if nothing had happened. Toombs had dismounted and placed himself at the head of his small force, and led them like a captain to the encounter. He and they soon placed themselves in front of the remainder of the line, and dashing forward in the most impetuous manner, soon recaptured McIntosh's battery and drove the enemy pell-mell across the bridge. The ground was strewn with the Federal dead, but our own loss in this charge was not heavy, owing to the furious rate at which the men moved. The conflict of infantry on the right at this point, as on the left early in the day, was unusually severe—probably as severe as any that has occurred since the war. [William] Pender's and Field's brigades of A. P. Hill's division, and other forces, co-operated gallantly in the charge.

It was now near night. The combatants with slight exceptions in our favor, occupied the positions they did in the morning; and when it had become quite dark, the firing ceased on both sides. It is probable that the enemy would not have renewed the contest at 4 o'clock, had the Confederates remained quiet. Many of the houses in Sharpsburg were riddled by the enemy's balls, which, passing over the heads of our men, entered the buildings on the rising ground behind. Many of the women and children had sought refuge in the cellars and behind the stone walls of the houses and enclosures, others had fled to the country on horseback behind husbands and parents; whilst others had boldly stood it out, saying the Federal friends were not ignorant of their sentiments, and would spare them as far as possible. Some of the houses, and many hay ricks and stacks of wheat, and straw, were set on fire, and added no little to the sublimity and fearfulness of the scene. During the combat, three pigeons wheeled wildly over the battlefield, and rising higher and higher, disappeared in the clouds and ascending smoke. Alas! how many brave spirits did they accompany in their upward flight from that bloody field of death!

The results are easily summed up. It was McClellan's battle. He made the attack, and was repulsed with very heavy slaughter. His losses are variously estimated at from 15,000 to 20,000 killed, wounded, and missing; ours from 5,000 to 10,000. These figures may be wrong; I am disposed to think they are too flattering to our own side, and offer them as rough estimates of others. We took but few prisoners—not more than six or seven hundred. The enemy captured as many, as you will see hereafter. Indeed, it was nearly a drawn battle—the enemy having the advantage to position and numbers; we the superiority in fighting, and in repulsing his assault. The only prisoner of distinction we took was Col. [Francis W.] Palfrey of Massachusetts, who was wounded and fell into our hands.

But I must close for the present. I write at a hospital, in the midst of the wounded and dying, amputated arms and legs, feet, fingers, and hands cut off, puddles of human gore, and ghastly, gaping wounds. There is a smell of death in the air, and the laboring surgeons are literally covered from head to foot with the blood of the sufferers. The wounded are lying in the house, on the piazza, under the trees, in the sun. Some have died; others are begging for water, though but few complain of their sufferings.

I turned aside yesterday in the midst of the battle to see how a true soldier can die. He was of twenty-two or three summers—of clear skin and mild blue eyes—John S. Hudson, of Elbert county, Ga. His thigh had been torn by a shell, and hung only by a thin piece of skin. He was calm and resigned, though his struggles were severe and protracted. Finally, as the dread hour of dissolution approached, he gathered up all his remaining strength, and turning to his brother, who hung over him in dumb agony, he said, "Tell mother I die rejoicing, and die a soldier's death." There was not a dry eye among the dozen spectators who, strangely enough, had stopped to witness the last moment of the youthful hero. May Heaven have mercy upon his soul, and upon our bleeding land!

Instances of the sternest heroism occur every hour, not among the troops of any one State, but all of them. I more frequently mention those among the troops from my own State, because, being known to officers and men, they come oftener under my observation. A case of the kind is that of Brig. General [Ambrose] Wright, who, having been disabled by a painful though not serious wound, begged his men to carry him on a litter at the head of his command, that he might still participate in the fray.

The battle has not been renewed to-day, as we all expected it would be. McClellan has been busy shifting the position of his forces, preparatory, perhaps, to the renewal of the conflict tomorrow. We shall see—that is, if the army remains on this side of the river.

P. W. A.

Official casualties for the Battle of Sharpsburg or Antietam were: Federals, 2,010 killed, 9,416 wounded, and 1,043 missing for a total of 12,469; Confederates estimated at 2,700 killed, 9,024 wounded, and 2,000 missing for a total of 13,724.

WINCHESTER, VA., September 26, 1862 [10-4-62]

My condition is such as to render it impossible for me to rejoin the army for the present. I was not prepared for the hardships, exposures and fastings the army has encountered since it left the Rappahannock, and like many a seasoned campaigner, have had to "fall out by the way."

No army on this continent has ever accomplished as much or suffered as much as the army of Northern Virginia within the last three months. But great as have been the trials to which the army has been subjected, they are hardly worthy to be named in comparison with the sufferings in store for it this winter, unless the people of the Confederate States, everywhere and in whatever circumstances, come to its immediate relief.

Do you wonder, then, that there should have been straggling from the army? That brave and true men should have fallen out of line from sheer exhaustion, or in their efforts to obtain a mouthful to eat along the roadside, or that many seasoned veterans should have succumbed to disease and been forced back to the hospital? I look to hear a great outcry raised against the stragglers. Already lazy cavalry men and dainty staff officers, who are mounted and can forage the country for something to eat, are condemning the weary private, who, notwithstanding his body may be covered with dust and perspiration and his feet with stonebruises, is expected to trudge along under his knapsack and cartridge box on an empty stomach and never to turn aside for a morsel of food to sustain his sinking limbs.

The men must have clothing and shoes this winter. They must have something to cover themselves while sleeping, and to protect themselves from the driving sleet and from storms when on duty. This must be done, though our friends at home should have to wear cotton and sit by the fire. The army in Virginia stands guard this day, and will stand guard this winter, over every hearthstone in the South. The ragged sentinel who may pace his weary rounds this winter on the bleak spurs of the Blue Ridge, or along the frozen valley of the Shenandoah and Rappahannock, will also be your sentinel, my friend at home. It will be for you and your own household that he encounters the wrath of the tempest and the dangers of the night. He suffers and toils and fights for you, too, brave, true-hearted women of the South. Will you not clothe his nakedness then? Will you not put shoes and stockings on his feet? Is it not enough that he has written down his patriotism in crimson characters along the battle-road from the Rappahannock to the Potomac, and must his bleeding feet also impress their mark of fidelity upon the snows of the coming winter? I know what your answer will be. God has spoken through the women of the South, and they are his holy oracles in this day of trial and tribulation.

Whatever may be done by the people, should be done immediately. Not one moment can be lost that will not be marked, as by the second hand of a watch, with the pangs of a sufferer. Already the hills and valleys in this high latitude have been visited by frost, and the nights are uncomfortably cool to the man who sleeps on the ground. Come up, then, men, and women of the South, to this sacred duty. Let nothing stand between you and the performance of it. Neither pride, nor pleasure, nor personal ease and comfort, should withhold your hands from the holy work. The supply of leather and wool, we all know, is limited; but do what you can, and all you can, and as soon as you can. If you cannot send woolen socks, send half woolen or cotton socks; and so with under clothing, coats and pants. And if blankets are not to be had, then substitute comforts made of dyed osnaburgs stuffed with cotton. Anything to keep off the cold will be acceptable. Even the speculator and extortioner might forego their gains for a season, and unite in this religious duty. If they neither cloth the naked, nor feed the hungry, who are fighting for *their* freedom, and for *their* homes and property, what right have they to expect anything but eternal damnation, both from God and man.

If the army of Virginia could march through the South just as it is—ragged and almost barefooted and hatless—many of the men limping along and not quite well of their wounds or sickness, yet cheerful and not willing to abandon their places in the ranks—their clothes riddled with balls and their banners covered with smoke and dust of battle, and shot into tatters, many of them inscribed with "Williamsburg," "Seven Pines," "Gaines' Mill," "Garnett's Farm," "Front Royal," "McDowell," "Cedar Run," and other victorious fields—if this army of veterans, thus clad and shod, with tattered uniforms and banners, could march from Richmond to the Mississippi, it would produce a sensation that has no parallel in history since Peter the Hermit led his swelling hosts across Europe to the rescue of the Holy Sepulchre.

I do not write to create alarm, or to produce a sensation, but to arouse the people to a sense of the true condition of the army. I have yet to learn that anything is to be gained by suppressing the truth, *and leaving the army to suffer.* If I must withhold the truth when the necessities of the service require it to be spoken, I am quite ready to return home.

P. W. A.

Alexander's commentary on the poor condition of Lee's army after the Battle of Sharpsburg was well calculated to fan the patriotic fires which burned so brightly in Southern hearts. This appeal brought public attention to the army's plight and was his single most important contribution to the war effort. Naturally the letter received much editorial comment throughout the South.

Editorial—October 9, 1862—Richmond *Daily Dispatch*

True eloquence, coming from the heart of a man who not only sees what he describes, but is himself a participant.

Editorial—October 20, 1862—Savannah *Republican*

His letter has been copied, without exception, by every exchange that comes to this office, and probably by every newspaper in the Confederate States, in every instance arousing the people to a sense of their duty to the suffering soldiery. We believe that one letter will do more towards clothing the army and making them comfortable than all the legislation of Congress in the past year.

And yet some people would profess to sneer at army correspondents, saying they do more harm than good!

Editorial—October 10, 1862—Rome *Southerner*

"P. W. A." is certainly exerting a wonderful influence, especially in Georgia. His letters are in almost every newspaper. He says our soldiers must be clothed by the people at home—the government can't do it. Almost instantly benevolent societies spring into existence as by magic. Money is contributed by the hundreds and thousands of dollars... .

Editorial—November 11, 1862—Savannah *Republican*

The letters of "P. W. A." are read by everybody, and he has given a connected and truthful account of the campaign in Virginia and on the frontier. With him it has been a work of the field and not of the fireside—being almost as often exposed to shot and shell and fatiguing marches and privations as the soldiers. The public are also indebted to him for giving true statements of the condition of our soldiers in the field—of their necessities, and his appeals in their behalf. Also, he has shown a fearless courage in exposing official delinquencies and inefficiencies, which might involve personal responsibility, were they not well founded, or of his being consigned to some such place as the "Old Capitol."

Letters to the Editor—Savannah *Republican* [11-5-62]

Your army correspondent, P. W. A., deserves a statue of gold, with inscriptions worthy to commemorate his unequalled services to the South. His appeal in behalf of our suffering troops I regard as the most eloquent thing I have read for years. It is eloquent without rhetoric, any attempt at it. He is truly able. His sense and breadth of views are equal to his rare descriptive powers. I read all I see under his signature—sure ever to be rewarded, and never meeting chaff where I expected grain. He is truly an honor to the profession, and his single pen might well sustain its equality, in competition with either army or State, with the Confederate Legislature and President and all the local centres of legislative wisdom.

"P. W. A." —A Proposition

November 19, 1862 [11-23-62]

Mr. Editor:

I take it for granted that your special army correspondent, who has served you so ably and faithfully since the commencement of the war, is fairly compensated by you for that service. There is another debt, though due him—a debt from the Public, who are under obligations to his vigorous and patriotic pen which they will never be able to cancel. In my judgment, he has done more for the army and the public in this war, than any other man in the Confederacy.

To respond, in part, to that claim is the object of this note, and I propose to be one of ten citizens of Savannah to pay into your hands one thousand dollars, to be expended in the purchase of a service of plate, to be presented to him as a feeble testimonial of our admiration and gratitude. Others beyond the limits of our city might be willing to subscribe, and thus swell the amount into a handsome contribution to distinguished merit.

Yours truly,   AN OLD SOLDIER.

In a private note to the editors of the Savannah Republican, *Alexander expressed his gratitude to those who had offered such a costly award, but added that he preferred that the one thousand dollars be invested in shoes and clothing and sent to the needy soldiers in Virginia.*

Alexander was not finished; while recovering from his illness in Winchester, he commented on the state of Confederate health care.

What the Government has done and is doing for the Sick, Wounded, and Destitute Soldiers

WINCHESTER, VA., October 12, 1862 [10-22-62]

It is customary after a battle has been fought to collect the wounded together in temporary hospitals or send them to the rear. At Richmond, they were placed in the hospitals in that city; after the second battle of Manassas they were sent back to Warrenton and other towns in the vicinity, and at Sharpsburg they were sent across the river to Shepardstown and thence to this place and Staunton. The regimental surgeons dress the wound, and set or amputate the limb, as the case may be, before the patient passes from their hands to the rear. Some of these operators perform their work skillfully and conscientiously; others do it hurriedly or ignorantly; whilst a few do it in a manner that can only be properly characterized as brutal. I have known of cases of amputation where the lapping part of the flesh was sewed together over the bone so stupidly, that the thread would disengage itself and the bone be exposed in less than twenty-four hours. The object of many of the surgeons seems to be to get through with their work, in some sort of fashion, as soon as possible, and turn their subjects over to the hospital surgeons. While engaged at the amputation table, many of them feel it to be their solemn duty, every time they administer brandy to their patient, to take a drink themselves. This part of their work is performed with great unction and conscientiousness. In a majority of instances, however, I am glad to say, the field surgeons do quite as well as could be expected of young men who have had but little practical experience in the art of surgery.

But it is when the wounded man falls into the hands of the hospital surgeons that his greatest sufferings begin. I do not mean such surgeons as those in the Richmond hospitals, which are located in a large city under the eye of the Government, and are provided for with careful matrons and nurses and an ample supply of hospital stores; the circumstances surrounding these officers, if nothing else, would constrain them to perform their duties. But I allude to the surgeons in those hospitals which are improvised in the rear of the army, as at this place and Warrenton, and who being of but little value at Richmond and other central points, are sent to the country. Shall I daguerreotype two of these surgeons for you? Sam Weller would call them "Sawbones," and perhaps that is a more appropriate term for them than surgeons.

Nearly two weeks after the battle of Sharpsburg, two young gentlemen, of irreproachable moustaches, were introduced into my room at a hotel in this place by the landlady, who informed me that they would be my room-mates for the present. It appeared from their conversation that they had just arrived from Richmond—that they had been acting in the capacity of assistant surgeons there for nearly a year, and that they had been dispatched to Winchester to assist in taking care of the wounded in the battle of Sharpsburg. Two questions of much magnitude occupied their attention for half an hour or more—to wit: 1st, whether they should report to the surgeon of the post in person or by note; 2nd, whether, in the event they report in person, they should "dress up" or go as they were. They finally decided to dress first, and then send up their report in writing. The consideration which brought them to this conclusion arose from the fact that they were without paper, and the idea of going into the street to purchase a supply in their present plight, could not be entertained for a moment. Nearly two hours were devoted to their toilet. After washing and scrubbing ever so long, their hair and moustaches had to be carefully cleaned and oiled, their uniforms, covered all over with gold lace, neatly dusted, and their boots duly polished. One of them put on a ruffled calico shirt with a large diamond pin and immense gold studs, a pair of white linen pantaloons, and a handsome black cloth coat made up in the extreme military style. He first thought he would wear a pair of gaiter shoes, but on consulting "Jim" (his companion,) it was finally agreed that boots would become the set of his pants better. So he put on the boots. Having finished their elaborate toilets and started out of the room, the following laconic dialogue ensued:

Boots—I say, Jim, don't you think we had better take a drop before going out?
Jim—Yes, I *do* think we had. I feel rather shaky after last night's affair.

They courteously inquired, after a moment's hesitation, whether I would not join them; but I was suffering at the time from fever consequent upon a chill, and a still fiercer fever of indignation that such stupid creatures should be sent here to attend to the wounded, and I declined to participate. They returned to the room after an hour's absence, complained that they had to walk so far through the heat and dust to get a little paper, prepared their note to the Chief Surgeon of the post, and sent it up to him in due form. The Chief Surgeon, who is represented to be a man of industry and energy, replied promptly, ordering them to a certain hospital, which they proceeded to take charge of next morning—nearly twenty-four hours after their arrival in town!

You are ready to inquire, of what use can such dainty gentry be in a dirty hospital filled with stern sufferers—men with broken bones and ghastly wounds, whose bodies are covered with filthy rags and alive with vermin—with nothing to lie upon but a little straw, and the air they breathe poisoned by exhalations from the festering wounds and feverish bodies around them? The answer is, they are of no use whatever. If ever so skilled in their profession, the neatness of their toilet and the delicacy of their noses would totally disqualify them for such work as this. A hospital at best is not a desirable place to abide in; but when filthy and filled with vermin, and crammed with sick and wounded men, whose wounds are seldom dressed and whose necessities require them to submit to the most disgusting practices, they fall but little, if any, short of purgatory. The buildings selected for hospitals, instead of being in a quiet, pleasant locality, are almost invariably located in the most noisy, dusty and dirty part of the town. It was so at Corinth, and it is so in Winchester. In the former place, they were located immediately around the depot, where the cars were running day and night, and where the wagons from the camps were constantly arriving and departing, whilst the houses in the rest of the town which the owners had been required to vacate, were occupied by Generals and their butterfly staff officers.

There are several hundred sick and wounded men here; and yet, if I am correctly informed, the Surgeons did not bring with them a single cot, bedsack, sheet, or towel, or a solitary change of clothing for the wounded! Some of the men are now lying on a scant supply of straw, with a foul blanket over them, who are otherwise naked as when they first came into the world! The little clothing they had was torn off when their wounds were dressed, and it was impossible to recover their knapsacks after they were wounded.

One thing has impressed me more painfully than all others connected with the army. It is the little concern which the government, its officers and surgeons show for the preservation of the lives of their troops. A great parade is made over a single piece of artillery captured from the enemy; and yet what is such a trophy compared with the life of an able-bodied man, even when considered as to its military value! We have none too many men in the South that we should adopt a system so disregardful of life. The whole country is interested in the life and health of every man in it, and if some of the energy displayed in forcing feeble and unhealthy conscripts into the service, were shown in taking care of the sick and wounded, the army would be all the better for it. A planter who would take as little care of the health of his slaves as the government does of its soldiers, would soon have none to care for, while he would be driven out of the community by his indignant neighbors.

P. W. A.

After sufficiently recovering from his illness, Alexander returns to Richmond.

HELP NEEDED AT ONCE! LET NO ONE WAIT!

RICHMOND, VA., October 18, 1862 [10-27-62]

There being but slight prospect of any more fighting on the line of the Potomac this fall, and a good opportunity offering to get from Winchester to Staunton, I decided to come on to Richmond, especially as my physician had advised me to that course. Typhoid fever and chills and fever were prevailing to a considerable extent in the lower Valley of the Shenandoah, and the supply of medicines and of suitable food for the sick was so limited, and the weather so raw and damp, that when one is once attacked with chills, or fever, he finds it exceedingly difficult to get rid of them.

I am glad to learn that my appeal in behalf of the army has been received with so much favor throughout the Confederacy. It has been a coal of fire even upon the back of the Government, which has already begun to send forward supplies of clothing and shoes. Thirty wagons loaded with winter supplies reached Winchester the day before I left, and I met others *en route* for the same destination. I called at the Clothing Bureau in this city this morning, for the purpose of improving my own wardrobe, which is none the better for the Maryland campaign, but was told that there was not a yard of officer's cloth in the establishment, the supply having been exhausted some time since. There was a considerable stock on hand of coarse strong cloth, which is being made up for the troops as rapidly as possible. An officer connected with the Bureau informed me that 33,000 garments had been sent up to Gen. Lee's army within the last twenty days, and that clothing for the army was being made up at the rate of 9,000 garments per week. The Government has fifty-eight tailors in its employ, whose business is to cut out the garments, and two thousand seven hundred women who make them up. The scraps of woolen cloth left by the cutters are sent to the Penitentiary, where they are converted into quilts, &c., for the use of the army, whilst those of the cotton fabrics are disposed of to the paper manufacturers.

Allowing three garments to a man—coat, pants and shirt—the 33,000 pieces sent up to the army will furnish an outfit for 11,000 soldiers. This will afford very great relief as far as it goes; yet it will fall far short of the necessities of the army. Estimating the clothing manufactured at all the government establishments in the country at 20,000 garments per week, and the number of troops in the field at 850,000 men, it would require more than a year at this rate to furnish each man with one suit of clothes. I do not include in this estimate blankets, shoes, socks and gloves, which are absolutely indispensable in a climate like this.

I have no means of knowing how many complete suits of clothing the government will be able to provide; but estimating them at 100,000, including a blanket, pair of shoes, two pairs of socks and one pair of gloves, there will still be left 250,000 men, who must perish unless they are supplied by the people at home. If we suppose the Government will be able to furnish winter outfits to 200,000 men, there will yet be 150,000 men who must look to the open hearts and willing fingers at home. The government, however, will not be in a condition to supply so many of the troops either with blankets, shoes, socks or gloves. Indeed, I am not aware that any provision has been made to secure a supply of either of these indispensable articles. Possibly some action was taken by Congress to have the shoemakers in the army detailed temporarily for the purpose of making shoes; *but the shoes are needed now.* This step, to have been of any benefit, should have been taken months ago. It is too late now to procure supplies of leather, thread and pegs; and even if we had an abundant supply of each, it would be months before a sufficient number of shoes could be manufactured to meet the present wants of the army.

These facts will enable the people of the country to appreciate the magnitude of the labor before them. All my figures are merely rough estimates, especially in regard to the number of men in the field; but they are sufficiently accurate for the purpose for which they are offered. Whilst the country will be amazed that no more effort has been made by those in authority to provide the army with suitable clothing, it will readily perceive the necessity of the most prompt and energetic measures on the part of the people, if they would meet the shortcomings of the Government. If every man, woman and child in the South were to exert themselves to the utmost in this good work, still there would be many a brave fellow in the field who would suffer all the pains of a rigorous winter, if not of death, before the much-needed relief could be received.

A statement appeared in one of the Richmond papers yesterday, based upon the report of "a passenger by the cars," to the effect that the condition of the troops was excellent, and that all they needed to render them entirely comfortable was a supply of blankets. Such statements as this may be gratifying to the public, but they are *a cruelty to the army.* I know, as every other observing man who has been with the army knows, that the condition of a vast number of our troops is deplorable. A few regiments and companies may have an adequate supply of clothing and shoes, but a large majority are in no condition to encounter the rigors of the approaching winter. Why, there are men in the hospitals of Winchester who are as naked as babes just born, and I saw here in the heart of Richmond this morning a poor emaciated soldier, who was hardly able to drag his bare feet along the cold pavement! In the army I know there are thousands of as true men as ever fired a musket, who have neither shoes nor stockings, nor more than one suit of clothes, and that a summer suit, and dirty and ragged at that.

P. W. A.

Alexander greatly overestimates the number of Confederate troops in the field—possibly in effort to deceive the enemy; at no time in the war did the Confederate armies number over 400,000 men.

RICHMOND, VA., November 4, 1862 [11-16-62]

Battle and disease have made sad inroads in the ranks of the Confederate army this year. Go where you will, whether on the battlefield, to the hospital, along the railways, or where the army has rested on its weary marches, and there you will find the evidence of death. The trenches where numbers have been placed together, and the little hillocks with the rude head-boards and simple inscriptions which mark the resting places of those who have been buried separately, greet you on every hand, and tell their own melancholy tale.

Our loss in killed and wounded at Fort Donelson may be roughly estimated at 3,500; at Roanoke and on the North Carolina coast, 600; at Elkhorn, 3,500; at Shiloh, 10,000; at Williamsburg, Seven Pines, and before Richmond, 20,000; in the Valley of the Shenandoah, 5,000; at Cedar Run 1,200; at the second battle of Manassas, 6,000; at Boonsboro' and Crampton Gaps, 4,000; at Sharpsburg, 10,000; at Corinth, 4,000; at Perryville, 3,000; and 5,000 for those who have fallen at outposts, skirmishes, &c. These figures added together make the frightful sum of 75,800! Of this number it would be safe to say that one-third, or 25,000, are now in their graves, having either been killed outright or died from their wounds. Quite as many—probably more—have died from sickness. To this should be added 25,000 more for those who have been maimed, and whose health has been ruined for life. Thus our losses in ten months of the present year may be estimated at 75,000 men, who have either perished or been disabled. If the whole truth were known they would probably reach 100,000 by the end of the year, for the deaths from disease, in the hospitals, in camp, and at home, generally exceed those in battle. For every year the war continues we must expect our casualties to be quite as heavy as they have been in the present.

These heavy losses fall entirely upon the young shoulders the country rests its hopes of present independence and wise statesmanship in the future. The effect of such a drain as this upon the population of the country, though painful and deplorable, cannot yet be fully realized. The withdrawal of one hundred thousand laborers from the industrial pursuits of life, and of one hundred thousand husbands and marriagable men from the walks of society, and with the loss of a vast amount of physical and mental energy, is a calamity from which it will require generations to recover. The loss of one hundred or two hundred thousand marriagable men, as the case may be, carries with it, of course, virtual loss of an equal number of marriagable women. This fact, taken in consideration with the policy of restraining foreign immigration in the future, especially from the United States, cannot fail to attract the attention of every reflecting mind.

It would seem as if the time spoken of by Isaiah was about to be realized by the women of the South:

"And in that day seven women shall take hold of one man, saying: We will eat our own bread, and wear our own apparel, only let us be called by thy name, to take away our reproach."

They will have the priceless consolation of knowing, however, that they have done more than any other race of women ever did since the foundation of the world towards the establishing of their country's independence. Neither the wisdom of our leaders, nor the valor of our soldiers, could ever have wrought out our liberties but for their unceasing prayers and labors. If their husbands and brothers deserve immortal honors for their deeds on the field, so also do they merit eternal happiness in that bright world beyond the sun.

P. W. A.

RICHMOND, November 8, 1862 [11-15-62]

The course pursued by the newspapers in the interest of the Government, and the unpardonable misrepresentations of officers in the Quartermasters' Department, have had the effect, I fear, to mislead the people in regard to the deplorable condition of the Army in Virginia. With every disposition to give the authorities credit for what they are doing, I have accepted their statements since my return to Richmond for the truth, and have felt the sincerest satisfaction in notifying to the public that sufficient supplies of shoes and clothing had been forwarded to the army to afford at least temporary relief to the more destitute. It would now appear that not only the people at a distance, but the residents of Richmond, who are in daily intercourse with Government officials, have been deceived, and that whilst partial supplies of clothing and blankets have been sent up to the army, the condition of thousands of troops is still as wretched as it can be.

I suppose it will be necessary to sustain this assertion by some show of proof; for it would appear that the speculations and extortioners who are growing fat and rich by an unholy traffic in the life and blood of their own defenders, require every statement which involves an appeal to their sordid souls to be supported by incontrovertible evidence before they will open their swollen purses and flinty hearts.

Let us proceed with the proof:

1. The Secretary of War, who ought to be well informed upon the subject, in answer to an inquiry from the Editor of the Savannah *Republican*, says the government wants all the clothing, blankets and shoes the people can furnish.

2. An officer, just arrived here from the army, makes an earnest appeal through the morning papers for shoes and clothing. *He says there are 2,600 men in a single corps of the army who are now barefooted!* This, too, at a time when the snow was four inches deep in Richmond, and possibly a foot deep in the mountains upon whose bleak spurs these barefooted men were keeping guard! And this, too, notwithstanding the supplies the government has sent up to the relief of the army! An appeal is now made to the people of Richmond for their old shoes and clothes to put on the frozen feet and naked backs of our defenders!

Such is the evidence. Is it sufficient to reach the hearts of the speculator and extortioner? Of course it is not. They are the bitter enemies of the army—the enemies, indeed, of the Confederate States, and of freedom itself—and it would require the same proof to make them our friends that it would to win over the Abolitionists themselves. These soulless extortioners—these scheming, hard-hearted speculators—who go up and down the earth, buying all the wool and leather and other necessaries of life they can lay their greedy hands upon, and hide them away for enormous profits, they are the most dangerous and implacable enemies with whom the South has to contend in this fearful struggle for liberty. They are fast destroying our currency, and are now doing all they can to put it out of the power of the people to cover the naked feet and shivering limbs of the army.

Nor can the Government be held blameless for the condition of the army. No one questions the good intentions of President Davis or Secretary [George W.] Randolph; but that they have shown a singular want of foresight, and their agents and officers been guilty of the most cruel neglect cannot be truthfully denied. It would have been an easy matter last Spring and Summer to obtain supplies of all kinds from abroad, but the government seems never to have given one thought to the future wants of the army. In Summer, our rulers appear to think there will never be Winter again; and in Winter that Summer will never return.

P. W. A.

RICHMOND, November 27, 1862 [12-5-62]

If the battle around the city elevated Gen. Lee in the public estimation as a military leader, his conduct of affairs since his return from Maryland should stamp him as one of the greatest living masters of the art of war.

By the skillful disposition of his forces in front of Winchester, he rendered it impracticable for McClellan to invade the Valley of the Shenandoah, and forced him to adopt the route on the East side of the Blue Ridge. The Federal commander accepted this alternative the more readily since he hoped, by an ostentatious display of a part of his forces near Shepardstown, to deceive Gen. Lee and gain his flank and rear at Warrenton. On his arrival at this latter place, however, much to his surprise and dismay, he found our far-seeing General quietly awaiting him on the South bank of the Rappahannock.

This unexpected discovery rendered it necessary for the enemy to change the plan of the campaign, and to adopt a new base of operations and a different route to Richmond. Accordingly, McClellan having been superceded by Burnside, the latter officer, after consultation with Halleck, the General-in-Chief, who visited his headquarters at Warrenton, caused a series of imposing demonstrations to be made along our front, as if he intended to give battle at an early day. In the meantime, he put the main body of his army in motion and marched it rapidly down the North bank of the Rappahannock, with the view of throwing it across that stream at Fredericksburg, gaining Lee's rear and descending by forced marches upon Richmond before our army could get into position to check his advance. But if McClellan was surprised to find Lee awaiting him at Warrenton, Burnside was *amazed* upon his arrival at Fredericksburg, to learn that the sagacious Confederate commander had not only anticipated his movement, but had completely blocked the passage of the Rappahannock.

So confident was Burnside and his army of the successful issue of his clever strategem, that the army correspondence undertook to furnish the Federal press with minute and glowing accounts of the triumphal march. Public expectation was raised to the highest pitch. The Government, the press, and even officers in the field, so far forgot the bitter disappointments of the past as to indulge the pleasant hallucinations of the early downfall of the "rebel capital." When Burnside reached the heights overlooking Fredericksburg, therefore, and cast his anxious eyes across the river, great must have been his astonishment when he discovered the Confederates, who he vainly supposed, were still awaiting his attack near Warrenton, drawn up on the opposite hills, and the gateway to Richmond completely closed.

The Abolition press, in its disappointment and mortification, indulges in charges of treason against its own people, and says some one in the confidence of Burnside must have communicated his plans to Gen. Lee. But this is not true. Gen. Lee, by superior genius and penetration, was enabled to fathom his adversary's designs, and baffle his well-laid plans; and that, too, without the assistance of traitors from the Federal camps.

As was remarked in a former letter, the Confederacy is fortunate in having such a man as Gen. Lee in its service. He is still in the prime and vigor of physical and intellectual manhood, being about forty-five [55] years of age. He is six feet in height; weighs about one hundred and ninety pounds; is erect, well-formed and of imposing appearance; has clear bright, benignant black eyes, dark grey hair, and a heavy grey beard. He is exceedingly plain in his dress, and one looks at his costume in vain for those insignia of rank for which most officers show a weakness. He wears an unassuming black felt hat, with a narrow strip of gold lace around it, and a plain Brigadier's coat, with three stars on the collar, but without the usual braiding on the sleeves. He travels and sleeps in an ambulance when the army is in motion, and occupies a tent when it is stationary, and not the largest and best house in the neighborhood, as is the custom of some officers. In a few words, he cares but little for appearances, though one of the handsomest men in the Confederacy, and is content to take the same fare his soldiers receive.

In character and personal deportment, he is all that the most ardent patriot can desire. Grave and dignified, he is yet modest and painfully distrustful of his own abilities. The descendent of a gallant officer of the elder revolution, the husband of the grand-daughter (by adoption) of Gen. Washington, the inheritor of a large estate, and the trusted leader of a great and victorious army, he is nevertheless accessible to the humblest and most ragged soldier in the ranks, courteous to his officers, just and kind to the citizens, and withal and above all, a meek and humble Christian.

During the time the army was in Maryland, an officer of high position in the country suggested a number of reasons to Gen. Lee in support of a grave measure then under discussion. Among others, he remarked to him that he was trusted by his government, had the hearts of his soldiers, and possessed the entire confidence of his country, and that the Army, the Government and People relied implicitly upon his patriotism and genius. Tears rushed to his eyes, and he exclaimed—"Do not say that—do not say that. I am sensible of my weakness, and such a responsibility as your remark implies would crush me to the earth." He said in the same conversation that there was nothing he so much desired as peace and independence. All he had, and all he hoped for—all that ambition could suggest or glory give— he would freely surrender them all to stop the flow of blood and secure freedom to the country. He did not doubt that these blessings would come in due season; but he wanted them now, and would readily sacrifice every thought of personal aggrandizement to save the life of even one soldier.

Gen. Lee, though not possessing the first order of intellect, is endowed with rare judgment and equanimity, unerring sagacity, great self-control, and extraordinary powers of combination. Like Washington, he is a wise man, and a good man, and possesses in an eminent degree those qualities which are indispensable in the great leader and champion upon whom the country rests its hopes of present success and future independence. In simple intellect there are other officers in the service who are equals, and perhaps his superiors, and as a mere fighter there are some who may excel him. But in the qualities of a commander, entrusted with the duty of planning and executing a campaign upon a broad scale, and with the direction and government of a large army, whether scattered over a wide extent of territory, or massed together as at Richmond, he surpasses them all, and is the peer of any living chieftain in the New World or the Old. The country should feel grateful that Heaven has raised up one in our midst so worthy of our confidence and so capable to lead. The grand-son of Washington, so to speak, let us hope that the mantle of the ascending hero has fallen upon the shoulders of the wise and modest chief who now commands the army of Northern Virginia.

P. W. A.

RICHMOND, VA., November 29, 1862 [12-5-62]

The Government organ says Gen. [Joseph] Johnston will leave to-day to assume command of the Department of the Mississippi. His department embraces the States of Kentucky, Tennessee, Alabama, Mississippi, and that part of Louisiana lying east of the great river. His restoration to health and assignment to duty have given much satisfaction here, where considerable concern is felt at the condition of affairs in the South-west. Gen. Johnston would have preferred to remain in Virginia. He has great admiration for the old Army of the Potomac, which he commanded for nearly a year, and which he is reported to have said is the finest body of troops in the world. But there are good reasons for sending him to the West, where an officer of superior abilities is needed, and for keeping Gen. Lee here, where his great engineering skill and knowledge of the topography of the State are of the utmost importance to the successful defense of the Capital.

Gen. Johnston, as you are aware, is a native of the proud old commonwealth of Virginia, and a little turned fifty years of age. He weighs about one hundred and sixty pounds, is five feet ten inches in height—though he looks taller on account of his erect carriage—has a florid complexion, short grey hair and closely cut side whiskers, moustache and goatee. His manners are rather quiet and dignified, and his general appearance and deportment highly military. Indeed, everything about him—his bearing, style of dress, and even his most careless attitudes—betoken the high-toned, and spirited soldier, who loves his profession, and whose soul revels in the din and uproar of the battle-field. His short hair and beard, high color, close fitting uniform, striking air and self-possession, remind one of the game cock, the most courageous of all "the fowls of the air," when clipped and trimmed and prepared for the ring.

Intellectually, Gen. Johnston is the equal of any of the five Generals in the army, and in the opinion of many, is superior to them all. His reports are written with great vigor, and a degree of elegance which shows that in the turmoil of the camp, he is not unmindful of the graces of literature.

As a strategist, he enjoys a very high reputation among military men. In his operations he regards masses and general results, rather than isolated bodies and mere temporary effects. And hence the opinion prevails, with some, that he lacks energy and enterprise. This, however, is a great mistake. No man is more watchful of his adversary, or more ready to strike when the right time comes; and when he does strike he delivers the blow of a giant. He sees but little advantage of picking off a man here and there, or in precipitating small bodies of men against each other. Instead of frittering away his strength, he seeks rather to husband it until the auspicious moment arrives, and then he goes to work with an energy and resolution that is wonderful.

For the same reason he is considered one of the best fighters in the whole army. Gen. Lee fights a good deal by maneuvers. One step is made to lead to another. An advantage gained here is the prelude to another on a different part of the field; until having attained certain positions and accomplished certain results, he presses forward against the vital point with a vigor and resolution that carry everything before them. Johnston orders the battle after the same fashion, and enters the field with the same purposes; but when he gets fully into the fight, and his blood is once up, he strikes right and left, and with a rapidity and skill that are perfectly irresistible. He is not content with commanding on the field, but like the deceased Irishman, when the bottle was passing around at his own funeral, he insists upon taking a hand himself.

When Jackson got into position and the battle was fully joined in front of Richmond, certain victory was the assured results of Lee's masterly combinations. And at the second battle of Manassas, when Jackson was hard pressed on the left and asked for assistance, Lee, instead of sending it to him and thus weakening his forces elsewhere, pressed Longstreet forward on the right, threw the enemy's left wing into confusion, and thus relieved Jackson more effectually, and in less time than if he had sent him reinforcements. Johnston, on the contrary, had a well matured plan of battle at the Seven Pines, but it was simple and direct. He struck right at the center of the enemy, intending to pierce his lines, capture the forces on this bank of the Chickahominy and then drive the remainder on the east side into the York and Pamunkey rivers.

When McClellan moved his army to the Peninsula last Spring, it is said that Johnston, then in command of the Army of the Potomac, was in favor of taking up his position behind the Chickahominy and not going to Yorktown at all. The President preferred the position at Yorktown, however, and accordingly the army was moved down to Magruder's lines. The night of his arrival there Johnston held a council of war, at which Toombs said: "We must fight to-morrow, or retreat to-night." All our forces had then come up, whilst McClellan's army, already enormous, was receiving fresh additions every day. Johnston agreed with Toombs, but kept his army there fourteen days, chiefly in deference to the wishes of the President, until McClellan got ready to offer him battle, when he broke up his camp and marched back to Richmond. It was during this retreat that the battle of Williamsburg was fought by Longstreet, who brought up the rear.

In a previous letter in relation to the contest before Richmond, and the parts taken by Johnston and Lee, a mistake occurred, which it is proper to correct. Persons who participated in that contest, and who were in a position to be well informed, say Johnston did ask that Jackson might be sent to him from the Valley of the Shenandoah, and [T. H.] Holmes from the south side of the James river. If this be true, then Johnston is entitled to the credit of having first suggested that master stroke of the campaign. To Lee, however, belongs all the honor and glory due to his brilliant plan of battle and the manner in which it was executed.

Important movements are about to be made on the Rappahannock, but it would be improper to state what they are. Jackson is in the right place, and everything is prepared for the enemy. The hawk does not care how many birds there are in the flock, nor does the wolf stop to count the sheep in the fold. When Lee does strike, his blow will be a crushing one.

The weather continues cold and raw. The health of the troops is good. Winter supplies continue to arrive from the Southern States, and the Quartermaster-General advertises that he is ready to pay for all that may be furnished by the people.

P. W. A.

RICHMOND, VA., December 4, 1862 [12-12-62]

Opinion, both here and in the Army, is divided in regard to the intentions of the enemy. In some quarters it is believed that Burnside contemplates an early attack upon Lee's position; in others, that he will not seek to cross the Rappahannock at this late period of the year, or if he does, that he will limit his operations to the occupation of Fredericksburg from whence he will seek to march on Richmond next spring. The weather has been raw and misty for some days, but is now clear and frosty, and invites the invader to active works. The pickets of the two armies occupy the opposite banks of the river, but by agreement between the respectable commanders, do not fire on each other. Our pickets are relieved at night, and are not permitted to speak above a whisper. The enemy's are changed during the day. The heights on the North bank are covered with Federal batteries, whose wide-mouthed guns are pointed down upon the town and the fords above and below. A number of field works have also been constructed by the enemy, the labor being performed at night. Whether these works have been thrown up to guard against attack by Gen. Lee, in the event they should decide to evacuate their present position, or to cover their advance should they attempt to cross the river, is a question of considerable doubt and speculation. A short time will decide, if the present good weather continues.

Our army seems to be very sanguine of success, should a battle be fought. The men feel the most implicit confidence in Gen. Lee, and the galaxy of officers by whom he is supported. Among these officers, no one possesses more of their respect and admiration than Lieut. Gen. Longstreet, the next in command.

Gen. Longstreet is, I believe, a native of South Carolina, and looks to be about forty years of age. He is at least six feet high, weighs about two hundred and twenty pounds, wears a heavy brown beard, and is withal one of the finest looking men in the army. He is a man of simple habits and modest deportment; seems anxious to do his duty without stopping to consider what the public will think of him; and never does or says anything to catch the popular applause or cut a figure in the newspapers. Thus far he has never been entrusted with a separate command, as Jackson was in the Valley of the Shenandoah last spring, and, consequently, he has never had an opportunity to display his abilities as a commander. It is only as a fighter that he is known, and even in this respect less is known of him by the people than of any other officer who has rendered the same important services. Whether this ignorance is justly ascribable to the singular reticence of the Press towards so meritorious an officer, or to his own modest behavior, I am unable to decide. This much, however, may be asserted with absolute certainty: He is satisfied, like Gen. Lee, to discharge his duty, and leave the public to judge of his performances as they please, believing their final judgment will be just and truthful.

As a fighter, General Longstreet stands second to no man in the army; indeed, I have heard that General Lee considers him the best fighter in the world. He reposes the most unlimited confidence in his coolness, skill and courage, and leans upon his broad shoulders and clear, strong judgement with a sense of the utmost security. This feeling is shared by his entire corps and by the whole army. It is but just to add, that Longstreet combines in an eminent degree the qualities of a great soldier, viz: the spirit and dash to storm a formidable position; the stubborn courage and cool judgment to maintain his ground against superior numbers, and make the best disposition of his own forces; and the skill and ability to control and direct a grand army.

General Longstreet has been attached to the Army of the Potomac, or of Northern Virginia, as it is sometimes called, ever since the war commenced. He first commanded a brigade under Beauregard, was subsequently made a Major General under Johnston and now holds the position of Lieutenant General under Lee—all of them masters of the art of war, though in different degrees. This admirable schooling has been of great advantage to him, and of equal importance to the country, since it has prepared and fitted him to take command of the army should anything occur to deprive it of its present unrivaled leader.

It is said that Longstreet was willing to cross the Potomac and march upon Baltimore with an army of 70,000 men. Gen. Lee found it necessary owing to the rapidity of his march, the intensity of the heat, and the unfavorable condition of the troops, to cross with a smaller number, and to fight the battle of Sharpsburg with less than 40,000 men. If he had had the 70,000 requested by his able lieutenant, he might have driven McClellan back upon Washington, and maintained his ground in Maryland.

The just and liberal spirit manifested by the people and authorities of Georgia and Alabama in regard to the troops they have sent to the field and especially the disposition they have shown to keep them properly supplied and to take care of their families, has had a happy effect upon the army, and indeed upon all classes.

P. W. A.

Probably for his recent criticisms of the Confederate War Department, Alexander was refused a pass to enter the lines at Fredericksburg, and had to initially report the battle from Richmond.

RICHMOND, VA., December 14, 1862 [12-23-62]

A great battle was fought on the Rappahannock yesterday, and the Confederate arms are again victorious. The fight commenced at 9 o'clock in the morning, and continued until six in the evening. Nothing was known of the battle here until late last night, after my letter of yesterday evening had been posted. The War Office has taken complete possession of the telegraph, and one can hardly order a bushel of salt by the wires without first getting permission from the authorities. This will explain why you have received nothing from me of late by telegraph, and why you may not in the future.

The enemy made the attack, moving first against our right wing, and as the fog lifted from the valley, it extended along the entire line to our extreme left. The conflict raged without intermission until night set in, and resulted in the complete repulse of the enemy at all points.

Our success was not so decisive as to preclude the idea of a renewal of the battle to-day. Indeed, in his dispatch to the War Office, Gen. Lee expresses the opinion that the fighting would be resumed at daybreak this morning. If so, Burnside has greater confidence in his troops than McClellan had at Sharpsburg, where he declined to return to the attack, notwithstanding his vast superiority in numbers.

We have to mourn the loss of many brave officers—among whom are Brig. Gens. T. R. R. Cobb, of Georgia, and Maxcy Gregg, of South Carolina. Though they had not many opportunities to display their qualities for command, these gentlemen were conspicuous for skill, courage and gallantry. Bartow and Bee fell side by side at the first battle of Manassas, and now Cobb and Gregg lock arms in death. For the second time the bloody marriage of South Carolina and Georgia has been celebrated upon the field of battle and to the harsh music of artillery.

Doubtless many gallant officers of the line and hundreds of brave men in the ranks have also been slain or wounded. The enemy had decidedly the advantage in numbers, and the lists of casualties, when they come to be published, will carry grief to many a stricken home in the Confederacy.

LATER

12 *m*—A telegram has just been received at the War Office from Gen. Lee, dated at half-past eleven this morning, in which he says the battle had not been renewed up to that hour. It is thought here that Burnside will not return to the attack. A few hours will decide.

I hope to be able to go up to the Army to-morrow morning. A passport was granted to the correspondent of the London *Times*, and why should one be refused to the correspondent of the Savannah *Republican*? Is it because the one is an Englishman and the other a Confederate?

STILL LATER.

8 p.m.—Passengers who left the Army at 1 p.m. to-day, say the fighting was renewed this morning, and continued up to the time they left. Dispatches to the War Office, on the contrary, speak of heavy skirmishing, especially this afternoon, but say nothing of any general engagement.

I have just been to see they body of Gen. Cobb, which was brought down this evening, and will be sent south by to-morrow morning's train. His brigade was posted behind a stone wall at the base of the hill, this side of Fredericksburg, and but a short distance from the town. Our batteries were placed on the elevation just behind and above the brigade, and fired over them. When the enemy charged upon Cobb's position, he reserved his fire until they got within one hundred yards, when his men poured into their ranks a fire which seemed literally to sweep them from the earth. The enemy retired, and having reformed their broken lines and been heavily reinforced, they returned to the charge at the double quick. The Georgians again reserved their fire until they had come within easy range, when they gave them another volley like the first and with the same result. A third charge was finally made, this time in still greater force, but in this instance, as in the first and second, the enemy were driven back with tremendous loss. Persons who participated in the fight say that 1,000 dead Yankees were left on the field in front of Cobb's position. Gen. Cobb himself displayed great courage and judgement. His mother was born in the town of Fredericksburg, and he acted as if he were fighting to rescue her birth-place from the clutches of a hated foe. His men were protected behind the stone fence, and he and Gen. [John] Cooke of North Carolina, were standing behind a house, from which point they could conveniently issue their orders. A shell passed through the house, and fragments of it struck both of them. Gen. Cobb was hit on the thigh, which was terribly mangled, about two o'clock, and died at four. It is reported that Gen. Cooke is also dead. A piece of the same shell struck Capt. [W. S.] Brewster, of the 24th Georgia, a most gallant officer, in the leg, and inflicted a severe, but not mortal wound.

It is feared that Capt. Lord King, son of the Hon. T. Butler King and aid to Gen. McLaws, was killed. He is missing, and a telegram to his father says his spurs had been found on the field near a pair of shoes. He had on cavalry boots, and the presumption is that he was wounded, and that some vandal relieved him of them and left his old shoes behind. Capt. K.

was brave to a fault, and has always conducted himself in battle with great gallantry and fearlessness.

P. W. A.

After appealing directly to Secretary of War James Seddon, Alexander finally received his pass.

The Battle of Fredericksburg

HEIGHTS OF FREDERICKSBURG, VA., December 16, 1862 [12-25-62]

The unexpected difficulties I had to encounter in reaching this place, have rendered it impossible for me to send you an account of the late battle as soon as could have been desired. The fault is not mine, however. All my arrangements have been made to return to the army the moment it became certain that a battle would be fought, and had a passport been granted me, I should have arrived in time to witness it. But without stopping to indulge in unavailing complaints, let us proceed with the work in hand, in the hope that the following sketch, late as it may be in reaching you, will not be without interest to your readers.

On Wednesday night, the 10th inst., the enemy commenced to throw three pontoon bridges across the Rappahannock—two at Fredericksburg, and one about a mile and a quarter below, near the mouth of Deep Run. The plain on which the town stands is so completely commanded by the northern [eastern] heights, and the river is so narrow and crooked, and its bed so deep, that it was found impossible to prevent the construction of the bridges. At the mouth of Deep Run our skirmishers were without shelter, and exposed to a destructive fire at short range, which rendered it necessary for them to retire. The completion of the bridge at that point was effected about noon on the 11th, and [William B.] Franklin's corps [Grand Division] immediately commenced to cross.

In the town, however, where [William] Barksdale's sharpshooters had the protection of the houses near the riverbank, the enemy were repeatedly driven back, notwithstanding their desperate efforts to lay the bridge, and the tremendous fire they concentrated upon the town from the opposite heights. Some idea may be formed of the terrific nature of the cannonade, when it is stated that eighty shots were fired to the minute for nearly two hours. This fire was directed against the town, and particularly that portion near the river, where our men had taken shelter.

And yet Barksdale and his brigade of brave Mississippians maintained their position against these repeated assaults until dark, when he was ordered to retire. During all this fierce engagement, not one shot had been fired by our batteries. The way being left open, a portion of Sumner's corps [Grand Division] crossed over on the night of the 11th, (Thursday) and occupied the town and a part of the plain below next to the river. Other columns were pushed over Friday night above and below; so that early on Saturday morning the 13th, the day of the battle, a large Federal army was in position on the south [west] bank of the river.

Burnside had largely the advantage in numbers; Lee, in position and the fighting qualities of his troops. The former moved to the attack, not skillfully, but as if impelled by a controlling force behind; the latter awaited the onset in position, calmly and serenely conscious not only of the superiority of his veterans and the impregnableness of his position, but of the righteousness of his cause.

A heavy fog rested upon the valley and concealed the movements of the enemy. At 9 o'clock they had advanced near enough to be distinguished by Stuart's keen eyes, and in less time than it requires to write it, the latter moved up a section of his horse artillery and poured a galling fire into their left flank. In a short time the right of Jackson's front line, under A. P. Hill, became hotly engaged, and a furious and protracted struggle ensued. Two of Hill's brigades were forced to give back before the immense columns precipitated against them, but not without offering a gallant resistance. A part of Ewell's old division, now commanded by [Jubal] Early, was dispatched to their assistance, and finally drove them back from the point of woods they had seized, and pursued them into the plain, until arrested by their artillery.

As the fog lifted from the valley, the battle ran along to the extreme left, but it was more an affair of artillery in many portions of it than an engagement of infantry. The batteries beyond the river joined the fire, which is represented to have been more rapid and deafening even than that at Sharpsburg. The Federals handled their artillery superbly. Their aim was so accurate that it required only a few minutes to kill nearly every horse attached to one of our batteries. It is but proper to remark that the enemy speak in the same terms of the Confederate artillerists.

The attack on the left was chiefly directed against that part of the line occupied by McLaws' splendid division. As the fog rolled away and the sun shone out, the enemy were seen advancing from the town in great force. Cobb's and Kershaw's brigades, posted at the base of the hill about a fourth of a mile from the edge of the town, and supported by Cooke's North Carolinians, were the first to receive the shock. Cobb's position was behind a stone fence, while the heights in his rear were occupied by the New Orleans Washington Artillery, under command of the veteran Col. [J. B.] Walton. These batteries poured a devouring fire into the ranks of the multitudinous foe as they advanced across the open plain. The enemy made a desperate effort to gain these heights. Assault after assault was made, each time with fresh troops and increased numbers. At no time, however, did they succeed in getting nearer than seventy or eighty yards to the stone wall, from which they were saluted with a fire that no mere human force could face and yet live. Our men did not pull a trigger until they got within easy range, and then taking deliberate aim, they gave them volley after volley right in their faces.

The enemy displayed great courage at this point. They advanced frequently at a double quick, though exposed to a tremendous fire in front, an almost equally fatal cross fire from the batteries posted on the heights to the right and left. This terrible fire was kept up not only while they were advancing, but after they were broken, and were retreating.

It is believed that the enemy brought up against this position, first and last, near 40,000 men; and yet these two heroic brigades, or rather portions of them, (for all the regiments belonging to them were not engaged,) with the powerful aid of the Washington Artillery, not only maintained it, but repulsed the foe with a slaughter that is without a parallel in this war. I went over the ground this morning, and the dead still remaining there, after two-thirds of them had been removed, lay twice as thick as upon any other battlefield I have ever seen. On a piece of ground not exceeding two hundred yards square, it is estimated that the enemy left between thirteen and fourteen hundred dead! Allowing five wounded for every one killed, (the usual proportion,) and it would be safe to put down their loss in killed and wounded on this bloody square of two hundred yards, at 6,500! The blood may still be seen in puddles on the ground, as in a butcher's pen, and the way along which their wounded were carried back into the town, is still red with blood, notwithstanding the rain this morning.

Just in front of our line is a thin plank fence, behind which the enemy sought shelter as they advanced up the hill. Some of the planks in this fence were literally shot away from the posts to which they were nailed, and one can hardly place his hand upon any part of them without covering a dozen bullet holes. At the foot of the stone wall behind which the Confederates fought, thousands of flattened musket balls may be seen, whilst the hills behind it have been converted into a partial lead mine.

Upon the fall of Gen. Cobb, the particulars of which were given in a former letter—the command of the brigade devolved upon Col. [R. E.] McMillan of the 24th Georgia. From 2 p.m.—the hour at which Gen. Cobb fell—until the last gun was fired, this officer, thus suddenly called to the command, firmly held this ground upon which his chief had perished. Regardless of personal danger, and conscious only that he held, in part, the key to our position, he handled his brigade with coolness and judgment and stood bravely up to his work throughout the iron rain that swept over and around those bloody heights.

Intelligent prisoners, taken this morning, estimated their loss at 19,090, and observations made by officers who were in a position to form a correct opinion, do not vary the figure much. I understand Gen. Lee thinks their loss exceeds 15,000. This includes the killed, wounded and missing. Under the last head may be placed 1,000 prisoners, many of whom were taken to-day, including a full brass band, the members of which had overslept themselves, and hence left behind.

I have often read of the scenes attending the sacking of a city, but was never able to realize the full import of the term until this morning when I rode into Fredericksburg. The number of houses destroyed by fire is not so great as at first reported, but otherwise the ruin is complete. Chimneys were knocked down, roofs torn away, great gaps made in the walls, streets barricaded, furniture hacked to pieces or used for firewood, store-houses opened and rifled of their contents, table-ware stolen, mattresses taken into the streets and alleys for the vandals to sleep upon, books, paintings and looking-glasses scattered over the ground, provisions consumed, cellars ransacked, and the enclosures around private residences and lots pulled down and used for firewood or to rest upon. There is hardly a structure in the whole city that does not bear some traces of the fearful struggle in the streets and suburbs. The floors of many of the houses into which the wounded were taken, are covered with blood, and in some instances the dead still remain in the silent chambers, their eyes fixed in death, yet glaring wildly up at blackened and blood-stained walls. A few of the inhabitants concealed themselves in cellars, and now and then they may be seen timidly peeping out from their hiding places, of flitting across the streets like mysterious shadows. The churches and better buildings seem to have been the mark of the enemy's greatest spite. But nothing escaped their fury, and it will be a long while before the town can recover from the terrible ordeal through which it has passed.

Among our trophies are two or three thousand stand of arms, and a number of flags, including that of the Sixty-ninth New York regiment.

P. W. A.

Official casualties for the battle of Fredericksburg: Federals, 1,284 killed, 9,600 wounded, and 1,769 missing for a total of 12,653; Confederates, 595 killed, 4,061 wounded, and 653 missing for 5,309.

The Late Battle—Further Particulars

HEIGHTS OF FREDERICKSBURG, VA., December 17, 1862 [12-27-62]

Each party continued to occupy his former line of battle on Monday [December 14]. Burnside, desirous of avoiding the appearance of defeat, refused to ask for a truce to bury his dead, though he permitted some of his officers to do so. Gen. Lee very properly refused the application, though twice renewed, until made by the Federal commander himself, which was finally done during the afternoon, and promptly granted. A large number of the dead still remained unburied this morning; but burying parties have just come over from Burnside for the purpose of assigning to each of their fallen comrades a snug little farm—not such, however, as had been promised to them by their officers, but a dirty little hole in the ground.

Monday afternoon I witnessed a spectacle that has seldom, if ever, been seen in any age or country. As was stated in my letter of yesterday, our lines were drawn up along the base of the hills and back on the heights in the timber, and the enemy in the open plain in front. The latter had three lines, and in some places four. The front one was posted just beyond the range of our muskets, and the others at short distances in the rear. There they stood—the two armies—in full view of each other, and in hailing distance, and yet not a gun was fired. The plain was black with the heavy masses of the North and their far-reaching lines. The innumerable small arms of the opposing hosts glistened in the sunlight, whilst their field batteries in the valley below, and their heavy batteries on the heights on either side of the river, wide-mouthed and ready for action, met the eye wherever it turned. Such a vast array was probably never seen before at a single view, either in ancient or modern times. The manhood of the continent was assembled here, and swarmed along this valley and over these hills. What vast power! What a network of muscle! Neither the lever of Archimides, nor any other engine or contrivance ever devised by man, was equal to the strength that for the moment slept in those brawny arms and fiery hearts.

Gen. Lee did not order his batteries to open upon the enemy's lines, for the reason that it was his obvious policy not to make the attack, but to await it. He could but desire that

Burnside would renew the attack, for his position, naturally very strong, had been rendered more so by a series of defensive works, any further allusion to which might be improper.

It were but uttering the simple truth to say, that a better army was never seen than that which Gen. Lee now commands. The men have attained to a degree of health and seasoning which cannot be improved upon, and which gives to them the appearance of trained gladiators or bronzed statues. The effects of the exhausting summer campaign have disappeared; whilst the rest at Winchester and the bracing winter air have imparted new vigor to their limbs and fresh courage to their hearts. Their confidence in their peerless chief is unlimited, their spirits cheerful, their purpose fixed. If such a thing were possible as that the government could desire to abandon the contest or reconstruct the Union, there can be no doubt that the Army would resist it to the death. It is a grand Army; and Lee may say of it—as Frederick the Great said of his—the world does not repose more securely upon the shoulders of Atlas, than the Confederate government upon such an army.

A few hundred men are still without shoes and proper clothing. These are permitted to remain at the campfires and take care of the baggage. How long shall the state of things continue? The condition of the great body of the troops, however, is much improved, thanks to the timely action of the people at home; but it might be rendered yet more comfortable. There should be no relaxation, therefore, in the patriotic work of furnishing supplies; for clothing and shoes soon wear out in a rugged campaign like this. Very few men have gloves, or more than one pair of socks.

The enemies batteries still occupy the Stafford Heights, and his pickets may yet be seen on the northern [eastern] bank of the river; but with these exceptions, and a few wagons and tents scattered over the distant hills, nothing remains in view of the "Grand Army." If Burnside thinks to decoy Gen. Lee across the river, and have him repeat the blunder committed by himself, he has but little conception of the character of the man with whom he has to deal. The most foolish thing the Federal Commander could possibly have done, was to pass the river, and attack our position; and the wisest thing he ever did was to retrace his steps. He is no match for the wise and modest hero who leads the Confederate Army; nor has he any such Lieutenants to lean upon as Longstreet, Jackson, McLaws, Stuart, and the Hills.

P. W. A.

HEIGHTS OF FREDERICKSBURG, December 19, 1862

Everything remains quiet in this quarter. Burnside would seem to have abandoned all idea of again trying to reach Richmond from the base of the Rappahannock. Indeed, the indications are that Washington, and not Richmond, is his present destination. His beaten and demoralized masses will, doubtless, find winter quarters more pleasant than the bleak heights and frozen flats of Fredericksburg.

The effect of the terrible disaster upon the people of the United States was most stunning, because it was most unexpected. The army was so large, its equipment so complete, and the press so confident and unanimous in the assertion that the "rebel capital" would certainly be taken this time, that the people were not prepared for any other result than that of victory. The Washington *Republican* admits that "the failure at Fredericksburg has taken the public, and possibly the military authorities, so much by surprise, that opinions are hardly yet formed as to what ought either now to be done, or what is likely to be done." It further adds: "For ourselves, we hope that as a few weeks will terminate the Winter of this latitude, the army designed for the defense of Washington will go at once into Winter quarters."

And into Winter quarters it will go; and that, too, notwithstanding the dangers which threaten the Federal government from abroad, the growing discontent of its own people and the mountain load of debt under which it already begins to stagger. With an army on hand of six or eight hundred thousand men, with a formidable war fleet afloat, with thousands of contractors and manufacturers employed, and a vast horde of robbers fattening on the public treasury—it must have been the most dire necessity that, under such circumstances, could have induced the government to withdraw its largest and best army from the field. Whence came that necessity? From the bloody banks of the Rappahannock—from the unrivaled valor of the Confederate army and the genius of its peerless leader.

An incident occupied during the battle, in which a private in the Fourth Georgia regiment, [George] Doles' brigade, participated, that deserves to be mentioned. The man had been wounded at Sharpsburg, and fell into the hands of the enemy. During his confinement he was tenderly nursed by a Federal soldier, who found and took him from the field. Having recovered from his wound and been exchanged, he rejoined his regiment, and is now in this vicinity. The day after the battle his attention was arrested by the groans of a wounded man, and proceeding to where he lay, he was astonished to find it was the Federal soldier who had been so kind to him at Sharpsburg. The Georgian returned immediately to Gen. Doles, informed him of the circumstances, and asked permission to remove the wounded man. The General not only granted his request, but charged him to take special care of his friend and nurse him until he got well.

The bread cast upon the water had returned.

P. W. A.

Effect of the late Battle in Washington—Sketch of Stonewall Jackson

RICHMOND, December 23, 1862 [12-29-62]

The blow administered to the invader at Fredericksburg would seem to have demoralized, not only the Federal army, but the Federal Government also. Our bomb-shells, it appears, fell in Washington as well as in Fredericksburg, and it is difficult to say whether they produced more effect on the Rappahannock or the Potomac. The army, cut to pieces and driven back like the waves of the sea from a rock-bound coast, is now seeking shelter—not from the winter's blast, but Lee's victorious legions—behind the fortifications at the Federal capital; whilst the members of the cabinet, defeated in their wicked purposes and overwhelmed in the sea of blood they have wantonly shed, are already searching for places in which to cover up their shame and confusion. The time will yet come when they will call upon the rocks and mountains to fall upon them, and hide them from the wrath of the infuriated mob and the gaze of the indignant world. Verily, "the rider and his horse hath He thrown into the sea."

The enemy attribute their defeat in part at least to the thick fog that hung over the Valley of the Rappahannock on the morning of the 13th, *and which was not lifted until all our preparations against their attack had been completed!* And well they may; for "it was a cloud and darkness to *them*, but it gave light to *them*." If Gen. Lee had been scene shifter in that rugged amphitheater of hills, he could not have rolled up the misty curtain that hid his army from the enemy, at a moment more opportune for his purpose. He had been reserved for another duty, however. The "cloud" had been placed between the camp of the North and the camp of the South by an Unseen Hand; but at the proper time, that same Hand gathered up its folds and pointed the way to victory.

The details to hand are too meagre to enable me to understand fully the extent of the troubles at Washington. The telegram I sent to you last evening came from Fredericksburg to Governor Letcher, and contained all the information received here up to this hour. Seward and his son (Assistant Secretary of State,) had thrown up their portfolios, in consequence of the action of a majority of the Senate, and it was generally concluded that the other members of the Cabinet would follow his example. It was believed, also, that Halleck would be displaced, and a new man put in his place, and that the command of the Army of the Potomac, made vacant by the reported resignation of Burnside, would be given to Fremont or McClellan. If given to the former, then the gulf between the Democrats and the Abolitionists would indeed become impassible; if the latter, then the party which was strong enough to drive Seward out of the Administration, might turn upon Mr. Lincoln himself, and force him to abdicate the Presidential chair.

If the war be continued, without the intervention of some power not now foreseen, the dissolution of both government and society cannot be far distant. There must be peace, or the monster Republic of the North will go to pieces. Like the dying whale, it may be that it will be more formidable in the struggles of death, than it has been in life. Such was true of France during the Reign of Terror that swept over that beautiful land.

The questions occurs, shall Gen. Lee seize the occasion of the military and political troubles that now distract the army and Government of the United States, to resume the offensive and march upon Washington? This inquiry can best be answered, perhaps, by another, to-wit: whether a movement of that kind would not strike the scales from the eyes of the enemy, show them the folly of their dissentions, and unite them in a common effort to resist a common foe? If this be not answer enough, then the misfortunes which have almost invariably attended campaigning in the winter, should teach us the necessity of avoiding them. The army, moreover, requires rest; but if it did not, the outfit of the troops is not of a character to prepare them for the vigors of a campaign in January, in this high latitude.

Let me conclude this letter with a brief sketch of Stonewall Jackson.

It is said that the hero of the Shenandoah made his appearance on the field at Fredericksburg in a brand new uniform, including a fine dark blue overcoat, and a handsome cap, with the requisite quantity of gold lace about it. His disguise was complete—so much so, indeed, that he was hardly recognizable by his intimate associates. This suit was, doubtless, the gift of some admiring friend; since his ordinary apparel is very plain, and his tastes and habits exceedingly simple.

Gen. Jackson is not quite yet forty years old. He is of medium size and height—weighs about one hundred and forty-five or fifty pounds—has dark, not black, hair, and wears short side whiskers. His complexion is rather pale, and his features, when at rest, are destitute of expression. His manners are wholly devoid of grace, especially among strangers, when he is both awkward and embarrassed. On horseback his appearance is anything but prepossessing, as it is under almost any circumstances; and one who should meet him on the road, would be apt to take him for a quiet farmer, with full barns at home, and no creditor abroad, going to the Court House; or better still, for a country school master who, though all unused to the saddle, had undertaken to ride over to a neighboring patron's house on Saturday, and was meanwhile engaged in some difficult mathematical calculating as he jogged along. But place him on the battle-field—let the cannon begin to thunder, the small arms rattle, and the sabres to flash in the sunlight—and the quiet farmer, the awkward, calculating pedagogue, becomes a hero—calm and self-possessed, it is true—but full of fire and energy, quick as lightning and terrible as the thunderbolt.

Though it is the boast of Gen. Jackson's friends that he has not a spade in his whole army, yet it would be doing him injustice to suppose he is unmindful of the advantages of a strong position, or that he neglects any honorable means which may contribute to his success. No officer in the army is more attentive to his duties, or labors harder and longer than he does. He is very careful to ascertain the strength and position of his adversary; and having done this, he swoops like the eagle upon his prey.

There is some diversity of opinion among military men in regard to Gen. Jackson's qualities as a strategist and commander of an army, but none as to his ability as a fighter. In his battles he has been attended with a larger degree of success than any officer in the army. He is the idol of the people, and is the object of greater enthusiasm than any military chieftain of our day. And this, too, notwithstanding the fact that he marches his troops faster and longer, fights them harder, and takes less care of them than any other officer in the service. Indeed, some go so far as to say that if he had no enemy to encounter, and nothing to do but march his troops about the country, he would yet lose one third of them in the course of a year. This indifference to the comfort of his men is only apparent, however—not real. No man possesses a kinder heart or larger humanity; but when he has anything to do, he is so earnest, so ardent and energetic that he loses sight of everything but the work before him. If, for example, he were required to move his corps from Fredericksburg to Richmond and had two weeks to do it in, he would be almost sure to perform the march in four days, or one fifth of the time, because he does [not] know how to [do] anything slowly. His style of campaign, as he is reported to have told Gen. Lee just after the second battle of Manassas, is to seek for the enemy, and to strike him whenever and wherever found, in season and out of season, and whatever his position or numbers.

Gen. Jackson is a member of the Presbyterian Church, and a sincere and humble Christian. He considers himself an instrument in the hands of God, and never arrogates any credit to himself when victory perches upon his banners, but ascribes all the praise to Him, without whose knowledge not a sparrow falls to the ground. Many apocryphal stories have been set afloat in regard to his religious practices after a battle—such, for example, is that he is in the habit of drawing up his troops in line and returning thanks to God for the victory. I am assured that nothing of this kind has ever occurred. He is too sincere a Christian to indulge in such ostentatious displays of his piety.

It is said that the bold chieftain has but one weakness, and that relates to his middle name. It is generally supposed that his name is Thomas Jefferson Jackson; but this is a mistake. The J. does not stand for Jefferson, not Johnson, nor Jeremiah, nor Jeroboam, but for a name more ugly and hated than either or all of them. What, then, do you suppose it is, reader? Why *Jonathan!* the name (Uncle Jonathan) by which the United States are personified. The General does not want it to get out that he bears any such name, and it is hoped, Mr. Editor, that your readers will say nothing about it.

P. W. A.

1863

Unholy War

To Alexander, Lee and his Lieutenants seemed invincible; but the New Year promised little else but more of the same—battlefield success, coupled with irreplaceable losses. Alexander firmly believed that only a victory on northern soil could achieve independence for the Confederacy.

While Alexander was once again laid low with "camp fever," a young friend, and protégé, Capt. Virgil A. S. Parks of the 17th Georgia Infantry, supplied army correspondence to the Savannah Republican *as "V. A. S. P."*

Special Correspondence from V. A. S. P.

NEAR FREDERICKSBURG, Dec. 19, 1862 [1-1-63]

Mr. Editor: My indisposition, and consequent dullness, have rendered me totally unequal to the task of writing such letters as your readers expect, or such as the stirring events of this remarkable period demand. I will attempt this morning an imperfect account of the late conflict.

In viewing the battleground, one who had not participated would conclude that the carnage was truly terrible. The hillsides are dotted, even yet, with the enemy's slain. Before they accepted Gen. Lee's offer, or before permission was granted to them to bury their dead, they lay in heaps. Hundreds of dead horses can be seen in every direction.

From sources entirely trustworthy, as well as by their own confession, the enemy's loss in killed and wounded will not fall far short of twenty thousand! They were so badly cut up that they positively refused to advance again a third time. There was a mutinous spirit in their camps which forced Gen. Burnside to withdraw his army to the North bank of the Rappahannock.

There can be nothing more puzzling than the analysis of one's feelings on the battlefield.—You cannot describe them satisfactorily to yourself or others. To march steadily up to the mouth of a hundred cannon while they pour out fire and smoke, and shot and shell in a storm that mows men down like grass, is horrible beyond description—appalling. It is absurd to say a man can do it without fear. During [Winfield S.] Hancock's charge at Fredericksburg, for a long distance the slope was swept by such a hurricane of death that we thought every step would be our last, and I am willing to say, for one, that I was pretty badly scared. Whatever may be said about "getting used to it," old soldiers secretly dread a battle equally with the new ones. But the most difficult thing is to stand up against is the suspense while waiting, as we waited drawn up in line of battle on the edge of the field, watching the columns file past us and disappear in a cloud of smoke where horses and men and colors go down in confusion, where all sounds are lost in the screaming shells, the cracking of musketry, the thunder of artillery, and knowing our turn comes next, expecting each moment the word "Forward." It brings a strange kind of relief when "Forward" comes. You move mechanically with the rest. Once fairly in for it, your sensibilities are strangely blunted, you care comparatively nothing about the sights that shock you first; men torn to pieces by cannon shot becomes matter of course. At such a time, there comes a latent sustenance from within us, or above us, which no man anticipates who has not been in such a place before, and which most men pass through life without knowing any thing about. What is it? Where does it come from?

Only a small portion of Hood's Division was engaged, the 54th and 57th North Carolina, of [Evander] Law's Brigade. A heavy force of the enemy had advanced in our immediate front and possessed a small copse of wood. A regiment of Law's Brigade was very near the point in a good position, and it was thought they would hold the ground against the superior numbers of the enemy; but to their shame and the astonishment of all beholders, they gave the Yankees one terrible volley, which staggered the advancing foe, and ran from the field! A few brave men remained, and keeping up such a brisk and deadly fire, the enemy were held in check until the 54th and 57th came up. These gallant regiments, led by brave officers, charged the Yankees with a yell, who fled in terror, leaving their numerous dead and wounded in our hands. Verily, if *some* North Carolinians will *run*, there are many noble, brave soldiers from the Old North State to redeem her honor. No troops have fought better than Branch's Brigade. The North Carolina regiments in Hood's Division have always fought well. He would have none other than brave troops.

I regret to learn that the 31st Georgia, [Alexander] Lawton's Brigade, suffered very much in a gallant charge upon the enemy's batteries. Lieutenant Daniel McNair, a paroled prisoner, met some members of my company, and told them that his regiment charged the enemy several hundred yards, and that getting very near the battery, he discovered a very heavy force of infantry coming to its support. He said Lieut. Judson Butts was the only officer he saw at that time, whom he told that if they did succeed in taking the battery they would not be able to hold it. Whereupon Lieut. Butts ordered a retreat. Soon after he (Lieut. McNair) was struck by a fragment of a shell or something of the sort, which momentarily paralyzed him. He was captured, and after two days was paroled. He knew nothing of what become of the regiment after the retreat; and I have not seen any one belonging to the regiment or Brigade.

McLaws' division played a conspicuous part in the bloody drama. His post was a good one, but his list of casualties show that the men and officers of his command did their whole duty. The enemy's loss on that part of the line—Longstreet's left—is five to our one. Indeed, it must be, in killed and wounded alone, nearly or quite *ten to our one* on the whole line. Our casualties will not exceed eighteen hundred or two thousand. "Why this great difference?" you will naturally ask. I can give the noted instance which may serve to explain. When the Yankees advanced upon the center with an object of breaking our lines, they came up in *columns—massed*, while our troops were in one column, and were protected by the railroad. They advanced for two miles over the broad level field without a shrub or tree to turn a bullet or protect a man. Our best batteries and bravest cannoneers poured a storm of iron hail into their dense ranks, each well directed shot killing numbers of men. When they came within rifle range, every shot which its object took effect upon those in the rear. In this way few shots were wasted and the mortality in the enemy's ranks was appalling.

Our pickets, until forbidden by Gen. Lee, held familiar conversations with the Yankees, who came over in little batteaus to trade coffee, bacon, &c., for tobacco. They acknowledged they were badly whipped. When asked if there was a mutiny in their camps on Monday, when ordered to renew the attack, they gave evasive answers, which confirmed the report.

The Medical Corps of Hood's division deserves favorable mention for the promptitude displayed in making ample arrangements for the wounded, and their kind treatment of the unfortunate sons of Mars, who were struck by balls or bombs.

An officer of Anderson's brigade which was stationed in the old field in advance of our line of defense and to the left, asked me if "that was not Toombs' brigade which charged so beautifully across the field and made the Yankees run at the point of the bayonet, to the tune of a genuine Southern yell?" I replied that our brigade had not been engaged, although we were under fire. I supposed it was a portion of Law's brigade. "Well," said he, "it was done so pretty that I thought it was your brigade." I thanked him for his good opinion of our veteran brigade, and remarked that we always liked to close with the Yankees, who always "get further."

The army was absolutely disappointed when it was announced that Burnside had recrossed the river. But a small portion had engaged the enemy, and they felt slighted. So confident were they of totally routing the Yankees that they often said they could whip the whole Yankee nation if they would come up in front of our *impromptu* works. Gen. Hood remarked in my hearing that we could whip all the forces the enemy could bring against us.

On Tuesday morning when the whole army was alive with excitement consequent upon the enemy's retreat, a loud shout was heard away down upon our right. The shout swelled in volume and drew nearer and nearer. "What can be the cause?" was the anxious query. I strained my eyes in the direction, and soon saw a man in full gallop. I understood it then. "Jackson! Stonewall Jackson's coming! Hurrah for General Jackson!" His cap was off, and the old hero presented a fine spectacle as he galloped by with his noble, manly brow and slightly bald head exposed. In this way he rode the whole line, receiving the homage of an admiring soldiers; and, doubtless, was glad to see the road turn off from the men who loved so much to do him honor. He never appears before the army without exciting the liveliest enthusiasm. Whenever the boys begin to cheer he pulls off his cap and puts spurs to his horse as if anxious to get out of sight. None but a good man could receive the plaudits he does without becoming puffed up and vain.

The General had so completely metamorphased his *personel* by wearing an entirely new suit of Confederate grey that many failed to recognize him at first. He is really a fine looking man.

Gen. Lee is looking much better than he did last summer. He reminds one of Washington, whose virtues he possesses in an eminent degree. He is organized, quiet, kind, Christian-like, and is accessible to the humblest private in the ranks.

This morning we were in lines and started to take our position, supposing the enemy to be advancing again. The two signal guns were heard. Everybody heard them, but they were Yankees firing at one of our wagons going for forage. All quiet now as before.

V. A. S. P.

Letter from P. W. A.

RICHMOND, February 14, 1863 [2-18-63]

An attack of camp fever, contracted at Fredericksburg, has detained me from the 27th of December until the present time. Fortunately, there has been but little news of a military nature to communicate since the battle upon the banks of the Rappahannock—the brilliant but bloody *finale* of the most glorious campaign of modern times.

It is not at all probable that any offensive movement will be undertaken by either party at Fredericksburg for some time to come. The impassible condition of the roads, the difficulty of procuring and distributing supplies over said roads, the sharp, sudden changes of temperature in this latitude—the rains, the snows and chilling mists—will compel the two armies to remain stationary, or, if they move at all, it must be without artillery, and with but little baggage. And you may be sure the enemy will never engage our troops without artillery. Indeed, there would have been no fighting at all before next Spring, if McClellan had remained in command of the Federal army. It was his policy to assemble in camps the 600,000 fresh troops called out by his government, and to drill, discipline, and prepare them for the campaign of the present year. He imagined that the questionable laurels he gathered at Sharpsburg would satisfy his government and people, and enable him to carry out the very judicious plan he had formed. The political necessities of the Federal Government were most urgent, however; the military reasons against a forward movement were forced to yield to the demands of state, and the commander of the army was superseded. But he should be content with the result, since the wisdom of his policy was abundantly vindicated by the Confederate at Fredericksburg.

While it was McClellan's plan to remain in Maryland and prepare his raw troops for this year's hard work, it was General Lee's most fervent desire to fight him as soon as possible—anyhow this winter, and before the Federal recruits had learned the art of war. It being left to him to select the ground where he would receive the enemy's attack, he felt sure that his veteran troops, after their rest at Winchester, would be able to dispose of any army, however numerous, that his opponents could bring against him.

The Congress is still hammering away upon the Currency and Exemption and Impressment bills. It is doing but little good however—indeed, almost nothing to help the Cause which should engage every heart and hand in all the land. Whilst there are a few able, and many earnest men in our Supreme Legislature, it must nevertheless be conceded that as a body it is weak and inefficient, capable neither of holding up the hands of the Government, or of restraining it within legitimate bounds. The army has absorbed most of the talent and energy of the country, leaving to the people but a limited choice in the selection of their representatives.

The country is afflicted with a redundant currency; yet Congress does not act; it only debates. Every additional note issued either by the Confederate or State governments, only cheapens the value of money and increases the cost of every article of production. Why not, then, at once adopt some plan to retire, as rapidly and safely as possible, such Confederate notes as are now in circulation, in anticipation of the fresh issue now preparing at the Treasury Department? The expenses of government are frightful—owing, in part, to the abundance of money and the consequent appreciation of all other values. A pair of shoes that could have been bought for two dollars before the war, now costs the Government eight dollars. This enormous difference in prices will apply to all the beef, bacon, flour, clothing, arms, ammunition, and every other article required for the use of the army. A fact always to be remembered in the connection is, that every note issued by the Government to meet this vast expenditure, will have to be redeemed at some future day with gold or its equivalent! It is impossible to reduce prices to their former standard so long as the blockade remains in force— even if our inflated currency consisted entirely of specie; yet the adoption immediately of a sound financial system would bring great and instant relief to the country. If taxation be a necessary part of such a system, then let taxation be resorted to. If the man who has on hand $100,000 in Confederate notes, were required to pay $20,000 of it in taxes, (and all others were called on to pay in like proportion) his remaining $80,000 would be worth almost as much, and would buy almost as much, as the original sum of $100,000; just as an ascertained crop of 3,000,000 bales of cotton would, in times of peace, sell for nearly, if not quite, as much money as a crop of 4,000,000 bales.

The solution of the Impressment question is both easy and simple. The property of the citizen should never be seized for public use without just compensation; nor should it ever be taken except in strict accordance with law, and by officers of discretion appointed for that purpose. The property of alien enemies cannot be sequestrated except by law, and why should the property of loyal citizens be treated differently?

In regards to exemptions from military duty, the whole question, like the last, lies in a nutshell. The Government's entitled to the service of every able bodied man in the country, whatever his age may be. If, however, the public welfare require that a portion of the arms bearing population be left at home, then let such as fall under this head be exempted by law. The public good is the only true standard by which to determine the matter, and to that alone the Congress should look. There are certain able bodied men whose services are worth more at home than in the field. Such men, whether rich or poor, whether mechanics, overseers, or planters, should be exempted from military duty—not as a favor to them, but because they can do more for the Cause at home than they could in the army.

There are only two classes now in the country—the fighting class and the producing class. The former, which constitutes the army, must be fed, clothed and shod, and men enough to do so must be left at home, with the help of patriotic women, to perform this necessary work, and to control and govern our slave population, and keep the machinery of the State governments in operation. It may be that the producer, the manufacturer and shoemaker, no less than the speculator and extortioner, have ground the face of the poor and plundered the Government; but if, in consequence of the blockade and the nature of our social system, the public will require that they, or any part of them, be left at home, then, however disagreeable it may be to the feelings of every patriotic heart, they should be suffered to stay where they are. When the war is over, and the men who have achieved our liberties shall have returned to their homes, then let a brand be set upon their ignoble foreheads, and the scorn of the brave and just heaped upon them and their ill got wealth.

The questions alluded to here all call for early action, and yet members stand day after day debating these and other matters, without coming to a resolution. Their duty is plain; yet a month has elapsed, and nothing has been done. The regular Congressional elections are next fall, and there are not wanting persons who are uncharitable enough to believe that some members are more interested in that event than the legislation before them.

What a time to think of self, when a Country is at stake, and Liberty itself trembles in the balance!

P. W. A.

With both armies inactive and settled in winter camp along the Rappahannock, Alexander travels elsewhere to find war news. Rumors were that a Federal attack on Charleston Harbor was planned.

P. W. A. in Charleston

CHARLESTON, S. C., March 2, 1863 [3-4-63]

There being no prospect of any more fighting in Virginia before May, I decided to visit this city and Savannah, in anticipation of the attack which it is believed will soon be made by the formidable Federal armada now on the coast. The latest intelligence in military circles here would indicate that your city is to be the first to receive the shock. In view of this probability, permit me to say, the opinion has obtained wide circulation, in some way or other, that neither Charleston nor Savannah will be allowed to fall into the hands of the enemy. It is believed that the troops and citizens have resolved to defend them literally to the last ditch, and to dispute the possession of them street by street, even though every street should be made to run with blood of the brave, and the last house should be given to the flames. Is such your resolution? The country looks for a noble example of heroism—an exhibition of dauntless courage and unselfish patriotism that shall fire the hearts of the people and set the land in a blaze.

Such appears to be the fixed determination of the people here. Whilst they hope the thunderbolt will not fall upon their city, nor upon yours, they seem to have made up their minds that it were better to imitate the Russians at Moscow than the Confederates at New Orleans. A heap of ashes, is better than a city in chains, and liberty and poverty better than slavery and riches. But the destruction of Charleston and Savannah will not become necessary so long as the people are animated by this high resolve. A people determined never to yield is seldom ever conquered, or driven by dire necessity to apply the torch to their own houses.

We have but little news here which it would be proper to communicate. The strength of our works and the disposition and number of our forces are of course contraband topics, and there is but little else at this time to write about. The blockading fleet hovers off the bar just within sight from the city. Fifteen vessels, it is said, were counted in the offing this morning. Though they are strung along in close proximity to each other, a daring, sharp-eyed craft will now and then elude them, and pass in and out without their knowledge. Two vessels of this description arrived here in safety yesterday morning, with valuable cargoes on board. If the enemy's ships could come to anchor nearer the bar, where the channel is narrow, they would be able effectually to close the port; but, unfortunately for them and fortunately for us, the sand is so loose in the vicinity of the bar that the anchors will not take hold; and hence the fleet has to seek anchorage further out.

P. W. A.

CHARLESTON, March 6, 1863 [3-10-63]

There is no change to report in the position of affairs in the vicinity of Charleston. The Federal blockaders still hover off the bar in the vain hope of closing this splendid gateway to the Confederate States. They must have a dreary time of it with the winds and water and might possibly be able to answer them in the song:

"What are the wild waves saying?"

Their black funnels and sharp tapering masts are distinctly outlined against the eastern sky; and now and then a vessel is seen to approach and disappear; but beyond this their labors would seem to be as monotonous and lonely as they are fruitless. It may be that they have instructions not to interfere with our export of cotton, since every bale that reaches England is bread and meat to her suffering operatives, and to that extent is an argument in favor of British neutrality. There is no reason to believe, however, as has been suggested, that there has been any unauthorized contrivance at our commercial adventures on the part of the officers of the Federal fleet, as, in that event, Capt. [D. N.] Ingraham would hardly have "pitched" into them so unceremoniously as he did some weeks ago.

Our southern railways are beginning to feel the wear and tear of the war to an extent that must give rise to serious apprehensions for the future. The locomotives and rolling stock, as well as the rails on many of the roads, are fast wearing out, and but little effort is being made in any quarter to replace them. So far has this deterioration proceeded, that it has been found necessary to adopt a new schedule on the lines between Richmond and Montgomery; the object of which is to reduce the rate of speed and allow more time for the trains to make connections. The change, while it lessens the speed and increases the time, will render the connections more certain, and thereby really expedite both travel and the mails.

You will remember that the attention of railway companies and the government was called to this subject, nearly a year ago, in one of my letters from the West. The evil has been allowed to continue, however, and now the roads are barely able to do the transportation of the government. What will be their condition a year hence? Iron bars and iron locomotives, like human hearts and muscles, will wear out in the course of time. If something be not done soon the enemy, whose means of transportation are abundant both by land and water, will have greatly the advantage of us in the rapid movements of troops.

The roads in Georgia have not been so heavily taxed as those in other States, and are therefore in comparatively good condition. In this, as in her freedom from invasion, the State has been singularly fortunate. The Charleston and Savannah road, and the Charleston and North-eastern road, were just completed when the war broke out, and with certain lateral lines in other States, are in good condition; but with these exceptions, the condition of the railroads in the Confederate States is of a character to excite the serious concern, and call for prompt action, both of the government and the people.

If some other plan should not be adopted, it may become necessary for the companies owning the lines chiefly used by the government, to buy the iron, locomotives and cars on the branch roads, in order to repair their tracks and keep up their rolling stock. The government itself may intervene, and require the parties to come into such an arrangement.

P. W. A.

CHARLESTON, March 10, 1863 [3-11-63]

It is not probable that the enemy will abandon the Southern coast without making an attack upon Charleston or Savannah. Their expenditures of money have been too heavy, and their preparations too elaborate to admit of such a supposition.

There is good reason, doubtless, for the hesitation which has characterized the movements of Gen. [David] Hunter. First, his differences with Gen. [John] Foster, as to the command of the Federal army, and next, the reports of spies and deserters as to the strength and character of our defenses, have almost certainly operated to produce the delay. It is understood that there are five iron-clad vessels of the Monitor class now on the coast. These, it was feared, would not be sufficient to effect the reduction of either city, and three others— some say four—were sent for. It is the arrival of the additional Iron monsters that the enemy are waiting. One or two of them are reported to be now on the way to Port Royal.

Five of these Monitors—the number understood to be now on the coast—would be quite sufficient to protect the water base of any movement by land. Indeed, the wooden gunboats and other vessels of war now blockading this harbor, would be equal to that service. Why, then, should the enemy be waiting for additional iron-clads? There can be but one answer to this question: Their purpose is to operate by water. If Charleston is the point at which they are aiming, then they will enter the harbor and engage the ports and batteries by which it is defended. They may even hope that the iron armor with which their vessels are protected, will enable them to run the gauntlet of the forts, and reach the city, as they did at New Orleans, and with like results.

But this is mere speculation, founded upon imperfect information, which a few days may suffice to dissipate. It may be, too, that no attack will be made upon Charleston or Savannah, and that Wilmington or Mobile is the destination of the Federal fleet. The possession of either one of these cities would be a greater advantage to the enemy, and a heavier blow to us than the fall of both Savannah and Charleston. Indeed, the capture of these latter cities would be a positive disadvantage to the enemy, except in that it would enable them more effectually to close their ports.

P. W. A.

CHARLESTON, April 6, 1863 [4-10-63]

I sent you a telegram to-night to the effect that all was quiet here, but that it could not remain so long, and that the public mind was in a state of intense suspense. For military reasons, it was deemed unadvisable to telegraph, in detail, the actual condition of affairs, lest the intelligence should be sent over the wires to Virginia, where it would not be long in finding its way to Norfolk, and thence to Fortress Monroe, where the enemy has a considerable fleet. If it be a part of the enemy's plans to reinforce Charleston, or to undertake a co-operative movement at more than one point on our coast, nothing would please him more than information of the progress of affairs here. The same reasons do not apply to a correspondence by mail, since the express boats of the enemy, one of which is sent to Fortress Monroe, every day or two, would carry the intelligence northward sooner than our railroads could take it. Upon my arrival here to-day, I found the military authorities and the people perfectly calm and confident. A few ladies had left town, and all classes manifested deep interest in the state of affairs; but beyond this, the people continued to prosecute their usual avocations with wonderful composure, and as if the most imposing armada the world has ever seen, was not hovering off their city.

When Hannibal's legions had overrun Italy and were thundering at the very gates of Rome, the land on which his men were encamped was sold at the Forum within the walls at undiminished prices. No Roman citizen allowed his action to be swayed for a moment from the undying confidence that a foreign conqueror, no matter how far he had succeeded in penetrating into the country, could ever seize and keep the soil of a people who had resolutely determined, for themselves and their posterity, not to be slaves. Charleston has now to confront a danger as great and as near to her doors as Rome did then, and she does it with a confidence as unshaken as that which animated the haughty conquerors of the old world. And her women, too, like those of Aquileid, are ready, if necessary, to surrender their sunny tresses to make ropes for the military engines.

As you have already heard, a large number of vessels of various size appeared off the bar yesterday. At once it was thought the attack might be made last night, as the moon was shining brightly, and if not, that it would probably be made this morning at high tide, which was about 9 o'clock. But the night and the day have passed away, and with them the tide which was to bring the armada to the gates of the city. The enemy contented himself, however, with sending five iron clads over the bar in the afternoon, as if to commence the assault, but after moving about in a singular manner for some time, they returned to their former anchorage. Gen. [Roswell] Ripley, who was in Fort Sumter at the time they came inside the bar, hoisted all the bunting in the Fort, and gave them a national salute, both with his guns and his flags, by way of expressing his gratification, I suppose, at their appearance.

At sunset this evening there were eight turreted Monitors, the [New] *Ironsides*, man-of-war, and thirty-four transports in Stono river, southeast of the city. Six thousand troops had been landed on Cole's Island, due south from and near Morris' Island, up to last night, it is supposed the enemy was engaged in debarking men and landing ammunition until day light this morning. Cole's and Goat's Island, which are small and beyond the reach of our guns, have probably been selected as depots of provisions and ammunition, and possibly with the hope that the enemy, by means of pontoons, might reach Morris' and James' Islands. It is not believed, however, that he can lay his bridge across to those islands, not that he would be able to accomplish anything if he were to do so. Two Monitors crossed ship bar to the southward of Morris' Island Point late this afternoon.

April 7th, 9 A. M. The enemy's fleet continues a position just beyond the bar. No change at other points as far as reported. Sunday next is the anniversary of the Battle of Fort Sumter, and possibly the enemy are waiting for that day to "wipe out" the disgrace put upon their flag two years ago.

P. W. A.

CHARLESTON, April 7, 1863 [4-8-63]

The day of trial and blood to Charleston has at last arrived, and the blow so long impending over the goodly city, like the sword of Damocles, has at length fallen. It has taken no one by surprise however, and especially the military authorities. Gen. Beauregard had received information some days ago, from a source and by means which must for the present be nameless, that the attack would probably be made to-day, and to-day it has been made. Having already sent you a full statement of the affair by telegraph, there is but little left me to add.

It was observed at half-past 2 P.M. that the Federal fleet, which had been lying off the bar since Sunday afternoon, was approaching in hostile array. Eight turreted iron-clads and the famous iron covered war steamer *Ironsides* were put in motion and advanced to the assault by what is known as "Ship Channel." Gen. Beauregard, whose headquarters are in the city, was promptly notified of the movement by telegraph from Fort Sumter. It may be stated that there are wires running from all the forts and batteries in and around the harbor to the city, and that telegraphic communication is frequent and expeditious between the forts and batteries, as well as with Charleston.

The *Ironsides* and five of the Monitors participated in the engagement. Fort Moultrie was the first to open fire, at five minutes past 3 o'clock. The double-turreted *Keokuk*—the most formidable vessel of the Federal armada—quickly responded. Fort Sumter took up the tale, and poured a broadside into the assailing squadron, and she was followed in turn by Fort Beauregard and Battery Bee, on Sullivan's Island, and Fort Wagner and Cummings' Point Battery, on Morris Island. In a few minutes the battle became general and the cannonading terrific. The iron-clads had entered the outer circle of fire, and from every fort and battery by which the outer harbor is girdled they were assailed with great ardor and coolness. The conduct of the enemy was equally spirited, and his fire deliberate and well directed. The principal attack was directed against Sumter, though all the forts and batteries came in for a share of the enemy's attention. But one shot, as far as I could see, passed over Sumter. The *Ironsides* threw monster shells, which burst over and around the fort without precision.

The *Keokuk* led the attack, and took the post of danger and of honor. And dearly did she pay for the distinction, as will be seen in the sequel. About forty-five minutes after the engagement commenced, a shot from Fort Wagner took effect in the stern of the *Ironsides*. It is believed she was also penetrated in the side, as steam could be distinctly seen issuing from her side next to the city. She soon withdrew out of range of our guns, and for the remainder of the time was a silent spectator of the conflict. This was a great triumph, as she was manifestly looked to, to test the strength of Fort Sumter. About five o'clock the *Keokuk* also withdrew, evidently badly injured. The others followed soon, and by half past five the entire fleet had retired, and when last seen was rounding Morris Island to the southward.

The practice of our gunners, after they got the range, was excellent. The enemy's vessels, (which were sunk by pumping water until the decks were nearly level with the water,) were frequently struck, and nearly all their smokestacks were perforated. This too, not withstanding they kept shifting their positions. Occasionally they would steam up within 1,000 yards of Sumter, but for the greater part of the time they maintained the fight at a distance of 1,500 to 2,000 yards. Late in the evening the *Ironsides* and three monitors were seen moving off slowly around Morris Island, as if they might be going to Port Royal for repairs.

The casualties on our side were slight, considering the nature of the conflict and the monster projectiles used by the enemy. In Fort Sumter, a drummer boy and five men were wounded, two of the men and the boy seriously. One 10-inch Columbiad was dismounted, and one 8-inch was bursted. The former will be remounted to-night. The Fort was struck 34 times, and the flag had a hole shot through it. No casualties occurred on Sullivan's Island, except the shooting away of the flagstaff and the accidental fall of a man who was trying to replace it, and from which he died soon afterwards. On Morris Island (at Fort Wagner,) six men were wounded by the accidental explosion of an ammunition chest, two of whom have since died. Two others are badly injured and will probably die before morning.

The conflict was witnessed by thousands of spectators from the Battery promenade and from the housetops. Among the vast throng there assembled I did not encounter one who expressed any doubt as to the result. It was a magnificent spectacle. The white puffs of smoke issuing from the port holes of the iron-clads with a tongue of fire in the center, the solemn waltz kept up by these huge monsters as they wheeled past the forts, the fantastic festoons of smoke that garlanded the heads of the forts and slowly floated off to the north, the bursting of 15-inch shells in mid-air and the deep booming of the titanic guns engaged in the conflict, the appearance of the Confederate rams *Chicora* and *Palmetto State* steaming energetically up and down their chosen fighting position, the silent city, and the breathless multitude who crowded its house tops and promenade, made up a spectacle at once grand and imposing.

But it is long after midnight, and I must cease.

P. W. A.

CHARLESTON, April 13, 1863 [4-15-63]

My telegraphic dispatch of last night informed your readers of the withdrawal of the Federal armada, and the abandonment of the siege of Charleston by the enemy. The movement has taken all classes here, civil and military, by surprise and many intelligent people, unable to account for it, still refuse to accept the general interpretation—viz: that the boasted iron-clads have retreated because they were too much disabled to renew the fight. They cannot understand how the most formidable fleet the world has ever seen, should abandon the contest and acknowledge itself beaten after a conflict of a little over two hours' duration. The foe had done all that science could suggest or ingenuity invent to render the attack successful. He had lavished 1 millions of money and a vast amount of labor upon the nondescript marine monsters that were to cover our flag with dishonor and reduce our homes to ashes. He had provided himself with a fleet formidable not only in numbers and the metallic armor in which it was incased, but in the enormous calibre of his guns and the novel and destructive character of his projectiles. He came boasting like Goliah, rejoicing in his "helmet of brass" and "coat of mail," and like Goliah he has been befelled and overthrown.

The result was expected, but it was believed that the contest would have been more prolonged, more desperate and bloody, and that our own loss would have been greater. If, however, we could examine the returns sent up to Admiral [Samuel] Dupont by the commanders of the iron-clads the night after the battle; if we could inspect the condition of his battered vessels and their crews, and read the dispatch which he immediately forwarded to Fortress Monroe for his government, we might readily understand the reasons why he retired from the conflict. It has frequently happened during this war that we inflicted a heavier loss upon our enemies than we were aware of at the time. This was particularly the case at the first battle of Manassas, at Shiloh and Fredericksburg, and it is venturing but little to affirm that the same thing will be found to be true in regard to the battle in Charleston harbor. The battle was short and sharp, but it was also terrific while it lasted. The enemy had entered only the first circle of fire; yet not less than a hundred well served guns poured rapid shot upon his devoted iron-clads; had he reached Fort Sumter he would have encountered a second more formidable circle, whilst still another lay between him and the city which, had he passed the other two, would almost certainly have proved fatal to his hopes.

At the time of the departure of the fleet yesterday afternoon, it was observed that the *New Ironsides* had careened considerably to one side, and that she set higher on the water than on the day of the battle, as if a portion of her armament had been removed. Her pumps had been kept in continuous motion since the battle, and a steam flat with a derrick on board was seen near her several times. The men were engaged all day in passing out something having the appearance of buckets or boxes. It is not unlikely that the enemy had expected to pass Fort Sumter, and that an extra supply of ammunition for the monitors had been placed on board of her to be used when they got inside. The *Ironsides* was towed outside the bar to her former anchorage, where she now remains as the flagship of the blockading squadron.

About the same time the six monitors crossed the bar, three of them being in tow of other vessels. The crew of one of them was transferred to the blockading steamer *James Adger*, and the crew of another to the blockader *Powhatten*, when both vessels steamed off in the direction of Port Royal with the two iron-clads in tow. Another iron-clad was also towed off, followed by the three Monitors which were able to get off without assistance. Twenty-four transports left the mouth of the Stono about the same time, and when last seen were going towards Port Royal. This evening only six remained behind. The steam derrick alluded to was observed to be along side of the three Monitors towed off repeatedly during the morning. Fewer blockaders were in sight at sunset yesterday than at any other time for several weeks, and hence it is inferred that it was important to remove the disabled iron-clads last night. Forts Sumter and Moultrie bade the ugly creatures adieu by firing a parting salute as they passed over the bar.

But why have these vaunted war dogs retired from the conflict, which they had so eagerly fought for? The answer may be read in the facts detailed above, and which have reached me to-day from an entirely trustworthy source. The truth is, the turretted iron-clads have been proven to be a failure. The demonstrations of this fact was begun at Fort McAllister, and has been completed at Charleston. The want of proper ventilation, the concussion produced by their own guns, and especially the pluck and excellent practice of our artillerists have shown that brick and mortar, as well as earthworks, are more than a match for them. Admiral Dupont was not far wrong when he said, as reported by a Federal correspondent, that "Ericsson, when he built the iron-clads should also have invented iron men to fight them."

Once again the star of Beauregard is in the ascendant. It was on these classic shores two years ago to-day that Fortune, stooping from the skies, first placed upon his brow the laurel wreath of Victory; and now he returns to celebrate the anniversary with a triumph still more glorious to himself, to the brave army which he leads, and the country which he serves. But let us not forget in the hour of rejoicing that there are others who are entitled to the gratitude of the country. To no one are we more indebted for the success of our arms than to the brave and energetic Ripley, to whom was confided the defences of the harbor. How well he has performed his work may be seen in the victory which now crowns our standard and fills all hearts with joy. To the gallant officers and men in gray old Moultrie and Sumter, and on Morris Island and Sullivan's Island, should we also accord the meed of our praise and admiration. They fought a good fight, and their deeds will be embalmed in the hearts of their countrymen.

It is very rough outside to-night, and the *New Ironsides* may yet find her way to the bottom. The steamer *Beauregard* arrived here yesterday morning, with a valuable cargo, including two Blakely guns, mainly for the government. The *Stonewall Jackson*, Capt. Black, after receiving three shots in her hull, was run ashore Saturday night through a mistake of her pilot, who failed to make the necessary allowance for the high rate of speed at which she was going, and burnt, otherwise she would have got in safely. Her cargo was very valuable, including 40,000 pairs of shoes.

P. W. A.

More Special Correspondence from V. A. S. P.

FREDERICK HALL, VA., May 11, 1863 [5-19-63]

At 4 P.M. on the 6th, the date of my last letter, the brigade took the train for Petersburg, where we arrived about sunset in a drenching rain. By the time we reached camps, two miles north of the city, it was dark and disagreeable enough, for the pitiless rain continued to pour down in torrents until 10 o'clock. The next day we marched to our old camps three and a half miles south of Richmond.

While at Ivor Station, Sidney C. Shivers of company K, was seized with several very severe fits or convulsions—epilepsy—which soon deprived him of consciousness, and lasted for hours. Our kind-hearted Assistant Surgeon, Dr. J. T. Palmer, did everything in his power to save his life, and succeeded in creating an artificial respiration. At Petersburg he took Shivers to the Ladies' Hospital, superintended by Mr. P. D. Woodhouse. The hospital is intended for officers. Dr. Palmer being a stranger, and unacquainted with the localities of the general hospitals asked Woodhouse to take Shivers in for the night, promising to remove him early next morning to some other hospital; but Woodhouse would not give him even this temporary shelter from the cruel rain! He said the hospital was intended only for officers, and that his orders would not allow him to take Shivers in even for one night. Dr. Palmer then asked permission to lay Sidney in the passage, but no, be could not do that even! "Well," said Dr. Palmer, "you prefer then to let a man dying with epilepsy lie out in this pitiless storm!" "I cannot help it," was his heartless reply, "it is against orders!"

Sidney C. Shivers, a noble young man, of good family connections, did die! Any common rake with gingerbread work on his sleeves, and bars on his collar, because he happens to hold a commission, would not have been turned away. Enlightened public opinion will condemn such *charity!*

Leaving Richmond at sunrise Friday morning, 8th instant, Gen. Hood's division reached Frederick Hall in Louisa county, yesterday by 1 p.m.—making a distance of fifty-five miles the way we came. The bridge across the South Anna being burned, we had to make a bridge detour to the left on Saturday. The country passed through is by far the prettiest of Virginia we have seen. The beautiful residences, the extensive plantations, capacious barns, and waving fields of grain argue a wealthy, prosperous and highly cultivated region.

To this division was assigned the duty of driving out Gen. [George] Stoneman's formidable cavalry force, said to number ten thousand. But Stoneman was here, because he could not be elsewhere. [Maj. Gen. Joseph] Hooker's defeat and the possessions of the upper fords by Stuart's cavalry, forced him to remain for a short time in this region. He has found a way of escape, and ere we reached here, had gone. I hear something of a cavalry fight near Gordonsville, but the reports are so meagre and uncertain that I will not attempt a recital. Citizens report that the Yankees were in such a strait that they tried to swap their blue coats to negroes in order to facilitate their escape.

Gen. Lee's victory was complete. It was wanting in nothing. He has registered over seven thousand prisoners, and states that he captured more small arms than have been taken in any previous battle of the war. The disappointed Yankees have raised a howl of despair. Joe Hooker is an imbecile—a brainless braggadocia, and ought to be hung for his blunders! On the other hand, our papers give Hooker credit for fighting well, and say he has done better than any general who has fought us. His plan was a masterly one, but was not deep enough to overthrow our great Captain.

In the absence of interesting news your readers may be entertained by the relation of two or three rich anecdotes. I will make the venture at any rate.

Col. C****, commanding brigade upon a certain march in February, made his headquarters at a wealthy citizen's house, and ordered rooms, entertainment, &c., for himself and staff. The proprietor, his wife and daughters were all attention, doing everything in their power to entertain their honored guests, feeling flattered by the presence of such distinguished visitants. In the course of the evening the conversation turned exclusively upon literary subjects. The eldest daughter, cheered by the distinguished consideration shone her family, put on her best looks, her pretty face beaming with the sweetest smiles, assumed the pleasing task of entertaining the Colonel.

"Well, Colonel," asked his fair entertainer, "how do you like Shakespeare's plays?"

"Oh, delightful, delightful!" said the Colonel. "I think they are incomparable. I have read them all several times, and have had the double advantage and pleasure of seeing them enacted upon the stage by the best actors in America."

"Indeed!" ejaculated the lady, whose opinion of the Colonel's erudition was considerably raised; "Which piece do you like best?"

"Oh! Romeo and Pocahontas, Madame!" "Very beautiful, indeed!" (Exit lady in paroxysm of laughter.)

A good story is told upon Major [John E.] Rylander. When his battalion joined Gen. Anderson's brigade, he loved to show off their perfection in the drill, and had them out very often. Large crowds from the other regiments collected to witness the performance, and out of a spirit of mischief would tease the Major by hollowing "hurrah for Maj. Laplander! That's a good maneuver for Maj. Lowlander! Wheel 'em again, Maj. Greenlander!" The Major feeling himself aggrieved, made complaint to Gen. Anderson.

"General," said the Major, "I wish you would make your men quit calling me Laplander, Lowlander and Greenlander. It is very disagreeable."

"Look here, Major," said the General, and turning his grey eyes upon the Major like he was going to look clear through him, "Are you any better than I am?"

"No, no! of course not, General."

"They call me '*Old Tige*' and I don't get mad about it. I can't stop their fun, and don't mean to try!"

The Major went away looking like he wished he had not made the complaint.

Among other good camp jokes is one told on the band of the 20th Georgia. In Gatesville they serenaded several families, who gave them good things to eat and drink. At one place in lieu of brandy and wine, butter milk was sent out, and was drunk by the boys of the Seventeenth! They are now known as the "*Butter Milk Band!*" This new *sobriquet* teases them no little.

The army and nation are shrouded in deep mourning on account of the sad intelligence of Gen. "Stonewall" Jackson's death. How heavily has the hand of affliction been laid upon this infant Republic! How are the mighty fallen!

A great calamity has befallen us. But God's will be done! He will rise up another Gideon to do battle for us! The defeat of our army would not have cast a deeper gloom over our army and people, than the death of this incomparable leader and great Christian soldier. He was a host within himself. He was not less a Christian than a soldier.

Whilst we are bowed in mourning our infamous foe will soon send up a shout of fiendish delight! Their greatest terror is now removed by death!

May the God of Battles, the God of Right and Justice succor us in this dark hour of affliction!

V. A. S. P.

Jackson's loss was felt keenly throughout the South; the following newspaper clipping was found among Alexander's papers.

The Last Days of General Stonewall Jackson [5-22-63]

The *Central Presbyterian*, whose editor had peculiar means of obtaining correct information, gives the following narrative of the closing scenes in the life of the great and good Jackson:

The secular papers have already conveyed to most of our readers the sad intelligence of the death of this brave and beloved man, which took place on Sunday, the 10th inst., at the house of Mr. Chandler, near Guinea's Station. The blow is so heavy and stunning that we have not the heart to dwell upon it, or to give him the tribute which his memory deserves. A braver, better man has never laid his life on the alter of human liberty, and his death, as far as a man can see, is an irreparable loss. His high religious character, his courage, skill, rapidity of motion, and marvelous success, had given him a hold on the army such as no other man had, and it was felt that his very name was a symbol of victory. There was no man who inspired the enemy with so much terror, or for whom they had in their secret hearts a more unbounded respect.

But it may be that we had begun to rely on his great name instead of that of the Lord our God, and to teach us the lesson of absolute reliance on himself, God has removed our beloved and idolized General. We cannot now attempt to fathom this great sorrow, or interpret its meaning, but we know that it is right, and we bow in silent and sad submission.

The immediate cause of death was pneumonia, which his system, prostrated by the wounds and amputation, was unable to cast off. And it is a characteristic fact that the cold which issued in this pneumonia was contracted by his unselfish anxiety for the health of some young members of his staff. The night before the battle was spent on the field, and having no extra covering at all, after great urgency, he accepted the cape of one of his aids, but in a short time arose and gently laid it over the young man, and spent the night just as he was. This exposure produced a cold which ended in pneumonia.

A few nights before this battle an equally characteristic incident occurred that is worthy of record. He was discussing with one of his aids the possibility and issue of a battle, when he became unusually excited. After talking it over fully, he paused and with deep humility and reverence said, "My trust is in God," then as if the sound of battle was in his ear, he raised himself to his tallest stature, and with flashing eyes and a face all blazoned with the fire of conflict, he exclaimed, "I wish they would come." This humble trust in God, combined with the spirit of the war-horse whose neck is "clothed in thunder," and who "smelleth the battle afar off, the thunder of the captains and the shouting," made that rare and lofty type of martial prowess that has shrined Jackson among the great heroes of the world. Trust in God and eagerness for the fray were two of the great elements of that marvelous success that seemed to follow him like a star, so that he was never defeated, or failed in anything that he undertook.

After he was wounded he retained his cheerfulness and remarked to a friend the pleasurableness of the sensation in taking chloroform; stating that he was conscious of everything that was done to him, that the sawing of his bone sounded to him like the sweetest music, and every sensation was one of delight.

Conversing with an aid he pointed to his mutilated arm and said, "Many people would regard this as a great misfortune, I regard it as one of the greatest blessings of my life." Mr. S. remarked, "All things work together for good, to those that love God." "Yes, yes," he emphatically said, "that's it, that's it."

When General Lee wrote him that beautiful note, so characteristic of his own generosity and worth:

"*General:*—I have just received your note informing me that you were wounded. I cannot express my regret at the occurrence. Could I have dictated events, I should have chosen for the good of the country to have been disabled in your stead."

"I congratulate you upon the victory which is due to your skill and energy."

After hearing it read he said with his usual modesty and reverence, "General Lee should give all the glory to God." He always seemed jealous for the glory of his Saviour.

When it was told him that Gen. Stuart led his old Stonewall Brigade to the charge with the watchword, "charge and remember Jackson," and that inspired by this they made so brilliant and resistless an onset, he was deeply moved; and said, "it was just like them. They are a noble body of men." He was deeply affected by Gen. [E. F.] Paxton's death.

His mind ran very much on the Bible and religious topics. He inquired of Lieut. S. [J. P. Smith], a Theological student on his Staff, whether they had ever debated in the Seminary the question, whether those who were miraculously [cured] by Jesus ever had a return of the disease. "I do not think," he said, "they could have returned, for the power was too great. The poor paralytic would never again shake with palsy. Oh! for infinite power!"

He endeavored to cheer those who were around him. Noticing the sadness of his beloved wife, he said to her tenderly, "I know you would gladly give your life for me, but I am perfectly resigned. Do not be sad—I hope I shall recover. Pray for me, but always remember in your prayer to use the petition, thy will be done." Those who were around him noticed a remarkable development of tenderness in his manner and feelings during his illness, that was a beautiful mellowing of that iron sternness and imperturbable calm that characterized him in his military operations. Advising his wife, in the event of his death, to return to her father's house, he remarked, "You have a kind and good father. But there is no one so kind and good as your Heavenly Father." When she told him that the doctors did not think he could live two hours, although he did not himself expect to die, he replied, "It will be infinite gain to be translated to Heaven, and be with Jesus." He then said he had much to say to her, but was too weak.

He had always desired to die, if it were God's will, on the Sabbath, and seemed to greet its light that day with peculiar pleasure, saying, with evident delight, "it is the Lord's day," and inquired anxiously what provision had been made for preaching to the army; and having ascertained that arrangements were made, he was contented. Delirium, which occasionally manifested itself during the last two days, prevented some of the utterances of his faith which would otherwise have doubtless been made. His thoughts vibrated between religious subjects and the battlefield, now asking some question about the Bible, or church history, and then giving an order, "Pass the infantry to the front," "Tell Major Hawks to send forward provisions to the men. Let us cross over the river and rest under the shade of the trees," until at last his gallant spirit gently passed over the dark river, and entered on its rest where the tree of life is blossoming beside the crystal river, in the better country.

Thus has passed away, the high souled, heroic man, falling like Sidney and Hampden in the beginning of the struggle to which his life was devoted, bequeathing to those who survive him a name and memory that under God may compensate for his early, and to us apparently, untimely fall. A little child of the family, when the hero was dying, was taunted with Jackson's wound by some of the prisoners who were collected there, awaiting transportation. "We have a hundred Jackson's left if he does die," was the heroic reply of the child. And so we trust it will be. The spirit of Jackson will be breathed into a thousand hearts which will emulate his bravery, and seek to make up for his loss, and in the end his memory and glory, his holy life, his manly piety, and his glorious death may be a richer blessing to us than if his life had been spared. He has shown the way to victory; and we trust that many a gallant spirit will come forward eagerly to tread it, and that our dead hero shall be worth to us more than a host of living ones. It will be if we copy his piety as well as his bravery, and like him cherish that feeling that he so strikingly expressed as he paced his tent before the battle. "My trust is in God—I wish they would come on."

Having missed the battle of Chancellorsville, Alexander returned to the Army of Northern Virginia in time to witness its high water mark.

"P. W. A." En Route to Gen. Lee's Headquarters

RICHMOND, VA., May 25, 1863 [5-28-63]

As the accounts heretofore published of the late battles on the Rappahannock were partial and disjointed, I had intended to devote my first letter from Virginia to a full and connected narrative of the operations which culminated in the glorious victories of Chancellorsville and Fredericksburg. But I find it impossible to prepare such an account here, without accepting in all cases the statements of others, and shall therefore have to postpone the work until my arrival at Fredericksburg, whether I shall proceed as soon as I can provide myself with a horse and an outfit for the campaign. Almost any kind of horse is selling here for eight hundred dollars, and a horse, saddle, bridle, blanket and saddle bags cannot be had for much less than one thousand dollars. This horse and outfit one is compelled to sell at the close of the summer's campaign for about one half of their original cost, or else remain here and take care of them himself through the winter months.

There are certain facts, however, connected with the late battles in the vicinity of Fredericksburg which have not appeared in print and which, if it were not improper to publish them, would still further increase our admiration for the peerless chieftain and the unconquerable army who have carried the Southern Cross victoriously through the fight. The enemy pretend that Gen. Lee was surprised by the suddenness and secrecy of their movement, and certain New York papers even, claim that the Federal commander had obtained exact information as to the position and strength of our forces before he crossed the Rappahannock. They assert (which is true,) that Longstreet was absent with two or more divisions of his *corps d'armee*, and that other forces, including artillery, cavalry and infantry, were not in a position to participate in the fight. The precise number of muskets which Gen. Lee had within reach, and which these voracious abolition organs affect to have obtained from the most authentic sources, was just 49,800, whilst the Federal forces are admitted to have exceeded 150,000 men.

Conceding the correctness of these figures, how should our hearts swell with gratitude and admiration when we reflect that our brave brothers in arms attacked three times their numbers of Federal troops, upon their own chosen ground and behind elaborate field works, and beat them and drove them back to the north bank of the Rappahannock, from whence they had come as boastful as Goliah. One is at a loss which to admire the more, the genius of our great Captain who instantly penetrated the designs of the enemy, hurled his small band first against one of his wings, and then against the other, and routed and defeated him in detail before he could concentrate his immense army; or the valor and endurance of the invincible veterans who bore him on their breasts to victory and to glory. We may well give thanks to Almighty God for such a leader and for such an army.

Could that spirit of flame, the immortal Jackson, have survived the field he had done so much to win, then there had been little left us to desire. His loss, while it fills every Southern heart with bitterest grief, may well be accepted by the North as a full equivalent for their ignominious defeat. When Mrs. Jackson reached Gen. Lee's headquarters in search of her wounded husband, she is said to have remarked: "I am told that Gen. Jackson has lost his left arm." "Yes, madam," was Gen. Lee's reply; "and I have lost my right." What a just and touching tribute to the then suffering, and now dead hero!

But Jackson's death is said to be not the only regretful thing in connection with the battle. I am informed by an officer of engineers that if Gen. Lee had possessed accurate information in regard to the approaches to the United States ford, he might have intercepted the retreat of the right wing of the Federal army, and captured or destroyed a large portion of it. The country in the vicinity of the ford, and especially that part of it known as the Wilderness, is intersected by numberless roads, many of which lead in the direction of the ford and unites a short distance from it. The river at this point is bounded on both sides by high rocky bluffs, between which and the water the road passes down some distance to the ford below and then up to the opposite point on the north bank. There was only one road by which Gen. Lee could hope to advance and cut off the retreat of the flying foe, as he passed between these overhanging bluffs, and that road was nowhere laid down on the maps, furnished him by his engineers! When Gen. Lee discovered, too late, that there was just such a road as he desired, you may well believe that, mild as he is, he gave the delinquent engineer who had been charged with the operations in that vicinity, "a regular blowing up." It was a similar error that prevented Beauregard, just one year ago, from getting his army into position to attack Halleck near Corinth, and which prevented him, as I have always believed, from achieving a signal victory.

It is currently reported that Generals Ewell and A. P. Hill have been made Lieutenant Generals, and that Ewell has been assigned to the command of Jackson's corps. The latter officer, you may remember, lost a leg at the second battle of Manassas. I saw him to-day, and learned that he will proceed to Fredericksburg to-morrow. He is able to ride on horseback, but will travel on wheels when the army is not in presence of the enemy.

Gen. Lawton has not yet been assigned to a command. Gen. Lee, it is reported, waited as long as he could, upon the wound of General Lawton, and at length felt it to be his duty to place another officer (General [John B.] Gordon) in command of his brigade. This step, I am persuaded, was dictated by regard for the good of the service, and did not proceed from any want of confidence in General Lawton, who enjoys the reputation of a meritorious officer. It is not probable, however, that his sword will be suffered to remain idle long.

                                                                                                    P. W. A.

RICHMOND, June 1, 1863 [6-5-63]

Everything remains quiet on the Rappahannock, though there is reason to believe this quiet will be broken ere long. A good deal of publicity has been given to a rumor that Gen. Lee is preparing for a forward movement—from which the newspapers of the United States infer that it is only a ruse to cover a demonstration in some other quarter, since they affect to believe that we would be more reticent if an advance were really in contemplation. The month of June, upon which we have this day entered, will unravel the mystery. In the meantime, the Confederate army and people can well afford to possess their souls to patience, and to leave their cause in the hands of that kind Providence which has guided us thus far through this bloody wilderness.

It is said that Gen. Lee is more than usually reserved in regard to his future plans and operations. He has been constrained to adopt this course in consequence of certain disclosures recently made by McClellan. It appears that General D. H. Hill, during last year's Maryland campaign, dropped in his tent, probably when he retired from Boonsboro' Gap, Lee's general order to his corps and division commanders, in which he set forth the whole object and plan of his advance across the Potomac, and that this paper was found and carried to McClellan. In this way, it is alleged, the Federal commander was informed of the strength and disposition of our forces, and knew that D. H. Hill, with his single division, was left to hold the gap at Boonsboro', whilst Jackson had turned off to Harper's Ferry, and Longstreet had taken position near the Pennsylvania line at Hagerstown. This disclosure explains the rapid movements of McClellan, and the confident manner in which he followed us up and delivered battle at Sharpsburg. Without this knowledge, it is not probable he would have sought Gen. Lee so soon and so eagerly; and thus the latter would have had more time to concentrate his forces, rest his troops, and prepare for the conflict. We can never know what would have been the result if that order had not fallen into the hands of the enemy; and yet it is not impossible, had it not reached the Federal general, that we should this day be in Maryland.

Great anxiety is felt here for the safety of Vicksburg. The possession of that stronghold is considered far more important to us than the possession of Richmond. Should the Confederates be able to maintain their position, then it is believed that all will go well in other quarters during the remainder of this year's campaign. Our banner thus far has been crowned with victory upon the land and upon the sea. It was triumphant in April, in the beautiful bay of Charleston, and again in May on the historic banks of the Rappahannock; whilst the paths of [Raphael] Semmes and [J. N.] Maffitt on the ocean, and of Morgan, Forrest and [Joseph] Wheeler on land, have been marked by the wrecks and dead of a discomfitted foe.

I leave for the Rappahannock to-morrow.

P. W. A.

HEIGHTS OF FREDERICKSBURG, VA., June 3, 1863 [6-8-63]

I arrived here yesterday from Richmond, and will leave this afternoon for Raccoon Ford, thirty miles above this place on the Rapidan, but for what reasons I need not now stop to state. The enemy persist in believing the Confederates contemplate a forward movement of some kind, and they very anxiously reconnoiter our position every morning from their safe and elevated perches in the balloons. Two balloons were up this morning—one just below Fredericksburg on the opposite side, and the other higher up the river. The *Herald* of Saturday [May 28], a copy of which fell into my hands last evening, says that these aerial reconnaissances have thus far developed no change in the position of the Confederate army around Fredericksburg. The opinion still prevails in Washington however, that Gen. Lee means mischief; and the *Herald* affirms that he even has designs upon Harrisburg and Philadelphia. Gov. [Andrew] Curtin and Gen. [Robert] Schenck would seem to participate in this opinion; since they took the trouble to go all the way to Washington to consult with Mr. Secretary [Edwin] Stanton on the proper plan to be adopted for the defense of the Pennsylvania border. It is admitted in the Federal newspapers that the defenses of Washington city, of both sides of the Potomac, are being made stronger, in anticipation of an attack by the pestiferous rebels. We know that General Hooker has planted heavy batteries at all the fords up the Rappahannock, so as to completely sweep the approaches and command the crossings. This looks as if he too were expecting a flank movement.

The rumor which prevailed some days ago that the enemy were withdrawing in the direction of Washington, is believed to be premature. Gen. Lee is doubtless well informed in regard to the position of his beaten adversary; but to an outsider, who has to trust to his own eyes and a pair of good field glasses, there is every indication of the presence of a large army on the opposite side of the river. The main body of the army lies back of the Stafford hills and out of sight; but there is enough visible on the crests of the hills, in the gorges between them, and on the slopes which sweep down to the river bank, to relieve one of all doubt on the question of the enemy's whereabouts. How long Gen. Hooker will remain where he is now encamped, is a very different matter, and one upon which I shall not undertake to express an opinion.

The scene from Lee's hill—so called because it was from that point Gen. Lee directed the first battle of Fredericksburg—is imposing and suggestive. The valley of the Rappahannock, with its wide-sweeping plains and cannon-crowned hills, is spread out before the beholder like a vast panorama. To the left are Marye's bloody heights, were McLaws made his gallant fight in December, and where Cobb offered up his life in defense of his mother's birth place. In front of those heights is the half ruined town of Fredericksburg, now garrisoned by Barksdale's impetuous Mississippians and occupied by a few miserable inhabitants who still cling to their homes under the very muzzles of the Federal guns. To the right and below is the wide, fan-shaped plain upon which Burnside deployed his immense host, and where Jackson fought and Gregg perished. On this side of the plain and far down to the right sweeps the range of hills occupied and successfully defended by the Confederates in the first great battle. In front and beyond the river, above and below, loom up the bare hills of Stafford, their crests crowned with batteries and their slopes checkered by a hundred camp roads and pathways, and covered with rifle pits and breastworks. Wagon trains and detachments of artillery, cavalry and infantry show themselves in the gorges between these hills and maneuver on their slopes. Beyond the heights a thousand spiral columns of pine smoke ascend from the campfires below, and here and there in the far distance great bands of dust are outlined against the northern horizon like immense yellow rainbows. Tents and white wagon tops dot the hills and glisten in the evening sunlight, whilst squads of teamsters and idle soldiers stroll listlessly about, and their hard served horses pick such scant herbage as the wasted and trampled soil offers. These pickets, the eyes and ears of the two armies, are guarding either bank of the river; the signal men wave their mysterious alphabets from the hills, and high over all soar the monster balloons of the inquisitive and anxious enemy, who have not yet recovered from the last stunning blow given them by Gen. Lee and his invincible legions. Meanwhile, the two armies lie back of the hills in the timber, like tigers in the jungle, ready to spring upon each other as opportunity may occur.

In this valley and behind these hills are gathered the muscle and manhood of the continent. What vast power! what engines of destruction! Thus far the smaller, but more active and intelligent combatant has had the best of the conflict. Better led, and with a better cause and more hardy and enterprising material, let us hope that Triumph will continue to crown our standard, and that the enemy we have so often beaten, will ere long lay down his arms and give us peace. Lee's army was never in better condition, or so well prepared to maintain the combat, if the adversary shall so decide.

P. W. A.

CULPEPPER COURT HOUSE, VA., June 6, 1863 [6-12-63]

Having rested one day at Raccoon Ford on the Rapidan, we came on to this place this morning, and will move again in a few hours. This is all I feel at liberty to say at this writing.

We hear that General Hooker threw a small force across the Rappahannock yesterday morning at the mouth of Deep Run, three miles below Fredericksburg. Possibly, he had information through his spies or balloonists that Gen. Lee had made some changes in the disposition of his forces, and this demonstration was intended as a counter movement, the effect of which would be to delay us until the Federal army could be withdrawn in the direction of Washington. This however, is a mere surmise; for I am too far removed from the immediate scene of operations to speak advisedly. If Hooker were as bold a man as Gen. Grant, he might cast all upon the hazard of the die, and attempt to reach Richmond. It is known that he asked permission of Gen. Burnside, upon the arrival of the latter at Fredericksburg last November, to cross the river and occupy Bowling Green, and that he has always been anxious to gain that important position and to make Rappahannock the base of operations.

It has also been ascertained that a large number of transports have been sent to the Potomac in the vicinity of Aquia Creek, Hooker's present base of supplies, and this fact encourages the supposition that he is preparing for a retrograde movement. Another fact of equal significance has this minute been communicated to me, viz: that the town of Morrisville, in the extreme southern corner of Farquir county, and between the Rappahannock and Deep Creek, has been recently occupied by a Federal infantry force of 20,000 men, and that Stoneman and his cavalry are posted beyond the Rappahannock, above and below the railroad, in the direction of Manassas. Would Hooker detach this large force from his main army if he expected to march upon Richmond? And would he have sent this force up the river to guard his flank, if he did not anticipate a serious demonstration upon his right?

Your readers will be glad to hear that Gen. Lee's army is in excellent condition and spirits. The health of the men was never so good; and they are well clothed and pretty well shod. Thus far I have seen but two barefooted men, and they may have laid aside their shoes merely for the march. The horses, wagons and harness are also in better condition than they have been for twelve months past; whilst our supply of ordnance and ordnance stores is abundant. The people at home, however, should persevere in their patriotic efforts to manufacture all the clothing, leather and shoes they possibly can; for they will all be needed by or before next December. I am not informed of what the Government is doing to procure supplies for the army; but it may safely be concluded that with all their efforts, they will not be able to obtain sufficient supplies for the men in time for next winter. Let the people never forget that but for their prompt response to the appeal for clothing and shoes last fall, Gen. Lee could not have fought the battle of Fredericksburg in December. That was one of the most brilliant and decisive victories of the whole war; and every man and woman, every boy and girl, who gave a pair of shoes, a yard of cloth, or a pair of socks to the brave men who defeated the enemy on the frozen plains of the Rappahannock, help to win the battle, and is entitled to a part of the honor conferred by the victory.

But I must close. I write in a pine thicket overlooking the town, and the mail boy is impatient for my letter.

P. W. A.

CULPEPPER COURT HOUSE, VA., June 8, 1863 [6-15-63]

Gen. Lee and his staff arrived here yesterday from Fredericksburg.

Whether Gen. Hooker will contest the crossing of the river in our present front, or make a stand behind our works at Manassas or Centreville, or fall back upon Washington, it is too early to say. Lee's flank movement, like a coal of fire upon the terrepin's back, has had the effect to put his army in motion, and this is all we do know. Our cavalry are at work, however, and will probably flush the game in a few days.

Gen. Stuart has assembled a heavy cavalry force here, and his men and horses are in such condition as to inspire the hope that he will be able to accomplish more than he has been doing lately. He was surprised at Kelly's ford last winter, and again this spring by Stoneman, and it is time he were doing something to keep green and fresh the laurels he has heretofore won. Some of the ladies yesterday adorned him and his horse with flowers, and in this condition he presented himself before General Lee, who, it is reported, having surveyed him from head to foot, quietly remarked: "Do you know General, that Burnside left Washington in like trim for the first battle of Manassas. I hope your fate may not be like his." Unfortunately Stuart was too much occupied with his flowers to take the hint.

Frequent and disastrous as have been the defeats sustained by the Federals at the hands of Gen. Lee, they nevertheless entertain the highest respect for his lofty character and splendid genius. Just at the close of the battle of Chancellorsville, he passed along the road where several thousand prisoners were assembled. Our troops greeted the victorious chieftain with deafening cheers, whilst the prisoners, eager to see him, crowded forward, and silently and respectfully removed their hats as he rode past them. Well might they and their whole nation indulge in such a mark of respect for one who had overthrown four of their chosen leaders, and who is never more modest than in the hour of triumph.

Having returned from Chancellorsville to Salem Church, where McLaws, Anderson and Early had enveloped [John] Sedgwick in their lines, an aid-de-camp inquired of Gen. Lee what he supposed the enemy's next movement would be. The old Chief responded that it made but little difference what it might be—that their position could not be stronger than it was at Chancellorsville. "If I can but get at them with my infantry," he added, "all will be well." He feels unbounded confidence in his infantry, and the greatest admiration for their steadiness and courage. And well he may; for not better troops ever went forth to battle.

P. W. A.

More Special Correspondence from V. A. S. P.

CULPEPPER, VA., June 10, 1863 [6-17-63]

Editor Republican: Great activity has characterized army movements since my last. From the best information we have, the enemy is in very strong force on the Rappahannock, opposite Culpepper. Yesterday morning was ushered in by the heavy booming of cannon at Hays' [Beverly's] Ford, nine miles from the town. The firing was rapid, and betokened an early and desperate fight. Soon we were in line and drawn up in order of battle in the broad level plains east of Culpepper.

By ten o'clock, straggling cavalry men, as is usual, came "limbering to the rear" with various reports. Col. [Williams] Wickham's regiment of cavalry was surprised, completely flanked, but gallantly cut its way through the enemy. Gen. [William] Jones, says rumor, was also surprised, permitting the enemy to get into his rear. He, too, cut his way out, capturing some artillery in the meantime. I have this upon the authority of participants.

Our worthy and efficient Postmaster, Mr. A. McCardie, informs me that he saw three hundred prisoners brought into Culpepper, many of whom were wounded with *sabre cuts.* This substantiates the reports of the cavalry, and shows very plainly the desperate character of the fight. This was one of the *few* encounters in a hand-to-hand fight in which the sabre was the arm used. Our cavalry are too often satisfied with a few discharges of their pistols and carbines, and then "retire" to give the infantry a chance. An idea that cavalry are only fit for spying out the enemy's position, picketing, and opening the fight, seems to prevail. There seems to be good reason for this belief, for they rarely ever meet the enemy in a general arm of the service. In the ways of raids they have accomplished wonders. But where have they ever broken a column, or decided the fate of a battle? Forrest's, Van Dorn's and Morgan's cavalry have perhaps imitated the brilliant exploits of Murat's horsemen; but they have not equaled their impetuous charges upon the enemy's massed columns.

Col. [Frank] Hampton is reported mortally wounded. I have no more reliable reports of the fight. It is not believed that the enemy's infantry are on this side of the river in any considerable force. Our friends may feel assured that Gen. Lee has a force here sufficient to meet any movement of Hooker. You may prepare to hear of the most stirring events of the campaign. Something grand is in pickle—whether an advance upon Washington or an invasion of the enemy's country, I will not venture to say; for it is impossible for one in a subordinate position, possessing limited means of information, to speak prospectively of our army movements. All may rest assured that whatever is done, will be done well, as long as our veteran Chief, Gen. Lee, is at the head of affairs. God will bless whatever he does.

The cavalry review of which I spoke, came off last Friday [June 5]. It was an imposing sight. One hundred and forty-four companies passed in review in the most splendid order. I counted twenty-six stands of colors, exclusive of those belonging to Stuart's horse artillery. After the review, there was a sham fight, in which the artillery fired over one hundred and sixty rounds, and the cavalry made several brilliant charges. The horses were generally good, and everything indicated a good degree of discipline. Many ladies, blooming in health and beauty, were present. Gen. Hood marched out his whole division to witness the review.

On the next evening we made a hasty march to Kelly's ford in a drenching rain, slept soundly and sweetly upon the wet ground, and retraced our steps the next morning. I have failed to ascertain the meaning of the movement.

I visited Gen. [Paul J.] Semmes' veteran brigade Monday evening, and spent a most pleasant night with Capt. W. O. Flemming, and company, whom I found to be in excellent health. Gen. Semmes has one of the best commands in the army of Northern Virginia. At the battle of Salem Church they displayed a heroism and devotion to our holy cause not surpassed by any brigade in the army. In an open field, without protection other than the protecting arm of the Almighty, they met and repulsed four or five columns of Yankees, vastly superior in numbers, with terrible slaughter. In the heroic "Fiftieth," twenty-two brave Southrons sealed their lofty devotion to our cause by yielding their lives upon that bloody field. A hundred and sixty were wounded. I did not learn the casualties of the other regiments, though I learn they were proportionately heavy. Gen. Semmes set his men a noble example by leading in the sanguinary work. Lt. Col. [Francis] Kearse, after his regiment had filed into line, waving his sword, called upon the men to follow, to which they responded with a yell which made the craven hearted vandals quake with fear. Prisoners and wounded report the fire of Semmes' men to have been the most terrible and destructive they had ever faced. Fine columns melted away before the sheet of flame and torrent of leaden hail which swept the field.

Evening before last all the Captains in Lee's army, from Decatur county, met at Maj. [Boliver H.] Gee's quarters, and as you may imagine, had a pleasant chat. Will a favoring Providence ever permit them to meet again? God has signally favored them. Gordon's (Lawton's old) brigade had the honor of retaking Marye's Heights. Capt. Geo. W. Lewis tells a good anecdote in connection with the charge. A prisoner reports that one of the men said to the Yankee Colonel: "Do you hear that yell? We had just as well get away, for them d—d rebels will take this hill as sure as h—l." That "yell" had as much to do, perhaps, with the retaking of the Heights, as the musketry, for very few shots were fired.

On several occasions "that hyena yell of the rebels," at the "critical moment," has decided the fortunes of the day. It inspirits our men and strikes terror into the hearts of the enemy.

I hear a good joke in camps in this wise: A soldier of the Ninth Georgia, passing General Hood's quarters, said to him, "General, will you take a drink with me?" The General took the drink. The soldier, swinging the canteen over his shoulder, and feeling he had a right to be more intimate, thus addressed the General:

"General Hood, when you want a drink, 'here's your mule!'" Gen. H. thanked him for his kind offer. "General Hood, when you want any fighting done, 'here's your mule!'" The General, unable to control his risibles, laughed heartily, and assured the Georgian that he would call upon him.

I could amuse your readers with many jokes, but in times like these they want news.

AFTERNOON—But little is yet known of the fight. Two officers, participants, represent our loss as not exceeding two hundred; others estimate it as much larger. About four hundred and fifty prisoners have been brought in. It was a general battle, all of Stuart's and Stoneman's [Alfred Pleasonton] cavalry being engaged, and lasted from early dawn until near night. In the morning the Yankees repulsed our men at every point, but were in turn repulsed and driven across the river in the evening, with heavy loss. Some infantry were on this side near Waterloo bridge, and fired upon our cavalry. One of Cobb's Legion says there were numerous charges, hand-to-hand fights, in which the sabre was used. He says our men were outnumbered at all points, and crossed sabres with the enemy several times.

At one time General Stuart, says the report, was surrounded, and escaped by cutting his way through the enemy. One of his staff officers lost a leg, and has since died. From all we can hear, it was a desperate fight. The enemy had five days' rations, and evidently intended to make a raid, but unexpectedly met Stuart.

V. A. S. P.

P. W. A. in Northern Virginia

CULPEPPER C. H., VA., June 12, 1863 [6-17-63]

My telegram and letter of the 10th will have put you in possession of the general facts touching the late cavalry engagement near Brandy Station. Those facts were derived from intelligent and candid persons who witnessed or participated in the fight; and yet it is reported that the telegraphic censor in Richmond, when my telegram reached that place, expunged that portion of it which related to the surprise sustained by General Stuart at the hands of the enemy. The folly of this act of the authorities is seen in the fact, that the morning after my telegram passed through, all the Richmond papers contained full accounts of the surprise. To be consistent, the government should establish a censorship over the mail bags, over the railway trains, and over the minds and tongues of men; for hardly a letter was sent from the army the day after the battle that did not admit the surprise, nor was there an individual, white or black, who left here by the railroad, that had not heard of it and who would not speak of it. The telegraphic lines are the property of private individuals; the mail routes and post offices are the work of the government. If either one, therefore, is to be subjected to official scrutiny and supervision, it should be the latter—the confidential letters and sealed communications of the citizen, rather than the messages which he may entrust to the wires of private parties. But to do either would be a great wrong, and such as is practiced only by despotic Powers, like Austria, Russia and the United States.

If the authorities were to attempt to silence the voice of the winds, or to put chains upon the waves of the sea, the act would not be more stupid, in a country like this, than an effort to destroy the freedom of speech and of the press. And it is well that it is so, since, without these great bulwarks, there could be neither personal nor national liberty. Deny the people the right to candidly criticize the conduct of those in power, and the latter will soon come to regard themselves as a close corporation, irresponsible to those upon whose broad shoulders they had mounted to office. Where Silence reigns there Ignorance and slavery hold their leaden sway.

The truth is, Gen. Stuart's pickets were surprised or circumvented at every point where the enemy made the attempt, and nothing but the superior fighting qualities of his men, and the ability of such officers as [Wade] Hampton, saved him from defeat and disgrace. Why should not this fact be published? Will it do any harm? Will it not rather do good by bringing him and his command to the bar of public opinion, and making them more vigilant in the future?

No official returns have yet been received of our casualties, but I see no reason to change the estimate contained in my last letter. There are still many contradictory reports afloat in regard to the number of prisoners we lost. Our captures were more numerous than at first reported, and will fall but little short of 400 prisoners. The gun we lost was subsequently retaken. Our loss in horses, killed and captured, was considerable. In Cobb's (cavalry) Legion alone, which went into action with 220 sabres, 33 horses were killed.

The number of horses in this army, including the cavalry, artillery, quartermaster's department, and field and staff, is not far from 35,000. And this, notwithstanding the transportation has been reduced to the lowest possible standard. To supply these horses with the usual rations of corn and hay, would require 7,500 bushels or 420,000 pounds of the former, and 490,000 pounds of the latter, per day. The labor and expense of supplying so large a quantity of forage are necessarily very heavy. Fortunately for us, as well as for the horses, neither army has occupied this part of the State since last fall, and consequently the supply of grass, clover and timothy is abundant, otherwise it would be impossible to subsist so many animals with our limited wagon and railroad transportation, and at a time of so much scarcity as the present. You will not be surprised to hear, therefore, that the horses receive no hay at all, and very seldom any fodder, and only one third the usual ration of corn. And yet I have never seen them in better condition. It is reported that the grazing in the counties between the Rappahannock and the upper Potomac is equally as good as it is in this vicinity. Many of the farms have been abandoned, and much of the fencing destroyed, but it is believed that the supply of grass, though not as abundant as in times of peace, is ample for our wants, should the army advance. The farmers are allowed ten cents per day for the grazing of each horse, which would make the total cost of grazing 35,000 horses, $3,500 per day.

Nothing has been said about the supply of provisions for the troops, but you will see from the foregoing how difficult it would be to subsist such an army as this in one of the cotton States. Indeed, it could not be done in ordinary times, without a large increase of our means of transportation and full granaries elsewhere to draw from. No State in the Confederacy is so well prepared to sustain a large army as Virginia. She produces a vast amount of beef, mutton, wool, leather, wheat, hay, coal and iron—is fruitful and well watered, and grows the best horses on the Western Hemisphere. But at least one-third of her territory is now in possession of the enemy; a large portion of her laboring population is in the army, and her supply of food and animals has been so much reduced as to make it necessary for the quartermaster and commissary department to look elsewhere for the means of subsistence.

Every man in the Confederate States, therefore, who has the ability, should diversify his pursuits, at least so far as to devote somewhat of his time and means to the raising of horses, cattle, sheep, and the production of small grain and fruit—everything, indeed, that will help to feed, clothe and move an army. No people or State can be said to be truly independent which relies upon other communities for the necessary articles of food and raiment.

P. W. A.

JUNE 13th—All quiet in front. Important movements, which it would be impolitic to mention, are on the eve of execution. My next letter may be dated from the top of the Blue Ridge, or the lovely valley of the Shenandoah, in which event, I shall have to rely upon couriers to communicate with the post office. It is believed that Hooker has changed his base from the Rappahannock to Bull Run, notwithstanding the show of strength he keeps up from the Stafford Hills.

P. W. A.

Lee's Grand Movements in Northern Virginia— Stuart's Cavalry Fights.

PARIS, ASHBY'S GAP, VA., June 19, 1863 [6-30-63]

I write from the town of Paris, which is situated in Ashby's Gap in the Blue Ridge, and just on the boundary line between Fauquier and Clarke's counties, in the vicinity of which and Snicker's Gap, Longstreet's corps is now encamped. Hill's corps was at Culpepper Court House, two days ago, with orders to follow on and it is supposed that he will reach Chester's Gap near Front Royal to-day, should he take that route; or this vicinity, if he took the route by which Longstreet came.

A courier just in from the Potomac, informs me that Ewell was at Williamsport last night. One of his divisions (Edward Johnson's) had crossed the river at Shepardstown, and was holding the ford at that place. Another division (Robert Rodes') had crossed at Williamsport on the 16th and was holding the ford at that point. Early's division of the same corps was in the vicinity of Martinsburg, in supporting distance of the two fords.

Such is the present position of the army, except the cavalry, which occupies a line passing through Middleburg and between Ashby's and Snicker's Gaps on the west, and Manassas and Centreville on the east. An Aid-de-camp of Hooker was captured yesterday with important dispatches, by [Col. John S.] Mosby, far in the rear of the enemy's cavalry forces, and the report he makes and the dispatches found upon him, induce the belief that the Federal army is near Manassas and Centreville, and in daily expectation of an attack from us. There can be no impropriety in communicating the foregoing facts, since our whole position will have been completely changed long before this letter can reach your readers.

Allusion was made in one of my last letters from Culpepper to the brilliant strategy of Gen. Lee, and by which he was actually maneuvering Hooker out of the State of Virginia without a battle. This letter will inform you how successfully the plans of the great Confederate leader have worked. First, he moved Longstreet's corps from Fredericksburg up to Culpepper Court House, forty miles above. This move on the military chess-board, called for a counter move on the part of Hooker; but he had just begun to make it, when Ewell was ordered to Culpepper also, whence he advanced by rapid marches across the Blue Ridge, and fell like a clap of thunder upon [Robert] Milroy at Winchester and Martinsburg, capturing the greater part of his forces, many guns and heavy supplies of grain, ammunition and other military stores. Having done this, he moved promptly up to the Potomac and occupied such fords as we may desire to use, in the event it shall be deemed proper to advance into the enemy's country. The sudden appearance of Ewell in the Valley of the Shenandoah, coupled with the demonstration at Culpepper, made it necessary for Hooker to abandon Fredericksburg entirely, and to occupy the strong positions at Centreville and Manassas, so as to interpose his army between us and Washington, and thus prevent a sudden descent from the Blue Ridge by Gen. Lee upon the Federal capital. Meanwhile, Longstreet and Hill were following fast upon Ewell's track, the former reaching Ashby's and Snicker's Gaps in time to prevent any movement upon Ewell's rear, and the latter (Hill's) getting to Culpepper in good season to protect Longstreet's rear, or to co-operate with him in the event of an attack upon his flank, or to guard against any demonstration in the direction of Richmond.

Thus you will perceive that Gen. Lee, having got the start on his antagonist, has managed to keep it, and that whenever and wherever Hooker approaches our lines, he found Lee not only in advance of him, but the head of his column still pushing forward. It is a noteworthy fact in this connection that Gen. Lee moved along the foot of the Blue Ridge on the eastern side, and continued to make demonstrations by his cavalry as if he intended to move upon Manassas by the same route that he took last year. These feints embarrassed and delayed Hooker's movements, and kept him in a state of uncertainty at a time when the head of our column was advancing swiftly and secretly upon the fords of the upper Potomac.

You may feel assured that Gen. Lee's operations have occasioned great excitement and consternation throughout the United States. Late Federal papers inform us that Gov. Curtin has called out 50,000 militia for the defense of the borders of Pennsylvania—the Executives of other States, including New York, had issued similar calls, and that Mr. Lincoln had directed that 100,000 additional militiamen to be raised for the Federal service.

My telegram sent back to Culpepper some days ago, if received, will have informed you of Ewell's operations in the Valley. But lest it may not have reached you, I would now state that he attacked Milroy in his strong entrenchments at Winchester on Sunday last, the 14th, and after a fierce bombardment of an hour and a half, the works were stormed in handsome style by Early's division, composed of [W. S.] Smith's Virginia brigade, [Robert] Hoke's North Carolinians, Gordon's (late Lawton's) Georgians, and [Harry] Hays' Louisianans. Milroy escaped with a remnant of his forces, leaving in our hands 3,040 prisoners with their arms, 22 guns, 200 wagons, 1,200 horses, a large amount of commissary and quartermaster's stores, and many sutler's wagons which had been taken into the works as a place of safety. The captures, exclusive of prisoners and arms, are valued at $1,000,000. A single fact will show how completely Milroy was surprised. Before opening upon the garrison, Ewell sent in a demand of surrender, to which Milroy replied that if Gens. [John] Imboden and [Albert] Jenkins desired to communicate with him, they had better address him over their own signatures, instead of Gen. Ewell's. Milroy effected his escape, according to report, through the assistance of a Union man in the neighborhood who acted as his guide.

Immediately upon the reduction of Winchester, Rodes who had marched around the latter place, fell upon Martinsburg, where he took 200 prisoners and a large amount of military stores including a fine lot of ammunition. Among the prisoners were many officers. Our loss at this place was only one man killed and one wounded. It was very slight at Winchester also, not exceeding 20 killed and wounded.

I failed to mention in the proper connections that the dispatches found upon Major [William R.] Sterling, Hooker's Aid-de-camp, contained full instructions to Gen. [Alfred] Pleasonton, the commander of the Federal cavalry in the absence of Gen. Stoneman. Among other things, he was instructed to occupy and hold Snicker's Gap, and from that point to watch the movements of the Confederates in the Valley. These dispatches show conclusively that Hooker was wholly ignorant of our position, and that he supposed the main body of Lee's army had not advanced so far.

P. W. A.

PARIS, ASHBY'S GAP, VA., June 20, 1863

My letter of yesterday and telegrams of to-day will have put you in possession of the latest intelligence from Gen. Lee's army up to date. At last accounts, Gen. Ewell, who is showing him well to be a worthy successor of the lamented Jackson, had advanced his whole corps into Maryland, and occupied Boonsboro' Gap, and probably Crampton's Gap. We have reports that one of his divisions (Rodes') was at Hagerstown, and that our troops held Harper's Ferry, but thus far they are without confirmation.

The march from Culpepper Court House to this place was very tiring, the roads being dry and dusty and the weather excessively hot. Many of the men fell by the way side from sun-stroke, and had to be left behind to be brought on by the ambulances. Some of them died in a few minutes after they were struck down; others who had simply fainted away, recovered after a night's rest, and resumed the march.

BERRY'S FERRY, SHENANDOAH RIVER, June 21st.

At four o'clock yesterday afternoon, the forces at Paris received orders to cross the Shenandoah and go into camp on the west bank. The rain was pouring down in torrents when the column commenced the descent of the mountain but when we reached the Valley and crossed the river, we found that there had been but little rain in the Valley during all the time it had been storming on the mountain. The men waded the river, which came up to their armpits, some with their clothing on, others carrying it on their bayonets, and all of them shouting and enjoying the scene. Meanwhile the bands drawn up on either bank, played Dixie and other spirited airs.

At 3 o'clock this afternoon couriers came in from the front and reported that Stuart had been hotly engaged all day with a large Federal force of cavalry and infantry, and that he had been compelled to retire upon Ashby's Gap, badly cut up. In a short time several wounded men were brought back, and they confirmed the previous reports. But few details have been received, but it would appear that the conflict was hot and severe for cavalry. Many of our own wounded and of such prisoners as we took bore the marks of the sabre upon their hands and arms. The greater part of our wounded however, and all our dead, fell into the hands of the enemy. The Confederate loss was considerable, and our forces admit that they got the worst of the fight. The contest was unequal however, in this, that the enemy had an infantry force to support his cavalry.

Immediately upon the receipt of the above intelligence, McLaws was directed to recross the Shenandoah and defend Ashby's Gap, to which point our cavalry had fallen back. He now occupies the Gap with his whole division, and should the enemy attempt to storm it, they will catch a terrible punishment. It would have done your heart good to see with what alacrity his brave Georgians, South Carolinians and Mississippians sprung to their arms, upon the receipt of the intelligence of the Federal advance. Semmes, Wofford, Kershaw and Barksdale are "ugly for a fight," to use a vulgar expression.

We hear also that Hood was engaged at Snicker's Gap to-day, thirteen miles below, but we have no details. The enemy is probably trying to ascertain our real position, and possibly to pass the Gaps and cut off Hill's corps above, or Ewell's in Maryland; but he is too late. Our forces are already in a position to be concentrated when it shall be deemed advisable. We have remained here thus long only to enable Hill to get up, which he has done.

P. W. A.

MILLFORD [MILLWOOD], CLARKE CO., VA., June 22, 1863 [7-4-63]

The report adverted to in my letter of yesterday that the enemy had engaged Gen. Hood at Snicker's Gap, was without foundation. He attacked Gen. Stuart, however with a mixed force of infantry and cavalry, but principally the latter, drove him back from Middleburg through Upperville to Ashby's Gap, a distance of thirteen miles—our dead, and nearly all of our wounded, falling into his hands. The affair is considered quite discreditable to the Confederate cavalry, or rather, to Gen. Stuart. The people of Upperville say only one brigade of cavalry, unaccompanied by infantry, made its appearance at that place, and yet this single brigade attacked Stuart's whole division, drove him from the town, and forced him to seek shelter in Ashby's Gap, his officers discouraged and mortified, and his men bordering on a state of demoralization.

It is reported that Stuart sent back word that the enemy was advancing in very heavy force. Be this as it may, it is true that McLaws' division was to recross the Shenandoah yesterday afternoon, to defend the Gap, and that Hood's division marched several miles back to Berry's ford for the same purpose.

McLaws got into position about sunset, and early this morning Wofford's brigade of his division advanced in line of battle in the direction of Upperville, the cavalry following behind, when the enemy, who had been informed by a negro of our return to the Gap, retired in the direction of Middleburg. At last accounts, Stuart had reached the vicinity of that place, and was busy procuring proof of the employment by the enemy in the late affair of a heavy force of infantry. But in this he will hardly be successful; since the people residing along the road affirm that they saw only two or three regiments of infantry, and that they did not come as far as Upperville, where the last engagement was fought. It is agreed on all sides that our officers generally conducted themselves with gallantry and courage, and that Hampton and his brigade distinguished themselves, as they always do where an opportunity is presented.

Officers under Stuart declare that the effort to give him a large command and maintain him in his position is working great mischief to the cavalry service. Both officers and men have come to regard him as unequal to the duty of wielding and fighting so large a force as that now subject to his orders. He has the rank of a Major General, and all the cavalry belonging to Gen. Lee's army has been massed together and placed under his command. The extent of this force it would be impolite to mention, though Federals say it numbers 15,000 sabres. Be this as it may, it would be safe to affirm that no one but an officer of ability and experience, like Ewell or Hood, both of whom had distinguished themselves in the old U. S. Dragoons, is capable of handling efficiently so large a body of cavalry. If some change be not made, either in the organization or command of this branch of the service, the country need not expect much benefit from it in the future. Neither the men nor the horses have received proper training, and without some change, it is feared they will not. Indeed, the cavalry service, which was so efficient under Frederick the Great, and in Napoleon's time, has come to be regarded by all other departments of the army in Virginia, with contempt, and the appearance of a dragoon is the invariable occasion of disparaging remarks by infantry men and artillerists. Thus far I am unable to recall any pitched battle in Virginia, in which the cavalry took no active part. It has, however, been repeatedly surprised, as at Drainsville, Kelly's Ford, in the Stoneman raid, and recently at Brandy Station. The material of which it is composed could not be better; all it requires to be made efficient and terrible in battle, is proper training and discipline, and able leadership.

The artillery service has been re-organized and greatly improved since last year. We now have battalions of artillery, one of which with proper reserves, is attached to each division of the three corps into which the army is divided. It has been suggested that a similar change in the organization of the cavalry service would be advantageous. This may well be doubted, however. What the latter arm of the service needs most is a leader—a man like Morgan or Forrest, one flash of whose sword on the banks of the Potomac would be worth a thousand sabres.

You may be sure it gives me no pleasure to indite such a soldier as this. There is no braver or gallant spirit than Stuart. As a Colonel of cavalry he rendered important service at Mason's and Munson's hills near Washington, and as a Brigadier he displayed commendable spirit and energy, especially as an executive officer; but the heavy force now under his command is too large for him, in that it requires a head that can conceive and combine as well as execute the orders of others. His circuit around McClellan's army before Richmond and in Maryland, was the suggestion of another brain than his; but it is due to him to say that no one could have performed the work more gallantly or successfully than he did. I might add much more, and yet not tell all; but I forbear.

June 23rd.

Longstreet's and Hill's corps will move tomorrow morning at 3 o'clock, crossing the Potomac at Williamsport and heading for Hagerstown. They halted here for a few days to ascertain the exact position of Hooker, who was last reported at Manassas, digging and entrenching, and to guard against attack upon our right flank and rear. The army will march by the left flank, as it did last year, and hence Ewell marched first, his position being the left, Hill's the center, and Longstreet's (the senior Lieut. Gen.) the right. Should the enemy attack us, therefore, from his present position, each of our *corps d' armee*, by facing to the right, would be in its proper place. It was for this reason that Ewell marched first, as Jackson did last year.

Gen. Lee has issued a most excellent order for the government of the army "while in the enemy's country." The troops will be disappointed when this order is published; and yet the dullest intellect in the ranks cannot but admit that a license to plunder and pillage indiscriminately, after the manner of the enemy, would ruin the troops and bring the army to shame and defeat. Last year the army crossed the Potomac to remove the yoke from the neck of "My Maryland," this summer it goes to avenge the wrong inflicted upon the helpless men and women and defenseless cities, and to retaliate upon a barbarous foe the violence and blood shed with which his own track has every where been marked. Such, at least, is the spirit by which the men are animated, and it is to check this spirit and direct it into a proper channel that Gen. Lee has issued the order to which allusion has been made.

The telegraphic wires will soon be put up as far as Winchester, and that is the point to which the army will send back its letters to be mailed. When we cross into Maryland, and probably into Pennsylvania, we shall be beyond the reach of the telegraph and the post office. If, we should pass for a season from your view, and if you should see only the lightning flashing luridly along the northern horizon, and hear the deep roar of thunder when you put your ear to the ground, you may know by that flash and that sound that we are there, battling as men ought to battle for the right and the loved ones at home. Will not those who are left behind remember this? And will they not remember, when they approach the footstool of the Giver of all victories, to ask for our safe deliverance—for peace and independence?

P. W. A.

More Special Correspondence from V. A. S. P.

MARTINSBURG, VA., June 25, 1863 [7-14-63]

As our Postmaster, Mr. A. McCardle, leaves this evening or tomorrow, I will improve a short time allowed me for rest, by writing you a short letter.

Anderson's brigade did not meet the enemy at Snicker's Gap, nor did Benning's follow; but the next morning, Monday, we retraced our steps up the Shenandoah to the ford at Ashby's Gap; thence we went to Millwood, where A. P. Hill's corps was encamped. Here we rested until Wednesday morning, washed up and prepared rations.

Gen. Lee's recent order enjoining upon the troops non-interference with private property *in the enemy's country*, was published. Nothing is to be touched except by the proper officers designated for that purpose, who are to buy what the army needs, or take it, if the inhabitants will not sell; and in every case to furnish the parties from whom supplies are received or taken, with a certificate of the quantity and kind. How different is this from the way our foes treat us! They not only take what they want, promising to pay upon evidences of loyalty produced by the inhabitants, but give their brutal soldiery license to pillage and rob. The question whether we should not retaliate upon their citizens, by burning houses and laying waste the whole country of the enemy, is discussed with a great deal of earnestness. For one, I say we should not. We would degrade ourselves to the low, despicable character of the Yankee, as developed by this war, were we to retaliate in such a way. What! imitate the Yankees! God forbid that our fair national fame for chivalry and honor should be blurred by so foul, so brutal, so barbarous a mode of warfare as characterize our foes! Thank God, we have no Butlers, Milroys or [John] McNeils! Our leaders are southern gentlemen—theirs are *Yankees!* I trust our government will never make war upon women and children, as the puritanical heathens of New England do.

We are within twelve miles of Williamsport, Md., where we will probably cross the Potomac to-morrow morning.

The whole of Gen. Lee's veteran army will have crossed the "Rubicon" in a few hours. Great events, vital interests to our beloved sunny South, hang tremblingly in the balance. "The wheeling sabre" of Ewell, like the sword which was suspended over Jerusalem, has already filled the hearts of our persecuting foe with dreadful apprehensions. Lee's victorious legions follow closely in his wake; and God blessing us, they will be made to feel the bitter curse of war. They will be enabled to form some idea of what we have suffered, though they will not be visited with the fire grand, the vindictive cruelty, the warfare upon women, the desecration of churches, the demolition of grave yards—in a word, the heartless barbarity which distinguishes their own soldiery.

We expect, of course, to fight bloody battles. By these, and those alone, do we expect to accomplish the great object of our mission—the bringing about a speedy peace. The army is in high hopes. God forbid that we should be disappointed. It is much stronger, by half, perhaps, than it was last summer. The men are healthier. Our excellent Surgeons, Drs. [W. D.] Hoyt and [John] Palmer, assure me that sickness is rapidly decreasing. It is so in other brigades.

The Yankee army, on the contrary, is much weaker, and greatly demoralized. An invasion is meditated, and it is believed, will be successful.

Gen. Hood is reported to have said that if he were a betting man he would stake all he is worth that peace would be made by Christmas. Gen. Longstreet evidently entertains the same opinion, as one might infer from his recent order exhorting men and officers to a faithful and rigid discharge of their duties as tending to bring about a speedy peace. It is an eloquent, touching appeal, and found its way to every true soldier's heart of the *corps d'armee.*

This hope is strengthened by the reports we have from Vicksburg, that Grant has been killed and his army defeated. I have not seen this in the Richmond papers, but it is reliably reported by army officers who say they saw the statement in the Washington *Chronicle* and Baltimore *Sun*. I have not seen these journals, and therefore, give the report as I heard it. I hope that it is true.

I had the pleasure of seeing the "Prince of correspondents" "P.W.A." on Tuesday. He is looking unusually well. Through his able letters, your readers will be well posted in the movements of the army.

More anon.   V. A. S. P.

P. W. A. in Maryland

HAGERSTOWN, MD., June 27, 1863 [7-6-63]

Once more has the Confederate army crossed the Potomac, and once more does it hold out the helping hand to Maryland and throw down the gage of battle upon her soil. Will she clutch the hand that is cordially extended to her, and thus save herself and her latest posterity from the ungodly rule of the infidel and the Puritan? And will the enemy seek us as he did last year, and again deliver battle? These are questions which Maryland and the despot beneath whose heel she writhes, alone can answer.

Our reception has been much the same as it was in September last. The natives of the country—the descendants of Lord Baltimore and his colonists—almost universally sympathize with us, and ardently desire our success. The Dutchmen and the Northmen, and their children, on the contrary, as unanimously wish for our defeat. In those counties which border on Pennsylvania, and where the humanizing institution of slavery can exert but little influence, a majority of the inhabitants affiliate with our enemies, but in all other portions of the State the friends of the Confederate cause are believed to be in the ascendant. This view of the state of public sentiment will, I think, be shown to be the true one, should our stay and movements be of such a character as to justify the people in openly espousing our cause. It is unjust to expect a people nearly equally divided, without arms in their hands, who have been held in chains for more than two years, and much the larger portion of whom, and especially our friends, are still enveloped within the Federal lines, to move as promptly as we could desire, and before they have some guarantee that they will not again be left to the rod of the smiter. If we could recall two years, when we were first entering upon the conflict there would be no excuse for their delay and indecision; but, two years of bondage produce unwholesome fruits, and such as we who have never felt the yoke of the oppressor, are slow to realize. Let us, then, bear with Maryland yet a while longer. If there be but ten righteous men and women within her borders, we should for their sakes strive to save her from the Dead Sea of Federal despotism.

Longstreet's corps crossed the Potomac yesterday, and Hill's the day before. Both are now moving upon Chambersburg, Pa., twenty miles distant, in the direction of Harrisburg, the capital of the State, which is sixty miles distant. Reports say that Gen. Jenkins was within three miles of Harrisburg two days ago, and that Ewell was not far off.

It is not known what Gen. Lee's plans are, whether to occupy Harrisburg, or to establish his camp in the vicinity of Chambersburg and along the Pennsylvania line, and there await the enemy. Nearly all the troops crossed the Potomac at Williamsport, and it will be through that place, Winchester and Staunton we shall endeavor to keep up our communication with the rear. This line may be cut now and then by the enemy; but we shall be in a fruitful and opulent country, abounding in everything necessary for the subsistence of the army, and shall not find it difficult to take care of ourselves. Already large numbers of horses, wagons, beef cattle and sheep have been secured, and immense stores of grain and flour. The horses cost us from $150 to $200 in Confederate money, and the wheat about $1.60 per bushel.

Gen. Lee's order has acted like a charm. While some of the people have fled into the interior of Pennsylvania with their cattle and horses, many others have remained, deeming it wisest to stay at home and make the best terms possible. In this they have shown their good sense. Our impressing officers pay the market price for everything the army needs, where the parties will receive payment, or give them scrip if they prefer that. In all purchases of articles of subsistence and clothing, payment is made in Confederate funds at par value. Thus, the enemy who has been counterfeiting Confederate Treasury notes and scattering them wherever they have penetrated into our territory, now we have "the poisoned chalice" put to their own lips, at least so far as to compel them to receive our genuine notes as if they were gold and silver. And thus, too, for the first time Confederate money is at par in the U. States.

We are not without friends in Pennsylvania, and especially in those districts which the army has occupied. The impressing officer is an effective missionary, and has already converted many a fat Dutchman and blind fanatic from the error of his ways. Men who were indifferent before, are now clamorous for peace; and it is reported that some of them are willing for the troops to take their wives and children, but beg hard for their sleek cattle and well fed horses and bursting granaries. But we prefer the latter, and will let them keep the former and all their pestiferous progeny. Imboden brought 2,500 horses out of Fulton county and about 30 volunteers, young men who are really friendly to us and mean to make our cause their own. Several students in the College near this place, and volunteers from other parts of Maryland, have joined our standard and entered the lists against the common foe. Their parents and others who have been made to feel the yoke of the tyrant, are not slow to give us useful information, and to point out the cattle pens and wheat houses of those Unionists who have been lording it over them. They have rendered important aid to the people of Virginia also, many of whom have accompanied the army in search of their stolen negroes and horses. Yesterday I met several gangs of negroes going to the rear who had been captured in the mountains in Maryland and Pennsylvania. Many of the owners of these slaves had procured wagons and other conveyances this side of the Potomac, which they had filled with goods and groceries at the market prices in Confederate money or gold, and were carrying into Dixie. There is another class of traders however, who follow the army like vultures with sharp beaks, and who are likely to be sent to the rear, if not punished by our military authorities. I allude to those dealers who have heretofore been running the blockade across the Potomac, and who have done so much to depreciate our currency. These people have no right to take shelter behind the army, and buy up articles necessary to the troops, to be sold again at heavy profit.

All honest men throughout the world will be rejoiced to hear that that malignant demagogue and abolitionist, Thaddeus Stevens of Pennsylvania, has received some of the punishment due for his enormous crimes against the happiness of the human race. He owns large iron works and mills in Adams [Franklin] county on the border, which I am informed have been utterly destroyed. His machinery, aqueducts, buildings, and supplies for his operatives, including, it is said, 20,000 pounds of bacon, have been swept away. *Amen!* will be the involuntary exclamation of every lover of justice and every foe of hypocrisy. An effort is made, in the work of impressment, to distinguish, as far as possible, between friends of peace and the aiders and abettors of Mr. Lincoln. Thus the red hand of war is made to fall heaviest upon those who were first to lift it. Some of the troops complain, however, that they are not allowed to appropriate and destroy as they go. If permitted, they would avenge Mississippi, Tennessee, and the Carolinas and Virginia, and leave behind a track of desolation as barren and enduring as the desert of Sahara. They give Gen. Lee high praise as a fighter and strategist, but they say "he has not a good pillaging mind." Gen. Lee is right, however, as all will acknowledge after a while.

P. W. A.

P. W. A. in Pennsylvania
CHAMBERSBURG, PA., June 28, 1863 [7-13-63]

General Lee's army has crossed Mason and Dixon's line, and is now encamped in Cumberland Valley, one of the most fertile and lovely districts in the large and populous State of Pennsylvania. The Southern Cross now floats in triumph in the second State in wealth and population in the whole Federal Union. This great success has been accomplished almost without the shedding of one drop of blood. Having attracted the attention of the enemy to Culpepper, assembling a large cavalry force there, and which it was adroitly reported, was about making a raid into Pennsylvania, Gen. Lee put his army in motion, and then interposing the cavalry between himself and the enemy on his right so as to effectually conceal his movements, he passed swiftly and secretly along the foot of the Blue Ridge, through Chester's, Ashby's, and Snicker's Gaps, crossed the Shenandoah, captured Winchester, swept rapidly down the Valley of Virginia to the Potomac, and launched his army into Maryland and Pennsylvania, before the boastful and beaten leader of the Federal forces was aware of his doings.

This is the first instance in which the Confederate army has penetrated into the territory of our enemies. What will be the result of this invasion, it is impossible yet to say. We only know that the tables have been turned, and that the invaded party has now become the invader. The people along the line of march are overwhelmed with grief and surprise, and exact one's pity and contempt by the unresisting and abject manner in which they receive us. They remind one of a flock of sheep terrified and bewildered by the howl of the wolf, and are astonished and slavishly thankful that we do not murder, burn, and ravage as we go, which they expected we would do, and which they acknowledge they fully deserve. The women alone have manifested any spirit, and even they confine themselves to such harmless exhibitions of loyalty to their government as the wearing of Federal colors, "making mouths" at the troops as they pass, and declaring their conviction that we will return soon and faster than we came. The chief concern of the men is about their property—their horses, cattle, grain, provisions and growing crops. They close their houses and barns, and hide themselves and their effects wherever they can; but the women, overcome by curiosity, will look out from the windows and assemble at the corners of the streets.

This is a strong democratic country, and peopled chiefly by Dutchmen and their descendants. In a conversation yesterday with a farmer, he remarked that all his horses and cattle had been taken, but he would willingly give them up if the war could only be brought to a close. He said war was a dreadful evil—that he had always been opposed to it, and that the people of Pennsylvania had never felt the effects of it before, except in the prices of a few articles of necessity and the absence of a fraction of the laboring population.

Confederate—How long is it since the enemy entered this State?

Farmer—It will be two weeks day after tomorrow since Gen. Jenkins and his cavalry passed up the road.

C.—Did he murder your people, burn your houses, or destroy or take your property without paying for it?

F.—He did not. He paid for everything he found it necessary to seize. Indeed, your troops have behaved more justly and kindly than our own; for they would steal our chickens and sheep, and sometimes threaten and even fire upon citizens who remonstrated with them. But, sir, war is a mighty evil, and we feel it sorely.

C.—If such be your feelings after a brief invasion of not quite two weeks in which the rights of person and property have been respected, what do you suppose is the condition of a large portion of the Confederate States whose territory has been ravaged with fire and sword for two years—whose homes have been desolated, whose property has been carried away or wantonly destroyed, whose churches have been closed or burned unless the people would ask the blessing of heaven upon the head of their oppressor, and whose women, and children and old men have been seized at the dead hour of night and hurried off to prison to herd with felons and outlaws? Old man, you know nothing of war. This is the peace of Eden compared with the sufferings of our people. When our track shall be marked by burning towns and smoking homes, your land laid waste, and your grey-haired men, and wives and daughters shall be stripped of their goods and driven from their pleasant homes into exile, then you will be able to realize what we have suffered at the hands of your government and people for two years past.

F.—It is too horrible to think of! If you were to do unto us, as we have done unto your people, we could not justly complain. I am astonished at the moderation of your army, and that it does not kill, ravage and imprison, as ours has done. We deserve it all, and cannot be too thankful for the mercy that has been shown to us.

Similar sentiments were expressed by many others whom we met along the march.

While such is the effect of the invasion in the district occupied by the Confederate army, it remains to be seen what influence it will exert in other portions of the State and Union. It cannot be disguised that Gen. Lee has taken a most important step, and one that must lead to a great triumph or a great disaster. It is true, also, that we have surrendered all the advantages possessed by an invaded people, and have incurred all the disadvantages which have ever attended the invader. To be successful, an invasion should be conducted, as a general rule, by an army twice as numerous as that brought into the field by the country invaded, or by forces whose superior courage and genius, as in the case of the invasion of Russia by Charles XII, of Sweden, and of our invasion of Mexico, are more than a match for the superior numbers of the enemy. In the present instance, we have advanced into a rich and densely populated country, in which we have no friends, and of the topography of which we possess but little accurate knowledge. Every man and woman we meet is ready to do us a wrong, or to mislead us by erroneous statements. All these adverse elements should be taken into consideration when we come to calculate the chances of success. The army, however, which has tried the metal of the enemy, and which reasons closely and shrewdly in such matters, feels no doubt of its ultimate triumph.

Of the political consequence of the present movement it is too early yet to speak, except to-day that intelligent men of the peace party—at least, such as I have talked with—do not believe it will affect their prospects injuriously. They express the opinion, on the contrary, that it will afford them material assistance, and enable them to wrest the State from the hands of the war men and abolitionists. The invasion of Southern territory, and indeed the history of all other invasions, teaches a different lesson, and it remains to be seen whether the people of the United States will form an exception to the general rule.

It is reported that the mail carrier of Gen. McLaws was captured by a squad of Federal cavalry yesterday at Hagerstown, with the mail he was bringing from Winchester. It becomes necessary therefore, for us to be cautious in our correspondence until our communications with the rear shall be placed beyond danger. It may be stated, however, that Gen. Ewell, at last accounts, was at Carlisle, and was about advancing upon Harrisburg, where, it was reported, the enemy was concentrating a heavy force of militia and some old regiments which have been mustered out of service, and which had enlisted again for the term of six months for the special defense of Pennsylvania. It is also reported, but upon doubtful authority, that McClellan has taken command of these forces and is throwing up works for the defense of the city. It is difficult to believe that an officer of his acknowledged ability would risk his reputation upon so frail a reed as the militia. The call for the militia will bring into the field a class of men who have felt none of the hardships of the service, and in this respect it may be of advantage to the Confederates. Great consternation prevails at Harrisburg and throughout the State. The people in the districts threatened by our forces are removing their goods and property to places of safety.

You will see by the order enclosed herewith, that General Lee has deemed it necessary to adopt a more stringent rule in regards to the impressment of private property. The troops, many of whose homes have been desolated by the enemy, regard these orders with much disfavor, and it may be that the people at home will sympathize with them in their disappointment; but personal observation constrains me to say that the success of our movements and the safety of the army itself require that this restraint be imposed. It is not out of consideration for the people that the sword and the torch are withheld from their persons and property, but for the discipline and welfare of the troops. License to plunder and destroy would soon beget demoralization, and demoralization would lead to ultimate ruin. Enough has already occurred to justify this unqualified assertion. The army is healthy, eager and well disciplined, and there has been no straggling; and to keep it in this condition, these wholesome restraints are absolutely necessary. The troops themselves will soon come to regard the matter in the same light, as many of them are already.

P. W. A.

P. S. A part of runaway negroes captured by Gen. Jenkins and sent to the rear some days ago, were rescued by the people of Greencastle on their arrival there, and concealed. Gen. Rodes reached that place soon after the release, and hearing of the affair, he notified the authorities and people of the town that if the negroes were not forthcoming in a certain number of hours, he would not leave one brick standing upon another. The kidnappers took the hint; the negroes were produced in the time specified, and were sent on to Virginia whence they had escaped.

GREEENWOOD, FRANKLIN CO., PA., July 1, 1863

My letter of the 28ᵗʰ ult. was not sent forward at the time, owing to the presence in Hagerstown of a small force of Federal cavalry, by whom one of our mail carriers was taken prisoner the day before. The route back to Winchester is reported to be again open, but even now there is no assurance that letters from the army will go through safely; and hence one has to be very particular as to what he writes. If my communications, therefore, should be as frequent as heretofore, and contain but little news in regard to the movements of our forces, you will know to what cause to ascribe my reticence.

Greenwood, whence this letter is dated, is seven miles east of Chambersburg on the turnpike leading to Gettysburg, and thence by one route to York, Pa., and by another in the direction of Baltimore. If it were Gen. Lee's object to cut the Northern Central railroad running from Baltimore to Harrisburg, this is the route he would take from Chambersburg; or, starting from the same place, if he desired to go to Baltimore, or to approach Washington in the rear, he would probably proceed by the same road. The same turnpike would take him into the upper valley of the Monocacy, if he desired to cross the South Mountain.

These Dutchmen here are good farmers and livers, but otherwise they are a stupid set, but little superior to their sleek cattle and well-fed horses. They know nothing beyond their immediate neighborhood, and fall far below the people of the Confederacy in spirit and intelligence. Their beef and mutton are excellent, but their horses are clumsy monsters, and good for little but for draught and the plow. The army has impressed several thousand horses of this kind since its arrival in Pennsylvania, and a large number of beef cattle for which payment is tendered in Confederate money at par value, and if this be declined then a receipt is given, to be used by the owner of the property in his reclamation upon his own government. If he prefer to rely upon his own government to reimburse his losses, instead of receiving Confederate notes, of course we do not object. In the one case the Confederate government pays for the property taken; in the other, the Federal government pays for it. I need not say that it is perfectly admissible, under the rules and usages of war, to impress horses, wagons, &c., in the hands of private parties, and to make requisitions upon the inhabitants for supplies of provisions and forage.

News has just come in that Ewell, after destroying the Cumberland Valley railroad about Carlisle, and threatening Harrisburg, swung suddenly round to York, an important point lower down the Susquehanna, where Rodes [Gordon] dispersed a flock of two or three thousand militia, who fled across the river at Columbia, destroying the splendid bridge behind them. This was very kind of them, as the destruction of the bridge was doubtless one of the objects of Ewell's [Early's] visit to that quarter. York is the point of intersection of the Northern Central and the Hanover, York and Lancaster railroads. Ewell will doubtless pay his respects to all of these roads by tearing up the tracks and destroying the bridges, as Longstreet has done with the Cumberland Valley road, leading from Hagerstown through Chambersburg and Carlisle to Harrisburg. The Baltimore and Ohio road was cut on the south side of the Potomac and at the Point of Rocks, in Maryland, as the army came on; so that there is now left but one road for the support of the Federal capital—the Baltimore and Washington road, with the Annapolis branch. The Potomac is still open, but can be easily closed against transport vessels. Thus the web is being drawn by a skillful hand around Washington city.

I omitted to say it is also reported that Ewell [Early] had levied a contribution upon the inhabitants of York of $100,000 worth of clothing and shoes, and had given them a specified time in which to fill the requisition. You will see from this and other facts mentioned in this communication, that we have made the enemy our quartermaster and commissary since we came into Pennsylvania.

We hear also that "Fighting Joe Hooker" has gone up, and that General [George G.] Meade, late in command of the Fifth Army Corps, has been appointed to succeed him. This is all right, though the Confederates did want to give Hooker another whipping before he went overboard. Meade is said to be an old army officer of ordinary capacity, but a gentleman, which is a good deal to say of a Yankee officer. I have heard that he is a native of one of the West India Islands, Bermuda, perhaps.

General [Ambrose] Wright, of Georgia, came near being captured last week in the vicinity of Sharpsburg. The division to which his brigade is attached, (Anderson's, of Hill's corps,) had crossed at Shepardstown and gone into camp near Sharpsburg. Wright was ordered to move his camp some three miles further up the Antietam to a small village, and being unwell he went out to select his camp and to rest, being accompanied by his son, who lost a leg at the second Manassas, and two couriers. Upon reaching the village he was attacked by a squad of Federal cavalry, dressed in Confederate uniforms, who fired upon him and his party at a few paces distant, but, strange to say, without effect. The General finally effected his escape, owing to the superior speed, of his horse, but his son who could not control his horse so well, fell into the hands of the enemy.

P. W. A.

Special Pennsylvania Correspondence from V. A. S. P.

CHAMBERSBURG, PA., June 26, 1863 [7-19-63]

Gen. Longstreet's corps crossed the Potomac Friday morning [June 26], and proceeded to within three miles of Greencastle, Pennsylvania. We ate breakfast in Virginia, dinner in Maryland, and supper in Pennsylvania. It is but a short distance across Maryland from Williamsport—say 11 miles.

At Williamsport, Gen. Hood halted his division an hour and issued a whiskey ration. While I believe a too free use of the "ardent" is injurious, particularly to the soldier, I believe the troops were benefited this time; for all the previous night and until 3 o'clock that evening they were exposed to a cold, drizzling rain. Furthermore, we had to wade the Potomac, and were not allowed to strip. In thirty minutes after the whiskey was issued, Hood's division presented the liveliest spectacle I ever saw. Good humor and wit ran high, and it was difficult even to hear one's self talk. But, as was to be expected, a few made "use and abuse" synonymous terms. Some men don't know when they had too much of a good thing. Cases of intoxication were, however, very rare.

We passed through Greencastle yesterday morning and Chambersburg at 6 o'clock in the evening—distant 11 miles. Greencastle is a considerable town, numbering about 4,000 inhabitants. The doors were all closed. They looked sad and down cast. A few, however, talked cheerfully and expressed a hope that peace would soon be made. The "Rebs" replied that "peace would certainly be made as the rebel army had *got back into the Union!*" We saw but one family that was really bitter against us, and they were renegade Virginians.

The Second Georgia band played "Dixie" as the long column with flying banners marched through Greencastle. The air was played so well that it called forth long, loud cheers from our boys. A young man standing on the side walk, remarked, "That's what we need to play going down South." The Rebs took fire at his taunt like a tinder box, and had not the fellow "dried up" quickly, he would have been handled roughly.

Chambersburg numbers about 8,000 inhabitants. It is decidedly a handsome town, and can boast a number of superb public and private buildings. The tower of the city hall was crowded with eager spectators, and many beautiful ladies, and handsomely dressed gentlemen, thronged the side-walks and balconies, gazing in wondering amazement at the host of rebels passing through.

Many old farmers expressed their surprise at our numbers, saying they did not think there were as many men in the entire South! When they ask our strength, the boys reply that we number about 300,000!

One fellow in Chambersburg replied to the question, "Where is Milroy our commissary?" that he was at Harrisburg, and would feed us on powder and lead! He had no answer for the question, "Why are you not there to help him?" Some of the citizens are glad we are here, as the conscription law is suspended. Anything to avoid being drafted.

The country thus far is unsurpassed for fertility and beauty. The wheat, oat, barley and clover fields resemble the prairies of the West. The farmers have the most magnificent barns I ever saw. A Dutchman's pride is in his large well-filled barns. All the residences are neat, but substantial buildings of stone and brick, about one-fourth the size of their magnificent barns.

Our quartermasters and commissaries have impressed a great many fine horses, mules and beef cattle. Very little private property—that is, poultry, vegetables, bee hives, &c., and no household furniture, no pantries or milk houses have been disturbed by the soldiers. Orders are very strict in this respect.

The inhabitants say McClellan is in command at Harrisburg, and has a regular and militia force of 60,000. Gen. Ewell is at Carlisle, 15 miles this side of Harrisburg. We hear nothing of Hooker's whereabouts. By "grapevine" dispatch I learn that he is still hugging his breastworks around Washington and doing picket duty in the gaps of the Blue Ridge, momentarily expecting Gen. Lee to attack him! Poor tool of a crack-brained despotism, he is not less jeered and abused by his own kith and kin than by the impudent rebels. He is surely moving somewhere—perhaps towards Philadelphia. We are in the heart of their country with a large and formidable army. They must, of necessity, make some counter move or abandon their country to subjugation.

Much breath is spent in speculating about Gen. Lee's plans. It is difficult to fathom his designs; and it is well for us that it is so, as the enemy would soon check mate him if his plans were loosely laid or apparent to every body. It is evident though, that one part of his grand programme, is to transfer the seat of the war to their own country, and let them feel for a while what war is. If successful, Washington will, of sheer necessity fall into our hands. But I will not speculate. It becomes me better to speak of accomplished facts.

5 p.m.—Our mail carrier has arrived with letters and Richmond papers, but no *Republicans*. He will return to Winchester to-morrow.

Since the preceding pages were written I have seen and heard enough to change materially the character of one paragraph therein contained. The 38th Virginia, on duty in town last night, entered the stores and took everything they wanted. Members of this brigade [Benning's] went to town this morning, and finding the stores open, took what they wanted. Chickens, bacon, vegetables, honey, butter, &c., are coming into camps in large quantities. Much of it was bought, the citizens readily taking Confederate money; while hundreds of soldiers are scouring the country, taking everything they can appropriate. Virginians and North Alabamians are retaliating upon the Pennsylvanians for the depredations committed upon their homes. Report says that the citizens shut themselves up and the soldiers have everything their own way. A respectable young man in the 15th Georgia says the streets of Chambersburg are strewn with gloves and fragments of goods. General Lee should and will punish such vandalism, even against our enemies.

V. A. S. P.

"V. A. S. P." wrote no more letters; Capt. Virgil Parks was killed on July 2, at Gettysburg.

The Great Battle of Gettysburg by P. W. A.

GETTYSBURG, PA., July 4, 1863 [7-20-63]

The bloodiest and most desperate battle of this bloody and desperate war, has just been fought here, on the soil of Pennsylvania. It commenced on the evening of Wednesday, the 1st inst., was renewed on the 2nd, and again on the 3rd, and the two armies still face each other in line of battle, worn, battle-scarred, and severely punished. The Confederates have had the best of the terrible conflict, yet their success has been purchased at a cost that will carry grief to many thousand hearts in our suffering land. I forwarded a full telegraphic synopsis of the battle to Winchester, and trust it was received in due season. Below you have a more detailed account, written under every possible disadvantage:

The two armies moved with great rapidity from the banks of the Rappahannock across the Potomac, and through Maryland into Pennsylvania. Federal prisoners say they marched, on an average, twenty-five miles a day, and that they stripped themselves of all surplus baggage and transportation that might impede their movements. The two leaders seemed to understand the designs of each other; at least, there is good reason for believing that Gen. Lee expected to encounter his antagonist not far from the place where he finally met him. It is probable, however, that he would have chosen a different field, and one somewhat nearer both to Baltimore and Washington; but the rapidity with which General Meade advanced, left him no alternative but to accept battle here or to maneuver for a more advantageous position. As it was, General Meade had the choice of ground, and most excellent use did he make of it. A position more favorable to himself and more unfavorable to Gen. Lee, (should the latter make the assault,) could hardly have been selected. His line extended along a range of hills just in front, and a little to the right of Gettysburg, and nearly parallel to the Gettysburg and Emmitsburg turnpike, and the South Mountain in our rear. His right wing rested upon Cemetery Hill, opposite to the town, and his left upon two very high hills or mountain spurs, one of which was covered with timber, and the other with immense rocks, behind which his men were protected as under a wall of adamant.

General Lee's position was also a strong one, but in no respect equal to that of the enemy. His line extended from a point above the town along a gently swelling ridge to the right. The space between the two lines, which was some four miles in length, was undulating, and, for the most part, free of timber and other obstructions, except an occasional stone fence and farm-house. The distance from one line to the other, or rather from one line of hills to the other, varied from a thousand to fifteen hundred yards; so that the party that should make the assault, would be subjected to a murderous artillery fire before his infantry could get within musket range. The enemy decided to receive the attack, and thus he secured all the great advantages which his position gave him.

Hearing of Meade's approach, Gen. Lee, on the 30th ult., put the forces about Chambersburg in motion. [William] Pender's and [Henry] Heth's divisions of Hill's corps were the first to cross the South Mountain by the Cashtown turnpike. They approached Gettysburg on the 1st instant, and finding the enemy in position between himself and the town, Gen. Hill proceeded at once to give him battle. The attack was made with vigor and success; the enemy was driven back with heavy loss through the town to the range of hills which he finally occupied during the remainder of the conflict. The battle did not open until after midday. Late in the afternoon Early and Rodes of Ewell's corps came up on the left from York, and contributed largely to the success of our arms. Several flags, including the colors of the 104th New York regiment, nearly all of the enemy's wounded, and about 3,000 prisoners, fell into our hands. General [John] Reynolds, who commanded the Federal forces (Gen. Meade with the main body of the army not having then arrived) and Gen. [Gabriel] Paul were killed [Paul survived]. Had not night put an end to the conflict, we should have gained the strong position which the enemy finally occupied. We lost a few prisoners on our part, including Brigadier General [James] Archer of Maryland, who commanded the Tennessee brigade.

Johnson's division of Ewell's corps, and Anderson's division of A. P. Hill's, reached the ground just at night, but not in time to participate in the conflict. Longstreet's corps, except [George] Pickett's division, arrived within three miles of the battlefield late at night, preceded a few hours by General Lee. The whole of the Federal army, largely reinforced by the troops stationed at Washington, Baltimore, Harper's Ferry, and other available points, came up the same night; and Gen. Meade assumed immediate command of the Federal troops as Gen. Lee did ours. Thus concentrated, the two armies were ready for the second day's fight.

It was late in the afternoon of the 2nd before either army got fully into position. Gen. Lee desired to make the attack immediately, feeling confident that his infantry were able to carry any position however strong. But little disposition was shown to undertake a proper reconnaissance of the ground—an omission which every man in the army now deeply regrets. It was well known that Meade had chosen a formidable position, but the extent and strength of his line bore to the mountain spurs on the right, were but little understood.

Longstreet was posted on the right, Hill in the center, and Ewell on the left. It was deemed advisable to make an effort to turn the enemy's left flank, and Longstreet was charged with that important duty. For this purpose McLaws' and Hood's divisions were put in motion, but the latter discovered, after proceeding some distance by a circuitous route, that he could go no further in that direction without bringing his column within view of the enemy, and thus disclosing the whole movement. It became necessary, therefore, for him to retrace his steps, and to advance by another route. In this way much time was lost before the movement upon the enemy's flank could be executed, and which might have been avoided by a previous examination of the ground. McLaws' proper position was on the extreme right, but in the hurry to make the attack Hood was placed on the right of McLaws next to him. Both of these excellent officers desired that a reconnaissance of the ground should proceed the assault, in order to ascertain, if possible, whether the enemy occupied the high hills in their front, and in what force; but the decision of Generals Lee and Longstreet was against it, and the assaulting column was ordered to move forward.

It is a fact not generally known, and which it may not be improper to state in this connection, that in all his famous flank movements Gen. Jackson was careful to examine the ground and to learn the exact position of the enemy, and hence his blows were always well aimed and terrible in effect. Such, too, is Gen. Lee's practice, but in the present case it was probably supposed that an immediate attack before the enemy could get into position, would more than counterbalance the disadvantages resulting from inexact knowledge of the ground.

But four o'clock had arrived, and the first gun from [M. W.] Henry's battalion of artillery announced that the assault had commenced on the extreme right. [Lt. Col. Henry] Cabell's battalion, of McLaws' division, opened next, and in a few minutes the artillery fire became general along our entire line. The splendid divisions of Hood and McLaws swept on to the charge in admirable style. An officer who was present said it was worth ten years of ordinary life to witness the manner in which McLaws' division rushed across the field and assaulted the almost impregnable position in front. It was soon discovered that the enemy was in strong force upon the mountain spurs on the right, and that it was impossible to turn his position and get in his rear, without passing around the mountains, which was impracticable; but it was then too late to pause, and onward the column moved in the face of a terrible fire of musketry and converging batteries. If the position could not be turned, the only alternative left was to dislodge the foe by hard blows. These blows were given freely; he was pushed from the wooded mountain, and his line bent back until it rested upon the high rocky hill or eminence. Indeed, his line all along Longstreet's front was driven back with immense loss; battery after battery was silenced or carried by storm, and a large number of flags taken and about 1,800 prisoners captured chiefly by McLaws' division. It is estimated that Wofford's Georgia brigade alone killed, wounded and captured more men than he had in his whole command. He brought off four splendid flags, taken by the infantry of Tom Cobb's Legion and Phillips' Legion, and passed so many prisoners to the rear that at one time he feared the enemy had turned his own position.

It was during this brilliant charge that Major General Hood, one of the best officers in the service, received a painful, though not dangerous, wound in the left arm, which made it necessary for him to turn the command of his division over to that rising young officer, Brig. Gen. Law of Alabama, whose excellent brigade formed a part of the division. Brig. Gens. [G. T.] Anderson of Georgia, and [Jerome] Robertson of Texas, were also wounded in the same charge, the former in the thigh. Gens. Law and Benning escaped without a bruise, though many of their field officers were killed or wounded, and their regiments badly cut up. In McLaws' division, Gen. Barksdale, one of the bravest and noblest spirits that have fallen in all the war, was killed, and Gen. Semmes, as true a knight as ever drew a blade, and who never says to his command "go on," but always "come on," was seriously wounded. An effort was made to save Gen. Barksdale's body, but it could not be done. He had led his brigade, hat in hand, and had first carried a heavy battery, when he was shot down by one of the enemy's retreating sharpshooters. Other batteries bore upon the position he had taken, and their terrible converging fire rendered it necessary for his brigade, which was also thrown into temporary confusion by his fall, to retire somewhat to the rear. The enemy waved their flag over his prostrate body when they re-occupied the eminence from which he and his brave Mississippians had driven them. Gen. Barksdale's last hasty words were: "Give my love to my dear family and tell them I died at my post."

Gen. Semmes had carried a tourniquet on his person since the beginning of the war. The fire of the enemy becoming more fearful than any he had ever witnessed in the many battles through which he had passed unscathed, he took the tourniquet from his bosom and was holding it in his hand, when he was struck in the thigh by a minie ball and the femoral artery cut. He applied the tourniquet with his own hand and stopped the hemorrhage until a surgeon could take up the artery; otherwise he must have died in a few minutes.

It is but justice to the dead and the living that the names of the brigades composing the divisions in Longstreet's corps, which participated in this brilliant work, should here be given, and it is to be regretted that time and space do not allow me to record the names of the regiments and officers also. The brigades are: In McLaws' division, Semmes' and Wofford's from Georgia, Barksdale's from Mississippi, and Kershaw's from South Carolina; and in Hood's division, Law's brigade from Alabama, Robertson's from Texas, and Benning's and Anderson's from Georgia. There is no better material in all the army than in these noble brigades. The Twenty-fourth Georgia, whose Colonel (McMillan) was absent on leave, wavered for a moment; but Gen. Longstreet placed himself at the head of it and led it forward, when the men gave him three rousing cheers and rushed upon the foe in most gallant style. Kershaw and his Carolinians always behave well, and their conduct on the present occasion, as well as that of the other officers and brigades in the corps, was all that could be desired.

It is proper to add that though Hood and McLaws captured a number of batteries, they were able to bring off but few guns. Gen. Meade, who belonged to the corps of Topographical Engineers, had chosen his ground, and posted his artillery so wisely that one battery bore upon another; so that when a battery was taken, it was found impossible to bring off the guns on account of the fire from other batteries bearing upon the position. In most instances too, the horses were killed, and the intervening stone fences prevented our men from drawing the guns from the field by hand.

But I must hurry on, even though my account should be meager and unsatisfactory; for the courier has saddled his horse and is ready to leave. I trust he may get through safely, and that my letter may reach you in due season.

The attack on the center, unfortunately, was not made simultaneously with that on the right. The same may be said of the attack on the left. The artillery opened about the same time all along the line, but McLaws and Hood had been engaged some time before Hill's infantry advanced to the charge; and when they did advance, their movement was not regular and systematic as it should have been. For instance, Anderson's division of Hill's corps, which was posted on the left of McLaws, never did get fully into action, while Pender's division did not fire a gun until late in the day. Anderson's division, for example, was posted in the following order: [Cadmus] Wilcox's brigade on the right, [William] Mahone's on the left, [Ambrose] Wright's in the center, [Edward A.] Perry's on the right center, and [Carnot] Posey's on the left center. Wilcox was to advance first, to be followed by the other brigades in their order to the left. Wilcox and his unconquerable Alabamians moved out at the appointed time and fought long and desperately. Perry's brigade (Perry was not present himself) advanced a short distance, but did not become fully engaged. Wright went boldly forward, and excelled, if possible, all his previous performances, though at a fearful cost to his command, as will be seen when a list of his losses shall come to be published. His brigade captured a battery of 20 guns, and two of his best officers—Maj. [George] Ross and Capt. [C. R.] Redding, of Macon—were shot down while endeavoring to move off the guns. The first was badly wounded and left on the field; the other was killed. But Posey, who was to move next in order, was unwilling, it is reported, to advance, contending that his left flank would be uncovered, and that Mahone should move first. Mahone, on the other hand, declined to proceed unless Posey and Pender's division on his left should do so at the same time. Upon this fact being made known to Pender he rode forward to examine the ground, when he received a wound and was disabled. The question then arose among his Brigadiers as to who was the senior officer, and this point was not settled until about sunset. Meanwhile, Wilcox and Wright were struggling with mortal odds against them; but their valor and blood were expended to little purpose, since the effect of their courageous efforts was defeated by the unpardonable conduct of other portions of the division. Wilcox's loss, as well as Wright's was very heavy. Among the killed in the brigade of the latter was Col. William Gibson, of the 48th Georgia.

I am not yet well informed in regard to the order in which Ewell's corps became engaged, and cannot, therefore enter into details. It is reported, however, that the attack on the left was made a little late, and not with even and well sustained lines. I know not whether this account is entirely correct; but it may be safely affirmed that the corps fought well, and was skillfully handled after it did become engaged. It is said that on the left, as on the right and center, the enemy was driven from several strong positions; but that it was found impossible to hold them, owing to the commanding fire of batteries posted in the rear, and to the right and left.

The results of the second day's fight may be summed up in a few words: The Confederates inflicted a tremendous loss upon the enemy, drove him a mile and a half on the right, captured about two thousand prisoners, a large number of flags and batteries, and won the ground on which the conflict for the most part had been waged, but owing to the great strength of the enemy's position—far exceeding that at Malvern Hill—the skillful arrangement of his numerous and admirably served artillery, and the want of previous knowledge on our part of the precise nature of the ground, they found it impracticable to hold the positions or bring off many of the guns they had taken. Law's brigade, of Hood's division, carried one of the batteries on the mountain, and turned the guns upon the enemy; but being raked by a cruel fire from other positions, he found it necessary, finally to abandon it. For the most part, however, Longstreet maintained the ground he had won on the right, until late next day, when he voluntarily withdrew from it to his original line. Our own loss was very heavy, especially in Hood's and McLaws' divisions, and Wright's and Wilcox's brigades of Anderson's division.

General Lee did not renew the attack next day—Friday, the 3rd—until ten o'clock, when he opened upon the enemy from all parts of his line with over a hundred and forty guns. The enemy responded promptly and vigorously, using a great deal of round shot, his supply of shell, it may be, having been exhausted. So heavy an artillery fire was probably never heard before. Our guns were well served, as was shown by the ground around the Federal batteries, which was covered with dead men and horses. At a quarter to three o'clock, and after the artillery had prepared the way, Pickett's Virginia division, Longstreet's corps, which had only arrived the night before, was ordered to assault Cemetery Hill, which was considered the key to the enemy's whole position. He was supported by Heth's division, commanded by [J. Johnston] Pettigrew, (Heth having been wounded in the first day's fight,) and Wilcox's brigade, of Anderson's division—both belonging to Hill's corps. Pickett's charge was made in excellent order and gallant style, and he succeeded in wresting a portion of the hill and the guns in that quarter from the enemy; but the enfilading fires which were brought to bear upon him, and the failure of Pettigrew to get up simultaneously with himself, rendered it necessary for him to retire with great loss. Of his brigadiers, Gens. [Richard] Garnett was killed, and left on the field; Gen. [James] Kemper mortally wounded [wounded and captured], and since dead, and Gen. [Lewis] Armistead wounded (since dead). All of his field officers were struck, except two or three, and many of them killed.

Today all has been quiet along the lines. Gen. Lee has endeavored to provoke the enemy to make an assault upon his position, by throwing his skirmishers forward; but Gen. Meade, who has displayed much skill and judgement, is too well aware of the strength of his own position and the madness of attacking Lee. Besides, if not nearly annihilated, he is certainly too badly crippled to undertake so hazardous an enterprise. If he can but save his army and get it away, he will doubtless be more than content.

It would have been better for us, perhaps, if our attack had been delayed until the next day, and the interval had been devoted to a careful reconnaissance of the ground. The delay would have enabled Gen. Lee to get his army into proper position, would have given the troops time to rest and prepare rations, and have insured a systematic combined and simultaneous attack from all parts of his lines. If this plan had been pursued, it is believed that the enemy would have been dislodged from his formidable position before now, and driven ignominiously back upon his capital. It was probably Gen. Lee's desire however, to fall upon his adversary before he could get into position, confident that his troops were equal to any demand upon their courage and constancy. But no person, much less one who, like myself, is unskilled in military affairs, can safely criticize the operations of such a commander as Lee, and I forbear, not for his sake, but my own.

July 5—Gen. Meade withdrew his army last night to the direction, it is supposed, of Frederick. It is said that Gen. Lee was aware of the movement, or guessed that it would be made, and commenced to put his own army in motion about the same time. No pursuit has been attempted, or any demonstration made by either party. We are now moving down the South Mountain towards Hagerstown, with a view probably to reopen our line of communications and to prepare for further efforts. There are other satisfactory reasons for returning to Hagerstown, which it would be improper to state, but which would be considered good if made known. But more of this hereafter.

I have made all necessary arrangements to procure lists of the killed and wounded, and hope to be able to forward them in a day or two.

I have omitted to state that while the battle was raging on Friday, the enemy's cavalry made an effort to pass round our right wing. To foil the movement, General Law, who had detached a battery, [M. W.] Henry's battalion, and the First Texas and Eleventh and Fifteenth Georgia, the latter for the time under command of Maj. Henry McDaniel, of the Eleventh. The artillery engaged the attention of the enemy in front, while the infantry passed around to his rear, and opened a murderous fire from that quarter. The end is soon told. Of two regiments of Federal cavalry engaged only 18 men escaped, all the others were killed or captured.

P. W. A.

Further Details of the Great Battle of Gettysburg

HAGERSTOWN, MD., July 7, 1863 [7-21-63]

The army reached this point yesterday, and has gone into camp. This apparent retrograde movement may occasion some surprise in the public mind, especially in view of Meade's withdrawal and Lee's failure to pursue him. If so, I can only express the decided conviction that the reasons for returning to Hagerstown were conclusive and satisfactory, though the time has not yet come when they may be safely declared. One thing, however, cannot escape the attention of intelligent men, to wit: that no army, whatever may be its triumphs in the field, and however successfully its commissariat may be supplied and its transportation conducted, can long maintain itself in an enemy's country without a well established base and safe and easy communication. In the present instance Gen. Lee's line of communications had been interrupted to a degree which rendered it difficult, if not impossible, to correspond with the government, or to receive supplies of any description. The army has not suffered for want of excellent food since it crossed the Potomac, though it cannot well remain in any one locality beyond four or five days at a time, in consequence of the scarcity of provisions. The farmers upon the approach of the army not only remove their horses and take off one or more wheels from their wagons, but they drive the beef cattle into distant districts and conceal them in the mountains; so that it is impossible to subsist the troops and animals employed in necessary transportation at one point for any considerable period. The supply of bacon and corn is limited, but little comparatively being produced in Maryland and Pennsylvania. There is a great abundance of wheat and flour and hay however, and of these the army has made very free use. The merchants and manufacturers also have sent into the interior—in some instances as far as Philadelphia—their stocks of clothing, shoes and hats. To such an extent has this policy been carried, that the troops in Ewell's corps, which led the advance, and had, therefore, better opportunity to supply themselves, are in worse condition in regard to shoes, (owing to their longer marches) than those in Longstreet's corps which brought up the rear. The reader will thus perceive some of the disadvantages attending an invading army, and how a policy like this on the part of farmers and merchants can be made as effective against Gen. Lee as the burning of Moscow by the Russians was against Bonaparte. But let us return to the late battle.

The success of our arms on the first day of the battle, when we inflicted a loss upon the enemy, according to his own admission, of 10,000 men in killed, wounded and prisoners, demonstrates the fact that if the Confederate army had been concentrated twenty-four hours sooner than it was, it could have destroyed Meade, and put his government and capital in the greatest jeopardy. Only four divisions were engaged on our part, one of which (Early's) arrived on the ground late in the afternoon; whilst the enemy had present three, or parts of three, army corps, all of which were represented by the prisoners captured. Had the whole army, or the greater part of it even, been on the ground on the 1st inst., when the battle commenced, it would have been an easy matter to dispose of the three Federal corps alluded to, and then to have fallen upon the remainder of Meade's forces before they could possibly get into position. If this be true, was not the march of Ewell upon Harrisburg unfortunate and ill-advised, in that it lost us precious time? It is understood that it was no part of Lee's plan to reduce Harrisburg; he could not afford to fritter away his time and strength upon harmless militiamen, while the main army of the enemy remained in the field. Having first disposed of the army, he might then march wheresoever he pleased, whether to Washington, to Baltimore, to Harrisburg or Philadelphia.

As has already been stated, Early's division of Ewell's corps reached the field late in the afternoon, but in time to contribute largely to the success of the Confederate arms. He came by the York turnpike, and took position on the left of Rodes' division, also of Ewell's corps, then hotly engaged—Pender's and Heth's division of Hill's corps being on the right, and the only other forces present. The enemy yielded easily to the impetuous charges of our men, and was thrown into much confusion and suffered more heavily, in proportion to the numbers engaged, than on the two following days. Gordon's (late Lawton's) brigade, for instance, counted 270 dead on that part of the field where it fought (being on the extreme left), and took more prisoners than his whole command numbered! His own dead was just 40. The brigade is one of the best in the service, and it has acquired fresh renown by its conduct in the late battles. It was known that Longstreet's corps would come up that night, and hence the enemy was not pressed after dark, after the fashion of Jackson; otherwise, it is not improbable the Federals might have been driven entirely from the field, and the advantageous position subsequently taken by Meade would have been secured for ourselves.

The strength of this position cannot hardly be exaggerated. The enemy not only occupied a range of hills, but along much of the rocky ridge was a stone fence, behind which his infantry were as well posted as ours were at Fredericksburg. He had also strengthened his position by abattis and throwing up field works wherever they could be of advantage. He even constructed works on the bald rocky hill on the right [Little Round Top], impregnable as the position seemed to be, and dragged artillery up its rugged sides to repel our assaults.

The artillery practice throughout the three days conflict was superb on both sides. The enemy's guns were served with great skill and judgment, and some of their shots were surprisingly accurate. The same may be said of the Confederate batteries, in the service of which there has been a decided improvement since last year. The policy of placing sections and single batteries in isolated positions, where their fire, however accurate, can produce but little effect upon the general result, has been abandoned, and a number of batteries are now massed together in commanding position—and a heavy fire concentrated upon the point of attack. There has also been much improvement in the character of our projectiles.

The loss on both sides was much heavier than in any battle of the war, and the wounds inflicted, as a general thing, more serious. The Washington *Chronicle* of the 5th, the mendacious organ of the Federal Administration, estimates our entire casualties in killed, wounded and prisoners, at 40,000, and admits that its own side suffered more than in any previous engagement. Our loss was heavy enough, though nothing like as much as the *Chronicle's* figures would had one to believe. It will not exceed 16,000, nor fall below 12,000. Say 2,000 killed, 10,000 wounded, and 1,200 missing or prisoners—making altogether 13,200. If the wounded who were left behind, be counted both as wounded and prisoners, then our loss will exceed this estimate somewhat. All the available transportation was brought into requisition to remove the wounded, and yet it was found necessary to leave a considerable number behind, and especially those whose injuries were serious. They were placed in houses and tents, and surgeons, nurses and cooks were left with them, and several days rations provided. The enemy, malignant and unprincipled as he is in other respects, has generally treated our wounded with kindness; and the friends, therefore, of those who may have fallen into his hands at Gettysburg, should not indulge in needless apprehensions in regard to the treatment they will receive.

The enemy's loss may be safely put down at 25,000, including 6,000 prisoners. Such is the opinion of impartial persons who examined different parts of the field. His infantry gave us but little trouble, it was his numerous and well served artillery and the strength of his position that enabled him to make such an obstinate resistance.

The ambulance train, with such of our wounded as could be moved, is now at Williamsport, unable to cross the Potomac on account of a freshet in the river. There has not been a whole day of sunshine since we left the top of the Blue Ridge, nearly three weeks ago. It has rained, more or less, every day or two, and the roads have been very heavy. Last year we had dust and drought; this year mud and rain. The wounded will, probably, be placed in hospitals at Winchester, Staunton and other convenient points in the Valley.

About 4,500 prisoners taken at Gettysburg are also at Williamsport , on their way to Richmond. Some 1,500 were paroled near the battlefield, but the Federal authorities are reported to have declared that they would not recognize the parole, and required that the prisoners should be taken to City Point, below Richmond, since that and Vicksburg were the only places at which an exchange could be properly effected under the agreement of the two governments. Of course this was not the true reason for withholding their consent to an exchange at Gettysburg. They were afraid that the temptation to their troops to surrender themselves, in order to get home, would be too strong for many of them to resist. They, doubtless, desired also to force Gen. Lee to detach a large force to guard the prisoners to Richmond, and to impose upon him all the expense of provisioning them, as well as all the risk of conducting them safely back to Virginia. The objection was well taken, however, and we have no just cause of complaint for their refusal.

My letters and telegrams of the 4th and 5th insts. have just been returned to me, the courier not being able to cross the Potomac, on account of the freshet. Until yesterday, the line was interrupted by the presence of Federal cavalry, and when they were driven off it was ascertained that the river could not be forded, and the ferry chain had been broken. This is indeed vexatious, but all has been done that could be done to get my communications through.

P. W. A.

Official casualty figures for the Battle of Gettysburg were: Federals, 3,155 killed, 14,529 wounded, and 5,365 missing for a total of 23,049; Confederates, 2,592 killed, 12,709 wounded, and 5,150 missing for 20,451.

Another Soldier Correspondent, "Tout-le-Monde" who served in Benning's Georgia Brigade contributed to the Savannah Republican *soon after the Battle of Gettysburg.*

Special Correspondence from TOUT-LE-MONDE

HAGERSTOWN, July 7, 1863 [7-22-63]

The last letter we wrote you was from Chambersburg, Penn., which, in all probability, you have never received, for our communication has been cut off for the last eight or ten days by the enemy's cavalry hovering about the rear of Lee's army. However, from that point we will continue, as nothing of importance came before, unless it was the actual invasion.

Having rested well, General Lee turned his course towards Gettysburg, which lay in an easterly direction on the way to Baltimore. Near a little town called Fayetteville, a gap in a small range was passed, and on the night of the 2nd of July rested within a few miles of Gettysburg. News came to us that General Ewell had been fiercely engaged the same day, and that the enemy were in large force before us. Early next morning we passed on to our lines, which had already been formed just beyond the town, from which the enemy had been driven the day before; and our suspicions were correct, for the enemy's skirmishers were in full view. The dead of the battle which had been fought the day before lay in many places over the ground, and also a large number of the wounded of both armies were seen lying about the farm houses which we passed. These unmistakable signs of blood left us no longer in doubt of the path that was before us. Behind the position which the enemy held was a small range of mountains, which, it seem, was purposely selected to fall back into, in case our troops forced them from the low hills already occupied. The advantage lay largely in the enemy's favor, and the probabilities of forcing him beyond the range were very much questioned by many who thought anything of the coming battle. The morning was occupied in maneuvering and waiting for the enemy to advance. This, it seemed, he would not do, and Gen. Lee had come for the purpose of giving him battle. As soon as everything was adjusted the advance was ordered.

General Hood formed his line on the extreme right of the line of battle. At the command the line advanced to carry the right, at which point it seemed Gen. Lee had aimed as the weak point in the enemy's position. Every man had nerved himself for death; for as the skirt of woods, in which the line had been arranged previous to advancing, was passed, beyond lay a field a mile in width running to the foot of the range which contained 13 pieces of artillery, making a gradual ascent until the foot was reached. As soon as we came in sight a furious blast of cannon broke from the tops of the hills and mountains around and the terrific cry and screams of shells began. Slowly the line moved in order forward, such of it as we saw, and that was Gen. Benning's brigade, undismayed by the terrors that seemed to awake from the infernal regions. Our batteries now began to open in the rear, sending the hissing shot over, answering to the enemy's guns in front. They hardly attracted the fire of any of his, but all seemed concentrated on the advancing lines. Down the plunging shot came, bursting before and around and everywhere tearing up the ground in a terrific rain of Death. Still the old brigade moved on in its solid and beautiful line, the red star gemmed cross floating defiantly in the midst. As it approached the guns, the rain of grape and canister began, mingling their sharp cries with the shrill whistle of the mad minie balls which seemed to come in showers. The ranks began to melt away, but springing forward with a shout the undismayed line steadily rushed on, determined this time to sacrifice every life or carry the cannon crowned hill before them.

The artillery raged with its fiercest fury, till now the very air seemed covered with the missiles of death. The storm of musketry that followed was the most terrific ever listened to by mortal man. The line reached the foot of the hill—that portion of it embraced by the 15th and 20th Georgia, the 2nd and 17th being forced into a gorge that lay between it and the mountain on the right. The 15th and 20th clambered over the rocks and pressed forward, and the 17th and 2nd plunged through the raking fire that now, more terrific than before, swept the gorge like a furious torrent. The enemy dismayed at such daring began to break before the fire which was now hurled through his ranks, and began a hurried flight to the mountain side which was lined with hundreds of minie rifles. The gunners [Smith's Battery] fled from their guns, leaving the three splendid Parrot pieces which had been pouring death into the old brigade for one mile. The hill and its artillery was ours. The inaccessible mountains still lay before it, but its steep rocky sides were beyond the ability of our men to carry, under the awful hail storm that came like a torrent, from its summit. But secreting themselves behind the rocks, our men defied the plunging fires that vainly tried to drive them back. The enemy formed his lines and swept down the hill to recapture the guns, but the steady fore of the old brigade swept him away and broke his ranks in every futile effort. Again and again he formed and desperately stormed at the hill which contained his guns, but at each time his ranks were broken and hurled back on the mountain heights. All the while the summits were blazing with cannon. The shells and shrapnel shot descended, exploding in the earth and hurling the rocks to an amazing heighth, but in spite of all, our men held their places firmly. A part of the Texas brigade were mingled in with the Georgians, and a braver lot of men never bit a cartridge. Coolly and deliberately every one waited till some favored one of the foe came within his range and sent the message of death to him. The attack commenced at near 3 o'clock, and raged until dark closed the horrors of that awful day. Then we stepped out from our hiding places to take away our dead and wounded. Silence reigned, except the wails of the maimed which rose dismally in the gloom and darkness. What an awful scene it was, there where everything was wrapt in night, with scarcely a thing visible, except the solemn mountains which rose darkly on the horizon, among the dead! The whole night was employed in removing the wounded for the next day's terrors. Those costly guns were rolled away, with the price of blood on them; the men placed in position to sleep away the hours which would bring on another grand day. So the day dawned.

But it seemed the idea which had infatuated our leaders to try these mountain passes had gone. The day before had taught a different lesson; for wherever General Lee had hurried his forces, they had driven the enemy until he reached the mountain passes. There he held his ground. Everywhere we had inflicted injury on the enemy, but our loss was terrific.

Gen. Hood was wounded, Barksdale killed, Semmes wounded, [G. T.] Anderson, Robertson wounded; Armistead wounded, Kemper and Garnett killed, all favorite generals of their commands, and perhaps others of whom we have not heard up to this moment. In our brigade Col. [John] Jones of the 20th Georgia, was killed, and also Lt. Col. [William] Harris, 2nd Georgia, besides numbers of other officers. Such mortality among officers was never known in the history of this war. So the day passed off with cannonading and some fighting on the right with cavalry, which resulted in capturing some two or three hundred. Our list of prisoners was swelled, so it was said, to 7,000. In the evening of the 4th the enemy came near flanking this brigade, but by a timely movement it barely escaped. The lines were drawn up behind and to the right of Gettysburg, where on the 4th Gen. Lee awaited the advance of the enemy. Except skirmishing he never came. At night Gen. Lee began to withdraw, and by the morning of the 5th was among the mountains on the turnpike towards Hagerstown. The enemy followed feebly, for it began now to be ascertained that he was withdrawing towards Washington. Now, this is written near Hagerstown, through which we passed last night. There was considerable cavalry fighting in the streets yesterday, hurting very few that we have learned. Everybody seemed frightened to death, for no lights were on the streets, and the city appeared like the residence of the dead. There is still some game and defiant residents who dare to maintain repugnance to Yankeeism. They report that after our army left last year no insult which their infamous enemies could heap upon them were spared them and some even arrested. But some are firm to the end.

It is much regret that our information would not allow us to give a more detailed account of the fighting of troops, but this will be excused when you learn we were busy all the while. But P. W. A. was on the ground. Your correspondent, V. A. S. P., was killed. He died nobly in the ranks, a brave and honorable soldier.

TOUT-LE-MONDE.

P. W. A. in Maryland

HAGERSTOWN, MD., July 10, 1863 [7-21-63]

There is one thing which it seems impossible for our military men to learn, and that is the advantage of a corps of pioneers and pontooners to go before the army, clear the way of obstructions, repair roads, construct bridges, and do whatever else may be necessary to facilitate the passage of troops. The necessity for such an organization has been abundantly demonstrated within the last four days. The army returned to this place with 4,500 prisoners, who had to be conducted to Richmond to be exchanged, and with an exhausted ordnance train that could be replenished only from the south side of the Potomac, which has been and is now so much swollen at Williamsport ford as to render it impassable to man or horse; and yet the only means at hand to cross over the prisoners and wounded brought off from Gettysburg, and receive supplies of ammunition, are a few ferry flats, which are drawn to and fro by the aid of a chain that was broken two days ago.

We have been here four days, and still we have neither pontoons, rafts, or other helps to cross, except such as have been mentioned. And all this, too, at a time when the army is in the country of the enemy, and just from a field where, while it was not beaten, it cannot claim to have been victorious.

True there is a body of about twenty-eight men, called pioneers, attached to each division of the army, who are furnished with axes, picks, and spades; but they are of little service, and do little else than lay a few rails across swollen branches, and pull down fences for the troops to march through the fields where the roads are rough or muddy. It is said that an Engineer corps is about to be organized, numbering one hundred men to each division, and having one captain and three lieutenants—the whole to be under an officer with the rank of Colonel. It is hoped that this is so, and that the corps will be commanded by practical engineers, and made up of carpenters, mechanics and blacksmiths, and that will be provided with portable forges and saw mills, and bridge timbers pitted together and ready to be laid down.

Pontoon boats, sufficient to lay one bridge across the Potomac, were hauled from Rapidan Station to the vicinity of Williamsport, but being left without a guard to protect them they were found by the enemy's cavalry scouts, during the absence of the army in Pennsylvania, and floated down to Harper's Ferry. If the same negligence and want of forethought are to prevail in the future, the Engineer corps which it is proposed to organize will accomplish but little good in moving the army. Under the superior energy and mechanical skill of our foes, the way of march is made smooth, and bridges and field works spring up like mushrooms in a night. As far back even as the beginning of the Christian era, Julius Caesar and his Roman legions knew how to throw a military bridge over the Rhine without the use of iron material, and in a space of time in which the Confederate engineers, with their present appliances, could hardly perform a similar feat.

It is reported that the last of the prisoners and many of the wounded have passed over the river; but it is questionable whether they will reach Winchester without an attempt to capture them being made by the enemy, who has had ample time to prepare for such an enterprise. Gen. Semmes crossed over some days ago and reached Martinsburg, where it is reported, he died last night of the wound. If the report is true, then the State of Georgia and the Confederate army have lost as true a gentleman and brave a soldier as ever graced a parlor or shed his blood on the field of battle. Of him it may be said as Marshal Ney, that he was "the bravest of the brave," and like the Chevalier Bayard, was without fear or reproach. He said to me the day after receiving his death wound, with tears of gratitude in his clear blue eyes, that his brigade had behaved with unsurpassed gallantry, and that he considered it a privilege to lay down his life for the liberties of his country. Like Bartow and Cobb, Gregg and Barksdale, Johnston and Jackson, and "the unknown and unrecorded dead" who have fallen in this war, he has quit this army and gone to join that grand army of martyrs who have shed their blood for the freedom of their race. What a precious contribution the people of these States have made to that heroic throng! How great is the price of liberty! How dearly should we prize the boon, and how reverently and affectionately should we regard the memory of those who have purchased it with their blood!

There has been heavy skirmishing in front to-day. Stuart's cavalry have been driven in, and they bring reports that the enemy is advancing along the Boonsboro' and Sharpsburg turnpikes. Kershaw and Col. Goode Bryan, commanding Semmes' brigade, were sent to meet him, and it was between their decimated commands and the Federal advance that the skirmishing took place. The opinion is prevalent that Gen. Meade intends to cross swords with Gen. Lee again. Knowing that there is a freshet in the Potomac which would render escape impossible in the event of a disaster to our arms—hoping that we have not yet replenished our advance train—and believing, since we too abandoned the battle field nearly as soon as he did, that we are in no condition to renew the conflict—he may hope, with the aid of fresh reinforcements, to take Gen. Lee at a disadvantage, and by one fell blow to end him. Whether the trial will come to-morrow or next day, or whether, finding that the river is falling, and Lee prepared to receive him, the Federal commander may not reconsider the matter, remains to be seen. Men are abundant and of but little value in the United States. In the Confederacy, on the contrary, where the population is less dense, even the surgeons have come to regard life of an able-bodied soldier as worth preserving. Under such unequal conditions, Mr. Lincoln may hope by rapid and repeated blows so far to disable us as to place us at his mercy.

The names of casualties come in slowly. Both officers and men are fatigued by recent trials, and busily engaged with other pressing duties; for the reasons already assigned, many of them have not found it convenient to prepare the lists.

P. W. A.

P. W. A. in Virginia

MARTINSBURG, VA., July 14, 1863 [7-27-63]

The army has re-crossed the Potomac into Virginia, and the time has come when the truth may be spoken, in candor and moderation, in regard to the late unfortunate campaign in Maryland and Pennsylvania. Up to the present time there has been no assurance that my letters would not fall into the hands of the enemy; and hence, as you must have observed, I did not deem it prudent to tell the *whole* truth, lest our mail carrier should be captured again and important information communicated to the Federal commander. A succinct and faithful narrative, bringing events down to the present date, will place your readers in possession of all the material facts, and show that the term "unfortunate," as applies to the operation of the army in Maryland, is not inappropriate, unless it be too mild.

No one with that part of the army left near Chambersburg suspected, on the morning of the 1st inst., that the great battle would begin on that day. I was sitting on the wet ground with my back against a tree writing to you and your readers, when Gen. Lee and his escort passed by in the direction of Cashtown and Gettysburg. He seemed to snuff the battle in the breeze, and for the first time it occurred to me that the enemy was approaching our lines. In a few minutes Anderson's division of Hill's corps marched down the same road, followed an hour or two later by Johnson's division of Ewell's corps, which had retraced its steps from Shippensburg. In the course of the morning orders came for Longstreet's corps, except Pickett's division left behind in Chambersburg, to follow on in the same direction, as soon as Gen. Ewell's train, sent back from Carlisle, should pass. This was an immense train, as long almost as a tail of a comet, and far more ominous of evil. It occupied four hours in passing, and moved so slowly through the Cashtown Gap (in the South Mountain) that Longstreet's corps was delayed until near midnight in reaching a point four miles distant from the battle ground. Pender's and Heth's divisions alone were in position to engage the enemy's advance column on the morning of the 1st. Early's and Rodes divisions of Ewell's corps arrived on the ground late in the afternoon, having marched down the Susquehanna from Carlisle to York, and thence to Gettysburg. These last two divisions joined the former, and together they drove the enemy back inflicting heavy loss; but Anderson's and Johnson's divisions, though near enough, were not put into the fight that evening. The enemy had, according to the statements of prisoners, three army corps present on the 1st, and that night and early next morning the remainder of Meade's forces were brought up and put in a very strong position. We did not press the enemy after nightfall.

The following deductions flow from the foregoing facts: Had Gen. Lee concentrated his forces twenty-four hours sooner, he might have dispersed, captured or destroyed the three Federal corps engaged on the first day, and have fallen upon the remaining forces then coming up and not yet in position, and driven them pell-mell back upon Baltimore or Washington. Or, if Anderson's and Johnson's divisions had been put in immediately upon their arrival and our advantage pressed with vigor that night, the enemy might have been driven beyond the formidable position he finally occupied, and from which we subsequently found it impossible to dislodge him. The same result would probably have followed, if Ewell's train had have turned out on the side of the road, and Longstreet's corps allowed to move rapidly to the front; or if the attack had been renewed early on the morning of the 2nd, instead of at a quarter to four in the afternoon.

It is understood that the reduction of Harrisburg constituted no part of General Lee's programme, since he could not afford to fritter away his strength and time upon the militia so long as an unbeaten army remained in the field. Having disposed of the army, he could then march wherever and whenever it suited him. The question then recurs, whether the distribution of his troops at different and distant points was not unfortunate, in this that it required more time to concentrate them when the time of battle had arrived. It was similar dispersion of his forces, after much hard fighting and marching, that prevented him from beating McClellan at Sharpsburg last year. His object then was the capture of the garrison at Harper's Ferry, in which he was successful. In the present instance it was his desire, doubtless, to place his army at convenient points for attack by cutting such railway lines as might be used against him, and to draw the enemy as far into the interior of the country as possible. But let us proceed.

Were we compelled to accept battle at the time and place we did? We were not. Having the start of the enemy from Fredericksburg, and the whole country before us, we might have chosen our own ground and time for making and receiving the attack. We might have occupied the pass at Cashtown, or remained on the north side of the South Mountain, or fallen down to Boonsboro' Gap. Having no base to protect, and no line of communication to keep open, but relying upon the districts we occupied for the means of subsistence, we were free to go where we pleased and to fight when we pleased.

But the battle was joined at the time and place selected by the Federal commander. The place, strong by nature, was rendered still more formidable by a number of stone fences which crossed the field, by the open ground we had to move over to reach it, and by field works thrown up by the enemy during the night. The attack was renewed by ourselves on the evening of the 2nd, without proper reconnaissances, and not simultaneously along the whole line, but irregularly and spasmodically, first by one corps or division, and then by another, reminding one of a team of ill-matched horses, which, refusing to pull together, are unable to move the load which a simultaneous and common effort might certainly accomplish. The troops never fought better or inflicted greater loss upon the enemy; and strong as the position of the latter was, they surely would have carried it, though at a heavy loss, if the attack had been differently planned. As it was they pushed the enemy back, ran over numberless batteries which they were unable to bring off, captured many flags, and killed and wounded more men than in any previous battle. Indeed, the more successful our assaults were up to a certain point, the greater was our loss; for the further an attacking column drove the enemy, not being supported by a combined attack, the more fearfully were its flanks raked by the oblique and enfilading fire of the batteries which were not assaulted. The enemy's left, which rested upon a mountain, McLaws and Hood, of Longstreet's corps, were ordered to turn his right wing, which rested upon open and less difficult ground.

On the 3rd, Pickett's division of Longstreet's corps, (which had come up the evening before), supported by a portion of Hill's corps, was ordered to assault Cemetery Hill near the center, believed to be the key to the position of the enemy. The order was executed in gallant style, and some of the batteries on the Hill were carried; but his success was temporary, though purchased at a fearful cost. The want of proper support, the movement of the enemy upon his exposed and bleeding flanks, and the terrible cross and oblique fires concentrated upon him from batteries not otherwise occupied, made it necessary for him to retrace his steps across the open ground over which he had advanced, his ranks torn and bleeding, and still suffering from the iron hail of shell, grape, canister and shrapnel that swept over the field. McLaws and Hood, Wright and Wilcox, Johnson and Early, had performed similar feats the day before, followed by similar results. Johnson slept upon the field within the enemy's entrenchments; Wright and Wilcox carried the ridge in their front, capturing numbers of guns, and driving the enemy from their covert behind stone fences and from his perch upon the hill; whilst Hood and McLaws had driven him a mile and a half on the right, wrested from him the wooded mountain upon which his extreme left rested, doubled his lines back, captured nearly 2,000 prisoners, many flags and several batteries. The brave and impetuous Barksdale was killed within the enemy's works, and some of Wright's boldest and best—[William] Gibson, [Joseph] Wasden, [George] Ross, Redding, [George] Jones, Campbell, Freeman, [Edward] Granniss, and others—were shot down on the very top of the ridge whilst trying to bring off the guns their valor had silenced. But these charges across the wide open fields and up the bristling hills were made at irregular intervals, which left the enemy free to direct his converging fires upon the heads of the assaulting columns; whilst the configuration of the ground, than which nothing could be more unfavorable to us or more favorable to the enemy, presented every military advantage that could be desired—an open, undulating space in front with occasional stone fences, orchards and patches of woods; a high ridge, not straight but concave in form, with advancing and retreating hills of lesser height, and on the left two very high hills or mountains, one of which was covered with timber and the other with immense boulders. This ridge was depressed here and there, and cut by ravines, but its curve was sufficient to enable the foe to direct a concentric fire from his numerous artillery upon any force which should dare to tread those open spaces or storm those cannon crowned heights.

The repeated assaults made by Confederates therefore, though made with the greatest valor and successful up to a certain point, failed to dislodge the enemy from his strong position. It is but simple justice to add, that in no single instance that now occurs to me did our troops retire except under orders; nor did the enemy ever make the least attempt at pursuit. They advanced and withdrew alike under orders and that too in face of a fire far more furious than that which greeted the advancing columns of the French at Waterloo. In no sense of the word were they beaten. All that can be justly claimed by the enemy is that he maintained his ground against our assaults, though at a fearful cost of life and limb. This touch, with the advantages he possessed in numbers and position, he ought to have done. If our position at Fredericksburg was such as to make Gen. Lee's army equal to a force of 300,000 men, as Gen. Longstreet is reported to have said it was, then Gen. Meade, who already had a superior force at Gettysburg, possessed an advantage in position which was quite as preponderating. There was the difference, however, in the two positions: at Gettysburg the Confederates had to charge over a much wider field than the Federals did at Fredericksburg, whilst the line of hills at the latter place trended off to the right and did not present a concave force as at the former.

Why, then, you are ready to inquire, did Gen. Lee fight at all at Gettysburg, when it was in his power to accept or offer battle at a different time and place? He acted, probably, under the impression that his troops were able to carry any position however formidable. If such was the case, he committed an error, such however, as the ablest commanders will sometimes fall into. No general can be always successful. The Confederate troops can do what any other troops in any period of the world's history have done; but there are some things which even they cannot accomplish. It may be, too, that the Supreme Ruler has chosen this means to teach us the iniquity of all invasions, and to impress upon our minds the justice and wisdom of defending our cause upon our own blood baptized soil. Indeed, there are some things connected, with the late battle which would seem to justify the belief that this punishment was inflicted by a Divine Hand and for some wise purpose. It is but just to add that Gen. Lee does not pretend to lay the responsibility upon his troops or officers, but takes it upon his own broad shoulders. In this, as in all other things, he is frank, and just, and magnanimous. Let us not be guilty of the folly, then, of withdrawing any part of our confidence from him, but let us rather imitate the Hebrew patriots and hold up his hands that he may prevail in the fight.

On Saturday, the 4th of July, nothing was done beyond a little skirmishing by either side. The enemy did not even fire a salute in honor of the day. Both armies withdrew about the same time—Gen. Lee in the direction of Hagerstown, and Gen. Meade in the direction of Washington. All of our wounded who could be removed, were sent back through the passes at Cashtown and Monterey Springs on Saturday, and that night and next morning the army followed, taking the road that crosses the South Mountain at Monterey Springs, and reaching Hagerstown Monday evening, the 6th. There is no doubt that the enemy commenced to retire quite as soon as we did. He had suffered such incalculable loss, and was so fearful lest Gen. Lee would eventually turn his left wing, or get around him and pass rapidly down towards Frederick and Washington, that he found it necessary to retreat, independently of a similar movement on our part. Indeed, if Gen. Lee had simply remained on the ground a few hours longer, what now can be regarded only as a drawn battle, in which both parties suffered terribly, and especially the enemy, would be considered a crushing victory.

Why, then, did Gen. Lee retire? First, because he did not know the enemy would retreat; secondly, because he had been checkmated and failed by the stubborn resistance of his antagonist, and had suffered heavily; and lastly, because he did not have ammunition enough left to fight a half day longer, and could not get it without taking it from his adversary or re-opening his communications with Winchester. These reasons for his withdrawal I did not feel at liberty to mention in my letters from the battlefield. It was impossible to take with us ammunition for the entire campaign, and a sufficient force to keep open our communications could not be spared from an army, already inferior in numbers to that of the enemy. Our only resource, therefore, was to take it from the enemy, and failing to do this, no alternative was left us but to retire towards our base of supplies. It was found impossible also, to subsist the army long at a time in any one place, the inhabitants having driven off as many of their beef cattle and horses as they could, taken one or more wheels from their wagons, and removed their stocks of shoes, hats and medicines far into the interior.

There are certain well known conditions upon which alone an invasion can be successful. The invader must have an army twice as numerous as that of the invaded country; or, if it be only equal or inferior to it, it must make up by its superior courage and genius what it lacks in numbers. He must have also a firmly established base of supplies and open communications, or he must be able to exact contributions of food, forage, animals and clothing from the inhabitants, and to supply his ammunition trains by captures from the enemy. We possessed none of these elements of a successful invasion, except the superior courage and fighting qualities of our troops. And hence our failure; and hence, too, we shall always fail, unless we can command the elements or enforce the conditions necessary to a successful invasion. This we can never do. Our army is too small, and our resources and transportation too limited for us ever to conduct a victorious campaign in a populous country like the United States, abounding in supplies of all kind; reticulated by railway lines and navigable streams, and having a numerous army and a dense population from which to recruit its wasted ranks. Let us, then, dismiss all further thought of invasion, and make up our minds, sore as the trial may be, to fight the battle of freedom upon our own soil and in front of our own hearthstones, with our mothers and wives, maidens, children and old men looking on as spectators from the doors of our own homes. In such a struggle as this a righteous God will give us the victory, and with it peace and independence.

Gen. Lee remained in the vicinity of Hagerstown one week, waiting for Gen. Meade to attack him. He (gave) up a strong position, with his right resting on the Potomac some distance below Williamsport by the river, and his left on the road from Hagerstown to Williamsport. The enemy threw forward forces along the roads from Boonsboro' and Sharpsburg, which were occupied up to the time of our departure in entrenching themselves. Finding it impossible alike to support himself within his restricted lines in Maryland, or to ford the Potomac which was much swollen by recent rains, or to draw the enemy out, Gen. Lee determined to recross the river; and to that end his engineers went to work and constructed a substantial pontoon bridge at Falling Waters, at a sharp bend in the river four miles below Williamsport. The river having subsequently fallen somewhat, a portion of the troops and nearly all the wagons except the ordnance trains, forded it at Williamsport Monday night the 12th and yesterday morning; whilst the great body of the army, all of the artillery and the ambulance train crossed on the pontoon bridge below. The army was withdrawn from Maryland, as it was from Pennsylvania, without molestation by the enemy, with banners flying and drums beating, and now rests on the Virginia side. It is reported that Meade was pushing a column across the river at Harper's Ferry, but it is impossible to vouch for the truth of the report.

I have just heard that some of our troops who had fallen asleep, and thus got behind, were attacked by a small body of cavalry this morning not far from Hagerstown. The cavalry was easily repulsed, or captured, except some fifteen or twenty. Unfortunately Gen. Pettigrew received a mortal wound, and has since died. His Adjutant General and some other officers were also killed or wounded.

P. W. A.

BUNKER'S HILL, VALLEY OF VIRGINIA, July 18th, 1863 [7-30-63]

A few observations remain to be made in regard to the campaign in Maryland and Pennsylvania, and the battle of Gettysburg, which may not be without interest to your readers. Gen. Meade, for example, in his address to his troops and in a dispatch to Gen. Halleck, shows that he, like Pope and Hooker, is a great economist of truth. In the address to the army, bearing the date July the 4th, he says that the Confederates, "utterly baffled and defeated, have now withdrawn from the contest." This declaration, to use a mild term, was simply untrue at the time it purports to have been made. In his dispatch to Gen. Halleck, dated "1:20 a.m., July 5." he is equally unfortunate, in that he says the Confederates "retired under cover of the night and a heavy rain, in the direction of Fairfield and Cashtown," and that his "cavalry were in pursuit." His cavalry made no pursuit at all, at any time; no part of our forces, except the wounded, withdrew by the Cashtown road; and at one o'clock and twenty minutes Sunday morning, July 5th, the Confederate army, though preparing to retire, had not done so. On the contrary, the whole army at that identical hour still held its position on the battlefield, or was in its immediate vicinity. Gen. Wofford's scouts actually captured two prisoners on the battlefield after midnight on Sunday morning, and reported that the enemy, except a few plunderers, was nowhere to be seen. The same report was made by Gen. Benning, of Hood's division, who was left behind with his brigade to observe and note the movements of the enemy in front of our right wing. He remained until 9 o'clock Sunday morning, July 5th, up to which hour the enemy had not shown himself upon that, or any other part of the field, so far as he could see.

The truth is, General Meade commenced to withdraw his own army on the 4th. So evident was this that Gen. McLaws reported to Gen. Longstreet on the afternoon of that day, through an intelligent aid-de-camp, Capt. G. B. Lamar, Jr., that the forces in his front were then retiring; and I am informed that a similar report was sent up from Hood's division on the extreme right. The same fact was noticed by officers at other points along the line. How, then, shall we account for the pretensions set up by the Federal commander? The inquiry finds its solution in the fact that he discovered some time on the 5th that Gen. Lee had certainly retired, just as Gen. Lee discovered that Gen. Meade had done; and with the hope of giving some color to his claim of having won a victory, he put on a bold front, with the address to the army and this dispatch to Halleck, and dated them back so as to cover the time alluded to. His assertions, therefore, can only be properly characterized as deliberate falsehoods, too transparent to deceive any one who was conversant of the facts.

While it is true that the people in Pennsylvania ran off many of their horses and cattle, removed wheels from their wagons, and transported their supplies of medicines, shoes, hats and clothing to points in the interior; yet it should not be inferred that the army returned empty handed. A large number of horses and wagons, a considerable number of beeves, and a small supply of medicines, shoes and hats, were brought away; though the number of shoes and hats fall far below the loss sustained by the troops in the same articles during the campaign. Payment was tendered for everything the army took, and where this was declined, a receipt was given. The supply of beef and flour was adequate to meet all the wants of the troops, though the course pursued by the inhabitants rendered it impossible to procure subsistence for a longer period than a few days at any one place.

An interesting episode of the campaign occurred at Williamsport about the time the army returned to Hagerstown. A considerable force of Federal cavalry made a dash at the ambulance train which was taking the wounded across to Virginia. The train consisted of ambulances proper, and such baggage and forage wagons as could be spared for the use of the wounded. The Confederate cavalry, which, with few exceptions, is regarded with little favor either by the enemy or ourselves, made but slight resistance, and soon fled the field. The teamsters, however, and much of the wounded as could lend a hand, seized the muskets in the wagons belonging to the wounded, formed into line between the train and the cavalry, and with the help of the guards, drove the enemy from the field, and saved the train and the wounded. The affair is known as the "teamsters' battle." Many of them had been disabled in the infantry service, and fought well, but not without considerable loss, as several of them were killed and wounded.

I have just been told by one who is in a position to be correctly informed, why it was that Gen. Lee fought the battle of Gettysburg. It appears he had been led to believe that the Federal army had not all arrived on the scene of action, that at least two *corps d'armee* were still absent, and he hoped, by falling suddenly upon the enemy before all his forces had been concentrated, to win an easy victory. The truth is, however, that the Federal army had been kept well together, and had marched very rapidly from the Rappahannock to Pennsylvania. The success of Hill's and Ewell's corps, portions of which had easily driven the enemy on the first day of the fight, had its influence, doubtless, in bringing Gen. Lee's mind to the conclusion to accept battle at Gettysburg. Here we have a practical illustration of one of the difficulties attending an invasion—the want of correct information of the operations of the adversary army, and that too at a time when the slightest movement on your own part is immediately known and reported.

It rained or was cloudy every day from the time the army crossed the Blue Ridge until it returned to Virginia. The men slept in the rain, got up in the rain, cooked and ate in the rain, and marched and sometimes fought in the rain. For the last three days they have been resting at this place, cooking rations, washing their clothes, and drying their blankets; all of which was much needed.

P. W. A.

CULPEPPER C.H. VA., July 20, 1863 [8-3-63]

There is no change to report in the position of Affairs in this quarter. Meade's headquarters, according to rumor, are now at or near Warrenton, some twenty-five miles distant. Rumor has it also that his army is encamped on the north bank of the Rappahannock, above and below the railroad crossing, and that the bridges and track have been repaired and the railroad put in running order from Alexandria to Catlett's station, a few miles beyond the river. No aggressive demonstration has been made since our return to this place, and it is not believed that any important movement will be attempted for some weeks to come. The Federal army is in no condition to assume the offensive, even if it should be decided to advance upon Richmond by this long and much exposed line. Its loss at Gettysburg was frightful. A Confederate soldier who was taken prisoner and carried within the Federal lines, from which he subsequently made his escape, says our artillery played terrible havoc with the enemy, and that he never saw so many dead men and horses, and such destruction of artillery carriages and caissons, as he witnessed in front and around Cemetery Hill. It is confessed on all hands that our guns were never served so effectively. The batteries were massed together at eligible points and their execution surpassed anything that has occurred during the present war. The practice of the Federal guns was equally good, and our own loss from their artillery fire was greater than on any previous occasion. Indeed, in no other battle of the war has the artillery on either side inflicted such heavy loss as at Gettysburg. Conspicuous on the Confederate side for accuracy of fire and energetic service, were Cutt's battalion of artillery, attached to Anderson's division, Hill's corps; Cabell's, Henry's and [James] Dearing's battalions, belonging respectively to McLaws', Hood's and Pickett's divisions, Longstreet's corps, and Alexander's battalion of reserves attached to the same corps.

One is left to conjecture as regards the future movements of the enemy, both in Virginia and the southwest. If it be the purpose of the Federal government to enforce the draft, as it doubtless is, then it is not probable that its armies will undertake any offensive movement on a broad scale for some weeks to come, unless it be in Tennessee. The draft cannot be enforced without the assistance of the military, and to render that assistance the military force of the United States must remain near the border for the present. In other words, active operations or the draft must be suspended for the time being. In the southwest, however, it is not improbable that Grant will leave strong garrisons at Port Hudson, Vicksburg and Memphis, with heavy reserves at Cairo and Louisville, and that with the remainder of his army he will join [William S.] Rosecrans and make a bold push for Knoxville, Chattanooga, and possibly Atlanta. The reserves left at Louisville and Cairo will be used, if necessary, to enforce the draft in the northwestern States, and to intimidate [Clement] Vallandigham and his friends; and in the event of an attack by the Confederates upon any of the fortified positions on the Mississippi, they will be sent to reinforce the garrisons at those points, or to Rosecrans and Grant in Tennessee, as the emergency may require. Such, at least, would seem to be the programme of the enemy.

I have endeavored in former letters to speak in fitting terms of the service and soldiery qualities of the lamented Gen. Semmes, and of the important parts performed by the South Carolinians, Georgians, Alabamians and Mississippians in Longstreet's corps at the great battle of Gettysburg. The following eloquent tribute, however, from Maj. S. P. Hamilton, of Cabell's battalion, will be read with melancholy. You will see that it is incorporated in this communication at the request of Maj. Hamilton, who, you will also observe, not only fights well, but writes well.

CAMP NEAR CULPEPPER C. H., VA., July 26th, 1863.

P. W. ALEXANDER, ESQ.,
Dear Sir: That distinguished soldier, Brig. Gen. Paul J. Semmes, who received the fatal shot finally terminating his life, while storming the rocky heights near Gettysburg, charged me, upon the battle-field, with a duty become sacred by reason of his death. I propose to make public, through you, the interview between Gen. Semmes and myself on that occasion. I believe that it was his desire and expectation that I would so do in case of his death. As your most excellent correspondence is everywhere read in the Confederacy, and with especial interest in Georgia, of which Gen. Semmes was a citizen, I have to request that you incorporate this communication in one of your earliest letters. It will be a mournful pleasure to the friends and family of this noble spirit to know, when the green wounds of sorrow shall be somewhat healed, that in the excitement of the hour, his mind turned with undying love to those at his far distant home. It will be matter of pride to the people of Georgia to hear how one of her many sons whom she has sent forth, performed the trust committed to him, and how, in his last charge and in his last hours, he illustrated the fame of his native State.

I was standing at the gun where the gallant [Capt. J. C.] Fraser had just before been struck down, when I observed a wounded man being borne from the field in a blanket. By the number of attendants I soon perceived that it was an officer of rank, and in a moment after recognized that officer as Gen. Semmes. Almost at the same instant he saw me, and called me to him, whither I had already started. I found him weak and exhausted, shot through the thigh, the femoral artery being almost severed. He caused himself to be lowered into a reclining position, and his eye brightening with a fire of peculiar brightness, he said:

"Major Hamilton, I am glad to see you. I am badly wounded, (pointing to the spot), and I believe I shall die. Perhaps, I may not; but something warns me that the chances are against my recovery. You and I are from the same State, and I wish you, and charge upon you, to bear testimony to the fact that I fell at the head of my brigade, leading them in a charge which up to that time was successful. I love my country as devotedly as any man ever has or can do. I had hoped to be spared to continue my endeavors (of whatever value they might be), to secure her independence. My love for those I leave at home is beyond expression; you will understand and appreciate those to be the most sacred and holiest emotions of the human heart. But as much as these considerations weigh with me, and make me cling to life, with an assured trust and reliance in the goodness and mercies of God, I will die with perfect resignation if it be known where my death-wound was received; that it was in my appointed place, where a soldier should, and where my State and Country had a right to expect."

I bear willing testimony to all of this and much more. I saw the charge of his brigade; the Tenth Georgia passed over the left of our battalion of artillery where I had command. No ordinary ordeal was it theirs to meet: a plain swept by thirty pieces of cannon first to be passed—a precipitous mountain, jagged with rocks, to be scaled in the face of brigade upon brigade of the enemy strongly posted on its side. In the divisions of McLaws and Hood, South Carolina was there, led by the cool, calm, intrepid Kershaw; Mississippi by the hard fighting Barksdale, who that day fought his last fight; Alabama by the dashing Law—the renowned Texans side-by-side. Georgia had strong representation there. The fiercely vigorous Wofford; Benning the fast fighter, and the unwavering G. T. Anderson, all marched with unfaltering tread to the work of death. The most precious blood of these Southern brothers was poured out in that charge. But among all the brave men who there fought and there fell, I venture to assert that no more complete soldier, more faithful officer, or more heroic spirit there received his doom than Paul J. Semmes. At Malvern Hill he went nearer to the enemy's guns than any other general officer in the field. At Salem Church his brigade and that of that gallant officer, General Wilcox, bore the brunt of the whole attack of Sedgwick's corps with unflinching resolve. I knew Gen. Semmes well. We commenced service in Georgia together; we came to Virginia at the same time; we were in the same brigade—he as Colonel of the 2nd Georgia, and I as Captain of artillery. Since our promotion, we have served in the same division. I have known him in the camp, on the march, and on the battlefield. If the faithful punctilious, and scrupulous discharge of every duty makes the soldier and officer, then was he one of the first.

The tender affection of those he loved so well may rear the cypress and the myrtle around his final resting place of Paul J. Semmes, but the laurel which crowns the living hero will spontaneously spring from the sod covering his manly breast—as it could not grace his brow, at least to shade his grave.

> I remain, very, respectfully,
> S. P. HAMILTON,
> Major of Artillery, Longstreet's Corps, A. N. V.

I was led into an error in regard to the cause of the delay of Pender's division in going into the action on the second day at Gettysburg. The delay did not arise from any squabble among the brigadiers after his fall as to seniority in rank. On the contrary, that point had been settled at Fredericksburg to favor of Gen. [James] Lane, to whom General Pender turned over the command immediately after receiving his death wound. The responsibility of the delay therefore rests with Gen. Lane. Gen. Pender was from North Carolina, and so was General Pettigrew—two most excellent officers, both of whom have perished.

> P. W. A.

ORANGE COUNTY, VA., August 7, 1863 [8-14-63]

I write from Mason's Farm, Orange county, about midway between Orange Court House and Fredericksburg, and nearly equal distant from the latter place and Culpepper by Somerville ford. It is not a favorable position for obtaining news of army operations, but it was not known at the time we were ordered here that we should remain beyond a day or two.

Both armies are quiet however, and there is but little that it would be proper to communicate. The position of our forces is such as to render it next to impossible for the enemy to cross the Rapidan, or gain possession of the heights of Fredericksburg, if he were inclined to make the attempt. He has thrown a small cavalry force as low down as Stafford Court House, and a few mounted men have made their appearance a short distance from Fredericksburg; but up to this time no serious demonstration has been made in that quarter. Frequent indecisive collisions take place between the Confederate and Federal cavalry beyond Culpepper along the upper Rappahannock, in which the advantage is claimed by both sides; but as far as is known here, the enemy's infantry have not crossed the river either above or below.

I still adhere to the opinion, expressed in a former communication, that Gen. Meade will not attempt, without considerable reinforcements, to move upon Richmond for some weeks to come, if at all. Professional pugilists who have battered each other for two or three hours, require many weeks to reduce their contusions and restore their bruised and distorted features to their wonted appearance. But in the case of large armies that have battled for three days; that have been hurled against each other with all the fury that malice or patriotism can inspire, and that have alternately watched and slept and fought beneath the scorching sun and amidst violent storms, more time and patience and labor are necessary to bind up the bruises, set the broken limbs, bury the dead, procure fresh supplies of subsistence and ammunition, repair the dilapidated transportation, and restore the wasted energies of men and animals. War is no child's play; it is the work of giants, and calls for the highest exercise of force, the most painful sacrifices, the most patient and unflinching endurance, of which mortal man is capable. Gen. Meade's army has not yet recovered from the injuries it received at Gettysburg. Its dislocated joints and broken bones have not all been reunited; its swollen eyes and battered skulls have not been reduced to their normal condition, nor its wasted ranks recruited. Time or reinforcements alone can effect this cure, and if the Federal general is a wise man, he will be a quiet man also.

The rest at Culpepper, as was remarked in my last letter, was of great service to the troops and animals of the army. The men not only had time to rest their weary limbs and sore feet, but to wash and repair their tattered garments, and to receive partial supplies of new shoes and clothing. More time is necessary to restore thirty or forty thousand horses employed in the service of the army to the condition in which they were when they started from Fredericksburg. From the 1st of July until our return to Culpepper, their work was very heavy and the supply of forage scant. The cavalry horses were on duty all the time, and those in the artillery service, whose work is hardest of all, suffered no little. There is but little opportunity to water or feed the latter during a battle, whether it last for one day or for three days, as at Gettysburg. When the army is in line of battle and in the immediate presence of the enemy they sometimes stand for a week, day and night, in the dew, the rain and the sunshine, with their heavy harness on, and with but little water or feed. And on a march, the only time when the horses can be watered is early in the morning or when they stop at night, unless there will be what is known as a noonday halt, which is long or short according to the exigencies of the service. It is customary to march an hour, and then rest ten minutes, but it is impossible to find shade sufficient on the road for an entire corps or division; and hence the horses, and sometimes the men, have to stand and swelter in the hot sun during those brief intervals of rest. If the drivers were to stop to let their horses drink when they cross a stream on a march, it would delay the rear of a single corps nearly a half of a day.

Horses suffer as much from want of shoes as men, especially on the turnpikes and rough, rocky roads in Virginia and north of the Potomac. It is almost impossible for them to travel on such roads without shoes, and when they are forced to do so, as they frequently are, they suffer severely. It is not easy to replace shoes on a march, though the army is provided with a number of farriers and portable forges and a supply of ready made shoes and nails. I have found it necessary myself to rise at day-break and tug away at the bellows of a village blacksmith shop for three weary hours, in order to have a shoe replaced which my horse had lost the day before.

Jomini lays down the following maxim: "The two great problems of warfare are, perhaps, how to find a harness that will not hurt a horse's back, and shoes that can be used by the men without causing sore feet." He adds the following advice: "Horsemen, give all care to the putting on of the bridle and saddle; always keep on hand four spare horse shoes, with as many nails as are necessary to fix them on and have more besides. Foot-soldiers, look for shoes that will fit you easy."

Having in a previous letter spoken of shoes for the men, I need only add now that they should be made of the best leather to be had, and they should be roomy, have wide substantial bottoms, and fit snugly around the ankles. Their clothing should also be roomy. Close-fitting garments not only chafe the wearer on a march, but they soon wear out. In regard to horses in the army, there is nothing from which they suffer more than harness and saddles that do not fit them. They are frequently wounded in battle, and seldom have sufficient forage; the service required of them is the hardest to which they can be put, and the drivers are often unfeeling wretches who take but little thought of their condition. But when to all these ills which horse-flesh is heir to, is added saddles and harness improperly constructed, and bare feet on flinty turnpikes, it will be perceived that the animals in the army have a hard time of it. There are probably 20,000 horses here to-day which have sore backs and shoulders such as a man at home never saw. In a majority of cases, neither the collars, nor the harness and saddle-trees fit well. The wood of the latter is not properly seasoned, and will spread and let the whole weight of the rider down on the fleshless backbone of the horse, while the collars and harness are for the most part manufactured out of leather not properly cured, and soon cease to fit the animal that has to carry them.

The horse is the noblest animal subjected to the dominion of man. He has rendered most valuable services in this war, and has to a considerable extent supplied the want of water and railway transportation. I raise my voice then in behalf of these willing, noble creatures, and bespeak for them better treatment in the future. The service in which they are employed is necessarily severe, and they have their camp diseases like the men; but their condition might be greatly improved by the exercise of a little forethought in regard to forage and shoes, in the manufacture of the harness, and in the preparation of the wood used in the harness and saddle trees. It is not an unusual thing to see these hard workers standing on the roadside, too lame to proceed, or unfit for further duty. They gaze at you wistfully as you pass along, and seem to beg for assistance. But they cannot travel, and are left behind to perish. The charger whose glories are reflected from many a battle field, and the artillery horse which has stood faithfully to his place amidst bursting shells and hustling cannon balls, are wounded or worn-down in the service, and left to share the same inglorious end. What would you not give to have one of these disabled creatures at your home where you might nurse him and care for him, and restore him to health! The parting between the rider and his charger is often painful and touching, and I have known the latter to remain behind with his faithful animal for many days, though environed with dangers, and all to save the friend who had borne him so often through the battle unscathed. "Take my horse home to my wife, my mother, or my aged father," is the last request of the dying warrior.

P. W. A.

ORANGE COURT HOUSE, VA., August 10, 1863 [8-24-63]

There is nothing which occurs so much surprise and indignation in this army as the reports that come to us from the southwest in regard to the temper of a portion of the people. It would appear as if some of them had already abandoned themselves to despair, and were debating among themselves whether it were not better to bow their craven necks to the yoke of the enemy, than to offer further resistance. That such a question should have ever arisen among any portion, however small, of the high spirited people of Mississippi and Alabama—a people to whom the country has been accustomed to look for examples of patriotism and courage—is the cause of inexpressible amazement in all this part of the Confederacy, where every valley has flowed with the blood of the brave, and every hill been crowned with the unmarked graves of the patriot dead. Capitalists are proverbally timid, but no one was prepared for the submissive spirit evinced by the wealthy planters and speculators whose princely estates border on the Gulf and the Father of Waters. They had been supposed to be men of high resolve and undaunted courage—men who would rather perish now and hereafter than become "hewers of wood and drawers of water" to the execrable race which now seeks their subjugation.

But is there any foundation for the reports that reach us? Has any man, "native to the manor born," gotten his consent to parley with the enemy as to his future duty and relations? If there be such a one, then it were better for him that a millstone were hanged about his neck and he cast into the bottomless sea. No terms can be made with the enemy against whom we contend. He seeks our blood, our property, and our eternal ruin. To accomplish his inhuman designs, he has already enslaved his own people; and can we, who have been warring against him, expect better conditions than he grants to his own subjects? Is there any reason to believe that if we were to lay down our arms to-day, he would receive us back into the Union upon terms of equality? Is there not, rather, abundant proof that the pillory and gibbet, confiscation and banishment, are the penalties held in reserve for us, and that, too, whether we voluntarily abandon the contest, or the fortunes of war prove adverse to our arms? What is the fate of Missouri and Kentucky, of Tennessee and Maryland? These are regarded by the enemy as border States which may be ultimately reclaimed to the cause of the Union; and yet they are dragged at the wheels of his brazen chariot like captive slaves. But Louisiana and all those portions of Virginia which are overrun by the invader—how humiliating their fate! how hopeless their condition! The people of Mississippi and Alabama have not even tasted the cup which Virginia has drained to the bitter dregs. And still her people have not been able, by oaths of allegiance extorted in dungeons and under the gallows, nor by submission to the woes of slavery, nor by quietly yielding up all they possess, to obtain permission of their implacable masters to drag out the remnant of a miserable existence by the graves of their forefathers. Their lands have been desolated, their houses reduced to heaps of ashes, their property confiscated, and their old men torn from their homes and immured in prisons. Large and populous districts have been converted into deserts, and the people, old and young, male and female, driven into exile. But the thought of yielding has never once entered their minds. On the contrary, the brave men and women of this proud old Commonwealth are more resolved than ever, never to ground their arms as long as a man is left to wield a musket or a woman to ply a needle and offer up a prayer. They have tried the enemy and know him well. They know he will keep no pledge, however sacred, and observe no oath, however solemn. The war cry of the great apostle of the elder revolution is still the rallying call of his undaunted descendants: *"Give me liberty, or give me death!"*

No, let the people of the Southwest dismiss all thought of compromise. Victory, or all the horrors of a hell on earth, are the only alternatives left them. If they fail on the field, or sue for peace and forgiveness at the footstool of Federal power, their fate will be alike the same; in either event, they will be stripped of their possessions, and by hostile legislation reduced to the condition of serfs or driven into banishment. Of all the tyrants known to history, the Puritan is the most implacable. More cruel than the Spaniard, more treacherous than the Italian, more blood-thirsty than the Turk, there is no wrong or humiliation however atrocious, than his malignant ingenuity would not devise, and in which his savage nature would not find a diabolical pleasure.

Liberty is not a fruit of spontaneous growth. It is, rather, a hardy plant which grows only when it is watered by the blood of brave men and the tears of widows and orphans. So great a blessing is the reward alone of suffering, of patient endurance, of high resolve and bloody sacrifices. Are the people of the Southwest shrinking from the trial. The Army of Northern Virginia was never more resolute in its holy purpose to quit the field only when our peace and independence shall have been secured; and it sends greeting to the army in Mississippi and Tennessee, and to the people everywhere, and bids them be of good cheer. We had grown arrogant and self-confident and were punished with defeat, as we have been before, and as we shall ever be when we forget the Giver of all victory.

It remains to be added that the poor have done their whole duty in this war. They have sent no substitutes to the army; they fill but few offices of honor or emolument; they do not hide themselves in safe places in nitre bureaus and the departments at Richmond, and they reap but little benefit from the Exemption Act; yet, confiding their wives and little ones to the justice of the government and the charity of the rich, they have gone forth to meet the storm, and have bared their heads to the battle's blast upon every field from Manassas to Vicksburg. Can the same be said of the capitalists and timid proprietors whose unmanly croakings now come up to us from the waters of the Gulf and the Mississippi? The latter should remember that a Red sea now flows between them and their enemies, and that their grief after the flesh-pots they have left behind comes too late. They should remember also that

> "Our doubt are traitors,
> And make us lose the good we oft might win
> By fearing to attempt."

There is no change to report in the situation of affairs in this quarter. The weather continues intensely hot. A few letters have been received under flag of truce from the wounded left at Gettysburg, but they will be addressed to friends at home and their contents have not transpired. One letter to an officer speaks of the treatment of the prisoners as kind and considerate.

P. W. A.

ORANGE COURT HOUSE, VA., August 21, 1863 [8-30-63]

Since the Richmond papers have made it public there can be no longer any impropriety in furloughs. These furloughs are granted, in the first instance, at the rate of two to every one hundred men present for duty, and subsequently at the rate of one for every one hundred present for duty. This system will be continued as long as the exigencies of the service will permit. Should the effect not be found prejudicial, commanders of regiments and battalions are instructed to forward the most urgent and meritorious cases from those recommended by the company officers for the approval of their superior commander. The men thus furloughed are "authorized to bring back stragglers and recruits who may come in their way."

The opinion expressed in one of my recent letters would seem, in view of the order, to have been well grounded, to wit: that General Meade is in no condition to advance, and that there is little prospect of active work in this quarter for some time to come. Gen. Lee would not have instituted this system of furloughs at this time if he had believed that he would again be called upon at an early day to cross swords with the Federal commander. That the latter has withdrawn his cavalry pickets to the north bank of the Rappahannock there is no longer any doubt; but it should not be inferred from this, as some seem inclined to do, that the enemy is about to retire to Bull Run or Alexandria. Furloughs have been granted on a liberal scale to the troops in the Federal army, or rather detachments have been sent home for the purpose of taking charge of the conscripts and bringing them to the regiments to which they may be assigned. These detachments will be on hand also to lend assistance in the enforcement of the draft, should resistance be offered by the people. The army has been further depleted by the withdrawal of these regiments whose terms of enlistment have expired. This reduction of his effective force has led Gen. Meade, doubtless, to mass his troops in the vicinity of Warrenton Junction, and to place himself strictly on the defensive until their ranks shall have been sufficiently recruited to enable him to assume the offensive again. He hopes, probably, to be in this condition some time in October, when, if the Federal draft be carried out, a resumption of active hostilities may be expected.

In the meantime what line of policy will Gen. Lee adopt? The answer to this enquiry will depend very much upon the success of the efforts now being made to recall the absentees from the army back to their posts of duty. During the Maryland campaign last year there was much unavoidable straggling. The weather was dry and hot, the supply of food insufficient, and a large number of troops without shoes. This year the men were better clad and shod, the supplies abundant, and the weather wet and cool. And yet there were many stragglers after the army recrossed the Potomac. Why was this?

Many causes might be assigned for the evil complained of. It might be truthfully affirmed that the march was badly conducted, that the commissariat department was inefficiently administered, that the army was without an engineer corps, that the men had to straggle over high roads and wade creeks and rivers with pontoon boats in sight, and that corps, division, brigade and regimental commanders were not as rigid in the enforcement of general orders as they should have been. But when all this has been affirmed and admitted, there is still something wanting to complete the explanation. While every officer of the army is responsible, with the sphere of his authority, for the discipline and behavior of his command, yet it cannot be forgotten that all needful power for the enforcement of his orders and the proper government and control of both officers and troops is lodged in the hands of the commander-in-chief. This power is given him for wise purposes, and it carries along with it responsibilities as well as honors, from which there can be no escape. The proper discipline of an army rests with every one who exercises authority, however limited, in that army; but since all officers and agents are, by the rules and articles of war, made answerable for the discharge of their duties to the chief commander—who is clothed with authority to have punishment inflicted upon all delinquents and violators of his orders—it is to him we must chiefly look for the good conduct and behavior of his troops and the efficiency of his subordinates.

To this general rule for fixing the responsibility in the matter of the discipline of an army there are certain exceptions as applied to the Confederate army, which deserve to be noted. In the first place, the army is not purely military in its spirit and organization. It contains a strong civil element, which must ever impair its discipline and efficiency so long as officers are permitted to become candidates for civil stations at home, and to look to the very men whom they command for the votes by which they hope to be elected. I do not question the justice of the measure which secures to the soldier the right of suffrage in matters of a political nature—though it must be confessed that the arrangement is both novel and anomalous; but I do doubt the wisdom of allowing officers to run for civil offices so long as they hold commissions in the army. Such an officer will neither enforce obedience, nor command the confidence of his men; and the latter will neither obey him, nor respect him.

In the next place, our military system is peculiar in that it is neither volunteer nor conscript in its character. For the first year of the war the army was composed wholly of volunteer regiments, the officers of which, when organized under State laws, were chosen by ballot. Since then a new rule has been adopted, and the principle of conscription has been engrafted upon the volunteer system. In some regiments (those organized by the President) vacancies are filled by promotion, and sometimes by Executive appointment; in others, by election; whilst the conscript is stripped of all choice in the matter except that of designating the regiment from his own State to which he will attach himself; and even this privilege is granted him only on condition that he proceed at once to join the regiment without waiting for the enrolling officer. It is too late now to change this system, mixed and incongruous as it is; but the reader will perceive, without further remark, how difficult it is to bring an army, thus organized, to a high state of discipline, and to keep it there. It is but just to add that the only particular in which the troops in this army are wanting in discipline relates to straggling and the evils consequent there upon. And this branch of good conduct is contained chiefly to marches and camps, and exists to a very limited extent during battles.

In determining the responsibility, therefore, and apportioning the blame for any want of discipline in our armies, it becomes us to take into consideration the nature of our military system, the elements that enter into the organization of the army, the superior personal character of the troops, and the further fact that arms is the profession of but few of them, either officers or men.

But no army, however wise the principle upon which its organization rests, or excellent the material that enters into its composition, or consummate the genius that leads and wields it, can ever be brought to the highest point of efficiency and discipline without an educated staff. I do not mean a staff that can read and write correctly—though that is important; but a staff that understands its duties, and that has been educated practically in those duties. But this is an important subject, and must be reserved for a future communication.

P. W. A.

Light for the People

WALLER'S TAVERN, Spottsylvania Co., Va., August 26, 1863 [9-4-63]

The rumors that prevailed last week to the effect that the enemy was withdrawing his forces in the direction of Bull Run and Alexandria, have all been dissipated, as was intimated in my last letter they would be. Gen. Meade may have caused some changes to be made in his camps, just as Gen. Lee has done, with a view to the health and comfort of his troops and the subsistence of his animals; but beyond this, the "situation" remains substantially the same as it was two weeks ago. The Federal army is encamped near the Warrenton Junction along the Orange and Alexandria railroad, and their pickets extend along the north bank of the Rappahannock from the foot of the Blue Ridge, down to Fredericksburg.

There are other rumors which will be dissolved into thin air by the return of the autumnal equinox; such, for instance, as that the Federal army is in a state of demoralization, that the men are deserting the service in unusual numbers, and that but few troops will be raised under the late Conscription law. Desertion is an every day occurrence in both armies; and after a bloody battle, whether the result be disastrous or otherwise, there is always more or less disorder and irregularity, or demoralization if you please. In these respects we cannot boast of better fortune than our enemies; and we only deceive ourselves when we indulge in hopes to the contrary. It were wiser, then, to remove the beam from our own eyes, ere we volunteer to pluck the mote from the eye of our adversary.

As for the Federal draft, it will be enforced, and the 300,000 conscripts called for will be raised—if not in one way, then in another; if not at one time, then at some other time. There are more than three times 300,000 men in the United States who have waged a life-long battle with hunger and nakedness—enemies far more cruel and relentless than the Confederate soldier; and this beggarly horde will be glad enough to exchange the fruitless struggle with the grim, gaunt, fleshless forms of Famine and Disease, for a contest with those warm-hearted, impetuous and less implacable foe who fight under the Southern Cross. When they enter the Federal service, they may be, and probably will be, stricken down by disease or killed in battle; but as long as they survive these dangers, they will receive abundant supplies of food and clothing. This is something—an important something, too—to a man who has rarely known what it is to have enough to eat or clothing sufficient to keep himself warm in winter. Such men are now presenting themselves as substitutes; and even diseased men, totally unfit for service, are offering for a consideration to take the places of those who have been drafted. Should there be any lack of this kind of material out of which to manufacture an army for our subjugation, the want can be, and will be, easily supplied by the needy hamlets, the dungeons, the poor-houses and hospitals of the Old World. Shiploads of these human vermin are now being wafted to Northern shores by every gale that sweeps from Europe. Such wretches make but indifferent soldiers, and many of them may desert in the future as they have done in the past; but however raised, and of whatsoever material composed, the fact still remains; there will be an army in the field for the Confederates to meet and beat back, until Mr. Lincoln's term of office shall have expired, or some foreign Power shall intervene to stop the effusion of blood.

It is worse than folly to attempt to hide these unwelcome truths under a bushel. From the beginning of the war the people have displayed greater firmness in the presence of danger, more patience and fortitude under adversity, and a higher type of patriotism, than those in authority; and yet the latter have on divers occasions, evinced an unwillingness, if not a downright fear, to divulge to them the true condition of affairs. The truth, when known to be the truth, never alarms a brave man or a brave people. It is darkness, doubt and falsehood that create dismay and confusion, and not the sunlight of truth. The same dangers lurk in the dim woods by day as by night, and the same spectres haunt the graves of dead men by the noonday sun as by the moon's pale ray; and yet men of firm nerves would prefer to tread those gloomy solitudes by the light of day, when they can see and understand for themselves the whole extent of the dangers by which they are surrounded. So in times of great national peril people, when permitted to look their true situation squarely in the face, instead of giving way to unmanly fears and wasting their energies in combating imaginary foes, go to work like courageous men, and measure their efforts and their sacrifices by the dangers which threaten them.

The truth has found many illustrations during our present struggle. At this very moment we find the people in some parts of the country abandoning themselves to a feeling of despondency and ready to exaggerate recent disasters, simply from a want of correct information; distance and doubt lend wings to their fears; whereas the veterans of many a battlefield, who sleep nightly on their arms in front of the enemy, who have met that enemy again and again, and know exactly how strong he is, and how great the danger, feel no uneasiness whatever. All the latter require is that they may be fed and clothed, and their decimated ranks filled up by willing spirits from home; let this be done, and all will be well in the end.

It is not contended that all the movements of armies and affairs of state should be made public. Secrecy, and even mystery, are elements of success in the field as well as in the cabinet. But it is believed and asserted that in times of manifest peril, when the only hope of relief rests upon the people, nothing should be hidden from them, a full knowledge of which is necessary to prepare them for the work expected at their hands. For this reason, they should be informed that they have an incomplete Cabinet at the head of affairs, to the end that they may prevail upon the President to change it; and a weak, plodding Congress that they who alone have the power, may send wiser and better men to the national legislature. They should be told also that the cause which engages their hearts and hands, has suffered serious damage at Vicksburg, Port Hudson and Gettysburg—that our loss of men and arms has been heavy— that the enemy is raising another large army—that there is but little prospect of foreign recognition or intervention—that no terms can be obtained from our foes short of confiscation and slavery, and that the only alternatives left us are victory or bondage and beggary. Let them know also, on the other hand, that while the despots at Washington, and the contractors and speculators at the North, are clamorous for a continuance of the war, and affect to be confident of final success, the great mass of the people ardently desire peace—that our enemies can never be successful so long as we are true to ourselves—that the Federal Government, rotten to the core, is ready to tumble into perdition—that we have the sympathies and good wishes of the friends of national freedom throughout the world, and that the Judge of all the earth has never forsaken those who love and fear Him, and are resolved, with His help, to be free.

When the people understand and appreciate all this, they will prepare their bodies and souls for the dangers that environ them; and when this is done, our peace and independence are secured.

P. W. A.

A Chapter on Stragglers, etc.

WALLER'S TAVERN, SPOTTSYLVANIA CO., VA. August 28, 1863 [9-4-63]

Attention has been called from time to time, in the course of this correspondence, to that great vice of the army, *straggling*.

There are stragglers on the march—those who move in advance of the army, make short cuts across fields, visit farm-houses, and plunder gardens and orchards. There are stragglers to the rear—barefoot men, (who are excusable,) lazy men, and bad soldiers, who drag along in the wake of the army, loiter on the way, and besiege dwelling houses for something to eat, being too careless to preserve their own rations, or too indolent to cook them when they have any. There are stragglers on the day of battle—those who affect to be unwell, who separate themselves from their commands under one pretense or other, congregate about the camp fires and wagon yards, and yet are well enough to scour the battle-field and gather up loads of plunder when the fight is over. There are other stragglers still—those who for a mere scratch or slight disorder manage to procure furloughs or sick leaves, go to the hospitals, and thence to their homes, where, through the assistance of county officers and resident physicians, and the neglect of enrolling officers, they are permitted to skulk behind certificates of continued disability, from week to week, and month to month. These last mentioned stragglers are designated, in polite phrase as "absentees," and are described in the muster rolls as "absent without leave." Their proper designation is *deserter*.

Is it not so? The soldier who runs away from the battlefield, who hides himself in the clefts of the Blue Ridge, who goes over to the enemy—is he not a deserter, and so denounced by all the world. And why not the man who, by false pretences, fraudulent practices, and the connivance of physicians and officers at home, abandons his post, and remains away long after the scratch has healed up and the cough disappeared?

One admires an open enemy, and execrates a false friend. Cornwallis, the British General, was the one, and Arnold, the American traitor, the other: which occupies the better position in history? So with these deserters in the hour of their country's need: while we cannot admire the man who openly quits his standard, yet we detest him less than the wretch who, by the aid of fraud and falsehood, steals into a hospital, purloins a furlough, and hides himself at home, at a time when our armies, reduced by the absence of such characters, are struggling against mortal odds, and forced to abandon ground which may be vital to our success. Under the calls of President Davis and General Lee, many of these men are returning to duty; at least, the newspapers say so; and it is hoped their report is true. But there are others who still lag behind. What shall be done with them? Will not the woman, without whose aid we should ere this have been subjugated, apply to them the lash of their indignant scorn? The contractors and speculators are too busy with their ill-gotten gains, and the croakers and cowards, with their dismal imaginings, to give any assistance. To the heroic, self-sacrificing women, to the fathers who have given their sons to their country, and to the rigid enforcement of military laws alone, can the country look in this supreme hour.

The reader will understand that this denunciation does not fall upon such as are really unfit for duty, and whose absence is properly accounted for. True economy requires that the wounded and sick should not be hurried back into the ranks until they are made whole, and are able to do the work of a soldier. But the men who slink away from the field and leave the burden to fall upon the brave and true, who pretend to be sick when they are sound, who deceive their officers, and abuse the weakness of physicians and magistrates at home, or, what is worse, *purchase* from them certificates of disability—it is upon such skulkers and deserters that the scorn of woman and the wrath of man should be heaped.

And what shall be said of those able-bodied men who take refuge in local offices, in bureaus and departments, and resort to all kinds of shifts and subterfuges to procure exemption from the service of *their* country? If they are fit for service, and yet do not render it, how much better are they than the man who hides in the hour of battle? Are men worthy of liberty who will not themselves strike for it? What can they know of the joys of patriotism? of the feeling experienced by that model soldier, Paul J. Semmes, who said to the writer in the agony of his death wound, his bright blue eyes filling with tears of exultant joy: "I consider it a privilege to die for my country." Their deliverance will be the work of other hands than theirs, and can they find in it happiness when they have performed no part of the labor? The soldier's life is indeed a hard one; but it is also a glorious one. He is exposed to heat and cold, to battle and tempest, to hunger, disease and death; but the supreme happiness, which is his when he has fought his last fight, when "He dies 'midst shouts of victory"—victory too, which he has helped to achieve for his country, for friends and family, for freedom and holy religion, and the generations that are to come after him in the far distant future—one moment of such happiness, "when triumph weeps above the brave," is worth a whole lifetime of those ignoble joys which brutish natures derive from gain, from shame and selfish indulgences. Who would not prefer the fate of Jackson, mourned by a whole nation, his early grave bedewed by the tears of a grateful people, yet radiant with the light of virtue, of heroism and of heaven, rather than that of the richest prince the world has ever known?

There are persons who can better serve their country in civil occupations than in the field; these should remain where they are. There are others who are capable, and yet do not render this service, either at home or in the army. These may not carry the brand of shame upon their foreheads--hey many even acquire the riches of Dives; but when the war is over, and "white-robed Peace shall have stretched her stainless hands in benediction over our beloved country," their wealth, like Dead Sea fruit, will turn to ashes upon their lips, and they will become aliens in the land, entitled to no lot or part in the glorious inheritance of freedom, which others, not they, have purchased with their blood.

P. W. A.

ARMY OF NORTHERN VIRGINIA, September 1, 1863 [9-11-63]

Nothing could be quieter than the two armies which confront each other along the banks of the Rappahannock. Even the cavalry, that prolific source of rumor and excitement, seem to have subsided into the involuntary armistice which prevails throughout the lines. The condition of affairs affords them ample opportunity to indulge in their favorite pastime of swapping horses, and scouring the country, in search of buttermilk and other good things. Should the article the trooper desires be a fine saddle horse, if he is an honest man, he will purchase him, or exchange his own for him. If he is not an honest man, he will conceal himself until night, and then take the horse without saying a word or paying a cent. So with the bridle, saddle, halter and blanket, if they happen to be convenient. Milk and butter in the spring house, honey in the bee hive, vegetables, fruits and green corn are appropriated with the same unscrupulous disregard of the rights of others. The good things are consumed; the horse and his accoutrements are put into service, or sold to some unsuspecting infantry officer in want of "a mount." The following night the horse disappears. The infantry officer supposes he has strayed off; the cavalryman knows better. But should the horse not disappear in this way, the farmer, or rightful owner, comes along after awhile, claims the horse, proves his property and takes him home, and the unwary purchaser, like the innocent lad in the Vicar of Wakefield, finds himself "sold."

You must not infer from this unvarnished statement that all of the cavalry, or a majority of them, or even a considerable portion, are guilty of these disreputable practices. On the contrary, the material of which this arm of the service is composed, is in the opinion of many superior to that of the infantry, and equal to the artillery. Nevertheless, there are enough bad men among them to bring partial discredit upon the whole service, and to call for this public exposure of their conduct.

For my own part, I see but little difference in the material which enter into the composition of the several arms of the service. In the beginning of the war, the sons of wealthy country gentlemen, especially in this State, preferred the cavalry. The young men in the cities and towns, including professional characters, selected for the most part the artillery; whilst the great body of the people throughout the country, including many professional men, and the rich, as well as the poor, generally chose the infantry. To this general rule there were at the time many exceptions; and now, when the call of the President embraces the whole country, we find every profession and condition well represented in the several branches of the public service, except in the departments at Richmond. In this latter service clerks and men who write good hands, are apt at figures and possess a certain amount of clerical skill, are generally employed. Constituted in these departments, but it has been found impossible to do so to any considerable extent, owing to the want of previous training for the duties required at their hands.

How is it then, you are ready to inquire, that any portion of the cavalry, however inconsiderable, should engage in these discreditable practices? The answer is simple: The cavalry man (leaving out of consideration the fact that there are bad men everywhere,) is allowed only nominal compensation for the loss of his horse, unless he is actually killed in battle. The horse cannot be replaced except by an outlay of from five to fifteen hundred dollars. It is not always convenient or possible to raise this large sum; and hence a temptation is presented to the man. In addition to this, there is a lamentable want of discipline in the cavalry service. Hampton's brigade, and some other commands, are distinguished for their good conduct in camp, as for their gallantry in the field; but it cannot be disguised, however often it may be denied, that Gen. Stuart has failed to give his men that training, and to subject them to that degree of discipline, without which it were folly to expect of them either obedience or efficiency.

There seems to have been no foundation but the public desire, for the report that prevailed some weeks ago in regard to the appointment of Gen. Hood to the command of all the cavalry forces in Virginia. Such a change would have given almost universal satisfaction to the army, including the cavalry themselves, not withstanding the letters and communications to the contrary with which the Richmond press was recently flooded. These unconscionable puffs deceived nobody, and least of all the army. With Gen. Hood in command, the cavalry in Virginia, with its excellent material and the accurate knowledge which the men now have of the topography of the country, might be made to equal, if they did not excel, the brave cavaliers of the South west, the followers of Morgan, Forrest, Wheeler, and [William] Adams.

P. W. A.

ARMY OF NORTHERN VIRGINIA, September 4, 1863 [9-12-63]

Spring and Summer have come and gone, and Autumn, with her glowing fingers, is now painting the skies and fields in those gorgeous hues produced only by her skillful hand. We have entered upon the ninth month of 1863, and three acts of the bloody tragedy have passed in review. The first was played at Chancellorsville; the scenery, a sterile soil and a dark wilderness; but the light of victory, reflected back from the Southern Cross, proclaimed the conqueror. The scene shifts, and the second act is ushered in among the rugged hills of Gettysburg. Blood flows in torrents and the slain lay in heaps, but Triumph, unable to decide in favor of either party, turns to Fortune, who warns us to return to our own soil, and fight the battle there.

From the Potomac we pass to the Father of Waters—to Vicksburg and Port Hudson—where the third act is performed, and where Fortune, less kind than she was wont to be places the crown of victory upon the standard of our enemies. From the great river we step to the sea, and, as the curtain rolls up to the lurid sky, the fourth act opens, and Charleston, and Sumter, and Wagner rise to view. When the curtain, all torn and bloody, and soiled from the terrible conflict, ascends again, it will be upon the fifth and final act in this horrid tragedy of 1863. It may be upon the Rappahannock, and it may be upon the Tennessee. If here, then the actors are ready; they have studied their parts, they have learned them well and are ready, with the assistance of that kind Prompter who stands above the clouds, to play them through to the bitter end.

Meanwhile, the army is not idle here. The interval between the acts is not left wholly unemployed. Fresh supplies of ammunition have been obtained; newer and better arms have been distributed where they are needed; clothing and shoes have been supplied; the men are exercising and drilling; the animals are resting and improving, and the whole army is preparing for other struggles and other triumphs. Not the least important subject which now engages the attention of the chiefs, relates to the organization of a corps of engineers. This necessary adjunct of an army should have been provided at the beginning of the war, but better late than never. The corps is intended to embrace pioneers, pontooniers, sappers and miners, as well as engineers proper.

The duties of the engineer is important, and often laborious. If it be necessary for the traveler to be informed beforehand of the roads over which he is to pass, the streams he is to cross, the mountains he is to scale, the defiles he is to thread, and the robbers he is to encounter; how much more important is it that the commander of an army and his chief officers, upon whom depend the safety of their troops, the welfare and honor of their country, and the success of the campaign, should possess the same information? This information cannot be had without the aid of engineers, a part whose business it is to thoroughly reconnoiter and map the whole country occupied, or expected to be occupied by either army.

This duty is usually performed by a party detailed by the chief of the Engineer Bureau. It should be done early, and the maps deposited in the office of the chief of the bureau in Richmond, where copies are prepared and sent to the department, corps, and division commanders in the field. These maps are on a sufficiently large scale to show accurately the roads, streams, cleared and uncleared land, elevations and depressions of ground, fords, bridges, mills, residences, towns, &c. Particular care is taken to show not only the direction but also the condition of roads, which are classified and each class shown by a different line or mark. It is necessary that all neighborhood and private ways, as well as public roads, should be laid down, as frequently a proper knowledge of roads will enable a General to save much marching by sending his train on one road and his troops on another, thus making the march more rapidly and with less fatigue to his troops. The maps should also go sufficiently into details to enable the General to know where he may encamp his troops on a march. Leaving out of consideration the question of attack and defense, camps on a march should always if possible, be located convenient to wood and water.

This duty, as above stated, belongs to the party specially detailed by the chief of the bureau; but the engineer acting with the army in the field should take every opportunity of proving the accuracy of the maps, acquiring through their assistance a thorough knowledge of the country. It is his duty, after the line of battle is established, to lay out all works for the strengthening of the line; and it is the duty of the engineer troops, with the aid of such details as are necessary, to construct such works under the superintendence of the officers of their corps. It is also the duty of the engineer, when the line of battle has been established, to acquaint himself most thoroughly with every rod of ground in the neighborhood, it is safe to reconnoiter. He should know not only where the strong and weak points of his own line are, but also those of the enemy. his knowledge should be such that he could inform his general of the country to be passed over, either in an advance or a retreat; and roads, forts, bridges, &c., should be prepared for both as far as practicable.

As has already been stated, an engineer corps for the field is now being raised. Its organization will be the same as that of the regiment, with a Colonel, Lieut. Colonel, Major, company officers and men. Perhaps it would be more proper to speak of the men as engineer troops. Officers have been detailed to go home to raise volunteers for this inviting service.

P. W. A.

ARMY OF NORTHERN VIRGINIA,
September 7, 1863 [9-15-63]

Ten men were shot near Orange Court House Saturday [September 5] for desertion and murder. They were from North Carolina, and were arrested near the James river on their way back to their homes. They resisted the officer who arrested them, and inflicted a mortal wound upon him, from which he subsequently died—thus adding the crime of murder to the crime of desertion, and thus proving that one step in crime invariably leads to another, and another, until the poor wretch is lost forever. Indeed, when a soldier makes up his mind to abandon his flag, he makes up his mind, though he may not think so at the time, to commit all the crimes known to the penal code. Having forfeited his life and incurred the condemnation of the law and of society, he must prepare to defend himself with any weapon that comes to hand, whether murder, arson, forgery or perjury. Having by the act of desertion declared war upon his government, and his government having placed the brand of DESERTER upon his brow, as long as life shall last every man's hand will be against him, because his hands have been raised against all mankind. I say all mankind, because crimes such as those named above, wherever and whenever and by whomsoever committed, are crimes against all men, since it is the interest of all men that there should be no such thing as desertion, arson, murder, forgery or perjury.

Into what an abyss, then, does the soldier plunge who deserts his post? Tired of fighting the enemies of his flag, he enters upon a life long conflict with his own kindred and country, his own government and society, and indeed with the good and virtuous in all lands and climes. Instead of a war of a few years' duration with the invaders of his soil, he invites a conflict with his own friends which must last as long as life, and in which he cannot possibly be successful. For if he should escape the judgement of a court martial, he need not expect the judgement of society and of his own conscience. He may hide from the law, and from the face of men, but not from conscience.

What is said of the North Carolina deserters will apply to the deserters from all the other States. Let wives and mothers, then, who write to their husbands and brothers beseeching them to come home, remember this, and the sad fate of the ten men who have just been shot. It is natural that friends at home should desire to see the loved ones who have gone forth to battle; but they should be careful not to write them letters which will unsettle their minds, and tempt them to commit the greatest crime of which a soldier can be guilty. Those who are at home should forbear and suffer as long as possible, and withhold their troubles and embarrassments from the soldier who already has enough to occupy his hands and heart.

But what shall be said of the Raleigh *Standard* and other papers, whose course has been calculated, if not designed, to produce disaffection among the troops from North Carolina? North Carolina is one of the staunchest States in the Confederacy, and her people among the bravest and most virtuous in the world. Why, then, do they tolerate these vipers in the bosom of their noble old Commonwealth. The bitter fruits of such teachings may be read in the records of the courts martial of the army, and in the awful sentence which has just been executed upon those ten unhappy men who perished on Saturday.

You will not be surprised to hear that deserters will be treated with more severity in the future than they have been in the past. Mild means having failed, Gen. Lee, like the old man in the spelling book, is disposed to try what virtue there is in stones. Hereafter, when a man deserts his colors, he may make up his mind to be shot, if caught, and caught he will be some time or another. It may be that the system of furloughs recently instituted will have the effect of checking desertion. If it does, its effect will be doubly beneficial in this, that it will banish this heinous crime from the army, and at the same time encourage the men to become good soldiers, since by the terms of the order, furloughs will be granted to those only who conduct themselves well.

In course of a recent letter attention was called to the injurious effect upon the discipline of the troops resulting from the practice, now quite common, of running officers holding commissions in the army for civil stations at home. The object of the letter was simply to point out one of the causes of any want of discipline that might be apparent, and not to condemn such officers as might have announced themselves as candidates for the State Legislature or Congress. It was to the policy of the law or practice, and not the officer who might become a candidate, that public reprobation was intended to be directed. So far as I am informed, the army candidates are worthy men. Their services in the field certainly entitled them to the favorable consideration of the people. The rule should be to elect the man who can render the country most service, whether he be a civilian or a soldier. If any distinction be made, it should be in favor of men beyond the military age who are distinguished for prudence and patriotism. Young men for arms; old men for counsel. No man, however, whether old or young, should be chosen for the Legislature or for Congress who is not in favor of a vigorous prosecution of the war, and opposed to any settlement which does not secure to us and our posterity complete independence. Men of courage and patience, of high character, experience and ability, are needed everywhere, and especially in Congress. Above all, let no young man who has been staying at home all this time, take refuge in civil and political employments. The man who is able, and yet unwilling to serve his country in the field, is unfit to serve it anywhere.

P. W. A.

On September 10, the Raleigh Standard *newspaper office was sacked by Confederate soldiers, destroying the presses owned by W. W. Holden—a Unionist and peace advocate.*

RICHMOND, September 10, 1863 [9-18-63]

There being but little prospect of active work on the Rappahannock for some time to come, I have decided to change the scene of my labors from Virginia to the vicinity of Chattanooga. There are other reasons for this step which it would be impolitic to disclose just now, I would say to the people of North Georgia, however, be of good cheer; the enemy will never be permitted, if you are but true to yourselves, to gain a permanent foothold upon your soil. But to prevent such a calamity, every man and woman will be expected to do his and her duty. The exigency of the times will admit of no exempts and no laggards now. The man in Georgia who is able and not otherwise serving the cause and yet holds back now, cannot be regarded as a friend to his country.

But Georgians have other duties before them besides those of a military character. They have a Governor, members of the Legislature, and members of Congress to elect. Are there any candidates running who are in favor of reconstruction, or of any terms of settlement short of a separate nationality and absolute independence? Are there any who refuse to declare themselves openly and unequivocally, for the Confederate cause, now and forever, in adversity as in prosperity, in the hour of defeat as in the hour of triumph? If there are such candidates for the Legislature, or for Congress, or for the Gubernatorial chair, then the red hot abolitionist whom our soldiers meet in battle array from Massachusetts, is less a foe to us and our cause than such candidates will be if elected.

And here let me say a word in regard to President Davis. The recent discussions in the newspaper press have led us to make enquiry in the Army of Northern Virginia, as to the feelings and opinions of the troops in regard to the President. My investigation has not been limited to officers, but has extended to the privates as well. Disclaiming emphatically any partisan feeling for the President, candor nevertheless constrains me to say it is the almost universal sentiment of the army that the President is entitled to the cordial support of the country. Without approving of all the acts of his administration, and indeed condemning many of them, they still believe it to be the duty of the army and of the people to frown upon all factious opposition, and to encourage a feeling of harmony and fraternity. The right to discuss measures of public policy, and to approve or condemn as may be thought best, will ever be maintained; but that kind of opposition which considers neither time nor circumstances, and which can have no other effect but to weaken the government, endanger the cause, and sow the seeds of discord and death, meets with universal condemnation in the army. A free people will always maintain the right to scrutinize closely the acts of persons in authority, but the exercise of this right should be characterized by a spirit of candor and fairness, and the faults and shortcomings of our rulers pointed out with a view to their correction and not for the purpose of bringing discredit upon the government. To organize a party in opposition to the President now, is to organize a party in opposition to the government, to the cause itself for which we are struggling, and indeed to ourselves. The President is by no means the government, nor is he infallible; indeed, most of his advisers are feeble men with a feeble and timid Congress to back them; but the circumstances of the country are such, the dangers which environ us are so formidable, and the foe against whom we fight so multitudinous and powerful, that every blow struck at him is a blow at the Confederate people and their government. Such at least is the feeling of the army of Northern Virginia.

Major General Hood and Brigadier General Anderson, both of whom were wounded at Gettysburg, have so far recovered as to be able to report for duty. It is probable that they will be heard from at an early day and upon an important field.

P. W. A.

On September 9, Longstreet's corps was detached from the Army of Northern Virginia and sent to assist Bragg in north Georgia. Alexander made arrangements to follow, but a delay in Savannah caused him to arrive on the battlefield of Chickamauga only after the fighting was over.

Great Battle of the Chickamauga

NEAR CHATTANOOGA, TENN., September 23, 1863 [9-28-63]

The most important battle of the war, after that of the first Manassas, has just been fought and won by the Confederate arms. The result is told in a few words: There is no longer an armed enemy on the soil of Georgia! Only the Federal dead, wounded and prisoners now remain.

The multitudinous host, swelling with confidence and pride, who lately invaded that powerful State, threatening to overrun her territory and devastate her homes, has been defeated and forced to seek refuge behind barricades and breastworks along the banks of the Tennessee river. Let every heart in all our suffering land give thanks to Almighty God for His great kindness—for this signal deliverance!

Having been detained on the route I arrived upon the field too late to witness the battle. I am also almost wholly uninformed of the organization of the various corps, division and brigades which compose the Army of Tennessee. Under these circumstances I am constrained to rely upon the statements of others who were in a position to be well informed, and do not pretend to speak with absolute certainty, or to enter much into detail. But there is one fact which may be affirmed with great confidence and emphasis—to wit, that the Confederate troops never fought better; nor did any other troops upon any other battlefield ever conduct themselves with higher courage or more distinguished gallantry. Longstreet's veterans and Bragg's braves entered into a generous rivalry, and each strove to set an example of daring, and to out do the other. The one rushed to the conflict with their old battle flags, bearing upon their ample folds the inscriptions of the first and second "Manassas," "Seven Pines," "Malvern Hill," "Fredericksburg" and "Chancellorsville," and fully resolved to wave those glorious standards in triumph over a western, as they had already done over an eastern foe. The other, conscious of their own manhood, and yielding to none in high resolve and dauntless courage, yet stung by the memory of former disasters, went upon the field with their minds and hearts fully made up, never to quit it but as victors, nor until they had proven to all the world that they were the worthy brothers of the heroes of the Chickahominy and the Rappahannock. Before men thus animated and thus resolved, many of whom (the Georgians) fought in view of their household gods, nothing could stand and live. Their fierce battle cries rung out above the din and uproar of the mighty strife, the trumpet note of victory to Confederate arms, and the knell of defeat and death to the enemy. Great clouds of yellow dust and blue smoke from the guns and burning woods enveloped the field and the struggling combatants, and ascending from the plains settled upon the crests of the hills and mountains in festoons of fantastic shape; but, deep as was the gloom, there were flashing eyes there that saw through it all, and followed with a steady gaze the path that led to victory.

Nor were Bragg and Longstreet insensible to the feeling which animated their followers. To the one, it was the last opportunity to reverse the decrees of a hitherto unpropitious fortune; to the other, it was a new field of hope and ambition, where another blow might be struck for his country, and fresh laurels gathered for his own brow. Each did his duty nobly, as did all their officers and men, and the rewards of a grateful country await them. Only portions of Longstreet's divisions arrived in time to take part in the fight, but they were a host within themselves. They were Benning's, Law's and [J. B.] Robertson's brigades of Hood's division, and Kershaw's and [Benjamin] Humphreys' brigades of McLaws' division. But let us proceed with the battle.

It is already known that Gen. Bragg deemed it prudent to withdraw his forces from Chattanooga and East Tennessee, and to retire into the State of Georgia and there await reinforcements. The enemy's cavalry penetrated as far as Ringgold and Tunnel Hill, on the Western and Atlantic railroad, our own cavalry, unfortunately, setting fire to the bridges as they retreated. Several affairs between outposts followed on Thursday and Friday, the 17th and 18th inst., and on the 19th a heavy skirmish ensued, amounting almost, if not quite, to a general battle, in which Hood and his veterans displayed great spirit and resolution. General Bragg advanced upon the enemy, driving in his outposts and skirmishers, and gaining important advantages. He considered it best, probably, to strike before Rosecrans could be reinforced, and even before all of his own reinforcements could arrive. The Federal commander was evidently surprised by the vigorous movements of Bragg, from whom he expected only a feeble resistance. Even as late as Sunday morning; when the Confederate deployed on the west bank of the Chickamauga, he was hardly prepared for a serious attack from an army which he supposed would be only too glad to effect its escape.

The great battle was fought on the west bank of the Chickamauga, on Sunday, the 20th day of September. The line of battle extended east and west, across the boundary line between Walker and Catoosa counties, resting here and there on the bends in the Chickamauga river, a very crooked stream, running east and northeast, and emptying into the Tennessee above Chattanooga. D. H. Hill commanded on the right, Polk in the center, and Longstreet on the left. The command of Longstreet was composed of such of the brigades of Hood's, McLaws' divisions as had come up, and [Thomas C.] Hindman's, [William] Preston's, [Alexander] Stewart's and Bushrod Johnson's divisions, of the army of Tennessee, the three last constituting the corps of that intrepid officer, Major General [Simon B.] Buckner. These forces held the extreme left, and were opposed to the right wing of the enemy, which rested upon the mountains and occupied a strong position. Hill's corps, on the right, was composed of Breckinridge's and [Patrick] Cleburne's fine divisions. I am not yet informed of the composition of Polk's command, which occupied the center, nor of [W. H. T.] Walker's corps, which was held in reserve.

By order of Gen. Bragg, the attack was commenced about 10 o'clock Sunday morning on the extreme right, and was taken up by each succeeding division to the left, reaching Longstreet's left at 11 o'clock, and thus taking one hour for the wave of battle to roll from one end of the line to the other. On the right and in the center that attack was not successful in the early part of the day. The enemy had massed a heavy force on this part of the field, and maintained his position with so much stubbornness that Walker was ordered up with his reserves to the support of Hill and Polk. He moved forward in superb style, and fell upon the enemy like a thunderbolt; but the Federal columns still stood the ground, and fought with desperate gallantry.

In the meantime Longstreet had been steadily pushing back the enemy on the left, meeting no check, and carrying everything before him. Under his orders, Buckner executed a successful flank movement, whilst Hood and others made a vigorous assault in the front. The effect of the combined attack was to force the Federals to abandon that part of the field, and to seek a position on a high ridge. They had not more than formed their lines, however, before the brigades of Kershaw and Humphreys, of McLaws' division, under command of Kershaw, (McLaws not yet having arrived with the remainder of his division), were ordered to assault the ridge. Here a desperate struggle ensued. Kershaw carried the position again and again, and lost it as often. It was evident that the enemy had the advantage both in position and numbers, but the brave Carolinians and Mississippians did not stop to count the odds against them. Gen. Longstreet very properly, however, sent [Archibald] Gracie's, [J. H.] Kelly's and [Robert] Trigg's brigades of Preston's heroic division, to their support. A vigorous and simultaneous assault was then made, and the enemy finally driven, with great slaughter, from the crest of the ridge and down its side. Preston and his entire command behaved with distinguished gallantry, and like the veteran Kershaw and his loyal followers, excited the admiration of all who witnessed their conduct. Kershaw captured nine guns, a number of small arms, and some prisoners; and Humphreys took 435 prisoners, four regimental standards, and one headquarter flag.

Hindman, whose position was next on the left, was not idle while this struggle was going on. He engaged the enemy in his front, and after a fierce encounter, compelled him to retire along with the rest of the Yankee forces.

The advantages which Longstreet had gained on the left could not but arrest the attention of Rosecrans, who consequently detached a heavy force from his left wing and center, and sent it to the support of the right. This important movement did not escape the vigilant eyes of the Confederates. Gen. Law, who had succeeded to the command of Hood's division after the latter was dangerously wounded, ordered a battery of ten guns to be pushed forward to a position from which it could enfilade the reinforcing column as it advanced. This was late in the afternoon, and at a time when Preston's and Johnson's divisions of Buckner's corps, and Kershaw's and Humphreys, of McLaws' division, had again become engaged with the enemy in a desperate conflict. After gaining possession of the ridge, as heretofore described, they had continued the pursuit until they came up with the retiring foe, who turned upon his pursuers and once more attempted to make a stand. The reinforcing column was about to wheel into position, when the battery of ten guns opened upon a terrific enfilading fire. About the same time, Lieut. Col. [Gilbert Moxley] Sorrel, of Longstreet's staff, ordered Stewart's division to advance and fall upon the flank of the column. The shock was terrible. The enemy halted, staggered backwards, fell into confusion, and finally fled, followed by those to whose assistance they had gone. Indeed, they were badly whipped on this part of the line, and lost largely in prisoners and killed and wounded. About 3,000 prisoners were taken. In addition to the guns captured by Kershaw, Hood's division took twenty-one—thirteen of which were brought off by Law's brigade and eight by Benning's. Each of these last named officers was conspicuous for good conduct. But this was true of all the officers and men, and I need not stop to particularize one more than another.

Gen. Hood's wound, which has resulted in the amputation of his thigh, is deplored by the whole army. A more useful and gallant officer is not to be found in the Confederate service.

But the maneuver by which the Federal commander sought to reinforce his right wing, did not escape the notice of Polk, Walker and Hill. They detected the movement, and again reduced by the reinforcements sent to oppose the victorious advance of Longstreet. This time their assault was successful. The foe was driven back at every point, on the right, center and left. The day had been won; the enemy were flying from the field. Night alone put an end to the conflict, and saved him from a ruinous defeat, if not from annihilation. Gen. Hill speaks in high terms of Breckinridge and Cleburne, and their brave commands. Polk and Walker acquired fresh renown; and the bold and intrepid Forrest, and the gallant Wheeler, with their hardy troopers, were omnipresent; at one moment harassing the flanks of the enemy; at another beating back his advances; now hovering on the hill and mountains, and anon swooping through the valley like eagles upon their prey. Indeed the universal report is that every man did his duty, and none more than Gen. Longstreet. The result speaks for itself, and is the eulogy of all, of the privates as well as the officers.

Of the loss sustained by either side, I am not sufficiently informed to speak with any degree of certainty. The number of killed is small compared with the number of wounded, which is unusually large, and the wounds are unusually slight. Many of the wounded of the enemy fell into our hands, and all of his dead together with about forty pieces of artillery, several thousand small arms, between six and eight thousand prisoners, and between twenty-five and thirty stands of colors. Among our own casualties were several general and field officers.

Monday was devoted to the care of the wounded, the burial of the dead, and the gathering up of the arms and other trophies of the battle. The enemy withdrew to Missionary Ridge Sunday night, and on Monday night continued his retreat to Chattanooga and the Tennessee river. Yesterday the Confederates followed up and took position in front of the town, where they still remain. The Federals are crouching on the riverbank behind entrenchments, and are busily engaged in erecting additional defences. They have a good position in a bend of the river, strongly fortified in front, and their flanks well protected. It is hoped Gen. Bragg, will find some way to maneuver them out of their hole without a direct attack. Possibly an energetic pursuit Monday morning would have compelled them to cross the river; but this is not certain. Their rear was pushed into Chattanooga yesterday evening by McLaws, who had arrived with the remainder of his command.

P. W. A.

Official casualties for the Battle of Chickamauga: Federals, 1,657 killed, 9,756 wounded, and 4,757 missing for 16,170 casualties; Confederates, 2,312 killed, 14,674 wounded, and 1,468 missing for 18,454.

Rosecrans' Position at Chattanooga

LOOKOUT MOUNTAIN, TENN., September 28, 1863 [10-5-63]

Rosecrans has not evacuated Chattanooga, nor is there any reason to believe that he has any such intention. The long lines of infantry, cavalry and artillery reported by the signal corps some days ago to be crossing the Tennessee to the north side, are now believed to have been forces sent out for the purpose of escorting provision and forage trains to Stevenson and McMinnville, whence the Federal army obtain their supplies. Their wagon trains have been sent across the river and parked only for greater safety. A few brigades of infantry have also been transferred to the north bank with a view to guarding Butler's ford, four miles below the northern end of the mountain, and Kelly's ford, some nine miles further down. The river at the town is in the form of a letter S, in the northern curve of which, but on the southern side of the river, the Federal army is encamped. A heavy battery has been planted on the tongue of land on the north side and in that part of the curve which sweeps around to the south. This position gives them an enfilading and oblique fire upon an attacking column moving against their front, which is also defended by three lines of breastworks running from one curve of the river to the other. These lines form a semi-circle in front, and are the complement to the bend of the river in the rear.

Within the circle thus formed by the river in the rear and the lines of entrenchments in front, there are a number of hills or elevations which are crowned by formidable earthworks and batteries. Some of these defences were erected by Gen. Bragg, but they have been greatly strengthened and multiplied by Gen. Rosecrans since the battle. There is a star-shaped fort [Fort Negley] of large extent in front of the railroad depot and near the center of the second line of breastwork. Eight hundred or a thousand yards to the right of this, on the line of the East Tennessee Railroad, is another work of equal dimensions, but different in form. This seems to be a redan. Back of these two works, on an eminence near the river and between them, is a strong redoubt. On the high hill behind the town are other batteries admirably located. Indeed, the entire curve of the Tennessee occupied by the enemy is covered with a net work of forts, breastworks, masked batteries and rifle pits. Many of them can be seen distinctly from Lookout Mountain, whilst only portions of others can be detected among the trees and behind the hills. When viewed from our picket lines in front, as I saw them this morning, they look formidable enough.

Can this stronghold be taken by a direct assault? Were Vicksburg and Fort Wagner thus taken? Strong as the position is already, Rosecrans shows no disposition to relax his efforts to render it really and absolutely impregnable. Day and night his engineers are at work. Possibly the place could have been carried by storm, though not without heavy loss, had we pressed forward from the victorious field of Chickamauga. If any mistake has been committed, it was in not making the effort at that time. It is too late now I fear. It may be, only two alternatives are left us: either to dig up to the place as the enemy did at Vicksburg and Fort Wagner, or to maneuver him out of it. To do the former, will require time and labor; to do the latter will be difficult and hazardous, as will be apparent to the most casual observer of the map of Tennessee.

This is not the only disagreeable truth we have to record. Reinforcements have reached Rosecrans since the battle, and others are expected. Prisoners and citizens report the arrival of Burnside's column, and late Federal papers hint that other troops are on the way. The retention of Chattanooga is considered as of the first importance, not only as regards Tennessee, but as a *point d'appui* in the future conduct of the war; and it will be held if possible. The papers admit the defeat of Rosecrans, but ascribe it to the large reinforcements which they say were sent to Bragg.

Rosecrans sent in this morning, under a flag of truce, one hundred and ninety-two ambulances and several wagons with supplies for his wounded in our hospitals, who have been paroled and will be returned to him this evening and to-morrow. The ambulance train was met at a point between the two picket lines, and there turned over to Confederate drivers who will go for the wounded, bring them back to the same point, and there deliver them to the Federal authorities.

It is believed that 10,000 will cover our loss in killed, wounded and missing, and that 20,000 will cover the enemy's, including 7,000 prisoners, of whom 5,000 were well men taken in battle. There seems to be some doubt about the wagons reported among the spoils of the victory, and the number of flags taken is twenty not forty, as reported to me by one of the highest officers in the army. Of the 25,000 stand of small arms picked up on the battlefield, a portion of them, of course, were dropped by our own killed and wounded.

It is reported that a few more guns have been found, in addition to those captured in the fight. The number is now said to be forty-three. The flags taken have been sent on to Richmond by the brave men who captured them and such company officers as greatly distinguished themselves. It is not probable that our killed will exceed 1,000. Of the remaining 9,000, it is not believed that more than 2,000, if so many, were severely wounded— all the rest receiving comparatively slight wounds.

There has been no rain here for eight weeks. It is exceedingly dry and dusty, and the supply of water scant.

P. W. A.

Further from the Battle of Chickamauga
ARMY OF TENNESSEE
In front of Chattanooga, September 25, 1863 [10-1-63]

There are some additional facts and circumstances connected with the battle of Chickamauga which deserve to be recorded.

The battlefield lies on the west bank of West Chickamauga, and is about eight miles from Ringgold, Ga., and about the same distance from Chattanooga, Tenn., being nearly due west from the former and nearly due south of the latter. It is some four miles below the Tennessee line, and is bounded on the west by Missionary Ridge (a continuation of Walden's Ridge, in Tennessee), and on the east by the Chickamauga, or "river of blood," as the Indian name implies. Rossville, the former home of John Ross, the celebrated Chief of the Cherokees, is two miles north from the battlefield, and situated at the foot of a pass in Missionary Ridge. It was in this lovely valley of the Chickamauga, and along these mountain passes, that the hostile tribes were wont to meet in battle array and settle their disputes. It was here that the dusky maiden was wooed and won by her forest-born lover, and questions of boundary, and dominion, and revenge found their bloody solution. This was in the years that are gone, when the untutored Indian held undisputed sway in these wild glens and caves, and among these rocky fastnesses. And yet how faithfully does the civilized white man of this day repeat the history of the savage red man of that! The same passions animate his heart, the same policies engage his councils, and the same field now drinks up his blood. The River of Blood—if this was so appropriate name for the crooked, gliding, serpent-shaped river given to it a yet stronger claim to that sanguinary title.

The ground upon which the battle was fought is slightly undulating, except where it approaches the mountain spurs and ridges on the west, and is covered with heavy timber, with occasional patches of cleared land here and there. The timber is not so thick as that around Chancellorsville, where the undergrowth is almost unpenetrable, but resembles more the woods about Shiloh, where the troops were maneuvered with comparative ease.

The artillery could take but an inconsiderable part in the battle, in consequence of the timber and the level character of the ground. On the left, next to Missionary Ridge, the ground is broken into hills and valleys, but the primeval forest still remains, and consequently the most skillful artillerist could accomplish but little.

It is said that Gen. Bragg's plan of attack was designed to be the same as that of General Lee on the Chickahominy, viz: a movement down the left bank of the Chickamauga by a column which was to take the enemy in flank, and drive him down the river, to the next ford or crossing below, where a second column was to cross over and unite with the first in punishing the enemy still further down the river, until all the bridges and fords had been uncovered and our entire army passed over. This plan was frustrated, according to reports, by a counter movement, which is explained in the following order of the Federal General [George] Thomas. This order was found upon the person of Adjutant General [Jacob] Muhleman, of Gen. [John] Palmer's staff, who subsequently fell into our hands:

HEADQUARTERS 14TH ARMY CORPS
Near McDonald's House
Sept. 19, 1863.—9 a. m.
Major General Palmer:

The Rebels are reported in quite a heavy force between you and Alexander's Mill. If you advance as soon as possible on them in front, while I attack them in flank, I think we can use them up.

Respectfully, your obedient servant,
Geo. H. Thomas, Major General Junior comd'g.

This was Saturday morning. The counter attack upon the front and flank of our flanking column was made with vigor soon after it crossed the river, and in accordance with the plan suggested by Gen. Thomas; and, if not entirely successful, it was sufficiently so to disarrange our plans and delay our movements.

The inquiry may arise in the mind of the reader, why Gen. Bragg did not postpone the attack until all his reinforcements could get up? It is said, but with what truth I cannot determine, that he acted under the belief that only three Federal corps had advanced up the valley of the Chickamauga, and that the remainder of Rosecrans' army was still on the north side of the Tennessee and Chattanooga, and that Burnside had not yet formed a junction with the main body. If such was his belief, he was deceived, except as to Burnside, as Gen. Lee was at Gettysburg when he supposed on the morning of the 2nd of July that the whole of Meade's forces had not then arrived. And yet it must be admitted that Gen. Bragg acted wisely in giving battle when and where he did. Delay was full of danger; it might bring heavier reinforcements to his antagonist than any he could count upon. Moreover, Rosecrans was not on his guard, and did not look for an attack from an enemy who he had supposed would be only too glad to effect his escape. At one time he was wary and active, combining the cunning of the fox with the sudden energy of the panther springing upon its prey; but he had become intoxicated by success, and had grown proud and confident and incautious. Gen. Bragg did well, therefore, to strike his boastful foe as soon as he did. His blow was given with skill and crushing effect. If it had only been followed up with other rapid blows upon the arrival of his remaining reinforcements, possibly still more gratifying results might have been accomplished. But this is not certain, and let us not be too fast to find fault.

As it is, let us see what were the fruits of our victory. In the first place we captured 7,000 well prisoners; these will go far toward equalizing our losses at Vicksburg and Port Hudson. In the next, we took 40 stands of colors, 38 guns, (of which Longstreet's command brought off 27,) 25,000 small arms, 150 wagons, and several thousand cartridge boxes and knapsacks with their contents. This is a good showing—one that speaks for itself—and will pass for a great victory in any country. But this is not all; indeed, it is the least part of the glorious result. By a single battle we succeeded in expelling the invader from the soil of Georgia, the teeming Egypt of the Confederacy, at a time of much solicitude in the public mind, and under circumstances which seemed propitious to the successful advance of the enemy into the very heart and stronghold of the country. Our success can be measured only by what our grief and loss would have been if the enemy had reached Atlanta and overrun the State.

I have endeavored heretofore to pay due homage to the skill and gallantry by which this great victory was achieved. Officers and men all did their duty, and to each and all is due next to the Giver of all victory, the deep gratitude of an imperiled people. But the truth of history, as well as simple justice, requires it to be stated here, that no one officer or body of men of the same number could have contributed more to the triumph of the Confederate arms, than did Gen. Longstreet and the brave veterans who followed him from Virginia. They had traveled from the Rappahannock in crowded box cars, upon open platforms, and upon the tops of cars, in the rain, in the dust, and in the sun, and with but little food or sleep. They had passed by their own homes without stopping to embrace the loved ones there—homes which some of them had not seen since the commencement of the war; and had rushed to the scene of action without rest or transportation, halting only long enough to clear their eyes of the dust of travel and replenish their cartridge boxes. The officers were without horses, and the men without wagons to transport their supplies. There was not time to furnish either; the battle was about to be joined. Arrived in front of the foe, these veterans were placed in the van, and led in every attack by the left wing, where our success was most signal, and where the day was recently won. All honor, then, to the modest chieftain and his invincible command! Their praises freely proclaimed by the Army of Tennessee, between whom and themselves there can be only a generous rivalry in heroic action and patient endurance.

Passing from the battle to the present situation, there are some important changes to report since the date of my last letter. We have wrested Lookout Mountain from the enemy, and now command the Nashville & Chattanooga Railroad below Chattanooga, the only channel, except by wagon trains, by which he can receive supplies from the rear. His forces occupy a bend in the Tennessee, which is spanned by two wide substantial pontoon bridges. His flanks are well protected—the right by Chattanooga creek, a deep stream with steep banks, and the left by a curve in the river above; while his front is defended by outer and inner lines of entrenchments and a series of redoubts and earthworks which crown every hill within the circuit of his fortifications and command every approach to the town. To attack the enemy in such a position were worse than madness. Many of these works have been prepared or strengthened since the battle.

But does Rosecrans intend to hold Chattanooga? A reconnaissance was undertaken last night at half-past 10 o'clock, when his pickets and skirmishers were chased back to the fortifications; but he was found to be in strong force, and not yet evacuating the place. To day however, our signal men on Lookout Mountain report that his wagons have been taken across the river and parked, and that long lines of infantry, cavalry and artillery, accompanied by forage wagons loaded with hay, could be seen moving over the bridges and across the mountains to the north. Whether this is a ruse, intending to countermarch at night, or the beginning of the final evacuation of the town, it is impossible to decide. Prisoners and citizens who have escaped out of their lines report that the whole army is moving towards Murfreesboro'. It may be a part of the plan of Rosecrans to leave a sufficient force behind to hold Chattanooga while he moves the main body of the army to some other point.

I have written and telegraphed you regularly since my arrival here.

P. W. A.

LOOKOUT MOUNTAIN, TENN.,
October 6, 1863 [10-12-63]

The dull monotony which has prevailed in camp since our arrival in front of Chattanooga, was relieved yesterday by a bombardment of the enemy's works. Several of our longest range guns were placed in position—some of them on the side of Lookout Mountain—and a slow but regular fire was kept up from 11 o'clock this morning until 5 in the afternoon. This fire was maintained at intervals during last night. The guns put in position on the side of the mountain were the 20 pounder Parrotts of Col. E. P. Alexander, chief of artillery in Longstreet's corps. The enemy replied to our fire from three points only—their extreme left up the river, the star fort in the center, and the moccasin works on their right. These last works are on the north side and in a bend of the river opposite our left and are so designated because the ground in the bend of the river assumes the shape of an Indian's moccasin. They are in the lower part of the S which sweeps around towards our lines at the foot of Lookout. The ground in the moccasin is elevated and irregular, and gives the enemy a enfilading fire upon a column moving across the plain against their center or right. There are three casemated batteries of rifle guns on the moccasin, and they are known among the Confederates as the Moccasin Batteries.

The star fort is situated about the center of the Federal lines, and is an extensive and formidable work. We have not yet been able to ascertain the number of guns it mounts, though we could see that four of its guns replied to our fire. None of their guns, however, were able to reach our batteries on the mountain, on account of their great elevation.

The distance was too far for our guns to produce any particular effect. Several of our shot were seen to explode above the star fort and over the Federal lines; but as far as I could see with the aid of an excellent glass, an unusual commotion was created thereby in the camps of the breastworks, and stood firmly to their posts throughout the day. A few of our 12 pounder howitzers were placed within twelve hundred yards of the Federal lines, but the guns chiefly relied upon were not nearer than two and two and a half miles.

Our casualties were few and slight, not exceeding five or six wounded from shells. The enemy doubtless suffered a heavier loss, inasmuch as his troops were more closely met in an open plain.

The freshet produced in the Tennessee by the late thirty hours' rain, carried away the enemy's lower bridge night before last. This was a hastily constructed tressle work, slight and frail, the pontoon bridge being higher up the river and opposite the town. Several parties were out yesterday, in flats and batteaux, trying to save the wreck of the bridge, but they met with indifferent success. The enemy have secured a small steamboat—probably one that had been plying up the river from Chattanooga—and this they are using as a ferry boat.

A deserter, who swam the river yesterday and delivered himself up to our pickets, says that a report prevailed in their camps that our cavalry has destroyed between four and five hundred of their wagons with their contents. He says also that the Federals suffered very much for food for a week after the battle of Chickamauga, but that they were now receiving full rations, a supply train having arrived.

With the exceptions noted above, no change has occurred since the date of my last letter. There is still some doubt felt in regard to the reinforcements alleged to have been received by Rosecrans. One day we hear that the force lately in East Tennessee under Burnside have certainly arrived, and again that several trains loaded with troops have been seen by our pickets below to arrive at Stevenson; and or the next it is affirmed most positively that no reinforcements whatever have come up, either from Burnside, Grant or Meade. My own opinion is that additional forces have been received, and that the time has passed when we could hope to force Rosecrans out of Chattanooga, except by a flank movement upon Nashville or the destruction of his line of communications to the rear. Twenty thousand men, if properly provisioned, can hold the place indefinitely.

Gen. Forrest, unwilling, it is said, to report to Gen. Wheeler, has been granted a leave of absence. There is but little harmony or unity in the Army of Tennessee; whilst its organization is less perfect, and its discipline less effective, than that of Gen. Lee's army.

P. W. A.

LOOKOUT MOUNTAIN, TENN., October 8, 1863 [10-13-63]

More rain, followed by frosty mornings, deep blue skies and a bracing atmosphere. The change is acceptable to the two armies, both of which have resumed their work of fortifying and strengthening their positions with fresh energy. If the position of Rosecrans is strong, so is Bragg's. The batteries of the latter, however, do not command the works of the former, as has been stated in several of the public journals. The fact was abundantly demonstrated a few days ago when an effort was made to shell the enemy's lines. Neither our splendid 20-pounder Parrotts, nor our best 24-pounder rifle guns, produced any appreciable result, so far as could be discovered, owing to the distance at which they were fired. If Bragg were provided with siege guns of the requisite caliber, he might drive the enemy out of Chattanooga, but field artillery is unsuited for such heavy work. Even the latter might be moved forward in the plain which spreads out before the town and brought within easy range; but in that event the ground would be in favor of Rosecrans, whose forts and batteries crown every eminence within the limits of the town and its immediate vicinity. It is estimated to be two miles from the base of Missionary Ridge and the side of Lookout Mountain, where our batteries are placed, to the enemy's main works. Our Parrott guns will carry that distance, but not with sufficient accuracy to accomplish much.

Scouts just in from East Tennessee report that one division only of Burnside's forces had gone to the relief of Rosecrans, and that the remainder—estimated at 12,000 muskets—was still at Knoxville, and as actively engaged in fortifying that place as Rosecrans is at Chattanooga. This, if true, is an important and significant fact.

If time be allowed Rosecrans and Burnside, or his successor, to render their position impregnable, and to accumulate supplies, for the winter they will be enabled not only to hold us at bay, but to "laugh a siege to scorn." I fear, we but flatter ourselves when we imagine that the condition of the roads in the winter will lead to the evacuation of those strongholds. One railroad was found sufficient for the transportation of the supplies for Johnston's army at Centreville and for Lee's army at Fredericksburg; and the road from Nashville to McMinnville and Bridgeport will probably be found capable of performing the same service for Rosecrans. The mountainous country between those points and Chattanooga, and the condition of the wagon roads crossing it, may oppose serious obstacles to the transportation of supplies; but those obstacles hardly deserve to be named in comparison with those which Hannibal surmounted under infinitely more adverse circumstances, nearly two thousand years ago, when he conducted his army of the Alps and drew his supplies after him. What Hannibal did for the subsistence of his army in Italy, Rosecrans, though a pigmy by his side, may do in Tennessee—a country that presents no such difficulties as those which opposed every step of the great Carthagenian General. The Federal commander has another advantage in the vast resources and means of transportation which his government possesses, and of which it is now availing itself with all its immense energy.

I was in error in saying that in the late battle, Polk commanded on the right, Hill in the center, and Longstreet the left. There were but two grand divisions of the army: the right wing, commanded by Polk, and the left wing commanded by Longstreet. Hill was under Polk, and Buckner was under Longstreet; and it is said that Hill is the officer who is really responsible for the failure to attack at sunrise on Sunday morning, and not Polk, who, it is affirmed, issued orders for his command to move at that hour. Gen. Bragg, however, could not, it is said, look beyond Gen. Polk to his subalterns, especially since he neither complained of their delinquency nor put them under arrest.

President Davis arrived in Atlanta this evening, and is expected here to-morrow.

P. W. A.

IN FRONT OF CHATTANOOGA, October 16th, 1863 [10-20-63]

The heavy rain adverted to in my last letter continued to pour down in torrents until last night. Chattanooga Valley, lying between Lookout Mountain and Missionary Ridge, is flooded with water. Our lines extend across this valley, which is drained by Chattanooga creek, now very much swollen; and, as you may imagine, the condition of the men, especially those in the trenches and on picket, is exceedingly uncomfortable. None of them have more than one blanket, and nearly all belonging to Gen. Bragg's original army, are without shelter of any kind. Longstreet's corps is somewhat better off, his men having provided themselves with Yankee flies, India rubbers, &c., at Chancellorsville and other battlefields.

Enquiry at the Quartermaster's Department, in Richmond, and personal observation in the armies of Gen. Lee and Gen. Bragg, leave no doubt that the greatest want of the troops this winter will be for blankets. It is not probable that there will be an adequate supply of either clothing, shoes, or hats, or even of provisions, unless we recover East Tennessee; but the chief want, as already stated, will be blankets. Arrangements were made sometime since to procure supplies of clothing and shoes, and if our adventures are attended by auspicious gales, the army will be able to get through the winter, with such help as the people at home can, and doubtless will, render. Their responses to the call made upon them last winter was the sublimest incident of the war, and will be recorded in history, as it has already been in "the books" which are kept beyond the sun, and in which all our accounts, whether for good or evil, are entered with an unerring hand.

As in the past, so at this time, I would address my appeal chiefly to the women of the Confederacy. The men have always done their duty in this respect, but the women have done more than their duty—they have helped their husbands, fathers, and brothers to do theirs. True, they do not enter the field, nor brave the blast of battle, nor use cannon, minie rifles and swords; and yet the vast army of heroic women who have given their hands and hearts to the cause, have done their parts as well as their brave brothers in the field. The weapons they employ are the Needle, the Spinning Wheel and the Loom, Words of Encouragement to the weary and faint-hearted, and kind and generous Deeds in the hospital and by the wayside. With these arms they have done as much to defeat our wicked enemies as an army of resolute men. If they have not met these enemies in battle, they have met them at the loom and around the couch of the wounded and sick. If they have not gone to the field in person they have ever been there in spirit. In every blanket they have given to the soldier, in every pair of socks they have put upon his bleeding feet, in every garment they have woven for his manly-limbs, they have been present in the hour of battle, and have given blows for the freedom of their race. It is to these heroines of the needle, the loom and the spinning wheel that brave veterans who have for three years stood between them and danger, not turn for relief. Shall their appeal be made in vain? Not as long as there is a blanket, a yard of carpeting or of cloth, or a sheepskin, that can be spared.

P. W. A.

ARMY OF THE TENNESSEE
Near Chattanooga, October 20, 1863 [10-26-63]

One month ago yesterday and to-day, the great battle of Chickamauga was fought. The victory of the Confederates, though not so regarded by the public, was a decisive one, in this that it prevented the enemy from again sundering the Confederacy and reaching the heart of the country, then apparently almost within his grasp. The invasion of Georgia already commenced, was defeated ere the enemy's columns had gone a day's march within her borders, and an army and a General hitherto triumphant were beaten back with great slaughter, and with a loss of nearly 8,000 prisoners, over two score of cannon, nearly as many flags, and many thousand small arms.

Such a victory would have been considered decisive in Europe where the cause of quarrel related to the rectification of a boundary line, or some supposed diplomatic insult. The French and Sardinians, though victorious at Magenta and Solferino, could boast of no such spoils that graced the triumph of Bragg on the Chickamauga; and yet a few days thereafter we find the defeated Austrian Emperor purchasing his peace by the cession of a large and important portion of his territory. Indeed, such victories as the Confederates have repeatedly won, would have led to an arrangement between almost any other belligerents in modern times; and the reason why they do not bear the same fruits for us, is because our cause of quarrel is different. The Confederates contend for independence; the Federals for domination. If we are successful, the Union is sundered forever, and the Federal government shorn of half its power, and more than half its wealth. If the North is triumphant, then we lose everything--life, liberty, property—and become the minions of a domination more foul than that of the Turk. Nothing, therefore, but the exhaustion of one of the parties, the success of the advocates of peace in the popular elections, or the intervention of one or more of the great powers, is likely to bring such a contest to a close.

Looking at the contest in this light, we find no cause for despondency. The United States are quite as nearly exhausted of native soldiers who go willingly to the field as we are;

there is already a large and increasing peace party in all of the Northern States; and if there should be any intervention by foreign powers, it is universally agreed that it will be in our behalf.

If it be said that our victories are resultless as compared with those of Napoleon and Frederick the Great, the reply is that in Europe the roads are numerous and good, the country open, and supplies abundant, thus rendering it easy to pursue a beaten enemy, whereas the reverse of all these is true of this country. In addition to this, the Federals outnumber us so far, that our Generals find it necessary to carry their last man into the fight in order to win the day, and can keep back no reserves to be put in at the critical moment, and to render the victory decisive and crushing. Their troops having already become exhausted in the struggle which preceded their triumph, are unable to press the advantages like a body of fresh reserves who would have been held back for that very purpose.

It is owing to this fact, perhaps, that Bragg and Rosecrans occupy the positions they do to-day. If the former had had 20,000, or even 10,000 fresh troops to put forward at 5 o'clock Sunday afternoon, he would in all probability have captured all the artillery and wagons of the latter, and slain and taken the greater part of his army. At it was, Rosecrans managed to get his forces back to Chattanooga, where he now remains. He has not only had time to render his position impregnable to assault, but to receive reinforcements who have traveled more than a thousand miles to get to the Tennessee river. A portion of these reinforcements—those from Meade's army—are reported to have crossed the river at Bridgeport, as if preparatory to another advance upon our flank and rear.

If we were to imitate their example, and call together our forces now scattered along a double line by the seaboard and in the interior from the Potomac to the Rio Grande, and mass them together in two compact and powerful armies, and control and direct each by a single clear head and steady hand, we might look for results such as we have never accomplished before.

P. W. A.

ARMY OF THE TENNESSEE,
MISSIONARY RIDGE, November 9, 1863 [11-13-63]
Four consecutive days of uninterrupted sunshine and a good prospect of a continuance of it—what a blessing! The Persians were not far wrong when they worshiped the Sun, without whose light and heat neither animal nor vegetable life can be sustained. One step further would have carried them to the First Great Cause of all, the Supreme Creator, alike of themselves, and the Sun. But the warm, gentle, blessed sunshine does not come alone: it is accompanied by high, drying winds by day, followed by sharp frosty nights. Under the influence of the former, the roads and trenches and muddy flats are rapidly drying. Under the influence of the latter, the forest is fast disappearing before the axe of the stalwart soldier, who must make up by fire what he lacks in the way of blankets, clothing and shoes. In the absence of tents, he is forced to provide himself with bivouacs either of brush, boards, wicker work, corn stalks or broom straw, ingeniously arranged to turn the water and shut off the wind from his humble bed on the ground. Some of the men display much ingenuity in the construction of these shelters, and avail themselves of means which would never have been dreamed of but for the hard school of Necessity in which they have taken their lessons.

But the effect of this change in the weather has not been less beneficial upon the animals employed in the army. They have had a hard time of it for some weeks past, the supply of forage being limited and irregular, the rains heavy and frequent, and the roads almost impassable. It must be admitted, moreover, that in many instances they have been sadly neglected, and the result of this neglect is a waste of horses, which must occasion alarm, if it do not create indignation, in all reflecting minds. The supply of horses in the Confederate States is limited and rapidly diminishing, and every effort should be made to preserve the lives of those we have, and to increase the stock. The loss of Kentucky and Tennessee deprives us not only of the usual supplies of bacon and flour obtained from those quarters, but of large numbers of horses and mules, which are almost as indispensable to an army as food itself. Instead, therefore, of impressing horses, in the hands of farmers and producers, it would be wiser and better economy to take the best care possible, under the circumstances, of those already employed in the service. To that end the roads in the neighborhood of the camps should be kept in repair, and not allowed to be worked into quagmires, and cut into great holes and ruts, in which the struggling and famished teams sometimes sink and perish, as some of them have actually done on the horrid road from here to Chickamauga station. Shelters and troughs of some sort should also be provided for them; anything, however rude and rough, is better than leaving them to take the snows and rains of winter, and to eat their scanty allowance of shelled corn in the mud, where they have been trampling for days and nights together. The forest here abounds in trees suitable for board timber and troughs. The stables or shelter should be located on the south side of a hill, when it can be done, and the ground dug down to nearly a level. By pursuing this plan, the animals can be effectually protected from the cold north-west winds, and will get the benefit of the Southern sun, while the stables can be more conveniently drained. A place of this sort with only a few pine tops thrown around it, is a great protection to the horse. Economy alone, if nothing else, should constrain the proper authorities to look after the welfare of army horses; for it is well known that an animal that is under shelter and provided with a trough, will do better on half rations than one that is exposed to the weather and fed on the ground, on a full allowance.

The loss of horses in this army since the battle of Chickamauga has already been very heavy, owing to the want of forage and the criminal neglect of quartermasters, teamsters and artillery drivers. In some instances, they have had to go from one to four days without a grain of corn or a blade of fodder, and no inconsiderable number have perished for want of something to eat. It was not to be expected, under the circumstances, that full rations would be served out to them, but that more could have been done than has been done, will hardly be disputed.

It is but proper to add that some of the more provident quartermasters and artillery officers, appreciating the services of these dumb but faithful co-workers in our war of independence, have begun to erect shelters, and have done all they could to overcome the difficulties of procuring forage for their teams. Execrating, as all human minds must do, the wretch who either abuses or neglects his horse, the noblest creature next to man in the whole range of animated nature, it affords us a corresponding pleasure when we find a person of an exactly opposite disposition. But more upon the subject of the Horse on some future occasion.

Except the exchange of an occasional shot between the batteries, the two armies continue to gaze at each other in quiet. Yesterday afternoon the enemy fired a shell at one of Gen. Walker's regiments which was going out to relieve another regiment on picket, disabling twelve men, one of whom subsequently died and another had his leg amputated. Our pickets had been previously warned by the enemy's that they would be fired upon if we continued to send the reliefs out in a body. As a general thing, the pickets are on very good terms and seldom fire upon each other, and especially without previous notice.

The weather has changed and become quite cold since this letter was commenced.

P. W. A.

On November 23 Grant began a series of attacks on the besieging Army of the Tennessee; the battle of Chattanooga had begun.

ARMY OF THE TENNESSEE
Missionary Ridge, November 23rd—9 p.m. [11-30-63]

Gen. Grant has made a move upon the military chess-board today, and one that is likely to effect military operations in this quarter. At an early hour this morning, when the fog had lifted from the valley below, it was discovered that the Federal commander was massing a heavy force on his left and opposite our right. As the morning advanced, this force grew denser and larger, until it covered the slopes this side of Cemetery fort, which is near the river above and the last work the enemy has on his left. At 12 p.m., three masses deployed into two lines of battle, with heavy reserves. This movement completed, the guns of the fort opened at 2 p.m., when the heavy lines of the Federals advanced rapidly against our pickets, and drove them in after a sharp resistance on their part. At 3 o'clock the enemy had gained Indian hill [Orchard Knob], an eminence which stands about midway between Cemetery fort and

Missionary Ridge, being between his left wing and our right. He advanced upon no other part of the lines, and rested after gaining possession of the hill.

In the meantime, Major [Felix] Robertson, brought up a few guns of his reserve artillery, and with other batteries posted on Missionary Ridge to the right, opened upon the enemy—with what effect is not yet known. We only know that he maintained his new position notwithstanding our fire. No report has been received of our casualties beyond a surmise in official quarters, that they will read from one to two hundred in killed and wounded. Only our pickets were engaged, the enemy not coming within range of our line of battle.

When this movement was going on, it was observed that the enemy threw a considerable column up the river further to our right, as if he intended to overleap our line and compel us to stretch it out to a length that would render it very long and very weak. Can it be that he means to threaten our depot of supplies at Chickamauga Station, and at the same time to draw us away from Lookout Mountain?

The first result of such a movement will be to compel Gen. Bragg to weaken his forces on Lookout Mountain, (his left) to reinforce his right which is comparatively weak. Indeed, orders to this effect have already been given, and are being followed. It will never do to let the enemy get possession of our depot at Chickamauga. The demonstration to-day was intended, doubtless, to force him to make his selection between the two. If he decides to hold Chickamauga, then he must yield the mountain and throw his army between the enemy's increasing left wing and the railroad. If he gives the preference to Lookout then the railroad and his depot of supplies must go.

The natural effect of the affair to-day, as has already been intimated, will be to force Gen. Bragg to weaken his left in order to strengthen his right wing, now threatened by a formidable and largely superior force. Therefore, I expect an assault upon Lookout to-morrow. Then it will be less able to resist an attack than it was to-day. Our artillery on the mountain will be of no assistance after the enemy shall have reached the foot of the mountain, it being impossible to depress the guns sufficiently. The importance of the mountain ceases with the loss of Lookout Valley. The possession of the Valley reduces the wagon transportation of the enemy to two or three miles at furthest, and gives him the use of the river besides. The voluntary abandonment of the mountain, therefore, should occasion no regret, since its longer retention is not only of slight importance, but will be attended with much difficulty, on account of the great length of our line.

P. W. A.

The following day, November 24, Lookout Mountain fell, and on the 25th Bragg was routed from Missionary Ridge; the road to Georgia was open.

Official casualties for the battle of Missionary Ridge: Federals, 753 killed, 4,722 wounded, 349 missing for a total of 5,824; Confederates, 361 killed, 2,160 wounded, 4,146 missing (mostly prisoners) for a total of 6,667.

ARMY OF THE TENNESSEE,
Dalton, Ga., November 27, 1863 [12-1-63]

It is only with great difficulty that letters can be written and forwarded from a retreating army. Postponing for the present, therefore, some additional particulars and observations concerning the battle on Missionary Ridge, I resume the thread of my narrative, with the remark that I have telegraphed you regularly, as occasion seemed to require it. It may be that the messages have not reached you in due season, as it is reported the wires are down at several places between Dalton and Atlanta.

But Major Tilton, the excellent Quartermaster of Walker's division, has just informed me that he had orders to put his train in motion on the road to Resaca, and as he has been kind enough to give me transportation for my blankets and valise, I must stop short with my letter here, with the remark that this sudden and unexpected order is an illustration of the difficulties which beset an army chronicler who remains with the troops, and sees and judges for himself. It is now seven o'clock and night is upon us; so with a mouthful of half cooked beef, I saddle my horse for the weary march before us.

RESACA, GORDON CO., GA., November 28th.

Returning to the narrative of events alluded to above, I would take the reader with me to the close of the battle of Missionary Ridge, which was fought on Wednesday, the 25th inst. General Hardee, who commanded the right wing, had repulsed every attack of the enemy, had inflicted heavy loss upon him, and he and his men were congratulating themselves upon their complete and brilliant victory, when Gen. H., who had passed to his left (the center of the army), discovered that [A. W.] Reynolds' brigade of Hindman's division, commanded by General Patton Anderson, had given way, and thus allowed the enemy to get a foothold upon the mountain. Having defeated the foe in his front, he immediately ordered his left to form into line across, or at right angles to the ridge, and to drive the intruders from his flank. This order, like all others that he had given, was carried out to the letter by his brave command, thus repulsing the enemy in front and on his left flank. Had the same skill and energy been displayed at other points on the line further to the left, the Confederates would not have been driven from Missionary Ridge. Reynolds' brigade is composed of the 54th and 63rd Virginia regiments, and the 58th and 60th North Carolina, troops who have always done well heretofore.

And here let me add, at the risk of becoming tedious, that [Carter] Stevenson's division, composed wholly of "Vicksburg troops," behaved with unsurpassed gallantry. These troops are Tennesseeans, Alabamians and Georgians. Gen. [Alfred] Cumming's Georgia brigade never fought so well. The fact here stated should silence forever the thoughtless tongues that have been ridiculing and maligning the heroes who fought at Vicksburg.

After night set in, the whole army was withdrawn to the east side of the Chickamauga, the trains having preceded it the night before. The roads were in bad condition, and there are but three bridges over which the troops could retire. But the enemy was too badly crippled, to make pursuit; only a small detachment of cavalry followed on the road by Bird's Mills. At Chickamauga station rations of hard bread and bacon were served out to the men from the depot, and the trains sent forward. Some of the stores were shipped off by the railroad; the remainder was destroyed. The army was put in motion by two o'clock at night on the road to Ringgold, and Gen. Bragg and Gen. Hardee left at daylight next morning. The road was bad as it could be, and but for the friendly light afforded by the moon on that and the preceding night, the army could not have effected its escape.

Thursday, the 26th. After a fatiguing march, the army with its long trains arrived at Ringgold during the afternoon and night. The enemy had thrown forward a mixed column of mounted infantry, artillery and cavalry, which was harassing our rear guard, under command of Gen. [States Rights] Gist, considerably. At one time, Gen. Bragg ordered the wagons towards the rear to be moved out of the road and parked, with a view, it is said, of having them burnt rather than let them fall into the hands of our enemies. Gen. Gist was repeatedly pressed back against the wagons, but managed finally, with the aid of his brave command, (Walker's division) to save them all. At one time, the enemy got in between him and the main column, but he took a neighborhood road and thus escaped destruction. Unfortunately, [T. B.] Ferguson's battery of four guns, belonging to Walker's division, was captured. The horses were in very bad condition, and unable to keep up with the column; hence the disaster. The greater part of the men and horses escaped. You will be astonished to hear that the horses in the artillery service, the most important in the whole army, are the most neglected—a fact, however, which quartermasters, and even artillerists, seem incapable of comprehending. The loss of the battery occurred soon after dark and not far from Ringgold. The trains were brought out three miles this side of Ringgold and the teams fed, while the army occupied the pass just outside the town. Three companies of the 16th South Carolina, acting as a special guard to Ferguson's battery, were dispersed and many of the men taken prisoners.

Nov. 27th—The trains were now put in front and directed to take a left hand road to Dalton, passing near Catoosa Springs. They moved at midnight—the troops at daylight following the direction of the railroad by Tunnel Hill, so as to cover the trains. Roads very bad for some miles; the teams overworked, and suffering for forage and rest. I saw a mule lie down when the harness was removed and go as soundly to sleep in two minutes as an infant, and that while hundreds of wagons and thousands of men were marching by within a few paces of where it rested.

Cleburne was entrusted with the command of the rear guard to-day, Walker's division having been relieved. The Federal pursuing column, numbering, it is estimated, about 10,000 men of all arms, assaulted him before he reached Tunnel Hill. This column consisted of picked troops who moved rapidly and fought gallantly; but Cleburne succeeded in restraining them whenever he encountered them. But they were becoming quite troublesome; so he ambuscaded them by concealing his forces, including his artillery, until the enemy got within a few paces of his guns, when they poured grape and canister into them with the most destructive effect. The road was filled with their dead and wounded. Our infantry then sprung forward from their covert on either side of the road, and literally mowed them down by their well directed shot. The enemy fled in confusion, leaving 250 prisoners and three flags (the latter taken by the artillerists,) in our hands, and from 1,000 to 1,500 killed and wounded in the road. The Federals kept at a respectful distance from Pat Cleburne after that, and were five hours marching one mile on our track.

A prisoner taken near Ringgold reports that [Peter J.] Osterhaus [actually Gen. Joe Hooker], of Sherman's corps, is in command of the pursuing column. He says that Osterhaus crossed the Chickamauga on a hastily constructed bridge, and that Grant was building a wide, substantial military bridge at Red House ford, by which to cross over his whole army, and that he intended to make a clean sweep of the Confederates. This last achievement, the beaten hero of Shiloh will find more difficult than he imagines.

The trains reached Dalton in the afternoon, and were parked and the teams fed. The troops arrived soon thereafter and went into camps. It was just at this point where my frugal meal was being prepared, and the first paragraph of this rambling letter was being indited, that an order came for the trains to move on to Resaca. The roads to this place are pretty good, though almost impassible in places. Several wagons were lost and a good many mules killed on the way, not by the enemy, but by the great holes or gulfs and quagmires in the road. I saw no pioneer corps with the trains; the teamsters were left to take care of the wagons as best they could. I am not certain that it would not be an eventual benefit if we should some day lose a train; perhaps, the authorities would then see the necessity, recognized in all other countries, of organizing an efficient corps of engineers, including pioneers, bridge and boat builders, &c. it commenced to rain at 11 o'clock, and by day it was pouring down in torrents. The roads, already heavy enough, now became indescribably bad. It was a horrid night. But a poor woman, the mother of ten children, her husband and oldest son in the army, gave me shelter at one o'clock, a fire to dry myself by, and a bed to rest upon, not forgetting a bundle of fodder for my horse. A dozen others, attracted by the cheering light seen through her window, applied for admittance, and room was found for all in that humble cabin. God bless that good woman and shield her husband and son from the dangers of the battle field! The light in her window was not hid under a bushel. Alas! how the poor do shame us by their charities!

It is now three o'clock, and the army has not yet come up. The rain will probably stop the pursuit of the enemy, at least for the present, unless his well-organized pioneer corps enable him to keep it up. Our future line will probably rest on the Coosa and its eastern tributaries.

But in conclusion: The battle of Missionary Ridge was a great misfortune, not on account of the loss of men, which was inconsiderable, nor the loss of territory, which is far more serious; but chiefly on account of the loss of the moral strength and confidence of the army and the country. Let us not, then, add to our calamities by beginning a war of abuse and condemnation against the Chief of the beaten army or the head of the government. Let us rather strive to reanimate the hopes of the people and the army, bring forward all our strength, and pray that Heaven will yet give us the final victory.

In a few days I shall prepare a review of the whole campaign in Northern Georgia, beginning with the evacuation of Chattanooga in September, and closing with the present retreat; and while I shall not gloss over the errors of any one, I shall be able to show that General Bragg has had a most difficult task to perform—that he behaved with unsurpassed courage on the field, and that if he has been unfortunate, he has also been devoted to the cause.

P. W. A.

THOMASTON, GA., December 20, 1863 [12-24-63]

I resume the pen for the purpose of disabusing the public mind of an erroneous impression in regard to the future movements of the Army of the Tennessee. I allude to the belief said to be entertained very generally in Georgia, that the army was engaged in repairing the roads and constructing bridges in its rear with a view to falling back upon Atlanta. Having heard that some uneasiness was felt upon this subject, I called upon Gen. Hardee before leaving Dalton, and I have his authority for saying that he has not the least thought of retiring from his present position; but on the contrary, if the enemy should advance this winter, which he does not believe they will do, he will dispute every foot of ground from Tunnel Hill to Atlanta. He believes moreover, that if the absentees will return to duty and the people at home will continue to supply the army with the means of subsistence, the Federal army will never succeed in reaching Atlanta any more than it has succeeded in reaching Richmond. It is now reported that General Johnston has been assigned to the command of the army; but there is no reason to believe that he will withdraw in the direction of Atlanta at a time when there is no prospect of an advance by the enemy.

But will Gen. Grant make a forward movement this winter? To do so, he must first accumulate large stores of subsistence at Stevenson or Chattanooga, and procure a fresh supply of horses and wagons to be used in conjunction with the railroad in the transportation of them. To complete these preparations, will require, not days nor weeks merely, but months. An army is an immense machine which can be moved only with much difficulty and expense. In the present instance, Grant would first have to repair the railway bridge at Bridgeport and Running Water (no easy matter at this season of the year,) reconcentrate his army at Chattanooga, bring up supplies, increase his trains and wagons, repair the Western & Atlantic railroad as he advances, and bring with him cars and locomotives to do his transportation. It is known that thousands of his horses perished or were disabled at Chattanooga, and that Wheeler destroyed and captured over a thousand of his teams, and four or five times as many mules and horses, a few days after the battle of Chickamauga. It is known, too, that the Federal army encamped around Chattanooga was reduced to greater extremity for food than the Confederates have ever been, not because they did not have the supplies in the rear, but because they could not get them up. And the recent intelligence that portions of the army have gone towards Stevenson and Nashville, is all explained, it is believed, by the suggestion that they have been distributed along the railroad to the rear with a view to lessening the pressure upon Chattanooga, and for greater convenience to supplies. If any troops have been sent to Virginia, they are probably the two Potomac corps which Hooker took to the assistance of Rosecrans, and which he is now returning to the Rappahannock.

For these reasons, in connection with the facts that the enemy has destroyed the Western and Atlantic railroad from Ringgold back to Chickamauga, and the Georgia and East Tennessee road from Cleveland for the distance of several miles towards Dalton, one may safely conclude there will be no forward movement undertaken by the Federal army this winter.

I would acknowledge the receipt, from the editor of the Savannah *Republican*, the day before I left Dalton, of a box of English russet half boots, and a few blankets and socks, all of which were immediately distributed to bare-footed and needy Georgians. The articles were much needed, and were received with many expressions of gratitude. There are several hundred men still left who are without shoes, while the thermometer is down to 12 deg.! How long shall this crying shame continue? If not, that officer can never find a time when they will be needed more.

Your printer, who seems to take a malicious pleasure in perverting my letters, makes me say in the *Republican* of the 18th that our killed at Missionary Ridge was 800 instead of 300, as I wrote it. I would overlook this and other errors which occur in the publication of nearly all my letters, but for the fact that I may not live to gather up the letters and correct these errors. I pray the future historian, therefore, should he design to consult your columns when he comes to write a history of this unholy war, not to visit his condemnation upon my head, but upon the fingers of those who will not print my letters as I wrote them.

P. W. A.

1864

Attrition

For the first few months of 1864, Alexander did little writing; much of his time was spent recovering from the rigors of previous campaigns. Crisis loomed ahead. Overall Federal commander and newly appointed Lieutenant General Ulysses S. Grant planned a multi-front assault against the Confederacy. During a six-week period in Virginia, Grant's forces suffered nearly 68,000 casualties, while inflicting 42,000 on Lee's army. Grant's losses were replaceable; Lee's were not.

Recent Movements of the Enemy—Their Object and their Defeat

MONTGOMERY, ALA., February 26, 1864 [3-3-64]

The vital part of the great combined movement by the Federal armies against our defensive positions has failed, and with it the whole plan must come to naught. The advance of Sherman's army was full of danger, as, in the event of success, he would have been in a position to derange all our plans and render the fall of Atlanta only a question of time; but this, like many previous combinations of the enemy, failed, because too much was attempted. The objective point at which the enemy aimed was beyond all doubt the great railway center of the Confederacy, and the naval attack upon Mobile, the advance of Sherman upon Meridian and the forward movement upon Dalton were all parts of the plan by which that point was to be reached. The scheme was a bold one, and showed great originality, if not soundness of judgment. Gen. Grant is a bold man, and if he had succeeded in his combinations, the North might well have claimed that he was really a great Captain.

There is reason to believe that Gen. Sherman expected, when he marched out of Vicksburg, to reach Selma, in Alabama. The heavy column of cavalry that started from Memphis and constituted an important part of his forces, was to move rapidly across Mississippi and Alabama, cut all interior railway lines, destroy the bridges and government workshops, lay waste the country, and gain the rear of General Polk, harass and delay his retreat, and, if possible, force him down towards Mobile, while Sherman rushed upon him in front. Had Gen. Polk retreated upon Mobile, the attack upon which by the Federal fleet was calculated, if not designed, to draw him in that direction, Sherman would have occupied Meridian, Demopolis and Selma, and thus have rendered his escape impossible, and the fall of Mobile, from lack of provisions and without a blow, a matter of absolute certainty. The possession of Mobile and Selma would have given the Federal commander two important water bases—the one on the Mississippi at Vicksburg, the other at Mobile on the Gulf. Indeed, a successful lodgment in this fertile region of Alabama would not only have carried with it the fall of Mobile, Montgomery, and secured to the enemy points of great material and strategic importance, but it would have been equivalent to the removal of the Mississippi river, if such a thing were physically possible, from Vicksburg and New Orleans to Montgomery and Mobile. Nay, more—it would have been a grand flank movement, as it was designed to be, against Gen. Johnston, which, if successful, would have resulted, as has already been intimated, in the fall of Atlanta and the occupancy by the legions of the enemy of the northern half of the great State of Georgia. Every man we might have sent to Mobile would only have enhanced the victory of our foes, as it did at Vicksburg. Had Gen. Polk retired upon Mobile, Sherman would have thrown himself in his rear and cut off his supplies, as Grant did at Vicksburg when he threw his army between Pemberton and all hope of succor. There could have been no escape by water; for there was [Adm. David] Farragut's fleet already hurling its thunder at Fort Powell; nor through Mississippi, for there was Banks and his column marching up from New Orleans. If Johnston should send reinforcements to the scene of action, as it was doubtless expected he would do, then Grant would fall upon him at Dalton and force him back upon Atlanta, against which it was finally hoped Sherman would be able to advance from the west, while Grant pressed down from the north. Indeed, the telegraphic wires inform us that Grant [Thomas] has already moved out from Chattanooga and that a battle is imminent at Dalton; but when he hears, as he must in the course of a few hours, that Sherman has been foiled and that his part of the combined movement has failed, he will probably retire to Chattanooga as the latter has to Vicksburg.

But how was the formidable combination defeated? It failed because too much was attempted, and because it was met by the Confederates with consummate skill and courage. The co-operating columns were too widely separated, were exposed to too many chances of failure, and were entrusted to too many different hands. The column of cavalry, though far outnumbering the Confederate horse, met with more than a match in those superb soldiers, [S. D.] Lee, Forrest and [Philip] Roddey, and their brave followers.

This combined movement was undertaken after mature deliberation and elaborate preparation. Its failure given us two months more time in which to prepare for the great campaign of 1864. The middle of April, perhaps the 1st of May, will have come before a new campaign can be devised and the necessary preparations made for its successful execution. In the meantime, the ranks of the foe are becoming thinner every day by reason of the expiration of the terms for which his troops enlisted, whilst our numbers are growing larger each successive day. That our civil authorities in Richmond and our Generals in the field will take advantage of these favoring circumstances, the country may feel assured. The prospect before us is encouraging, and gives promise, under the benign favor of Heaven, of eventual success and independence. Let each and all of us, then, work and fight as we have never worked and fought before. "A long pull, a strong pull, and a pull together" will carry us through, and give us peace and liberty for our reward.

P. W. A.

In April, Alexander returned to Virginia for the upcoming spring campaign.

Letter from Virginia

RICHMOND, May 2, 1864 [5-10-64]

Official information leaves no room to doubt that Burnside had made, or soon will make, a junction with Meade, on the upper Rappahannock. One account has it that his forces are now well on the way to Culpepper Courthouse, and another states that he has already reached that place, and will soon be ready to unite in the attack upon Lee's position along the south bank of the Rapidan. This position is represented by military men to be very strong—stronger indeed than any position, including the heights of Fredericksburg, heretofore held by the Army of Northern Virginia. It remains to be seen whether Grant will make a direct attack, or attempt to turn the position.

Meade's force before the junction of Burnside did not probably exceed 65,000 men, and the latter does not bring him more than 15,000 sorry troops—making altogether 80,000 opposed to Lee. This number may be further increased by Western troops and garrisons doing duty along the frontier and Northern cities. The force assembling on the Peninsula under Gen. [William F.] Smith—not Beast Butler, as stated in a previous letter—is estimated at 15,000, and is made up of troops heretofore stationed in North Carolina, South Carolina, Georgia, Florida and Eastern Virginia. This added to Meade's army, will make a force of 95,000, or allowing 15,000 additional troops that may be gathered in the West and from the military posts on the frontier, the whole force now marshaled against Richmond under the supreme guidance of Gen. Grant may be put down at 110,000 seasoned troops, 90,000 of whom will attempt to move down from the line of the Rappahannock, while 20,000 will operate on the Peninsula and south side of James river. This is a large army—larger than either the French or the Allies had at Waterloo—larger, indeed, than the armies with which Napoleon won a majority of his victories.

It would be obviously improper to go into any estimate of the forces which General Lee has, or soon will have, to meet the legions of the invaders, though it may not be amiss to state that the change in General Grant's plan of campaign from what it was understood in official circles some days ago to be, has produced no uneasiness here. Our forces had been so disposed as to enable General Lee to meet the foe on the Rapidan, on the Peninsula, or on the south side of the James, either simultaneously or in succession.

The chief uneasiness felt here is in regard to the question of supplies. The Danville extension will be completed by the 1st of June, and this will give the Government a shorter and better route from the capital to Georgia, the granary of the Confederacy. Railway men inform me also, that the railroads, though much deteriorated, are in quite as good condition as they were eight months ago, and that it is not probable they will become much worse in the future. The necessities of the times have forced railway companies to rely upon their own efforts to keep their roads and rolling stock in running order, and many of them have gone vigorously to work, and have been successful to an extent that is highly gratifying. But should Government be guilty of the folly of taking military control of the railroads in the Confederacy, all these improvements would be stopped, and the roads, and the country with it, would soon go to ruin. The railway business is not learned in a day or a year; it requires time and experience, and great energy and administrative capacity, to enable a man to conduct a railroad corporation with success.

P. W. A.

The Battle of the Wilderness
ARMY OF NORTHERN VIRGINIA
Battlefield, May 7, 1864 [5-23-64]

Again it becomes my grateful task to chronicle another Confederate victory. While it cannot be regarded in its military aspects as a decisive battle, since the enemy was neither routed nor driven back across the Rapidan, yet when we consider the circumstances under which it was fought, the elaborate preparation made by the enemy, the large army of veteran troops with which he advanced, and the common consent with which both sides had come to regard the present campaign as probably the last act of the bloody drama which has convulsed the North American continent for the last three years, we cannot but look upon it as one of the most important battles of the whole war. The boasted leader of the Federal army chose his own time and place to deliver battle; he made the attack and was repulsed with heavy losses; his combinations were penetrated and defeated, and his whole movement check-mated, at least for the present. These are results of great consequences, and for them the country should be grateful to the Giver of all victory, and to the brave army by whose valor they have been achieved. But let us take up the narrative at the beginning and bring it down to the present time, and thus see what was done and how it was done.

Arriving at Gordonsville Wednesday, the 4th instant, at one o'clock, and learning that Grant had crossed the Rapidan below Germanna and Ely's fords, and was endeavoring to turn Lee's right flank, I took horse and pushed to the point to which both armies seemed to be approaching. The moment General Lee ascertained that Grant had really cut loose from his base at Culpepper, Hill's and Ewell's corps were withdrawn from their position on the Rapidan and ordered to advance upon the enemy's line of march, the former taking the plank-road and the latter the turnpike, both leading from Orange Courthouse to Fredericksburg. Longstreet, who was encamped in the vicinity of Gordonsville, ready to move upon any point, was ordered to march down the Catharpin road. The main body of Grant's army crossed at Germanna ford and took the road leading thence in the direction of Bowling Green and Richmond, and known in the neighborhood as Brock's road, by which name I shall speak of it hereafter. The first object at which he aimed, doubtless, was to reach the point where that road intersects the Orange and Fredericksburg plank-road and turnpike. These highways run nearly parallel to each other, the distance between them varying from one mile to three miles and more. There is an unfinished railroad which runs nearly parallel to the other two roads, and extends from Orange Courthouse to Fredericksburg. The turnpike lies on the north side or next to the river, the railroad on the south side, and the plank-road between the two. These roads do not cross Brock's road, along which Grant was moving, at right angles, but diagonally, the distance between the points where they cut Brock's road being as follows: between the railway bed and the plank-road about five hundred yards, and between the plank-road and the turnpike nearly 4 miles. The enemy's line of battle extended along Brock's road from the unfinished railroad across the plank-road to the turnpike, and was consequently about four miles in length. Chancellorsville is four miles below on the plank-road, and Fredericksburg about fifteen miles. The surrounding country is very appropriately called the Wilderness, the people being ignorant, the soil destitute of fertility, the supply of water scant, the ground broken and covered with a dense and almost impenetrable growth of stunted bushes, pines and black jacks. It is a blasted region, adjoining the district known as the "poisoned fields of Orange," and providing but little for the subsistence of man or beast. So thick are the woods in some places, that it is impossible to distinguish a man at the distance of fifty paces. The reader can readily imagine that it would be difficult to select more unfavorable ground for a battle between two great armies. It only remains to be added, that the battle was fought near the western boundary of Spottsylvania county, the line of battle being nearly at right angles to a straight one drawn from Fredericksburg through Chancellorsville to Orange Courthouse.

If the reader will keep these points in his mind, and will place a good map before him, he will find but little difficulty in forming a satisfactory conception of the battle.

As has already been stated, Ewell moved down the turnpike, which is on the left and nearest to the river, and Hill down the plank-road. Stuart passed still further to the south, and marched down the Catharpin road, so as to throw his cavalry in front of the head of Grant's army and retard his march. His troopers did their duty well, especially [Thomas] Rosser's brigade of Hampton's division, and forced the Federal cavalry, which was marching up the road by which he was advancing, back into Brock's road, with considerable loss in men and horses. Indeed, Grant threw his cavalry up the turnpike, plank-road and Catharpin road, in the vain hope that he might be able to interpose a screen between himself and the Confederates, and thus both protect and conceal his movement. But Lee was not slow in penetrating his designs, and immediately sprung upon his flank like a tiger upon the side of an ox. Ewell and Hill pushed rapidly down the turnpike and plank-road, encountered and drove the cavalry and their infantry supports, which had been thrown forward to block up these highways, and compelled the whole army to halt and defend itself. Stuart in the meantime had reached Brock's road in front of the enemy, and thus opposed another obstacle to his further advance. It is not known that Grant especially desired to give battle here, but he saw the danger of his position, and immediately formed into line of battle and advanced nearly two miles to meet the threatened attack. This, it will be seen hereafter, was all that saved him from a most disastrous defeat, since it gave him time to send his trains to the rear, and throw up strong entrenchments parallel with and in front of the road by which he had been marching, and behind which he might rally his troops in the event they were beaten back. This was Thursday, the 5th, one year and one day after the great battle of Chancellorsville.

It was about four in the afternoon when both armies encountered each other. Grant attacked heavily and repeatedly along the whole line, and especially on our right, which he showed a disposition to turn and thus place himself between Lee's army and Richmond; but in every instance he was repulsed with heavy loss. He was persistent, however, in his efforts to break our lines, and continued his assaults until night. His last advance against Hill's front was made just before dark, and was handsomely repulsed by Wilcox's and Heth's divisions. His final attack upon Ewell was made after night against that part of the line held by Edward

Johnson's division. Here too he was beaten back leaving many dead and wounded on the ground. During these operations Ewell captured 2,000 prisoners, nearly all of whom were taken by Gordon's Georgia brigade and Hays' Louisianians, both of whom behaved with distinguished gallantry.

Longstreet had not yet reached the ground. Leaving Gordonsville at 4 o'clock, Wednesday afternoon, he marched fifteen miles that night. The next day he marched down the Cartharpin road (so called from a run which it crosses); he halted during the afternoon within eight miles of the battlefield, but owing to the peculiar condition of the atmosphere and the density of the forest he could not hear the guns of Hill and Ewell, and was not aware the battle had commenced until the receipt of a dispatch from Gen. Lee at midnight, ordering him to cross over to the assistance of Hill. His corps was put in motion immediately, and reached the field Friday morning soon after sunrise. Hill's troops were aware of the approach of Longstreet's corps, and that it would take their place in the line. They had a hard fight the previous evening and rested but little that night, and when the head of McLaw's division (now commanded by that noble soldier, Brig. Gen. Kershaw,) came in sight, they relaxed somewhat their vigilance and were preparing to withdraw, when they were attacked in front with a great fury by a very heavy force. Under these untoward circumstances, Gen. Wilcox's and Gen. Heth's divisions, which had done so well the evening before, were thrown into confusion and gave way, just as Kershaw double-quicked it to the front in column. The latter succeeded in throwing three regiments of his old brigade into line while Heth's and Wilcox's men were falling back over his troops, and with this small band he confronted the heavy masses of the enemy now flushed with the hope of an easy victory, and pressing rapidly forward. These regiments suffered severely but they maintained their ground until the remainder of the division could be got into some sort of line under the terrible fire to which it was exposed. Gen. Lee witnessed the unfortunate and unexpected confusion and withdrawal of the divisions of Wilcox and Heth, in both of which he had reposed so much confidence and which had behaved so handsomely on former occasions, and tears rushed into his eyes. He at once placed himself at the head of [John] Gregg's Texan Brigade, [Charles] Field's division, formerly Hood's and prepared to lead it in person. The heroes of the Lone Star who had made the circuit of the Confederacy under Longstreet remonstrated against such an unnecessary exposure of his life—a life so important and precious to the Confederacy and to all friends of liberty throughout the world. He replied that he must win this battle at every hazard—that we must whip the fight. The Texans who had not yet moved from their tracks, answered that they could whip the fight without his leading them and would do it. In the meantime appeals were made by several officers to Longstreet as the only person who could probably dissuade Gen. Lee from so rash a proceeding. He went immediately to Gen. Lee, and begged him to restrain himself and not to think of exposing himself and the cause which he had so much at heart to such terrible chances. The Texans, finally gave him to understand, in the most respectful and affectionate manner, that they would obey any order he might give providing he remained behind, but that they would not budge an inch if he led them. Gen. Lee was at length prevailed upon to desist from the hazardous undertaking, and right gloriously did the heroic Texans redeem their pledge.

Kershaw has, by the unanimous voice of the army, won his spurs and Major General's commission. He has ever proved himself equal to the occasion, however critical, but yesterday he displayed a degree of skill, energy and intrepidity that elicited the admiration of all who witnessed, or have heard of, his performance. When he and Fields, another officer who behaved with great judgment and gallantry, at length got into position under these difficult circumstances, with their old leader, Longstreet, to guide and direct them, it would have done you good to see how they and their officers and men pressed forward with shouts that rent the skies, and finally repulsed the immense numbers that crowded down upon them, with terrible slaughter. They saved the day, which for nearly two hours trembled in doubt, and were at length enabled to assume the offensive. It was evidently Grant's object to turn our right wing, and if he had succeeded, it is impossible to say what might have been the result.

On the left we were equally successful. An attempt was made to pierce that part of Ewell's line which was held by [John] Pegram's brigade, but it was signally defeated. You will regret to hear that Gen. Pegram was severely wounded, and that Brig. Gens. [John M.] Jones, of Virginia, and [Leroy] Stafford, of Louisiana, were killed the evening before. With this exception, the left wing was not required to take any further part in the fighting of the day, the enemy's almost exclusive attention being given to our right.

About 11 o'clock, Longstreet was ordered to move upon the enemy's left flank, and if possible dislodge him from the railroad cut and the plank road, and drive him back upon Brock's road. The brigades selected for this movement were G. T. Anderson's and Jenkins' of Field's division, Mahone's and Davis', of R. H. Anderson's division, and Wofford's, and perhaps two others, of Kershaw's division. Anderson's division but lately arrived, having been left at Orange Court House to guard against any demonstration upon our rear. The flank movement was completely successful; the enemy was taken by surprise and driven back from the railroad cut, across the plank road, with heavy loss, a portion of his troops retreating rapidly down the plank road to Brock's road. Mahone's Virginia brigade, of Anderson's division, ran over the 4th United States Infantry, a regiment which boasted that it had never been broken before. The plank road being clear, Longstreet advanced down it at the head of Jenkins' brigade, and had hardly gone half a mile when he was fired upon in the dense woods parallel to the road, and not more than seventy-five paces from it. Mahone was waiting there to catch such of the enemy as might have been cut off up the road, and when Jenkins' brigade arrived opposite to him, his men, being unable to distinguish one man from another through the woods, very naturally concluded it was a body of the enemy retiring, and opened fire upon their friends, killing eight or ten and wounding several others. Capt. [Alfred E. Doby] Duffy of Kershaw's staff was killed instantly; the intrepid Gen. Jenkins of South Carolina, received a mortal wound in the head, from which he died a few hours afterwards, and Gen. Longstreet was shot in the neck. The ball struck him in front on the right of the larynx, passing under the skin, carrying away a part of the spine of scapula, and coming out behind the right shoulder. The wound is severe, but not considered mortal, the only danger apprehended being from secondary hemorrhage. Should he survive ten or twelve days and the carotid artery not become involved, it is the opinion of Dr. [J. S. D.] Cullen, his medical director, that he will be able to return to the field in a few weeks. He has lost the temporary use of his right arm, what surgeons call the cervical plexus of nerves being injured. He was carried to the rear this morning and was doing remarkably well when he left. Gen. Lee called to see him just before he was moved, and when he bade him farewell and came out of the tent where his great Lieutenant lay, his eyes were filled with tears. It is a remarkable coincidence that Jackson received his death wound just twelve months ago only four miles from the spot where his companion-in-arms fell, and just after he had completed a successful flank movement, and under almost precisely the same circumstances. Heaven grant that Lee may not lose his left arm now as he lost his right arm then!

Gen. Longstreet had just been congratulated by Gen. Lee, Gen. Kershaw and others upon the complete success of his attack upon the flank of the enemy, and he was sweeping down the plank road to pluck the rich fruits of his victory, then almost within his grasp, when he was struck down by his own friends. The delay of an hour which ensued, gave the enemy time to escape back behind his entrenchments on Brock's road. The command of the corps then devolved upon Maj. Gen. Fields, and today it was turned over to Maj. Gen. Anderson of Hill's corps, who had been reporting to Longstreet after his arrival, and who formerly belonged to the corps.

The enemy had thus been repulsed along our whole line, and left many dead and wounded in our hands. In many places his dead appeared to be five or six times as numerous as our own. Our loss was not so heavy as at first reported, and will not exceed 5,000 of whom not more than 500 were killed. Most of the wounds were comparatively slight, owing to the protection afforded by the trees and bushes. The enemy's loss cannot be much less than 15,000, inclusive of prisoners. The unfavorable character of the ground and the thick chaparral prevented both sides from using artillery, only a few guns being put in position. Among all the killed, no truer or braver knight ever fell in defense of the liberties of his country than the gallant and accomplished Col. [James] Nance, of South Carolina; and no harder fighter or more perfect gentleman ever received a wound on the field of battle than

Gen. Benning, of Georgia. The one has gone to the rest of the true soldier; let us pray that the other may long be spared to the country he has served with so much modesty and courage. Maj. Gen. [James] Wadsworth, of the Federal army, received a mortal wound in the head and is now in one of our hospitals. Brig. Gen. [Alexander] Hays of the same army was killed.

At half past 4 o'clock General Lee determined to feel of the enemy and ascertain his position on Brock's road. On the right where I had my position, the brigades of Kershaw, Humphreys and Wofford, of Kershaw's division, Anderson, Jenkins, Gregg and Law, of Field's division, and Mahone, of Anderson's division, moved forward in the form of the letter V, with the sharp point towards the enemy. G. T. Anderson, known in the corps as "Tiger Anderson," formed the apex of the line, and succeeded in reaching the enemy's entrenchments, two of them falling within the works. On the left Ewell was equally successful. The result of the attack or reconnaissance was the discovery that Grant had been driven back a mile and a half, to a strong line of entrenchments in front of Brock's road, and that his left wing rested upon a deep cut in the railroad along which he had posted a force that effectually protected it. His position is therefore a strong one, being rendered the more so by the dense woods through which his line runs. Lee's position is equally satisfactory.

Last night Gordon, of Early's division, threw his brigade around an exposed point in the enemy's lines, and took Brig. Gens. [Truman] Seymour, of Ocean Pond memory, and [Alexander] Shaler, and about 500 men prisoners. Seymour admits that Grant has been whipped, and that the Federal army will continue to be whipped until their ports are closed and the troops reduced to "parched corn and beans like the rebels." He says Grant drinks too much liquor, and that the war on the part of the North is conducted as if it were a matter of frolic and contract.

Our lines were withdrawn a few hundred yards last night from the enemy's immediate front for the purpose of improving their position. Not understanding exactly what the movement Grant advanced with heavy forces this morning at half past ten o'clock, but he soon discovered where the Confederate troops were. He was driven back with ease, and now at sunset is cowering behind his entrenchments in the Wilderness. His troops have not done as well as they did under McClellan, Burnside or even Hooker. The Confederates, on the contrary, never fought better—Gen. Lee had caused it to be circulated among them some days ago that they must not think of defeat as possible; it was a thing not to be even dreamed of. Nobly have his invincible legions responded to the call of their great chief. Oh, that we may ever have such a leader and such an army!

P. W. A.

Official casualties for the Battle of the Wilderness: Federals, 2,246 killed, 12,037 wounded, 3,383 missing for a total of 17,666; Confederate losses are estimated at around 7,500.

ARMY OF NORTHERN VIRGINIA
Spottsylvania C. H., May 9, 1864 [5-24-64]

The operations in this quarter continue to be of the most interesting character. On Saturday afternoon, the 7th inst., the date of my last letter, the cavalry reported that Grant while keeping up a threatening attitude in our front, was preparing to move still further to our right and to the direction of Spottsylvania Court House and Richmond. Having fortified his position, especially on the plank road and turnpike, he hoped that a small force would be able to hold it while the main body of his army was being moved on this place, the possession of which was a matter of the greatest consequence to Grant. The road from Germanna ford on the Rapidan, by which he advanced, leads directly to this point, and thence to Richmond. Other important roads, including one from Fredericksburg, intersect here, and render it a place of no little strategic value. In the present campaign against the Confederate capital, its consequence can hardly be over-rated.

Upon the reception of the intelligence alluded to above, orders were immediately issued by General Lee for Longstreet's corps (or Anderson's, as I shall designate it hereafter,) to move at 11 o'clock that night rapidly to Spottsylvania Court House, and if possible head off the Federal army then believed to be marching for the same destination. Our cavalry had behaved very well, and had beaten back the enemy's cavalry for two days. Late Saturday evening and early Sunday morning, however, it was ascertained that the cavalry were supported by infantry, and that the latter were advancing in considerable force. Their march was delayed as much as possible, in order to give Anderson time to get up; but they succeeded in occupying the Court House, and were in possession early Sunday morning when Kershaw's division (formerly McLaw's) arrived. With [Goode] Bryan's and Wofford's brigades, Kershaw immediately advanced against the enemy holding the village; his old brigade and Humphreys' were sent under Humphreys against the force then approaching down the road from the battle field of the Wilderness, pushing our cavalry before them. Kershaw cleared the village in a few minutes and made dispositions to hold it. Humphreys placed his command behind a fence and some rail obstructions which the cavalry had previously prepared. The enemy advanced with great confidence being ignorant of the presence of Confederate infantry and supposing the troops behind the line of fences and brush were dismounted cavalry. Humphreys reserved his fire until they got within a few paces, and then gave them a volley which covered the ground with their dead and wounded. A sharp combat ensued, the result of which was the rapid retreat of the enemy who left five hundred dead and many wounded in our hands, including a Brigadier General [John C. Robinson], who was mortally wounded [survived]. Our own loss was insignificant. Fields' division came up soon afterwards, and a portion of it (Law's brigade) engaged the enemy later in the day, repulsing him as usual.

The forces disposed of in this summary manner by Anderson was the Fifth Army Corps which Ewell had beaten so handsomely three days before in the Wilderness. Some two hundred prisoners and five or six hundred small arms fell into our hands.

Ewell's corps moved from the battlefield early yesterday (Sunday) morning, and Hill's corps Sunday night; the former got into position last evening, and the latter this morning.

Thus has Gen. Lee succeeded in throwing his whole army right across the path of his antagonist. Had the ground been more favorable to military operations, or had the enemy delayed his attack on the second day an hour longer until Longstreet could get in position, our victory at the Wilderness would have been decisive and crushing. As it was, General Lee repulsed all Grant's assaults with heavy loss, and held him there until he could throw his army in front of him and between him and the capital. This was a masterly performance, and renders it necessary for Grant to give us battle here or make a further detour to the right. There is but one road on the right between Spottsylvania Court House and the Mattapony by which he can move, that is known as the Telegraph road, and leads directly from Fredericksburg to Richmond, crossing the North Anna, South Anna and Little river a few miles above the point where they unite and form the Pamunkey. East of the Mattapony is another road which passes through Bowling Green; but if Grant should move by that, he would find it necessary to cross three considerable streams, the Mattapony, Pamunkey and Chickahominy. The importance of these observations will be apparent to the reader upon the inspection of a good map. The distance from the Court House to the Telegraph road is about eight miles, and to Fredericksburg it is eleven miles.

It must be confessed that Grant has shown a good deal of cleverness in one respect, and that was in avoiding the route by Fredericksburg which proved so disastrous to Burnside. At the time Burnside moved down the north bank of the Rappahannock and attempted to cross at Fredericksburg, it is known that Hooker pointed out the route by which Grant has advanced as the better of the two; and it will be remembered when he succeeded to the command of the army, then occupying the heights of Stafford, he added his original plan in part and succeeded in getting as far as Chancellorsville. The thing which we have chiefly to regret is the loss of the devoted town of Fredericksburg, which has passed, temporarily at least, into the hands of the invader. We hear that Grant brought twenty days' supplies with him, the men carrying seven days' supplies on their backs and the remainder being transported in wagons, of which there are 800 to each corps. It was evidently his purpose to make a rapid march upon the capital, just as Sherman did upon Meridian from Vicksburg. From information derived from prisoners, one is led to believe that he expected when he crossed the Rapidan on Lee's right, that the latter would fall back by Gordonsville towards Richmond.

The two armies now confront each other on the north side of the Court House, and a battle may take place at any time. There has been considerable skirmishing and maneuvering all day. Twenty-four hours will decide whether Grant will deliver battle here, or seek to turn our position again.

I have not gone much into detail in my account of the late battle, being prevented by the constant changes in the positions of the army, and the difficulty of visiting the several brigades in such a wilderness as that in which they have been operating. I have also been deferred somewhat by my recollection of the squabbles in which certain officers engaged just after the battle of Gettysburg in regard to the performance of themselves and their commands. Let it suffice then to say that the battle of the Wilderness should inspire every State in the Confederacy with additional pride in its heroic soldiers. Virginia did her duty, as she always does; and so did modest North Carolina, chivalric South Carolina, gallant little Florida, hard fighting Alabama, impetuous Mississippi, dashing Louisiana and unflinching Texas. As for your own proud State, she has written her eulogism in blood upon the person of her enemies. She never showed more conspicuous on any battlefield, if we except Chancellorsville. Gordon, Benning, Anderson, Wright, Wofford, Doles, [Edward] Thomas, Bryan and [Pierce] Young and their intrepid brigades, did their whole duty nobly. Wofford was especially complimented by Gen. Lee for the successful manner in which he reached the rear of the enemy and rifled the camps of the *corps d'armee*. Special application was made by Wofford to be allowed to make the attempt; his success was complete, and if he had had a large force he might have put the whole army to route and captured much material.

P. W. A.

ARMY OF NORTHERN VIRGINIA,
Spottsylvania Court House, May 10, 1864 [5-20-64]

I have written to you regularly since my arrival at this headquarters of the army, but fear some of my letters have not reached you. The Federal Cavalry have been in our rear, and may have captured some of our mail carriers. But little is known here of the operations of the raiding party that passed down the Telegraph road towards Beaver Dam station of the Central railway; we have heard that they destroyed the houses at the station and a large quantity of the army supplies, and that they recaptured 300 prisoners and a few hundred guns on the way to Richmond. It is a matter of surprise here that the party was able to pass to the rear without the knowledge of our own cavalry.

We have had more bloody work to-day, and again, as at the Wilderness, our losses are miraculously small. It has been a singular battle, not only in its results, but especially in regard to the manner in which it was delivered by the Federal commander. The greater part of the forenoon was consumed by him in an attempt to make Gen. Lee develop his position and plans. Artillery was used freely, and skirmishers and sharpshooters were pushed forward along the lines, and vigorous efforts made to provoke Lee to unmask his batteries and show his hand. At length Grant seemed to grow weary of this kind of work, and ordered an assault to be made. His infantry came up to the work in handsome style, and yet they seemed to have no stomach for the fight, for three separate assaults upon Anderson's corps (late Longstreet's) were repulsed by his skirmishers and sharpshooters alone. The results were not dissimilar in front of Ewell. The heavy masses of the enemy were pushed back with the ease with which one puts a drunken man away from him. The Confederates fought behind field works thrown up hurriedly, and they appeared to relish the fun amazingly. The last assault made upon Anderson's position was late in the afternoon, and was headed by a regiment of the old U. S. Army. The enemy succeeded after a hard struggle in gaining a salient in the lines occupied by Gregg's Texan brigade; but of all who cleared the entrenchments, not one lived to return; they were all either killed or taken. They met with a temporary success also in front of Rodes' division, Ewell's corps, where they captured a portion, if not all, of the guns belonging to the Richmond Howitzers of Gen. Alexander's artillery command. The guns were soon recovered however, and the assailants beaten off with heavy loss.

Towards noon it was ascertained that the enemy were moving upon our left and rear with cavalry and infantry. Early was sent with Heth's division to drive them off and repossess us of the bridge over the Po, one of the branches of the Mattapony river. He accomplished the object of his mission in gallant style. Heth's men were glad of the opportunity to prove to all that the temporary confusion into which they were thrown at the Wilderness, was the result of accident, rather than of a lack of spirit. The enemy were punished well, and driven entirely from that part of the field.

I have spoke of our casualties as miraculously small. They were less than 1,000, and including the loss resulting from the heavy skirmishing yesterday, they will not exceed 1,200. The enemy's loss, on the contrary, since our arrival here, is estimated as high as 15,000, and at the Wilderness as high as 30,000, including prisoners. These figures are probably too large, though they reflect the opinion which obtains in high official circles here. The calculation rests upon the number of the enemy whom we buried—2,700—and the 4,000 prisoners who fell into our hands. It is proper to add that papers have been captured since the battle of the Wilderness which admit a loss there of 20,000. These papers confess also that Grant was beaten badly on his right (our left) where Ewell commanded, and that Gordon in his night attack inflicted great loss; but they claim that he was successful on his left, our right. The first is true, but the last is not; our victory was complete on every part of the field.

It is reported that Grant, just before opening the battle this morning, issued an order, in which he announced to his army that Butler had taken Petersburg and was then investing Richmond, with every prospect of reducing it at an early day, also that Johnston had been defeated at Dalton, leaving his dead and wounded in the hands of Sherman. We have not heard from Dalton for some days, but we know that the order utters a falsehood when it claims that Butler has occupied Petersburg or invested Richmond. The courage of Grant's army, however, like that of the man in the play, is oozing out at their finger ends, and it needs to be stimulated. In other words, their feeble assaults, though made with heavy lines, and the unanimous confession of prisoners, show that the army is ready to abandon the contest. They report that Grant says he will never recross the Rappahannock as long as he has one soldier left who will follow him. He is a determined man and having got the better of his army, it only remains for us to get the better of him.

Wednesday, May 11th.

Almost unbroken quiet has reigned to-day. The two armies still confront each other, lashing their sides and glaring upon each other like lions about to engage in mortal combat. A report prevailed in high quarters this afternoon that Grant was retiring in the direction of Fredericksburg and Germanna ford, but it is probably without foundation. He is not the man to yield so easily. Some things that have come to my knowledge to-day satisfy me that he did not mean to offer battle yesterday, but rather sought to feel of our lines, and ascertain their direction and strength with a view to a real attack to-morrow or next day, and that the great battle is still to be fought. There can hardly be any doubt but that he has made up his mind to fight us here. The chief danger to be appreciated, arises from the impaired morale of some of the brigades which lost heavily in officers at the Wilderness, and which occupy the weakest part of our line of entrenchments, embracing the salient angle that was lost temporarily yesterday. It has been Gen. Lee's opinion for the last two days, that the real attack will be made on the right wing, and all Grant's maneuvers and demonstrations on the left have failed to create any diversion from the right.

P. W. A.

ARMY OF NORTHERN VIRGINIA
Spottsylvania Courthouse, May 13, 1864 [5-27-64]

On yesterday was fought in front of this modest little village—henceforth to be famous throughout all coming time—one of the fiercest and most obstinate battles of modern times. It commenced at daylight, and raged and roared with tremendous fury until two o'clock in the afternoon, when the enemy retired from the bloody conflict. Grant made the attack again as he did at the Wilderness, and gained a considerable advantage by the suddenness and vigor of the assault early in the day; but with this exception, he was repulsed with a loss that will carry mourning to thousands of Northern and European hearthstones, and dismay and confusion to the tyrants and demagogues, whose hosts he leads. The Confederates failed at one point only—partly from accident, partly from mistake, and partly, I fear, from lack of spirit; but on all other parts of the field they were victorious, and as firm and resolute as ever. The enemy was beaten, but not routed or driven from the field.

It is not my purpose to go much into the details of the battle—first, because the letter, if captured between this place and Richmond, might give the foe desirable information in regard to the strength and position of our forces; and second, because it is almost impossible to prepare any account of a battle that will give satisfaction to subordinate officers, and if one makes the attempt and fails, as he certainly will, he is almost sure to have his motives impugned and become involved in a controversy in the newspapers.

The battle was fought on the north side of Spottsylvania Court-house, on undulating ground diversified by fields, pine thickets and patches of woods. Our line is crescent shaped or, perhaps it will be more correct to say that it is nearly in the form of a horse-shoe, and extends around the court house, or village, on the north or north-western side, so as to cover all the approaches from those quarters. Slight entrenchments had been thrown up along our entire front, extending from near the Shady Grove (or Catharpin road continued,) on the west, around to and beyond the Fredericksburg road on the northeast side of the village. At one point on the right is an eminence a few hundred yards in advance of the general direction of our line, and in order to prevent the enemy from getting possession of it for his artillery, a sharp angle was projected so as to include the hill within our entrenchments. The result shows that this was an unfortunate piece of engineering. Past the foot of the hill, on the north side, sweeps a ravine, which presents a convex line to the hill, the two approaching each other like circles that touch but do not cut each other. The enemy availed himself of this ravine in his assault upon the angle, which was the weakest point in our lines, being considerably in advance of the general line, and beyond the reach of support from the forces operating on the right and left.

Information was received night before last that Grant was retiring in the direction of Fredericksburg and Germanna Ford; a report to this effect was noised abroad through the army, though subsequent events show that it was without the least foundation. Through a mistake, which I cannot trace to its source, but which grew out of this mischievous report, the artillery, which had been posted on the hill, in the angle alluded to above, was withdrawn during the night. This left Maj. Gen. Johnson, of Ewell's corps, whose division, heretofore considered one of the best in the army, occupied this part of the line, without any artillery support. He communicated this fact to the corps commander at midnight, with the additional intelligence that the enemy was massing a heavy force in his immediate front for the purpose, as he believed, of assaulting him next (yesterday) morning. The guns, or others, were sent back, and were just moving into the angle at 4 o'clock yesterday morning when the force which Johnson reported to be massing in his front, made a vigorous assault upon his position and carried it. The assaulting force had been assembled in the ravine at the foot of the hill, was very strong, and advanced, one report says, in column of regiments. It had rained the evening before, and considerable fog prevailed, under cover of which the attack was made. One or two guns were got into position and fired, but the horses attached to the other pieces were shot down before they could be unlimbered and most of the cannoniers captured. Jones' Virginia brigade, whose commander was killed at the Wilderness while trying to rally his men, was the first to break; the old Stonewall and other brigades belonging to the division, becoming involved, soon followed its example, and the last seen of Gen. Johnson, the hero of Alleghany, he was standing almost alone with a musket in his hand contesting the ground single-handed with the multitudinous foe. The brigades composing the division are the Stonewall brigade, Gen. Jas. M. Walker, and Jones' brigade, both of this State, Steuart's brigade of Virginians and North Carolinians, and Stafford's brigade of Louisianians. Jones and Stafford fell at the

Wilderness, Walker was wounded yesterday. Steuart, and Johnson, the commander of the division, were taken prisoners, and the Colonel [William Witcher] commanding Jones' brigade is reported killed, with many other officers. The guns left on the field, but which neither party has been able to secure on account of the fire of the other—some eighteen or twenty—are said to belong to [W. E.] Cutshaw's and [R. C.] Page's battalions. A thousand or twelve hundred prisoners were lost at the same time.

This occurred at a very early hour in the morning. If Jones' Brigade had not given away, it is possible, though not probable, that Johnson would have been able to maintain his ground. He is one of the best officers in the army, and the sublime spectacle presented when battling alone with the enemy, though deserted by his command, should excite our admiration, rather than provoke criticism. But it should not be imagined that the enemy gained the hill without opposition, sudden and vigorous as his assault was. He was received with volley after volley, and the ground was covered with his slain; but he had massed such a heavy force upon a single exposed point, some distance in advance of the general line and incapable of being instantaneously supported, that it was found impossible to repulse him. It is but just to add, too, that the enemy's charge was as spirited as it was successful, and reflects no little credit upon his troops. He was aware of the weakness of the point from its comparative isolation, having effected a temporary lodgment in the angle two days before, as detailed in my letter of yesterday, and it would have been wonder if he had not been successful with the preparation he had made.

The Confederates suffered severely as they retreated across the intervening space to our second line, or rather to the line which subtends the angle, and which may be considered the base of the triangle covering the hill. Even this line is somewhat in advance of the direction of the general line. But the broken division did not stop here; they continued their retreat far to the rear. Fortunately, the gallant Gordon, commanding Early's division, was in reserve, and swept to the rescue in a manner that excited the admiration of every beholder, including Gen. Lee. The enemy swarmed over the hill and rushed against the lines to the right and left, but Rodes and Gordon and Wilcox were there to meet them.

The battle was now fully joined, and for nine hours it roared and hissed and dashed over the bloody angle and along the bristling entrenchments like an angry sea beating and chafing against a rock bound coast. The artillery fire was the most sustained and continuous I have ever heard for so long a time, averaging thirty shots to the minute, or 1,800 to the hour, for six hours. The rattle of musketry was not less furious and incessant. At ten o'clock, when the din and uproar were at their highest, an angry storm cloud swept over the field, and thus to the thunders of battle was added "the dread artillery of the skies." It was now manifest that Grant's real assault, as General Lee had believed, would be launched against our right wing, and to that point the opposing forces gravitated from all parts of the field, just as when a cloud surcharged with electricity forms in the heavens, all the lesser clouds and racks drift to it, and are swallowed up in the swelling, angry mass.

Grant strove hard to hold us to other parts of the field, and prevent this concentration of force, and for that purpose he engaged Anderson on our left, and Early, who had been sent to the extreme right. He made three separate assaults against the former, but was repulsed each time with frightful loss by Field's division, formerly Hood's. Early, at the head of Hill's corps, hurled him back, as a mad bull would an incautious mastiff caught upon his horns, as often as he advanced upon him. But it was against Ewell, who held the right of the original line, that Grant expended his greatest efforts and made his most desperate assaults. Having gained a foothold in the angle or center of Ewell's position, he brought up line after line, and hurled it with tremendous violence, at one time against Rodes, at another against Gordon, and then against both. Wilcox was brought up and placed on Gordon's left, and Wofford and Humphreys, of Kershaw's division, and Jenkins' brigade, of Field's, Anderson's corps, were sent to the assistance of Rodes. Additional batteries were sent in the same direction. Heth went to the right, and all of Anderson's old division but Wright followed him. And thus the whirling, remorseless maelstrom drew everything into its angry vortex. The enemy exhibited courage and resolution worthy of a better cause. Grant seemed to have breathed into his troops somewhat of his own spirit and indomitable energy. But if the Federals fought well, the

Confederates fought better. From early dawn until far in the afternoon, with steady hands and unblanched cheeks, they faced the leaden hail that was poured upon them without intermission. At some points, the two armies fought upon opposite sides of the entrenchments, the distance between them not being more than the length of their muskets. Again and again would Grant marshal his men for the onset, and right valiantly did they respond; but as often as they returned to the assault, so often were they repulsed, as if they had rushed against a wall of iron. At no point of the line, and at no time during the long and terrible, and exhausting conflict, did the heroic children of the South falter or waver for one moment. Each man knew that he was fighting the battle for the possession of Richmond. The battle, indeed, for the independence of the Confederate States—and the thought of yielding to the foe never once entered his mind.

During one of the assaults, Gordon inflicted very heavy loss upon the enemy by moving around and striking the assaulting column in flank. The enemy was thrown into great confusion, and retired rapidly to the rear, leaving many dead and wounded on the ground.

The most important movement against the enemy's flank, however, was executed by Mahone's and Lane's brigade on the extreme right, under the direction of Gen. Early. The expedition was intended to operate, not against the flank of the assaulting column, but against the flank of the Federal army, and thus afford relief to our center and left wing, both of which were hard pressed. The two brigades were placed under command of Mahone, who passed around to the Fredericksburg road, and was about to engage the enemy, when he met the latter coming out, probably to take us in the flank. An engagement ensued immediately, and resulted in the defeat of the enemy, who retired back to the main army, where considerable commotion was produced by the fresh danger with which it was threatened. A division operating against our left, supposed to belong to Burnside's corps, was withdrawn and double-quicked across the field to check Mahone. Just before it reached the scene of action, it came within full view of Pogue's and [William] Pegram's guns, and not more than 1,200 yards distant. Twelve pieces were brought to bear upon it in less time than it takes to describe this brilliant episode in the battle. The enemy stood their ground for a moment, then staggered back, and finally broke in the wildest disorder. What with Mahone's fire in front, and the artillery plowing great gaps in their flank, their loss was terrible. A shell exploded just as it struck the ground right in their midst, and hurled one man in the air several feet above the heads of his flying comrades. His movement afforded instantaneous relief to our left, and from this time the assaults of the enemy grew more and more feeble along the whole line, and finally they ceased altogether at 2 P. M.

The men were anxious to follow up the enemy when he was repulsed. Gen. Lee's plan was to act on the defensive, and not to strike until the right time came. The Federal army far exceeded his in numbers; they had entrenched themselves, as his had done; and common sense, as well as military science, would teach the propriety of patiently awaiting, rather than rashly making, the attack. The result has shown the wisdom of the policy adopted. Grant has already well nigh exhausted himself, whilst Lee's army remains almost intact, ready to assume the offensive, or to continue to act on the defensive, as occasion may require.

Our loss in the rank and file is remarkably small, the men being well protected by the entrenchments. The casualties, however, have been unusually heavy among field officers, who were not protected, and had to move frequently from one point to another, under the terrible infantry and artillery fire of the enemy, which swept every part of the field in the rear of our entrenchments. The ground is torn and plowed up by the direct and cross fire of the Federal guns, as if it had been prepared by the farmer for the reception of spring seed. Three assistant surgeons were killed in the discharge of their duty on the field; and chaplain [William B.] Owen, of Texas, who carried the news to Gen. Lee at Chancellorsville that Sedgwick was moving on his rear from Fredericksburg, was severely wounded early in the morning, whilst on his way to the Richmond Howitzers to hold prayers. Including the battle of the Wilderness, we have lost the following General officers.

Killed: Brig. Gen. [Leroy A.] Stafford, of Louisiana; Jones, of Virginia; Jenkins of South Carolina; and [Junius] Daniel, of North Carolina.

Wounded: Lieut. Gen. Longstreet, of Alabama; Brig. Gen. [Harry] Hays, of Louisiana; Benning, of Georgia; [Samuel] McGowen, of South Carolina; [Stephen D.] Ramseur and [Robert D.] Johnston, of North Carolina; and James A. Walker, (Stonewall brigade,) Henry H. Walker and [John] Pegram, of Virginia.

Captured: Maj. Gen. Edward Johnson, of Georgia; and Brig. Gen. George H. Steuart, of Maryland.

Gen. Lee made more than one narrow escape, his clothing being covered with mud thrown upon him by bursting shells. He will persist in staying near the point of greatest danger. The whole country, with one voice, should protest against such rash exposure of a life in which we are all so deeply interested, and upon the preservation of which so much depends. Col. [Walter] Taylor, his Adjutant General, had his horse shot. Gen. Ramseur's wound is slight. Many field officers were killed and wounded, but their names will appear in the lists of casualties in their respective commands. I omitted to mention above that Maj. [A. S.] Hamilton, Commissary of Gregg's Texas brigade, and Capt. [Fountaine] Barksdale, Quartermaster of the 18th Miss. regiment, were killed at the Wilderness. They believed that the hour of supreme trial had come, and that the final battle for our independence was about to be fought, and feeling that every man who could wield a musket should be in the field, they procured arms, though against positive orders, went into the fight, and fell with their feet to the foe, battling manfully for the right.

The two armies, led by the most renowned chieftains on the western continent, if not in the world have now been wrestling with each other for the mastery for eight long days. Thank God the smaller combatant thus far has been marvelously successful, and has suffered comparatively little loss except in officers; whilst the larger, being the wrong doer, has been punished beyond all precedent in this war. His dead and many of his wounded *still* remain on the ground, being too near our entrenchments to be moved, and they tell their own melancholy tale. If half that prisoners report of their losses in battle, and from desertion, straggling and demoralization, be true, then the enemy's casualties are indeed frightful. The loss in prisoners here has been about equal—say 1,500 on each side; this gives us the advantage by 3,000 including those taken at the battle of the Wilderness. Of the prisoners captured here, two or three hundred were taken by Mahone, and four colors and one guidon, when he moved on the flank of the enemy.

Last night we rectified our lines near the angle which has given us so much trouble, retiring it somewhat and locating it where it should have run originally. The enemy still retains possession of the angle, but he has not been able to remove the guns of Cutshaw and Page, nor have we, the sharpshooters on either side preventing it. We brought away from the Wilderness 12,000 captured rifles and muskets.

Both armies have rested from the strife to-day. The dead have to be buried, the wounded have to be cared for, shattered regiments and brigades have to be reorganized, and fresh plans to be devised. This requires time, and the men require rest. There can be no doubt that Grant's troops were well supplied with liquor before they entered the battle; many of the prisoners, including more than one Colonel, were in a state of intoxication when taken. It rained last night and again to-day.

May 14th—There has been a good deal of shelling and picket firing to-day, and at one time a renewal of the strife seemed to be imminent. The New York *Herald* urges the recall of Grant and his army to the north side of the Rappahannock. Will he go? We hear that the movement upon Richmond from City Point and the Peninsula has failed to accomplish its purpose; that being true, what can Grant hope by pressing further in this direction? It is said he started with 92,000 muskets; if he can muster 50,000 of these now, he is more fortunate than prisoners, both officers and men, represent him to be.

It has been raining at intervals all day.

P. W. A.

Official casualties for the Battle of Spotsylvania: Federals, 2,725 killed, 13,416 wounded, and 2,258 missing for a total of 18,399; Confederate losses are estimated at around 10,000.

ARMY OF NORTHERN VIRGINIA,
Spottsylvania C. H. May 16, 1864 [5-28-64]

Our mail communications are so much exposed to the depredations of the enemy, that I do not feel at liberty to write you as fully as usual in regard to the movements of the army. You must rest satisfied for the present with the assurance that as far as human foresight can discern, all is well in this quarter. The army is in better spirits and better fighting condition than I have ever known it, and notwithstanding its recent important victories, the men say they will not be content until Grant is either completely overthrown or driven across the Rappahannock.

The announcement of the death of Gen. J. E. B. Stuart has been received with universal sorrow by the Army of Northern Virginia, of which he has been a conspicuous officer since the beginning of the war. However much men may differ in their estimates of his abilities as an officer, all accord to him the purest patriotism, an ardent zeal, a talent for organizing forces, great powers of endurance, and a cheerful and sanguine temper which he communicated to his whole command, and which never yielded to despondency under even the most adverse skies. Now that life's fitful fever is over, the gay and gallant cavalier sleeps well in his honored grave.

The rains continue and the roads are almost impassible.

P. W. A.

ARMY OF NORTHERN VIRGINIA,
Spottsylvania C. H., May 20, 1864 [5-30-64]

We had a little excitement last evening, but today all is quiet as a summer morning. It was ascertained yesterday that the enemy was again retiring from our left front where he had been so handsomely repulsed the day before by Gordon, and was moving towards the Richmond and Fredericksburg Railroad. Gen. Lee, not disposed to follow along in the same direction, nor allow his adversary to proceed alone, ordered Ewell to advance and strike him in the flank and rear, and thus compel him to return to his former position. Ewell marched out of the trenches late in the afternoon, and encountered the enemy a little before sunset. A sharp, brief combat ensued, the enemy being thrown into considerable confusion and retiring before our troops. It is believed that the attack would have resulted in important captures had all portions of the command behaved equally well, but Jones' [Witcher's] brigade of Johnson's division, which did not stand firmly at the Wilderness, and was the first to break in the great battle of the 12th, fled incontinently, and some report that the Stonewall brigade did not do as well as it might have done. The latter is composed of troops from the Valley of the Shenandoah, and the former from counties in Southwestern Virginia. Pegram's [J. S. Hoffman's] brigade of the same division, on the contrary, displayed much gallantry.

In consequence of the unsteadiness of a portion of the corps here alluded to, Ewell did not press his advantages, nor bring off some forty-five wagons which he captured. Indeed, finding that the enemy was receiving heavy reinforcements, and it being no part of his instructions to bring on a general engagement within the Federal entrenchments, he returned late at night to his former position, leaving his dead and a portion of his wounded behind. His losses were small, not exceeding 100 in killed and wounded. Through some oversight, the ambulances of the corps did not accompany it, or the wounded might have been removed. The real object of the demonstration however, was fully accomplished; the movement to the right was checked, and Grant reduced to the condition of the man who receives unexpected news on a journey and who stops to scratch his head, being in doubt which way to turn or what to do, whether to go on or return.

Since different accounts of the attack upon Johnson's division, of Ewell's corps, on the morning of the 12th, have been given to the public, and since all of these accounts, probably, have more or less of error in them, I have applied to an intelligent officer who was present throughout the battle, and who was in a position to understand what was going on as fully as Gen. Ewell himself, for the facts, so far as they fell under his own eye. The following is the substance of the statement of the officer to whom I made application:

On the morning of the 12th, Johnson's division occupied the right of Ewell's corps, Hays' brigade being on his left, then J. A. Walker's (Stonewall), next Jones' [Witcher's] and then Steuart's. At the junction of Jones' and Steuart's brigades the line of works made a bend at nearly a right angle, in which a battalion of artillery had been posted. The artillery had been withdrawn the preceding evening, and the line of Jones' brigade was extended to cover this gap. At 3 o'clock on the morning of the 12th Johnson asked for artillery, saying the enemy was massing heavily in his front, and Page's battalion was started to him. Jones' brigade, of six regiments, had but three in line when the assault was made at 4 o'clock; one had been detached to cover the gap of half a mile between Steuart's brigade and Lane's brigade, of Wilcox's division, on the right; one had been deployed as skirmishers, and another had just been sent out to relieve the latter. The enemy made their attack in mass, with a rush upon the point where the artillery had been, and the three regiments of Jones' brigade gave way, almost without firing a shot. The artillery which had been sent was just driving up to the works at a gallop as the enemy poured over, killing the horses and preventing the men from unlimbering the guns, and capturing the guns and Gen. Johnson who was endeavoring to rally his command. As the enemy rushed in the Stonewall brigade, on the left of the gap and part of Stewart's, on the right of it, received them with heavy fire, but the enemy closing down on Stewart on the flank, front and rear, succeeded in taking the larger part of his command in the works. In attempting to swing around his brigade so as to oppose the enemy in front, Gen. Walker was severely wounded and carried from the field. The senior Colonel not being aware of this, there was no head to the brigade, and each regiment, from right to left, continued to fight at the works until its flank was turned, inflicting heavy loss on the foe and losing much themselves. The enemy still pressing his advantages, Johnston's North Carolina brigade, of Gordon's command, was put in on the right of the Louisiana (late Stafford's) brigade, near the Stonewall brigade, and succeeded in checking the enemy for a time. The loss of Johnson's division was about 2,000 prisoners and eighteen pieces of artillery, besides the killed and wounded.

The enemy had now gained possession of a wood within our works and advanced nearly a quarter of a mile from the works to McCoul's house. At this point Gordon threw in three regiments of his Georgia brigade near McCoul's house, at a charge, who struck the enemy in front and on the left, and drove those they met out of the works and over them. The Federals being thus checked, he formed the other three of his brigade and Pegram's Virginia brigade, and put them in on the right of the other three regiments, and pushed back the enemy in splendid style, regaining Steuart's and parts of Jones' line and the artillery. This position they continued to hold during the day against repeated assaults, although their left was never supported by other troops. A little after Gordon had gone in, Ramseur's North Carolina brigade, of Rodes' division, made a magnificent charge upon the enemy's right as they poured through the works, driving them out with slaughter and retaking the line of the Louisiana and part of the Stonewall brigade, and here they stood all day.

Although these troops were doing splendidly, there was still a gap of some length between Ramseur's right and Pegram's left, where the enemy held our works, and through this they continued to press. To close this gap and regain our whole line and the artillery, there was desperate fighting. [Cullen A.] Battle's Alabama brigade, of Rodes' division, was thrown in on Ramseur's right, his center passing the McCoul house, and drove the enemy back some distance into the woods, gaining a foothold in the wood, which they resolutely held.

The enemy now occupied the outside of our works on the crest where Jones' brigade broke, and our line was along the works of the Stonewall brigade, and there, broke off towards the right through the wood, nearly to Pegram's left. Again and again the enemy made desperate efforts to drive out the Confederates and press through the gap still existing, but they failed. [Nathaniel] Harris' Mississippi brigade was sent up at this time and put in on Ramseur's right, over the same ground as Battle's, and it drove the enemy from another portion of the works, and the ground thus regained they held for the remainder of the day. Subsequently [Abner] Perrin's [Alabama] and McGowen's South Carolina brigades were brought up and put in on the right of Harris, and still later the remnant of Johnson's division moved up to close the gap between Pegram's left and the right of the other troops to about one hundred yards in the angle of the works, which the enemy continued to hold, and from which we did not succeed in ousting them. Our artillery was so far regained as to enable Major Cutshaw to take his artillerymen to the pieces and work them during the rest of the day with marked effect upon the enemy; but the horses having all been killed and the enemy's sharpshooters being near, these guns could not be withdrawn. During these operations we captured on this part of the lines about one thousand prisoners from every corps in the Federal army. Our captures during the day were quite equal to those made by the enemy.

It is apparent from this brief narrative that, while we did not regain the whole of our lines, we should probably not have lost any part of them if the artillery had been in position when the assault was made.

No one has been appointed to succeed Gen. Stuart. The cavalry, for the present, are, under an order from Gen. Lee, reporting to him by divisions. Hampton is the ranking officer of that arm of the service in Virginia.

I fear my letters have reached you irregularly, owing to the recent interruption of our communications. I have written promptly, however, and have done all in my power to get them through in time.

P. W. A.

ARMY OF NORTHERN VIRGINIA,
Slashes of Hanover, May 27, 1 p.m. [6-3-64]

At an early hour this morning it was ascertained that Grant had withdrawn his army under the cover of darkness last night to the north bank of the North Anna, and was moving down the east side of that river in the direction of West Point. As intimated in a former letter, Gen. Lee's lines extended along the range of hills on the south side of the North Anna, except on his flanks, where they took such a direction as to protect his position against any attempt that might be made against either wing of his army. This disposition of his forces left Grant room to throw the greater part of his own army across to the south bank. The latter had erected formidable works in his front, a short distance from the river, and behind which his troops could rally in case of disaster, and at least hold us in check until they could regain the north bank. These works he has now abandoned, whether because he has found the Confederate position too strong to encourage any hope he might indulge of being able to carry it by storm, or because they had accomplished the object of their construction in holding us at Hanover Junction until he could establish his base at West Point and put his army in motion for the lower Pamunkey, it is impossible yet to say. I only know that it is a cause of universal regret in the army that he did not attack us in our late position, which was stronger and better in every respect than that at the Wilderness or Spottsylvania Court House.

Unfortunately for the Confederates the late battles have taught Grant a wholesome lesson. The first ten days after crossing the Rapidan he evinced a disposition to fight us whenever he met us; since the 18th inst., however, the day on which he made his last effort to bring his dispirited troops up to the bloody work, he has shown quite as strong a desire to avoid battle. That he has found it necessary to change his whole plan of operations, there can be but little doubt. If it had been a part of his original design to make West Point or the lower James his base of operations, then he has committed a great blunder in marching across the country from Culpepper at a cost of forty or fifty thousand men, when by following McClellan's route he could have reached the same destination without the loss of a single man. Grant is a hard-headed man however, as well as a hard fighter, and like most hard-headed men, he has come very near having his head broken.

P. W. A.

ARMY OF NORTHERN VIRGINIA,
Battlefield of Cold Harbor, June 6, 1864 [6-15-64]

My last letter bore the date of the 31st inst., 4 p. m., and concluded with an intimation that the enemy, though badly beaten in the bloody battle of that morning, was probably preparing to make an assault at night. The assault was made, that night, soon after dark, against that part of the lines held by Generals Breckinridge and [Joseph] Finegan, as they were preparing to establish their skirmish line. The enemy was soon repulsed with heavy loss. Immediately afterwards an attack was made upon General [Robert] Hoke's front, with like result. These assaults were repeated on the nights of the 4th and 5th, and repulsed as often as made.

The assault last night was intended to cover another movement to the right in the direction of the James river. It was suggested in this correspondence, some days ago, that Grant was aiming for the James river, and probably the south side of it, his object being to throw his army between Richmond and the South. This is now the prevailing opinion in the Army of Northern Virginia and to high official quarters in the capital. Should he stop on the north side of the river, near City Point, he might easily throw a number of pontoon bridges across to that point, or across to Bermuda Hundred, which is between the two rivers, and at the point of their confluence. With his army thoroughly entrenched on the north side of the James, his bridges protected by his monitors, and a foothold already gained by Butler between the two rivers, he would be able to rush a raiding party across the river any dark night and cut the Petersburg and Weldon railroad, and probably the Richmond and Danville road also. Should he throw his army behind the Appomattox and across the Petersburg and Weldon road, with his left extending well up towards the Danville road, he might annoy us a great deal, if he did nothing more; while General Lee would find it exceedingly difficult, if not impossible, to dislodge him. The chief objection to this latter course is the danger to which his communications would be exposed by our artillerists and sharpshooters posted along the north bank of the James. Possibly he would endeavor to guard against this danger by drawing a portion of his supplies from Norfolk by the Petersburg and Norfolk railroad.

But will he be able to reach James river? If he continues to move down on the north side of the Chickahominy, he probably will be; but should he attempt to cross that stream, and march directly across the James, he will never reach his destination. But suppose he does reach the James, and establish himself on the banks of that stream or the Appomattox, what then—will he be able to carry Richmond by assault? He will not; his object will be to starve us out. Will he be able to do this? The future alone can give a satisfactory answer to this inquiry. I, however, if one may be permitted to venture an opinion so far in advance, I should say that under the leadership of Lee and Beauregard, and with the guidance of Heaven, which has never forsaken us, except to our own good, the enemy will be able to reduce the capital neither by battle nor starvation.

As already stated, the enemy commenced to move last night. It was discovered this morning that he had disappeared in front of our left wing, and the probability is that he is repeating the movement by which, like the crab, he has been advancing sideways since he left the Wilderness. In addition to the assault last night, Grant made further effort to conceal this movement by sending a communication to Gen. Lee, proposing that hereafter, when the armies are not actually engaged, either side may send out parties to bury its dead and remove the wounded. Gen. Lee replied in fitting terms, stating however that he preferred the custom common among military men, viz: when the commander of either side desired to succor his wounded and bury his dead, he should send in a flag of truce and ask permission to do so, and that the party sent upon the field to attend to this humane duty, should carry white flags. To this Grant sent a rejoinder this morning, affecting to understand that Lee agreed to his proposition, and adding that he would send out a force to look after his wounded and dead today between 12 and 3 o'clock, and that they should be accompanied by flags of the kind suggested by Gen. Lee. To this smart attempt of the Federal chief, Lee replied, informing him that he had misunderstood his former communication—that he meant to indicate the usual custom of a flag of truce as the proper mode of accomplishing his object as stated in his first dispatch, and notifying him that if he sent forward a burial party without conforming to this usage and first obtaining permission to do so, he would cause it to be warned off.

I am not informed whether any further communication has been received from Grant. His object was transparent enough. He desired to conceal his movement last night, to bury his dead and succor his wounded before leaving, and to void the confession of defeat implied by his asking permission to perform this humane duty. His dead and wounded still remain in front of our entrenchments, exposed to the rain and sun, the one poisoning the air by their stench, the other vexing it by their cries for help. The poor creatures—the wounded—may be seen appealing to their friends by waving their handkerchiefs or beckoning them with their pale hands. Grant left many of his dead and wounded uncared for at the Wilderness and Spottsylvania Court House, and he will be guilty of the same barbarity here, unless he smothers his pride and obtain Gen. Lee's leave to attend to them.

I am endeavored today to obtain an official statement of our casualties on the 3rd, but did not succeed. I learned enough, however, to venture to say that they do not exceed 1,000 and that in all the engagements, skirmishes, and picket firing that have occurred since we left Hanover Junction, they do not exceed 2,000. The loss of the enemy is probably ten times as great—say 20,000.

P. W. A.

Estimated Federal casualties for the June 3 battle of Cold Harbor, 7,000; Confederates under 1,500.

RICHMOND, June 17, 1864 [6-20-64]

The situation grows more and more grave. Grant is rapidly unfolding his plans, and thus far they are precisely the same that were foreshadowed in these letters some weeks ago. It is not known here whether he has moved the bulk of his army to the south side of James river, though it is well established that Hancock's and Smith's corps, and a portion, if not all of Burnside's, are across the river. He is building extensive wharves from Swineyard's to Wilcox's Landing on the north side and opposite to *Fleur de Hundred* on the south side, where the water is of sufficient depth to float vessels of the largest size. He has also a number of negroes engaged in throwing up entrenchments to cover the approaches to this part of the river from Richmond, and to prevent parties from getting below and firing upon his transports. It has been suggested that these works, being on the north bank, are a blind, and that the real movement will be made on the south side against Petersburg, and the railroads terminating there. But would Grant build such extensive works for the simple purpose of misleading his adversary, and then run away and leave them? His conduct at Cold Harbor, where he dug thousands of rifle pits, and threw up six parallel lines of entrenchments, intersected in some places by transverse lines, all of which he finally abandoned, furnishes an answer. He broke up the depot established at White House, and removed the cars, engines, railroad iron and bridge timber which he brought to that point, and changed his base from the York to the James river. What he has done once, nay three times, already in this rapidly shifting campaign, he can and will do again, if not prevented. He has moved on the principle of the screw, the next turn of which will carry him around behind Petersburg and the Appomattox, and across one of our chief lines of railway.

Indeed, he is already within three miles of Petersburg. On Wednesday morning, the 15th, the enemy, about 3,000 strong, advanced up the south side of the Appomattox by the City Point road and engaged our forces, consisting of the Fourth North Carolina [Cavalry] and Graham's (Petersburg) battery, at Baylor's farm, some six or seven miles from Petersburg, and finally compelled the Confederates to abandon their position. Later in the day it was discovered that the enemy was pressing his advantage and massing a heavy force, say ten or twelve thousand men against our outer line of fortifications, three miles out from the town. This force advanced up the City Point and Prince George Court House roads, next to the river, the fourth one was successful. The enemy gained Battery No. 5, when they poured over the works, capturing three of Sturdivant's guns and some of his men, (who stood to their pieces until they were run through by bayonets) and turned the captured guns upon the Confederates as they retreated toward the town. Captain Sturdivant and two of his Lieutenants (the latter wounded) were taken prisoners. The success of the enemy at this point exposed our forces at other parts of the lines to an enfilading fire, which at length forced them to yield and surrender an important section of the outer line of fortifications by which Petersburg is defended. It is said that all the batteries from No. 5 to No. 9, inclusive, being those next to the Appomattox on the south side, have fallen into the hands of the Federals.

On the Baxter road, which was defended by a portion of the Thirty-fourth Virginia, of Wise's brigade, and the Macon Georgia Light Artillery, Capt. C. W. Slater, we were more successful. These forces held Battery No. 16, which the enemy subjected to a heavy cannonade and then charged. They were repulsed, however, with considerable loss, and chased from that part of the field entirely.

While those operations were going on south of the Appomattox, the enemy pushed forward a force from Bermuda Hundred on the north-side and drove in our pickets near Chester Station on the Richmond and Petersburg rail-way. They also attacked a division of infantry that was marching along the turnpike towards Petersburg, but they were easily driven back upon the river and considerably punished. Between Port Walthall and Swift Creek they succeeded in cutting the telegraphic wires and tearing up a portion of the railroad track. The Federal cavalry on the north-side of the James were repulsed also on Wednesday in the vicinity of Malvern Hill, and driven back by W. H. F. Lee behind their work at Westover.

There was more or less skirmishing yesterday in front of Petersburg between the James and Appomattox. Last night Gen. Beauregard took some 500 prisoners, but under what circumstances, I am not informed. A prisoner taken by him this morning says that [Gouverneur K.] Warren's corps has gone to parts unknown. Possibly Grant has heard of certain movements on our part, and sent Warren out to check them, if possible. The Federals have occupied Howlet's House, four or five miles below Drewry's Bluff on the same bank of the river, and about four miles from the Richmond and Petersburg rail-way and have taken the guns that were there. The ground there is forty or fifty feet higher than it is at Drewry's Bluff. The configuration of the country however, as I have already explained to your readers, is exceedingly favorable to the enemy and unfavorable to us. But for this they would not have been able to reach the works in front of Petersburg in advance of the Confederates, and to gain the unfortunate advantage already described. This morning they threw three shells into Petersburg, one of which fell in the Court house yard, another near the S. Carolina Hospital, and a third near the Telegraph office. Prisoners say they are bringing up heavy guns and putting them in position, and the fear is that with these guns the enemy will be able at a distance of three miles to destroy the town.

I have this moment learned that the Confederates retook Howlet's House and the guns left there at 11 o'clock last night, and that our former lines between the James and Appomattox have been re-established this morning. Gen. Beauregard reports now to Gen. Lee, the latter being in command of all the forces in Virginia and North Carolina.

At 5 o'clock yesterday afternoon, Hunter's column reached New London, six miles south-west of Lynchburg, and drove away Imboden's and [John] McCausland's cavalry. Breckinridge was at Lynchburg, and help was near at hand. More than this I cannot say, as my letter has to run the gauntlet, and may fall into the hands of some of the daring raiders of the North. Longstreet left Campbell Court House before they arrived, and thus eluded their pursuit.

P. W. A.

Postscript, 3 p. m.—The enemy have taken to-day another one of the batteries on the outer lines in front of Petersburg, and seems to be concentrating on Beauregard's right. Citizens report that Grant crossed 30,000 over to the south side last night. It is a short march from their landing to Petersburg.

Postscript, 3 p. m.—The enemy have taken to-day another one of the batteries on the outer lines in front of Petersburg, and seems to be concentrating on Beauregard's right. Citizens report that Grant crossed 30,000 over to the south side last night. It is a short march from their landing to Petersburg.

The prisoners alluded to above were taken last night during a charge upon Beauregard's lines, which was repulsed handsomely.

The enemy has sunk five vessels at Trent's Reach, a few miles below Drewry's Bluff, to prevent our iron-clads from passing down the James river. This fact would seem to be conclusive as to his intention to strike at Petersburg from the south side of the James and Appomattox.

[Maj. Gen. Philip] Sheridan is beyond the North Anna, just above Hanover Junction, in considerable force. Hampton is watching him.

P. W. A.

ARMY OF NORTHERN VIRGINIA,
Petersburg, Virginia, June 19, 1864 [6-27-64]

I reached this place this forenoon—too late to enter much into detail in regard to the operations in this vicinity for the last few days. From all accounts, there has been more or less fighting day and night since Wednesday the 15th inst. It was during the night of that day that the enemy made his first serious assault, and carried a large section of our outer line, extending from the Appomattox far around to the right. Our force was very weak, consisting chiefly of Wise's brigade, and a few comparatively worthless citizens that had been dragged out to the lines and put in position for the militia. The remainder of Beauregard's troops, not many at most at that time, was holding the line in front of Bermuda Hundred between the James and Appomattox. Had the enemy pressed his advantage at the time, he might easily have occupied Petersburg. The fighting continued at intervals on Thursday and Thursday night, by which time Bushrod Johnson's division appeared on the field. With these two divisions, part of Gracie's brigade and the Sixty-fourth Georgia regiment which was not then attached to any brigade, but has to-day been added to Colquitt's, Beauregard maintained his ground until 8 o'clock yesterday (Saturday) moving against the greater part of Grant's army. What greater praise can be bestowed upon any commander than this simple statement proclaims.

About half-past three o'clock Friday morning, just after the moon had sunk below the western horizon, the enemy crept through the thick undergrowth in front of battery No 16 on the Baxter road, which is on our right, and got within a few paces of that work before they were discovered. They were in heavy force—too heavy to be resisted, and the result was they carried the battery or redoubt, and drove the Confederates away. Indeed, the wonder is that they did not carry all parts of the line, so great was the disparity between the forces of the respective armies. Our lines extended from a point on the Appomattox three miles below the town, around to the east and southeast, a distance of five miles, and to defend them we had only two divisions and a fraction. Col. Pohattan R. Page of the Twenty-sixth Virginia, commanding Wise's brigade at the time, received a mortal wound during the assault, and died soon thereafter. The battery of the Macon (Ga.) Light Artillery, consisting of four 12 pounder Napoleons, was lost, in spite of the gallantry of the officers and men. Twenty-one of their horses were killed, and their infantry supports having been forced back, it was found impossible to bring off the guns.

Skirmishing continued throughout the day along the greater part of the lines. At three o'clock the enemy assaulted Battery No. 17, an important position next to Battery 16, but they were driven back with considerable loss. An hour later they charged our works on the hill near New Market racecourse, and were again repulsed, but with still heavier loss. At 6 o'clock the assault was renewed in front of Batteries No. 17, 18, 19 and 20, and as night approached the cannonade became general along the whole line from No. 20 around to the Appomattox on the left. Aware of the comparative weakness of Beauregard's forces, and stimulated by the desire to get possession of Petersburg, Grant made a desperate effort to bear down all opposition and enter the town. He massed his forces, as he did at Spottsylvania Court House and Cold Harbor, and rushed them against our positions as if he believed that numbers and brute force could accomplish everything. His heaviest assault was made upon Wise's and [S. E.] Elliott's (late Evans') brigade, of Johnson's division. Wise at length gave way, and one regiment of Elliott's, and the enemy poured in through the gap in a stream that can be compared only to the Mississippi river when it breaks through the levee and submerges the adjacent plantations. Fortunately, [Matt] Ransom of the same division and Gracie were near at hand; Colquitt and [Thomas] Clingman, of Hoke's division, rushed forward also to close the gap which grew wider and wider every moment. The shock was terrible. Night had now set in, but the jets of fire from the musketry and the tongues of flame from the artillery lit up the earth and the sky and pointed the way to the warring hosts. If the enemy were successful, Petersburg must fall, and with its fall what other evils would befall us I need not now pause to enumerate; if, notwithstanding their late success, they were yet repulsed, all might be saved. Both parties understood the importance of the stake as they hugged each other in mortal combat. The one covered the ground with their swelling masses; the other was only a handful; and yet the latter, gathering itself up, and binding itself together like a ball, was hurled against the multitudinous foe with a skill and force which nothing human could stand before and live. The enemy were driven back and out of the works with great loss, and the guns belonging to Blount's (Ga.) battery, which had behaved with so much gallantry, but which was lost when the Federals broke over the works, were recaptured. The fight now ceased, and the women and children and old men, who had crowned the hills and housetops, tearful spectators of the unequal combat, retired to their beds with grateful hearts. At 3 o'clock Beauregard withdrew his forces and occupied a new and better line of entrenchments he had thrown up a short distance behind those he abandoned.

At 8 o'clock next morning (yesterday) Kershaw's veteran division reached the field after a rapid march all night, and relieved Johnson's which had been in the trenches, day and night, since Thursday morning. In a short time Field's and Pickett's divisions were placed in position, and still later other forces belonging to Lee's grand army made their appearance.

Feeble assaults were made at intervals yesterday, and were repeated last night; a brigade was brought up here and there and hurled against our steady lines, as one would cast a stone against a wall of adamant; but in every instance the enemy were repulsed with but little effort. Constant skirmishing and artillery firing have been kept up to-day, but without results. It was a strange commingling of sounds at 10 o'clock this morning—the soft, sweet tones of the church bells inviting the people to the house of prayer, and the boom of cannon and crash of shells summoning the unfortunate soldier to the dark abodes of eternity. The one was the gentle messenger of peace and life, the other the dread summoner of suffering and death!

Petersburg is now safe against assault, though it is within range of the enemy's long range guns. A number of shells have exploded in the streets, but thus far only eleven persons have been hurt, including one old negro woman killed. General Lee waited almost too long before he sent the much needed reinforcements, as but for the heroic resistance of Beauregard and his command the city must have fallen. The people have removed from the eastern part of the town to places of greater safety.

Grant's entire army is now in front of Petersburg and Lee's is where it should be. Warren's corps was sent around by water from West Point, but it is here, and parts of it have already been engaged.

We have just heard that Early and Breckinridge attacked Hunter yesterday, near Lynchburg, and beat him badly. At last accounts the latter, who is reported to be without supplies, was in full retreat.

P. W. A.

ARMY OF NORTHERN VIRGINIA
Petersburg, Virginia, June 29, 1864 [7-9-64]

I have not written you for several days, in consequence of the interruption of both of our lines of communication with the South. The Petersburg and Weldon Railway was cut at

Reams' Station, ten miles south of this place. No bridges were destroyed, and only a small portion of the track was torn up. The injury to the South Side road between Petersburg and Burkeville was also unimportant. The greatest destruction fell upon the Danville road, between Burkeville and Staunton river. It is reported that the road had been rendered unfit for service for a distance of thirty-seven miles. The track has not been destroyed continuously for that distance, but at intervals of every few miles. It will require some weeks to repair the track and replace the bridges that have been burnt. This work of destruction was performed by a force of four thousand Federal cavalry, under Brigadier Gen. [James] Wilson, who started out from Grant's army a week ago, taking with them ten days' rations. Gen. W. H. F. Lee went in pursuit of them, but the enemy having the start, kept out of his way until he reached the vicinity of Staunton river. Here the Federals were repulsed by the bridge guard, and Gen. Lee coming up soon afterwards, succeeded in putting them to rout. They committed numberless depredations on their march, such as forcing negroes from their comfortable homes, carrying off horses, killing hogs and cattle, and pillaging houses and barns. If they were not such incorrigible rogues, they would make better soldiers. In other words, if they had not stopped so frequently on the road to steal and destroy, they might have kept out of the way and inflicted more serious injury.

Communication by railway having been destroyed, I am compelled, for the present, to improvise a mail line of my own. It is not probable that this mail line will be as regular and punctual as Mr. [Postmaster-General John H.] Reagan's, but it will suffice, I hope, for the transmission of an occasional letter, until the railroad can be repaired. The enemy's left rests near the road—so near, indeed, that communication by the Weldon route must remain uncertain and hazardous until the enemy shall be dislodged from his present position. This latter work will be no easy task, since he has surrounded himself by formidable works and guarded every approach to his fortified position. We have a rumor that Burnside's corps has been sent to Washington to protect the capital from assault by some imaginary foe, and another account has it that after Burnside left, a second corps was sent on the same errand I know not what, if any, truth there is in these reports. We know that a number of regiments are returning home, their terms of service having expired, and that their places are being filled by "one hundred day men," and such recruits as can be obtained by love of money. The passage up and down the Potomac of these troops may have led to the rumors first alluded to, or it may be that there is good foundation for them, and that Mr. Lincoln has become alarmed for the safety of the capital. This supposition is not weakened by the fact of the late Presidential visit to Gen. Grant at City Point.

The expiration of the terms of service of the outgoing regiments, and the necessity, if it exist, of sending off troops for the greater security of Washington, may have made Grant to adopt the policy of entrenching his present position, and surrounding himself by strong defensive works, in the vain hope that he will be able to maintain his ground until he can force Lee, by destroying his communication and cutting off his supplies, to retire into North Carolina. That such was the policy that induced him to cross to the south side of James river, there can be no longer any doubt. The attempt to concentrate a formidable force at Lynchburg, to operate upon our railway lines, formed an important part of the plan. But fortunately for us, Hunter, [William] Averill and [George] Crook have been badly beaten and driven completely from the field, while Sheridan has been defeated twice by Hampton, first near Trevillian station, in the vicinity of Gordonsville, and second at Charles City Court House, low down on the James. Sheridan found it necessary, after the affair at the latter place, to take shelter under the Federal monitors, through whose assistance he finally gained the south bank of the James. We have reason for believing he joined Grant yesterday in front of Petersburg, and took position on his left near the Weldon railway. Hampton, I need hardly add, is in his proper place.

Nothing of special importance has occurred since the date of my last letter, which, I fear, has not yet reached you. There has been constant skirmishing day and night, in spite of the terribly hot weather and suffocating dust. For a time it was believed that the occasional shells that fell in Petersburg, were accidental and resulted from the inferior character of the enemy's ammunition, but this supposition will no longer stand the test of recent facts. A number of shells have been thrown into the town, during the last few days and nights, with a regularity and precision that precludes the idea that they were unintentional. Indeed, Northern letter writers admit that the town has been fired upon, the excuse for the barbarity being the unfounded supposition that the Confederate army were massed together in the streets of Petersburg. It is not probable that the present quiet will continue a great while.

P. W. A.

ARMY OF NORTHERN VIRGINIA,
Petersburg, Va., July 4, 1864 [7-12-64]

Grant will not dine in Richmond today. He will not dine in Petersburg today. He is lying behind his elaborate entrenchments, apparently unconscious that this is the Fourth day of July. It is now 12 o'clock, m. and he has not even fired a national salute. What would be a national salute for the United States in these days of revolution? Would it be a number of guns equal to the number of States in the old Union? Or would it be necessary to add one more gun for the new State of Western Virginia, which the Northern authorities pretend they have organized out of the territory of Virginia?

Those who have appreciated the condition and position of Grant's army, are not surprised that he has not signalized the day by a fresh assault upon our lines. His future hopes and plans will be directed, probably to an effort to starve us out; and failing in that, but two alternatives will be left him—either to remain ensconced behind his present entrenchments, or return to the north side of the James, and possibly to Washington. His army has already been depleted by the withdrawal of regiments whose terms of service have expired, and by sickness. His troops have had an arduous campaign, and the almost unparalleled hot weather which has prevailed for some weeks, with the accompanying dust and meagre supply of bad water, has told fearfully upon their health. Numbers of transports daily pass down the James and up the Potomac loaded with sick and retiring men. The numbers thus returning gave rise to the unfounded report that Burnside's Ninth Army corps had been sent to Washington. The new troops sent to Grant do not, it is believed, more than fill the places of the sick and those who have gone home.

The Federal Congress has just passed a bill to call out 200,000 additional men, and to repeal the act by which conscripts were exempt upon the payment of three hundred dollars. This measure has been rendered necessary by the falling off in the numbers of recruits obtained from Ireland and Germany. These 200,000 men, if obtained, will not be available before next spring and in no event will they do more than supply the places of those who have perished already this summer and retired from the service. This estimate includes the armies on both sides of the Mississippi. The repeal of the $300 exemption has created much excitement in the North, and may convert many a noisy advocate of war into an advocate of peace. The shoddy aristocracy, who have hitherto been able to keep out of service upon payment of $300, are now reduced to the unpleasant dilemma of shouldering their muskets, or opposing the further prosecution of the war.

The enemy continue to throw shells into Petersburg at regular intervals, day and night. The lines at the nearest point are not more than a mile and a half from the center of the town, and from that point his long-range guns can throw shells into every part of the city. Everybody has left, or is preparing to leave, who is able to get away. The houses and even the woods and fields for miles around Petersburg, are filled with women and children and old men who have fled from their homes. Some have provided themselves with tents; others have erected bush arbors and others are bivouacking under the trees. This is a sad fate for a town so distinguished for hospitality, refinement, and cultivated men and women. There is no excuse for the barbarous extremity to which Grant has proceeded, and of which he gave no notice whatever either to Gen. Lee or the town authorities. We have no military establishment in the place, no troops, no magazines, and the town is of no sort of advantage to the Confederates in maintaining their present position. In other words, it contributes nothing to the strength of our position, which would be quite as strong if there were no town here as it is now. Upon what ground, then, will the Federal commander justify his wanton destruction of life and property? Yesterday a shell struck one of the churches in which the people had just assembled for worship. The minister proposed to proceed with the service, but upon consultation with the congregation, it was finally determined to withdraw. The people retired quietly and without confusion. If the enemy is permitted to remain where he is, the inhabitants must be exposed to much suffering, whether they continue at their homes or fly to the country.

Gen. Lee, whose estimates are always below those of other people, puts down the total loss sustained by Wilson and [August] Kautz during their recent raid against the railroads, besides their killed and wounded left on the field, as follows: 1,000 prisoners, 13 pieces of artillery, 30 ambulances and wagons, many small arms, horses, ordnance stores, and several hundred negroes taken from the plantations on their march. The number of negroes is estimated at about 700, and the killed, wounded and prisoners at quite 2,000. Prisoners state that their plan contemplated a division of their forces after they had destroyed the bridge over Staunton river; one party was to push on to Danville and Raleigh and thence to Weldon, destroying the railways, bridges and public stores, while the other was to visit the Roanoke country, and lay waste the plantations.

Having despaired of conquering us in battle, the present policy of the enemy is to despoil the country and render it incapable of supporting an army. That beautiful and fruitful region extending from the Rapidan to the Potomac has been laid waste, and more recently Hunter has swept up the Valley of Virginia from Martinsburg to Lexington, the richest and most inviting portion of the State, and destroyed whatever he could lay his vandal hands upon, including mills, forges, bridges, growing crops, cattle, horses, houses and provisions. The policy of his government has been to interpose a desert between us and the Federal capital, and thus prevent the possibility of another invasion of Maryland and Pennsylvania. With a barrier of this sort, it would no longer be necessary for Mr. Lincoln to maintain any about Washington. Such, at least, was the object proposed by the barbarous course which his officers have pursued.

What then must have been his surprise when he heard a few days ago, as reported in Northern papers of the 30th ult., that Early, with a considerable force, was at Winchester, preparing to swoop down upon Washington! Such a report has certainly reached the North, and consequently gold continues to advance. Hunter had reached Wheeling, and Sheridan the Southside, but notwithstanding each one reports that he had accomplished all he had in view when he undertook his expedition, the Congress found it necessary to call for 200,000 more men and to repeal the $300 exemption clause.

Let the people of the Confederate States take heart; the day begins to break in the east.

P. W. A.

ARMY OF NORTHERN VIRGINIA,
Petersburg, Virginia, July 7, 1864 [7-14-64]

Gen. Grant continues to indulge in his favorite pastime—shelling Petersburg—otherwise there is no change to report in the position of affairs. He uses both mortars and Parrott guns, and keeps up the fire day and night, sometimes at intervals of ten and fifteen minutes, with occasional intermissions of an hour or more. Last night the shelling was more rapid than usual, up to the time I went to sleep; this morning I have not heard a gun. But it is just four o'clock; the sun is not yet risen, the time at which he is accustomed to open the batteries, and one of which consists of 32-pounders. The Parrott guns will send a ball not only into the heart of town, but clear beyond it. Indeed, the prevailing opinion among the soldiers is that a Parrott ball, if fired at a sufficient angle, never stops until it comes against something!

It is only at this early hour in the morning that a distant view of the Federal lines can be obtained. As soon as the horse trains begin to move, the clouds of dust shut out every object except at very short distances. There have been only one or two passing showers since the army left Spottsylvania. The roads and paths about an army are as numerous as the streets and lanes in a city. They run in every possible direction, and cut each other at all possible angles. This is especially the case where the ground, as in the front of Petersburg, is cut into ridges and ravines where over a man can climb or a horse can walk, or a wagon, an ambulance and an artillery carriage can move without upsetting, there you will find a footpath or a road. The number of these ways is increased where hostile armies are drawn up near each other, as in this event it becomes necessary for the troops and trains to avail themselves of every inequality in the ground to shield themselves from the fire of the opposing sharpshooters. With a drought of eight weeks, a thin, light soil, and thousands of men, horses and vehicles moving to and fro from early dawn until late at night, grinding the earth into powder, you may form some idea of the dust which they create and in which we have lived since we came to Petersburg. Everything partakes of the color of dust—the woods, the fields, the corn, the grass, the men, the horses and the wagons. We breathe it; we sleep in it; we eat and move in it. It is thicker than the darkness that overspread Egypt in the days of Pharaoh; so thick, indeed, that Gen. Butler from his lofty lookout will be able to descry but little else except—dust. If there is no wind to blow it away, the dust raised by a solitary horseman is so great that it is impossible at the distance of a few paces to tell whether it is produced by a man, a horse or a vehicle. It might be an elephant and you would be none the wiser for it. All you can see is a moving column of dust, the cause of which remains a mystery, being concealed, like the cuttle fish, by a curtain of its own creation.

The important bridge over Staunton river was saved by the successful defense made by the militia reserves and the convalescent sick and wounded from the hospitals at Lynchburg. I mention this fact with the most perfect confidence that the reserves in Georgia, and the inmates of the hospitals in the rear of Johnston's army, will emulate the heroic example of their brethren in Virginia. There is another example worthy of record and imitation. I refer to the gallant exploit of Capt. [A. J.] White of Brunswick county, who was wounded at Gettysburg, and had not been able to return to the field. A detachment of 32 Federal horsemen from Wilson's raiding column passed by his home during the late expedition. Capt. White gathered together six citizens from the neighborhood, followed the enemy, and next morning while the party were at breakfast, he so arranged his small force as to create the belief that he was supported by one or more companies. He then advanced boldly and demanded a surrender. After a short parley, the enemy complied; and thus seven resolute Confederates marched thirty-two Yankee cavalrymen, with their horses, equipments and plunder, into camp. Can't the good people between Atlanta and Chattanooga imitate these examples of courage and enterprise?

But is Gen. Grant to be allowed to remain in easy cannon range of Petersburg all summer? It would cost many valuable lives to drive him away. Gen. Lee's defensive policy has worked admirably well thus far, and he can afford to continue it a while longer, especially since his own army is not suffering for food, while Grant's is melting away by sickness and the withdrawal of those regiments whose term of service have expired. Meanwhile a coal of fire has been prepared for the back of the Federal terrapin. He may feel it tomorrow or next day. He might feel it today. I cannot be more explicit; my letter might be captured before it can reach one of Mr. Reagan's mailbags between this place and Weldon. Early has gone to—. He is the coal of fire.

P. W. A.

RICHMOND, July 11, 1864 [7-20-64]

All quiet at Petersburg yesterday afternoon when I left. Nothing of importance has transpired since as far as is known at the capital. The enemy shelled the town from four o'clock Friday afternoon until ten at night. The same thing was done Saturday afternoon. Both sides commenced to reconnoiter the position of the other at the same time Friday afternoon, and the artillery fire commenced at that time was kept up by the enemy until late at night. Grant's object is manifest. He knows that Petersburg is of very little, if any, military advantage to Gen. Lee, but he intends to force the inhabitants to quit their homes and seek refuge in Richmond and other crowded localities. Every non-combatant he can drive into Richmond, increases the number of mouths to be fed, and to that extent embarrasses government in its efforts to defend the city. The Federal plan is to lay waste the country and cut off supplies; and to that end, raiding parties have been sent out in almost every direction, with instructions to cut the railways, burn the mills, foundries, factories and bridges, kill the cattle, carry off the horses, strip the people of their scanty supplies, and ravage the land generally. Not only has Grant driven many of the people of Petersburg from their homes with the hope that they would fly to Richmond and help consume supplies designed for the army, but his cavalry have been pursuing the same policy in all those portions of the State where they have been able to penetrate. In the Valley, in that productive region lying between the Rapidan and the Potomac, in the eastern or tide water counties, and more recently along the line of the Danville railway, these marauders have destroyed everything they could lay their hands upon, and many of the most fertile districts in the commonwealth are now a waste, producing next to nothing for either man or beast.

The object sought to be accomplished by this system of military brigandage, is the eventual evacuation of Richmond by the Confederates. Having despaired of his ability to drive them from the capital and the State by open combat, Grant and his government now seek to reduce them to such extremities for food as to leave them no alternative but to retire further to the South. It is not believed here that he will be successful in his efforts either to whip us or starve us.

The morning papers contain the latest information to hand from Maryland and Northern Virginia. It is hoped that the commander of the Confederate forces on the Potomac will be equal to the situation, and that he may soon have the co-operation of the prisoners confined at Point Lookout. If the expedition should do nothing else but force Grant to abandon his position at Petersburg and go to the defense of his own capital, that would be a most important success. Grant will not leave however, as long as it is possible to maintain his ground.

This morning papers contain full accounts also of the naval combat between the *Alabama* and the *Kearsarge*, and the sinking of the former. The result of the conflict is the cause of universal sorrow here. It seems that the *Kearsarge* had the largest crew, the heaviest guns, the strongest machinery, and a partial armor of chain cable, which protected its more vital parts. It appears, also, that Capt. Semmes was not aware of this great superiority of his adversary. While we regret that the *Alabama* should have fought at all, since the enemy could better afford to lose ten vessels than we could one, yet it is a matter of universal congratulation that the wild rover of the seas went to the bottom rather than fall into the hands of an insolent foe.

The information received this morning that Sherman had crossed the Chattahoochee and was entrenching himself, has produced the most profound and painful impression in official circles here. It was known that Johnston had a sort of passion for retreats, or maneuvers and strategy, but it was hoped he would be able to get his consent to make a stand somewhere. Lee had found it necessary to retire almost as far as Johnston has done, but in doing so, he has disabled his antagonist; whereas Johnston has not fought a battle—only heavy skirmishing, and what in Virginia would be called pretty sharp engagements. A commander who waits to get a dead thing on his opponent, may never fight a battle, and though he may never lose one, he will rarely ever accomplish any good.

P. W. A.

RICHMOND, July 13, 1864 [7-24-64]

There is no change in the military status around Richmond and Petersburg. The opinion obtained in military circles at Petersburg that Grant has sent the Sixth corps to Washington, and it is believed by some persons that either forces have been, or will be, sent in the same direction. One thing, however, is highly probable: If Grant does not go to Washington, nor send reinforcements, the safety of the Federal capital will be in danger.

It must be confessed, however, that the position of the Confederates is not without danger. If Grant has sent reinforcements to Washington, upon their arrival at the Federal capital they would be in the rear of the Confederates, should the latter press on to Baltimore.

It must be remembered, also, that Hunter is moving around from Wheeling and will soon be, if he is not already, near the scene of operations. But if Grant despatches reinforcements to Maryland, Lee can do the same, though the former by reason of their water facilities, can accomplish the distance in much less time than we can. All the railway bridges beyond Orange Court House were destroyed by the enemy before they left Culpepper, and the bridge over the South Anna, near Richmond, has not yet been replaced. It has been a part of the policy of our foes to protect their capital by creating a desert throughout Northern Virginia, so that an army can neither be subsisted there nor transported rapidly to the Potomac.

That Grant's troops would be glad to exchange the Appomattox for the Potomac, there can be but little doubt. They are now encamped in what is considered an exceedingly unhealthy locality, especially in the months of August and September, now near at hand. Their supply of water is very limited and inferior at that; and the greater part of what they do get has to be hauled in barrels from the James and Appomattox for considerable distances. All the sewers in Petersburg empty their contents into the Appomattox, and all the sewers in Richmond empty their contents into the James; so your readers may form some idea of the character of the water with which the Federal army is chiefly supplied.

No mail has reached the army from the South for the last three weeks, owing to the interruption of our communications by the enemy. It is hoped that a small part of the mail matter that has been accumulated on the route will reach Richmond tomorrow, but it is not certain. In no event will the roads be opened for the regular transmission of the mails for some time to come.

P. W. A.

RICHMOND, July 16, 1864 [7-23-64]

The telegraphic wires keep you well informed of the progress of events in Maryland. At past accounts the Confederates had invested Washington City. Before this hour they have entered the Federal capital, or their daring expedition has come to grief. Neither event is improbable. But can we hold Washington after it is taken? Without a fleet and the hearty co-operation of Maryland it would seem to be impossible. Indeed, the control of the rivers and bays of Maryland and Virginia by the enemy, has been and continues to be until the end of the war, worth more to the enemy than the services of one hundred thousand veteran troops. When Grant cut loose from his railway base at Culpepper Court House, the Rappahannock furnished him a safer and better water base at Fredericksburg and Port Royal. When he abandoned the latter he found a still better one at West Point, on York river, and when he moved upon Petersburg, nature, who seems to have done her best for our enemies and her worst for us, provided him with one infinitely better than either at City Point, on James river, and distant only eighteen miles from his present encampment.

The advantages which the topography of Eastern Maryland and Virginia gives to the enemy are seen in the facility with which he can forward reinforcements to Washington and Baltimore. There is reason for believing that considerable bodies of men have been sent down the James and up the Potomac to the relief of Washington and Baltimore. In this way troops can be moved to those cities in one day, can fight a battle on the second, and return to City Point on the third; meanwhile, the Confederates, with their broken railways and dilapidated wagons, engines and cars, could not even reach the scene of action.

But if the physical geography of the country gives the enemy advantage over us, the power of steam has increased that advantage a hundred fold. For the last eighteen months we have derived but little benefit from this prodigious aider and abettor of mankind, and at no time has it been available to us except upon our railways. The enemy, on the contrary, has used it in transporting troops and supplies by land, in conveying arms and recruits from countries beyond the sea, in bombarding our seacoast cities and fortifications, in penetrating our rivers, and throwing large bodies of armed men upon exposed points, in protecting the retreat of his beaten armies, in digging canals, and even pumping up water from contiguous streams as at City Point, and forcing it through hose to the distance of two miles or more for the use of his troops. We possess but few of these advantages. For three years and more we have had to fight against nature, against the art and science of man, and against a foe three times as numerous as ourselves—a foe, too, who has had access to the markets of the world, and who has been able to close all of our best ports. And yet we still hold our own, and to-day our arms are thundering at the gates of his Capital!

But the advantages here referred to may enable the enemy to concentrate a force in Maryland that will leave the Confederates no choice but to retreat. It may be they will find some difficulty even in extricating themselves. We hear that a good many of them, tempted by the spoils of the country, have straggled from the ranks; these will probably be taken prisoner. Let us, however, hope for the best. Should the Federal Capitol and public buildings be devoted to destruction, or failing in this, should the Confederates mount themselves at the expense of their enemies, and sweep through Pennsylvania, leaving a dark trail of smoking ruins behind them, the government and people of the United States at least would have no just cause of complaint.

Grant shelled our lines heavily yesterday morning, and threw the usual number of shells into Petersburg. He was replied to with vigor. He will endeavor to hold on to his present position by his teeth, while he fights us with his hands in Maryland and along our railway lines. When a Yankee army once imbeds itself in the ground, like a cancer in the human body, it extends its roots in every direction, until it becomes exceedingly difficult, if not impossible, to expel it.

It is reported here that the belief prevails generally in Georgia that Johnston, in his retreat from Dalton to Atlanta, has acted in obedience to instructions from Richmond. If such belief is entertained, it is without the least foundation in fact. The authorities here have given him all the aid in their power. If they have not done more for him, it was because they could not do more. His force of all arms, as compared with his adversary, has been greater than Lee's as compared with Grant's. The President and his military advisers here have desired that he would make a stand and fight the enemy, and his failure to do so has caused much disappointment and dissatisfaction. His friends, of whom he has many, still hope he will vindicate his great reputation.

P. W. A.

RICHMOND, VA., July 19, 1864 [7-31-64]

There is no change to report in the position of affairs at Petersburg.

Gen. Early, who commanded the expeditionary forces lately operating in Maryland, has recrossed the Potomac at White's Ferry, near Leesburg, in good order and without molestation from the enemy, and bringing wagons and their other spoils. His reasons for returning to the south side of the Potomac have not yet transpired. It is supposed, however, that his withdrawal from the front of Washington was rendered necessary by the large force which the enemy's facilities of water and land transportation enabled him to concentrate in an almost incredibly short time. The Washington *Chronicle* admits that there was a period of thirty-six hours during the late operations when the Federal capital might have been taken. This is probable, though the result shows conclusively that it could not have been held. The enemy's superiority in numbers and his control of the lower Potomac would have enabled him in a short time to cut off all supplies from the city and compel the Confederates to retire. It may be that Gen. Early did not, as at Lynchburg, move as rapidly as could have been desired; but it should be remembered that he had to collect supplies, and impress horses, wagons, etc., as he advanced; and to do this, it was necessary for him to disperse his forces and move slowly. It must be added, however, that we have lost in all probability the only chance we shall ever have of capturing the capital of our enemy. In other respects the expedition has proven a failure, especially in this that it did not occasion the withdrawal of Grant's army from Petersburg. I need not inform you that this was the principal object sought to be accomplished by the movement. Early's force consisted of Ewell's corps, Breckinridge's command, and Imboden's and Bradley Johnson's cavalry, and he was supported by such officers as Rodes, Gordon and Breckinridge.

You have already been informed by telegraph of the removal by the President of Gen. Johnston from command of the army in North Georgia, and the appointment of Gen. Hood, as his successor with the temporary rank of full General. The interest and importance which attach to the change in the command of one of the principal armies of the Confederacy, will render any excuse unnecessary for the space I may occupy in detailing some of the causes and circumstances that led to this important step. My information is derived from sources which leave no room to doubt its correctness.

Gen. Bragg, you will remember, three times made application to the President to be relieved of the command of the Army of Tennessee—the first time just after the battle of Murfreesboro'; the second time, after the battle of Chickamauga, and the third time, after the retreat from Missionary Ridge. On the last occasion he desired permission to withdraw from his position and to turn over the command to Lieut. Gen. Hardee, the next in rank. Gen. Hardee modestly declined to take permanent command of the army, but consented to occupy the position from which Gen. Bragg had retired until his successor could be appointed. In the meantime, Gen. Hardee being unwilling to assume the responsibility, Gen. Bragg requested the President to place Gen. Johnston in command, and as an inducement to the appointment of that officer, he offered to take the position of Chief of Staff under Johnston, or any other position in which the President might believe he could be useful to the army or the country. The troops, the people and the press united in the desire that Johnston might be placed at the head of the army. Such indeed seemed to be the universal wish of the country. It is no secret that the President did not place the same estimate upon Gen. Johnston's abilities for command that the people and the army did. But he yielded his conviction to his own judgment. Johnston and Bragg were then and are now warm friends, but the former having intimated no wish to avail himself of the services of the latter, the President, in conformity to an act of Congress, called Gen. Bragg to his present office at Richmond, with the approval of Gen. Lee, Johnston and Beauregard, and the Secretary of War and the Adjutant and Inspector General.

Johnston's administration of the army under his charge, so far as I know or have heard, left nothing to be desired. He was eminently successful in infusing a spirit of confidence into his troops and the people. He had the support of government, the co-operation of his officers, the confidence and affection of his men, and the unanimous approval and encouragement of the press, and the opinion was almost universal that he would not only hold Northern Georgia, but would recover Chattanooga, and in the course of the winter, it became manifest that the policy of the enemy was to mass three large armies—one of which was to operate in Virginia against Richmond, another in Georgia against Atlanta, and the third in the Trans-Mississippi country. This policy left the President no alternative but to concentrate his own forces and meet the enemy upon his chosen ground. To this end, every man that could be spared from other points on the east side of the Mississippi, was sent to Lee and Johnston, and every preparation made to defend the great strategic points about to be assailed. The country is too familiar with the efforts of the President, the Secretary of War and Gen. Bragg to increase the effective strength of our forces, to require further remark in this connection. It was ascertained that the enemy would assemble his largest army in Virginia, and consequently the forces under Lee were made somewhat, though but little, stronger than those under Johnston. But even when this had been done, the difference between Lee and Grant was greater than the difference between Johnston and Sherman.

Grant crossed the Rapidan with at least 125,000 men, and was subsequently reinforced including Butler's command, by 40,000 additional troops—making 165,000 men. In the course of the rapid and bloody campaign that followed, Lee found it necessary to move along with his adversary, like two desperate wrestlers, from the Rapidan to the Appomattox, but in doing so, he fought him at the Wilderness, at Spottsylvania, on the North Anna, on the Pamunkey, at Cold Harbor, and at Petersburg. His communications were cut again and again, his cavalry had to be detached from the main army, and though they could not prevent the foe from tearing up the railway, they succeeded in beating him away from Richmond, at Trevillian's station, in Charles City, and at Reams' depot. The ground over which the terrible conflict was waged, was favorable to the enemy, in that it enabled him to change his base whenever he desired, gave him short and safe lines of communication, and left his cavalry free to operate upon the rear of the Confederates. But this is not all. The enemy pushed a formidable column up the Valley of Virginia, and made it necessary to detach Breckinridge's command, and then Early's, from the main army. This latter force cleared the Valley of the enemy, and then swept across the Potomac to the very gates of Washington, creating the greatest dismay and consternation throughout the United States.

The result is told in a few words: Of the 165,000 men who poured down upon the devoted capital of the Confederates, one half now rot in the soil of Virginia, and roll and suffer in the hospitals of the North and the prisons of the South, while the army that remains has been disabled from further aggressive undertakings.

In Georgia the campaign has resulted less favorably. Johnston had a fine army. It was well fed, well shod, and well clothed, and was ready to follow wheresoever he might lead. The theater of operations was as favorable for defensive purposes almost as nature could make it, being crossed by rugged mountain ranges and deep unfordable rivers. Abandoning his strong position at Dalton, Johnston retreated across these rivers and over these mountains, from one position to another, for one hundred miles, without delivering battle or attempting to cut the communications of his adversary. He fought a combat at Resaca, and repulsed an assault at Dallas, and another at Kennesaw mountain; but there was no general engagement, nor was any disposition shown to seek the enemy, as Lee did at the Wilderness and Cold Harbor, though his troops are represented to have been keen for the encounter. In the meantime, Sherman made no attempt against his communications with Atlanta. This left Johnston's cavalry at liberty to operate upon the lines of his adversary. He chose, however, to keep Wheeler upon his own flank, notwithstanding, the latter had a body of fine cavalry, well disciplined, and capable, as their enterprising chief believed, of inflicting great injury upon the enemy's lines and depots of supplies. Johnston desired that Forrest might be sent to the rear of the enemy, and made repeated applications to that effect. It was the desire and expectation of the authorities here that Forrest should join him, and orders to do so were sent from Richmond. But heavy reinforcements were moving out from Memphis to Sherman, and Forrest being on the spot, and believing he could render Johnston more essential aid by driving them back than by going to Georgia and leaving them to follow, attacked and beat them. He soon discovered that the enemy was not disposed to abandon the undertaking. A good portion of the *debris* of Banks' army was got together and marched for the same destination; and it was only four days ago that S. D. Lee and Forrest met this force upon the old battleground of Tupelo, and defeated and drove back this second reinforcing column. In all this Forrest has been aiding Johnston as effectually as if he had been in Georgia. Of this fact Johnston must have been aware. He continued to call for reinforcements, however, even after he had been informed that he had received the last man that could be sent to him.

Of Johnston's general abilities there cannot be two opinions. Military men say he is superb in action, and handles an army with great skill. He is considered a cautious man, fond of maneuvers, strategy and retreats, preferring, it is thought, to circumvent his adversary by his wit, rather than strike him with his fist. The army believed, the country believed, and the press nearest the scene of action reiterated it day after day, that he retreated only to draw the enemy into a trap; that when he got him where he wanted him, he would fall upon and destroy him. The object was to get the incautious Sherman in his grasp, when he would crush him as he would an eggshell in his hand.

The President, it seems, did not share in this confidence. He did not like this sort of strategy, it gave up too much territory, and exposed to capture the great railway center of the Confederacy. I am informed, not by the President, for I do not know him, but by persons who can hardly be mistaken, that he heard with regret and dissatisfaction of Johnston's successive retreats. He did not order him to make a stand, knowing that a man who fights against his will, is not likely to fight successfully, but he was careful not to leave him in ignorance of his dissatisfaction. When, however, Johnston permitted Sherman to maneuver him from Kennesaw Mountain, and allowed the Federal commander to cross the Chattahouchee simultaneously with himself, and that too without an effort to prevent him, he felt that the time had come to interpose his authority, and if possible save Atlanta and the State of Georgia.

It is understood that he inquired of Johnston by telegraph what his plans were; and that Johnston's reply indicated no change from his former policy. Satisfied that he would not, or could not, make a stand behind some of the mountains and rivers across which he retreated, he would not do so now that he had reached the level country, where his antagonist had an equal chance with himself—satisfied, indeed, from all the information he could obtain that Johnston did not believe he could hold Atlanta, and that he would abandon it, he determined to remove him, and since Hardee's modest estimate of his own abilities forbade his acceptance of the command, to turn it over to Hood. Gen. Bragg's visit to Georgia had nothing whatever to do with bringing the President to the resolution. It is not improbable that he desired the President to give Johnston a further opportunity. It is known that he, like the President, desired Johnston to give the enemy battle.

The change in command may have been made too late to save Atlanta. The President had to choose between what he believed would be the certain abandonment of that place under Johnston, and the possibility of saving it under a new commander. Was he right to remove the former? Johnston's friends cannot complain that he has not had a fair opportunity and an open field. The President, while not disguising his own opinions, left him free to act as he thought best. Did Johnston do the best that could be done? If Lee had been in his place, would Sherman now be on the east side of the Chattahoochee with such an army as he has? The feeling here is that the President did right to remove him. Upon one point there can be no difference of opinion: I refer to the necessity upon the part of the army and country to give Gen. Hood every possible aid and encouragement. He is a gallant soldier, and is not afraid to risk his reputation in a battle.

P. W. A.

The rigors of the previous three months' campaign brought on another attack of recurring fever, disabling Alexander on and off for nearly two months.

RICHMOND, August 11, 1864 [8-16-64]

Grant has again contracted his lines on our right, withdrawing them still further from the Weldon railway towards City Point. This change has been rendered necessary by the withdrawal of additional forces for the defense of Maryland and Pennsylvania. With this exception, and the fact, now become manifest, that he is putting himself on the defensive, nothing worthy of note has occurred in the vicinity of Petersburg since the date of my last letter.

At last advices, Early had recrossed the Potomac from Hagerstown, and was between Winchester and the river. This may be part of a combined movement, of which you will probably hear more hereafter. McCauseland and Bradley Johnson had also retired to the south side of the Potomac, and were subsequently surprised, through gross negligence, it is reported, in the vicinity of Moorefields, [West Virginia] losing over four hundred, in killed, wounded and missing, a considerable number of horses and four guns. I fear their troopers were overloaded with booty brought out of the fertile Cumberland Valley and from the burning houses of Chambersburg.

The idea some entertained in certain quarters in the South, that the forces now operating on the Potomac might be better employed in Georgia. This is an error. Had Early, after the defeat of Hunter near Lynchburg, gone to Atlanta instead of Maryland, he might have rendered Hood important service, but it would have been at the great hazard, if not the loss, of Richmond. Lee might have held his ground at Petersburg, but he could not have provisioned his army. The forces dispersed at Lynchburg, like wolves driven from a carcass, would have returned and occupied the place in less time than it would have taken Early, in the present condition of our railroads, to reach Atlanta. With Hunter at Lynchburg and Grant at Petersburg, it would have been impossible for Lee to defend and keep open the railway lines by which his army was supplied. By moving across the Potomac however, Early has not only enabled our people to bring out large supplies of wheat and hay from the Shenandoah Valley, but he has changed the theatre of operations to Maryland, and thus relieved that part of Virginia of an active and enterprising foe, placed the railroads out of danger, and forced the enemy to subsist his army as well as their own. If he were to withdraw from the Potomac even now, 25,000 troops now occupied in Maryland, would soon swarm up the Shenandoah and Grant's hold upon Petersburg, now being relaxed, would soon tighten again.

I do not know that the statement I am about to make is true, but if it is, it shows that Early's operations, though not crowned with the capture of Washington, have nevertheless borne good fruit. Intelligence has just reached here, through the most reliable channel by which we can communicate with the enemy's country, that Grant and staff arrived at Washington on Sunday last, the 7th inst., and that he took with him a considerable portion of his army. We hear also, that Grant's total losses since he crossed the Rapidan have been 115,870 men. In this number are included the killed, the wounded who have not yet returned to their commands, prisoners, deserters, sick, and those whose terms of service have expired. Grant's original force was estimated at 125,000. He received at Spottsylvania some 15,000 more, making 140,000. To this should be added Butler's command, and the troops sent him from New Orleans and other points, say 35,000, making the grand total 175,000. If we subtract from this, 115,870, he would have left as his present effective force, 59,130 men. These figures show what Lee and Beauregard and their brave commands have done for the enemy.

P. W. A.

RICHMOND, August 18, 1864 [8-24-64]

There has been more or less skirmishing and fighting below Richmond for nearly a week past. The accounts which reach here are conflicting, some representing the conflict to have been severe and the loss of the enemy heavy, whilst others treat it as just the reverse. Unfortunately, I am unable just now to visit the scene of action and verify the accounts, my horse having more than ten days ago been sent to the Valley of Virginia, in anticipation of important movements in that quarter. Such a thing as hiring a horse in Richmond is utterly impossible, though one should offer as much for one as King Richard did.

There is a prospect of the early resumption of the exchange of prisoners. The exchange will be conducted on the principle of giving man for man, and officer for officer, any surplus of either not to be paroled, but held for future exchange. It is not probable that objection will be made by the Confederate authorities to including the exchange such free negroes, inhabitants of the Northern States, as may have fallen into their hands. Free blacks are enlisted in the English and French armies, and are exchanged like white prisoners. Negroes who have been seduced or forced from their Southern homes by the emissaries and armies of the North, will not, of course, be exchanged, but will be returned to their former owners.

P. W. A.

PETERSBURG, August 20, 1864 [8-26-64]

It is difficult to understand Grant's strategy. About a week ago he embarked a considerable body of cavalry on transports and started them down the James, as if for Washington. They were landed on the north side of the river however, and were soon joined by a heavy force of infantry and artillery, under Major General Hancock. This combined force moved cautiously up the river, and made it necessary for Gen. Lee to send additional troops to that quarter, to hold it in check. The enemy was easily defeated and driven away.

Before Hancock had been recalled and while he was yet on the north bank of the James, Warren was sent with a heavy column against the Weldon railway on our extreme right. Grant thus stretched on his right wing across the James and his left across the Weldon Railroad. This dangerous extension of his lines, under ordinary circumstances, would have exposed him to certain destruction, but in the present case the James and Appomattox and the heavy works in front of Petersburg may save him from the punishment which his rashness would seem to deserve. As it is, you will perceive by the following account that he has not escaped without serious loss.

As soon as it was reported to Gen. Beauregard, early yesterday morning, that Warren had moved out with his own corps, reinforced by cavalry and artillery, and placed himself across the railroad two miles south of Petersburg, he ordered Lieut. Gen. Hill to march against him and dislodge him. Hill took with him two brigades of Heth's division, Mahone's old brigade, of Mahone's division, Colquitt's and Clingman's brigades, of Hoke's division, and [James] Dearing's brigade of cavalry. Heth commanded on the right and Mahone on the left. Hill's orders were to turn the enemy's right—that is, to drive through his lines and throw himself between Warren and the main body of Grant's army, and thus cut him off. He came up with the enemy three o'clock in the afternoon, drawn up across the railway and protected by breastworks of logs and rails, and dirt thrown up during the proceeding night.

The assault was made in most gallant style. Heth occupied the attention of the foe in front, while Mahone moved around to the left and endeavored to insert his brigade between Warren's corps and the main body of the Federal army. The enemy received our charge with a heavy fire of artillery and musketry, but he failed to check the onset of the Confederates. We used but little artillery, owing to the heavy roads and dense undergrowth, but moved right in upon them with the musket and bayonet, and carried their works. As soon as Warren felt Mahone tugging at his flanks, and hear the war shout of his old brigade, he retreated. He made as good a fight as he could get out of his men, and disputed the ground with some degree of stubbornness. He had not expected an attack upon his right, and consequently he found it necessary to withdraw the moment he was struck in that unprotected quarter; but he moved slowly, yielding no ground except under compulsion. He was driven from two lines of breastworks, and had just taken shelter behind the third when night put an end to the conflict.

No return has yet been made of our losses, but it is not believed that they will exceed 600 men. The losses of the enemy, on the contrary, are estimated at 5,000, including 3,000 prisoners, of whom 2,400 are well men, the remainder being wounded. Among the prisoners taken is Brig. Gen. [Joseph] Hayes. All our troops behaved well.

It has been remarkably quiet to-day. It is not probable that the enemy will be left in possession of the railway. Indeed, I hear that an effort will be made to-morrow to dislodge him. In the meantime, he is doubtless at work, burrowing in the ground, and when we renew the attack we shall probably find him strongly intrenched.

Gen. Lee returned to this part of the lines this morning at an early hour.

P. W. A.

Casualties for the battle of Weldon Railroad: Federals, 198 killed, 1,105 wounded, and 3,152 missing for 4,455; Confederate losses are estimated at about 1,600.

RICHMOND, August 25, 1864 [8-31-64]

Your correspondent, like a large number of men in Lee's army, is on the sick list. This will account for the brevity of this letter. There is as much sickness in the Army of Northern Virginia, in proportion to numbers, as there has been at any time since the first year of the war. The sickness if not of a malignant type, however, being chiefly intermittent fever and disorders of the bowels. The terrible campaign in which the men have been engaged, the recent almost unparalleled term of drought and hot weather, constant duty in the trenches, absence of vegetable food and fruit, as well as the lack of good water, and the chill and fever producing district in which the troops are encamped, have all conspired to impair the health of the army. It will be readily understood from this state of things that many of those men who were wounded in the late engagements in front of Petersburg are not doing as well as could be desired. Their vital powers have been impaired by the constant exposure and hardships that persons of feeble health do not recover from wounds as certainly or rapidly as men of robust constitutions. It is some consolation to know that the enemy is suffering far more than we are in this respect. His hospitals are crowded with sick, and many of his men whom Grant refused to let go upon the expiration of their term of service, are hourly receiving their final discharges at the hands of death, that great liberator whose certificate neither surgeon nor generals can dispute.

Our casualties in the affair of Sunday, the 21st, have been exaggerated. [Gen. Johnson] Hagood's brigade suffered most, both in prisoners and killed and wounded; but our entire loss on Friday and Sunday does not exceed fifteen hundred. I doubt whether it is so much. A Federal colonel [Capt. Dennis Dailey] seized the flag of one of Hagood's regiments, and insisted upon the surrender of the command, whereupon he and Hagood got into an altercation, the result of which was that the Yankee was slain by a pistol shot, and the flag taken from him.

The possession of the Weldon Railroad by the enemy interrupts one of our lines of supply and brings Grant three or four miles nearer to the Danville road, distant about forty-five miles. This is all. We have in the Danville connection a shorter and better line than that by Weldon, which was found sufficient for the wants of the army for the first three years of the war. It was with some reluctance that Gen. Lee consented, and the instance of his Chief Quartermaster, to repair the Weldon road, when it was first cut by Wilson and Kautz, about the 1st of July. It was as evident then as it is now, that we could not prevent the enemy, whose lines approached it very near, from cutting it whenever he felt inclined to do so, and had a dark night to cover his movements.

P. W. A.

RICHMOND, VA., September 1, 1864 [9-6-64]

A slight attack of fever, and attendance upon a wounded brother, who has answered to his last roll call upon this earth, have prevented me from writing for several days past. There has been but little to communicate, however, except the particulars of the affair on the Weldon railway on the 25th ult. Two thousand prisoners, nine pieces of artillery and seven stand of colors, together with a heavy list of killed and wounded, on the part of the enemy, and a relatively small loss on our part, makes a very handsome affair and reflect no little credit upon Gen. Hill and his command. The gallant conduct of Hampton's cavalry, who drove the enemy's infantry out of one line of entrenchments and took about eight hundred prisoners, is particularly gratifying. Hampton has accomplished a great deal since he succeeded to the command of this arm of the service. His success has been continuous and unbroken, the credit of which is no longer monopolized by the regiments and officers from Virginia, as was too frequently the case in former campaigns. Some of the papers here still speak of "Fitz Lee's and Hampton's Cavalry," as if these officers possessed separate and equal commands, or as if Fitz Lee were the chief of cavalry and not Hampton. Such solecism was never perpetrated in Stuart's day.

But Virginians have much to excite their pride and stimulate their patriotism. They have a magnificent domain, superb scenery, a productive soil, immense resources, a devoted race of men and women, and a long line of patriotic ancestors. Their sons have been conspicuous in the Senate and in the field, and their women lack no virtue that can add grace or dignity to their sex. It is difficult, if not impossible, therefore, for a Virginian, whatsoever may be his position or circumstances in life, ever to cease to be a Virginian. Some of Gen. Lee's warmest admirers have thought that even he, great and good as he is, has not been always quite able to rise superior to this feeling, which, however much its excellence in the breast of the Commander of an army or the Chief Magistrate of a nation may be regretted, nevertheless lies at the bottom of much of the excellence and renown to which any community or State may attain. I know not how much truth there is in the supposition in regard to our great chief; but if there is any foundation for it, I can only say it is the only defect that mars the otherwise perfect symmetry of his character.

But to return to the cavalry of the Army of Northern Virginia: It is not probable that it will ever be brought to that state of efficiency to which it might have attained if it had been subjected to a more rigid and judicious discipline in the first year of the war; but that Hampton and the accomplished officers under him will do all in their power to make this arm of the service what it should be, there is every reason to believe. The improvement already made, and which is manifest to the whole country, is only an earnest of what may be expected in the future. At the onset of the war, the material of which the cavalry was composed was as good as it could be. Since then a goodly number of persons formerly attached to the infantry service, who were tired of walking and desired to ride, have exchanged the musket for the sabre, in thought of having an easier time of it. These recruits require a commander with a clear head, and especially a firm hand; and these, it is believed, they now have.

The morning papers contain an address from the Confederate Commissioner of Exchange, to the friends and relations of our prisoners in the hands of the United States, in which he exposes the duplicity of the Federal authorities in their persistent refusal to carry out the cartel for the exchange of prisoners of war. A short time ago, there was reason to believe that the exchange would be resumed at an early day, but at the time there is no prospect of it whatever. The reason the United States do not abide by their agreement is too obvious to admit of any differences of opinion. We have the larger number of prisoners, but nearly all of those in our hands are men whose terms of service have expired, or hundred days men whose brief enlistments will have soon come to an end. If these prisoners were exchanged, therefore, but few, if any, of them would be available for further service; whereas the Confederate prisoners at the North are in for the war, and if released, would soon be in the field again. Mr. Lincoln may have some doubts, too, whether the inmates of Belle Isle and Andersonville would vote for him, if exchanged. At all events, he knows they have mouths to fed, and require a considerable force to guard them. Under these circumstances, he is "smart" enough to believe he would gain nothing by the change; and when was a Yankee ever known to do anything, unless he saw a prospect of gaining some advantage, or tricking somebody?

There is no foundation for the report that peace commissioners or agents have arrived at Richmond from the northwestern States, or from any other quarter. [James] Jacquess and [James] Gilmore were here, and they went away with a flea in their ears. It is to be regretted that Confederate journals devote so much space to the discussion of peace prospects and the Presidential election in the United States; since the greater the anxiety we manifest in this regard, the stronger will be the reason on the part of the enemy to continue the war.

P. W. A.

RICHMOND, September 9, 1864 [9-14-64]

Grant calls for one hundred thousand more men—only one hundred thousand—to finish up the rebellion at once. Two millions and more have been mustered into the armies of the North, of whom hundreds of thousands now sleep in the soil of the land they invaded, or creep about their homes on crutches and with enfeebled frames, while only a small remnant of the multitudinous host confronts us in the field of battle. This vast army has not been found sufficient for the work at hand. At first the famous "anaconda" principle was tried; these immense forces were scattered over the country, and an effort made to envelop us in their fold and crush us to death. This plan having failed, the policy at present relied on is concentration, the mustering together of the Federal armies, and an attempt to reach particular points supposed to be vital. In order to carry out this policy, it was found necessary to abandon the Trans-Mississippi country, to give up nearly the whole of the States of Mississippi and Tennessee, and to withdraw entirely from the mainland of the Atlantic States, except in Georgia and Virginia. And even in those States they hold in the one only James river, the waters around Fortress Monroe and Norfolk, and the ground on which they stand at Petersburg; and in the other, only Atlanta and the line of railway leading thence to Chattanooga.

Their present policy has been crowned with success at Atlanta only. In Virginia it has cost the United States 125,000 men in four months, without bringing the army nearer to success, and in the Red river country it has proved a bloody and disastrous failure. No Yankee foot now treads the soil of the great State of Texas, and Arkansas, Louisiana, Mississippi, Alabama, Florida, South Carolina and North Carolina, except along the coast and some of the rivers, are almost equally free from the presence of the foe.

But suppose Grant gets the 300,000 men for whom he frantically calls—200,000 of whom are to be distributed along the railways and rivers, and 100,000 to be placed in the field for offensive operations—what then? Will these 100,000 men enable him to capture Richmond and reach Macon? If they do, will the occupation of those points be followed by the results which he seems to anticipate? Having succeeded thus far, will he not then find it necessary to revert to the original plan and distribute the remaining remnant of his forces throughout the country, in order to hold it? Perhaps he may consider Macon and Richmond as vital points, the holding of which will so far disable us as to render the subjugation of the people and the confiscation of their property an easy matter. If such are his hopes, then they are destined to be disappointed. The truth is, the South, like Milton's archangel, has no vital point, but its instinct with equal life and resistance throughout all its members and parts, and "cannot, but by annihilating, die." The possession by the enemy of Macon, Augusta, or Richmond, would be a serious misfortune, but not an irreparable disaster. In such an event, our lines of communication would be cut and our armies separated from each other, but the parts, still remaining the principle of vitality and the means of subsistence, would continue to fight on as heretofore. When Vicksburg and the Mississippi river passed into the hands of our enemies, the faint hearted believed we were doomed, and yet the loss of the father of waters has been a slight misfortune to us and a doubtful benefit to them; while the Confederate army, on its western side, has not only been able to hold its ground, but has actually driven the invader out of the country.

But if Grant increases his army, we must increase ours also. If he brings 300,000 fresh men into the field, we must also bring at least half of that number. How are we to do this? By calling out every detailed man that can be spared, and placing a disabled soldier in his place, by sending to the field all able-bodied men in the Quartermaster's, Subsistence and Medical Departments of the army whose duties can be performed by men who have lost an arm or a leg in the service, substituting colored for white drivers, and by revoking the exemptions of the greater part of the six or seven thousand civil officers in each one of the States of the Confederacy. There are many men hid away in all the departments, civil and military, both of the Confederate and State Governments; and there is hardly a General or Field Officer in the army, or a major quartermaster or commissary, surgeon, military court, ordnance, or signal officer, who is not protecting or keeping out of the service some relation or friend, contrary to the laws of Congress and the Army Regulations.

Here is the work for the Press. Some of the best friends of the Press do not believe that it has done its duty the last two years as it did in the first two years of the war. Some of its numbers have grown querulous and censorious, and are given to finding fault and sowing the seeds of dissension. They no longer speak of the mistakes of government and commanding officers as one friend should point out to another of his errors. They do not mean to be factious, or to cripple or embarrass those in authority; yet such is the natural effect of their course. By returning to its former patriotic policy; by exercising its ingenuity to find a good motive, rather than assign a bad one or the actions of those from whom it differs; by abstaining alike from unmerited praise as well as undue censure; by circulating with candor and justice, and pointing out the errors of public men with a view to the correction of them rather than a course of this kind, the Press may accomplish incalculable good, add much to the effective strength of our military establishment, and do much to repair the injury which certain well meaning but indiscrete journals in different parts of the country have done to the army of Tennessee. These journals at one time allowed themselves to become the organs of particular officers in that army, and permitted their correspondents in the field to heap fulsome praise upon their favorites, while they pursued others with unsparing pens. In this way the seeds of discord were planted in the army, modest merit was overlooked, the ambition of incompetent men to command the army unduly stimulated, and the General commanding brought into disrepute, and his wisest combinations often frustrated.

I might here reproduce a remark made by Gen. Lee, whose moderation is well known in regard to the class of newspapers referred to; but the remark may not have been intended for the public, and I refrain. I would not have you think, however, that I desire to read any portion of the Press a lecture; on the contrary, I do not feel guiltless myself. It is because I mean to practice my own precepts, and because I am connected with the Press, and interested in its success and the great cause it has done so much to uphold, that I have ventured to speak thus plainly. The Press should be patient and just, and at all times fearless and independent.

P. W. A.

RICHMOND, September 12, 1864 [9-18-64]

It would seem as if the interest in this war were once more about to center in this bloodstained commonwealth. Sherman, it seems, is not yet ready for a forward movement. His line of communication requires attention; his army needs rest; several old regiments whose terms have expired, have to be sent home; Atlanta has to be emptied of its inhabitants; supplies have to be accumulated, and fortifications must be constructed, before he will feel safe to undertake to penetrate further into Georgia. It maybe that some of his brigades will be sent to Grant, who is believed to be preparing for some fresh enterprise against Richmond. He is certainly building a railway from City Point around to Ream's Station on the Weldon road, when completed will be of great aid to the Federal commander, not only in the transportation of supplies during the winter months, when the country roads become almost impassible, but in the rapid movement of troops from one part of his lines to another. It will run behind his intrenchments, believed to be the most elaborate and formidable ever constructed, and will be as safe from Confederate attack as the Richmond and Petersburg road is from Federal assault. The railway completed to Ream's Station, his next movement will probably be directed against the Southside road, which hugs the southern bank of the Appomattox as it passes from Petersburg out to Burkesville. The success of this movement would endanger the Danville connection, the only remaining line of communication between Richmond and the South.

The hundred days men and raw recruits are sent to Grant as fast as they are obtained, and will be used to hold the fortified lines in front of Petersburg, while the veteran troops operate on our wings and engage in fresh enterprises. Can we not adopt a similar policy? Cannot some of the seasoned regiments on the coast of South Carolina be relieved by the spirited reserves of that State? It is hardly possible that any considerable reinforcements can be brought across the Mississippi, the panic discussions and reprehensible disclosures in Georgia having thus far defeated all efforts to that end. We must look nearer home for assistance. It were an easy matter, if the men who are hiding at home and hiding in the army, under the partial protection of the civil, military and medical authorities, were sent to the front to defeat all of Grant's purposes and repossess ourselves of Atlanta.

Meanwhile there is reason to believe that the enemy is preparing a formidable expedition against Wilmington, the only remaining port through which we are enabled to keep up anything like certain communication with the rest of the world. Having closed the ports of Charleston, Savannah, Pensacola, Mobile, and New Orleans he hopes, by turning all his attention to Wilmington, to close that also. It is even doubtful, under this view of the situation, whether any further serious effort will be made against the city of Mobile, though if the enemy could capture that place and ascend the Alabama river to Selma, he would inflict a blow quite as serious as the fall of Atlanta.

The possible loss of the port of Wilmington makes it necessary that no effort should be spared to save the workshops, foundries and manufacturing establishments still in our possession. If we were cut off entirely from the rest of the world, no resource would be left us, but to rely upon ourselves for all we would wear, and for all our munitions of war. If some convalescents from the hospitals and untrained militia could hold the Staunton river bridge, on the Danville railway, against a formidable body of cavalry, why may not the reserves and detailed men of the counties where these foundries and factories are situated, be able, with one or two pieces of artillery previously put in position, to defend them against raiding parties sent out to destroy them?

The letter of Gen. Butler in reply to Col. [Robert] Ould, printed in the morning papers, effectually closes the door upon all hope of a renewal of the exchange of prisoners. The Federal authorities require that our slaves who have been taken with arms in their hands, shall be treated as prisoners of war, and exchanged as they were white men or free blacks; and they do not say, even if that were done, that they will agree to carry out the cartel. Indeed, it is now evident that Mr. Lincoln does not mean, under any circumstances, to release the Confederate prisoners in his hands, since they, if released, could return to the army and add materially to its numbers, while the Federal prisoners in our hands, their terms of service having expired, would return to their homes and not to the field.

P. W. A.

RICHMOND, September 15, 1864 [9-20-64]

Grant shelled Petersburg furiously yesterday, but with the exception of knocking a few ugly holes into the houses, he did no damage; no lives were lost. Our batteries replied vigorously, but with as little effect. Late in the afternoon, the Confederate gunboats and land batteries opened on Butler's canal at Dutch Gap, but with what effect is not known. Deserters say the work progresses slowly, owing to the fatal effects of our shells. The new railway has been finished to the Jerusalem plank road, and is being pushed forward to the Weldon Railroad. We have nothing further from Early. Large quantities of wheat and flour are being forwarded from the Valley of Virginia as fast as they can be prepared for shipment. The corn crop in this State will fall short of the usual yield, as it has done since 1861; nevertheless, with the James river canal and Virginia Central Railway in our possession, we should be able to maintain our position in Richmond for several months, even if the enemy should get possession of the Danville road, of which there is not the least probability. He may cut the Southside and temporarily interrupt the Danville line, but it is utterly impossible to hold the latter with his present force.

The *Examiner* states that Major John C. Maynard, Quartermaster of this post, "having need of a great number of shoes for the negroes employed in his department, determined last Fall to utilize some of the Yankee skill lying idle in the Libby. He fitted up a shoe shop at the Government stable yard on Navy Hill, and procuring some forty odd shoemakers from among the Yankee prisoners at the Libby, who were willing to practice their trade during their captivity, set them to work. These men have made all the shoes and boots required by the Quartermaster's Department in Richmond, and done besides a large amount of work for our army and for citizens. The quality of the work turned out at this establishment is superior to any done in the Confederacy. The prisoners here employed are so delighted with their condition as to be unwilling to be exchanged: they desire nothing better than to live as they are till the end of the war. They are well fed and comfortably lodged and clothed. The report of their happy condition having spread among the prisoners at the Libby and Belle Isle, the artisans of all kinds among them have become anxious to be similarly employed at their respective trades. The guard required for the prisoners thus employed is very small, and the whole experiment has been so successful that Major Maynard has it in contemplation, with the assent of the authorities to enlarge the establishment and increase the number of his workmen to one hundred or more.

The success of this experiment deserves more than a mere passing notice. Since the appearance of Gen. Butler's letter, and the refusal of Gen. Sherman to exchange Confederate prisoners for the men of his own army in our hands, whose time is up, all hope which Federal prisoners may have indulged of being exchanged is extinguished. Why, then, should not the artisans and mechanics among them be put to some employment and required to support themselves? Such employment would promote their health and happiness, would furnish ample compensation for the expense of clothing, feeding and physicking them, and would liberate a large number of detailed men now engaged in skilled labor at home and enable them to go to the field.

This is not all. There is a considerable number of Irishmen among the prisoners in our hands who were inveigled into the Federal army by foul means. Many of them were seduced by the offer of large bounties, only a small part of which was ever allowed to reach their hands; others were drugged or drenched with vile liquor, and their names enrolled at a time when they were in no condition to exercise their free choice. These men, after having been tricked into the service and cheated of their bounty money, are now abandoned by the government they had undertaken to serve. What claim, either in law or morale, has that government upon them now? None whatever. Having first been cheated, and now forsaken, they are absolved from all obligations to serve further the government of the United States. Indeed, they are free to take up arms against a government that has been guilty of the great crime of abandoning its soldiers because their term of service had expired. It is not an unusual thing for prisoners, for far less provocation than this—indeed, without any provocation whatever—to enter the service of their captors. This practice has been common in all ages of the world, and at no period more so than during the wars of Frederick the Great. The prisoners here spoken of have no sympathy for the North and no prejudice against the South. Indeed they ought be our friends, since the Confederates, like the people of their own country, only ask for the right to govern themselves. If they ever believed that the British government was friendly to the South, and that the North would assist them in gaining their own freedom, after having deprived us of ours, their minds must have been disabused of this great error by this time. Earl Russell is now well known to be the cold, implacable enemy of the South, and the fast, fanatical friend of the North; and the United States will hardly send an army across the Atlantic Ocean to rescue Ireland from the thralldom of England, when they steadily refuse to rescue their Irish soldiers, and even their own countrymen, who have fallen into our hands as prisoners of war.

Why, then, should not the Irish prisoners at Andersonville and elsewhere form themselves into a division under Pat Cleburne or Joseph Finegan, or some other good officer, and tender their services to the Confederate Government? Their condition would be greatly improved thereby; they would be better clothed and better fed, and the mortality in battle would not be greater than it is now in prison. At all events, the subject is worthy of their consideration; and under any circumstances their action should be perfectly free and voluntary. If they have not been treated as well while in prison as they could desire, the fault has not been wholly ours. The public enemy by closing our ports and ravaging and devastating our country, deprived us of the means of taking such care both of our own soldiers and the unfortunate prisoners in our hands, as we would wish to do under more auspicious circumstances.

The iron-clad ram *Alexandria* has put to sea, followed by two vessels, one laden with her armament and the other with her ammunition. It is believed that she will be heard from in due time and in the right quarter. It is not known how she got out, the British government having done all it could to prevent her sailing.

A vessel belonging to the well-known Charleston house of John Fraser & Co., has just arrived at Wilmington with an important cargo.

The remains of Gen. Morgan, expected here this afternoon, will be received by the Kentuckians in town and deposited in a vault in Hollywood Cemetery until the war shall be closed, when they will be taken to his native State for final internment.

P. W. A.

RICHMOND, September 18, 1864 [9-24-64]

Grant has shown some activity within the last few days. On the 15th, the date of my last letter, he threw forward a considerate force both on his extreme right and left. The force on his right, near Deep Bottom, was easily driven back. On his left, however, he was somewhat, more successful, having captured forty or fifty men on our picket line, and advanced his own picket line a few hundred yards further to the left. Early the following day, the 16th, Gen. Lee made a reconnaissance in force, in order to ascertain the position and strength of the enemy, during which he took ninety prisoners. Finding the enemy in heavy force and strongly entrenched he withdrew his troops, but not until after they had driven in the Federal pickets along his front.

About the same time, Hampton, with a detachment of cavalry, turned Grant's left wing and passed around to his rear, where he captured three hundred prisoners, twenty-five hundred head of beef cattle, and a large number of wagons, horses, ambulances, &c. On his return, [David] Gregg, of the Federal cavalry, was sent out to intercept and cut him off; but instead of doing that, he got badly beaten by Hampton, who brought off his spoils without further molestation. His own loss was slight, not exceeding fifty, including killed, wounded and missing.

Yesterday, the two armies were quiet. To-day I hear some firing down the river, and the railway trains have been drawn out on the track ready to be sent to Petersburg at the first touch of the electric wire. It is now 5 p. m. , and no movement has occurred as far as is known here.

McClellan's letter of acceptance is just what might have been expected from him. With his antecedents, he could be nothing else than an Union man. Since he has declined the role of a Peace candidate, the political necessity of further military success on the part of Mr. Lincoln no longer exists. They are both war candidates. But Grant is an ambitious, energetic man. He has his own part to perform, and it is not likely that his restless nature will allow him to remain idle if he should think he saw an opportunity to strike an effective blow. In the contest, between his patron, Mr. Lincoln, and his rival, Gen. McClellan, the people here are very much in the condition of the woman in the fight between her husband and the bear; they do not care much which whips. Should the Chicago nominee be elected, of which there is not much prospect, he could not carry on the war, since he would have the support of the Peace men, who oppose any further prosecution of the war, nor of the Republicans except upon condition that he adopted, as he would put their policy of abolition and confiscation. The election of Mr. Lincoln, on the contrary, will, it is believed in very high circles here, bring about a bloody collision at a distant day between the Peace men and the War men, leading eventually to the withdrawal of the Northwestern States from the Federal Union.

In the event of the election of either, therefore, our duty is to continue to resist both until our independence has been acknowledged.

The New York *Herald* has lit upon "A New Plan for Peace—How to Divide the South." This new plan has the sanction also of General McClellan, and consists in opening negotiations with the States separately, for the purpose of detaching them from the Confederacy. The *Herald* says, "Let us divide the Confederacy, and split up the rebel armies; by negotiating separately with the seceded States." This plan of dealing separately with the States has worked well for the abolitionists in Kentucky, Missouri, and Maryland—too well, indeed, that it is hoped no other Southern State plunge into the gulf where they are all wailing and gnashing their teeth. As now we stand shoulder to shoulder, our elbows touching those of our neighbor, we are invincible. The moment we attempt to act alone, we shall sink, never to rise again. Heaven help the State that flies to the enemy for safety; the lamb may as well seek the protection of the wolf.

P. W. A.

RICHMOND, VA., September 24th, 1864 [9-28-64]

The Confederate arms have met with a fresh disaster in the Valley of Virginia. After his defeat at Winchester on the 19th, Early retreated up the Valley to Fisher's Hill, a strong position a short distance above Strasburg, and which, it was supposed that he would be able to hold. Not so, however. On the 22nd, Sheridan assaulted him in this strong position, turned his left, which soon gave way, followed by the entire line. We lost twelve pieces of artillery, though but few men. Such is Early's official report to Gen. Lee. The Confederates were retiring further up the Valley towards Staunton.

Do you ask for an explanation of these rapidly occurring disasters in a portion of the State where the Confederates, until the 19th, never suffered a defeat? It is simple and easily given: We have two enemies to contend with in the Valley, one of whom has never been beaten since Noah drank too much wine and lay in his tent. These enemies are the Federal army and John Barley Corn. Sheridan has been largely reinforced, and the Valley is running with apple brandy. Here is the key to our reverses. Officers of high positions—yes, of very high positions—have, to use an honored English word, been drunk—too drunk to command themselves, much less an army, a division, a brigade, or a regiment. And, where officers in high command are in the habit of drinking to excess, we may be sure their pernicious example will be followed by those lower grades.

Shall I call names? Not now. The names are known to the authorities, and shall be to the country, unless there be a speedy reformation. Let us wait a little to see whether the guilty parties will not reform their habits, and especially whether the President, Secretary of War, Gen. Lee and Gen. Bragg will take hold of those men and punish them as they deserve. Just think of a drunken man in command of a body of men in battle?

A drunken driver of a stage coach in a dark night over a mountain road, a drunken conductor of a railway train on a crooked line and out of time, and a drunken pilot in charge of a ship at sea in a furious tempest—these are horrible things, even to suppose or think of. But they are venial sins, insignificant faults, compared with a drunken general commanding an army, or any part of an army, fighting for liberty. There is no punishment too great for such men—no disgrace too deep to be affixed to their names forever. Will the authorities lay their hands upon them, punish them, cashier them, scourge them out of the service? We shall see.

But there are other unpleasant truths connected with the army in the Valley which require notice. That army comprises some of the finest divisions in the Army of Northern Virginia—veteran troops inured to hardship, to self-denial and battle. They knew not what it was to turn their backs upon an armed foe, and, what is equally gratifying, they knew as little of self-indulgence. They went into Maryland; they went near enough to Washington to throw shells into its streets. They tasted many good things beyond the Potomac; they burnt Chambersburg in Pennsylvania, and brought back many spoils with them. This excursion into the rich country of the enemy, the license allowed to officers and men, and the plunder that was secured, together with the free use of liquor since their return have borne their natural result. Some of this fruit was gathered by the enemy at Winchester and Fisher's Hill.

The cavalry forces that had been operating in the Valley, and flitting hither and thither along the Potomac and Shenandoah, were already demoralized, and, since their last visit to Maryland, they have been utterly worthless. They were in the habit of robbing friend and foe alike. They have been known to strip Virginia women of all they had—widows, whose sons were away in our army—and then to burn their houses. At Hancock, in Western Maryland, they stopped a minister of the gospel in the street, on the Sabbath day, and made him stand and deliver his watch and money. These monstrous truths are stated in the official report of the officers commanding a part of these cavalry forces, and which I have read. Do you wonder then that McCausland's and Bradley Johnson's commands, just returned from such an expedition and loaded down with plunder, should have been disgracefully surprised and dispersed as they were some weeks ago near Moorfield?

Rapine and pillage will ruin a Southern army, while they may not injure a Northern army. The men who make up the Federal armies are in the habit, even in peace times, of living by their wits; and they will march further, endure more and fight harder for personal spoils and promised homesteads, than they will for liberty or glory. Licenses to steal and burn and rob do not demoralize them, nor does the free use of ardent spirits have the same pernicious effect upon them as upon us. They will drink as much as is good for them and sell the balance, whereas the Southern man would drink it all, he and his friends. The material of our army being superior the troop cannot engage in such practices without suffering greater demoralization than the enemy. Indeed, there is no surer way of destroying a Confederate army than to march it into the enemy's country and allow the men to help themselves to whatever they want. And yet there are high officers and influential newspapers in the South who are constantly urging the policy of sending Lee's army across the Potomac with license to burn towns and plunder the inhabitants to their heart's content!

It is now believed that Grant has sent considerable reinforcements to Sheridan, and that a few regiments may have reached him from the Mississippi, but none from Sherman's army. It is known that only a small part of Grant's cavalry is now in front of Petersburg. Indeed, we have intelligence that he has only seven regiments of cavalry with him whereas a few weeks ago he had over thirty. The absent regiments, with a considerable body of infantry, it is now understood, have been sent around to the Valley. In order to effect this transfer of troops with secrecy, an order was issued two or three weeks ago by Grant for the arrest of all male citizens living within five miles of James river. This barbarous order has been carried out in most instances at a late hour at night, and the men and boys arrested have been sent to Fortress Monroe and points further North.

Sheridan either strikes for Gordonsville or Lynchburg—the latter probably. Should Lee weaken his army by sending reinforcements to Early, then Grant will make a bold push for the Danville road. With his army upon that, the last lines of communications, he would have some reason for saying he had his "hands upon the throat of the rebellion." In making this effort, he will endeavor to hold his works at Petersburg with his new recruits.

Meanwhile Lee is not idle.

P. W. A.

RICHMOND, VA., September 28, 1864 [10-3-64]

The Federal cavalry did not enter Staunton so soon by a few hours as was stated in my last letter; nor had Early reached Waynesboro' at the foot of the western slope of the Blue Ridge.

The precise position of Early's forces is not known at this time, but it is believed that they are on this side of the Blue Ridge and not far from Charlottesville. He may have sent a detachment to the railway tunnel, and may have left some of his cavalry at Brown's Gap, but the main body of his army, it is believed, is on the east side of the mountains.

Early has been reinforced by one of the best divisions [Kershaw's] in Virginia, and will soon be in condition to give battle to the enemy. Ordnance stores, guns to replace those lost at Winchester and Fisher's Hill, and Commissary supplies have been sent to him. His men are now, or soon will be, well in hand, and ready to dispute the further progress of the Federal army towards Lynchburg. Sheridan in the meantime, doubtless, is not idle. His dead have to be buried, his wounded sent to the rear, his men and animals fed, his ordnance trains replenished, and his forces rested and reorganized; and to do all these things requires more time than persons inexperienced in military affairs are aware of. The clash of arms will soon be heard again in the mountains, however; and then, especially if Sheridan be successful, we may look for Grant's last great movement against Richmond. For the present Grant is quiet, though active; whilst that pink of a soldier, Butler the Beast, "keeps pegging away" at his canal at Dutch Gap.

Their industry and enterprise are alike creditable to themselves and worthy of our imitation. We, being the weaker party in numbers, should have been the first to avail ourselves of defensive works and mechanical and scientific appliances; but instead of this being the case, the enemy, notwithstanding he largely outnumbers us, was the only party who employed the spade during the first three years of the war. Two years ago it was the fashion to laugh at McClellan and his army for the use they made of the spade. But we have got over all that now, and find the spade almost as good a weapon as the musket. This is the first campaign the Army of Northern Virginia ever fought behind breastworks, though not the first time it ever prepared such defenses. Just now it is fashionable to laugh at Butler's canal.

P. W. A.

RICHMOND, September 30, 1864 [10-4-64]

Late Wednesday afternoon, the 28th, the enemy opened fire on our right at Petersburg, and at length along the entire line around to the north side of the James. The fire was kept up until a late hour, and at some points it continued all night. An assault was expected yesterday morning, if not a formidable attempt to get possession of the Southside railroad. But when morning came it brought perfect quiet along the lines on the south side of the river; not so, however, on the north side. The enemy had availed himself of the darkness the preceding night to cross over a heavy column, with which, at a very early hour yesterday morning, he proceeded to attack the small force placed in observation in that quarter. He soon drove in our pickets, carried our outer line, held by a handful of men, and assaulted and took a small earthwork known as Fort Harrison, capturing at the same time a few prisoners and guns. I am unable to locate Fort Harrison, it having been erected quite recently. Gregg's Texan and Benning's Georgian brigades (the latter commanded by Col. [Dudley] DuBose) behaved very well, but found it necessary to retire to the next or intermediate line, where they received the second assault of the enemy, who attempted to carry Fort Gilmer, a small work similar to that of Fort Harrison, which they continue to hold. We took three or four hundred prisoners, including several negroes, and inflicted severe punishment upon the foe. Some negroes escaped from the enemy, who had forced them into the ranks, and came in and delivered themselves up, asking only that they might be sent home to their masters.

I hear artillery firing down the river as I write, 12 m. Whether it proceeds from an attempt on our part to shell the enemy out of Fort Harrison, or indicates a fresh move by Gen. Grant, I have no means of deciding. It is not believed that the Federal commander contemplates an advance on Richmond by the north side. He tried that experiment ineffectually on the 3rd of June, at Cold Harbor. It is more probable that he desires to divert Gen. Lee's attention from Petersburg and the southside rail way; or it may be he wishes to prevent his sending reinforcements to Early. A few days, perhaps a few hours, will decide.

As soon as it was known yesterday morning that the enemy was advancing up the left bank of the river Gen. Bragg issued orders to impress every able bodied man in the city between the ages of sixteen and fifty-five, to organize and arm them and sent them immediately out to the lines. The orders were carried into execution with great promptitude by Major Gen. [James] Kemper, and before night four thousand men were marched out to the scene of operations. Officers and men on furlough, citizens visiting the city on business, exempts and detailed men, clerks in the Departments, printers, newspaper men, Express men—all were required to take up arms for the defense of the capital. It is believed that three or four thousand more men will be obtained today. Only one of the newspaper offices—the *Whig*—was able to publish a paper this morning. By the way, why are not females employed in these offices? They can do nearly all the work now performed by men, and their employment would insure the certain and regular publication of the journals upon which they might be engaged.

These vigorous measures will doubtless bring down much censure upon the head of Gen. Bragg. It is fashionable in many parts of the country, and especially in Virginia, to deny him credit for the good that he does, and hold him responsible for the errors of others. But fortunately he is a cast-iron sort of man who is not afraid to do his duty. Just now he is striking at the glaring abuses in the Conscript Bureau and other branches of the service, and if he were properly supported, he would cut up by the roots many of the wrongs known to exist in almost every department of the Government. The moment he commences a reform, however, the parties smoked out of their hiding places rush into print or apply to a Congressmen or bureau officer; and thus much of the good he might do is defeated. Of course, the unthinking multitude are ready to believe everything said against him. There are thousands of men all over the country, and even many intelligent journalists, who even now believe that General Bragg's late visit to Atlanta led to the removal of Gen. Johnston; whereas, it is as well known as anything can be, that, so far from favoring the removal of that officer, he advised against it.

There is room for many reforms in every State in the Confederacy, and no where more than Virginia, where there is a very loose administration of the acts of Congress affecting our military establishment. In proof of this, I need only recapitulate some of the main points set forth in a "report," now before me "of the Thirteenth Congressional (Abingdon) District," as follows:

Whole number of active class and reserve class enrolled since 1st of January to the 31st of August of the present year, not including details in the Nitre and Mining Bureau, 3,233. Of this number 135 were exempt for light duty; 816 were exempted by the Medical Board, 1 was a Confederate officer; 39 were State officers; 53 were ministers of the gospel; 4 editors; 9 newspaper employees; 2 apothecaries; 7 overseers and agriculturists; 498 detailed farmers; 692 detailed mechanics, &c.; 85 detailed in conscript department; 30 detailed in quartermaster's department, 18 detailed in commissary department, and 560 in the Nitre and Mining Bureau! leaving only 433 who were sent to the army!

What a showing we have here! Out of 3,233 men enrolled, only 433 sent to the army. The reports are but little less unfavorable from other districts and from other States. The duties performed by many of these details can be just as well discharged by disabled soldiers and men beyond the military age. And yet how few disabled soldiers and men beyond the military age do we find performing these services for Government. With the exception of the Horse Infirmary in Georgia, and the guards at the depots and on the trains of a few of the railways, I have seldom seen a disabled soldier filling any of the stations or offices alluded to in the foregoing report. Why is this? If rigid reforms are not instituted, the army cannot be reinforced; and if the army is not reinforced, we are done for, and there is an end of it. Money and favor may secure exemptions from military service, but they will not secure liberty and independence. It is for the authorities and the people to choose which they will have.

P. W. A.

RICHMOND, VA., October 14, 1864 [10-19-64]

At 7 o'clock yesterday morning the enemy endeavored to advance between the Darbytown and Charles City roads below Richmond, but was repulsed in every attempt by Fields' division. Repeated attempts were made between 7 in the morning and four in the afternoon, to break through our lines, both by infantry and cavalry, but without success. The most strenuous effort was made about 4 p.m., after which the enemy withdrew, "leaving many dead," according to Gen. Lee's official dispatch. The same dispatch states that our loss is very slight, including, however, Maj. Willis Jones of Kentucky, the efficient Adjutant General of [C. W.] Fields' Division, who fell early in the action.

It is not believed that the enemy expected to gain any very important advantage by this movement. It was probably only a preliminary maneuver, and the real assault will follow hereafter, and it may be very soon. Indeed, it is now believed that Grant's last grand effort will be made within the next ten days—anyhow in time for the Presidential election the first week in November. Reinforcements of new recruits and convalescents from the hospitals continue to reach him, and transports laden with troops and supplies pass up and down the river daily and nightly. The Federal authorities are exerting themselves to the uttermost to forward the reinforcements called for by Grant, and without which, as was stated in my last letter, he is reported to have said that he would have to let go his hold here. Our last advices from beyond the Potomac state that he is expected to be reinforced by 40,000 men by the 25th of this month. The new troops will doubtless be placed behind the entrenchments, so as to give the veteran commands wider and freer range to operate against our flanks. It is not improbable that the figures here given have been exaggerated, since it is not unlikely that a portion of the reinforcements; originally designed for Grant, will be diverted to Georgia and Missouri, where there is more call for them at this time, than there is in Virginia.

The New York *Herald* states that "the total number of volunteers called for" by the United States Government since the beginning of the war "has been 3,040,637 for volunteer army; in regular army, December 1863, 43,332; in navy, July 1, 1863, 34,000. Total 3,113,969." Omitting from these figures all those who could possibly have been counted twice up to August 1, 1864—say 42,034—under first call for three years' men, and 300,000 nine months' men furnished under call of August 4, 1862, there would still remain, according to the calculation of the *Herald*, 2,811,935 as the number of men called for to put down "the rebellion." The immense force we have withstood for now nearly four years, and with a measure of success rarely equaled, and never exceeded, in any age or country. The enemy fully expected to be able, by mere force of numbers, to crush us during the campaigns now drawing to a close, but having failed to do so, he is now seeking, at the end of the bloodiest and most furious campaign of modern times, to recruit his wasted ranks by a large force hastily collected, and with one last desperate blow to put an end to the war.

But suppose we maintain our ground here and elsewhere, as we hope to do, and Mr. Lincoln should be re-elected, as he will be, and should make another attempt to bring a large army into the field, what then? Why, we must meet him in the future as we have met him in the past. But where are the men to come from? It has been suggested that we have them ready to our hands. If the worst comes to the worst, and no other resort is left us, neither the world nor our enemies can complain if we do as the latter have done, call upon the Negro.

This subject is attracting a good deal of attention at the capital and in the army, and but few persons are found who do not approve of the employment of the negro upon the happening of the contingency here alluded to. The Federal armies persist in enticing away all able bodied negroes within reach of their lines, and in forcing them to take up arms against us; and the question arises, whether it were not better that these blacks should remain here and help us fight our enemies, than join our enemies and help them fight us? The Southern slave will make a better soldier than the free negro of the North, because he is more accustomed to obedience and the restraints of discipline. If he fly to the enemy and survive the war, he can but obtain his freedom, and this he can and should obtain here, if he should be put in the army, and conduct himself as a good solider.

It is not believed that Mr. Lincoln will be able to raise another great army, and that consequently it will not become necessary for us to put the negro in the field as a soldier; but one thing is certain beyond all doubt, to wit, if we are subjugated or consent to a reconstruction of the Union under Mr. Lincoln, we will be required to give up the negro. If he is to become a freeman, therefore, and the necessity to use him as a soldier should arise, why not let him have his freedom by fighting our enemies instead of ourselves, and at the same time assist us in gaining our own freedom as well. The employment of the negro would enable the Government to dispense with the services of persons under eighteen years of age and over forty-five, and would remove the pressure from detailed men whose skill and services may be found advantageous to the army.

P. W. A.

RICHMOND, October 18, 1864 [10-25-64]

The prevailing quiet continues unbroken along the line in front of Richmond, and Petersburg. The enemy is hard at work, and so are we; but no new move has been made since the date of my last letter. Butler continues "pegging away" at his canal, and in order to facilitate his work, and especially to gratify his satanic passion, he has placed one hundred and ten Confederate prisoners "into the canal at Dutch Gap and put them at hard labor," and informs Col. Ould that he "shall continue to add to their number until this practice is stopped." He pretends that he has received information that we have employed a like number "of United States colored soldiers in the trenches near Fort Gilmer," this is the "practice" to which he alludes, and which he says must be stopped, or he will place the Confederate prisoners in the canal, where they will be exposed to the fire of our guns. What a "beast" he is!

The last flag of truce boat brought up over one hundred sick and wounded Confederate officers, who were exchanged only because they would never be able to render further service in the field. Most of them have been confined for several months. Captain [W. H.] Hatch of the Exchange Bureau, when he went down the river to receive them, took with him a band of music. When the prisoners reached the bluff preparatory to embarking for Richmond, the band struck up "Home, sweet Home"; whereupon they took off their hats and limped and hobbled on board the steamer with uncovered heads and streaming eyes. They had "faced the cannon's mouth," and encountered unmoved the shock of battle; but the sight of the flag under which they had fought, the thought of home, and the outstretched arms that waited to embrace them, were more than these pale and mutilated heroes could bear, and their hearts melted in tears. But the tears were soon succeeded by smiles, as the band commenced to play Dixie and the boat headed up stream, and at length their joy, growing and swelling, burst forth in cheers that would have done no discredit to a Confederate regiment charging in battle. When they reached the city, they were escorted up Main street by a large concourse of people, and welcomed by many a waving handkerchief. Hard must be the heart that would withhold the tribute of a tear and hearty welcome to those lame and halting veterans, henceforth the pride of a grateful country.

These men come back to us as firm, as brave, and as confident as when they first buckled on the sword. They bring cheering news also from the officers and men who still languish in northern prisons. They say with one voice, "fight on, never give up, better all die freemen than all live as slaves, and never yield a principle for our sakes." They desire to return to their homes, but rather than the government should sacrifice an important principle to procure their release, they are willing to remain and suffer where they are until the end of the war. How noble and self-sacrificing is their conduct! And how it should shame those people at home, who, because the enemy has gained some advantages and now threatens their homes, are ready to give up all as lost. These battle-scarred heroes have met our foes on the field and felt their devilish malice and ingenuity in prison—they have drained the cup of sorrow and suffering to the bottom; and yet their brave spirits do not quail; while others, far removed from danger, cry peace! peace! and are ready to bow the neck to the Puritan, the worst tyrant that ever cursed the earth.

Gen. Bragg has been ordered to Wilmington to take charge of the defenses at that place. The enemy are now preparing a formidable expedition at Fortress Monroe, the rendezvous of the vessels and force which are to engage in it. It is not supposed that the enemy will attempt to capture Wilmington, but will rather seek to isolate and possess himself of the forts at the mouth of the river, and thus close the port.

P. W. A.

RICHMOND, October 24, 1864 [10-31-64]

As you have already been advised, Confederate arms have suffered a fresh disaster in the Valley of the Shenandoah. The disaster was not so great as it was first represented however, while the loss of the enemy, though victorious, was far heavier, especially in officers and men, than ours was.

Officers who have arrived here since the battle, report that on the 18th our army lay at Fishers's hill near Strasburg, in front of the Eighth and Nineteenth Federal corps, which held a strong position on the north bank of Cedar Creek. The enemy's line extended across the Valley turnpike, and was strongly entrenched on the left, the works on the right, not having been completed. The Sixth corps was held in reserve between Middletown and Newtown, and the cavalry was posted still further to the rear. Early, smarting, it is supposed, under his recent defeats, determined to attack the enemy before daylight, on the morning of the 19th, and, if possible, to surprise him and capture his camp. Accordingly, his whole force was put in motion on the night of the 18th, and moved across Cedar Creek, when it was divided into two columns, the larger of which passed around to the right flank for the purpose of falling on the enemy's left flank, and the smaller turned to the left with a view to engaging his right. The column moving to the right had to take a circuitous route and pass through a narrow defile in a spur of the mountain, where two men could not march abreast. The plan was to make a simultaneous assault upon both wings of the enemy. Owing to the difficulty in passing the defile, the right column did not get in position as soon as the left, and consequently the assault on the left was delivered sooner than on the right by about twenty minutes; otherwise, it is believed our captures in prisoners would have been larger.

Our troops were all night getting into position and were much jaded when the battle commenced. The assault, nevertheless, was made with vigor, and the enemy, taken completely by surprise, were driven back with heavy loss upon Middletown. Two divisions fled without firing a gun, and eighteen loaded pieces of artillery fell into our hands, the cannoniers being too badly frightened or too hard pressed to discharge them. The Federal camp, rich with the fatal spoils, was taken, and the road and fields from the creek back to Middletown were filled with wagons, small arms, knapsacks and other articles abandoned by the enemy in his flight. Over fourteen hundred prisoners fell into our hands, and have since been safely lodged in the Libby prison in Richmond.

Unfortunately at Cedar Creek, as at Shiloh, there were many Achans among the victorious Confederates, who, the moment the enemy fled, went to straggling and plundering. The delay thus produced gave Sheridan, who had just reached Winchester on his return from Washington time to reach the field and bring up the Sixth corps. When, before, the Confederates, minus the stragglers and plunderers, advanced about 2 p.m., they found the enemy reinforced by the cavalry and the Sixth corps, and far superior to themselves in numbers, in position and ready to receive them. Prudence would have justified a cessation of battle at this point on the part of Gen. Early, but his recollection of past disasters, and his desire to render his victory decisive, and perhaps something else, urged him on to a renewal of the fight. The result was, he was repulsed when the Federal horse attacking his flanks, compelled his whole line to give way in confusion. He was pursued only to Cedar Creek and that far only by cavalry, the enemy's infantry too badly punished to take further part in the action. The prisoners were brought off safely, but the eighteen captured guns, and thirty of our own, with the enemy's camp, and nearly all of our killed and wounded, fell into the hands of the victors. Among the mortally wounded, was Maj. Gen. Ramseur of North Carolina, who fell into the hands of the enemy and has since died.

It is impossible to say what our loss was, but there is reason to fear it will reach quite two thousand. Northern writers admit a loss on their part of five thousand men. As Sheridan galloped forward to Middletown, he found the turnpike filled with wounded men and stragglers, and flying wagons and ambulances. He acknowledges, too, in his official dispatch, that his "left was turned and driven in confusion" at Cedar Creek, and adds—"in fact, most of the line was driven in confusion."

Early has retired thirty miles to New Market, and Sheridan now occupies Strasburg. There is a rumor that the former has been relieved of his command, and Breckinridge and Gordon has been appointed to succeed him. Gordon is regarded as the most promising young officer in the Army of Northern Virginia, and what is far better, he is a temperate man.

Col. [Leigh Richmond] Terrell, of the Forty-seventh Alabama, Law's Brigade, wounded on the 14th, below Richmond, died here on the 21st, and was buried yesterday with military and Masonic honors from St. Paul's Church. The most touching part of the procession that followed the deceased soldier to the grave was his charger, whose position was just behind the hearse. It was doubtless my imagination, but he looked as if he had lost his best friend, and that he too was a mourner.

P. W. A.

Official casualties for the battle of Cedar Creek: Federals, 644 killed, 3,420 wounded, and 1,591 missing for 5,665; Confederate estimates, 320 killed, 1,540 wounded, 1,050 missing for 2,910.

RICHMOND, October 27, 1864 [11-1-64]

The facts in regard to the late extraordinary battle at Strasburg are coming to light. The first accounts, as well as my letter written as late as the 24th, when, as was believed, we had obtained a full understanding of the affair, contained many errors. Even the press of this State finds it necessary to lift their voices against the bad management in the Valley, not withstanding the commander of the army there is a Virginian. It is true an article appeared in the Richmond *Enquirer* yesterday, prepared at the instance of certain friends of Gen. Early, in which an effort was made to defend him against the charge of drunkenness, contained in a late letter of mine and leveled at nameless officers high in command. It is admitted that he drinks, but it is claimed that he does not drink to excess, as if drinking at all, except for medical purposes, were not an excess on the part of an officer charged with the lives and fortunes of an army. But so rapidly has the evidence of Gen. Early's unfitness for a separate command accumulated, that the *Enquirer* of today is forced to confess that his campaign has proven a failure from the beginning to the end, and to call loudly and indignantly for his removal. Other journals in this State indulge in like plainness of speech, while some, as might have been expected, are quite as earnest in his defense.

Indeed, the danger now is that the press may go too far, and do Gen. Early injustice denying him the merits which he unquestionably possesses. We have but few as good divisional commanders, as his gallant services under Lee and Jackson abundantly demonstrate. Like many of the finest officers under Frederick the Great and Napoleon, however, when entrusted with separate commands and forced to rely upon their own judgments, he has invariably failed when acting alone. This was true at the battle of Chancellorsville, where he was left to command the forces at Fredericksburg; at Lynchburg, last summer, where he allowed Hunter to escape; in his failure to capture Washington; at the battle of Winchester, where he scattered his forces at a time when the enemy was concentrating against him; at Fisher's Hill a few days after; and again on the 19th inst., at Strasburg, where, by stopping the pursuit, he gave the enemy time to recover from his panic and wrench from him what a little more vigor would have made one of the most brilliant victories of modern times.

Writers and persons just from the Valley state that the plan of the late battle was Gordon's, and a most sensible and brilliant plan it was. It appears that on the night of the 18th, Gordon, commanding his own, Ramseur's and Pegram's divisions, moved to the right by a circuitous route a distance of seven miles, for the purpose of surprising the enemy in his camp. Rosser went to the left with his cavalry, with instructions to fall upon the enemy's right flank. Kershaw's and [Gabriel C.] Wharton's divisions, acting under the immediate orders of Gen. Early, were to attack in front, carrying the enemy's works, capture his guns and turn them upon his flying columns. All the accounts agree in giving Gordon great credit, not only for the plan of the battle, but for the superb manner in which he handled his corps; but also appears that every part of the army acted with great gallantry, that the combined movement was a perfect success, and that the enemy was driven in wild confusion from his camp, and back some four miles through Middletown.

But it was here that the fatal error was committed. Early now took command of all the forces, but instead of taking advantage of the panic and confusion among the enemy, and pressing the pursuit, he halted his troops, reformed his lines, and attempted to call in the men who had straggled. Here he waited four or five precious hours, when if vigorously employed after the fashion of Stonewall Jackson, would have secured such a victory as the Valley of the Shenandoah has never witnessed. Meanwhile, his men, attracted by the spoils of the enemy's camp, straggled worse than ever; so that at the expiration of the time thus lost he had fewer men in hand than at the beginning. Two Federal corps—the Eighth and Nineteenth—had been driven in confusion from the field, and the Sixth corps, held in reserve, was ready to give way when the pursuit was stopped. Sheridan, who had now come up, threw the last named corps across the line of pursuit, got together as many men of the Eighth and Nineteenth corps as possible, and finding that Early was not disposed to continue the conflict, and suspecting doubtless that our troops were plundering his camp, he assumed the offensive, when the senseless cry "we are flanked, we are flanked," was raised, our line began to undulate and give way, and finally broke in utter confusion. The enemy, amazed at our conduct, and unable to understand it, stood stock still for sometime, and thus gave the Confederates time to recross Cedar Creek. It was after they had crossed this stream, that a handful of Federal cavalry dashed forward through an opening, and produced such dismay that about forty cannon, and many wagons and ambulances filled with wounded fell into their hands, without an effort being made to prevent it. Rosser covered the retreat on his part of the field with much judgment. The men had lost confidence in Early, and this, with the cry that they were flanked, caused the stampede. Gordon had massed thirty more pieces of artillery at Middletown, and was just getting ready to open upon the Sixth corps, when Early took command and stopped the fight.

Gen. Early, in an order, which was published here before it was read to the army, lays all the blame upon his men; if they had not abandoned their posts to plunder the camps of the foe all would have gone well. This is probably true; but it is equally true that if he had not recalled his troops from the pursuit, they would have won a glorious victory. A lack of discipline led to demoralization, and a lack of generalship, lost the victory already within his grasp. It is reported that Gen. Lee opposes the removal of Early, and if this be so, there will be no change in the command of the Army of the Valley.

P. W. A.

RICHMOND, October 28, 1864 [11-3-64]

Intelligence had been received here that the enemy would yesterday attempt to get possession of the Southside railway west of Petersburg, and would at the same time attack the works by which the water approaches to Wilmington are guarded. Up to this hour we have heard nothing from Wilmington confirmatory of the information alluded to, though we know that a formidable movement was made against the Southside railroad, which happily failed.

As you were advised by my letter of yesterday, Grant put both wings of his army in motion at an early hour in the morning. His left wing pushed across Rowanty creek below Burgess' mills, and occupied the Boydtown plank road at the mills where it crosses the creek [Hatcher's Run], having driven our cavalry back. In the afternoon Gen. Heth attacked, and at first drove the enemy, but found them too strong a force, and at length desisted. Afterwards, the enemy attacked Heth, and endeavored to cut their way through to the railroad, but were heavily repulsed, leaving some colors and prisoners in our hands. They still hold the plank road at Burgess' mills, however. The enemy is thus brought somewhat nearer to the Southside road, though at a point further removed from Petersburg. We have no report of the probable loss on either side.

Simultaneously, with his advance on the south side of the James, the enemy moved out on the north side, and made an attempt to turn our extreme left. Two attacks upon our lines were made; one to the left of Fort Gilmer, between the Henrico county Poor House and the Charles City road, and the other further north on the Williamsburg road. Both attacks were repulsed and between six and seven hundred prisoners and four stands of colors taken. Our own loss did not exceed twenty.

The attack on the Williamsburg road was an attempt to completely turn our left. General Longstreet penetrated the enemy's design, and despatched Brig. Gen. [Martin] Garey, with his cavalry and some light artillery, to hold the works in that quarter until he could send forward an infantry force. There was a ruse as to which party should reach the threatened point first, brave, however, and Garey arrived on the ground in time to get his troopers and artillery in position. With this force he held the lines until reinforcements came up, soon after which there the enemy moved forward in heavy masses and with a loud yell against our works. The Confederates reserved their fire until they got within short range, when they poured a terrific volley of grape, canister and minie balls into the faces of the advancing foe, who, reeling and staggering back, finally broke in wild confusion, leaving many dead and wounded on the ground. So great was the impulse of the charge, however, that the head of the assaulting column was carried forward to the ditch on the outside of our entrenchments, and leaping into it, the men immediately threw down their arms as a token of surrender. Nearly a hundred of them were killed and wounded in the ditch before their intention was understood and the fire stopped. Over five hundred prisoners and four stands of colors were taken at this point. The prisoners were brought to town last night by Major [John W.] Fairfax, of Longstreet's staff, and lodged in the Libby.

The Federal officers made two attempts subsequently to bring their men up to this work, but failed; after which the fighting ceased along the whole line, and has not since been renewed. It commenced to rain about noon yesterday, and continued until 9 o'clock last night, accompanied by high winds which still prevail. The condition of the weather, and the consequent difficulty of moving artillery may have had some effect in discouraging the enemy from further operations today, though it is now bright and clear.

P. W. A.

RICHMOND, October 29, 1864 [11-3-64]

The details as they come in leave no doubt as to Grant made his grand assault on Thursday, the 27th. He may make another effort between this and the day of the Presidential election; but that he took his measures and prepared his plans with a view to the speedy capture of Richmond or the Southside Railway, or both of them, is now manifest to the dullest apprehension. As it is, he took nothing by his last move; on the contrary, his defeat was complete at all points, on the right, on the left and in the center. The importance and extent of our victory do not appear so much from Gen. Lee's official report, as from trustworthy persons who were present and participated in the battle. Indeed, Gen. Lee has an inveterate habit of understating the losses of his adversary and of refining away his own victories; whereas it is the practice of the enemy to magnify his triumphs, and not unfrequently to claim a victory where he has suffered a defeat. The effect of these diverse policies is as different as the policies themselves; in the one case, the enemy is encouraged and the war spirit stimulated; in the other, neither our army nor our people receive the encouragement which should be derived from our success. The re-publication here of the war bulletins of the enemy even, have a bad effect, notwithstanding he is known to be a great economist of truth, and in many instances to set up claims which are preposterous as they are unfounded. If the positions of the two armies had been reversed, and we had been the assaulting, and the enemy the assaulted party, the whole North would be ringing with the paeans of victory.

It now seems that our success beyond Petersburg was quite as complete as it was below Richmond. The enemy got possession of the Boydton plank road at Burgess' mills, on Rowanty Creek [Hatcher's Run], when Mahone moved against him in the rear. Though he was not then dislodged, Mahone took over four hundred prisoners, three stands of colors, and six pieces of artillery. The latter could not be brought off, however, the enemy having possession of the bridge over the Creek. In the attack subsequently made by the enemy, Mahone broke three lines of battle, and inflicted a heavy loss upon the foe, who retired during the night from the plank road, leaving many of his wounded and between two and three hundred dead on the field. Including those made on the north side, quite a thousand well prisoners were taken during the day.

During these operations on the extreme left and right, a considerable demonstration was made on our center, between the James and Appomattox. This was done to prevent reinforcements from being sent either to the right or the left. Having failed at all other points, and supposing doubtless that Gen. Lee had weakened his wings, the enemy, about 9 o'clock at night, advanced against our works on the Baxter road, and took possession of them; but they were soon driven out. The two armies, therefore, now occupy the same relative positions they had held before the fight. As already remarked, Grant took nothing by his last move, but lost more than a thousand men for every hundred that Lee lost. In other words, his loss will not fall short of six or seven thousand; while Lee's does not exceed five or six hundred.

I am glad to have it in my power to state that, in view of the fact that a large number of prisoners will probably be held in captivity by both belligerents during the coming winter, Judge Ould, Confederate Commissioner of Exchange, has proposed to the Federal Secretary of War and Maj. [John E.] Mulford, the assistant commissioner on the part of the United States, that each government shall have the privilege of forwarding for the use and comfort of such of its prisoners as are held by the other, all necessary articles of food and clothing, and that Gen. Grant has notified Gen. Lee of the acceptance of the proposition. The details of the agreement have not yet been fixed, but it is understood that it will include necessary clothing and blankets, and rations of meat, bread, coffee, sugar, pickles, vinegar and tobacco. Judge Ould suggested that it would be necessary that the Confederate authorities should make purchase of these articles outside the limits of the Confederate States, and then ship them to one of the Federal ports, since it would be impracticable to send the stores by flag of truce boats—the supplies thus sent to be considered as being in addition to such rations as are furnished by the government which has the prisoners in custody. To this Gen. Grant replies: "in the proposition submitted by Judge Ould, I see no one thing to object to. I shall be perfectly willing to receive at any place held by the Federal troops, all clothing or delicacies sent for the use of prisoners in our hands, provided the same privilege is extended for supplying the wants of those held by Confederate authorities. No objection will be urged to receiving supplies for like distribution at any of our Northern ports, direct from Europe, or to allowing purchases in Northern cities for the same purpose."

Such is the spirit of the entire correspondence, which is highly honorable to all the parties concerned in it. Gen. Grant suggests that a commissioned officer of each party be selected from among the prisoners of war, whose duty it shall be to receive and receipt for all articles sent for distribution, and who shall see that they are distributed according to the wishes of those sending them; and to this suggestion Gen. Lee gives his ready assent.

Upon consultation with Gen. Lawton, the Quartermaster General, it was ascertained that clothing cannot be purchased in Europe and delivered to our prisoners in the North before the middle of January or first of February next; and in that view, as blankets are their first and greatest need, Judge Ould has recommended to Mr. Seddon, the Secretary of War, the immediate purchase of thirty thousand pairs, to be made in a Northern city. He suggests also that the Federal authorities be asked to allow us to ship an amount of cotton from Wilmington, or some other port, to make the purchase. Mr. Seddon approved of the recommendation and suggestion, and has authorized Judge Ould to proceed at once to their execution.

The correspondence between Gen. Lee and Gen. Grant is now before me, and I have been much struck by the handwriting of these two ablest Generals the war has brought forward on either side. Gen. Lee's handwriting is bold and rather stiff, his letters being large, round and very distinct. He bears heavily upon the pen—probably a goose quill—and abbreviates many of his words, as if writing were a labor to him. The following is an exact transcript of the first sentence in his letter to Gen. Grant:

"GEN'L

I have rec'd your letter of the 18th inst. accomp'g copies of letters from Judge Ould Comm'r of Exchange of Pris'rs on the part of the Conf'ate States, & the Honb'le E. M. Stanton Sec'y of War and Lt. Col. Mulford Asst. Comm'r of Exc. Of the U. States."

He does not, as you perceive, punctuate closely; and no where in his letter does he write out the word *and*, but invariably uses the abbreviation, &. And yet he pauses long enough to dot all his *i's* and cross all his *t's*. All his letters are drawn nearly straight up and down the paper; in other words, they are like himself, round, full, bold and upright, inclining neither to the right nor the left, and standing firmly on their base as if they disdained all assistance. They are so clear and precise, so round and weighty, and distinct, that each letter reminds one of a solid cannon ball, and each word of a cluster of grapeshot.

Gen. Grant's handwriting, on the contrary, though not so bold and distinct, nor the letters so large and round and erect, is, nevertheless, very legible and very striking. It is full of energy and action, and his letters all incline to the right, and follow one another with a little space between them, as if they represented an equal number of his brigades on a rapid march around Lee's right. Among chirographers his hand would be called a running hand. The words occupy much space from left to right, and still they are very clear and legible. He pays more attention to punctuation than Gen. Lee, abbreviates less, and is equally careful of his *i's* and *t's*. It may be the work of imagination, yet in reading his letter I cannot but picture the writer as a restless, nervous, energetic man, full of fire and action, always in motion and always in a hurry.

The handwriting of both these great men is what would be denominated as experienced and characteristic. Neither of them writes well, and neither would be selected to take charge of a country school, if their selection depended upon their chirography. Thus we have two more witnesses, in two men who occupy more of this world's attention at this time than any other two living, that "great men write poor hands."

P. W. A.

RICHMOND, November 4, 1864 [11-9-64]

Our armies seem to be resting upon their arms everywhere except on the Tennessee river and in Missouri. Combats between small bodies of men at distant and isolated points and along the skirmish line, may take place from day to day; but beyond these unimportant conflicts, which are as often accidental as otherwise, nothing has occurred in this part of the Confederacy since Grant's disastrous defeat of the 27th ult.

The Congress which is to assemble here next week, will be charged with the gravest and most responsible duties touching the reorganization and increase of the army. It is understood that Mr. [William P.] Miles, the energetic and enlightened Chairman of the

Committee on Military Affairs in the House of Representatives, has already addressed a letter to Gen. Lee, soliciting his opinion as to the most advisable means to be adopted to increase and re-organize the army and improve the discipline of the troops. I understand also that Gen. Lee's reply is about ready for delivery. It is not known what plan he will recommend for the better disciplining of the troops and the reorganization of the army; but it is not improbable that Congress will find it necessary, owing to the reduced numbers of the various commands into which the army is divided, to consolidate not only companies and regiments, but even brigades and divisions. In regard to the reinforcement of the army, it is reported, and very generally believed, that Gen. Lee is in favor of enlisting a sufficient number of negroes to enable us to meet whatever force the enemy may bring against us next year. If the enemy does not increase his force, then it will not be necessary for us to increase ours, by the enlistment either of white men or black men. But if he does come against us next spring with armies like those with which he assaulted us last spring, then it is believed that it will become necessary to send every white man in the Confederacy under sixty years of age to the field, or enlist one or two hundred thousand negroes, or abandon the contest and bow our necks to the yoke of our northern masters.

I am informed that Gens. Longstreet, Ewell, and many other distinguished officers in the Army of Northern Virginia and the Army of the Valley concur with Gen. Lee in the matter. Such, too, is said to be the prevailing sentiment among officers of lower grades, as well as among the rank and file of these two armies. The negroes, if conscribed, will never be placed on an equality with white Southern troops, and the men thus far have manifested no objection on that score. They will be organized, doubtless, in separate commands, and placed under our best white officers; and in this way, officers who might be displaced by the consolidation of existing regiments and brigades, would be retained in service.

But whatever decision the country and the Government may come to, it behooves us to discuss this great delicate question with perfect freedom from prejudice and passion. Happily, such is the spirit with which it has been treated thus far by the press. We are all embarked upon the same bottom, and must sink or swim together. In this spirit, I would remark that, with a single exception among leading men, the persons I have met who oppose the measure are generally quiet men—men who are retiring in their nature and habits, who stay a good deal in their closets and have particular theories, and who have not been much in the rush and whir of this great revolution. The men who favor it, on the contrary, are, for the most part, men of action, who have been actively engaged in our mighty struggle, who have rubbed against the army and against the enemy, and who have felt much as well as thought much. Both classes are equally candid and equally patriotic.

P. W. A.

RICHMOND, November 15, 1864 [11-21-64]

The military situation remains without change, except in the Valley, where Rosser's cavalry repulsed two divisions of the enemy's, with considerable loss, on the 10th. About the same time, the enemy attacked McCausland's Virginia brigade of cavalry, and drove it off, as usual. Sheridan has withdrawn his lines a few miles back towards Winchester, and two days ago was entrenched eight miles south of that place between Newtown and Kernstown. Late Northern papers state that he will retire to Winchester or to Martinsburg, in consequence of the difficulty of procuring forage for his animals. He has torn up the iron on the Manassas Gap railway, from Strasburg eastward to Manassas Junction, and will use it, it is reported, to repair the branch road leading from Harper's Ferry up to Winchester. A few weeks ago Sheridan was trying to repair the Manassas Gap railroad, and, in order to protect the trains from the fire of Mosby's troopers, he found it necessary to place prominent Southern men on the locomotives and platforms of the cars, to draw the fire of the Confederates. But Mosby proved too much for him; he could not keep the road open, and has been compelled to abandon it and rely upon the Baltimore and Ohio road.

I regret the election of Mr. Lincoln; and yet it is but just to add, that a majority of public men here seem to think it better for us that he should have been chosen President of the

United States than McClellan. They believe if the latter had been elected, that a proposition from him to the South to return to the fold of the Union as it existed at the beginning of the war, would have carried off the Unionists who still remain firm in their principles, the secessionists who have fainted by the way, the traders and speculators, who, having amassed large fortunes, are anxious to save them, and the reconstructionists, as well as a large number of the advocates of a convention of the States, who are regarded as reconstructionists in disguise; and that the object sought to be gained through so much bloodshed and suffering and loss, if the whole country had yielded to these timid counsels, might have been defeated, the Union restored, high tariffs, corrupt legislation and slavery agitation revived, and, established upon a footing that would enable it to enjoy the spoils of office for generations to come, and all at the expense of the South.

However this may be, it is certain that Mr. Lincoln has been re-elected by a large majority of the electoral vote, but not by a large majority of the popular vote. For the present, therefore, whatever may be the object of the advocates of a convention of the States—whether it be loyal and praiseworthy as the friends of the measure declare, or factions, and designed to embarrass the government and eventually to restore the Union, as its opponents maintain—it is now evident that no such convention can be got together. We might as well make a proposition for a convention to the men in the moon as to Mr. Lincoln, flushed as he is with political success, and clothed for another four years with all the power that the sword and purse of a rich and populous nation can give him. I preferred the election of McClellan, simply because I did not believe he could carry on the war at all beyond a few months, and also believed that the people, seeing this, would be firm and wise enough to resist his seductive offers.

There appears to be no foundation for the rumor that Mr. Lincoln has issued another call for troops to reinforce his beaten and wasted armies. Grant has been calling for four months for one hundred thousand men, and has not been able to get them, even to help to carry the Presidential election, if not the works around Richmond. Every effort has been made to increase the Federal armies since August, and every influence existed in full force that could stimulate the Government, the people, and especially the supporters of the war, to bring forward reinforcements. And yet reinforcements were not raised, except in small numbers, as compared with the force called for by the President. Will he be more successful now, that the pressure has been removed, now that his election has been secured, and now that the contractors and speculators have voted themselves another four years' of spoils and power? I doubt it. Indeed, there is a reason to believe that we shall encounter no more grand armies like those with which the enemy marched to battle in the second, third and fourth years of the war.

For this reason, the opinion was advanced in my first letter touching the conscription of the negro, that the necessity did not yet exist for the employment of our slaves as soldiers. That necessity may never arise, if the present Congress will do its duty fearlessly, and the Secretary of War will close the back door to his office and enforce the laws without fear, favor or affection. The enemy outnumbers us already, and he will be able by one means or another, to add to his forces by next spring, though not to the same extent as heretofore. We must do the same. Absentees must be brought back to their commands, and the exemption law revised, if not repealed, or we shall not be in a condition to meet these increased forces of the invader. If proper laws are enacted, and executed with the necessary vigor and fidelity, there will be no necessity, at least for the present, to bring the negro into the army.

Such, too, seems to be the judgment of Congress. The measure recommended by the President for the raising of a corps of forty thousand negroes, to act as teamster, cooks and pioneer and engineer laborers will probably be adopted, omitting the emancipation features. Beyond this, it is not believed that any action will be taken at this time, and in advance of a necessity that may never arise. The resolutions now before the House will be referred to the Judiciary Committee as soon as they come up again, and there will be allowed to remain.

Brigadier General Battle, of Alabama—whom some anonymous writer has recommended for the position of Major General—comes out in a card, to the Richmond *Whig*, in which he takes occasion to express his opinions upon the matters and things generally.

Among other topics, he refers to the Army of the Valley, to which he is attached, and says the charge of drunkenness against the army has been "virtually withdrawn," &c. In this General Battle is mistaken. I made the charge, and have not withdrawn it, and shall not withdraw it, *because it is true*, as applied to the high officers in that army; and I am sorry that one who should be considered by any one worthy to be a Major General, should attempt to screen them.

P. W. A.

With the Richmond-Petersburg area relatively quiet, and Sherman advancing upon Savannah, Alexander heads south, stopping long enough to report on the attack at Fort Fisher which guarded the Cape Fear River and the port of Wilmington.

WILMINGTON, N. C., December 19, 1864 [1-4-65]
There has been considerable excitement here for the last two or three days, and especially yesterday, when the local forces were called out and other measures taken to resist the reported landing of the enemy. Without giving the authority upon which the statement is made, I may remark that intelligence has been received to the effect that a land force, estimated at 20,000 men, together with the fleet of monitors and gunboats which has for some time been assembling at Fortress Monroe, sailed on Friday, the 16th, for the South, with the intention of making a descent on the coast in the vicinity of Newbern and Wilmington. Other facts and circumstances were reported in connection with the expedition, which I need not stop to relate. The weather, which is rough outside, may have made it necessary for the monitors to put into port at some point further North, or the fleet may have kept on to Charleston or Port Royal. Beast Butler is reported to be in command of the expeditionary force, and this leads to the belief that their destination is the South Carolina coast. At this inclement and stormy period of the year, it would be a dangerous operation for the enemy to attempt to land an army by surf-boats upon the open beach, and it would be quite as difficult to subsist it there after it had landed. It is out of the question to land artillery and cavalry.

Trustworthy accounts from Georgia are sufficiently discouraging. Some woeful blunders have been committed there, and some in Richmond. Sherman's movement will be finally and fully successful. A base will be secured on the sea, from which our lines of communication will be assailed, and an effort made to isolate Lee's army in Virginia and cut off its supplies. The grand objective he has in view, however, is not the destruction of railway lines and the reduction of Savannah and Charleston; these are only means to help him to an end; and that end—which is the real object of his advance to the sea and of Grant's present comprehensive combinations—is the complete isolation of Lee's army and the enforced evacuation of Virginia by the Confederates.

It may well be doubted, therefore, whether the President and Gen. Lee, looking alone to the security of Richmond and Virginia—which it is feared engrosses too much the attention of both—did not lose an opportunity to place the safety of Virginia beyond the future danger, and at the same time to strike the foe a fatal blow, when they declined to send 10,000 seasoned troops to Georgia. With this force, added to the force already there, the destruction of Sherman would have been assured. There has not been the least danger of an attack upon Richmond and Petersburg since the last assault on the 27th of October. All of Grant's great maneuvers were undertaken for the purpose, doubtless, of producing a different impression, and to prevent reinforcements being sent to Georgia. This is not more evident now than it was two weeks ago; and the wonder is that everybody did not see it.

P. W. A.

WILMINGTON, N. C., December 22, 1864 [1-6-65]
At the date of my last letter, the 19th, the Federal fleet reported to have sailed from Fortress Monroe for this port, had not arrived. It has since made its appearance off New Inlet,

the eastern entrance to the harbor of Wilmington. It came to anchor during the night of the 19th, and the morning of the 20th, and consists of, all told, of about forty transports and the steam frigates *Wabash* and *Colorado*. No monitors or gunboats have been seen, and, if any started, they were compelled by stress of weather to put into port at some point north of this, or have gone down in the gale that has swept the coast for the last three days.

The policy of the enemy is manifestly the same in North Carolina as it is in Georgia: It is to destroy our railway lines and devastate the country. The movement against the Weldon railroad some ten days ago was part of the plan of operations at present being undertaken against this place and the railway leading hence to Weldon. The fate of Richmond and Virginia—as I hope Gen. Lee and Mr. Seddon will discover in time—will not be decided alone on the banks of the James and Shenandoah. Should the enemy be permitted to gain possession of Charleston, the great battle for the Old Dominion and for Confederate independence will be fought early next Spring, probably near Branchville, South Carolina, and at all events somewhere on the single and all-important line of railway from Kingsville to Augusta. For four years the enemy has sought in vain to overrun the country from the Ohio and the Potomac, and to defeat us in battle. Henceforth his policy will be to operate from the sea by short lines against our railways. This Grant is now doing, and such will be the future policy of Sherman. Having failed to take Richmond by marching overland, Grant now hopes to effects its fall by cutting off its supplies.

The time has come, therefore, for the President and Gen. Lee to elevate their telescopes and take a wider view of the situation.

P. W. A.

WILMINGTON, N. C., December 27, 1864 [1-7-65]

The enemy, checkmated and defeated at all points, has abandoned the strip of ground on which he was crowding above Fort Fisher, and under cover of his powerful fleet, re-embarked on board his transports. His monitors and numerous other ships of war have hauled off from Fort Fisher, and for the present, at least, have abandoned the attempt to carry that stronghold. Such is the result of three days' fighting, and of the fiercest bombardment to which any fort or town was ever subjected. But let us take up the thread of events where my last letter left it.

As soon as the Federal infantry had gained a footing on the mainland, Sunday afternoon [December 25], they threw themselves across a narrow spit of sand, on the southeastern extremity of which Fort Fisher stands, and thus got between [William] Kirkland's brigade and the fort, while Kirkland was between them and Wilmington. They moved forward immediately against Fisher, and attempted to carry it by a *coup de main*; but the brave garrison, quitting their guns and taking up their muskets, easily repulsed them. A second assault was made, and with the like result; after which the enemy withdrew up the beach beyond the reach of the Confederate fire, and went to work entrenching themselves under cover of their protecting fleet. They made some prisoners among the Junior Reserves when they advanced down against the fort; but beyond this our loss was insignificant, not exceeding fifty killed and wounded. Nearly all of our casualties consisted of slight wounds, but few having been killed.

Another account states that the credit of repelling the assaults against the fort belongs to the Junior Reserves of this State. It is certain that these youthful soldiers have played an important part in the defense of the fort, and have acquitted themselves with much credit. The fleet continued its fire until the infantry were ready to begin the assault, when, at a signal from the shore every vessel ceased its fire, and the men on the water became spectators of the conflict on the land. Very little damage was sustained by the fort, which is probably the strongest earthwork in the world. Mortar firing was kept up against the fort during the night, doing no damage however beyond interrupting the rest of the men.

Meanwhile reinforcements, which should have reached here two days sooner, began to arrive. Some of these reinforcements, we are informed, were sixty hours in going from Danville to Greensboro, a distance of less than fifty miles. It is not improbable, indeed, that not for the providential detention of the Federal fleet off the bar for three entire days by the severe gale which set in about the time it made its appearance, Fort Fisher would now be in the hands of the enemy, and with its fall the last open port in the Confederacy would have been hermetically sealed.

The situation, though not desperate, has now become extremely critical; and consequently General Bragg determined to clear the road to Fisher and reopen communications by land with the garrison. This he succeeded in doing yesterday, as well as pushing the enemy back upon the beach, where they were huddled together under their fleet. I neglected to say that every available man was thrown into Fisher Sunday night, or sent down to Sugar Loaf Hill, on the mainland. All places of business were closed, and every man who could carry a musket was put in the field.

It was the situation of the enemy that had now become critical. Having failed to carry the fort, and having been driven back upon the beach, if a gale should set in for a few days and communication be cut off with the fleet, he must either surrender or perish for want of food. It is reported that Gen. Bragg, comprehending their condition, ordered them to be shelled through the night to prevent them from receiving supplies, as well as from re-embarking on board their transports. If such an order was given, it failed to accomplish its object; indeed, if it had any effect, it was only to hasten the retreat of the baffled and beaten foe, who took to his ships last night and this morning, and left the Confederates masters of the field.

Such is the finale of the Christmas campaign of Beast Butler and Admiral Porter. It is not supposed that they have wholly abandoned their designs against North and South Carolina; but for the present their attack upon Wilmington and its defenses is checked and baffled.

P. W. A.

Fort Fisher finally fell on January 15, 1865.

1865

The Cause Lost

The grim war of attrition was fast coming to a close. With Sherman in the Carolinas, Thomas in Tennessee, and Grant at Petersburg, the end of the Confederacy was one campaign away. Ironically, Alexander spent the final months of the war in the city where it all began.

CHARLESTON, S. C., January 10, 1865 [1-24-65]

One is surprised and pained, on returning to Charleston after an absence of twelve months, to find many of the most furious advocates of secession in 1860, as well as many of the most confident and resolute supporters of our holy cause in 1863, now the most querulous and despondent. The reverses which have overtaken our arms, and the demoralizing influence of the blockade-running trade, have wrought this great change, so that the Charleston of to-day is no longer the Charleston of former days. The "cradle of the rebellion," the "hot-bed of secession," as the Yankees were wont to designate the town, and as the Charlestonians themselves were glad to have it designated, no longer presents the bold front with which it entered upon the conflict. I do not mean to insinuate that the people of Charleston are canvassing the propriety of abandoning the contest, and of running up the white flag in place of the Southern cross. Far from it. I do mean to say, however, that the city abounds with prophets of evil, with croakers, with fault finders, with speculators who, having amassed large fortunes, are anxious to save them even if the Confederacy should fall, and with persons who, the moment a reverse occurs, run up and down the streets, saying to every passer-by, "I told you so; the President should have done that; we must have a change of rulers or we are lost; let us have a dictator." Men who would not stop to count the cost four years ago, and who did more than all others to inaugurate the secession movement, now hint at another revolution!

What a falling off there is here! The country has a right to expect better things of every man and woman in Charleston, a city of so much renown, and one which has made so noble a stand against her enemies and her country's enemies. The country looked to her for an exhibition of calmness in the hour of trial, of fortitude and patience in the presence of danger, and of that sublime repose which is the result of conscious strength and a good cause. That there should have been more or less despondency and faction in Georgia, a large portion of whose territory has been overrun and devastated by the public enemy, was to be expected, and especially in view of the amazing fact that the Executive of South Carolina refused to allow the militia of the State to cross Savannah river at a time when the militia of Georgia were fighting and winning the battle of Grahamville [Honey Hill]; but from Charleston, so differently situated we had a right to expect a nobler example.

I write thus because I feel a just pride in this "City by the Sea," and in all that appertains to it. Its past is secure, and I have not the least doubt that its fortitude in the future will be equal to its heroism in the days that are gone. The croakers and fault-finders, and the whole pernicious brood of timid speculators and traders, as well as the mild revolutionists who would fly from the ills we have to those we know not of, will be frowned down, and the city will hold its even way on the road that leads to independence. Already a better state of feeling prevails, and the timid begin to envince greater presence of mind. In a short time, when better counsels shall have prevailed, the city and State will strip for the great fight which is before them, and from which there is no escape. The struggle will be fierce and bloody and protracted, and will test the patriotism, self-denial and endurance of the people; but that they will be found equal to the trial, there is not the least ground for doubt.

There has been but little change in the military situation for some days. Sherman has sent a corps around by water to Beaufort, and has marched a force across Savannah river to Hardeeville, having his outposts well thrown forward to Grahamville. The strength of this latter force is not known; but there is as yet no authentic information that his main army has left Savannah. A winter campaign is practicable in this latitude, but thus far I have seen no cause to look for an immediate advance by the enemy. Time is necessary, after such a march as that of Sherman's, to refit, rest and bring up supplies of food, clothing, ammunition and transportation, and before any fresh enterprise can be undertaken with safety. In any event, there is no reason to believe that an effort will be made to carry the works by which Charleston is defended by a direct assault. The attack, it is believed, will rather be made by the west bank of Savannah river against Augusta, or upon Branchville. In other words, it is believed that the movement will be made against the line between Columbia and Augusta, so as at the same time to cut off supplies from Lee's army, and take Charleston in the rear, as in the case of Vicksburg and Savannah, and as Grant sought to do, and still seeks to do, with Petersburg and Richmond.

P. W. A.

CHARLESTON, S. C., January 15, 1865 [1-26-65]

Sherman has commenced his movement against Charleston and Branchville. Refugees from Savannah, who arrived here on the 12th, stated that he has sent one corps up the west bank of the Savannah towards Augusta, that a second corps had gone to Wilmington, and that two corps were moving around by water to Beaufort. The corps sent up the west bank of the Savannah, it has since been ascertained, was recalled after it had proceeded some fifteen miles.

From Pocotaligo to Branchville the distance does not exceed forty-five miles, and can be easily accomplished in three days. The enemy once firmly established on the railroad, either at Branchville or some point nearer Augusta, and the fall of Charleston becomes only a question of time, and a short time at that. We may leave it to the President and Gen. Lee to decide what effect such a movement would have upon Richmond and the Army of Northern Virginia. At Branchville Sherman's flanks would be protected by the Edisto and its swamps on the left, and by the Santee and its swamps on the right, whilst his base at Charleston would be unassailable either by land or water.

If the official telescope at the capital could be elevated just enough to take in that part of the Confederacy which lies beyond the boundaries of Virginia, it would be well. Leaving the military aspect of the question entirely out of consideration, the authorities cannot fail to understand that the failure to reinforce the army in Georgia and South Carolina is producing a very bad effect. The enemies of both the cause and the President are taking advantage of this omission, to call it by no harsher name, and are multiplying the difficulties in our way. The retention of Charleston is not, as many of its inhabitants imagine, indispensable to our success; but the retention of the railway line from Kingsville to Augusta is.

The project of abolishing slavery, on condition that England and France will lend us material aid in the war, while it would be rejected by those powers, is producing further mischief, by alienating the cotton States and forcing upon them the necessity of considering the propriety of readjusting their political relations. The employment of one hundred thousand slaves as suggested by the President, will be acquiesced in by the States, and the proposition even to put them into an army is growing in public favor; but the press and politicians of Virginia should be careful not to go further, and especially not to aspire to the place in the Southern Confederacy that Massachusetts occupied in the old Union.

P. W. A.

The Civil War came to an abrupt end beginning with the surrender of Lee's army on April 9, followed by the assassination of President Lincoln on April 14. Alexander's last dispatch was begun on May 15, and for unknown reasons went unfinished and unpublished; his handwritten final summation was found among his personal papers.

The State of the Confederate Cause
MACON, GA., May 17, 1865

Events of the most important character have followed each other with such startling rapidity in this country that it is difficult, if not impossible, for even intelligent men to appreciate fully either their causes or their effects. A few weeks ago the Confederate government, backed by considerable armies, still held sway at Richmond and preparations were making for a vigorous campaign this summer. Unfortunately however, these preparations were made too late. An act calling the negro to field and receiving freedom to him and of his family if passed twelve months ago would have averted the catastrophe which has overtaken the Confederate cause. But the prejudices of the people, and not a lack of patriotism, prevented the adoption of so wise a measure, and when the remedy was finally applied, it was too late, the patient being already in articuls morte.

It became evident to thinking men, as soon as Sherman reached the sea at Savannah, that Hood's army having been badly beaten and broken in Tennessee, that it would soon become impossible for the Confederates to maintain their hold upon Richmond, and difficult, if not impossible, for them to withdraw. The remains of Hood's army which was moved into North Carolina and the officer placed in command of it—Gen. Johnston— could not be relied on in the desperate emergency, and Gen. Lee himself made the mistake of looking too much to Richmond and Virginia, and too little to other parts of the country, in making his military dispositions. It was the opinion of sagacious persons more than a year ago, that Richmond should be abandoned, and the army withdrawn further south to some point nearer its supplies. The failure of the provision crops in Virginia for three consecutive years, made it necessary for Gen. Lee to draw the greater part of the subsistence and forage consumed by his men and animals, from states west of the Savannah river. His ammunition was obtained from the same distant sources; and all of these supplies of whatever kind, were transported by land over worn-out railways from four hundred to a thousand miles. In no instance, except for a short distance on the Alabama river, could the Confederates avail themselves of water carriage in moving troops or subsistence. The pressure upon these broken and dilapidated railway lines and limited resources was too great to be borne. The principal seat of war was at one end of the Confederacy, while the chief source of supplies was almost at the other, as was the case with Russia in the Crimean War, and the result has been the same in both cases.

If Gen. Lee gave too much attention to the defense of Virginia, his own State, and too little to other portions of the country, it was owing doubtless to a cause which has exacted a pernicious influence upon the conduct of the war on the side of the South, and which has been overlooked by European writers in their criticism upon the campaigns which have now come to an end. I allude to what is recorded in the political nomenclature of the country as State rights; in other words, to the local State governments, and the consequent prejudices and attachments of the people. These prejudices and attachments are the result of State lines and geographical divisions, operated very ingeniously against the South, since they rendered it necessary for the government to hold and defend the territory of each one of the States, however unimportant and even undesirable it might be in a military view, or otherwise the government could not hope to secure the hearty support and cooperation either of the people or the authorities of each of the States as might be abandoned. In order to hold the Virginians squarely up to their duty, therefore, it became necessary to hold their capital and as much of the territory of their commonwealth as possible.

Indeed, it was proposed by some of the more unscrupulous leaders to withdraw the six cotton States, east of the Mississippi, overthrow Mr. Davis and his government, elect a new President and a new Congress, reconstruct the Confederation by leaving out such border

States as Missouri, Kentucky, Tennessee, and perhaps Virginia and N. Carolina, and change the seat of government to a point further South, and take a fresh start on the bloody path of war and revolution. Other schemes equally impracticable and revolutionary, if not equally extreme, were suggested and discussed in event, and but for the fortunate appearance of Mr. [Francis P.] Blair at Richmond and the consequent appointment of commissioners to confer with the Federal authorities on peace, it is impossible to say what might not have been done by the factions and radical demagogues whom the revolution has floated to the surface.

Indeed, there never was a clearer case of self-destruction than that which is now presented by the exploded Southern Confederacy. Success and independence were certainly within its reach, and its failure to grasp them is due almost entirely to the divisions and dissensions of the people and to their lack of patience, fortitude and self-denial. The immense superiority of the Federal states in numbers and resources would never have enabled them to overrun and conquer the South, if the latter had but remained true to herself. The advantage professed by the North were largely increased by the illegal blockade to which the Confederate ports were inflicted, and the moral support given to it by certain European reactionary powers, conduct which the sad and beaten Confederates will not soon forget or forgive.

The European reader will have heard long before this letter can reach him that all the Confederate forces east of the Mississippi have laid down their arms and been paroled and that President Davis was captured on the 10th inst., in Wilcox County in Georgia while on his way to the Trans-Mississippi States. Mr. Davis was accompanied by his family, three or four members of his staff, the Postmaster General Reagan, and a small train of wagons and cavalry. He had been travelling separately from his family, but becoming uneasy about their safety, he determined to join them; and since his discovery and arrest upon his arrival in this town, the headquarters of Gen. [James H.] Wilson's cavalry corps, he was received by a large concourse of citizens in silence, and with heaving bosoms, and straining eyes. The people had been forbidden to approach him, or to speak to him, or to make any demonstration whatever. The fallen chief though in public healthy was as calm and erect and self-possessed as he was on the memorable field of Manassas and even the Federal soldiers who thronged the railway station where he took his departure for Washington, could not suppress their admiration for one who bore himself so manfully in his hour of misfortune.

Such foreign powers who have so long stood aloof from the struggle on this continent, will not look on with folded hands and see this great statesman and upright patriot executed, either for the part he has played in the great American war or on the bold pretext that he was in any ways connected with the unfortunate assassination of President Lincoln. Nor is it true that victory makes the hero and want of it the traitor?

It is quite as probable that Vice-President Johnson, or the Pope of Rome, or the great Mogul himself was concerned in the conspiracy for the murder of Mr. Lincoln as that Mr. Davis was. He is not that manner of man. (Indeed, many in the Confederate Congress and army, the fellow countrymen of the Federal Vice-President Johnson, predicted soon after the election of Mr. Lincoln and Mr. Johnson that the former would not survive his inauguration three months!) True as the Italian proverb has it, cosa fatta capola, but it is quite as probable that the chief conspirator as well as the assassin himself was furnished by the North. If not executed on one pretext or another, he will soon perish if placed in prison, owing to his very frail constitution and delicate health. It is believed that the excitement of the struggle alone kept him alive thus far, and if the war had accentuated in Confederate independence, instead of defeat, that he would not probably have survived it six months. But if he shall be executed and more blood must be spilled, then his grave and the graves of his fellow martyrs will become the rallying points for generations to come, and the conflict will be renewed again and again, until the South shall have conquered her independence, or shall pulled down the temple of American liberty upon the head of her oppressors as well as upon herself. The assassination of Mr. Lincoln much as it is deplored throughout the South, will not be permitted to stand alone in the history of this country, and the pistol and the bowie dagger will become the customary means for disposing of tyrants in America, as they are still in Russia.

Moderation and forbearance will accomplish far more towards the pacification of the country than a harsh and vindictive policy, such as the government at Washington now seem inclined to adopt. A general unconditional amnesty would secure the respect and goodwill of the people; while a repressive policy will just as certainly convert the states of the South into so many volcanoes, which will renew the firery eruptions from generation to generation until the whole political fabric shall have been buried as deep as Pompeii and Herculaneum. The people have been stunned and confused by the great disasters that have fallen upon them with such wonderful rapidity. They are quiet and dumb now, I should say immeasurably sad and unhappy. They could subsist without complaint to the process of disavowing them, but this cannot last always. The guillotine may reduce the number of heads in the Confederacy, but it will also hasten the rebound. The Southern people have been reduced to extreme poverty by the war. Four years of fire and scorn have left them with hardly clothing to hide their nakedness or food enough to sustain life. These four years have been devoted, not to the accumulation of wealth, but to its destruction—not to the improvement of their farms, but to their devastation—not to the increase of the stock of horses, cattle, and sheep, but to their consumption. There is hardly a household or hamlet in all of the South that does not bear the marks of the terrible conflict....

Endings

"The demand of them did not cease with the end of the war," recalled a fellow newspaperman citing the popularity of the "P. W. A." correspondence, "Alexander was frequently urged to collect as many of them as he could, and publish them in some permanent form." This was not to be, for Alexander had failed to maintain an archive of his work. "P. W. A." now looked to his former audience to supply him with his old correspondence and notices appeared in newspapers throughout the South:

Advertisement, Rome *Courier*, November 30, 1865
P. W. Alexander, the well known and much admired correspondent, "P. W. A.," is writing a History of the recent struggle, and will be greatly obliged to any one in this vicinity, having either any of his letters or other important information, to leave the same with Thos. Perry of this place.

In collecting material for his proposed History of the Lost Cause, Alexander looked to former Confederate leaders for assistance:

Lexington, Va., 11 Oct. '65
My dear Sir,
I have just rec'd your letter of the 25 ulto., I am sorry to inform you that all my papers & records, private & public, were destroyed on the retreat of the Army of N. Va., from Petersburg. I am unable therefore to comply with your request.
It is my desire to write the history of the Campaigns in Virginia provided I can procure the necessary information.
The work you propose, or any number of such, will in no way interfere with my purpose, and I hope you will prosecute it to completion. My only object is that a truthful record of our struggle should reach posterity & if this is done, it will answer my purpose.
If I can aid you in this object, either by a personal interview as you propose, or otherwise, it will give me pleasure.
Sympathizing sincerely with you in your losses, and wishing you every success in your undertaking.
I am with great respect your obedient servant.

R. E. Lee

Alexander spent the next two decades collecting his wartime correspondence, and for reasons unknown, never wrote the history of the Lost Cause; maybe, perhaps, it was a subject too painful to revisit, or more simply, life got in the way.
On September 27, 1870, Peter Alexander married Marie Theresa Shorter (daughter of former Alabama Governor John G. Shorter); the couple, settling in Columbus, had three children. Alexander then resumed his law practice with a partner, James Milton Smith who was elected governor of Georgia in 1872; Alexander then served as Smith's private secretary.
In 1877, Alexander moved to Marietta, where he died of heart failure on September 23, 1886 and is buried in Linwood Cemetery, Columbus, Georgia in the Shorter Lot.

Obituary, Atlanta *Constitution* September 24, 1886
"P.W.A." DEAD— Not only the people of Georgia will be saddened to hear of his death, but the noblest men of the entire South will receive the sad news with the profoundest regret. His life was a historic one....

Index